I0659452

(Frysian)
p193

p207

**Haarlem &
North Holland**
p101

Amsterdam ☆
p40

**Central
Netherlands**
p219

Utrecht
p135

**Rotterdam
& South
Holland**
p146

**Maastricht &
Southeastern Netherlands**
p236

Language

THIS EDITION WRITTEN AND RESEARCHED BY

Ryan Ver Berkmoes, Karla Zimmerman

welcome to the Netherlands

Art & Icons

In the world of art the Netherlands has given us Rembrandt and Van Gogh. Sure, there's also Frans Hals, Hieronymus Bosch and Piet Mondrian – but when you've got the first two, why mention the rest? (OK that Vermeer guy, he's big...). Then there are icons: classic windmills, the ultimate green machines that are back in vogue a century after the Dutch used these twirling beasties to pump the country dry. Clogs? Renewable. Affordable. Floatable (if the dykes break). Tulips? The Dutch have made a fortune from little bulbs that go in the ground, then burst forth with beauty that is universally loved.

Big in Size & Spirit

The Dutch themselves seem oversized (actually they are statistically the tallest nationality on the planet.) Gregariousness, thrift, good sense and wry humour are all national traits, as is no-holds-barred honesty. This is not the country for the neurotic to ask: 'Do you think I look fat in this?' (Not that this can be much of a worry in the best place to ride a bike on the planet.)

Essential Amsterdam

For Amsterdam – the entire city is also a Dutch icon – current upheavals will merely create more ripples in a city used to waves of change. Misunderstood by

Discover the many secrets of this gently beautiful country and its masterpieces, canal towns and windmills. Revel in the welcoming yet wry culture at a cafe, then bike past fields of tulips.

(left) Windmills, Kinderdijk, near Rotterdam (p181)
(below) Tulips, Bloemenmarkt, Amsterdam (p60)

many, the virtual heart of the Netherlands is not what many people expect on their first visit. The sex and drugs are mostly kept to one 'hood (convenient to the train station) while the rest of the city keeps to its own beauty along the murky canals.

And the Rest

Other places as old as Amsterdam have evocative beauty and come in a variety of sizes: Edam, Haarlem, Delft and Deventer to name just some of the smaller delights. Moving up the league tables in size, there's the canal towns of Leiden, Haarlem and Utrecht. And Rotterdam is a modernist feast all of its own.

Perhaps the best way to get to the heart of the Netherlands is to do as the Dutch do. Join them in the city centres of classic towns as far flung as Groningen, Maastricht and Den Bosch, lively places filled with cafes that heave with happy Dutch socialising on a sunny day. Or join them on the thousands of kilometres of bike routes as they add not a molecule of carbon to the atmosphere while riding through the lush countryside and past sweeping watery vistas at sea (or is it see?) level. You don't have to travel far to find a lot.

› The Netherlands

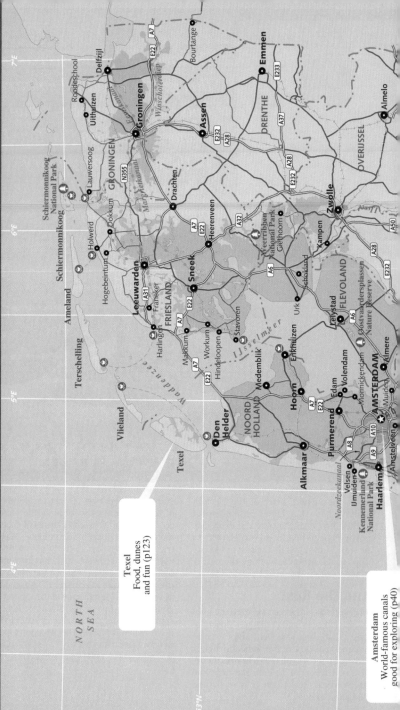

Texel
Food, dunes
and fun (p123)

Amsterdam
World-famous canals
good for exploring (p40)

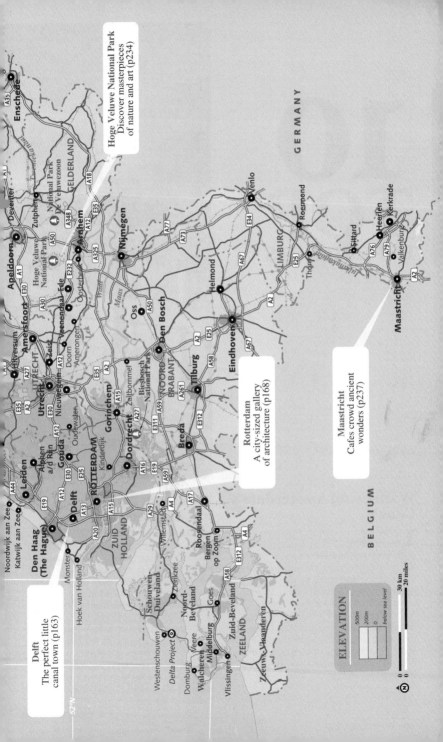

Delft
The perfect little canal town (p163)

Hoge Veluwe National Park
Discover masterpieces of nature and art (p234)

Rotterdam
A city-sized gallery of architecture (p168)

Maastricht
Cafés crowd ancient wonders (p237)

GERMANY

BELGIUM

GELDERLAND

LIMBURG

NOORD-BRABANT

ZUID HOLLAND

ZEELAND

Enschede
Deventer
Apeldoorn
Amersfoort
Hilversum
Zutphen
National Park De Veluwezoom
Arnhem
Nijmegen
Zeist
Doorn
Amerongen
UTRECHT
Nieuwegein
Gorinchem
Zaltbommel
Oss
Den Bosch
Helmond
Venlo
Roermond
Sittard
Heerlen
Kerkrade
Valkenburg
Maastricht
Eindhoven
Tilburg
Breda
Biesbosch National Park
Dordrecht
Kinderdijk
Oudewater
Gouda
Alphen a/d Rijn
Leiden
Den Haag (The Hague)
Noordwijk aan Zee
Katwijk aan Zee
Monster
Hoek van Holland
Delft
ROTTERDAM
Willemstad
Roosendaal
Bergen op Zoom
Goes
Zuid-Beveland
Zeeuws-Vlaanderen
Vlissingen
Middelburg
Walcheren
Domburg
Veere
Westenschouwen
Delta Project
Schouwen-Duiveland
Noord-Beveland
Zierikzee
Ede
Veenendaal
Zwolle

Hoge Veluwe National Park

Rijn
Lek
Waal
Maas
Julianakanaal
Thorn

A1 A2 A4 A7 A12 A13 A15 A16 A17 A18 A20 A27 A29 A30 A35 A44 A50 A58 A59 A67 A73 A76 A77 A79 A261 A325 A348
E19 E25 E30 E31 E32 E34 E35 E311 E312

52°N

ELEVATION
500m
200m
0
below sea level

N

0 — 30 km
0 — 20 miles

10 TOP EXPERIENCES

Wandering Amsterdam's Canals

1 Amsterdam has more canals than Venice, and getting on the water is one of the best ways to feel the pulse of the city. You could catch the vibe by sitting canalside and watching boats glide by: myriad cafes seem purpose-built for this sport. Or you could stroll along the canals and check out some of the city's 3300 houseboats. Better yet, hop on a tour boat and cruise the curved passages. From this angle, you'll understand why Unesco named the 400-year-old waterways a World Heritage site. Keizersgracht canal

Admiring Dutch Masterpieces

2 The Netherlands has produced a helluva lot of famous artists. In Amsterdam, the Van Gogh Museum (p65) hangs the world's largest collection by tortured native son Vincent. Vermeer's *Kitchen Maid*, Rembrandt's *Night Watch* and other Golden Age masterpieces fill the mighty Rijksmuseum (p65), while the Stedelijk Museum (p66) shows Mondrian, de Kooning and other homeboys among its edgy modern stock. Outside the capital, the Frans Hals Museum (p104) collects the painter's works in Haarlem, and the Mauritshuis (p155) unfurls a who's who of Dutch masters in Den Haag. Rijksmuseum

Day Tripping to Delft

3 The Netherlands has no shortage of evocative old towns. Haarlem, Leiden and Utrecht are just some of the more well known. With their old canals lined with buildings whose human-scaled architecture is nothing but characterful, these towns bring the beauty of the Golden Age into the modern age. But one old canal town shines above the rest: Delft (p163). Even if you're not staying here, an afternoon spent along its canals, churches, museums and just sitting in a cafe soaking it all in is essential time spent. Canal, Delft

Cycling Between Villages

4 Grab a bike and go. You can rent them anywhere and no nation on earth is better suited for cycling. Not only is it flat but there are thousands of kilometres of bike lanes and paths linking virtually every part of the country, no matter how small. From a bike road atop a dyke, you can see *polders* (areas of drained land) below the water in the canal, hear cows mooing in the fields and enjoy the view of old windmills. Soon you're at another cute little village ready to explore. Tulip field, North Holland

Enjoying Cheesy Delights

5 Whether it is cubed or melted, sliced on a sandwich or shaved onto a salad, you cannot escape Dutch cheese. Names like Gouda and Edam inspire more notions of curdled milk than images of the municipalities that spawned them. And forget the bland stuff you find in the supermarket, Dutch cheese comes in a vast range of styles and flavours. Start with the caraway-seed-infused variety. Next consider one of the aged goudas that is crystallised like a fine parmesan and is best had with a touch of mustard – and beer. Cheese at De Kaaskamer (p96)

Best Park in the Netherlands

6 A vast swathe of beautiful land that was once private hunting ground, Hoge Veluwe National Park (p234) combines forests, sand dunes, marshes and ponds. It's a bucolic escape from the densely packed cities and you can easily spend a day here just luxuriating in nature. But wait, there's more! At the park's centre, the Kröller-Müller Museum is one of the nation's best. Its Van Gogh collection rivals that of the namesake museum in Amsterdam, plus there is a stunning sculpture garden. Red deer, Hoge Veluwe National Park

Revelling in Maastricht

7 The city where Europe's common currency began (p237) has been a meeting place for centuries. The Romans built underground forts here you can still explore, and every generation since has left its mark. But 2000 years of history, monuments, ruins, churches and museums aside, where Maastricht really shines is in how it embraces the moment. Few places in the Netherlands have such a densely packed collection of alluring cafes great and small, filled with people enjoying every minute of life that's as good as the food and drink.
Nightlife with bikes, Maastricht

Rotterdam's Dramatic New Look

8 Unlike many European cities that emerged from the ashes of WWII with hastily reconstructed city centres, Rotterdam (p168) pursued a different path from the start. Its architecture is striking rather than functional and it has a rarity for Europe: an identifiable skyline. The world's best architects compete here for commissions that result in artful – often daring – designs. The Erasmusbrug, a birdlike bridge, is a city icon and is surrounded by buildings that are both bold and beautiful to contemplate. Piet Blom's Cube Houses

Island Charms on Texel

9 The vast Waddenzee region, where northwest Europe almost imperceptibly melts into the sea, is recognized by Unesco as a World Heritage site. These tidal mudflats with their hypnotic charm are punctuated by a string of offshore islands. The largest, Texel (p123), offers endless walks on beautiful beaches, almost limitless activities and a stark beauty you can appreciate on land or on a wildlife-spotting boat trip. And when you're ready for a pause, it has inspired places to stay and some very fine food – you won't believe the smoked fish. Mudflats, Texel

Savouring Brown Cafes

10 It means convivial but not quite. It also means friendly but still not quite. Snug, cosy and good-humoured all apply as well. Kind of. *Gezelligheid* is the uniquely Dutch trait that is best experienced in one of the country's famous brown cafes (p89). Named for their aged, tobacco-stained walls or just plain oldness, these small bars are filled with good cheer. It takes little time, on even your first visit, to be drawn into the cheery warmth and welcome of their *gezelligheid*. Hoppe, Spui

need to know

Currency
» Euro (€)

Language
» Dutch and English

When to Go

Texel
GO Apr–Oct

Amsterdam
GO Year-round

Deventer
GO Apr–Oct

Rotterdam
GO Mar–Nov

Maastricht
GO Year-round

Warm to hot summers, mild winters
Warm to hot summers, cold winters

High Season
(Jun-Aug)
» Everything is open.

» The odds of balmy weather to enjoy a cafe or a countryside bike ride are best – but not assured.

» Crowds fill the famous museums.

» Prices peak, book ahead.

Shoulder Season (Apr & May, Sep & Oct)
» Most sights open.

» Few crowds.

» Prices moderate, only book popular places in Amsterdam

» Weather mixes the good with wet and cold. Bring warm clothes for outdoors.

Low Season
(Nov-Mar)
» Many sights outside of major cities closed.

» It may just be you and a masterpiece at a famous museum.

» Weather cold and or wet, biking is only for the hardy.

» Deals abound.

Your Daily Budget

Budget less than
€100
» Dorm bed €22–35, private room under €60

» Supermarkets and lunchtime specials for food €15

» Free outdoor exploration

Midrange
€100– 200
» Double room €100

» Good dinner in casual restaurant €30

» Museums and trains €20

Top end more than
€200
» Luxurious hotel double room €160

» Dinner in top restaurant with drinks €60

» First-class trains, guided tours €40

Money

» ATMs widely available. Credit cards accepted in most hotels but not all restaurants. Non-European credit cards are sometimes rejected.

Visas

» Generally not required for stays up to three months. Some nationalities require a Schengen visa.

Mobile Phones

» Local SIM cards can be used in European and Australian phones. Most American smartphones will work.

Transport

» Drive on the right; steering wheel is on the left side of the car. Trains and buses go almost everywhere.

Websites

» **Expatica** (www.expatica.com/holland) Entertaining guide to life in the Netherlands, with daily news and listings.

» **Netherlands Tourism Board** (www.holland.com) Attractions, cultural articles and practical stuff.

» **Uitburo** (www.uitburo.nl) Events, in Dutch, but is easy to navigate.

» **Windmill Database** (www.molendatabase.org) Pick your favourite in advance.

» **Lonely Planet** (www.lonelyplanet.com/netherlands) Destination information, hotel bookings, traveller forum and more.

Exchange Rates

Australia	A$1	€0.76
Canada	C$1	€0.74
Japan	¥100	€0.79
New Zealand	NZ$1	€0.62
UK	UK£1	€1.16
US	US$1	€0.73

For current exchange rates see www.xe.com.

Important Numbers

Drop the 0 when dialing an area code from abroad.

Emergency	☎112
Country code	☎31
International access code	☎00
Operator	☎0800 04 10

Arriving in the capital

» **Schiphol Airport** Trains to Amsterdam Centraal Station depart every 10 minutes or so from 6am to 12.30am €4; taxi €45. Trains to Rotterdam depart often and take 30 minutes to one hour €11 to €15.

Getting Around the Netherlands

Depending how you travel, getting to your next destination in the Netherlands may not just be half the fun, it may be all the fun.

» **Bike** One of the best reasons to visit is to ride bikes. Short- and long-distance bike routes lace the country and you are often pedalling through beautiful areas. All but the smallest train stations have bike shops to rent bikes as do most towns and all cities.

» **Train** Service is fast, distances are short and trains are frequent. Buying tickets is sometimes a challenge but once aboard, the rides can be lovely; eg in the spring trains in and around Leiden pass through gorgeous bulbfields.

what's new

For this new edition of the Netherlands, our authors have hunted down the fresh, the transformed, the hot and the happening. These are some of our favourites. For up-to-the-minute recommendations, see lonelyplanet.com/netherlands.

Rijksmuseum, Amsterdam

1 After a 10-year renovation, the nation's premier art trove reopened in its entirety in 2013, splashing Rembrandts, Vermeers and 7500 other masterpieces over 1.5km of galleries. See p65.

Stedelijk Museum, Amsterdam

2 Amsterdam's modern art museum finally popped the top on 'the Bathtub', its new wing that nearly doubles the space for Monets, Mondrians, glassworks, posters and textiles. See p66.

EYE Film Institute, Amsterdam

3 It's ready for its closeup: the Netherlands' film centre (p44) opened its new complex in an architecturally stunning, waterfront space in Amsterdam-Noord, screening classics and art films for all ages.

Amsterdam Tattoo Museum, Amsterdam

4 Prepare for a wild array of inky artefacts, including pickled skin from 19th-century sailors. On the 2nd floor, resident tattoo artists apply the ultimate souvenir from your visit. See p67.

Motor Scooter Taxis, Amsterdam

5 Hopper – a fleet of lime-green, Vespa-style electric scooters – has taken to Amsterdam's streets as an ecofriendly alternative to sluggish autotaxis in the congested centre. See p100.

Rotterdam Centraal Station, Rotterdam

6 After years of chaos and construction, Rotterdam is finally getting a new main train station that can go toe to toe with any of the city's other stunning buildings. See p180.

Museum Broeker Veiling, Broek Op Langedijk

7 A great example of the interesting and idiosyncratic museums of Holland: new multimedia displays bring to life a region of 15,000 vegetable farms that were farmed by boat. See p118.

Oudeschild, Texel

8 This fishing port is a great place to get a boat tour, visit the amazing museum or feast on smoked fish, now it's getting a real centre on the waterfront. See p129.

Fyra

9 After a disastrous gestation, the high-speed rail service linking Amsterdam, Schiphol, Rotterdam, Breda and Brussels is finally up and running, cutting day-trip journey times even more. See p304.

Museum Aan Het Vrijthof, Maastricht

10 Right on the iconic Vrijthof, the medieval square, this lavish new museum traces Maastricht during the Golden Age. See p239.

Fries Museum, Leeuwarden

11 Friesland's premier museum opens in a starkly beautiful new building on a reinvigorated central square. The grand collection of silver and artworks has never looked better – nor have the cafes outside. See p195.

if you like...

Unique Architecture

The Dutch have always excelled at alluring architecture that you'll find nowhere else. Whether it was the canal house of the Golden Age or the sleek, modern and bold visual statements of today.

Amsterdam's canals Just like a crowd of people, each narrow canal house has its own distinct personality – from the gable down. (p78)

Rotterdam The entire central city is a showplace of modern architecture. Buildings show a daring lack of restraint; the Overblaak development is a cubist classic. (p168)

Rijksmuseum Pierre Cuypers' magnificent, iconic design from 1875 harks back to earlier times, with Renaissance ornaments carved in stone around the facade. (p65)

NEMO Renzo Piano's green-copper, ship-shaped science museum in Amsterdam is a modern classic. (p68)

ARCAM Amsterdam's Centre for Architecture is a one-stop shop for architectural exhibits, guidebooks and maps. (p68)

Netherlands Architectuur Institute In Rotterdam, has regular special exhibits on Dutch architecture. (p175)

Art

Powerhouse museums filled with masterpieces can be found across the Netherlands.

Van Gogh Museum The world's largest collection of the tortured artist's vivid swirls. (p65)

Rijksmuseum The Netherlands' top treasure house bursts with Rembrandts, Vermeers, Delftware and more. (p65)

Stedelijk Museum Renowned modern art from Picasso to Mondrian to Warhol stuffs this revamped building. (p66)

Hermitage Amsterdam This satellite of Russia's Hermitage features one-off, blockbuster exhibits showing everything from Matisse cut-outs to Byzantine treasures. (p60)

Mauritshaus The royal collection in the Den Haag encapsulates all that's great about Dutch art in a small package. (p155)

Museum Boijmans Van Beuningen Rotterdam's great museum has works from Bosch onwards. (p169)

Kröller-Müller Museum Hidden in the nation's most beautiful national park is an unsurpassed collection of Van Goghs and other masterpieces. (p235)

Frans Hals Museum Reason enough for any art lover to visit Haarlem. (p104)

Markets

Every city and town in the Netherlands has open-air markets at least one day a week. Some are specialised around organic foods or antiques; most are held on interesting central squares.

Albert Cuypmarkt Amsterdam's largest and busiest market has been selling flowers, clothing, household goods and food of every description for 100 years. (p66)

Waterlooplein Flea Market The city's famous flea market piles up curios, used footwear, ageing electronic gear, New Age gifts and cheap bicycle parts for bargain hunters. (p51)

Oudemanhuis Book Market Located in a moody, old, covered alleyway, this place is lined with second-hand booksellers and is a favourite with academics. (p95)

Den Haag Organic Farmers Market Foods of all kinds from Holland's breadbasket are sold here. (p158)

De Bazaar Beverwijk One of Europe's largest open-air markets has a truly international flavour. (p109)

Blaak Market Antiques and ethnic foods mix and mingle at this vast Rotterdam shopping carnival. (p180)

» Wooden houses on Marken, Zuiderzee (p111)

Cycling

While the entire country is a cyclist's dream, there are some good day-trip choices that won't leave you too pooped for a night out. It's easy to rent bikes for the following.

Waterland Easily reached by bike from Amsterdam, this region combines classic Dutch scenery in a compact package of cows, dykes, canals and lots and lots of green. (p29)

Bulbfields Get a bike from Leiden in the spring and ride west through a cacophony of colour as Holland's tulips and more explode in bloom. (p30)

Weerribben-Wieden National Park Bike routes circle through this old land of peat farming that is rich with birds. (p228)

Hoge Veluwe National Park Nature and beauty plus the country's best ice cream can be enjoyed while using the park's free bikes. (p234)

South Holland's Beaches Start in Scheveningen and ride north or south along dunes and beaches. You'll soon leave the crowds behind and enjoy the refreshing salt air. (p157)

History

With a history as rich as that of the Netherlands there's no shortage of historic sites.

Anne Frank Huis The secret annexe, Anne's melancholy bedroom and her actual diary are all here; chilling reminders of WWII. (p55)

Amsterdam Museum Intriguing multimedia exhibits take you through the twists and turns of Amsterdam's convoluted history. (p44)

Delfshaven Rotterdam's old neighbourhood still has many of the features that greeted the pilgrims when they passed through to America. (p169)

Lakenhal The ground floor of this excellent art museum recreates what a gallery would have looked like in Leiden at the peak of the Golden Age. (p149)

Hindeloopen A tiny former fishing village that feels like a time warp to the days when people eked out a living here. (p201)

Deventer The entire old part of the city still has a Hanseatic League echo 800 years on. (p221)

Airborne Museum Hartenstein Learn about the botched WWII battle Operation Market Garden. (p234)

Islands

With so much water around, at times much of the country feels like an island. But there are some real ones and they are worth a visit.

Texel The largest of the Waddenzee islands has excellent places to sleep and eat, plus myriad ways to access its beaches and natural places. (p123)

Vlieland The least visited of the Frisian islands is almost entirely natural and is an ideal true escape, especially the barren west. (p202)

Schiermonnikoog Beautiful beaches and dunes make the smallest Frisian island an excellent natural retreat – and a good *wadloper* (mud-walker) destination. (p205)

Marken Once an isolated fishing port on an island in the Zuiderzee this tiny village is now linked by a causeway, it's a real step back in time. (p111)

Noordereiland An island right in the middle of Rotterdam, stop here on our walking tour for good views of the stunning skyline. (p174)

If you like... shopping in
little shops and boutiques
that defy description and
where each door yields a
new surprise, spend a day
browsing Amsterdam's Negen
Straatjes (Nine Streets).

Cafes

Everybody in the Netherlands has a favourite cafe – or 10. The country has the concept of convivial places to drink, make friends, meet friends and maybe have a meal, nailed.

De Sluyswacht Swig in the lockkeeper's tilted quarters across the street from Rembrandt's Amsterdam house. (p89)

Cafe Belgique Pouring fine lambic beers and Trappist brews, this moody beer cafe saves you from a trip south. (p88)

't Oude Pothuys Generations of music students have performed at this ancient Utrecht pub, with fine canalside tables. (p142)

Take One A Maastricht institution that's everything a Dutch cafe should be: engaging, offbeat, eccentric and with a fab selection of brews. (p242)

De Zwarte Ruiter It seems everyone in Den Haag pops through the vast terrace of this über-popular cafe at least once a day. (p159)

Heksenketel An amiable Deventer crowd gathers at this cafe which has an excellent beer selection. (p223)

Windmills

Even a blonde girl in wooden clogs carrying a round of cheese is not more iconic than Holland's windmills. Travelling the country you'll see many of the 1200 surviving originals.

Zaanse Schans A must if you have even a slight interest in windmills. Along a pretty dyke you'll find six in operating condition. Tour their insides to see how they did far more than just pump water. (p109)

Kinderdijk The perfect day trip from Rotterdam, the 19 windmills are beautifully arrayed along a dyke and are recognised by Unesco. Get a bike and explore (p181).

De Valk A sort of beloved mascot of Leiden, this restored mill has a fine little museum explaining how they work. (p149)

Alkmaar You can dine in the shadow of a windmill at Abby's. (p117)

Windmill Ride By car or bike you can visit a clutch of mills near Alkmaar. (p116)

Adult Entertainment

Amsterdam's adult-oriented allure is both well known and celebrated. Few legitimate tastes won't find something to titillate here. And the pleasures don't stop here as there are others to be enjoyed countrywide.

Dampkring This coffeeshop stalwart has a comprehensive, well-explained menu; a Cannabis Cup winning product; and Hollywood pedigree. (p91)

Kokopelli Life gets a whole lot more colourful (literally) with a serving of magic truffles from this classy smart shop. (p95)

Condomerie Het Gulden Vlies puts the 'pro' back in prophylactic with its tasteful setting and huge array of condoms for sale. (p95)

Rotterdam No slouch in afterhour joy, it has a killer club scene, a bevy of bars with live music and some utterly enjoyable coffeeshops. (p178)

Groningen City The university town in the far northeast has a hopping nightlife. (p208)

month by month

Top events

1 **King's Day,** April

2 **New Year's Eve,** December

3 **Carnaval,** February

4 **Keukenhof Gardens,** March

5 **National Windmill Day,** May

January

Yes, it's cold and dark. Luckily the museum queue was nonexistent, and now you're in a cosy cafe in front of a fireplace.

Amsterdam International Fashion Week

Amsterdam's fledgling fashion scene takes flight biannually during Fashion Week (www.amsterdamfashionweek.com), with catwalks, parties, lectures and films around the city. Many events – both free and ticketed – are open to the public. There's a June festival, too.

February

It's still cold and the nights are long. Happily if you head south, the Catholic provinces are going to party.

Carnaval

Weekend before Shrove Tuesday. Celebrations with gusto that would do Rio de Janeiro or New Orleans proud, mostly in the Catholic provinces of Noord Brabant, Gelderland and Limburg. Maastricht's party means days of uninhibited drinking, dancing and street music. On occasion it occurs in early March.

March

If the weather complies, you can get a jump-start on tulip viewing in March, and since the season is still off-peak, you won't have to fight the crowds to enjoy them.

European Fine Art Foundation Show (TEFAF)

For 10 days in the first half of March in Maastricht. Europe's largest art show is your chance to pick up a Monet, or at least do some serious browsing.

Keukenhof Gardens

The world's largest flowering bulb show (www.keukenhof.nl) opens in midMarch and runs through mid-May near Leiden in the heart of Holland's bulbfields. Buy tickets in advance for weekends.

April

April is host to King's Day, the show-stopping highlight of Amsterdam's jam-packed calendar. You should be there.

King's Day (Koningsdag)

The biggest – and possibly the best – street party in Europe celebrates the monarch. Expect plenty of uproarious boozing, live music and merriment, plus a giant free market where everything under the sun is for sale.

World Press Photo

Stunning, moving, jaw-dropping: just a few words to describe this annual show (www.worldpressphoto.org) of pictures shot by the best photojournalists on the planet. On display at Amsterdam's Oude Kerk from late April to late June.

May

Alternating rainy and gorgeous weather and plenty of historic events make post-King's Day May a perfect time to explore the country. Hope for a balmy weekend to get out and blow with the windmills.

Herdenkingsdag & Bevrijdingsdag

(Remembrance Day & Liberation Day) On 4 and 5 May. The fallen from WWII are honoured in an Amsterdam ceremony, followed by live music, debate and a market the following day.

National Windmill Day

On the second Saturday in May, 600 windmills throughout the country unfurl their sails and welcome the public into their innards (www.nationalemolenengemalendag.nl). Look for windmills flying a blue pennant.

June

The promise of great weather and very long days draws people outside and keeps them there.

Holland Festival

For all of June the country's biggest music, drama and dance extravaganza (www.hollandfestival.nl) practically takes over Amsterdam. Highbrow and pretentious meet lowbrow and silly, with something for everyone.

Ronde om Texel

The largest catamaran race in the world (www.roundtexel.com) is held off Texel; spectators line the beaches for hours on end watching boats jive back and forth on the sea.

Oerol

In the latter half of June, this outdoor performance festival on Terschelling (www.oerol.nl) is revered nationwide as a perfect excuse for going to sea.

Parkpop

In late June some 350,000 ravers descend on Den Haag (www.parkpop.nl).

July

The days are long, the sun is shining, outdoor cafes are mobbed with locals and tourists alike. Nobody wants to be inside.

North Sea Jazz Festival

World's largest jazz festival (www.northseajazz.nl); attracts big names from around the planet, and even bigger crowds. Mid-July, in Rotterdam.

Vierdaagse

In late July, thousands go on a four-day, 120km- to 200km-long march held around Nijmegen (Four Days; www.4daagse.nl).

August

August is a surprisingly pleasant time to visit, with temperatures that are much milder than in many other European tourist, er, hotspots. Many Dutch decamp for holidays elsewhere.

Noorderzon

Eleven-day arts festival in mid-August in Groningen that is huge fun.

Amsterdam Pride Festival

The rainbow flag blankets Amsterdam on the first weekend of the month, with oodles of parties and special events (www.amsterdampride.nl). The climax, the Gay Pride Parade, is the world's only waterborne spectacle of the flesh-baring kind.

Lowlands

Mid-August, in Biddinghuizen (Flevoland): alternative music and cultural megabash, with campgrounds for the masses (www.lowlands.nl).

Grachtenfestival (Canal Festival)

This music festival (www.grachtenfestival.nl) delights, with classical concerts around the Canal Ring in the second half of August. The Prinsengracht Concert takes place on barges in front of the Hotel Pulitzer.

September

September is one of the best months to visit the Netherlands: there's mild, summer-like weather and fewer crowds.

Wereld Havendagen

In early September Rotterdam celebrates the role of the harbour, which directly or indirectly employs more than 300,000 people. There are boatloads of open houses, ship tours and fireworks.

 Nederlands Film Festival

The Dutch film industry may be tiny, but its output is generally good. Find out for yourself at the NFF in late September, culminating in the awarding of the coveted Golden Calf (www.filmfestival.nl).

October

While the mild weather may still persist, low-season prices kick in and queues thin out.

 Leidens Ontzet

Leiden grinds to a halt 3 October for Leidens Ontzet, commemorating the day the Spanish-caused starvation ended in 1574. It's a drinkfest the night before.

Amsterdam Dance Event

A club music powwow (www.amsterdam-dance-event.nl), with 700 DJs and more than 80,000 avid

dancers attending parties all over the city – all on one long, sweaty weekend late in the month.

November

A handful of fun cultural events make up for the possible cold and rain, although November is less cold than you'd expect. You'll find cheaper off-season rates everywhere.

Sinterklaas Intocht

In mid-November every year, the Dutch Santa Claus arrives at a different port 'from Spain' with his staff and Black Peter helpers.

International Documentary Film Festival

Ten days in late November are dedicated to screening fascinating true stories (www.idfa.nl) from all over the world in Amsterdam.

Cannabis Cup

Hosted by High Times magazine, this far-out

Amsterdam festival (www.hightimes.com) doles out awards for the nicest grass, biggest reefer and best 'pot comedian'.

December

Holiday magic blankets the Netherlands, even if snow does not (although a few recent white Christmases have given parts of the nation much to cheer about).

Sinterklaas

On 5 December families exchange small gifts ahead of religious celebrations for Christmas.

New Year's Eve

In Amsterdam: fireworks displays over the Amstel and elsewhere around town (try Nieuwmarkt). Big stages on the Museumplein host live bands and plentiful beer tents for a giant party. Other cities have impromptu raucous celebrations on main squares.

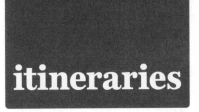

itineraries

Whether you've got six days or 60, these itineraries provide a starting point for the trip of a lifetime. Want more inspiration? Head online to lonelyplanet. com/thorntree to chat with other travellers.

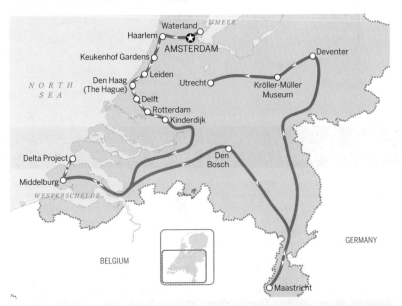

Three Weeks
Southern Sojourn

> Start in **Amsterdam**, stay three days, visit the city's big museums and relax in **Vondelpark**. Discover the **Jordaan** and the **Southern Canal Belt**, then take a load off in Hoppe, a grand cafe on the Spui. Plunge into the city's celebrated **nightlife**. Escape the city by bicycle to enjoy the classic beauty of the **Waterland** region.

Continue on as in the one-week tour to **Haarlem**, **Leiden** (and **Keukenhof Gardens**, in season), **Den Haag (The Hague)** and **Rotterdam**, but add a day for **Delft** and its Vermeer splendour. Take the ferry to see the windmills at **Kinderdijk**, then head for **Middelburg**, Zeeland's prosperous capital, and the nearby **Delta Project**. Take trains through the Netherlands' southern provinces, stopping for the hidden canals of lovely **Den Bosch**, before continuing to **Maastricht**, a city with more panache than most; two days should be enough to sample some great cuisine and meander through the medieval centre. Head north to visit Hanseatic **Deventer** and then head east to the excellent **Kröller-Müller Museum**. Polish off your trip in the cosmopolitan yet deeply historic city of **Utrecht**.

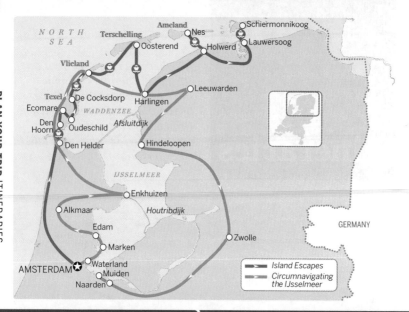

NORTH SEA

GERMANY

Island Escapes
Circumnavigating the IJsselmeer

Two Weeks
The IJsselmeer

A practical place to start this tour is **Amsterdam**; three days will whiz by in a blur of museums, parks, canal tours and nightlife. Head north along the IJsselmeer coast through the **Waterland region** to the tiny fishing village of **Marken**. Cycle the dykes to cute-as-a-button **Edam**. Stay overnight before reaching **Alkmaar** early to experience its kitsch but fun cheese market, then wander through **Enkhuizen's** enthralling **Zuiderzeemuseum**.

Next, catch a bus to **Den Helder**, and a ferry to **Texel**. Spend two days (or two weeks...) dividing your time between beach and bike exploration, then take another ferry to **Vlieland** to appreciate the wilder side of the Frisian Islands. From Vlieland, get a ferry to charming **Harlingen**, from where **Leeuwarden** is only a short train ride away. Friesland's capital is an entertaining place, as is the nearby chain of coastal towns highlighted by **Hindeloopen** on the IJsselmeer.

Break the train trip at Hanseatic **Zwolle** and add more stops in **Naarden** and **Muiden**, two historical fortress towns.

One to Two Weeks
Island Escapes

The necklace of low-lying Wadden Islands (Texel, Vlieland, Terschelling, Ameland and Schiermonnikoog) is recognised by Unesco and makes for good island-hopping. Some ferry links require advance planning; you might be able to link all five by boat but for most there will be connections via the mainland. From Amsterdam, head to **Texel**. Bike along the island's western coast from sleepy **Den Hoorn** through dark copses to the **Ecomare** seal and bird refuge. Comb the eastern side of the island, visiting the superb **Maritime & Beachcombers Museum** in **Oudeschild**.

From **De Cocksdorp** at the northern end of Texel, board the morning ferry to car-free **Vlieland** to explore its nature and hiking trails before catching the boat to **Terschelling**, Friesland's main tourist island. Hole up in peaceful **Oosterend** and cycle the untouched dunes, then hightail it by ferry to **Harlingen**, a pretty little port on the Frisian coast, and on to **Holwerd**, to ferry across to somnolent **Ameland**. Stay in the whaling port of **Nes**. Return via the ports of Holwerd and **Lauwersoog** and back on a ferry to **Schiermonnikoog**, the smallest of the Frisian Islands and featuring a windswept, evocative national park.

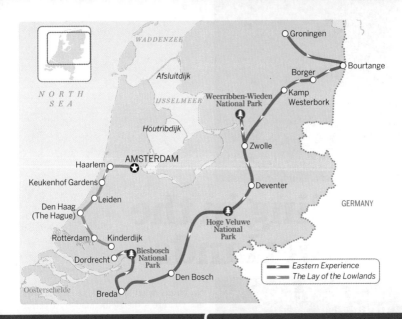

Legend:
- Eastern Experience
- The Lay of the Lowlands

One Week
Eastern Experience

The Netherlands' eastern expanse is largely ignored by tourists, but there is myriad highlights to discover.

Begin your trip in **Groningen**, a vibrant city filled with students, bars, cafes and a couple of fine museums. Cycle southeast to **Bourtange**, a perfectly preserved 17th-century fortified town, before moving on to **Borger** and its prehistoric **hunebedden**, stone arrangements once used as burial chambers. Cycle through the woods to **Kamp Westerbork** and encounter its moving, horrible heritage. Catch a train to **Zwolle**, an unhurried Hanseatic town that's ideal for backstreet meanders. A trip through nearby **Weerribben-Wieden National Park** should include renting a canoe.

From Zwolle it's only a short train ride to **Deventer**, one of the most appealing small towns in the Netherlands. Next, explore the **Hoge Veluwe National Park**, a natural oasis that's home to a renowned art museum. Then head for **Den Bosch**, which has a dynamite museum dedicated to its namesake artist. **Breda** is your next stop, where you can enjoy the city's cafe-filled centre. Go back to nature at **Biesbosch National Park** before finishing up on the lovely old streets and canals of **Dordrecht**.

One Week
The Lay of the Lowlands

Begin in **Amsterdam**. Visit the **Van Gogh Museum** and the **Rijksmuseum** and rent a bicycle to explore the pretty neighbourhood of **Jordaan**. On the second day board a **canal boat tour** and walk the **Red Light District** before hitting a brown cafe or coffeeshop. Or both.

Head west to the town of **Haarlem** – stroll the compact old quarter, and view the masterpieces at the **Frans Hals Museum** and the stained glass of the **Grote Kerk van St Bavo**. In tulip season (mid-March to mid-May) witness the unbelievable colours of the **Keukenhof Gardens**, north of Leiden. Then spend a day among **Leiden**'s old-world splendour. Next, take a day in **Den Haag (The Hague)**, being sure not to miss the **Mauritshuis** collection, with five-star works from everyone from Vermeer to Warhol.

In the remaining time take a harbour boat tour in **Rotterdam** and visit the **Museum Boijmans van Beuningen** and the **Maritiem Museum Rotterdam**. The next morning, do a walking tour of the city's **modern architecture** before departing for **Kinderdijk** and its gaggle of Unesco-recognised windmills.

Cycling in the Netherlands

Good Day Trips by Bike

Just a few of the many possible...

Amsterdam to Waterland Loop (37km loop) For more on this route see p29.

Amsterdam to Haarlem (50km to 70km return) A return trip to a great day-trip town that can include a side jaunt to the beach.

Den Haag to Gouda (70km to 80km return) A classic day trip through lush Dutch countryside to a cute little cheesy town.

Rotterdam to Kinderdijk (25km/50km one way/return) See the heritage-listed windmills. Ride one way and take a fast ferry back.

Dordrecht to Biesbosch National Park (25km to 50km return) A trip to a surprisingly natural park that is best appreciated by bike. Explore vast marshlands and see if you can spot a beaver.

No matter what shape you're in – or what age you are – the Netherlands is a perfect country to explore by *fiets* (bicycle). Even if it's only a day pedalling along Amsterdam's canals, or a couple of hours rolling through green *polder* (strips of farmland separated by canals) landscape, it's more than worth it, and you'll be rewarded with the sense of freedom (and fun) that only a bicycle can offer.

With more than 35,000km of dedicated *fietspaden* (bike paths), there's even more reason to hop on a bike and do as the locals do. And every local seems to be doing it; the Netherlands has more bicycles than its 16 million citizens. You'll see stockbrokers in tailored suits riding alongside pensioners and teenagers, and mutual tolerance prevails.

Major roads have separate bike lanes and, except for motorways, there's virtually nowhere bicycles can't go. That said, in places such as the Delta region and along the coast you'll often need a fair dose of stamina to combat the North Sea headwinds.

You can have a great holiday cycling in the Netherlands. Whether you spend an entire trip cycling around the country, or do a series of day trips, or even just the occasional jaunt, you'll find that riding a bike here can be the highlight of your trip. And there are many places where riding a bike is simply the only way to get around, such as the national parks, the coastal beaches and the Frisian Islands.

LF Routes

While the Netherlands is webbed with bike routes great and small, one series stands out as the motorway of cycling: the LF routes. Standing for *landelijke fietsroutes* (long-distance routes) but virtually always simply called LF, this growing network of routes criss-cross the country and (like motorways) are designed to get you from one locale to another. So far there are more than 25 routes comprising close to 7000km. All are well marked by distinctive green-and-white signs.

LF routes (also called 'national bike routes') mostly use existing bicycle lanes and rural roads, which often run beside dykes. A whole series of guidebooks has sprung up about them, including a range with one title for each route.

Important LF Routes

Among the nearly 30 routes are these:

» **LF1 North Sea** Following the coast of Holland from the Belgian border 280km north to Den Helder; it jogs inland briefly near Den Haag (The Hague) and Haarlem.

» **LF2 Cities Route** From the Belgian border (it starts in Brussels), this route runs via Dordrecht, Rotterdam and Gouda to Amsterdam.

» **LF3** A 500km marathon route that runs north from Maastricht through Nijmegen to Arnhem, then to Zwolle via Deventer and finally to Leeuwarden and the north coast.

» **LF4 Central Netherlands Route** Starts at the coast at Den Haag and runs 300km east through Utrecht and Arnhem to the German border.

» **LF7 Overland Route** Runs 350km northwest from Maastricht through Den Bosch, Utrecht and Amsterdam to Alkmaar.

Using This Book

In the Getting There & Away sections for cities, towns and attractions in this book, relevant cycling information is listed. This can include the following details:

» Whether the train station has a bike shop.

» Where to find useful independent bike shops.

» Which LF routes pass through or near the city.

» Cycling details and distances to nearby towns and attractions.

» Ideas for day trips.

Information

Cycling information is copious and widely available. Your biggest challenge will be limiting yourself.

Maps & Books

All tourist offices stock a huge range of maps and guidebooks for cycling. In addition they are adept at handling questions from cyclists about routes etc. The one exception is Amsterdam, where the sheer volume of tourists means that the tourist office doesn't have a lot of time. In the capital, head to one of the bookshops for your references. You can also purchase maps and books at ANWB (p302), the Dutch motor club's offices.

The best maps are found only in the Netherlands and not through international sources such as generic online bookshops.

The best overall maps are the widely available Falk/VVV *Fietskaart met Knooppuntennetwerk* (cycling network) maps, a series of 20 that blanket the country in 1:50,000 scale, and cost €8. The keys are in English and they are highly detailed and very easy to use. Every bike lane, path and other route is shown, along with distances.

Beyond these maps, there is a bewildering array of regional and specialist bike maps, some as detailed as 1:30,000. Many are only available at the local tourist offices of the region covered.

Websites

There are many online resources. Here are some excellent starting points (go to translate.google.com to instantly translate Dutch sites into English):

» **holland.cyclingaroundtheworld.nl** Superb English-language site with a vast amount of useful and inspiring information.

» **www.landelijkefietsroutes.nl** Dutch site that lists all the LF routes and gives basic details and an outline of each.

» **fiets.startpagina.nl** Dutch site that lists every conceivable website associated with cycling in the Netherlands.

Cycling & Smartphones

It's almost too easy: using your smartphone to navigate around the Netherlands by bike. You'll know where you are at any given time and you'll be able to make decisions about where to go next. Best of all, you can keep

» (above) Cyclists passing windmills at Zaanse Schans (p109)
» (left) Taking a break at Vondelpark, Amsterdam (p66)

BICYCLE ROAD RULES

Heavy road and bike traffic can be intimidating, but observe a few basics and soon you'll be freewheeling like a native:

» Watch for cars. Cyclists have the right of way, except when vehicles are entering from the right, although not all motorists respect this.

» Watch for pedestrians. Tourists wander in and out of bike paths with no idea they're in a dangerous spot.

» Use the bicycle lane on the road's right-hand side; white lines and bike symbols mark the spot.

» Cycle in the same direction as traffic, and adhere to all traffic lights and signs.

» Make sure you signal when turning by putting out your hand.

» By law, after dusk you need to use the lights on your bike (front and rear) and have reflectors on both wheels. If your bike does not have lights, you need to use clip-on lights, both front and rear.

» It's polite to give a quick ring of your bell as a warning. If someone's about to hit you, a good sharp yell is effective.

» Helmets are not required. Most Dutch don't use them, and they don't come standard with a rental.

track of distances using the route-planning features on the map apps to keep your ride manageable.

Google is now including a bike-specific route option on its map apps and website, although the data is not yet in-depth and it may suggest you use a bike lane along a road when a prettier option exists.

Planning

Experienced cyclists will know how far they are comfortable riding each day. In general, people used to being on their bikes say that 80km to 100km of riding each day is both comfortable and allows them plenty of time to stop and see the sights or, as is especially true in the Netherlands, smell the flowers.

If you have no idea how far you can or want to ride a day, then you need to find out! First-time tourers are often comfortable at 50km a day, which is easy in the Netherlands as you rarely even have to ride that far from one interesting town to the next. If you really have no idea what will work for you, then don't plunge in with an overly ambitious point-to-point itinerary. Rather, try a few circular day trips to start. The Waterland Route is 37km long and a perfect introduction to Dutch bike riding.

Clothing & Equipment

Wind and rain are all-too-familiar features of Dutch weather. A lightweight nylon jacket

will provide protection, and a breathable variety (Gore-Tex or the like) helps you stay cool and dry. The same thing applies to cycling trousers or shorts.

A standard touring bike is ideal for the Netherlands' flat arena, and for toting a tent and provisions. Gears are useful for riding against the wind, or for tackling a hilly route in Overijssel or Limburg – though the Alps it ain't. Other popular items include a frame bag (for a windcheater and lunch pack), water bottles and a handlebar map-holder so you'll always know where you're going. Very few locals wear a helmet, although they're sensible protection, especially for children.

Make sure your set of wheels has a bell: paths can get terribly crowded (at times with blasé pedestrians who don't move) and it becomes a pain if you have to ask to pass every time. Another necessity is a repair kit. Most rental shops will provide one on request.

Getting a Bike

Your choices are hiring a bike, buying a bike or using your own. Each has pros and cons.

Hire

Rental shops are available in abundance. Many day trippers avail themselves of the train-station bicycle shops, called **Rijwiel shops** (www.ov-fiets.nl), which are found in more than 100 train stations.

Operating long hours (6am to midnight is common), the shops hire out bikes from €3 to €12 per day with discounts by the week. Many have a selection of models. You'll have to show a passport or national ID card, and leave a cash or credit-card deposit (usually €25 or €100).

The shops also usually offer repairs, sell new bikes and have cheap secured bike parking.

Private shops charge similar rates but may be more flexible on the form of deposit. In summer it's advisable to reserve ahead, as shops regularly hire out their entire stock, especially on places such as the nearly car-free Frisian Islands where everybody arriving wants a bike.

You normally have to return your bike to the place you rented it. Given that distances are short, you can easily just hop on a train back to your starting point. Some Rijwiel shops do offer a one-way scheme to other shops for €10, so it is worth asking about.

Purchase

Your basic used bicycle (no gears, with coaster brakes, maybe a bit rickety) can be bought for around €75 from bicycle shops or the classified ads. Count on paying €100 or more for a reliable two-wheeler with gears. Stolen bikes are available on the street for as little as €15, but it's highly illegal and the cash usually goes straight into a junkie's arm. Good new models start at around €200 on sale, but top-of-the-line brands can cost €1000 or more. Bike shops are everywhere.

Your Own Bike

If you love your bike, it may be the ideal mechanical companion for your trip. But there are drawbacks. First, there's the hassle of getting your bike to the Netherlands. What do you need to take into consideration when flying with your bike or riding in over the border, or if you come from the UK on a ferry? Flying policies vary by airline, there's nothing to consider crossing the invisible border from Belgium and Germany, and ferries usually only have a small bicycle surcharge.

More importantly, the odds of your bike being stolen in Amsterdam, and to a lesser extent Rotterdam, are high.

On the Train

You may bring your bicycle onto any train as long as there is room; a day pass for bikes (*dagkaart fiets; €6*) is valid in the entire country regardless of the distance involved. There are no fees for collapsible bikes so long as they can be considered hand luggage.

Dutch trains often have special carriages for loading two-wheelers – look for the bicycle logos on the side of the carriage. Bicycles are prohibited on trains during the weekday rush hours (6.30am to 9am and 4.30pm to 6pm), except for the Hoek van Holland boat train. There are no restrictions on holidays, at weekends or during July and August.

Security

» Be sure you have one or two good locks. Hardened chain-link or T-hoop varieties are best for attaching the frame and front wheel to something solid.

» Even the toughest lock won't stop a determined thief, so if you have an expensive model it's probably safer to buy or hire a bike locally.

» Many train-station bike-hire shops also run *fietsenstallingen,* secure storage areas where you can leave your bike cheaply (under €2 per day).

THREE LONG-DISTANCE FAVES

Each of these can be done in a week by a rider of average ability, and you'll still have lots of time to stop off and see things along the way. Add more time to turn them into longer, circle routes, or do your return journey by train. Another option is to avoid the surrounding Amsterdam hassle, take the train to the first town and pick up your bike there.

» **Old Holland** Amsterdam–Haarlem–Leiden–the coast/tulips–Den Haag–Delft–Dordrecht.

» **North Holland** Amsterdam–Waterland–Marken–Edam–Enkhuizen–Alkmaar–the coast–Den Helder–Texel.

» **Classic Holland** Amsterdam–Muiden–Utrecht–Amersfoort–Hoge Veluwe National Park–Arnhem–Deventer–Zwolle.

Waterland Route

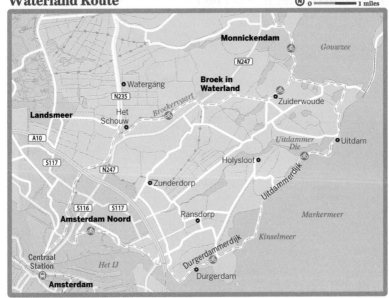

Map legend:

Monnickendam · Gouwzee · N247 · Watergang · Broek in Waterland · N235 · Zuiderwoude · Landsmeer · Het Schouw · Broekervaart · Uitdammer Die · Uitdam · A10 · Holysloot · S117 · N247 · Uitdammerdijk · Zunderdorp · S116 · S117 · Ransdorp · Markermeer · Amsterdam Noord · Kinselmeer · Durgerdammerdijk · Centraal Station · Het IJ · Durgerdam · Amsterdam

» Some places have bicycle 'lockers' that can be accessed electronically.

» Don't ever leave your bike unlocked, even for an instant. Secondhand bikes are a lucrative trade, and hundreds of thousands are stolen in the Netherlands each year. Even if you report the theft to the police, chances of recovery are virtually nil.

Tours

Amsterdam has several companies offering bike tours of the city. There are multiday trips around the country and many bike-touring operators.

Accommodation

Apart from the recommended camping grounds, there are plenty of nature camp sites along bike paths, often adjoined to a local farm. They tend to be smaller, simpler and cheaper than the regular camping grounds, and many don't allow cars or caravans. The **Stichting Natuurkampeerterreinen** (Nature Campsites Foundation; www.natuurkampeerterreinen.nl) has more than 130 locations throughout the Netherlands.

You may also wish to try *trekkershutten*, basic hikers' huts available at many camping grounds.

Many hostels, B&Bs and hotels throughout the country are well geared to cyclists' needs; often those on some of the more popular cycle routes, particularly along the coastline, market directly to tourists on two wheels. As always, tourist information offices can help here.

Routes

To give you an idea of what's possible, here are some of our favourite cycling routes.

Amsterdam to Waterland Loop (37km, 3½ to five hours)

This is an excellent start to your Dutch cycling experience: pretty scenery, cute towns and easy riding on good bike lanes and roads.

The eastern half of **Waterland** (p109) is culture-shock material: 20 minutes from central Amsterdam you step centuries back in time. This is an area of isolated farming communities and flocks of birds amid ditches, dykes and lakes.

It takes a few minutes to get out of town.

» First, take your bike onto the free Buiksloterwegveer ferry behind Amsterdam's Centraal Station across the IJ River.

Leiden to the Bulbfields Loop

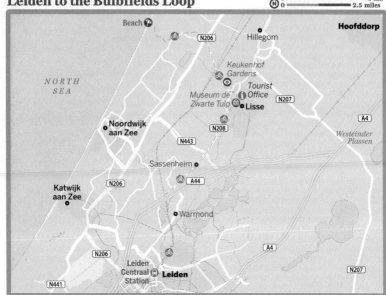

» Continue 1km along the west bank of the Noordhollands Kanaal. Cross the second bridge, continue along the east bank for a few hundred metres and turn right, under the freeway and along Nieuwendammerdijk past Vliegenbos camping ground.

» At the end of Nieuwendammerdijk, do a dogleg and continue along Schellingwouderdijk. Follow this under the two major road bridges, until it becomes Durgerdammerdijk, and you're on your way.

» The pretty town of **Durgerdam** looks out across the water to **IJburg**, a major land-reclamation project that will eventually house 45,000 people.

» Further north, the dyke road passes several lakes and former sea inlets – low-lying, drained peatlands that were flooded during storms and now form important bird-breeding areas. Colonies include plovers, godwits, bitterns, golden-eyes, snipes, herons and spoonbills. Climb the dyke at one of the viewing points for uninterrupted views to both sides.

» The road – now called Uitdammerdijk – passes the town of **Uitdam**, after which you turn left (west) towards **Monnickendam** (p110).

» Alternatively, you could turn right and proceed along the causeway to the former island of **Marken** (p111). After visiting Marken, you could take the summer ferry to **Volendam** (p112) and backtrack along the sea dyke to Monnickendam.

Or you could return over the causeway from Marken and pick up our tour again towards Monnickendam. These diversions to Marken and (especially) Volendam would add significantly to the length of your trip (55km, seven to 10 hours).

» From Monnickendam, return the way you came (if you came by the first route, not by one of the Marken diversions), but about 1.5km south of town turn right (southwest) towards **Zuiderwoude**. From there, continue to **Broek in Waterland** (p110), a pretty town with old wooden houses.

» Cycle along the south bank of the Broekervaart canal towards **Het Schouw** on the Noordhollands Kanaal. Cross the Noordhollands Kanaal (the bridge is slightly to the north); bird-watchers may want to head up the west bank towards Watergang and its bird-breeding areas.

» Follow the west bank back down to Amsterdam-Noord. From here it's straight cycling all the way to the ferry to Centraal Station.

Leiden to the Bulbfields Loop (50km to 60km, four to seven hours)

On this trip, you'll explore the heart of the world-famous bulbfields of Holland. The best time to do it is mid-March to mid-May when the tulips and daffodils are at their peak and the ribbons of bold colours are astounding. But it's a lovely ride at any time; it includes a stop at the beach so it's especially good in the summer if you want to take a break on the sand and a refreshing dip in the sea.

» Start in **Leiden**, where you can rent a bike at the train station or from one of the vendors in town.

» Head north from the station following bike lanes and paths along the east side of the train tracks. Stay with the tracks as they curve north. After crossing several bridges (about 3km), you'll see a fair bit of water and the village of **Warmond** to your right.

» Stay with the rail path *(spoorpad)* and cross under the A44. You'll be at the Rijksstraatweg. Turn right (northeast) and follow the road for 4km as it changes names to Hoofdstraat and reaches the pretty little village **Sassenheim**. You'll start to see tulips and the bulbfields. Stay on the little road as it passes the churches and you come to the busy N443.

» Cross the N443 and stay on the good bike paths along Heereweg for almost 4km to the middle of the village of **Lisse** (p153). Here you can pause at the tourist office for more detailed bulbfield bike info and you can visit the Museum de Zwarte Tulp, which has lots of interesting bulb stories.

» From Lisse, **Keukenhof Gardens** (p156) is just 1.25km west.

» After you've visited the gardens, head west 7.5km to the beach. Start on Delftweg amid bulbfields and stay on the bike lanes as the road crosses N206 (Oosterduinen). Here the bike route separates from the road. Stay with the bike route through the ever-more sandy landscape.

» The route will curve south and at Langevelderslag take the parallel path through the dunes. When you cross national bike route LF1, you're at the **beach**.

» Try some DIY routing to return. Once past the dunes, take little lanes through the bulbfields that take you due south towards Leiden. You'll be dazzled by the colours if it is spring. Eventually you'll run into some section of your initial route. Then simply retrace your course back to the train station.

PLAN YOUR TRIP CYCLING IN THE NETHERLANDS

Travel with Children

Best Regions for Kids

Amsterdam One of Europe's most kid-friendly cities, with an atmosphere that's cheerfully accommodating to children. In fact, most areas – except the Red Light District, of course – are fair game.

Haarlem & North Holland Cute old towns, lots of cows, some fun museums and the island of Texel, a huge sandy playground.

Utrecht Cool canals to explore and castles to bike to.

Rotterdam & South Holland The neatest old Dutch cities, a fun amusement park in Den Haag, cool things to do in Rotterdam, windmills and beaches in Zeeland.

Friesland More cows and sandy islands.

Northeast Netherlands Ancient stones and parks.

Central Netherlands Fun little towns and parks.

Maastricht & Southeast Netherlands The country's best amusement park.

The Dutch love kids and their beloved statistics show this: the Netherlands has one of the highest reproduction rates in Western Europe. It's a kid-friendly country where there's consideration and – yes – tolerance of people of all ages. Plus it's just a fun place. Read on.

The Netherlands for Kids

The Dutch have a country well suited for kids. The needs of younger people have been thought of at every turn.

Accommodation

Very few hotels have a 'no kids' rule; those that do are mostly in areas of Amsterdam that you wouldn't take kids anyway. Family rooms sleeping four are common. Upscale hotels often offer child-minding services.

Eating Out

Children are welcome in all but the most formal restaurants. In fact, the trend towards stylish bistro-style eateries with high ceilings and a slightly raucous atmosphere are all the better for little ones, who may enjoy a dish of raucousness with their meal. Everyone is pretty tolerant of any antics children may get up to when dining out. You'll see Dutch families enjoying meals inside and out at cafes, pubs and restaurants, as well as sitting on benches sharing a quick repast from a fish stall or *frites* (French fries) joint.

Kids menus are common and tend to have the deep-fried treats that always go down well. You can also reasonably ask for high chairs and even crayons in many restaurants.

Child-Friendly Facilities

Facilities for changing nappies are limited to the big department stores, major museums and train stations, and you'll pay to use them. Breastfeeding is generally OK in public if done discreetly.

On the Road

Most bike rental shops have kid-sized bikes for rent but few offer helmets (for any age); bike helmet use among the Dutch is very limited.

Trains have 'silent' cars where people can escape noise. In contrast the other cars can be that much more noisy.

Bargain-Hunting

Family tickets for attractions are common and can yield huge savings. Most museums have children's entrance rates which are 50% of adult prices. Even as government budget cuts have caused some admission fees to soar, many major museums are sticking to free admission for kids.

Children's Highlights
Outdoor Fun

Green spaces, parks, windmills and canals galore add up to plenty of fresh-air fun with the little (and not so little) ones. During winter kids will dig the skating rinks and outdoor merriment at the carnivals that spring up in many Dutch cities and towns.

» **Vondelpark, Amsterdam** This vast play space, replete with leafy picnic spots and duck ponds, has cool space-age slides at its western end and a playground in the middle.

» **Westerpark, Amsterdam** A great playground with wooden drawbridges.

» **Amsterdamse Bos** Tykes can feed goats and climb trees in the woods.

» **Keukenhof Gardens, Rotterdam** The millions of flowers might delight kids for a while but they'll really love the huge playground.

» **Canal Bike, Amsterdam** Take a unique pedal-powered ride through Amsterdam's beautiful canals.

» **Canals, Den Bosch** Most canal towns have canal boat tours which last a not-too-long hour

and offer lots of fun views. The ones in Den Bosch go through big underground canals. Neat!

» **Artis Royal Zoo, Amsterdam** The extrovert monkeys, big cats, shimmying fish and planetarium will keep young eyes shining for hours; teenagers and adults will love the beautifully landscaped historical grounds.

» **Ecomare, Texel** A nature centre with all sorts of animals from the islands, including injured seals recuperating, and lots of exhibits designed for kids.

» **Kinderdijk** Nineteen windmills in a pretty setting near Rotterdam; the whole family can rent bikes and explore.

» **Zaanse Schans** At these windmills north of Haarlem you can go inside to see all the wild gears, pulleys and more.

Sand & Surf

» **Beaches** Texel and the other Frisian Islands have excellent beaches for kids. Much of the west coast is a long beach; Scheveningen near Den Haag is well suited for families.

» **Surfing** Learn to surf on Texel, which has many other activities – such as horse rides – aimed at kids.

» **Mudflats** North of Groningen, you can spend a day playing out on the mud. *Wadlopen* (mudflat-walking) lets you head out to sea when the vast tidal areas are clear of water at low tide. It's hours of muddy enjoyment, and you're expected to get dirty.

Kid Cuisine

Pancakes, *frites,* cheese, ice cream. Even non-kids love fun Dutch food. Every city and town has at least one weekly outdoor market where there are often stalls selling all sorts of tasty items; don't miss the unique holiday treats, like *poffertjes* (tiny Dutch pancakes), that are served up in winter.

» **Pancakes!, Amsterdam** The capital is full of eateries serving this kid-pleasing delight.

» **De Pannenkoekenboot, Rotterdam** Eat pancakes sailing aboard a boat.

» **Albert Cuypmarkt, Amsterdam** For *stroopwafel* (syrup waffle), fruit smoothies, outlandishly topped waffles, chocolate, candy and fresh fruit.

» **Vleminckx, Amsterdam** This hole-in-the-wall is an old *frites* standby; part of the fun is deciding between dozens of sauces.

» **Reitz, Maastricht** A favourite for *frites*.

» **De Haerlemsche Vlaamse, Haarlem** Local *frites* institution; has a goofy stall with lots of clever sayings on the walls.

» **Ijs van Co, Hoge Veluwe National Park** Sure, the parents want to see the Van Goghs at the Kröller-Müller Museum, but there is also a huge lure near the Hoenderloo entrance to the national park – a simple storefront with the best soft ice cream in the country.

» **Talamini, Deventer** Over 50 varieties of ice cream made in the huge shop and sold year-round.

» **Ijssalon W Laan, Alkmaar** Watch the ice cream being made in enormous old machines.

Kid- & Teen-Friendly Museums

While dragging museum-resistant kids through an exhibit on the notoriously sombre paintings of the Dutch Masters might give any parent nightmares, there are plenty of museums that are accessible, educational and fun.

» **NEMO, Amsterdam** Tailor-made, kid-focused, hands-on science labs inside; an artificial beach with sand and ice-cream stands on the roof outside.

» **Tropenmuseum, Amsterdam** The children's section devoted to exotic locations is a hit in any language. Spend the afternoon learning to yodel, sitting in a yurt or travelling via otherworldly exhibits.

» **Het Scheepvaartmuseum, Amsterdam** Climb aboard the full-scale, 17th-century replica ship and check out the cannons.

» **TunFun, Amsterdam** Build, climb, jump, draw and more at this indoor playground; a great rainy-day option.

» **Rijksmuseum, Amsterdam** Lest the kids be left out of the masterpieces, children get their own audiotour to explore the museum's treasures.

» **Zuiderzeemuseum, Enkuizen** Has enough old stuff kids can play with to keep them amused for hours, and there's a cool playground right out the front.

» **Maastricht Underground** Explore 2000-year-old tunnels and caves underground. It's spooky and very cool – literally.

» **Maritiem Museum Rotterdam** More ship models than a hundred bathtubs could hold.

» **Dick Bruna House, Utrecht** Miffy is one of the most beloved cartoon characters in the Netherlands and you can see a lot of her and other characters at a museum dedicated to their creator Dick Bruna.

» **Dutch Railway Museum, Utrecht** Trains in all shapes and sizes.

Amusement Parks

The ultimate kid attraction.

» **Efteling, Kaatsheuvel** This is the most popular amusement park in the Netherlands and it seems every Dutch person of any age has memories of the fun they've had here. Thrill rides, cartoon characters and more. It's in the south near Breda.

» **Madurodam, Den Haag** See Holland in miniature outdoors at Madurodam; it's what a kid would build with unlimited time and cash.

» **Miniworld Rotterdam** See Holland in miniature indoors at Miniworld; a huge model train layout duplicates much of the country.

» **Euromast, Rotterdam** See all of Rotterdam from this observation deck filled with features aimed to thrill and delight kids.

» **Waterland Neeltje Jans, Zeeland** Amid the amazing and vast Delta Project, tells the story of how the Dutch have battled the sea, with exhibits aimed at kids. Plus there are seals, a water park and rides.

Junior Entertainment

» **Amsterdams Marionetten Theater** Puts on captivating shows such as Mozart's *The Magic Flute*.

» **Openluchttheater, Amsterdam** A free theatre in Vondelpark hosting musicians, acrobats, storytellers and more most Saturdays afternoons in summer.

regions at a glance

Amsterdam

Museums ✓✓✓
Canals ✓✓✓
Entertainment ✓✓✓

Museum Mania

Amsterdam's world-class museums draw millions of visitors each year. The art collections take pride of place – you can't walk a kilometre without bumping into a masterpiece by Van Gogh, Rembrandt or Mondrian. The Anne Frank Huis leaves an indelible impression with its claustrophobic rooms, their windows still covered with blackout screens. And a fine assortment of oddball museums educates on everything from tattoos to handbags to houseboats.

Golden Age Beauty

Amsterdam's remarkably preserved core enchants. The gabled homes look much as they did during the 17th century. Boats travel the same canals as they did 400 years ago. Brown cafes that poured drinks for Rembrandt's peers fill glasses for visitors today. The tower where Henry Hudson launched from still rises on the waterfront. Wherever you go, the aura of centuries past is never far away.

Wildly Entertaining

Little jazz cafes abound and you could easily see a live combo – from far-out improv to more traditional notes – every night of the week. The dance music scene thrives, with big-name DJs spinning at clubs around town. Amsterdam's packed classical venues put on a full slate of shows. Then there are the less savoury diversions: coffeeshops dispensing weed, magic truffles for tripping, and ladies selling sex from red-lit windows.

p40

Haarlem & North Holland

Old Towns ✓✓
Nature ✓✓
Adventure ✓✓

Cute Towns

Haarlem is like a little old Amsterdam and you can feel the middle ages and the Golden Age as you walk its compact centre. Smaller (and cuter) still are the enticing Edam, Marken, Alkmaar and more. You half expect to see an old merchant's ship sail into Hoorn's harbour.

Birds & Seals

Texel, the large Waddenzee island just off the coast of north Holland, is ringed by beaches and dunes. Birds of all feathers nest here; out on the water you'll find colonies of seals.

Blowing with the Wind

You can surf, hike, bike, sail a boat and more in the waters off Texel. On land, the cycling across the dykes and virescent countryside make for great days exploring.

p101

Utrecht

Old Towns ✓✓✓
Sights ✓
Day Trips ✓

Fine Old City

Now that it's fixing (at a cost of zillions) its unfortunate unwelcome into the city from the train station, Utrecht city stands ready to shine. Its canals are uniquely two-level, which only add to the interest as you wander the enticing old quarters.

Old & New

Utrecht city's sights include the Domtoren, a soaring surviving church tower with sweeping views. It's main museum includes a side trip to the a world-renowned Rietveld-Schröder House. Many other museums large and small provide diversions rain or shine.

Out & About

Holland's most famous painters didn't all die before the 20th century: Amersfoort was home to Piet Mondrian, the famous 20th-century artist. Visit his home, and consider side-trips to country castles and the bewitching town of Oudewater.

p135

Rotterdam & South Holland

Dutchiness ✓✓✓
Beauty ✓✓✓
Cycling ✓✓✓

Heart of Holland

Leiden symbolises a cute Dutch city, with its gently flowing canals and beautiful old buildings. Stately Den Haag symbolises the Dutch commitment to tolerance with the UN's International Court of Justice, where the intolerant are brought to trial. While Rotterdam, a stunning modern city, symbolises a bold future, not beholden to the past.

Feast for the Eyes

Strolling the canals of Delft on the same streets, that Vermeer once roamed, you can't help but be transfixed by the beauty of it all. And wait until you see the bulb-fields in spring.

Myriad Destinations

From Rotterdam it's a fun ride to Kinderdijk, the Unesco-recognised string of windmills. Or you can ride to quaint Gouda or the sandy seashore of Zeeland or...

p146

Friesland (Fryslân)

Islands ✓✓✓
Towns ✓
Adventure ✓✓

A String of Pearls

Since 2009, the Frisian Islands off the north coast of the Netherlands have been part of Unesco's recognition of the rich Waddensee environment. These mounds of sand and trees are popular for holidays if only because even on days when the ferries from the mainland all arrive full, there are still endless expanses of empty beach.

Old Dutch Towns

Calling Harlingen a ferry port is a disservice given how those places are so often dreadful. Instead it's a fascinating historic town. Leeuwarden also charms and has a stunner of a new museum, while Hindeloopen is a gem of an old fishing village.

Boats & Bikes

The Frisian Islands define outdoor fun and you can island-hop by boat while exploring by bike. In Sneek you can rent a boat and explore.

p193

Northeast Netherlands

History ✓✓✓
Parks ✓
Nightlife ✓

A Good & Bad Past
Some of the oldest finds in the Netherlands are in its far northeast corner: *Hunebedden* (old burial sites) date back 5000 years. The preserved fortress town of Bourtange is a 16th-century time capsule while Groningen still has echoes of the Golden Age. Much more recent and far more terrible, Kamp Westerbork was used by the Nazis for deporting Jews and others.

Green Lands
The region boasts national parks that preserve the ancient past like the *hunebedden* and the verdant lands of today. Explore old farms, forests and heaths on oodles of biking and hiking trails.

Party On
The ancient university town of Groningen has 20,000 students who ensure there is never a dull moment.

p207

Central Netherlands

Old Towns ✓✓
Outdoors ✓
History ✓✓

Primly Ancient
One of the unexpected pleasures of the Netherlands is randomly walking the back streets of Deventer and making your own discoveries. Old brick buildings unchanged since this was a Hanseatic trading city delight with carved stone details. Nearby Zwolle offers the same, as does compact little Kampen.

Land & Water
Water courses throughout the centre of the Netherlands. In fascinating Weertribben-Wieden National Park you follow canals and channels dug over the centuries by peat harvesters and farmers. Nearby, you can enjoy the canal-laced rural idyll of Giethoorn.

Past Glories & Horrors
Deventer, Zwolle and Kampen show the region's wealth centuries ago. In and around Nijmegen and Arnhem, monuments and museums recall the fierce battles of WWII and their awful aftermath.

p219

Maastricht & Southeast Netherlands

History ✓✓
Art ✓✓
Food & Drink ✓✓

Back to the Romans
Maastricht might as well be built on an old piece of gouda cheese. The land beneath it is a honeycomb of tunnels and underground forts dating back through centuries of wars and occupiers to Roman times. Above ground, almost every era since is represented by a landmark or building in its compact and beautiful centre.

Art, Observed
Hieronymus Bosch was a sharp observer of human frailties and his intricate paintings still ring true today. In his namesake city Den Bosch, you can learn about this genius. Maastricht is home to the world's largest annual sales fair of old art and its museums are artful pleasures.

I'll Have Another
Cafe culture is alive and thriving in Maastricht, Den Bosch and Breda. Pull up a chair and enjoy.

p236

> Every listing is recommended by our authors, and their favourite places are listed first

> Look out for these icons:

 Our author's top recommendation

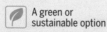 A green or sustainable option

 No payment required

See the Index for a full list of destinations covered in this book.

On the Road

Amsterdam

🎵020 / POP 780,600

Best Places to Eat

» Piet de Leeuw (p84)
» Gartine (p81)
» Latei (p82)
» De Kas (p87)
» Van Dobben (p84)

Best Places to Stay

» Cocomama (p77)
» Collector (p79)
» Backstage Hotel (p77)
» Hotel Résidence Le Coin (p73)
» Hotel Brouwer (p73)

Why Go?

Amsterdam works its fairy-tale magic in many ways: via the gabled Golden Age buildings, the glinting boat-filled canals, and especially the cosy, centuries-old brown cafes, where candles burn low and beers froth high. Art admirers will be hard-pressed to ogle a more masterpiece-packed city, thanks to rich collections at the Rijks, Van Gogh, Stedelijk and Hermitage museums. Music fans can tune into concert halls booked solid with entertainment from all over the globe. And hedonists? Amsterdam's risqué side beckons, from the women in the Red Light District windows to the cannabis-selling coffeeshops (though these pursuits are facing more and more restrictions).

The city is remarkably intimate and accessible, its compact core ripe for rambling. You never know what you'll find among the atmospheric lanes: a hidden garden, an antique book market, a 17th-century distillery – always worlds within worlds, where nothing ever seems the same twice.

When to Go

Summer is the peak time, when cafe terraces boom and festivals rock almost every weekend. Locals go on holiday in late July and August, so you might find your favourite restaurant closed. Visitor numbers start to taper in October, and by November off-peak rates begin in earnest. Ice skating, fireplace-warmed cafes and queue-less museums ease the chilly days from December through February. Crowds start coming back in March around Easter, and amass in full force around King's Day (27 April), Remembrance Day (May 4) and Liberation Day (May 5).

History

Around 1200, a fishing community known as Aemstelredamme – 'the dam across the Amstel river' – emerged at what is now Dam square. The town soon grew into a centre for sea trade. Unfettered by high taxes and medieval feudal structures, a society of individualism and capitalism took root. The modern idea of Amsterdam – free, open, progressive – was born.

The city flourished during the 17th century Golden Age. Merchants and artisans flocked in, Rembrandt painted, and city planners built the canals. By the next century though, international wars and trade competition stagnated the local economy.

In 1806 Napoleon's brother Louis became king of Holland. He eventually moved into the city hall on Dam square and transformed it into the Royal Palace. Infrastructure projects such as Centraal Station, the Rijksmuseum and harbour expansion followed later in the 19th century.

WWI and the Great Depression took their toll in the form of food shortages and increasing poverty. WWII brought hardship, hunger and devastation to the local Jewish community during the Nazi occupation. Only one in every 16 of Amsterdam's 90,000 Jews survived the war.

During the 1960s, Amsterdam became Europe's 'Magic Centre': hippies smoked dope on the Dam and camped in Vondelpark. In 1972 the first coffeeshop opened, and in 1976 marijuana was decriminalised to free up police resources for combating hard drugs.

By the 1990s the city's economy had shifted to white-collar jobs and a thriving service industry, while gentrification increased. The ethnic make-up had changed too, with non-Dutch nationalities (particularly Moroccans, Surinamese and Turks) comprising more than 45% of the population.

Two high-profile murders and protests over immigration marked the first years of the 21st century. Recently Amsterdammers have turned their attention to a new metro line, massive artificial suburban islands and other grand urban projects. The Red Light District clean-up and coffeeshop closures also occupy local politics.

◉ Sights

Amsterdam is compact and easy to roam on foot. Hop on the occasional tram if you need a rest. The major sights are clustered in the city centre or within a few kilometres, such as the Old South's art museums (3km from Centraal Station).

For more in-depth explorations, pick up Lonely Planet's *Amsterdam* city guide or *Pocket Amsterdam* guide.

MEDIEVAL CENTRE

Amsterdam's heart beats in its tourist-heavy medieval core. The Royal Palace rises up here, but the main thing to do is wander the twisting lanes past 17th-century pubs, hidden gardens and eye-popping speciality

AMSTERDAM IN...

Two Days

On day one, goggle at the masterpieces in the **Van Gogh Museum** and **Rijksmuseum**, side by side in the Old South. Spend the afternoon in the city centre getting a dose of Dutch history at the **Dam**, **Amsterdam Museum**, **Begijnhof** or **Royal Palace**. At night venture into the eye-popping **Red Light District**, then sip in a brown cafe like **In 't Aepjen**. Start the next day browsing the **Albert Cuypmarkt**, Amsterdam's largest street bazaar. Make your way over to the Southern Canal Belt and peek in **Museum Van Loon**, the **Kattenkabinet** or another opulent canal house before taking a **canal boat tour**. At night party at hyperactive, neon-lit **Leidseplein**. Check at the **Uitburo** for concerts or show tickets; **Paradiso** and **Melkweg** host the coolest agendas.

Four Days

On day three head to the Western Canals and immerse yourself in the **Negen Straatjes**, a tic-tac-toe board of oddball speciality shops. The haunting **Anne Frank Huis** is nearby, and is a must. Spend the evening in the **Jordaan** for a *gezellig* dinner and canalside drinks. Begin the following day at **Museum het Rembrandthuis**, then mosey over to the Plantage for the **Amsterdam Tattoo Museum** and **Brouwerij 't IJ**, an organic beermaker at the foot of a windmill.

Amsterdam Highlights

1 Admire the vivid swirls of a tortured genius at the **Van Gogh Museum** (p65)

2 Experience a young girl's hidden life at **Anne Frank Huis** (p55)

3 Visit the Golden Age painter's inner sanctum at **Museum het Rembrandthuis** (p50)

4 Feel *gezelligheid* (a cosy sense of wellbeing) in the lanes and cafes of the **Jordaan** (p53)

5 Trawl the exotic goods at **Albert Cuypmarkt** (p66), Amsterdam's largest street market

6 Plunge into the revamped **Rijksmuseum** (p65) and its trove of Vermeers, Rembrandts and other national riches

7 Wander the **Red Light District** (p48), a contradiction of charming cafes and near-naked women in windows

8 Kick back amid the ponds, lawns, thickets and paths of **Vondelpark** (p66)

9 Sip killer microbrews under an 18th-century windmill at **Brouwerij 't IJ** (p92)

shops. Centraal Station is the main landmark. Damrak, the core's main thoroughfare, slices south from the station to the Dam (Amsterdam's central square). The road then becomes Rokin (in the throes of metro construction) as it continues south.

Royal Palace
PALACE

(Koninklijk Paleis; Map p46; ☏620 40 60; www.paleisamsterdam.nl; Dam; adult/child €7.50/3.75; ☷11am-5pm daily Jul & Aug, noon-5pm Tue-Sun Sep-Jun) Built in 1665, the imposing structure initially served as Amsterdam's grand city hall. It became a palace in 1808 when King Louis, Napoleon Bonaparte's brother, ruled the land. DIY tours take in Louis' 1000 pieces of Empire-style furniture and decorative artworks, plus roomfuls of chandeliers, damasks and paintings by Ferdinand Bol and Jacob de Wit. While the palace is the official residence of the monarch, the property is primarily used only for ceremonies. Check the website for periodic closures. Free audiotours are sometimes available at the front desk.

Amsterdam Museum
MUSEUM

(Map p46; ☏523 18 22; www.amsterdammuseum.nl; Kalverstraat 92; adult/child €10/5; ☷10am-5pm; ☐1/2/5 Spui) The city's history museum keeps getting spiffier, thanks to ongoing renovations. Start with the multimedia DNA exhibit, which breaks down Amsterdam's 1000-year history into seven whiz-bang time periods. Afterward, plunge into the lower floors to see troves of religious artefacts, porcelains and paintings. Bonus points for finding Rembrandt's macabre *Anatomy Lesson of Dr Deijman*. Bring your smartphone to scan exhibit barcodes for extra features.

FREE Civic Guard Gallery
GALLERY

(Map p46; Kalverstraat 92; ☷10am-5pm; ☐1/2/5 Spui) This cool gallery is part of the Amsterdam Museum – consider it the free 'appetiser' – and fills an alleyway next to the museum's entrance. It displays grand posed group portraits, from medieval guards painted during the Dutch Golden Age (à la Rembrandt's *The Night Watch*) to *Modern Civic Guards*, a rendering of Anne Frank, Alfred Heineken and a joint-smoking Personification of Amsterdam.

FREE Begijnhof
HISTORIC BUILDINGS

(Map p46; ☏622 19 18; www.begijnhofamsterdam.nl; main entrance off Gedempte Begijnensloot; ☷8am-5pm; ☐1/2/5 Spui) This veiled courtyard of tiny houses and gardens was built in the 14th century for the Beguines, a lay Catholic order of unmarried or widowed women

---

WORTH A TRIP

NDSM-WERF & EYE FILM INSTITUTE

Free ferries depart behind Centraal Station and glide across the IJ to two avant-garde destinations in Amsterdam-Noord.

NDSM-werf (www.ndsm.nl) is a derelict shipyard turned edgy arts community 15 minutes upriver. It wafts a post-apocalyptic vibe: an old submarine slumps in the harbour, abandoned trams rust by the water's edge, graffiti artists roam the streets and a giant wooden tiki head watches over it all. Besides the thundering skateboard hall (www.skateparkamsterdam.com; admission €5.50, rentals €5; ☷3-10pm Tue-Fri, 1-8pm Sat & Sun) and groovy Cafe Noorderlicht (www.noorderlichtcafe.nl; TT Neveritaweg 33; ☷11am-late), set in a flag-draped greenhouse, the main thing to do is wander around and ogle the recycled-junk street art. The whopping IJ Hallen (www.ij-hallen.nl; admission €4; ☷9am-4.30pm) flea market provides a bonus for visitors who coincide with its one-weekend-per-month spread; check the website for the schedule. The NDSM ferry runs between 7am (9am on weekends) and midnight, departing Centraal Station at 15 minutes and 45 minutes past the hour.

The gleaming new EYE Film Institute (☏589 14 00; www.eyefilm.nl; IJpromenade 1; ☷10am-6pm) is a five-minute ride from the train station, accessed via the 'Buiksloterweg' ferry. Movies (mostly art house) from the 37,000-title archive screen in four theatres, sometimes with live music. Exhibits (admission €8 to €12) of costumes, digital art and other cinephile amusements run in conjunction with what's playing. View-tastic cafes and free Dutch film displays in the basement add to the hep-cat feel. The ferry runs continuously, 24 hours a day. One quirk to keep in mind: EYE does not accept cash; you must use a credit or debit card to pay for anything there.

who cared for the elderly. Two churches hide here: a 'clandestine' chapel (1671), where the Beguines worshiped in secret from the Calvinists; and the English Church (circa 1392), where English and Scottish Presbyterian refugees (including the Pilgrim Fathers) congregated. Both churches are usually open for browsing. The wooden house at No 34 (circa 1465) is the Netherlands' oldest.

Dam
SQUARE

(Map p46; 🚊4/9/16/24/25 Dam) The square is the very spot where Amsterdam was founded around 1270. Today pigeons, tourists, buskers and the occasional Ferriswheel-dotted fair take over the grounds. It's still a national gathering spot, and if there's a major speech or demonstration, it's held here.

Nationaal Monument
MONUMENT

(Map p46; Dam) The obelisk on the Dam's east side was built in 1956 to commemorate WWII's fallen. The 12 urns at the rear hold earth from war cemeteries of the 11 provinces and the Dutch East Indies.

Nieuwe Kerk
CHURCH

(New Church; Map p46; ☑638 69 09; www.nieuwekerk.nl; Dam; adult/child €8/free; ⊙10am-5pm; 🚊1/2/5/13/14/17 Raadhuisstraat) The Nieuwe Kerk (dating from 1408 and 'new' only in relation to the Oude Kerk) is the historic stage of Dutch coronations and royal weddings. Other than such ceremonies, the building no longer functions as a church, but rather a hall for art and cultural exhibitions. For a free peek, slip through the gift shop (by the entrance) and upstairs for a display on the church's history.

Spui
SQUARE

(Map p46) Inviting cafes and brainy bookstores ring the Spui, a favoured haunt of academics, students and journalists. On Fridays a book market takes over the square; on Sundays it's an art market. And so you know: it's pronounced 'spow' (rhymes with 'now').

Sexmuseum Amsterdam
MUSEUM

(Map p46; www.sexmuseumamsterdam.nl; Damrak 18; admission €4; ⊙9.30am-11.30pm; 🚊4/9/16/24/25 Centraal Station) The Sexmuseum is good for a giggle. You'll find replicas of pornographic Pompeian plates, erotic 14th-century Viennese bronzes, some of the world's earliest nude photographs, an automated farting flasher in a trench coat and a music box that plays 'Edelweiss' and purports

to show a couple in flagrante delicto. It's sillier and more fun than its Red Light District neighbour, the Erotic Museum. Minimum age for entry is 16.

Madame Tussauds Amsterdam
MUSEUM

(Map p46; www.madametussauds.nl; Dam 20; adult/child €22/17; ⊙10am-8.30pm Jul & Aug, to 5.30pm Sep-Jun; ♿) Sure, Madame Tussauds wax museum is overpriced and cheesy, but its focus on local culture makes it fun: 'meet' the Dutch royals, politicians, painters and pop stars, along with global celebs (Bieber!). Kids love it. Buying tickets online will save you a few euros and gets you into the fast-track queue. Going after 3pm also nets discounts.

Noord/Zuidlijn Viewpoint
VIEWPOINT

(Map p46; www.noordzuidlijn.amsterdam.nl; across from Rokin 96; ⊙1-6pm Tue-Sun; 🚊4/9/14/16/24/25 Rokin) Descend the stairs across from Rokin 96 and behold the North/South Metro line excavation in action. The massive engineering project is like a sci-fi movie: an abyss filled with muck and pipes and colossal digging machines. The whole place rumbles when a tram passes overhead. The displays and signage are in Dutch, but English-speaking guides are often on hand.

Centraal Station
ARCHITECTURE

(Map p46; Stationsplein) Beyond being a transport hub, Centraal Station is a sight in itself. The turreted marvel dates from 1889. One of the architects, PJ Cuypers, also designed the Rijksmuseum, and you can see the similarities in the faux-Gothic towers, the fine red brick and the abundant reliefs (for sailing, trade and industry).

Schreierstoren
HISTORIC BUILDING

(Map p46; www.schreierstoren.nl; Prins Hendrikkade 94-95; 🚊4/9/16/24/25 Centraal Station) Built around 1480 as part of the city's defenses, this tower is where Henry Hudson set sail for the New World in 1609; a plaque outside marks the spot. It's called the 'wailing tower' in lore – where women waved farewell to sailors' ships – but the name actually comes from the word 'sharp' (for how the corner jutted into the bay). Step into the VOC Cafe for a look inside the tower.

Beurs van Berlage
ARCHITECTURE

(Map p46; ☑530 41 41; www.beursvanberlage.nl; Damrak 243) Master architect and ardent socialist HP Berlage (1856–1934) built this financial exchange in 1903. He filled the

Amsterdam Centre

200 m
0.1 miles

Het IJ

IJpleinveer

Piet Heinkade

Open Havenfront

Droogbak

Oosterdok

Centraal Station

Stationsplein

Centraal Station

Prins Hendrikkade

Prins Hendrikkade

Prins Hendrikkade

Geldersekade

Geldersekade

Oudezijds Kolk

Sint Olofsst

Zeedijk

Nieuwebrugst

Nieuwezijds Voorburgwal

Singel

Singel

Singel

Keizersgracht

Herengracht

Herengracht

Prinsengracht

Prinsengracht

Noordermarkt

WESTERN CANAL BELT

Haarlemmer Houttuinen

Haarlemmerstr

Haarlemmerdijk

Brouwersgracht

Buiten Brouwersstr

Binnen Visserstr

Roomolenstr

Herengracht

Herengr

Korsjespsst

Langestr

Oude Nieuwstr

Blauwburgwal

Herenstr

Herenstr

Bergstr

Prinsenstr

Leliegr

Torensluis

Beursstr

Warmoesstr

Oudebrugsst

Mandenmakersst

Onze Lieve Vrouwest

Nieuwe Nieuwstr

St Nicolaasstr

St Geertruidenst

Beurspassage

Mosterdpolst

Museum Ons' Lieve Heer op Solder

Heintje Hoekst

60 Lange Niezel

Spooksst

Oudezijds Armst

Paleisstr

Nieuwendijk

Gouwenaarssst

Smaktst

Engelsesst

Spuistr

Stromkt

Teerketelst

Korte Kolkst

Nieuwezijds Kolk

D van Hasseltsst

Suikerbakkerst

Nieuwezijds Kolksst

Sint Jacobsstr

Karnemelksst

Haringpakkersst

Hesselssst

Martelaarsgr

Oude Brugst

Kolksst

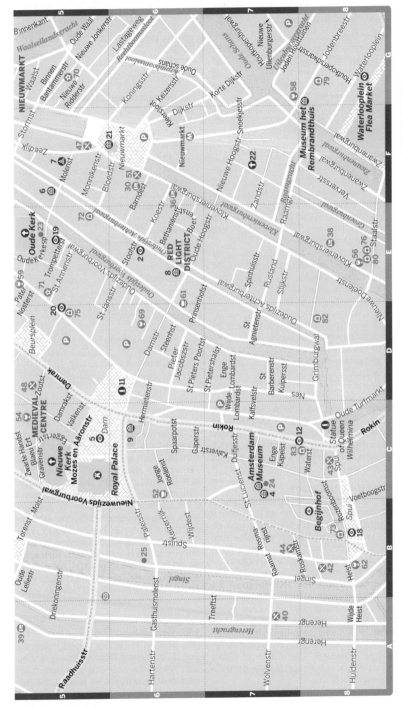

Amsterdam Centre

temple of capitalism with decorations that venerate labour – look inside the cafe to see tile murals of the well-muscled proletariat of the past, present and future. The building also hosts orchestra concerts and art exhibitions.

RED LIGHT DISTRICT

The city's famous Red Light District retains the power to make your jaw go limp, even if near-naked prostitutes beckoning passers-by from backlit windows is the oldest Amsterdam cliché. But far from being a no-go area, De Wallen (as the district is known locally) has some beautiful historic cafes and buildings. Zeedijk and Warmoesstraat are the main commercial thoroughfares chock-a-block with restaurants and shops (many with a hedonistic bent). For a seamier scene, walk along neon-lit Oudezijds Achterburgwal, past its fetish shops, sex shows and pot museums. The district is tightly regulated and safe for strolling on the main streets.

Oude Kerk   CHURCH
(Old Church; Map p46; ☎625 82 84; www.oudekerk. nl; Oudekerksplein 23; adult/child €8/6; ⊗11am-5pm Mon-Sat, 1-5pm Sun; 🚊4/9/16/24/25 Dam) Outside, Red Light windows surround the 14th-century church, which is Amsterdam's oldest building. Inside, the Müller organ, naughty choir stall carvings and famous Amsterdammers' tombstones in the floor (such as Rembrandt's wife Saskia) steal the attention; ask for a map when you enter. The church holds Sunday services at 11am, but generally it hosts exhibitions such as the World Press Photo Show (p72). You can also climb the tower (per person €7; ⊗1-5pm Thu-Sat Apr-Sep). The church was finishing extensive restoration work in 2013, so the interior will gleam.

Trompettersteeg   STREET
(Map p46) An intriguing place to view the Red Light action is Trompettersteeg, a teeny alley where the most desirable women are stationed. Claustrophobes beware: the passageway is only 1m wide, but it's plenty busy.

Look for the entrance in the block south of the Oude Kerk.

Museum Ons' Lieve Heer op Solder
MUSEUM

(Map p46; ☎624 66 04; www.opsolder.nl; Oudezijds Voorburgwal 40; adult/child €8/4; ☉10am-5pm Mon-Sat, 1-5pm Sun; 🚊4/9/16/24/25 Centraal Station) What looks like an ordinary canal house turns out to have an entire Catholic church stashed inside. Ons' Lieve Heer op Solder (Our Dear Lord in the Attic) was built in the mid-1600s in defiance of the Calvinists. Inside you'll see labyrinthine staircases, rich artworks, period decor and the soaring, two-storey church itself. The museum ws undergoing restoration in 2013, so some artefacts were put away temporarily.

Prostitution Information Centre
INFORMATION CENTRE

(PIC; Map p46; ☎420 73 28; www.pic-amsterdam. com; Enge Kerksteeg 3; ☉1-8pm Sat or by appointment) Established by a former prostitute, the PIC provides frank information about the industry to sex workers, their customers and curious tourists. The centre's small shop sells enlightening reading material and souvenirs, but best of all is its excellent hour-long walking tour (5pm Saturday, €15 per person, no reservations needed), which takes you around the neighbourhood and into a prostitute's working room. You can also peek in the mini-museum set up like a historic brothel (free with tour, otherwise €1 per person).

Cannabis College
INFORMATION CENTRE

(Map p46; ☎423 44 20; www.cannabiscollege.com; Oudezijds Achterburgwal 124; ☉11am-7pm) Assuming the country's restrictive new drug regulations don't put this nonprofit centre out of business, the college will continue to educate visitors on tips and tricks to having a positive smoking experience, and to provide the lowdown on local cannabis laws. Browse displays, try out a vaporiser (bring your own smoking material), or view marijuana plants growing sky-high in the basement garden (€3 to see them; photos permitted).

RED LIGHT DISTRICT FAQS

» **What year was prostitution legalised in the Netherlands?** 1810

» **When were brothels legalised?** 2000

» **What percentage of working prostitutes were born in the Netherlands?** 5%

» **What is the average rent per window?** €75 to €150 per eight-hour shift (paid by prostitute), depending on location.

» **How much money is generated by the industry?** About €650 million annually, according to the Central Bureau of Statistics.

» **Do prostitutes pay taxes?** Yes.

» **What happens if a patron gets violent?** Prostitutes' quarters are equipped with a button that, when pressed, activates a light outside. The police or other protectors show up in a hurry.

» **Why red light?** Because it's flattering. Especially when used in combination with black light, it makes teeth sparkle. Even as early as the 1300s, women carrying red lanterns met sailors near the port.

Guan Yin Shrine
BUDDHIST TEMPLE

(Fo Guang Shan He Hua Temple; Map p46; www.ibps.nl; Zeedijk 106-118; ⊙noon-5pm Tue-Sat, 10am-5pm Sun year-round, plus noon-5pm Mon Jun-Aug) Europe's first Chinese Imperial–style Buddhist temple (2000) is dedicated to Guan Yin, the Buddhist goddess of mercy. Make a donation, light an incense stick and ponder the thousand eyes and hands of the Bodhisattva statue.

Hash, Marijuana & Hemp Museum
MUSEUM

(Map p46; ☎623 59 61; www.hashmuseum.com; Oudezijds Achterburgwal 148; admission €9; ⊙10am-11pm) Simple exhibits in this recently renovated museum cover dope botany and the relationship between cannabis and religion. Highlights include an impressive pipe collection, an interactive vaporiser exhibit and a hemp-body guitar. Admission also includes the **Hemp Gallery**, filled with hemp art and historical items, in a separate building a few doors north. Visitors on a budget might prefer the Cannabis College (p49).

Erotic Museum
MUSEUM

(Map p46; www.erotisch-museum.nl; Oudezijds Achterburgwal 54; admission €7; ⊙11am-1am) Bondage exhibits, naughty photos and lewd cartoons titillate the eyeballs. Although the Erotic Museum has the advantage of location, it's less entertaining and more expensive than the Sexmuseum Amsterdam (p45) on the Damrak.

W139
ARTS CENTRE

(Map p46; www.w139.nl; Warmoesstraat 139; ⊙noon-6pm) Duck into this contemporary arts centre and ponder the multimedia exhibits, which often have an edgy political angle. Check the website for frequent artists talks.

NIEUWMARKT

Nieuwmarkt (New Market) is a district as historic as anything you'll find in Amsterdam. Rembrandt painted canalscapes here, and Jewish merchants generated a fair share of the city's wealth with diamonds and other ventures. The area's focal point is Nieuwmarkt square, just east of the Red Light District. This bright, relaxed place – ringed with cafes, shops and restaurants – is arguably the grandest spot in town after the Dam.

TOP CHOICE ### Museum het Rembrandthuis
MUSEUM

(Rembrandt House Museum; Map p46; ☎520 04 00; www.rembrandthuis.nl; Jodenbreestraat 4-6; adult/child €10/3; ⊙10am-5pm; ☐9/14 Waterlooplein) You almost expect to find the master himself at Museum het Rembrandthuis, set in the three-storey canal house where Rembrandt van Rijn lived and ran the Netherlands' largest painting studio between 1639 and 1658. The atmospheric, tchotchke-packed interior gives a real-deal feel for how Rembrandt painted his days away until bankruptcy forced him to leave for cheaper digs in the Jordaan. Highlights include his full etching collection (expect to see around 50 prints displayed) and etching demonstrations daily; his light-filled studio, where artists show how he sourced and mixed paints; and his mind-blowing cabinet of seashells, Roman busts, stuffed alligators and other curiosities. Ask for the free audioguide. You can buy advance tickets online, though it's not as vital here as at some of the other big museums.

Joods Historisch Museum
MUSEUM

(Jewish Historical Museum; Map p62; ☎626 99 45; www.jhm.nl; Nieuwe Amstelstraat 1; adult/child €12/3; ⊙11am-5pm; ✚; ⓜ9/14 Mr Visserplein) A beautifully restored complex of four Ashkenazic synagogues from the 17th and 18th centuries reveals the history of Jews in the Netherlands. It vividly captures the vibrant Jewish community erased by WWII. Pick up the free, English-language audiotour for extra insights. Admission tickets are in conjunction with the Portuguese-Israelite Synagogue.

Portuguese-Israelite Synagogue
SYNAGOGUE

(Map p62; www.portugesesynagoge.nl; Mr Visserplein 3; adult/child €12/3; ⊙10am-4pm Sun-Fri; ⓜ9/14 Mr Visserplein) This was the largest synagogue in Europe when it was completed in 1675, and it's still in use today. The interior features massive pillars and some two dozen brass candelabra. Outside (near the entrance) take the stairs underground to the 'treasure chambres' to see 16th-century manuscripts and gold-threaded tapestries. Admission tickets also provide entry to the Joods Historisch Museum.

Waag
HISTORIC BUILDING

(Map p46; www.indewaag.nl; Nieuwmarkt 4; ⊙10am-1am; ⓜNieuwmarkt) The multi-turreted Waag dates from 1488, when it was part of the city's fortifications. From the 17th century onwards it was Amsterdam's main weigh house, and later a spot for public executions. A bar-restaurant occupies it today. Out front, Nieuwmarkt square hosts a variety of events, including a Saturday farmers market and Sunday antiques market.

Waterlooplein Flea Market
MARKET

(Map p46; www.waterlooppleinmarkt.nl; ⊙9am-5pm Mon-Sat; ⓜ9/14 Waterlooplein) Covering

i RED LIGHT PHOTO ETIQUETTE

Your first instinct might be to take a photo of the barely clad women winking from the crimson-lit windows, but don't do it – out of simple respect, and to avoid having your camera tossed in a canal by the ladies' enforcers.

the square once known as Vlooienburg (Flea Town), the Waterlooplein Flea Market draws sharp-eyed customers seeking everything from antique knick-knacks to imitation Diesel jeans, pot lollipops and cheap bicycle locks. The street market started in 1880 when Jewish traders living in the neighbourhood began selling their wares here.

FREE Gassan Diamonds
DIAMOND WORKSHOP

(Map p62; www.gassan.com; Nieuwe Uilenburgerstraat 173-175; ⊙9am-5pm; ⓜ9/14 Waterlooplein) This vast workshop demonstrates how an ungainly clump of rock is transformed into a girl's best friend. You'll get a quick primer in assessing the gems for quality, and see diamond cutters and polishers in action. The one-hour tour is the best of its kind in town, which is why so many tour buses stop here. Don't worry: the line moves quickly.

Zuiderkerk
CHURCH

(Map p46; www.zuiderkerkamsterdam.nl; Zuiderkerkhof 72; adult/child €7/3.50; ⊙1-5pm Mon-Sat Apr-Sep; ⓜNieuwmarkt) Famed Dutch Renaissance architect Hendrick de Keyser built the 'Southern Church' in 1611. The interior is now used for private events, but you can still tour the tower. Guides lead visitors up lots of stairs every 30 minutes, past the bells and to a swell lookout area for a sky-high city view.

PUT OUT THE RED LIGHT?

Since 2007, city officials have been reducing the number of Red Light windows in an effort to clean up the district. They claim it's not about morals but about crime. Pimps, traffickers and money launderers have entered the scene and set the neighbourhood on a downward spiral. Opponents point to a growing local conservatism and say the government is using crime as an excuse, because it doesn't like Amsterdam's current reputation for sin.

As the window tally decreases, fashion studios, art galleries and trendy cafes rise up to reclaim the wanton spaces, thanks to a program of low-cost rent and other business incentives. It's called Project 1012, after the area's postal code, and how far the city will take the effort remains to be seen.

Jordaan & Western Canal Belt

N

0   200 m
0   0.1 miles

STAATSLIEDEN - FREDERIK HENDRIKBUURT

Kattensloot
Jacob Catskade

Willemsstr

Goudsbloemstr

Goudbloemdwarsstr

Lindengr

37

39

Noorderkerkstr

11

10

Lindenstr

1e Lindendwarsstr

27

Frederik Hendrikplantsoen

Frederik Hendrikstr

Singelgracht

Nassaukade

Marnixkade

Marnixstr

Lijnbaansgr

17

Karthuizersstr

2e Boomdwarsstr

12

33

34

Prinsenstr

Tichelstr

Westerstr

24

Prinsengr

Van Oldenbarneveldtplein

Marnixplein

Marnixstr

Anjeliersstr

1e Anjeliersdwarsstr

Van Oldenbarneveldtstr

Nassaukade

Marnixkade

Westerkade

Lijnbaansgr

JORDAAN

Tuinstr

2e Egelantiersdwarsstr

26

14

28

36

Egelantiersstr

Madelievenstr

3e Egelantiersdwarsstr

38

1

Egelantiersgracht

2e Egelantiersdwarsstr

Egelantiersgr

Nieuwe Leliestr

3

21

Leliegr

Prinsengracht

Anne Frank Huis

Ketersgracht

Keizersgr

3e Leliedwarsstr

20

Bloemgr

Bloemgr

2e Leliedwarsstr

13

5

Westermarkt

32

Pink Point

Raadhuisstr

19

Hugo de Grootgracht

Bloemstr

15

Rozengr

1e Rozendwarsstr

2e

Reestr

Hartenstr

47

To Moeders (100m)

Rozendwarsstr

Laurierdwarsstr

2e

Rozenstr

Laurierstr

Prinsengr

Keizersgr

Keizersgracht

Herengr

Lijnbaansgr

Marnixstr

Lauriergracht

Konijnenstr

35

30

Hazenstr

31

43

Berenstr

29

Wolvenstr

Lijnbaansgracht

Elandsstr

40

8

6

42

Lijnbaansstr

Elandsgr

9

22

41

16

Nassaukade

3e Looiersdwarsstr

45

25

18

Oude Looiersstr

Runstr

Huidenstr

23

Looiersgr

44

2

7

OUD WEST

46

7

4

Kinkerstr

Jordaan & Western Canal Belt

Scheepvaarthuis   ARCHITECTURE
(Shipping House; Map p62; Prins Hendrikkade 108; ☐4/9/16/24/25 Centraal Station) The grand Scheepvaarthuis, built in 1916, was the first true example of Amsterdam School architecture. The exterior resembles a ship's bow and is encrusted in elaborate nautical detailing. Step inside (it's a luxury hotel now) to admire stained glass, gorgeous light fixtures and the art deco-ish central stairwell.

De Appel   ARTS CENTRE
(Map p62; ☑625 56 51; www.deappel.nl; Prins Hendrikkade 142; adult/child €7/free; ⊙noon-8pm Tue-Sat, to 6pm Sun; ☐4/9/16/24/25 Centraal Station) See what's on at this swanky contemporary arts centre. The curators have a knack for tapping young international talent and supplementing exhibitions with lectures, film screenings and performances.

JORDAAN

If Amsterdam's neighbourhoods held a 'best personality' contest, the Jordaan would surely win. Its intimacy is contagious, with funky galleries, beery brown cafes and flower-box-adorned eateries spilling out onto the narrow streets. Originally a stronghold of the working class, the Jordaan is now one of the most desirable areas to live in Amsterdam.

FREE **Noorderkerk**   CHURCH
(Northern Church; Map p52; www.noorderkerk.org; Noordermarkt 48; ⊙10.30am-12.30pm Mon, 11am-1pm Sat, 1.30-5.30pm Sun) The Noorderkerk was a Calvinist church for Jordaan's 'common' people. It's shaped like a Greek cross (four arms of equal length) around a central pulpit. A sculpture near the entrance commemorates the bloody Jordaan riots of July 1934, when five people died in protests over government austerity measures. The church

WORTH A TRIP

WESTERPARK & WESTERN ISLANDS

Amsterdam doesn't get much cooler than these two enclaves, a stone's throw north of the Jordaan. You can easily idle away an afternoon checking out architecture and cafes in the hip, eco-urban mashup.

Start at the remarkable housing project **Het Schip** (☑418 28 85; www.hetschip.nl; Spaarndammerplantsoen 140; admission €7.50; ⊙11am-5pm Tue-Sun; 🚊22 Zaanstraat), the pinnacle of Amsterdam School architecture. Michel de Klerk designed the triangular block, loosely resembling a ship, for railway employees. It now hosts a small museum where you can poke around the old post office and an apartment.

From Het Schip, walk southeast along the train tracks and cut through a small underpass to Westerpark. The pond-dappled green space is a hep-cat hang-out that blends into **Westergasfabriek** (☑586 07 10; www.westergasfabriek.nl; Haarlemmerweg 8-10; 🚊3 Haarlemmerplein), a former gasworks transformed into an edgy cultural park, filled with bars, clubs and concert halls.

Toko MC (☑475 04 25; www.tokomc.nl; Polonceaukade 5; mains €17-20; ⊙from noon Tue-Sun; 🚊10 Van Limburg-Stirumstraat) is a good place to get the pulse of the scene. It's part Caribbean soul-food restaurant (think grilled sardines and baked pumpkin), part paper-lantern-lit bar pouring cane-sugar cocktails, and part late-night club where DJs spin world music.

Head east past the big stone Haarlemmerpoort (Haarlem Gate) to the Western Islands. They originally were home to shipworks and the West India Trading Company's warehouses, which buzzed with activity in the early 1600s. The district is a world unto itself, cut through with canals and linked with small drawbridges. It's worth a wander among the homes and artists' studios, and for dinner at Marius (p83).

Trams 3 and 10 swing by the area; bus 22 goes right to Het Schip. You can also walk or cycle from Centraal Station; it's 1.6km to the park.

hosts a well-regarded **Saturday afternoon concert series** (☑620 45 56; www.nooderkerk concerten.nl; tickets from €15; ⊙2pm Sat mid-Sep–mid-Jun).

Noordermarkt   MARKET
(Northern Market, Noorderkerkplein; Map p52; www. boerenmarktamsterdam.nl; ⊙8am-2pm Mon, 9am-4pm Sat; 🚊3 Nieuwe Willemsstraat) The Noordermarkt surrounds the Noorderkerk and hosts two bazaars. On Monday mornings it's a trove of secondhand clothing (great rummage piles) and assorted antique trinkets. On Saturdays, gorgeous produce and cheese from farmers from around Amsterdam take over the stalls.

Houseboat Museum   MUSEUM
(Map p52; ☑427 07 50; www.houseboatmuseum.nl; Prinsengracht, opposite 296; adult/child €3.75/3; ⊙11am-5pm Tue-Sun Mar-Oct, 11am-5pm Fri-Sun Nov-Feb, closed Jan; 🚊13/14/17 Westermarkt) The quirky Houseboat Museum, situated on a 23m-long sailing barge from 1914, offers a good sense of how cosy (or cramped, depending on your view) life can be on the water. The actual displays are minimal, but you can watch a slide show of wild-looking boats, and inspect the sleeping, living, cooking and dining quarters on board. In case you were wondering: most vessels have sewerage hook-ups.

Johnny Jordaanplein   SQUARE
(Map p52; cnr Prinsengracht & Elandsgracht; 🚊13/14/17 Westermarkt) The small square Johnny Jordaanplein is dedicated to the local hero and singer of schmaltzy tunes such as *'Bij ons in de Jordaan'* ('We in the Jordaan'). There are bronze busts of Johnny and his band, but the real star here is the colourful utility hut splashed with nostalgic lyrics.

Pianola Museum   MUSEUM
(Map p52; ☑627 96 24; www.pianola.nl; Westerstraat 106; adult/child €5/3; ⊙2-5pm Sun; 🚊3/10 Marnixplein) This is a very special place, crammed with pianolas from the early 1900s, as well as nearly 20,000 music rolls. Every month (except July and August) player-piano concerts are held, featuring anything from Mozart to Fats Waller and rare classical or jazz tunes composed especially for the instrument. The curator gives demonstrations with great zest.

Electric Ladyland
MUSEUM

(Map p52; www.electric-lady-land.com; 2e Leliedwarsstraat 5; adult/child €5/free; ⊘2-5pm Tue-Sat; 🚊13/14/17 Westermarkt) The world's first museum of fluorescence is a hippie-trippy treat. Even if you didn't eat a space cake before arriving, you're gonna feel like it, as grey-ponytailed artist and owner Nick Padalino takes you to his shop's basement and shows you all kinds of glow-in-the-dark objects, from psychedelic sculptures to luminescent rocks. Allow a good hour for the tour.

Amsterdam Tulip Museum
MUSEUM

(Map p52; ☑421 00 95; www.amsterdamtulipmuseum.com; Prinsengracht 112; adult/child €6/4; ⊘10am-6pm) A couple of bulb companies operate this small, clinical museum. It provides an overview of the tulip from its beginnings in Turkey to Dutch 'Tulipmania', bulbs as food in the war years, and present-day scientific methods of growing and harvesting. The gift shop offers oodles of tulip souvenirs.

WESTERN CANAL BELT

The Western Canal Belt is one of Amsterdam's most gorgeous areas. Grand old buildings and oddball little speciality shops line the glinting waterways. Roaming around them can cause days to vanish.

Anne Frank Huis
MUSEUM

(Anne Frank House; Map p52; ☑556 71 05; www.annefrank.org; Prinsengracht 276; adult/child €9/free; ⊘9am-7pm daily, later Sat, and mid-Mar–mid-Sep; 🚊13/14/17 Westermarkt) The house where Anne, her family and their friends hid from the Nazis from July 1942 to August 1944 draws almost a million visitors annually. The building originally held Otto Frank's pectin (a substance used in jelly-making) business, and on the lower floors you'll see the former offices. Then it's on to the *achterhuis* (rear house), where you step through the revolving bookcase of the 'Secret Annexe' and into the claustrophobic living quarters. It was in these rooms, preserved in powerful austerity, that the eight inhabitants observed complete silence during the daytimes, outgrew their clothes, pasted photos of Hollywood stars on the walls and read Dickens, before being mysteriously betrayed. More haunting exhibits and videos await after you return to the front house – including Anne's red-plaid diary itself, sitting alone in its glass case, and heartbreaking letters from Otto, the only occupant to survive the concentration camps.

Westerkerk
CHURCH

(Western Church; Map p52; ☑624 77 66; www.westerkerk.nl; Prinsengracht 281; ⊘11am-3pm Mon-Fri Apr-Sep, also Sat Jul & Aug; 🚊13/14/17 Westermarkt) This blue-crowned Protestant church, built in 1631, has become a symbol of the Jordaan. To be a true local, it's said, you must be born within earshot of the Westerkerk's carillon bells. Rembrandt supposedly lies here, in an unmarked pauper's grave. Climbing the 85m-high **tower** (per person €7; ⊘10am-5.30pm Mon-Fri, to 7.30pm Sat Apr-Sep), by tour only, reveals striking canal views, but it's steep and claustrophobic – not for the faint-hearted.

Homomonument
MONUMENT

(Map p52; cnr Keizersgracht & Raadhuisstraat) The three pink granite triangles behind the Westerkerk recall persecution by the Nazis, who forced gay men to wear a pink triangle patch. Citizens lay flowers on the monument on Liberation Day (4 May).

Het Grachtenhuis
MUSEUM

(Canal House; Map p52; www.hetgrachtenhuis.nl; Herengracht 386; adult/child €12/6; ⊘10am-5pm Tue-Sun; 🚊1/2/5 Spui) If you're intrigued by the canal ring and what a feat of engineering it is, don't miss the Canal House, which explains how the waterways and the houses that line them became an integral part of Amsterdam city planning. A 40-minute audiotour guides you through. Entry is via

---

ⓘ VISITING THE ANNE FRANK HUIS

» Come after 6pm to avoid the biggest crowds. Queues can easily be an hour-plus wait otherwise.

» Buying tickets in advance allows you to skip the queue entirely and enter via a separate door (left of the main entrance).

» Prebook two ways: via the website (€0.50 surcharge), though you must buy the tickets several days ahead of time and be able to print them; or via the tourist information office at Centraal Station (€1 surcharge), which you can do on shorter notice. Both methods give you a set time for entry.

» Download 'Anne's Amsterdam', a free app available in Dutch, English and German from the museum's website.

Southern Canal Belt & De Pijp

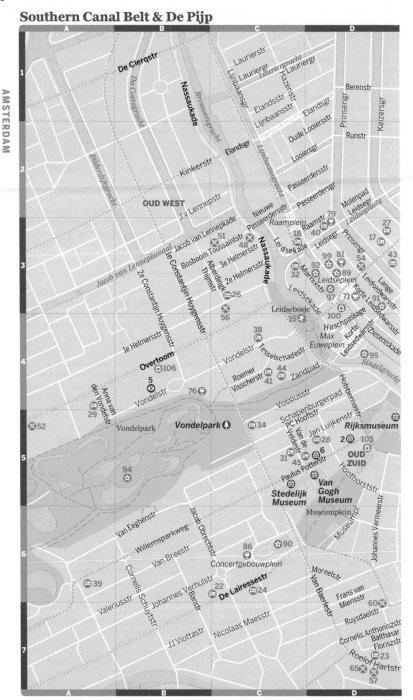

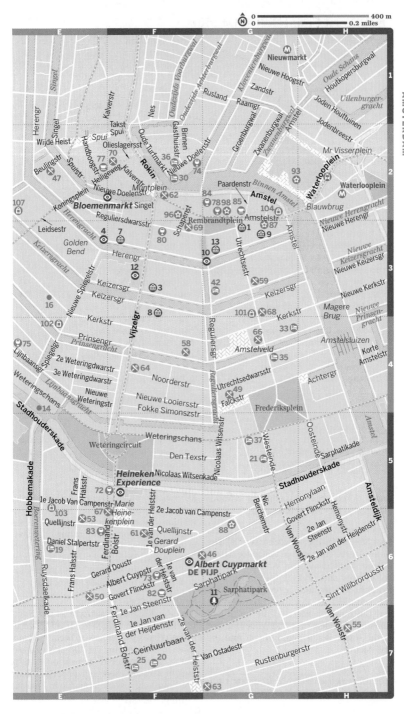

Southern Canal Belt & De Pijp

timed tickets; reserve online in advance (which also provides a discount).

Negen Straatjes   STREETS

(Nine Streets; Map p52; www.de9straatjes.nl) The Nine Streets comprise a tic-tac-toe board of wee shops dealing in vintage fashions, housewares and oddball specialities from toothbrushes to antique eyeglass frames. It's bounded by Reestraat, Hartenstraat and Gasthuismolensteeg to the north and Runstraat, Huidenstraat and Wijde Heisteeg to the south. Bonus points if you find the doll doctor!

Huis Marseille   MUSEUM

(Map p52; www.huismarseille.nl; Keizersgracht 401; adult/child €5/free; ⊙11am-6pm Tue-Sun; 🚊1/2/5 Keizersgracht) This well-curated photography museum stages large-scale, temporary exhibitions by international artists. Themes might include portraiture, nature or regional photography. The gallery space spreads over several floors of a historic home and spills into a tiny summer house in the garden. There's a terrific little library, too.

Reypenaer Cheese Tasting   CULINARY

(Map p46; ☎320 63 33; www.reypenaer.com; Singel 182; tastings from €10; 🚊1/2/5/13/17 Raadhuisstraat) Here's your chance to become a *kaas* (cheese) connoisseur. The 100-plus-year-old Dutch cheesemaker Reypenaer offers tastings in a rustic classroom under its shop. The hour-long session (available in English) includes six cheeses plus optional wine and port pairings. The staff leads you through them from young to old, helping you to appreciate each hunk's look, smell and taste. Call for the schedule.

Netherlands Media Art Institute
CULTURAL BUILDING

From the hilarious and ridiculous to the deep and experimental, there's always something interesting in NMAI's changing exhibits. Don't expect to see works by the hit makers or TV directors of tomorrow, though. The institute is specifically about video as art. At the time of print, NMAI had merged with Smart Project Space (SPS) to form New Art Space Amsterdam (NASA). NASA is operating from the SPS building at

Arie Biemondstraat 101, just north of Vondelpark.

Bijbels Museum
MUSEUM

(Bible Museum; Map p52; www.bijbelsmuseum.nl; Herengracht 366-368; adult/child €8/4; ⌚10am-5pm Mon-Sat, 11am-5pm Sun; 🚋1/2/5 Spui) Not just a museum of Bibles, this canal-house trove is more like a museum about the Bible's importance in 19th-century culture. It contains musty mummies, hand-carved models of the Tabernacle and the Temple in Jerusalem, as well as several antique Bibles (check out the 1477 Delft edition). Near the pretty garden, there's also a display of biblical smells (nicer than it sounds).

ℹ️ MUSEUM TIPS

Amsterdam's world-class museums draw millions of visitors each year, and queues at the Van Gogh Museum, Rijksmuseum, Anne Frank Huis and others can be outrageous, particularly in summer. Want to avoid the mobs and save money? Here's how.

How to Beat the Crowds

» **Take advantage of e-tickets** Most sights sell them and there's little to no surcharge. They typically allow you to enter via a separate, faster queue. Note you need to be able to print the tickets in many cases.

» **Go late** Queues are shortest during late afternoon and evening. Visit after 3pm for the Rijksmuseum and Van Gogh Museum (also open Friday nights), after 6pm for the Frank house (open late nightly in summer).

» **Try tourist offices** You can also buy advance tickets at tourist offices, but often the queues there are as lengthy as the ones at the sights.

» **Buy a discount card** In addition to saving on entrance fees, discount cards commonly provide fast-track entry.

How to Save Money

Museumkaart (Museum Card; www.museumkaart.nl; adult/child €45/22.50, plus €5 for first-time registrants) This card works well if you plan to be in the Netherlands a while. It provides free entry to some 400 museums nationwide for a year.

Amsterdam Card (www.iamsterdam.com; per 24/48/72hr €40/50/60) Good for quick visits to the city. It includes admission to many of the same venues as the Museum Card, plus a GVB transit pass, a canal cruise and restaurant discounts. You'll need to visit three or so museums per day to make it pay for itself.

Holland Pass (www.hollandpass.com; 2/5/7 attractions €28/44/54) Like the I Amsterdam Card but without the rush for usage; you can visit sights over a prolonged period. It gets a bit tricky to figure out how much money you're saving because you pick from 'tiers' of attractions (the most popular/expensive sights are top-tier).

Poezenboot BOAT
(Cat Boat; Map p46; www.poezenboot.nl; Singel 38; admission by donation; ⊙1-3pm, closed Wed & Sun) This barge began life as a shelter for hundreds of homeless cats in the 1960s. It's now a registered charity – pat and pet the current feline inhabitants for a small donation.

FREE **Multatuli Museum** MUSEUM
(Map p46; www.multatuli-museum.nl; Korsjespoortsteeg 20; ⊙10am-5pm Tue, noon-5pm Sat & Sun) Better known by the pen name Multatuli – Latin for 'I have suffered greatly' – novelist Eduard Douwes Dekker was best known for *Max Havelaar* (1860), about corrupt colonialists in the Dutch East Indies. This small but fascinating museum-home chronicles his life and works, and shows furniture and artefacts from his period in Indonesia.

SOUTHERN CANAL BELT

Two clubby nightlife districts anchor the Southern Canal Belt: Leidseplein and Rembrandtplein. Both are neon-lit, one-stop shops for partygoers. In between lie several intriguing museums, and restaurants, cafes and shops galore.

Hermitage Amsterdam MUSEUM
(Map p62; ☑530 74 88; www.hermitage.nl; Amstel 51; adult/child €15/free; ⊙10am-5pm; ☐9/14 Waterlooplein) This satellite of St Petersburg's State Hermitage Museum occupies the vast Amstelhof, an almshouse since the 17th century. Prestigious exhibits, such as treasures from the Russian palace or masterworks by Van Gogh and Gauguin, change about twice per year, and they're as blockbuster as you'd expect. You can visit the old kitchen and other historic rooms preserved behind the main galleries.

Bloemenmarkt MARKET
(Flower Market; Map p56; Singel, btwn Muntplein & Koningsplein; ⊙9am-5.30pm Mon-Sat, 11am-5.30pm Sun; ☐1/2/5 Koningsplein) The touristy Flower Market has been floating canalside since the 1860s, when gardeners used to sail up the Amstel and sell from their boats. Exotic bulbs are the main stock. If you're

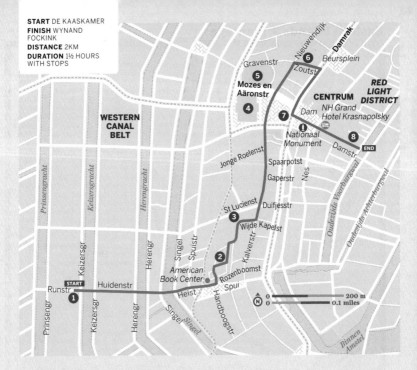

Walking Tour
Cheese, Gin & Monuments

> This tour is a hit parade of Amsterdam's favourite foods and historic sights.

The Dutch eat more than 14kg of cheese per person annually, and it appears much of that hunky goodness is sold in ❶ **De Kaaskamer**. Wheels of Gouda, Edam and other locally made types are stacked to the rafters. Get a wedge to go.

As you make your way through the Spui, keep an eye out just past the American Book Center for a humble wood door. Push it open and behold the hidden community known as the ❷ **Begijnhof** surrounding two historic churches and gardens. Cross the courtyard to the other entrance.

From the Begijnhof turn north and walk a short distance to the ❸ **Civic Guard Gallery**. Paintings of stern folks in ruffled collars stare down from the walls. Cross the gallery and depart through the Amsterdam Museum's courtyard restaurant onto Kalverstraat.

Kalverstraat deposits you by the ❹ **Royal Palace**, home to King Williem-Alexander and Queen Máxima. The sumptuous interior deserves a look. The palace's neighbour is the ❺ **Nieuwe Kerk**, the stage for Dutch coronations. After admiring its mightiness, get onto crowded Nieuwendijk, and walk to Zoutsteeg. C'mon, stop being shy about eating raw fish, and order the famed Dutch herring at ❻ **Rob Wigboldus Vishandel**, a wee, three-table shop. Then depart Zoutsteeg onto Damrak.

Cross Damrak so you're on the Nationaal Monument side of the ❼ **Dam** – Amsterdam's birthplace. Wade through the sea of bikes to see the urns behind the monument, which hold earth from East Indies war cemeteries. Now follow the street leading behind the NH Grand Hotel Krasnapolsky to ❽ **Wynand Fockink**. The Dutch gin-maker's tasting room dates from 1679. The barkeep will pour your drink to the brim, so do like the locals to prevent spillage: lean over it and sip without lifting.

Eastern Islands & Plantage

N

| 0 | 200 m |
| 0 | 0.1 miles |

15

Oosterdoksstr

3
22

Oosterdokskade

IJ Tunnel

Dijksgracht

8

Oosterdok

11

Prins Hendrikkade

Binnenkant

Oude Waal

Valkenburgerstr

Kattenburg

NIEUWMARKT

Oude Schans

Kattenburgerstr

Koningsstr

Lastageweg

Oude Schans

Peperstr

19

Rapenburg

Het Scheepvaartmuseum

Kattenburgerstr

Houtkopersburgwal

Oude Schans

Nieuwe Uilenburgerstr

1

Schippersgr

Nieuwevaart

Wittenburgergr

Nieuwe Vaart

5

Uilenburgergracht

Valkenburgerstr

Anne Frankstr

Kadijkspl

20

21

Hoogte Kadijk

Laagte Kadijk

Jöden

Houttuinen

Rapenburgerstr

Nieuwe Herengracht

Plantage Parklaan

Entrepotdok

Plantagekade

Binnenkadijk

Entrepotdok

Jodenbreestr

Mr
Visserplein

14

13

Henri Polaklaan

12

Wertheim
Park

Muldestr

17

Artis
Royal
Zoo

10

JD Meijerplein

**Joods Historisch
Museum**

Hortus Botanicus

2

Waterlooplein

PLANTAGE

6

Plantage
Kerklaan

Plantage Middenlaan

**Amsterdam
Tattoo
Museum**

Waterlooplein

Weesperstr

Hortusplantsoen

Plantage Muidergr

18

Plantage
Wester-
manlaan

Nieuwe Herengr

Nieuwe Keizersgr

Nieuwe Keizersgracht

Plantage Muidergr

Plantage Muidergracht

Plantage
Lepellaan

Plantage
Badlaan

**Hermitage
Amsterdam**

Nieuwe Keizersgr

Nieuwe Kerkstr

Managestr

Lepelkruisstr

Nieuwe Prinsengracht

Nieuwe Prinsengr

7

Amstel

Weesperstr

Nieuwe Achtergracht

Nieuwe Achtergr

Korte Lepelstr

Valckenierstr

Sarphatistr

Lepelstr

Roetersstr

Amstelsluizen

Korte Amstelstr

Valckenierstr

Spinozahof

Singelgracht

's Gravesandestr

Voormalige
Stadstimmertuin

16

Weesperplein

Sarphatistr

Spinozastr

Mauritskade

Sajetplein

Oosterpark

9

Eastern Islands & Plantage

planning to buy, ask lots of questions, since bringing bulbs into your home country can be prohibited. Vendors need to provide a special certificate to accompany most bulbs.

FOAM GALLERY
(Fotografie Museum Amsterdam; Map p56; www. foam.nl; Keizersgracht 609; adult/child €8.50/ free; ☺10am-6pm Sat-Wed, to 9pm Thu & Fri; ☐16/24/25 Keizersgracht) Simple, functional but roomy galleries, some with skylights or grand windows for natural light, make this museum an excellent space for all genres of photography. Two storeys of exhibition space create a great setting for admiring the changing exhibits from photographers of world renown, including Sir Cecil Beaton, Annie Leibovitz and Henri Cartier-Bresson.

Museum Van Loon MUSEUM
(Map p56; ☎624 52 55; www.museumvanloon.nl; Keizersgracht 672; adult/child €8/4; ☺11am-5pm Wed-Mon; ☐16/24/25 Keizersgracht) Arguably the best of the canal-house museums, this 1672 mansion was first home to painter Ferdinand Bol. In the 19th century the Van Loon family (descendants of Willem van Loon, cofounder of the Dutch East India Company) moved in, and they still occupy the upper floors. Take your time wandering through the shadowy rooms adorned with

rich wallpaper, worn carpets and well-used Louis XV furniture.

FREE **Stadsarchief** HISTORICAL ARCHIVE
(Municipal Archives; Map p56; ☎251 15 11; www. stadsarchief.amsterdam.nl; Vijzelstraat 32; ☺10am-5pm Tue-Fri, noon-5pm Sat & Sun) The Amsterdam archives occupy a monumental bank building that dates from 1923. When you step inside, head to the left to the enormous tiled basement vault and displays of archive gems such as the 1942 police report on Anne Frank's bike theft. Well-done temporary exhibits fill the gallery space upstairs; sometimes these have an entry fee (up to €6).

Kattenkabinet MUSEUM
(Cats Cabinet; Map p56; ☎626 53 78; www.kat tenkabinet.nl; Herengracht 497; adult/child €6/3; ☺10am-4pm Mon-Fri, noon-5pm Sat & Sun; ☐4/16/24/25 Keizersgracht) The offbeat Kattenkabinet devotes its Golden Bend real estate to cat-related art. A Picasso drawing, kitschy kitty lithographs and odd pieces of ephemera like a cat pinball machine cram the creaky old canal house. A few happy live felines lounge around on the window seats.

Museum Willet-Holthuysen MUSEUM
(Map p56; ☎523 18 22; www.willetholthuysen.nl; Herengracht 605; adult/child €8/free; ☺10am

-5pm Mon-Fri, 11am-5pm Sat & Sun; 🚊4/9/14 Rembrandtplein) This mansion has been a museum since 1895, when a wealthy widow gave the city her home and her husband's assorted treasures – furniture, paintings and loads of 18th-century china. It's a bit fussier than nearby Museum Van Loon, but the objets are lovely. The 3rd-floor 'collection room' impresses with its stained glass and red velvet wallpaper.

Tassenmuseum Hendrikje
MUSEUM

(Museum of Bags & Purses; Map p56; 🕿524 64 52; www.tassenmuseum.nl; Herengracht 573; adult/child €8.50/free; ⊙10am-5pm; 🚊4/9/14 Rembrandtplein) Dedicated entirely to handbags, this chic canal-house museum is surprisingly interesting even for nonfashionistas. You'll find everything from a crumpled 16th-century goatskin pouch to dainty art deco and design classics by Chanel, Gucci and Versace. Even if you don't see the '80s touchtone phone bag, the 17th-century interiors (and the tearoom's fragrant cake aromas) are worth the entrance price.

Golden Bend
ARCHITECTURE

(Gouden Bocht; Map p56; Herengracht, btwn Leidsestraat & Vijzelstraat) During the Golden Age, the Golden Bend was the 'it' spot, where the wealthiest Amsterdammers lived, loved and ruled their affairs. Look up at the mansions as you walk along the Herengracht. Many date from the 1660s, and thanks to some lobbying at city hall, the gables here were allowed to be twice as wide as the standard Amsterdam model.

Reguliersgracht
CANAL

(Map p56) The Reguliersgracht, aka the canal of seven bridges, is especially romantic in the evening when its humpbacked arches glow with tiny white lights. To get the money shot, stand with your back to the Thorbeckeplein, with the Herengracht flowing directly in front of you to the left and right. Lean over the bridge and look straight ahead down the Reguliersgracht. Ahhh...

Magere Brug
BRIDGE

(Skinny Bridge; Map p62; btwn Kerkstraat & Nieuwe Kerkstraat) The undeniably picturesque Skinny Bridge is the site of many a Dutch wedding photo. Dating from the 1670s, the nine-arched structure has been rebuilt several times in both concrete and timber. It's still operated by hand and remains photogenic even at night, when 1200 twinkling lights make the bridge look like a Christmas confection.

Ajax Experience
MUSEUM

(Map p56; www.ajaxexperienceamsterdam.com; Utrechtsestraat 9; adult/child €17.50/12.50; ⊙11am-7pm) Amsterdam's beloved football club has a museum on the Rembrandtplein geared mostly to youth and diehard fans. The interactive high-tech exhibits let you practise dribbling for speed and kicking for accuracy. You even get an automated pep talk from coach Frank de Boer in the reconstructed Ajax locker room. Displays have famous jerseys, trophies and other memorabilia as well.

OLD SOUTH

Often called the Museum Quarter, the Old South (Oud Zuid) holds the top-draw Van Gogh, Stedelijk and Rijksmuseum collections.

Van Gogh Museum

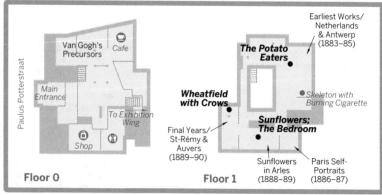

Paulus Potterstraat

Van Gogh's Precursors

Cafe

Main Entrance

To Exhibition Wing

Shop

Floor 0

Earliest Works/ Netherlands & Antwerp (1883–85)

The Potato Eaters

Skeleton with Burning Cigarette

Wheatfield with Crows

Sunflowers; The Bedroom

Final Years/ St-Rémy & Auvers (1889–90)

Sunflowers in Arles (1888–89)

Paris Self-Portraits (1886–87)

Floor 1

VAN GOGH MUSEUM ITINERARY

To see the core collection head to Floor 1 (not to be confused with Floor 0, aka the ground floor where you enter). Van Gogh's paintings hang in chronological order here.

» **Netherlands/Earliest Works Room** Shadowy, sombre images from Van Gogh's time in the Dutch countryside and in Antwerp fill the space. *The Potato Eaters* (1885) is his most famous piece from this period. *Skeleton with Burning Cigarette* (1886) was painted when Van Gogh was a student at Antwerp's art academy.

» **Paris/Self-Portraits Room** In March 1886 Van Gogh moved to Paris, where his brother Theo was working as an art dealer. Van Gogh wanted to master the art of portraiture, but was too poor to pay for models.

» **Sunflowers/Arles Room** In 1888 Van Gogh left for Arles in Provence to delve into its colourful landscapes. This room hangs an awesome line-up of *Sunflowers* (1889) and other blossoms. Also here is *The Bedroom* (1888), which depicts Van Gogh's sleeping quarters at the house where he intended to start an artists colony with Paul Gauguin. The year 1888 is perhaps most notorious as the year Van Gogh sliced off part of his ear.

» **Final Years Room** Van Gogh had himself committed to an asylum in St-Rémy in 1889. While there he painted several landscapes with cypress and olive trees. In 1890 he left the clinic and went north to Auvers-sur-Oise. One of his last paintings, *Wheatfield with Crows* (1890), is an ominous work finished shortly before his suicide.

» **Other Floors** Floor 0 shows paintings mostly by Van Gogh's precursors, such as Millet and Courbet, though Vincent's work is sprinkled in. Floor 2 houses temporary educational exhibits and works on paper. Floor 3 hangs Van Gogh's contemporaries and those he influenced. This is another bountiful level, where you might spy landscapes by Monet and Gauguin, or a room full of French fauvists.

» **Exhibition Wing** Reaching back towards the Museumplein, the Kisho Kurokawa–designed exhibition wing is commonly referred to as 'the Mussel'. It hosts blockbuster exhibitions.

They cluster around the Museumplein, a grassy, people-filled square that entertains with its skateboard ramp, ice-skating pond (in winter) and *I amsterdam* sculpture (everyone's favourite photo opp). The surrounding genteel neighbourhood is more residential than food and drink focused.

Van Gogh Museum MUSEUM
(Map p56; ☑570 52 00; www.vangoghmuseum.nl; Paulus Potterstraat 7; adult/child €14/free, audiotour €5; ☺10am-6pm Sat-Thu, to 10pm Fri; ☀; ☐2/3/5/12 Van Baerlestraat) The world's largest Van Gogh collection packs the building and offers a superb line-up of masterworks. Trace the artist's life from his tentative start through his giddy-coloured sunflower phase, and on to the black cloud that descended over him and his work. There are also paintings by contemporaries Gauguin, Toulouse-Lautrec, Monet and Bernard.

Entrance queues can be huge, as the museum is pretty much the top draw in town. Try waiting until after 3pm. Prebooked e-tickets and discount cards expedite the process with fast-track entry. Or visit on Friday evenings, when the museum stays open late, serves drinks and hosts free cultural events.

Rijksmuseum MUSEUM
(National Museum; Map p56; ☑674 70 00; www.rijksmuseum.nl; Stadhouderskade 42; adult/child €15/free; ☺9am-5pm; ☀; ☐2/5 Hobbemastraat) The Rijksmuseum is the Netherlands' premier art trove. After a 10-year renovation, it reopened in its entirety in April 2013, splashing Rembrandts, Vermeers and 7500 other masterpieces over 1.5km of galleries.

The Golden Age works are the highlight. Feast your eyes on meaty still lifes, gentlemen in ruffled collars and landscapes bathed in pale yellow light. Rembrandt's *The Night Watch* (1642) takes pride of place. Initially titled *Company of Frans Banning Cocq* (the militia's leader), the *The Night Watch* name was bestowed years later due to a layer of grime that gave the impression it was evening. Crowds mob the massive painting. Other must-sees are the Delftware (blue-and-white

DON'T MISS

RIJKSMUSEUM HIGHLIGHTS

» *The Night Watch* (1642) by Rembrandt van Rijn

» *Kitchen Maid* (1658) by Jan Vermeer

» *The Merry Drinker* (1628–30) by Frans Hals

» *The Merry Family* (1668) by Jan Steen

» Delftware pottery collection (late 1600s)

pottery), dollhouses (insanely detailed) and brand-new Asian Pavilion. The sculpture-studded gardens around the exterior are free to visit. To avoid the biggest crowds, come after 3pm. Or prebook tickets online, which provides fast-track entry.

Stedelijk Museum   MUSEUM

(Map p56; ☑573 29 11; www.stedelijk.nl; Museumplein 10; adult/child €15/free; ☺11am-5pm Tue & Wed, 11am-10pm Thu, 10am-6pm Fri-Sun; ♿; ☐2/3/5/12 Van Baerlestraat) Amsterdam's weighty modern art museum is among the world's best. It struts Matisse cut-outs, Kandinsky abstracts, Picasso drawings, Rodin sculptures, and a vivid collection of paintings by Dutch homeboys Piet Mondrian, Willem de Kooning, Charlie Toorop and Karel Appel. After a nine-year renovation, the Stedelijk reopened in September 2012 with a huge new wing (dubbed 'The Bathtub'), where uber-contemporary installations add to the show. The main building also displays textiles, glassworks, posters and cool industrial design pieces (Mies van der Rohe chair, anyone?). Ask about free tours.

House of Bols   MUSEUM

(Map p56; www.houseofbols.com; Paulus Potterstraat 14; admission €12.50; ☺noon-5.30pm Sun-Thu, to 9pm Fri, to 7pm Sat; ☐2/5 Hobbemastraat) An hour's self-guided tour through this *jenever* (Dutch gin) museum includes a confusing sniff test, a distilled history of the Bols company and a cocktail made by one of its formidable bartenders, who train at the academy upstairs. It's kind of Tom Cruise *Cocktail* cheesy, but fun. Come Friday after 5pm, when admission is only €7.50.

Diamond Museum   MUSEUM

(Map p56; www.diamantmuseum.nl; Paulus Potterstraat 8; adult/child €7.50/5; ☺9am-5pm; ☐2/5 Hobbemastraat) Almost all of the exhibits at the small, low-tech Diamond Museum are clever recreations, glinting in glass cases. Those who are economically minded might want to save money by just going next door to Coster Diamonds (the company owns the museum and is attached to it) and taking a free workshop tour, where you can see gem cutters and polishers doing their thing.

VONDELPARK

The city's bucolic playground unfurls next door to the busy Museum Quarter.

Vondelpark   PARK

(Map p56; www.vondelpark.nl; Stadhouderskade; ☺24hr; ☐2/5 Hobbemastraat) On a sunny day it seems the whole city converges on this sprawling equivalent to New York City's Central Park. Couples kiss on the grass, friends cradle beers at the outdoor cafes, while others trade songs on beat-up guitars. The people-watching is sublime. Named for 17th-century poet and playwright Joost van den Vondel, the 'Dutch Shakespeare', the park rolls out ponds, lawns, gardens and winding paths prime for pedaling. The closest bicycle rental shop is MacBike (www.macbike.nl; Weteringschans 2; ☐1/2/5/7/10 Leidseplein), across the Singelgracht from the main entrance. In summer, be sure to see what's on at the free Openluchttheater (p94).

FREE Hollandsche Manege   RIDING SCHOOL

(Map p56; www.dehollandschemanege.nl; Vondelstraat 140; ☺10am-5pm; ☐1 1e Constantijn Huygensstraat) Softly sunlit and smelling of hay and horses, the neoclassical Hollandsche Manege (1882) is an Amsterdam treasure. Buy treats in the shop to feed the creatures, or watch the instructors put them through their paces as you sip in the elegant cafe. To get there, enter through the long arcade on Vondelstraat, take a left turn and head up the stairs.

DE PIJP

With its narrow streets crowded by a lively mix of people – labourers, intellectuals, new immigrants, prostitutes, young urban professionals, gays, movie stars – De Pijp is often called the Latin Quarter of Amsterdam. What started as a 19th-century slum has gentrified into one of the city's coolest neighbourhoods. There aren't many sights. But free-spirited cafes on every block? That's where De Pijp rocks it.

Albert Cuypmarkt   MARKET

(Map p56; www.albertcuypmarkt.nl; Albert Cuypstraat, btwn Ferdinand Bolstraat & Van Woustraat;

⊘10am-5pm Mon-Sat; 🚊16/24 Albert Cuypstraat) The 800m-long Albert Cuypmarkt is Amsterdam's largest and busiest market. Here Surinamese and Indonesian immigrants mix with locals at stalls hawking rice cookers, spices and Dutch snacks like herring sandwiches and *stroopwafels* (two cookie-like waffles with caramel syrup filling). Graze as you gaze at the whirl of goods on offer.

Heineken Experience BREWERY
(Map p56; 🕿523 9435; www.heinekenexperience.com; Stadhouderskade 78; adult/child €17/13; ⊘10.30am-7pm Jun-Aug, 11am-5.30pm Sep-May; 🚊16/24 Stadhouderskade) Heineken used to be brewed in this very building. Now it's a glitzy, self-guided multimedia tour, the high price only slightly offset by the three beers you get out of the process. One nice touch, though: you can visit the brewery's sturdy draught horses in their original stables. Allow 75 minutes for the tour, and expect lots of company. Buying tickets online saves you a few euros. Under-18s only allowed entry with adult supervision.

Sarphatipark PARK
(Map p56; Centuurbaan; ⊘24hr; 🚊16/24 Albert Cuypstraat) While the Vondelpark is bigger and more famous, Sarphatipark delivers an equally potent shot of pastoral summertime relaxation, with far fewer crowds. In the centre you'll see a bombastic temple with a fountain, gargoyles and bust of Samuel Sarphati (1813–66), a Jewish doctor, businessman and urban innovator who helped define the neighbourhood.

PLANTAGE

Located next door to Nieuwmarkt, the Plantage was laid out as a garden district originally, and it still wafts a graceful, leafy air.

Amsterdam Tattoo Museum MUSEUM
(Map p62; www.amsterdamtattoomuseum.com; Plantage Middenlaan 62; adult/child €10/5; ⊘10am-

MORE RED LIGHTS

What the...? You're walking along Ruysdaelkade in De Pijp and suddenly there's a strip of red light windows between 1e Jan Steenstraat and Albert Cuypstraat. It's the usual scene of ladies in day-glo lingerie, but minus the stag parties and drunken crowds that prowl the main Red Light District in the city centre.

DON'T MISS

BEST OFFBEAT MUSEUMS

» **Amsterdam Tattoo Museum** Eye-popping array of inky artefacts (p67).

» **Kattenkabinet** Kitty-cat art, including a Picasso (p63).

» **Houseboat Museum** Vessel that gives a feel for the watery lifestyle (p54).

» **Tassenmuseum Hendrikje** Handbags and purses galore (p64).

» **Electric Ladyland** Trippy times at the fluorescent museum (p55).

7pm; 🚊9/14 Plantage Badlaan) This wild new museum has relics aplenty to back up its 'Tatican' nickname: the first electric tattoo machine, preserved pieces of tattooed flesh (check out the Boston whaler's skin from 1850) and painful-looking tribal implements from Borneo to Burma. Want a memento of your visit? Ascend to the 2nd floor, where resident tattoo artists apply the ultimate keepsake. Then show off your ink in the boisterous cafe. One caveat: as this book was going to press, a disagreement had erupted between the artifacts' owners and the building managers, so it's possible the museum will move.

Hortus Botanicus GARDEN
(Botanical Garden; Map p62; www.dehortus.nl; Plantage Middenlaan 2a; adult/child €7.50/3.50; ⊘10am-5pm; 🚊9/14 Mr Visserplein) Established in 1638, the Hortus Botanicus was the repository for tropical seeds and plants Dutch ships brought back from exotic voyages. Groovy greenery includes the Palmhouse's 300-year-old cycad, one of the world's oldest potted plants, and a semicircular garden representing the entire plant kingdom. Guided tours (additional €1) of the compact grounds are held at 2pm on Sundays.

Verzetsmuseum MUSEUM
(Dutch Resistance Museum; Map p62; 🕿620 25 35; www.dutchresistancemuseum.org; Plantage Kerklaan 61; adult/child €8/4.50; ⊘10am-5pm Tue-Fri, 11am-5pm Sat-Mon; 🚊9/14 Plantage Kerklaan) Intriguing exhibits detail how locals fought the German occupation during WWII. Learn how the illegal press operated and how thousands of people (like Anne Frank) were kept in hiding. It wasn't all noble: another chilling display articulates the

THINGS TO DO WHEN IT'S RAINING IN AMSTERDAM

It'll rain at some point during your stay (you can count on it) though it probably won't pour for long.

» **Amsterdam Museum** Learn about your favourite city without waiting in a rain-soaked queue (p44).

» **Cafes** Loaf over a newspaper, drink and/or bite to eat.

» **Centrale Bibliotheek** Check your email or read a book at the ubercool main library (p69).

» **Tropenmuseum** Learn about Dutch colonial activities, also sans soggy queue (p69).

» **Tuschinskitheater** Absorb the glorious architecture while watching a film (p94).

reasons many citizens refused to shelter Jews. A smaller wing covers the Resistance in the Dutch East Indies.

Hollandsche Schouwburg　　　MEMORIAL
(Holland Theatre; Map p62; ☑626 99 45; www.hollandscheschouwburg.nl; Plantage Middenlaan 24; suggested donation €2.50; ☺11am-4pm; ☐9/14 Plantage Kerklaan) After 1942 this theatre became a detention centre for Jews awaiting deportation. Up to 80,000 people passed through on their way to the death camps. Glass panels show the names of the deported, and upstairs a modest exhibit hall displays photos and artefacts from the period; look for the heartbreaking tale of Bram and Eva Beem.

Wertheimpark　　　PARK
(Map p62; Plantage Parklaan; ☺dawn-dusk; ☐9/14 Mr Visserplein) Opposite the Hortus Botanicus, this park is a willow-shaded spot brilliant for lazing by the Nieuwe Herengracht. On the park's northeast side locals often place flowers at the Auschwitz Memorial, a panel of broken mirrors installed in the ground that reflects the sky.

Artis Royal Zoo　　　ZOO
(Map p62; ☑523 34 00; www.artis.nl; Plantage Kerklaan 38-40; adult/child €19/15.50; ☺9am-6pm Apr-Oct, to 5pm Nov-Mar; ☗; ☐9/14 Plantage Kerklaan) Artis has an alphabet soup of wildlife – alligators, birds, chimps and so on up to zebras, but the lush grounds are the true delight, full of ponds, statues and verdant pathways.

Check out the aquarium's murky canal cross-section, featuring discarded bikes and creepy eels. If you prefer your nature stuffed, stop by the zoo's museum, a trove of taxidermy and other 19th-century relics.

EASTERN ISLANDS & EASTERN DOCKLANDS

In the past 15 years, the crumbling shipyard and warehouse district that used to be the city's fringe has morphed into a hub for cutting-edge Dutch architecture. Because the neighbourhood is more spread out than others, it's a good one to explore by bicycle, gawping at innovative structures along the way. *Eastern Docklands Amsterdam* is a good resource, despite being a bit dated, for history and DIY walking and cycling tours of the neighbourhood's mod structures.

TOP CHOICE Het Scheepvaartmuseum　　　MUSEUM
(Maritime Museum; Map p62; ☑523 22 22; www.scheepvaartmuseum.nl; Kattenburgerplein 1; adult/child €15/7.50; ☺9am-5pm; ☗; ☐22/43 Kattenburgerplein) The Maritime Museum puts on a helluva display. In the Oost entrance you'll find nifty collections of globes from the 1600s, oodles of ship models, and silver and porcelain brought back from Dutch voyages – all on the 1st floor. The 2nd floor has spooky ship figureheads and trippy time-worn navigation instruments. A full-scale replica of the Dutch East India Company's 700-tonne *Amsterdam* moors outside.

FARCAM　　　ARCHITECTURE
(Stichting Architectuur Centrum Amsterdam; Map p62; ☑620 48 78; www.arcam.nl; Prins Hendrikkade 600; ☺1-5pm Tue-Sat; ☐32/33/34/35/359/361/363 IJ-Tunnel) The Amsterdam Architecture Foundation should be the first point of call for architecture and urban design buffs. Exhibits vary, but you are sure to find books, guide maps and suggestions for tours on foot, by bike and by public transport. Check the website for digital resources and free apps about the city's buildings.

NEMO　　　MUSEUM
(Map p62; ☑531 32 33; www.e-nemo.nl; Oosterdok 2; admission €13.50; ☺10am-5pm, closed Mon Sep-May; ☗; ☐32/33/34/35/359/361/363 IJ-Tunnel) Jutting into the harbour like a ship, Renzo Piano's stunning green-copper edifice is an excellent science and technology museum with hands-on laboratories for kids. For adults, NEMO's stepped roof (admission free) is the city's largest

summer terrace and worth a stair climb for the fantastic view.

FREE **Centrale Bibliotheek Amsterdam**   LIBRARY
(Amsterdam Central Library; Map p62; ☎523 09 00; www.oba.nl; Oosterdokskade 143; ☺10am-10pm; ⍟25/26 Muziekgebouw) Inviting chairs and couches scatter around the nine floors of Amsterdam's mod main library, as do loads of internet terminals (per half-hour €1). The top-floor cafeteria provides terrific views over the city and water (you can go look without having to buy anything).

OOSTERPARK

Oosterpark is one of Amsterdam's most culturally diverse neighbourhoods, with Moroccan and Turkish enclaves, and sights that are off the everyday tourist path.

Tropenmuseum   MUSEUM
(Tropics Museum; ☎568 82 15; www.tropenmuseum.nl; Linnaeusstraat 2; adult/child €10/6; ☺10am-5pm Tue-Sun; 👶; ⍟9/10/14 Alexanderplein) You could spend all day in this utterly absorbing anthropology museum, watching Bollywood clips, strolling through recreated African markets and learning to yodel from old recordings. The museum began as a collection of colonial booty, so the areas covering former Dutch territory are particularly rich, with gorgeous Indonesian jewellery and enormous Polynesian war canoes.

Oosterpark   PARK
(Map p62; 's-Gravesandestraat; ☺dawn-dusk) Oosterpark was laid out in 1891 to accommodate the diamond traders who found their fortunes in the South African mines, and it still has an elegant, rambling feel, complete with regal grey herons swooping around the ponds. On the south side, look for **De Schreeuw** (The Scream), a silvery monument that honours free speech and, more specifically, filmmaker Theo van Gogh, who was murdered here in 2004.

Dappermarkt   MARKET
(www.dappermarkt.nl; Dapperstraat, btwn Mauritskade & Wijttenbachstraat; ☺10am-4.30pm Mon-Sat; ⍟3/7 Dapperstraat) The larger Albert Cuypmarkt in De Pijp may the king of street bazaars, but the Dappermarkt is a worthy prince. Reflecting the Oost's

---

WORTH A TRIP

AMSTERDAMSE BOS & COBRA MUSEUM

Goats in the forest and wild art reward those who venture southwest of the city to the quiet suburb of Amstelveen, near Schiphol Airport.

The jewel here is **Amsterdamse Bos** (Amsterdam Woods; www.amsterdamsebos.nl; Bosbaanweg 5; ☺park 24hr, bicycles 10am-6pm Tue-Sun; 👶), a vast tract of lakes, woods and meadows criss-crossed by paths. **Bike rentals** (€9.50 per day; 10am to 6pm Tuesday to Sunday) are available at the main entrance and are vital for park exploration. The **Fun Forest** (www.funforest.nl; adult/child €21.50/19.50; ☺10am-7pm Apr-Oct; 👶) tree-top climbing park is also by the main gate.

The park's most delightful attraction is about 4km into the woods. **De Ridammerhoeve** (www.geitenboerderij.nl; admission free; ☺10am-5pm Wed-Mon) is an organic, working goat farm where kids can feed bottles of milk to, well, kids (€8 for two bottles). The cafeteria sells goat's-milk smoothies and ice cream, as well as cheeses made on the premises. Several additional cafes, a farmhouse pancake restaurant, **canoe and kayak rentals** (per hour €6) and an open-air theatre round out the offerings.

The fascinating **CoBrA Museum** (www.cobra-museum.nl; Sandbergplein 1; adult/child €9.50/6; ☺11am-5pm Tue-Sun) lies near the park. Formed by artists from Copenhagen, Brussels and Amsterdam after WWII, the CoBrA movement produced semi-abstract works known for their primitive, childlike qualities. The two-storey building holds a trove of boldly coloured, avant-garde paintings, ceramics and statues, including many by Karel Appel, the style's most famous practitioner.

Take bus 170 or 172 from Centraal Station. It's about a 40-minute ride to the forest, and another 10 minutes to the museum. For the latter, you can also take tram 5 from Centraal Station to the end of the line in Amstelveen. It takes a bit longer and drops you about a kilometre from CoBrA, but you'll save money if you're using a GVB travel pass (which is not valid for bus 170 or 172).

diverse immigrant population, it's a whirl of people (Africans, Turks, Dutch), foods (apricots, olives, fish) and goods from sports socks to shimmering fabrics to sunflowers, all sold from stalls lining the street.

🏃 Activities

Cycling

Fiets (bicycles) outnumber cars in Amsterdam. Rental shops are everywhere. Vondelpark and the Eastern Islands and Docklands are easy destinations for DIY cycling.

Travel 20 minutes north of the city centre, and the landscape morphs to windmills, cows and wee farming communities – all accessible via an afternoon bike ride. To get there, take your wheels onto the free Buiksloterweg ferry behind Centraal Station, and cross the IJ River. The ride takes about five minutes, and boats depart continuously throughout the day. Then pedal north along the Noordhollands Kanaal. Within a few kilometres you're in the countryside. Cycling maps are available at the VVV main office by Centraal Station. Tour companies also cover the area.

Boating

Canal Bike　　　　　　　　　　BOAT RENTAL
(Map p56; www.canal.nl; per person per hr €8; ☉10am-6pm Apr-Oct, to 10pm in summer) These pedal boats allow you to splash around the canals at your own pace. Landings are by the Rijksmuseum, Leidseplein, Anne Frank Huis and the corner of Keizersgracht and Leidsestraat. Requires a €20 deposit. Affiliated with the Canal Bus hop-on, hop-off company.

Ice Skating

In winter the pond at the Museumplein becomes a popular ice-skating rink, and the scene looks like the top of a wind-up jewellery box. The rink is free; there's a modest fee for skate rentals.

Occasionally the canals freeze over for skating, but stay away unless you see large groups of people gliding. The ice can be weak, especially at the edges and under bridges.

Skateboarding

The half-pipe on the Museumplein brings out boards aplenty. There's also a skateboard hall (see p44) at NDSM-werf, though it's slated to close in 2014. Skateboarders are advised to bring their own gear to Amsterdam as rentals are thin on the ground.

Tours

Bicycle Tours

The companies following also rent bikes.

Mike's Bike Tours　　　　　　　　CYCLING
(Map p56; ☑622 79 70; www.mikesbiketours.com; Kerkstraat 134; tours €22) Fantastic four-hour tours take you around the centre of town and south along the Amstel river, past dairy farms and windmills. Reserve in advance.

Orangebike　　　　　　　　　　CYCLING
(Map p46; ☑528 99 90; www.orangebike.nl; Singel 233; tours €15-33) Orangebike offers several three-hour cycling jaunts, from a traditional see-the-sights Historic City Tour to themed options (Dutch snacks, beer, Eastern Harbour architecture, countryside journeys). Reserve in advance. There's another branch at Geldersekade 37.

Yellow Bike　　　　　　　　　　CYCLING
(Map p46; ☑620 69 40; www.yellowbike.nl; Nieuwezijds Kolk 29; city/countryside tours €19.50/29.50) Yellow Bike offered the original Amsterdam bike tour, so it's got it down pat. Choose from the two-hour city tour or the longer four-hour countryside tour through the pretty Waterland district to the north. Tours are less youth-oriented than Mike's. Reservations recommended.

Boat Tours

Sure they're touristy, but canal tours are also a delightful way to see the city. Several operators depart from moorings at Centraal Station, Damrak, Rokin and opposite the Rijksmuseum. Costs are similar (around €13 per adult). To avoid the steamed-up glass window effect, look for a boat with an open seating area. On a night tour, there's the bonus of seeing the bridges lit up (though these tours usually cost a few euros more).

Boom Chicago Boats　　　　　　BOAT TOUR
(Map p56; www.boomchicago.nl; Leidseplein 12; per person €15; ☉tours 2.45pm; ◌1/2/5/7/10 Leidseplein) The comedy club's 75-minute tours cater to a younger crowd; it uses smaller open-air boats (that can be covered in bad weather).

TOP
CHOICE **St Nicolaas Boat Club**　　　　BOAT TOUR
(Map p56; www.amsterdamboatclub.com; Leidseplein 12) The excellent tour is in an open-air, 10-seat vessel that can manoeuvre into the narrowest canals. There is no set fee, just a

AMSTERDAM FOR CHILDREN

Never mind the sex and drugs – think bikes and boats, puppet shows and pancakes. Amsterdam really is one of Europe's most kid-friendly cities.

Playful Museums

» **NEMO** Kid-focused, hands-on science labs inside; an artificial beach with sand and ice-cream stands on the roof (p68).

» **Het Scheepvaartmuseum** Climb aboard the full-scale, 17th-century replica ship and check out the cannons (p68).

» **Tropenmuseum** Spend the afternoon learning to yodel, sitting in a yurt or travelling via otherworldly exhibits (p69).

» **Rijksmuseum** Children get their own audiotour to explore the museum's treasures (p65).

Parks & Animals & Active Endeavours

» **Vondelpark** Space-age slides at the western end, playground in the middle, duck ponds throughout (p66).

» **Artis Royal Zoo** Extrovert monkeys, big cats, shimmying fish and a planetarium provide the requisite thrills (p68).

» **Amsterdamse Bos** Tykes can feed goats and climb trees in the woods (p69).

» **TunFun** (Map p62; www.tunfun.nl; Mr Visserplein 7; adult/child free/€8.50; ⊙10am-6pm, last entry 5pm; 🔊) Build, climb, jump, draw and more at this indoor, underground playground; it's a great rainy-day option.

» **Canal Bike** Glide through the city's waterways in a paddleboat (p70).

Kid Cuisine & Entertainment

» **Pancakes!** Even picky eaters will say yes to these giant spongy discs of goodness (p84).

» **Taart van m'n Tante** Fantastically decorated cakes in a whimsical parlour bring whoops of joy (p87).

» **Amsterdams Marionetten Theater** Puts on captivating shows such as Mozart's *The Magic* Flute (p93).

» **Openluchttheater** Vondelpark's free theatre hosts musicians, acrobats, storytellers and more most Saturdays afternoons in summer (p94).

suggested €10 donation. Departure is from Mike's Bikes. Alas, the club was on hiatus due to licensing issues at press time. Check the website for updates.

Canal Bus BOAT TOUR
(www.canal.nl; day pass adult/child €22/11) Offers a unique hop-on, hop-off service; has 17 docks around the city near the big museums.

Blue Boat Company BOAT TOUR
(Map p56; www.blueboat.nl; Stadhouderskade 30; ⊙every 30min 10am-7pm; 🚊7/10 Spiegelgracht) The main tour (adult/child €14/7.50) clocks in at 75 minutes. Blue Boat also offers evening cruises, kids' cruises and art cruises in conjunction with the Rijksmuseum.

Walking Tours

Prostitution Information Centre
Red Light District Tour WALKING TOUR
(Map p46; www.pic-amsterdam.com; Enge Kerksteeg 3; tours €15; ⊙5pm Sat) This nonprofit centre (see p49) offers fascinating one-hour tours of the Red Light District, where guides explain the nitty-gritty of how the business works and take you into a Red Light room. Proceeds go to the centre.

Randy Roy's Redlight Tours WALKING TOUR
(Map p46; ☎06 4185 3288; www.randyroysred lighttours.com; tours €12.50; ⊙8pm Sun-Thu, 8pm & 10pm Fri & Sat, closed Dec-Feb) In-the-know anecdotes about the city's sex life and celebrity secrets feature on Randy Roy's lively 1½-hour tour. Meet in front of the Victoria

Hotel (Damrak 1-5), opposite Centraal Station, rain or shine.

Sandeman's New Amsterdam Tours
WALKING TOUR

(Map p46; www.newamsterdamtours.com; donations encouraged; ☺11.15am & 1.15pm) Slick young guides lead an entertaining three-hour jaunt to the sights of the city centre and Red Light District. Meet at the Nationaal Monument on the Dam, rain or shine.

Drugs Tour
WALKING TOUR

(Map p46; www.drugstour.nl; tours by donation; ☺6pm Fri) The 1½-hour itinerary includes smart shops, a 'user room' (the tour doesn't go inside) and a look at fake drugs being sold on the street. Tours depart by the Oude Kerk. Reserve in advance. Private tours also can be arranged (€40 per four people) in multiple languages.

Mee in Mokum
WALKING TOUR

(Map p46; www.gildeamsterdam.nl; Kalverstraat 92; tours €7.50; ☺11am & 2pm Tue-Sun) Mee in Mokum's low-priced walkabouts are led by senior-citizen volunteers who often have personal recollections to add. The tours can be a bit hit or miss, depending on the guide, but are well worth the value. They depart from the cafe in the Amsterdam Museum.

✦✦ Festivals & Events

5 Days Off
MUSIC

(www.5daysoff.nl) Five-day electronic music festival in early March with dance parties at Paradiso and Melkweg.

King's Day
CULTURAL

(Koningsdag) On 27 April festivities let loose around the nation to honor the monarch, but Amsterdam parties hardest. Streets fill with orange-clad revelers, booming bands and a citywide flea market.

Herdenkingsdag
CULTURAL

(Remembrance Day) For the fallen of WWII. On 4 May the monarch lays a wreath on the Dam and the city observes two minutes' silence at 8pm. Bevrijdingsdag (Liberation Day) follows on 5 May with street parties and concerts, especially in Vondelpark.

World Press Photo Show
CULTURAL

(www.worldpressphoto.org) Pictures taken by the world's best photojournalists are displayed at the Oude Kerk from mid-April to June.

Holland Festival
CULTURAL

(www.hollandfestival.nl) The country's biggest music, drama and dance extravaganza takes over Amsterdam for most of June. Highbrow and pretentious meet lowbrow and silly.

Roots Festival
MUSIC

(www.amsterdamroots.nl) Paradiso, Bimhuis and other venues program fantastic world music over a long weekend in early July, highlighted by a free outdoor bash in Oosterpark.

Over het IJ Festival
CULTURAL

(www.overhetij.nl) Uninhibited theatre, music and fine arts shows take place over 10 days in early July in offbeat venues around the NDSM shipyards in Amsterdam-Noord.

Amsterdam Pride
CULTURAL

(www.weareproud.nl) On the first weekend in August the completely over-the-top gay shebang culminates with a waterborne parade of boats on the canals, followed by street parties.

Grachtenfestival
MUSIC

(www.grachtenfestival.nl) Classical musicians pop up in canalside parks and hidden gardens for this 10-day fest in mid-August. The highlight is the free concert on a floating stage in the Prinsengracht, attended by nearly every boat in the city.

Amsterdam Dance Event
MUSIC

(www.amsterdam-dance-event.nl) A club music powwow, with 700 DJs and 200,000 avid dancers attending parties all over Amsterdam during a long, sweaty weekend in mid-October.

Cannabis Cup
CULTURAL

(www.cannabiscup.com) Hosted by *High Times* magazine in late November, this far-out festival doles out awards for nicest grass, biggest reefer and best 'pot comedian'.

🛏 Sleeping

Book well ahead in summer and for weekends throughout the year. Any hotel with more than 20 rooms is considered large, and most rooms are on the snug side. Free wi-fi is nearly universal, but air-conditioning and lifts are not. Prepare to carry your luggage up steep staircases.

Rates listed are nondiscounted rack rates; they do not include breakfast unless stated otherwise. Prices usually drop from October to April. Most of the quoted rates also include a 5.5% city-hotel tax; however, this is sometimes added separately to the bill, so ask before booking. If you're paying by credit card, some hotels add a surcharge of up to 5%.

Take heed with lodgings in the centre, as they can be noisy and poor value for the money. Western Canal Belt places are near the action but more dignified and quiet. The Old South and Vondelpark offer quality digs that are close to the museums and only a short walk from the action at Leidseplein. Apartment rentals work well for local-life areas such as the Jordaan and De Pijp. Citymundo (www.citymundo.com) is a reliable apartment broker; there's a three-night minimum. AirBnB (www.airbnb.com) and Craigslist (www.craigslist.org) also turn up lots of Amsterdam options.

MEDIEVAL CENTRE & RED LIGHT DISTRICT

Hotel Résidence Le Coin   APARTMENT $$
(Map p56; ☏524 68 00; www.lecoin.nl; Nieuwe Doelenstraat 5; s €125, d €145-160, f €240; ☎) This shiny inn, owned by the University of Amsterdam, offers 42 small, high-class apartments spread over seven historical buildings, all equipped with designer furniture, wood floors and kitchenettes – and all reachable by lift. It's in the thick of things, opposite the popular Café de Jaren and just a five-minute stroll to pretty Nieuwmarkt. Breakfast costs €11.50 per person; wi-fi costs €5 per 24 hours.

Hotel Brouwer   HOTEL $$
(Map p46; ☏624 63 58; www.hotelbrouwer.nl; Singel 83; r €60-100; @☎) A bargain-priced favourite,

FREE THRILLS

It's possible to spend a fortune in Amsterdam, but many enjoyable sights and activities cost nothing.

Sights

» **Civic Guard Gallery** Stroll through the monumental collection of portraits, from Golden Age to modern (p44).

» **Begijnhof** Explore the 14th-century hidden courtyard and its clandestine churches (p44).

» **Stadsarchief** You never know what treasures you'll find in the vaults of the city's archives (p63).

» **Albert Cuypmarkt** Amsterdam's biggest market bursts with cheeses, bike locks and socks, as do the city's many other bazaars – all free to browse (p66).

Entertainment

» **Concertgebouw** Sharpen your elbows to get in for Wednesday's lunchtime concert, often a public rehearsal for musicians playing later that evening (p93).

» **Muziektheater** More classical freebies fill the air during lunch, this time on Tuesdays (p93).

» **Bimhuis** Jazzy jam sessions hot up the revered venue on Tuesday nights (p92).

Tours

» **Sandeman's New Amsterdam Tours** Young guides show you the centre's top sights (p72).

» **Gassan Diamonds** Don't know your princess from marquise, river from top cape? Get the shiny low-down here (p51).

DIY

» **Canals** Walk along the 400-year-old waterways and decide which old gabled house leans the most.

» **Ferry rides** Free ferries depart behind Centraal Station to NDSM-werf, northern Amsterdam's edgy art community 15 minutes up harbour, and to the EYE Film Institute, five minutes across the river.

» **Red Light District** Keep your eyes on the architecture and you needn't spend a cent.

GAY & LESBIAN AMSTERDAM

Information

Gay Amsterdam (www.gayamsterdam.com) Lists hotels, shops, restaurants and clubs, and provides maps.

Pink Point (www.pinkpoint.org; ☉noon-6pm Mar-Aug, limited hours Sep-Feb) Located behind the Westerkerk, Pink Point is part information kiosk, part souvenir shop. Get details on GLBT hang-outs and social groups, and pick up a copy of the candid *Bent Guide*.

Sleeping

Most hotels in town are lesbian and gay friendly, but some cater specifically to a queer clientele:

Amistad (Map p56; ✆624 80 74; www.amistad.nl; Kerkstraat 42; r without bathroom €100, s/d with bathroom from €130/160; @ ☎) Rooms at this bijou hotel are dotted with designer Philippe Starck chairs, CD players, chic soft furnishings and computers. The breakfast room (with ruby-red walls and communal tables) becomes a hopping internet cafe later, popular with the gay set.

Golden Bear (Map p56; ✆624 47 85; www.goldenbear.nl; Kerkstraat 37; r with shared/private bathroom from €75/100; ☎) The oldest gay hotel in Amsterdam has been operating since 1948. Straddling two 18th-century buildings, rooms are done up in bright colours, with mod furnishings and minifridges. Breakfast included.

Entertainment

Amsterdam's gay scene is among the world's largest. Five hubs party hardest. **Warmoesstraat** in the Red Light District hosts the infamous, kink-filled leather and fetish bars. Nearby on the upper end of the **Zeedijk**, bright crowds spill onto laid-back bar terraces. In the Southern Canal Belt, the area around **Rembrandtplein** (aka the 'Amstel area') has traditional pubs and brown cafes, some with a campy bent. **Leidseplein** has a smattering of trendy venues along Kerkstraat. And **Reguliersdwarsstraat**, located one street down from the flower market, draws the beautiful crowd (though financial and legal problems have

Brouwer has just eight rooms in a house dating back to 1652. Each chamber is named for a Dutch painter and furnished with simplicity, but all have canal views. There's a mix of Delft-blue tiles and early 20th-century decor, plus a tiny lift. Staff dispense friendly advice. Reserve well in advance. No credit cards accepted.

Hotel de L'Europe   LUXURY HOTEL **$$$**
(Map p56; ✆531 17 77; www.leurope.nl; Nieuwe Doelenstraat 2-8; r from €340; ❄@☎☰) Owned by the Heineken family, who recently gave it an $85-million renovation, L'Europe mixes classical elements (glass chandeliers, doormen in top hats) with whimsical Dutch design. The 111 rooms are grand, with iPads, canal views, heated floors and white marble bath-tubs; wi-fi is free. The on-site cigar lounge and Freddy's bar, with brass-topped tables and leather chairs, attract a professional crowd.

Hotel The Exchange   BOUTIQUE HOTEL **$$**
(Map p46; ✆561 36 99; www.exchangeamsterdam.com; Damrak 50; r €100-400; @☎) A newcomer to the city, the Exchange has 61 rooms done up in wild high style by students from the Amsterdam Fashion Institute. Anything goes, from eye paintings on the walls to a Marie Antoinette dress tented over the bed. If you like vanilla, this isn't your place. Rooms span one star (small and no view) to five stars; all have a private bathroom. Rooms fronting the Damrak can be noisy.

St Christopher's at the Winston   PARTY HOSTEL **$**
(Map p46; ✆623 13 80; www.winston.nl; Warmoesstraat 123; dm €34-42, r €80-120; ☎) This place is party central for touring bands, with rock 'n' roll rooms and a busy club, bar, beer garden and smoking deck downstairs; it hops 24/7. Dorm rooms (all en suite) sleep up to eight. Most private rooms are 'art' rooms: local artists were given free

taken a toll on many venues here recently; check www.reguliers.net for updates on openings and closings).

Some possibilities, in addition to favourites 't Mandje (p88) and Cafe de Barderij (p89):

FUXXX (Map p46; www.clubfuxxx.com; Warmoesstraat 96; ⊙from 11pm Thu-Sun) Lots of action here. It's men only for hardcore dancing and cruising Thursday through Saturday. Women join the ranks on Sundays.

Getto (Map p46; www.getto.nl; Warmoesstraat 51; ⊙Tue-Sun; 🚊4/9/16/24/25 Centraal Station) A younger crowd piles into this groovy, welcoming bar-restaurant for cheap food and fun people-watching. It's a haven for anyone who wants a little bohemian subculture in the Red Light District's midst.

Montmartre (Map p56; www.cafemontmartre.nl; Halvemaansteeg 17) Beneath outrageous ceiling decorations, patrons belt out Dutch ballads and Top 40 songs. It's like a gay Eurovision. Regarded by many as the Benelux' best gay bar.

Queen's Head (Map p46; www.queenshead.nl; Zeedijk 20) The beautiful, canal-view, old-world-style cafe was once run by legendary drag queen Dusty. It's a mixed gay-straight crowd now, with drag queen bingo on Tuesdays.

Saarein (Map p52; Elandsstraat 119; ⊙from 4pm Tue-Fri & Sun, from noon Sat; 🚊7/10/17 Elandsgracht) A one-time feminist stronghold, Saarein is still a meeting place for lesbians, although these days gay men are welcome too. The cafe dates from the 1600s. There's a small menu with tapas and soups.

Vivelavie (Map p56; www.vivelavie.net; Amstelstraat 7; ⊙from 4pm; 🕿) Just off Rembrandtplein, this lively place is probably Amsterdam's most popular lesbian cafe, with flirty girls, loud music and a buzzy outdoor terrace.

Festivals

The biggest single party is the **Roze Wester** thrown at the Homomonument (p55) on King's Day (27 April), with bands and street dancing. Amsterdam Pride (p72) puts on the only waterborne gay parade in the world, with outlandishly decorated boats plying the canals.

---

rein, with results from super-edgy (entirely stainless steel) and playful to questionably raunchy. There's no internet in the rooms, but the ground-floor wi-fi (lobby and bar) is free. Rates include breakfast.

Hotel Luxer　　　　　　　HOTEL **$$**
(Map p46; ☏330 32 05; www.hotelluxer.nl; Warmoesstraat 11; r €90-150; ❋@🕿) A pleasant surprise if ever there was one, this smart little number is probably the best option for your money in the thick of the Red Light District. Rooms are small but well equipped (air-con!) and at night the breakfast area becomes a chic little bar. Breakfast is €10.

Aivengo Youth Hostel　　　　HOSTEL **$**
(Map p46; ☏421 36 70; www.aivengoyouthhostel. com; Spuistraat 6; dm €18-26, r €80-100; @🕿) Aivengo spreads out across two buildings – one with a Middle Eastern interior, the other with exposed wood beams. Rooms come in a variey of shapes: there's a 10-bed female dorm, a 20-bed mixed dorm and a

couple of private en suite doubles among the stock. As far as in-the-thick-of-the-scene hostels go, Aivengo has a quiet, respectful vibe. There's no real common room though, and the 'lounge' area meant to fill the gap sits next to the bathroom (a bit too close for comfort).

NIEUWMARKT

Misc Eat Drink Sleep　BOUTIQUE HOTEL **$$$**
(Map p46; ☏330 62 41; www.misceatdrinksleep. com; Kloveniersburgwal 20; r €155-245; @🕿) Steps from Nieuwmarkt square, the Misc's six themed rooms range from 'baroque' (quite romantic) to 'the room of wonders' (a modern Moroccan escapade); two rooms contain quirky 'bumble-bee' ceiling fans. Canal View rooms cost more, but the Garden View rooms are equally charming (and bigger). There's free breakfast, and all in-room snacks and nonalcoholic beverages from the minibar are free. Rooms also come with a Nespresso coffee machine.

AIRPORT ACCOMMODATION

Need a bed by the Schiphol Airport? Citizen M (☎811 70 80; www.citizenmam sterdamairport.com; Plezierweg 2; r €79-139; ❄@☎) is a five-minute walk from the terminals. The *Starship Enterprise*–like rooms are snug but maximise space to the utmost, with plush, wall-to-wall beds, and shower and toilet pods. Each room includes a Philips MoodPad – command central for the lighting (purple, red or white), blinds, flat-screen TV (free on-demand movies), music, temperature and rain shower. Sushi, sake and self-service snacks are for sale in the lobby's clubby canteen.

Stayokay Amsterdam Stadsdoelen   HOSTEL $

(Map p46; ☎624 68 32; www.stayokay.com; Kloven-iersburgwal 97; dm €20-33, r €60; @☎) Efficient Stadsdoelen is always bustling with backpackers and we can understand why. Staff are friendly and the 11 ultraclean single-sex and mixed rooms (each with up to 20 beds and free lockers) offer a modicum of privacy. There's a big TV room, a pool table, laundry facilities, free lobby wi-fi, bicycle storage (€2 per day) and free continental breakfast. Laptop rental costs €3 per hour.

Christian Youth Hostel 'The Shelter City'   HOSTEL $

(Map p46; ☎625 32 30; www.shelter.nl; Barndes-teeg 21; dm €25-39; @☎) The larger branch of the squeaky-clean Shelter Jordaan (p76).

JORDAAN

TOP CHOICE **All Inn the Family B&B**   B&B $$

(Map p52; ☎776 36 36; www.allinnthefamily.nl; 2e Egelantiersdwarsstraat 10; r €95-140; ☎) This four-room B&B, in a charming old Amsterdam canal house, gets rave reviews. The spirited hosts speak five languages, there's a bountiful organic Dutch breakfast, and the property sits in a quiet location in the heart of the Jordaan. It's an ideal base for those seeking the *gezellig,* open-minded friendliness that travellers come to Amsterdam for. Bathrooms are shared.

Hotel Amsterdam Wiechmann   HOTEL $$

(Map p52; ☎626 33 21; www.hotelwiechmann.nl; Prinsengracht 328; r €90-210; @☎) The family-run Wiechmann occupies three houses in a marvelous canalside location, just a stone's throw from the Negen Straatjes. The cosy, lovingly cared for rooms are furnished like an antique shop, with country quilts and chintz, and the lobby knick-knacks have been here for some 60 years. Breakfast is included.

Christian Youth Hostel 'The Shelter Jordaan'   HOSTEL $

(Map p52; ☎624 47 17; www.shelter.nl; Bloemstraat 179; dm €25-39; @☎) OK, we'll put up with the no drinking and partying policy at this small hostel because it's such a gem. Single-sex dorms are quiet and clean; the free breakfasts – especially the fluffy pancakes – are beaut; and the garden patio is a relaxing retreat. The cafe serves cheap meals the rest of the day. Linens are free, but towels cost €1. Bible study is optional.

Hotel van Onna   HOTEL $$

(Map p52; ☎626 58 01; www.hotelvanonna.nl; Blo-emgracht 102-108; r €65-150; @☎) Even if the 41 utilitarian rooms won't win any design awards, they're reasonably priced and you're in a gorgeous section of the Jordaan, within earshot of the Westerkerk's bells (get a back room if you're sensitive to noise). Try to book one of the two attic rooms, which have old wooden roof beams and panoramic views over the Bloemgracht (Flower Canal). Continental breakfast is included. Rooms do not have phones or TVs.

Hotel Acacia   HOTEL $$

(Map p52; ☎622 14 60; www.hotelacacia.nl; Linden-gracht 251; r €65-145; @☎) If you simply want to park your bones after a day wandering the canals, the Acacia is just the ticket. It's in a sleepy corner of the Jordaan, and rooms in the angular corner building are larger than the norm. Ask about studios with kitchen-ettes. Rates include breakfast.

International Budget Hostel   STONER HOSTEL $

(Map p56; ☎624 27 84; www.internationalbudgethos tel.com; Leidsegracht 76; dm €18-40, r €65-80; @☎) Reasons to stay: canalside location in a former warehouse; close to nightlife; four-person limit in the rooms; cool mix of backpackers from around the world; clean rooms with lockers; printer access and bike rental; and staff who are more pleasant than they need to be.

WESTERN CANAL BELT

The Toren   BOUTIQUE HOTEL $$

(Map p52; ☎622 60 33; www.toren.nl; Keizersgracht 164; r €130-210, ste from €300; ❄@☎) A title-holder for price, room size and personal service, the Toren's communal areas mix 17th-century decadence – gilded mirrors, fireplaces and magnificent chandeliers – with a sensual flair that screams (or, rather, whispers) Parisian boudoir. The 36 guest rooms are elegantly furnished with modern facilities, including Nespresso coffee machines.

Sebastian's
BOUTIQUE HOTEL **$$**

(Map p46; 433 23 42; www.hotelsebastians.nl; Keizersgracht 15; r €100-230; ❄✳@🖙) The Toren's newer sister property rocks the same brand of dramatic cool, but skews more bohemian-Goth decor-wise. It's located a few blocks away, along the same canal.

Dylan
LUXURY HOTEL **$$$**

(Map p52; 530 20 10; www.dylanamsterdam.com; Keizersgracht 384; r from €350; @🖙) When George Clooney, Mariah Carey, Justin Timberlake and their ilk come to town, they check in at the uberstylish Dylan. Slink through the 17th-century canal house's courtyard garden entrance and past the gorgeous staff to ensconce yourself in the restaurant or the black-and-white lobby, where world beats don't so much play as fizz. The 41 sumptuous rooms each have a unique theme, whether you're after flamboyant colours, Zen minimalism or the Dylan Thomas suite's fully stocked cocktail cabinet.

Maes B&B
B&B **$$**

(Map p46; 427 51 65; www.bedandbreakfastamsterdam.com; Herenstraat 26hs; s €95-115, d €115-135, apt €135-260; @🖙) If you were designing a traditional home in the western canals, it would probably turn out a lot like this property: oriental carpets, wood floors and exposed brick. It's actually fairly spacious for such an old building. The kitchen (open all day for guests to use) is definitely *gezellig*. Coffee, croissants and other continental-style items comprise breakfast.

Sunhead of 1617
B&B **$$**

(Map p46; 626 18 09; www.sunhead.com; Herengracht 152; r €100-150, apt €120-150; @🖙) The fabulous and funny Carlos is your host at these lovely, cheerful rooms and suites along some of Amsterdam's prettiest stretches of canal. Expect a delightful balance of modern design and traditional Dutch charm, along with an excellent egg-filled breakfast. Spanish spoken.

Frederic's Rentabike & Houseboats
APARTMENT, HOUSEBOAT **$$**

(Map p46; 624 55 09; www.frederic.nl; Brouwersgracht 78; r/apt/houseboat from €75/115/120; 🖙)

Frederic offers nicely outfitted houseboats on the Prinsengracht, Brouwersgracht and Bloemgracht that are bona fide floating holiday homes with all the mod cons. On land, the company also offers various rooms and apartments in central locations. Additional fees (15% for cleaning, €7.50 for linens, 10% surcharge for a single-night stay) can add up.

Chic & Basic Amsterdam
BOUTIQUE HOTEL **$$**

(Map p46; 522 23 45; www.chicandbasic.com; Herengracht 13-19; r from €110; @🖙) Spread across three canal houses, the mod, all-white rooms are more basic than chic, though they strut their minimalism with flair (the generic photos above the beds notwithstanding). The key here is location: on a pretty canal, a 10-minute walk from Centraal Station, surrounded by eating and shopping options. Rates include a coffee-and-toast breakfast.

Hotel Nadia
HOTEL **$$**

(Map p52; 620 15 50; www.nadia.nl; Raadhuisstraat 51; r €70-160; @🖙; 🚊13, 14, 17) The handsome building has a precipitous set of stairs, but the energetic staff will tote your luggage up them. Rooms are small but immaculate; some have balconies, and the ones in front have great views of the Westerkerk (though tram traffic here means noise). Breakfast is included.

SOUTHERN CANAL BELT

TOP CHOICE Cocomama
HOSTEL **$**

(Map p56; 627 24 54; www.cocomama.nl; Westeinde 18; dm/r from €37/108; @🖙) Opened in 2010, Amsterdam's first self-proclaimed 'boutique hostel' plays up its tawdry past (the building was once home to a high-end brothel). Some of the themed bunk rooms are decorated with red curtains and naughty pictures; others are more demure with Delftware or windmill themes. Private rooms (check out the monarchy-themed 'Royal' room) come equipped with iPod docking stations and flat-screen TVs. Everything goes well beyond typical hostel quality, with en suite bathrooms, in-room wi-fi, a gorgeous back garden, a well-equipped kitchen, a book exchange and a super-comfy lounge for movie nights.

Backstage Hotel
HOTEL **$$**

(Map p56; 624 40 44; www.backstagehotel.com; Leidsegracht 114; r without bathroom €85-155, r with bathroom €125-205; @🖙) The seriously fun, music-themed Backstage is a favourite among musicians jamming at nearby Melkweg and Paradiso, as evidenced by the lobby bar's

CANALS OF AMSTERDAM

In Dutch a canal is a *gracht* (pronounced 'khrakht'), and the main canals form the central *grachtengordel* (canal ring). The beauties came to life in the early 1600s, after Amsterdam's population grew beyond its medieval walls, and city planners put together an ambitious design for expansion. Far from being simply decorative or picturesque, or even just waterways for transport, the canals were necessary to drain and reclaim the waterlogged land.

In 2010, Unesco dubbed the waterways a World Heritage site. In 2013, they mark their 400th birthday with a series of special events.

The core canals are the semicircular Singel, Herengracht, Keizersgracht and Prinsengracht. An easy way to remember them is that, apart from the singular Singel, these canals are in alphabetical order as you move outward.

» **Singel** Originally a moat that defended Amsterdam's outer limits.

» **Herengracht** This is where Amsterdam's wealthiest residents moved once the canals were completed. They named the waterway after the Heeren XVII (17 Gentlemen) of the Dutch East India Company, and built their mansions alongside it.

» **Keizersgracht** Almost as swanky, the Keizersgracht (Emperor's Canal) was a nod to Holy Roman Emperor Maximilian I.

» **Prinsengracht** Named after William the Silent, Prince of Orange and the first Dutch royal, Prinsengracht was designed as a slightly cheaper canal with smaller residences and warehouses. It also acted as a barrier against the crusty working-class quarter beyond, aka the Jordaan. Today the Prinsengracht is the liveliest of Amsterdam's inner canals, with cafes, shops and houseboats lining the quays.

» **Brouwersgracht** The Brouwersgracht (Brewers' Canal) is a radial canal that cuts across the others. It takes its name from the many breweries that used to operate along the banks. It's often cited as the city's most beautiful waterway.

band-signature-covered piano and pool table. Gig posters (many signed) line the corridors, and rooms are done up in mod-retro black and white, with iPod docking stations and drum kit overhead lights. Late at night, bands (and their fans) hold court in the lively bar.

Seven One Seven LUXURY HOTEL **$$$**
(Map p56; ☎427 07 17; www.717hotel.nl; Prinsengracht 717; r €450-650; ❋@☎) The nine hyperplush, deliciously appointed rooms come with that rare luxury: space. Step into the splashy Picasso suite – with its soaring ceiling, prodigiously long sofa, and contemporary and antique decorations – and you may never, ever want to leave. Rates include breakfast, afternoon tea, house wine and oodles of one-on-one service.

Hotel V BOUTIQUE HOTEL **$$**
(Map p56; ☎623 13 29; www.hotelv.nl; Weteringschans 136; r €80-160; @☎) Facing lush Fredericksplein and minutes away from Utrechtsestraat's fab dining, the 48-room Hotel V offers surprising style and location for the price. Artsy rooms done up in charcoal colours feature stone-wall bathrooms and

crisp, comfy beds. Grab a cocktail from the bar and curl up in the mod lobby around the gas fireplace with a magazine. A breakfast buffet is included.

Seven Bridges BOUTIQUE HOTEL **$$**
(Map p56; ☎623 13 29; www.sevenbridgeshotel.nl; Reguliersgracht 31; d €110-220; @☎) Private, sophisticated and intimate, the Seven Bridges is one of the city's most exquisite little hotels on one of its loveliest canals. It has eight tastefully decorated rooms, all incorporating lush oriental rugs and elegant antiques.

Hotel Freeland HOTEL **$$**
(Map p56; ☎622 75 11; www.hotelfreeland.com; Marnixstraat 386; r €70-150, without bathroom from €60; @☎) Freeland has the Leidseplein scene twigged. Think tidy rooms with themes (tulips, roses and sunflowers, and a few with Moroccan details) at an excellent canalside location. Add in a tasty breakfast and it pretty much kills the competition.

Hotel Orlando BOUTIQUE HOTEL **$$**
(Map p56; ☎638 69 15; www.hotelorlando.nl; Prinsengracht 1099; r €100-160; ❋@☎) Oh Orlando, how do we love thee? Let us count the

ways. One: seven biggish, high-ceilinged, canalside rooms at smallish rates. Two: hospitable, gay-friendly hosts. Three: a hearty breakfast. Four: impeccably chic, boutique style with custom-made cabinetry and satin curtains. We could go on...

Hotel Prinsenhof HOTEL $

(Map p56; ☎623 17 72; www.hotelprinsenhof.com; Prinsengracht 810; s/d without bathroom €55/75, with bathroom €75/95; ☎) Honest value, this 18th-century house features canal views, rooms with mismatched furniture and 'Captain Hook', the electric luggage hoist (no need to haul your luggage up the narrow steps). Breakfast is included.

OLD SOUTH

TOP CHOICE Collector B&B $$

(Map p56; ☎673 67 79; www.the-collector.nl; De Lairessestraat 46hs; r €80-115; @☎) This spotless B&B near the Concertgebouw is furnished with museum-style displays of clocks, wooden clogs, ice skates – things the owner, Karel, *collects*. Each of the three rooms has balcony access and a TV. Karel stocks the kitchen for guests to prepare breakfast at their leisure (the eggs come from his hens in the garden), and the kitchen is open all day if you want to cook your own dinner. There's also a couple of bikes Karel lends out to guests.

Hotel Fita HOTEL $$

(Map p56; ☎679 09 76; www.hotelfita.com; Jan Luijkenstraat 37; r €109-169; @☎) Family-owned Fita, on a quiet street off the Museumplein and PC Hooftstraat, has 15 handsome rooms with nicely appointed bathrooms; a bountiful breakfast of eggs, pancakes, cheeses and breads; and an elevator. The dynamic young owner has been making lots of upgrades (new furniture, fresh paint), and service could not be more attentive. It's one of the Old South's best-value digs, and tends to book up fast with older Americans. Breakfast is included.

Hotel Aalders HOTEL $$

(Map p56; ☎662 01 16; www.hotelaalders.nl; Jan Luijkenstraat 13-15; r €107-205; @☎) There are fancier hotels in town, but family-owned Aalders is homey and well situated near the museums. The 28 rooms are spread among two row houses and come in varying sizes and styles (some with wood panelling and leaded-glass windows). In the morning, munch homemade pastries in the chandelier-adorned breakfast room. Aalders also rents bikes.

Conscious Hotels Museum Square BOUTIQUE HOTEL $$

(Map p56; ☎671 95 96; www.conscioushotels.com; De Lairessestraat 7; r €120-190; @☎) This is your place to go green. It starts with the living plant wall in the lobby and the organic breakfast (€10 extra). Then come modern rooms – beds made with 100% natural materials, desks constructed from recycled yoghurt containers, and energy-saving plasma TVs. A second location is at Overtoom 519 near Vondelpark.

Xaviera Hollander's Happy House B&B $$

(☎673 39 34; www.xavierahollander.com; Stadionweg 17; r/ste from €110/130; @☎) The former madam and author of *The Happy Hooker* welcomes guests to her home in the ritzy Beethovenstraat neighborhood. The two rooms (which share a bathroom) are decked out with erotic photos, red heart pillows and books, such as her most recent *Guide to Mind-Blowing Sex*. There's also a garden hut with its own facilities (bathroom, refrigerator, terrace). The B&B is a good 1km south of the Museumplein. Two-night minimum stay required.

College Hotel BOUTIQUE HOTEL $$$

(Map p56; ☎571 15 11; www.thecollegehotel.com; Roelof Hartstraat 1; r from €225; ✴@☎) Originally a 19th-century school, the College Hotel has fashioned its 40 chambers – with high ceilings, tasteful furnishings and the occasional stained-glass window – from former classrooms. Hospitality-school students now staff the hotel to earn their stripes, while celebs from Brooke Shields to Fatboy Slim enjoy the swanky end product. The hotel is nicely situated between the Museum Quarter and De Pijp's sights and cafes (about 1km from both).

Van Gogh Hostel & Hotel HOSTEL, HOTEL $$

(Map p56; ☎262 92 00; www.hotelvangogh.nl; Van de Veldestraat 5; dm €20-45, r €90-160; ✴@☎) No false advertising here: it sits about 14 steps from the Van Gogh Museum, and every room has a Van Gogh mural. The set-up at the new property puts the 200-bed hostel on one side, the hotel on the other, and the common area for breakfast (€5) divides them. The hostel dorms have six to eight beds, en suite bathroom and flat-screen TV. The hotel rooms have balconies on the higher floors (ask for one when booking).

VONDELPARK

Hotel de Filosoof
BOUTIQUE HOTEL $$

(Map p56; 683 30 13; www.hotelfilosoof.nl; Anna van den Vondelstraat 6; s/d/ste from €90/130/200; @) The 38 rooms at this hotel are named after philosophers, ranging from Thoreau (with a mural of Walden Pond) to Nietzsche (lots of red, representing his book *Morning Red*). Decor can be posh or minimalist, depending on the room's honoree. Added perks include the elegant bar and the tranquil English garden that's a pastoral pleasure come summer.

Hotel Vondel
BOUTIQUE HOTEL $$$

(Map p56; 612 01 20; www.vondelhotels.com; Vondelstraat 28-30; r €125-235; @) The chic Vondel's rooms have a dark and subdued calm with comfy decor (lots of plush grey), and guests can lounge next to goldfish and koi ponds in the Zen-like back gardens. Downstairs, Restaurant Joost offers a brief menu of fish, meat and vegie options in a dramatic dining room, or just come to sip on a *caipirinha* (Brazilian cocktail) at the pretty bar. Wi-fi is €10 per 24 hours.

Hotel Zandbergen
HOTEL $$

(Map p56; 676 93 21; www.hotel-zandbergen.com; Willemsparkweg 205; s/d from €100/140; @) The Zandbergen stands out like sterling silver in a tray of plastic cutlery. The caring staff go overboard, and the rooms are absolutely faultless; those at the rear have balconies overlooking a quiet courtyard. The Vondelpark is just over the road, and the Museum Quarter is less than 1km along Willemsparkweg (which turns into Paulus Potterstraat). Tram 2 stops nearby to whisk you to the centre.

Hotel Piet Hein
BOUTIQUE HOTEL $$

(Map p56; 662 72 05; www.hotelpiethein.com; Vossiusstraat 52-53; s/d from €100/145; @) Overlooking the Vondelpark's fine old arbour, this immaculate hotel offers a startling variety of contemporary rooms (including snug, single 'business' rooms) in a quiet location, with a sublime garden and a relaxing bar.

Owl Hotel
HOTEL $$

(Map p56; 618 94 84; www.owl-hotel.nl; Roemer Visscherstraat 1; s/d from €90/115; @) Some guests love this place so much that they send in owl figurines from all over the world. Staff are warm and welcoming, and rooms are dapper, bright and quiet. The breakfast buffet (included in the price) is served in a se-

rene, light-filled room overlooking a garden. Wi-fi costs €10 per day.

Flynt B&B
B&B $$

(Map p56; 618 46 14; www.flyntbedandbreakfast.nl; 1e Helmersstraat 34; r €85-120; @) The spacious slate bathrooms feel more mod boutique hotel than neighbourhood B&B, but the cheerful colours, friendly owner, cosy breakfast nook and pet-friendly policy say otherwise. Single travellers will bliss out in the Buddha room.

Stayokay Amsterdam Vondelpark
HOSTEL $

(Map p56; 589 89 96; www.stayokay.com; Zandpad 5; dm €27-39, r from €60; @) A blink away from the Vondelpark, this 536-bed hostel attracts over 75,000 guests a year – no wonder the lobby feels like a mini-UN (with a pool table and pinball machine). The renovated rooms sport lockers, a shower, a toilet and well-spaced bunks. Chill out in the congenial bar-cafe. Breakfast is included.

DE PIJP

Between Art & Kitsch B&B
B&B $$

(Map p56; 679 04 85; www.between-art-and-kitsch.com; Ruysdaelkade 75-2; s/d from €80/90; @) Mondrian once lived here – that's part of the art – and the kitsch are bits like the crystal chandelier in the baroque room and the smiling brass Buddha nearby. The art deco room, meanwhile, has seriously gorgeous tile work and views of the Rijksmuseum. The husband and wife hosts, Ebo and Irene (and Hartje, their fluffy white cat), couldn't be friendlier. Rooms have private bathrooms. It's on the 3rd floor, so prepare to climb.

Bicycle Hotel Amsterdam
HOTEL $$

(Map p56; 679 34 52; www.bicyclehotel.com; Van Ostadestraat 123; r without bathroom €50-95, with bathroom €100-155; @) Run by Marjolein and Clemens, who love pedal power, this place is great if you're into the bed-and-bike thing. The casual, friendly, green-minded hotel has no-frills rooms that are comfy and familiar. It also rents low-cost bikes, and serves a big breakfast spread (included in the rate). Wi-fi is dubious on the upper floors.

easyHotel
HOTEL $

(Map p56; www.easyhotel.com; Van Ostadestraat 97; d from €49; @) If all you want is a cheap, tidy place to lay your head, easyHotel fits the bill. Rooms are sterile and tiny (you're screwed if you have much luggage), and absolutely everything costs extra: wi-fi (€7.50), TV (€5), room cleaning after the first day (€15), movie package (€12.50) and so on. The upside is if you don't care about any of this, you can get rock-bottom rates that are cheaper than a hostel. The only way to make a booking is online.

PLANTAGE, EASTERN ISLANDS & OOSTERPARK

Lloyd Hotel   BOUTIQUE HOTEL $$
(☎561 36 36; www.lloydhotel.com; Oostelijke Handelskade 34; r €90-400; @🖥) In 1921 the Lloyd was a hotel for migrants, and many of the original fixtures (tiles, cabinetry etc) still exist, now combined with triumphs of contemporary Dutch design. The niftily restored rooms span one star (bathrooms down the hall) to five star (plush, huge, grand piano included). The property is also a cultural centre and local gathering place.

DoubleTree Amsterdam Centraal Station   HOTEL $$$
(Map p62; ☎530 08 00; http://doubletree3.hilton.com; Oosterdoksstraat 4; r €210-330; ✳@🖥) Better deals are out there, but many visitors appreciate Hilton's reliably upscale DoubleTree brand, especially this one right smack by the train station. The 553 hyper-mod rooms (each with in-room iMac) fill a glassy new building that opened in 2011. Ascend to the rooftop Skylounge for sunset bliss.

Hotel Rembrandt   HOTEL $$
(Map p62; ☎627 27 14; www.hotelrembrandt.nl; Plantage Middenlaan 17; s/d from €75/95; @🖥) The Rembrandt has character and a leafy location between the zoo and botanic garden. Most of the unassuming quarters contain pop-art prints of the Golden Age master himself. Breakfast (€10) is an impressive affair, served in a wood-panelled room with chandeliers and 17th-century paintings on linen-covered walls.

Hotel Allure   HOTEL $$
(Map p62; ☎627 27 14; www.hotelallure.com; Sarphatistraat 117; r €109-139; @🖥) The scarlet-draped Allure often pops up on hotel booking sites. It's a decent, modest option less than 1km south of the Artis Zoo. Wi-fi costs €5 per day. Continental breakfast typically is included, but ask to make certain.

Stayokay Amsterdam Zeeburg   HOSTEL $
(☎551 31 90; www.stayokay.com; Timorplein 21; dm €21-37, r €30-100; @🖥) The sibling of Stayokay

Vondelpark and Stayokay Stadsdoelen, Zeeburg might be the best of the bunch. It has 508 beds spread over three floors; most of the spick-and-span rooms are four- or six-bed dorms, all with en suite bathroom and bright orange decor. Hot breakfast is included, wi-fi (lobby only) is free. Next door is Studio K, a cool arts centre/cinema/cafe, and a bike rental shop (€11 per day). Dappermarkt and Javaplein – with restaurants like Wilde Zwijnen (p88) – are a short stroll away. Take tram 14 from the Dam, a 15-minute journey.

🍴 Eating

Amsterdam's culinary scene has hundreds of restaurants and *eetcafés* (pubs serving meals) catering to all tastes.

Note that many restaurants do not accept credit cards – even top-end places. Or if they do, they levy a 5% surcharge. Be sure your wallet is filled before dining out.

Phone ahead and make a reservation for eateries in the middle and upper price brackets. Nearly everyone speaks English. Many places also let you book online.

MEDIEVAL CENTRE & RED LIGHT DISTRICT

Zeedijk holds several Thai and Chinese options. Spuistraat is another happy hunting ground.

TOP CHOICE Gartine   CAFE $$
(Map p46; ☎320 41 32; www.gartine.nl; Taksteeg 7; mains €6-12, high tea €12-21; ⏰10am-6pm Wed-Sun; 🍴; 🚋4/9/14/16/24/25 Spui) Gartine is magical, from its sly location in an alley off busy Kalverstraat to its mismatched antique tableware and its sublime breakfast pastries, sandwiches and salads (made from produce grown in its garden plot). The sweet-and-savoury high tea is a scrumptious bonus.

Vleminckx   FRITES $
(Map p56; Voetboogstraat 31; small/large €2.20/2.70, sauces €0.80; ⏰11am-6pm Tue-Sat, to 7pm Thu, noon-6pm Sun & Mon; 🚋1/2/5 Koningsplein) This hole-in-the-wall takeaway has drawn the hordes for its monumental *frites* since 1887. The standard is smothered in mayonnaise, though you can ask for ketchup, peanut sauce or a variety of spicy toppings.

'Skek   CAFE $$
(Map p46; ☎427 05 51; www.skek.nl; Zeedijk 4-8; sandwiches €3-7, mains €12-14; ⏰noon-10pm; 🖥; 🚋4/9/16/24/25 Centraal Station) Run by students for students (flashing your ID gets you

DON'T MISS

SNACK TIME

Whatever the pretext – before drinking, after drinking, for sightseeing sustenance – be sure to try these classic local snacks:

» *Kroket* from Van Dobben (p84).

» Fries with mayo from Vleminckx (p81).

» Herring sandwich from Rob Wigboldus Vishandel (p82).

» Aged gouda from De Kaaskamer (p96).

» Lamb roti from Roopram Roti (p88).

one-third off), this friendly cafe-bar is an excellent place to get fat sandwiches on thick slices of multigrain bread, and healthy main dishes with chicken, fish or pasta. Bands occasionally perform at night.

D'Vijff Vlieghen   CONTEMPORARY DUTCH $$$
(Map p46; ☎530 40 60; www.vijffvlieghen.nl; Spuistraat 294-302; mains €26-33, set menus from €45.50; ☺dinner; ⛟1/2/5 Spui) So what if every tourist and business visitor eats here? Sometimes the herd gets it right. 'The Five Flies' is a classic, spread out over five 17th-century canal houses. Old-wood dining rooms are full of character, featuring Delft tiles and works by Rembrandt and Breitner.

Thais Snackbar Bird   THAI $$
(Map p46; ☎420 62 89; www.thai-bird.nl; Zeedijk 77; mains €9-15; ☺1-10pm; ⛟4/9/16/24/25 Centraal Station) Don't tell the Chinese neighbours, but this is some of the best Asian food on the Zeedijk – the cooks, wedged in a tiny kitchen, don't skimp on lemongrass, fish sauce or chilli. The resulting curries and basil-laden meat and seafood dishes will knock your socks off.

Haesje Claes   TRADITIONAL DUTCH $$
(Map p46; ☎624 99 98; www.haesjeclaes.nl; Spuistraat 273-275; mains €16-25, set menus from €27.50; ☺noon-10pm; ⛴; ⛟1/2/5 Spui) Haesje Claes' warm surrounds, a tad touristy but with lots of dark wood and antique knick-knacks, are just the place to sample comforting pea soup and *stamppot* (mashed pot: potatoes mashed with kale, endive or sauerkraut). The fish starter has a great sampling of different Dutch fish.

Hofje van Wijs   CAFE $
(Map p46; ☎624 04 36; www.hofjevanwijs.nl; Zeedijk 43; mains €8.50-10.50; ☺noon-6pm Tue-Fri & Sun, 10am-6pm Sat; ⛟4/9/16/24/25 Centraal Station) The 200-year-old coffee and tea vendor Wijs & Zonen (the monarch's purveyor) maintains this pretty courtyard cafe. In addition to cakes, it serves inexpensive Dutch stews plus local beers and liqueurs.

Rob Wigboldus Vishandel   SANDWICH SHOP $
(Map p46; ☎626 33 88; Zoutsteeg 6; sandwiches €2.50-4.50; ☺breakfast & lunch; ⛟4/9/16/24/25 Dam) A wee three-table oasis in the midst of surrounding tourist tat, this fish shop in a tiny alley serves excellent herring sandwiches on a choice of crusty white or brown rolls.

NIEUWMARKT

Nieuwmarkt square brims with cafes where locals hang out.

TOP CHOICE **Latei**   CAFE $$
(Map p46; www.latei.net; Zeedijk 143; mains €6-16; ☺8am-6pm Mon-Wed, to 10pm Thu & Fri, 9am-10pm Sat, 11am-6pm Sun; ☂; ⛿Nieuwmarkt) Young locals throng groovy Latei, where you can buy the lamps (or any of the mod decor) right off the wall. The cafe goes ethnic, usually Ethiopian or Indian, for dinner Thursday through Saturday. Otherwise it serves sandwiches, apple pie and *koffie verkeerd* (milky coffee).

Lastage   FRENCH $$$
(Map p46; ☎737 08 11; www.restaurantlastage.nl; Geldersekade 29; set menus from €38; ☺dinner Wed-Sun; ⛟4/9/16/24/25 Centraal Station) Small, cosy Lastage is a rose among thorns at the Red Light District's seedy edge. The changing menu might start with, say, stuffed guinea fowl atop red cabbage, followed by halibut with nutty Camargue wild rice and beetroot purée. It's all beautifully presented, and the elegant wine list matches to a tee.

Toko Joyce   INDONESIAN $
(Map p46; www.tokojoyce.nl; Nieuwmarkt 38; mains €5-10; ☺4-8pm Mon, 11am-8pm Tue-Sat, 1-8pm Sun; ⛿Nieuwmarkt) Pick and mix a platter of Indonesian-Surinamese food from the glass case. The 'lunch box' (you choose noodles or rice, plus two spicy-coconutty toppings) is good value. To finish, get a wedge of *spekkoek* (moist, layered gingerbread). Take your meal upstairs to the handful of tables, or outside, where canalside benches beckon a few steps from the door.

JORDAAN & WESTERN ISLANDS

Convivial little places, including many Italian restaurants, are the Jordaan's hallmark.

At the northern edge, Haarlemmerstraat and Haarlemmerdijk have the latest hot spots. And there's a foodie favourite beyond in the Western Islands.

Koevoet
ITALIAN $$

(Map p52; ☑624 08 46; Lindenstraat 17; mains €12-23; ☺dinner Tue-Sun; ☑; ☐3 Nieuwe Willemssstraat) The congenial Italian owners of Koevoet took over a former cafe on a quiet side street, left the *gezellig* decor untouched and started cooking up their home-country staples. Don't miss its signature, drinkable dessert, *sgroppino limone* (€7): sorbet, vodka and prosecco whisked at your table and poured into a champagne flute.

Balthazar's Keuken
MEDITERRANEAN $$

(Map p52; ☑420 21 14; www.balthazarskeuken.nl; Elandsgracht 108; 3-course menu €29.50; ☺dinner Wed-Sat; ☐7/10/17 Elandsgracht) Balthazar's offers a fixed-price, three-course menu that changes weekly. With an open kitchen and only a few tables, it feels like eating at someone's house. It is consistently one of Amsterdam's top-rated restaurants, but don't expect a wide-ranging selection. The byword is basically 'whatever we have on hand'. Reservations recommended.

La Oliva
SPANISH $$

(Map p52; www.laoliva.nl; Egelantiersstraat 122-124; mains €21-26; ☺lunch & dinner; ☐3/10 Marnixplein) La Oliva's visually stunning food is inspired by the Basque region. Stroll by and you can see the colourful *pintxos* (tapas with a northern Spanish/southern French twist) skewered with wooden sticks and stacked on the gleaming bar, where hungry foodies sip cava (Spanish sparkling wine) and gaze lustfully at the stuffed figs, mushroom Manchego tartlets and Iberian ham with pear.

Marius
INTERNATIONAL $$$

(☑422 78 80; Barentszstraat 173; mains €26-38, set menu €47.50; ☺dinner Tue-Sat; ☐3 Zoutkeetsgracht) Foodies swoon over pocket-sized Marius. Chef Kees, an alumnus of California's Chez Panisse, shops daily at local markets, then creates his menu from what he finds (eg grilled prawns with fava bean purée). He also operates a sausage and wine bar a few doors west. Located north of the Jordaan in the Western Islands; take tram 3 to Zoutkeetsgracht.

Moeders
TRADITIONAL DUTCH $$

(Map p52; ☑626 79 57; www.moeders.com; Rozengracht 251; mains €15-19, 3-course menus €25-30;

☺5pm-midnight Mon-Fri, noon-midnight Sat & Sun; ☑; ☐10/13/14/17 Marnixstraat) When 'Mothers' opened over 25 years ago, staff asked customers to bring their own plates and photos of their mums as donations, and the result is still a delightful hotchpotch. So is the food, including *stamppot*, seafood and a rijsttafel-style presentation of traditional Dutch dishes in many small plates. Book ahead.

Hostaria
ITALIAN $$

(Map p52; ☑420 21 14; 2e Egelantiersdwarsstraat 9; mains €13-26; ☺dinner Tue-Sun; ☐3/10 Marnixplein) On a street bursting with excellent Italian food, the Tuscan classics, fresh stuffed pastas and sublime yet simple desserts here are among our favourites. We witnessed a diner so thrilled with her ravioli that she asked to kiss the chef; he graciously complied.

De Bolhoed
VEGETARIAN $$

(Map p52; ☑626 18 03; Prinsengracht 60-62; mains €13-15, 3-course menu €22; ☺lunch & dinner; ☑; ☐13/14/17 Westermarkt) The art-walled, bright-hued interior is a nice setting to tuck into enormous, organic Mexican-, Asian- and Italian-inspired dishes. In warm weather there's a verdant little canalside terrace. Remember to leave some room for the banana-cream pie. Vegetarians swear by it.

Festina Lente
CAFE $

(Map p52; www.cafefestinalente.nl; Looiersgracht 40b; sandwiches €4-8, small plates €5-10; ☺noon-10.30pm Sun & Mon, from 10.30am Tue-Sat; ☑) This canalside neighbourhood hang-out is typical Jordaan *gezelligheid*, packed with regulars playing board games, reading poetry, and snacking on small-portion Mediterranean dishes and big sandwiches.

DON'T MISS

BEST VEGETARIAN EATS

» **De Waaghals** The 'Daredevil' emulates a different country each month, but it's always a vegie delight (p86).

» **De Peper** The OT301 squat cooks vegan meals for the masses (p86).

» **De Bolhoed** Heaps of eclectic global options, and then banana-cream pie for dessert (p83).

» **Maoz** Mmm, piping-hot felafel served at branches around town (p85).

Brasserie Blazer
FRENCH $$

(Map p52; 620 96 90; www.brasserieblazer.nl; Lijnbaansgracht 190; mains €13-15; lunch & dinner, closed Tue) Amsterdam's simplest French brasserie sits inside the De Looier Antiques Centre. Fancy it's not, but it gets bohemian street cred for its winning combo of well-priced classic dishes – including *confit de canard* (preserved duck) and rib eye Béarnaise – outgoing staff and a certain *je ne sais quoi*.

Winkel
CAFE $

(Map p52; www.winkel43.nl; Noordermarkt 43; mains €4-14; breakfast, lunch & dinner; ; 3 Nieuwe Willemsstraat) This sprawling, indoor-outdoor space is great for people-watching, popular for coffees and small meals, and out-of-the-park for its tall, cakey apple pie. On market days (Monday and Saturday) there's almost always a queue out the door.

WESTERN CANAL BELT
Ridiculously cute cafes and small restaurants line the Negen Straatjes; Berenstraat is a bountiful lane.

Pancakes!
TRADITIONAL DUTCH $

(Map p52; www.pancakesamsterdam.com; Berenstraat 38; pancakes €6-10; 10am-7pm; ; 13/14/17 Westermarkt) Just as many locals as tourists grace the blue-tile tables at snug little Pancakes!, carving into all the usual options, plus daily creations like ham, chicory and cheese or chicken curry pancakes. The batter is made with flour sourced from a local mill.

Buffet van Odette
CAFE $$

(Map p46; www.buffet-amsterdam.nl; Herengracht 309; mains €8-16; 10am-8.30pm Wed-Sat, to 5pm Sun & Mon; ; 1/2/5 Spui) It's hard to get a seat in this tiny place on the weekend – it's packed with customers noshing on fat meatloaf sandwiches and omelettes with truffle cheese. Stay for sweets too: the sticky toffee and carrot cakes are delicious. Grab a seat by the window for one of the city's loveliest canal views.

Wil Graanstra Friteshuis
FRITES $

(Map p52; 624 40 71; Westermarkt 11; frites €2-3.75; 11am-6pm Mon-Sat) Legions of Amsterdammers swear by the crispy spuds at Wil's. The family-run business has been frying by the Westerkerk since 1956. Most locals top their coneful with mayonnaise, though *oorlog* (a peanut-sauce-mayo combo), curry sauce and *picalilly* (relish) rock the tastebuds, too. Wil is a character.

De Belhamel
FRENCH $$$

(Map p46; 622 10 95; www.belhamel.nl; Brouwersgracht 60; mains €24-26, set menus €33-43; lunch & dinner) In warm weather the canalside tables at the head of the Herengracht are an aphrodisiac, and the sumptuous art nouveau interior provides the perfect backdrop for excellent French- and Italian-inspired dishes like silky roast beef.

Lunchcafe Nielsen
CAFE $

(Map p52; 330 60 06; Berenstraat 19; mains €5-10; 8am-4pm Mon-Fri, to 6pm Sat, 9am-5pm Sun; 13/14/17 Westermarkt) Looking for where the locals go to lunch and brunch in the Negen Straatjes? Here it is. Under leafy murals, chow on speciality quiches, salads, and fresh lemon and apple cakes that disappear as quickly as they're put out.

SOUTHERN CANAL BELT
A few steps south of gaudy Rembrandtplein, Utrechtsestraat is a relaxed artery stocked with enticing shops, designer bars and cosy eateries – a prime place to wander (assuming the road construction gets completed).

Piet de Leeuw
STEAKHOUSE $$

(Map p56; 623 71 81; www.pietdeleeuw.nl; Noorderstraat 11; mains €13-20; lunch Mon-Fri, dinner nightly; 16/24/25 Prinsengracht) The building dates from 1900, it's been a steakhouse and hang-out since the 1940s, and the dark and cosy atmosphere has barely changed since. If you don't get your own table, you may meet folks from all over at a common table, eating well-priced steaks with toppings like onions, mushrooms or bacon, served with salad and piping-hot *frites*.

TOP CHOICE Van Dobben
SANDWICH SHOP $

(Map p56; 624 42 00; www.eetsalonvandobben.nl; Korte Reguliersdwarsstraat 5; items €2.75-6.50; 10am-9pm Mon-Thu, to 2am Fri & Sat, 11.30am-9pm Sun; 4/9/14 Rembrandtplein) Open since the 1940s, the venerable Van Dobben has white-tile walls and white-coated counter men who specialise in snappy banter. Traditional meaty Dutch fare is its forte: try the *pekelvlees* (something close to corned beef), or make it a *halfom* (if you're keen on that being mixed with liver). The *kroketten* (croquettes) are the best in town and compulsory after a late-night Rembrandtplein booze-up.

Beulings
FRENCH, ITALIAN $$$

(Map p56; ☎320 61 00; www.beulings.nl; Beulingstraat 9; 3-/5-course menu €36/49; ⏰from 6.30pm Tue-Sat) Beulings is one of those quintessential Amsterdam restaurants: passionate chef; lovely, understated, bite-sized space; flavoursome, fresh-from-the-market fare; small, rotating menu. Everything – sausage, bread, pasta – is made in-house. Spot-on wine pairings help wash it all down. Closed on Tuesdays in summer.

Loekie
SANDWICH SHOP $

(Map p56; www.loekie.net; Utrechtsestraat 57; sandwiches €5-9; ⏰9am-6pm Mon-Sat, to 1pm Wed; 🚋4 Keizersgracht) This delicatessen piles fresh, delicious ingredients into its takeaway sandwiches, such as smoked beef with egg and salt, or warm goat's cheese with pine nuts and honey. Ask for the English menu if it's not on the counter already.

Le Zinc...et les Autres
FRENCH $$

(Map p56; ☎622 90 44; www.lezinc.nl; Prinsengracht 999; mains €15-30, 3-course menu €34.50; ⏰5.30-11pm Mon-Sat; 🅿; 🚋4 Prinsengracht) This cosy old canal-house restaurant is an unapologetically old-fashioned affair, with candlelight, wine and romance to spare. The menu matches the vibe, with rustic dishes like pigeon and rabbit, and an option of matched reds and whites alongside each course. Vegetarians can fill up, too – maybe a dish with beetroot and goat's cheese or an oven-roasted tomato tart.

Tempo Doeloe
INDONESIAN $$$

(Map p56; ☎625 67 18; www.tempodoeloerestaurant.nl; Utrechtsestraat 75; mains €20-25, rijsttafel & set menus €28-40; ⏰dinner Mon-Sat; 🅿; 🚋4 Keizersgracht) Tempo Doeloe is one of Amsterdam's most respected (and hottest spiced!) Indonesian restaurants. It's a slightly formal place that gives solo diners a chance to try the sampler-plate *rijsttafel* (many places will do it only for a minimum of two people). But the à la carte options are arguably better. Reservations are required – or visit the owners' more casual Tujuh Maret next door.

Segugio
ITALIAN $$$

(Map p56; ☎330 15 03; www.segugio.nl; Utrechtsestraat 96; pastas €17-20, mains €24-36; ⏰dinner Mon-Sat; 🅿; 4 Prinsengracht) This fashionably minimalist storefront with two levels of seating is the sort of place other chefs go for a good dinner. It's known for risotto and high-quality ingredients combined with a sure hand. Book ahead – it's almost always busy.

Bouchon du Centre
FRENCH $$

(Map p56; ☎616 74 14; www.bouchonducentreamsterdam.com; Falckstraat 3; mains from €15; ⏰noon-3pm & 5-8pm Wed-Sat; 🚋4 Frederiksplein) A secret of meat fanatics and Francophiles in the know, this little restaurant isn't for everyone, and it doesn't want to be. There's a changing, daily menu of a few dishes only: bet on it being French, meat-oriented and divine.

Maoz
MIDDLE EASTERN $

(Map p56; ☎420 74 35; www.maozusa.com; Muntplein 1; mains €4-8; ⏰11am-1am Sun-Thu, to 3am Fri & Sat; 🅿; 🚋4/9/14/24/25 Muntplein) Felafel, saviour of vegetarians the world over, is perfected at this mini-chain. For around €5 you get four fried chickpea balls with pita and unlimited access to a massive salad bar. Other outlets have popped up around town, and they're usually open late-night.

FEBO
FAST FOOD $

(Map p56; ☎620 86 15; Leidsestraat 94; mains €3-6; ⏰11am-3am Sun-Thu, 11am-4am Fri & Sat; 🚋1/2/5 Prinsengracht) Plucking a deep-fried snack from the yellow automat windows at FEBO is a drunken Dutch tradition. We don't exactly recommend the fare, but it's there when you need it – especially in the wee hours. FEBO branches beckon from practically every street corner in the city.

OLD SOUTH & VONDELPARK
The streets north of Vondelpark, along Overtoom, teem with worldly options. They're not far – and are a nice escape – from Leidseplein's madness.

La Falote
TRADITIONAL DUTCH $$

(Map p56; ☎622 54 54; www.lafalote.nl; Roelof Hartstraat 26; mains €13-19; ⏰dinner Mon-Sat; 🚋3/5/12/24 Roelof Hartplein) Wee chequered-tableclothed La Falote is about Dutch home-style cooking, such as calf liver, meatballs with endives, and stewed fish with beets and mustard sauce. The prices are a bargain in an otherwise ritzy neighbourhood. And wait till the owner brings out the accordion.

Loetje
TRADITIONAL DUTCH $$

(Map p56; www.loetje.com; Johannes Vermeerstraat 52; mains €15-25; ⏰lunch Mon-Fri, dinner Mon-Sat; 🚋16/24 Ruysdaelstraat) This cafe's short menu may be written on the chalkboard, but everyone just orders thick steak, served medium-rare and swimming in delicious brown gravy. The staff are surprisingly good humoured, particularly considering the loud, meat-drunken mobs they typically serve.

Café Toussaint
FRENCH **$$**

(Map p56; ☑685 07 37; www.bosboom-toussaint. nl; Bosboom Toussaintstraat 26; sandwiches €5-7, mains €13-19; ◷9am-10pm; ☒3/12 Overtoom) On one of Amsterdam's prettiest streets, this casual neighbourhood gem feels like it's straight out of an Edith Piaf song. Come to sip cappuccino under the trees, or for creative twists on French classics in the candlelit evenings. The owners also have an Italian pizza place across the street, with gluten-free options.

Lalibela
ETHIOPIAN **$**

(www.lalibela.nl; 1e Helmersstraat 249; mains €8-12; ◷dinner; ☒1 Jan Pieter Heijestraat) Lalibela was the Netherlands' first Ethiopian restaurant, and it's still a favourite. You can drink Ethiopian beer from a half-gourd, and sop up your stews, egg and vegetable dishes using *injera* (a spongy pancake) instead of utensils. Trippy African music rounds out the experience. Located just north of Vondelpark.

Blue Pepper
INDONESIAN **$$$**

(Map p56; ☑489 70 39; www.restaurantbluepepper. com; Nassaukade 366; set menus €53-70; ◷dinner; ☒; ☒3/12 Overtoom) Chef Sonja Pereira elevates Indonesian cuisine to art in her dramatic blue dining room. The exquisite *rijsttafel* includes an array of Pacific Rim–influenced dishes such as crackly crab, lamb saté, grilled scallops with tropical fruit, blue pears and coconut flan. Vegetarian options abound, too.

Hap Hmm
TRADITIONAL DUTCH **$**

(Map p56; www.hap-hmm.nl; 1e Helmersstraat 33; mains €8-11; ◷4.30-8pm Mon-Fri; ☒3/12 Overtoom) Elsewhere €8 might buy you a bowl of soup, but at this wood-panelled neighbourhood place, it might buy an entire dinner: simple Dutch cooking (soup, plus meat, vegies and potatoes), served on stainless-steel dishes.

Restaurant Elements
INTERNATIONAL **$$**

(Map p56; ☑579 17 17; www.heerlijkamsterdam.nl; Roelof Hartstraat 6-8; 4-course set menu €24.50; ◷dinner Mon-Fri; ☒3/5/12/24 Roelof Hartplein) Students – the same ones who run the nearby College Hotel (p79) – prepare and serve contemporary international dishes at this mod restaurant. The result is white-glove service at an excellent price. There are usually two seatings per night (5.30pm and 7pm). Reserve in advance.

De Peper
VEGAN **$**

(Map p56; ☑412 29 54; www.depeper.org; Overtoom 301; meals €7-10; ◷7-8.30pm Tue, Thu, Fri &

Sun; ☒; ☒1 Jan Pieter Heijestraat) The friendly restaurant at the OT301 squat serves cheap, organic, vegan meals in a lovable dive bar atmosphere. Sit at the communal table to connect with like-minded folk. Same-day reservations are required; call between 4pm and 6.30pm. Located just north of Vondelpark.

DE PIJP
Albert Cuypmarkt offers good grazing, or browse the exotic ethnic eats west on Albert Cuypstraat and Ferdinand Bolstraat.

Firma Pekelhaaring
ITALIAN **$$**

(Map p56; www.pekelhaaring.nl; Van Woustraat 127-129; mains lunch €5-10, dinner €10-23; ◷10am-midnight; ☎☒; ☒4 Lutmastraat) Full of graphic-designer types having long lunches with wine, this joint offers an arty industrial vibe with loads of fun and little pretence. Social touches – like the communal table, strewn with magazines and board games to play over dessert – belie the focused attention on fresh Italian flavours. Kids will find a small stash of toys to play with.

Mamouche
MOROCCAN **$$**

(Map p56; ☑670 07 36; www.restaurantmamouche. nl; Quellijnstraat 104; mains €16-24; ◷dinner; ☒16/24 Stadhouderskade) Mamouche gets serious acclaim for its French-accented North African cuisine: think Morocco amid minimalism. The sleek design, with exposed flooring, mottled raw plaster walls and slat-beam ceilings, complements the changing selection of organic, seasonal *tajine* (Moroccan stew) and couscous dishes. It is one of De Pijp's most posh urban spots.

Op de Tuin
MEDITERRANEAN **$$**

(Map p56; ☑675 26 20; www.opdetuin.nl; Karel du Jardinstraat 47; 3-course menu €26-30; ◷from 4pm Tue-Sun; ☒3/25 2e Van der Helststraat) This is the kind of breezy, informal neighbourhood restaurant where you can while away an evening snacking on an antipasti platter (let the chef decide on a mix of Mediterranean standards) or a beautifully prepared three-course meal, and fantasise that you live across the street. Many of the regulars do. It's a few blocks south of Sarphatipark.

De Waaghals
VEGETARIAN **$$**

(Map p56; ☑679 96 09; www.waaghals.nl; Frans Halsstraat 29; mains €13-19; ◷5-9.30pm Tue-Sun; ☒; ☒16/24 Stadhouderskade) The popular white-walled 'Daredevil' is stylish enough that even non-vegies may re-examine their dining priorities. The menu concentrates on one country each month – say, Thailand or Italy – plus a rotating array of inventive seasonal, organic dishes. Book ahead (it takes online reservations, too).

Bazar Amsterdam
MIDDLE EASTERN **$$**

(Map p56; www.bazaramsterdam.nl; Albert Cuypstraat 182; mains €8-15; ⊙11am-midnight Mon-Thu, 11am-1am Fri, 9am-1am Sat, 9am-midnight Sun; ⚡🏠; ᩅ16/24 Albert Cuypstraat) Beneath a golden angel in the middle of the Albert Cuypmarkt, this one-time Dutch Reformed Church has fab-u-lous tile murals and 10,001 Arabian lights to complement the cuisine: from Moroccan to Turkish, Lebanese and Iranian. Fish and chicken dishes please meat eaters; eggplant and portobello mushroom dishes gratify vegetarians. Come for the gigantic breakfast spread, or just for a beer and baklava.

Burgermeester
BURGERS **$**

(Map p56; www.burgermeester.eu; Albert Cuypstraat 48; burgers €7-9; ⊙noon-11pm; 🏠; ᩅ16/24 Albert Cuypstraat) This sleek little bistro makes the finest burgers in town, bar none. It uses only organic beef (or lamb, felafel or fish), in huge portions that would pass as a main dish without a bun. Then come the toppings: feta, fresh mint, pesto, pancetta and more. You can also get a killer milkshake, but don't ask for chips or fries.

Taart van m'n Tante
BAKERY **$**

(Map p56; www.detaart.com; Ferdinand Bolstraat 10; items €4-7; ⊙10am-6pm; 🏠; ᩅ16/24 Stadhouderskade) One of Amsterdam's best-loved cake shops operates from this uber-kitsch parlour, turning out apple pies (Dutch, French or 'tipsy'), pecan pie and wish-your-mother-baked-like-this cakes. Hot-pink walls accent cakes dressed like Barbie dolls; or are they Barbies dressed like cakes?

PLANTAGE, EASTERN ISLANDS & EASTERN DOCKLANDS

Greetje
CONTEMPORARY DUTCH **$$**

(Map p62; ☎779 74 50; www.restaurantgreetje.nl; Peperstraat 23-25; mains €23-28; ⊙dinner; ⓂNieuwmarkt) Elegant Greetje will make you reconsider Dutch cuisine. Never mind *stamppot* – here you'll see dishes like leek soup, pickled mackerel and Dutch venison, all composed of market-fresh ingredients and beautifully presented. Sweet tooths can finish with the Grand Finale: a combo plate of six creamy, fruity, cakey desserts.

Fifteen
INTERNATIONAL **$$**

(☎509 50 15; www.fifteen.nl; Jollemanhof 9; mains €18-23; ⊙lunch Mon-Sat, dinner daily Sep–mid-Jul, dinner only Tue-Sat mid-Jul–Aug; ᩅ25 PTA) 'Naked chef' Jamie Oliver has brought to Amsterdam a concept he began in London: take 15 young people from underprivileged backgrounds and train them for a year in the restaurant biz. Results: noble intention, sometimes spotty execution. The setting, however, is beyond question: Fifteen faces the IJ, and the busy, open-kitchen space is city-cool, with graffitied walls and exposed wood beams.

Koffiehuis van den Volksbond
INTERNATIONAL **$$**

(Map p62; www.koffiehuisvandenvolksbond.nl; Kadijksplein 4; mains €16-19; ⊙dinner; ᩅ22/42/43 Kadijksplein) What began life as a charitable coffeehouse for dockworkers was later revived by squatters. It still has a fashionably grungy vibe – wood floors, tarnished chandeliers and a giant red-rose mural. The ever-changing menu has huge plates of creative comfort food with dishes like red onion tart with blue cheese and lamb with artichoke purée.

De Pizza Bakkers
ITALIAN **$**

(Map p62; ☎625 07 40; www.depizzabakkers.nl; Plantage Kerklaan 2; mains €7-13; ⊙lunch & dinner; ᩅ9/14 Plantage Kerklaan) 'Pizza and Prosecco' is the motto at this arty mini-chain, which means you sip the bubbly latter while waiting for the wood-oven-fired former. Generous toppings range from pancetta and mascarpone to ham and truffle sauce, though we're partial to the vegetarian with taleggio, aubergine and courgette. Be sure to take your ATM or credit card; the restaurant doesn't accept cash.

OOSTERPARK

Strike out east from the park down 1e van Swindenstraat, which eventually turns into Javastraat, and you'll strike a vein of delicious Moroccan and Turkish bakeries.

🍴 De Kas
INTERNATIONAL **$$$**

(☎462 45 62; www.restaurantdekas.nl; Kamerlingh Onneslaan 3, Park Frankendael; lunch menu €37.50, dinner menu €49.50; ⊙lunch Mon-Fri, dinner Mon-Sat; ⚡; ᩅ9 Hogeweg) Admired by gourmets citywide, De Kas has an organic attitude to match its chic glass greenhouse setting – try to visit during a thunderstorm! It grows most of its own herbs and produce right here, and the result is incredibly pure flavours with innovative combinations. There's one set menu each day, based on whatever has been freshly harvested. Reserve in advance. Tram 9 to Hogeweg gets you there.

 Wilde Zwijnen   CONTEMPORARY DUTCH **$$**
(☑463 30 43; www.wildezwijnen.com; Javaplein 23; mains €18-21, 3/4 courses €29.50/35.50; ⊘lunch & dinner Tue-Sun; 🛜🖉; 🚊14 Javaplein) The name means 'wild boar' and if it's the right time of year, you may indeed find it on the menu. The rustic, wood-tabled restaurant serves locally sourced, seasonal fare with bold results. There's usually a vegetarian option, and chocolate ganache with juniper berries for dessert. It's about 1km east of Oosterpark; take tram 14 to Javaplein.

Roopram Roti   SURINAMESE **$**
(1e van Swindenstraat 4; mains €4-10; ⊘2-9pm Tue-Sat, 3-9pm Sun; 🚊9 1e van Swindenstraat) There's often a line to the door at this barebones Surinamese place, but don't worry – it moves fast. Place your order – lamb roti 'extra' (with egg) and a *barra* (lentil doughnut) at least – at the bar, and don't forget the fiery hot sauce. It's some of the flakiest roti you'll find anywhere, super-delicious for takeaway or to eat at one of the half-dozen tables. It's located at Oosterpark's eastern edge.

🍷 Drinking

The city centre holds the mother lode of boozers. To drink with locals try the Jordaan or De Pijp neighbourhoods.

MEDIEVAL CENTRE & RED LIGHT DISTRICT

TOP CHOICE **Wynand Fockink**   TASTING HOUSE
(Map p46; www.wynand-fockink.nl; Pijlsteeg 31; ⊘3-9pm; 🚊4/9/16/24/25 Dam) This small tasting house (dating from 1679) serves scores of *jenever* (Dutch gin) and liqueurs in an arcade behind Grand Hotel Krasnapolsky. Although there are no seats or stools, it is an intimate place to knock back a taste or two with a friend. Guides give an English-language tour of the distillery every Saturday at 12.30pm (€9; reservations not required).

Hoppe   BROWN CAFE
(Map p46; www.cafehoppe.nl; Spui 18-20; 🚊1/2/5 Spui) Boasting the city's highest beer turnover rate, gritty Hoppe has been filling glasses for more than 300 years. Journalists, bums, socialites and raconteurs toss back brews amid the ancient wood panelling.

Most months the energetic crowd spews out from the dark interior and onto the Spui.

In 't Aepjen   BROWN CAFE
(Map p46; ☑626 84 01; www.cafeintaepjen.nl; Zeedijk 1; 🚊4/9/16/24/25 Centraal Station) Candles burn even during the day at this bar based in a mid-16th-century house, which is one of two remaining wooden buildings in the city. Vintage jazz on the stereo enhances the time-warp feel. The name allegedly comes from the bar's role in the 16th and 17th centuries as a crash pad for sailors from the Far East, who often toted *aapjes* (monkeys) with them.

Cafe Belgique   BEER CAFE
(Map p46; www.cafe-belgique.nl; Gravenstraat 2; ⊘from 2pm; 🚊4/9/16/24/25 Dam) Pull up a stool at the carved wooden bar and take your pick from the glinting brass taps. It's all about Belgian beers here. Eight flow from the spouts, and 30 or so are available in bottles. The ambience is quintessential *gezellig* and draws lots of chilled-out locals.

In de Olofspoort   BROWN CAFE
(Map p46; ☑624 39 18; www.olofspoort.com; Nieuwebrugsteeg 13; ⊘from 4pm Wed & Thu, from 3pm Fri-Sun; 🚊4/9/16/24/25 Centraal Station) The door of this brown cafe-tasting room was once the city gate. A crew of regulars has dedicated *jenever* bottles stocked just for them. Check out the jaw-dropping selection behind the back room bar. Occasional singalongs add to the atmosphere.

'T Mandje   BROWN CAFE
(Map p46; www.cafetmandje.nl; Zeedijk 63; ⊘Tue-Sun; 🚊4/9/16/24/25 Centraal Station) Amsterdam's oldest gay bar opened in 1927, then shut in 1982, when the Zeedijk grew too seedy. But its trinket-covered interior was lovingly dusted every week until it reopened in 2008. The devoted bartenders can tell you stories about the bar's brassy lesbian founder. It's one of the most *gezellig* places in the centre, gay or straight.

Brouwerij De Prael   BEER CAFE
(Map p46; ☑408 44 69; www.deprael.nl; Oudezijds Armsteeg 26; ⊘11am-11pm Tue-Sun; 🚊4/9/16/24/25 Centraal Station) Sample organic beers named after classic Dutch brewers at the multilevel tasting room of De Prael brewery, a do-gooder known for employing people with a history of mental illness. It's mostly a younger crowd that hoists suds and forks into well-priced stews and other Dutch standards

at the comfy couches and big wood tables strewn about. Bands plug in some nights.

Café de Barderij
BAR

(Map p46; www.barderij.com; Zeedijk 14; ⛴4/9/16/24/25 Centraal Station) This friendly, candlelit bar draws a mixture of local gay regulars and tourists. It has killer views of the canal out back and Zeedijk in front. Come on Mondays and Wednesdays when the bar serves a two-course homemade Dutch meal (€12.50) in the basement.

Café de Jaren
GRAND CAFE

(Map p56; www.cafedejaren.nl; Nieuwe Doelenstraat 20; ⏰from 9.30am; ⛴4/9/14/16/24/25 Muntplein) Watch the Amstel flow by from the balcony and waterside terraces of this soaring, bright and *very* grand cafe. The great reading table has loads of foreign publications for whiling away hours over beers.

NIEUWMARKT
De Sluyswacht
BROWN CAFE

(Map p46; www.sluyswacht.nl; Jodenbreestraat 1; ⏰from 11.30am; ⛴9/14 Waterlooplein) Built in 1695, De Sluyswacht lists like a ship in a high wind. The tiny black building was once a lock-keeper's house. Today the canalside terrace is one of the nicest spots in town to relax and down a Dutch beer (Dommelsch is the house speciality).

Café de Doelen
BROWN CAFE

(Map p46; Kloveniersburgwal 125; ⏰from 10am; ⛴4/9/14/16/24/25 Muntplein) Set on a busy canalside crossroads between the Amstel and the Red Light District, De Doelen dates back to 1895 and looks it: carved wooden goat's head, stained-glass lamps and sand on the floor. In fine weather the tables spill across the street for picture-perfect canal views.

JORDAAN
TOP CHOICE / ### Café 't Smalle
BROWN CAFE

(Map p52; www.t-smalle.nl; Egelantiersgracht 12; ⏰from 10am; ⛴13/14/17 Westermarkt) There's no more convivial spot than this canalside terrace on a sunny day, and the romantic 18th-century interior is perfect in winter. Proof of its powerful *gezelligheid*, 't Smalle remains a lively local place even while being gushed over in multiple guidebooks.

De Kat in de Wijngaert
BROWN CAFE

(Map p52; ☎620 45 54; Lindengracht 160; ⛴3 Nieuwe Willemsstraat) De Kat in de Wijngaert is the kind of place where one beer soon turns to half a dozen – maybe it's the influence of the

old-guard arts types who hang out here. Try soaking it up with what many people vote as the best *tosti* (toasted sandwich) in town.

Finch
DESIGNER BAR

(Map p52; ☎626 24 61; Noordermarkt 5; ⛴3 Nieuwe Willemsstraat) This funkalicious bar with its retro decor (deliberately mismatched yet somehow harmonious) is just the spot to hang out and knock back a few beers after a visit to the Noordermarkt. It's known for an arty-designy clientele and is always packed on the weekends.

De Pieper
BROWN CAFE

(Map p56; Prinsengracht 424; ⛴7/10 Raamplein) Small, unassuming and unmistakably old (1665), De Pieper features stained-glass windows, fresh sand on the floors and antique Delft beer mugs hanging from the bar. It's a sweet place for sipping a late-night Wieckse Witte beer as you marvel at the claustrophobia of the low-ceilinged environs.

De Twee Zwaantjes
BROWN CAFE

(Map p52; www.detweezwaantjes.nl; Prinsengracht 114; ⏰from 3pm; ⛴13/14/17 Westermarkt) To experience the Jordaan's famous (or infamous) tradition of drunken sing-alongs, duck into De Twee Zwaantjes. It's at its hilarious best on weekend nights, when crooners with big hair and ruffled shirts belt out nostalgic anthems with accordion accompaniment. Karaoke replaces the pros in summer.

WESTERN CANAL BELT
't Arendsnest
BEER CAFE

(Map p46; www.arendsnest.nl; Herengracht 90; ⏰from 4pm Mon-Fri, from 2pm Sat & Sun; ⛴1/2/5/13/17 Nieuwezijds Kolk) This gorgeous,

DON'T MISS

BEST BROWN CAFES

Atmospheric brown cafes are Amsterdam's crowning glory. The time-hewn pubs have candle-topped tables, sandy wooden floors and sometimes a house cat that sidles up for a scratch. Most importantly, they induce a cosy vibe that prompts friends to linger and chat for hours over drinks. These places cast a heady enchantment:

» Café 't Smalle (p89)
» In 't Aepjen (p88)
» De Pieper (p89)
» 'T Mandje (p88)

TILTED ARCHITECTURE

No, you're not drunk... Amsterdam's buildings *are* leaning. Some – like De Sluyswacht (p89) – have shifted over the centuries, but many canal houses were deliberately constructed to tip forward. Interior staircases were narrow, so owners needed an easy way to move large goods and furniture to the upper floors. The solution: a hoist built into the gable, to lift objects up and in through the windows. The tilt allows loading without bumping into the house front.

restyled brown cafe stocks only Dutch beers. The bartenders are evangelistic about the options from more than 50 breweries, including many small and hard-to-find suds makers – ask for the staff's expert recommendations.

Café Tabac   BAR
(Map p46; www.cafetabac.eu; 2e Brouwersgracht 101; ⊘from 11am Sat-Mon, from 4pm Tue-Fri; ⌖3 Nieuwe Willemsstraat) Is Café Tabac a brown cafe, a designer bar, or simply an effortlessly cool place to spend a few blissful hours at the intersection of two of Amsterdam's most stunning canals? No matter. Just enjoy the graceful views and kick back under the high-beamed ceilings to cool rock tunes.

Café Restaurant van Puffelen   GRAND CAFE
(Map p52; www.restaurantvanpuffelen.com; Prinsengracht 377; ⊘from 3pm Mon-Thu, from 1pm Fri, from noon Sat & Sun; ⌖13/14/17 Westermarkt) Sprawling Van Puffelen, popular among cashed-up professionals and intellectual types, has lots of nooks and crannies for nice, cosy drinks, and big communal tables for sharing meals like antipasto and large salads.

Café de Vergulde Gaper   BROWN CAFE
(Map p52; www.goodfoodgroup.nl; Prinsenstraat 30; ⊘from 10am; ☎) Decorated with old chemists' bottles and vintage posters, this former pharmacy has amiable staff and a terrace that catches the sun. It gets busy with 20- and 30-something media types meeting for after-work drinks and big plates of fried snacks.

SOUTHERN CANAL BELT
De Kroon   GRAND CAFE
(Map p56; www.dekroon.nl; Rembrandtplein 17-1; ⊘from 11am; ⌖4/9/14 Rembrandtplein) A

gem restored to its original 1898 lustre, De Kroon offers high ceilings, velvet chairs and the chance to wave at the little people below on Rembrandtplein from your 2nd-storey windowside perch. Or sit at the English-library-themed bar and admire its curious display of 19th-century medical equipment.

Eijlders   BROWN CAFE
(Map p56; www.eijlders.nl; Korte Leidsedwarsstraat 47; ⊘from 4.30pm Tue-Thu; ⌖1/2/5/7/10 Leidseplein) During WWII Eijlders was a meeting place for artists who refused to toe the cultural line imposed by the Nazis, and the spirit lingers on. It's still an artists cafe with classical music jams and poetry readings on varying Sundays.

Café de Spuyt   BEER CAFE
(Map p56; www.cafedespuyt.nl; Korte Leidsedwarsstraat 86; ⊘from 4pm; ⌖1/2/5/7/10 Leidseplein) Steps away from the bustling Leidseplein, the bar staff at this mellow, friendly cafe will happily guide you through the massive chalkboard menu of more than 100 beers, from Belgian Trappist ales to American Sierra Nevada.

Door 74   COCKTAIL BAR
(Map p56; ☑06 3404 5122; www.door-74.nl; Reguliersdwarsstraat 74; ⊘from 8pm; ⌖9/14 Rembrandtplein) Far and away Amsterdam's best cocktails, served in an elegant but unpretentious atmosphere, behind an unmarked door. For entry, you must make a day-of reservation; call before 8pm, or send a text message after.

OLD SOUTH & VONDELPARK
Café Vertigo   BAR
(Map p56; www.vertigo.nl; Vondelpark 3; ⊘10am-1am; ☎; ⌖1 1e Constantijn Huygensstraat) Of the Vondelpark's many cafes, Vertigo buzzes loudest. The terrace offers prime sunshiney seats to settle into, swig a brew and watch the action. A cinema theme prevails inside (Vertigo is located in the old film museum). Service can be spotty.

Welling   BROWN CAFE
(Map p56; www.cafewelling.nl; Jan Willem Brouwersstraat 32; ⊘from 4pm Mon-Fri, from 3pm Sat & Sun; ⌖3/5/12/16/24 Museumplein) Tucked away behind the Concertgebouw, this is a relaxed spot to unwind with a newspaper, sip a frothy, cold *biertje* (glass of beer) and mingle with intellectuals and artists. Don't be surprised if the cafe's friendly cat hops onto your lap.

DE PIJP

Kingfisher
DESIGNER BAR, CAFE

(Map p56; www.kingfishercafe.nl; Ferdinand Bolstraat 24; ⊘from 10am Mon-Sat, from noon Sun; ⌐16/24 Stadhouderskade) The communal table welcomes laptops, newspapers and lunching by day. By happy hour the place is kicking. Kingfisher is a lot of locals' 'local', and as it's on one of De Pijp's main streets, it offers a great view of the neighbourhood's action (creative bicyclists are just the start).

Café Berkhout
BROWN CAFE

(Map p56; www.cafeberkhout.nl; Stadhouderskade 77; ⊘from 11.30am; ⌐16/24 Stadhouderskade) Once a derelict spot, this beautifully refurbished brown cafe – with its dark wood, mirrors and shabby elegance – is a natural post–Heineken Experience wind-down spot (it's right across the street).

Café de Groene Vlinder
BROWN CAFE

(Map p56; www.cafedegroenevlinder.nl; Albert Cuypstraat 130; ⊘from 10am; ⌐16/24 Albert

COFFEESHOPS

Remember: 'cafe' means 'pub' throughout the Netherlands; a 'coffeeshop' is where one procures marijuana. After a precarious period when it seemed tourists would be banned from Amsterdam's coffeeshops, there was a collective toke of relief in late 2012 when the national 'weed pass' law fell by the wayside. The conservative Dutch government that passed the act – whereby coffeeshops could sell pot only to registered locals – lost power. The new government is letting individual municipalities decide for themselves whether to enforce it. In Amsterdam, where one in three tourists visits a coffeeshop, the city has decreed it will conduct business as usual.

So, keep in mind the following:

» Ask at the bar for the menu of goods on offer, usually packaged in small bags. You can also buy ready-made joints (€3 to €7). Most shops offer rolling papers, pipes or even bongs to use.

» Don't light up anywhere besides a coffeeshop without checking that it's OK to do so.

» Alcohol and tobacco products are not permitted in coffeeshops.

Dampkring (Map p56; www.dampkring.nl; Handboogstraat 29; ⊘from 10am; ☎; ⌐1/2/5 Koningsplein) You saw it in *Ocean's Twelve;* now see Dampkring up close. Wood-carved, hobbitish decor fills the moodily lit room. Consistently a winner of the Cannabis Cup, the coffeeshop is known for having the most comprehensive menu in town, including details about smell, taste and effect.

Abraxas (Map p46; www.abraxas.tv; Jonge Roelensteeg 12; ⊘from 10am; ☎) It's stoner heaven: mellow music, comfy sofas, thick milkshakes and rooms with different energy levels spread over three floors. The considerate staff make it a great place for coffeeshop newbies. Free wi-fi and computer terminals, too.

Greenhouse (Map p46; Oudezijds Voorburgwal 191; ⊘from 9am; ☎; ⌐4/9/16/24/25 Dam) One of the most popular coffeeshops in town. Smokers love the funky music, multicoloured mosaics, psychedelic stained-glass windows, and high-quality weed and hash. It also serves a breakfast, lunch and dinner to suit all levels of the munchies.

Katsu (Map p56; www.katsu.nl; 1e van der Helststraat 70; ⊘from 11am Mon-Sat, from noon Sun; ⌐16/24 Albert Cuypstraat) Flamboyant Katsu, De Pijp's favourite coffeeshop, brims with colourful characters. The front table with newspapers lends a bookish vibe, although the smoke inside probably won't make you feel any smarter.

Siberië (Map p46; www.coffeeshopsiberie.nl; Brouwersgracht 11; ⊘from 11am; ☎) Popular among locals, Siberië's inviting setting goes beyond marijuana – its owners regularly schedule cultural events like art exhibits, poetry slams, acoustic concerts, DJ nights and even horoscope readings. It also features a tobacco-friendly lounge.

Bulldog (Map p56; www.thebulldog.com; Leidseplein 13-17; ☎) The Bulldog is Amsterdam's most famous coffeeshop chain, with multiple branches around town. The over-the-top scene appeals mostly to stag parties and backpackers. The Leidseplein shop is the flagship. One side is for drinkers, the other for smokers.

Cuypstraat) The Green Butterfly strikes just the right balance between hip and cosy, meaning it's the perfect spot to go for a *koffie verkeerd* in the warm wood interior before meeting up for a *biertje* on the hopping patio.

PLANTAGE, EASTERN ISLANDS & EASTERN DOCKLANDS

TOP CHOICE **Brouwerij 't IJ**   BEER CAFE
(www.brouwerijhetij.nl; Funenkade 7; ⊙2-8pm; 🚊10 Hoogte Kadijk) A *de rigueur* photo op, plus beer! Amsterdam's leading microbrewery happens to be tucked in the base of De Gooyer Windmill, an 18th-century grain mill and the last of five that stood in this area. The organic house brews are excellent. Try a five-beer sampler (€6.50), and order the *skeapsrond* (sheep's cheese) alongside. Tours (€4.50, including one beer) run Friday through Sunday at 3.30pm and 4pm. The brewery is a short distance east of the Artis Zoo; walk along Hoogte Kadijk or take tram 10 to Hoogte Kadijk.

Café Orloff   BAR
(Map p62; www.orloff.nl; Kadijksplein 11; ⊙from 8am Mon-Fri, from 10am Sat, from 11am Sun; 🚊22/42/43 Kadijksplein) Join the ranks on the sprawling outdoor terrace or head inside, where folks chat around the magazine-strewn communal table. The kitchen turns out light breakfasts and cornbread sandwiches during the day, and light dinners with plenty of French wine in the evening.

☆ Entertainment

I Amsterdam (p98) lists all sorts of music and cultural goings on, as does the monthly magazine *Time Out Amsterdam* (www.timeoutamsterdam.com).

Live Music
ROCK & FUNK

Melkweg   LIVE MUSIC, CLUB
(Map p56; www.melkweg.nl; Lijnbaansgracht 234a; 🚊1/2/5/7/10 Leidseplein) A linchpin of the scene, this former milk factory off Leidseplein is Amsterdam's most vibrant club/gallery/cinema/cafe/concert hall. It's impossible not to find something to pull you in, from international DJ club nights to live punk bands to cutting-edge theatre.

Paradiso   LIVE MUSIC, CLUB
(Map p56; www.paradiso.nl; Weteringschans 6; 🚊7/10 Spiegelgracht) Worship rock 'n' roll in this gorgeous old church. Lady Gaga, the

Roots and other big names rock the Main Hall, while the Small Hall upstairs provides an intimate venue to see up-and-coming bands from around the world. Midweek Paradiso hosts club nights with low cover charges.

De Nieuwe Anita   LIVE MUSIC
(🖉415 35 12; www.denieuweanita.nl; Frederik Hendrikstraat 111; 🚊3 Hugo de Grootplein) A stone's throw west of the Jordaan (across the Singelgracht), De Nieuwe Anita is the neighbourhood clubhouse. It's an intimate living-room-like art lounge that's expanded for noise rockers, with a great cafe on-site.

Sugar Factory   LIVE MUSIC, CLUB
(Map p56; www.sugarfactory.nl; Lijnbaansgracht 238; 🚊1/2/5/7/10 Leidseplein) The vibe at this self-described 'cutting-edge multi-disciplinary night theatre' is always welcoming and creative. Most evenings start with live music, cinema, or a dance or spoken-word performance, followed by late-night DJs and dancing. The excellent midsize space also has a smoking lounge upstairs.

Winston Kingdom   LIVE MUSIC, CLUB
(Map p46; www.winston.nl; Hotel Winston Warmoesstraat 127; 🚊4/9/16/24/25 Dam) Here's a club that even nonclubbers will love for its indie-alternative music beats, smiling DJs and stage-diving cover bands. The scene can get pretty wild in the good-time little space.

JAZZ & BLUES

Bimhuis   JAZZ
(🖉788 21 88; www.bimhuis.nl; Piet Heinkade 3; tickets €10-22; ⊙closed Aug; 🚊25/26 Muziekgebouw) The core of Amsterdam's influential jazz and improvisational music scene since 1973, the Bimhuis has kept its focus even after merging (architecturally) with the classical Muziekgebouw. Tuesdays at 10pm from September to June are an open jam session in the cafe – fun and free (as is the preceding music workshop at 8pm).

Jazz Café Alto   JAZZ
(Map p56; www.jazz-cafe-alto.nl; Korte Leidsedwarsstraat 115; ⊙from 9pm; 🚊1/2/5/7/10 Leidseplein) Smack in Amsterdam's touristy heart, this gem of a club is so small you feel as though you're part of the musical conversation between the band members. Doors open at 9pm but music starts around 10pm – get there early if you want to snag a seat.

Badcuyp
JAZZ
(Map p56; www.badcuyp.org; 1e Sweelinckstraat 10; tickets €4-8; ☺Tue-Sun; ☐4/25 Stadhouderskade) From free jazz sessions (2.30pm Sundays) to salsa nights, this De Pijp music cafe combines an energetic community spirit with top-notch international performers.

Maloe Melo
BLUES
(Map p52; ☎420 45 92; www.maloemelo.com; Lijnbaansgracht 163; ☐7/10/17 Elandsgracht) Maloe Melo is the free-wheeling, fun-loving altar of Amsterdam's tiny blues scene. The dingy but atmospheric venue often adds bluegrass and soul to the calendar, too.

CLASSICAL

TOP CHOICE Concertgebouw
CLASSICAL MUSIC
(Map p56; ☎671 83 45; www.concertgebouw. nl; Concertgebouwplein 2-6; ☺box office 1-7pm Mon-Fri, 10am-7pm Sat & Sun; ☐3/5/12/16/24 Museumplein) Built in 1888, this acoustically pristine concert hall is one of the world's busiest venues. Free half-hour concerts take place every Wednesday at 12.30pm from mid-September until late June; arrive early. Those aged 27 or younger can queue for €10 tickets 45 minutes before shows.

Muziekgebouw aan 't IJ
CONCERT VENUE
(☎788 20 00; www.muziekgebouw.nl; Piet Heinkade 1; tickets €26-37; ☺box office noon-6pm Mon-Sat; ☐25/26 Muziekgebouw) The dazzling building plays host to everything from the Holland Symfonia, which typically backs the National Ballet, to the prestigious Metropole Orkest, which does smart arrangements of jazz and pop. People under the age of 30 can get €10 tickets 30 minutes before showtime at the box office, or online via earlybirds. muziekgebouw.nl.

Muziektheater
CLASSICAL MUSIC
(Map p56; ☎625 54 55; www.hetmuziektheater.nl; Waterlooplein 22; ☺box office from noon, closed Aug; ☐9/14 Waterlooplein) Located in the odd, mod Stopera building – which is half *stadhuis* (town hall) and half opera house – the Muziektheater is home to the Netherlands Opera and the National Ballet. Free classical concerts (12.30pm to 1pm) are held most Tuesdays from September to June in the Boekmanzaal.

Conservatorium van Amsterdam
CLASSICAL MUSIC
(Map p62; www.cva.ahk.nl; Oosterdokskade 151; ☐25/26 Muziekgebouw) The city's prestigious music school, set in a dramatic building

TICKET SHOPS

Not sure how to spend your evening? Head to the **Uitburo** (Map p56; ☎621 13 11; www.amsterdamsuitburo.nl; Leidseplein 26; ☺10am-7pm Mon-Fri, 10am-6pm Sat, noon-6pm Sun; ☐1/2/5/7/10 Leidseplein), in the corner of the Stadsschouwburg (City Theatre) on the Leidseplein. Tickets to just about anything – comedy, dance, concerts, even club nights – are available, for a small surcharge. In addition, the Uitburo's **Last Minute Ticket Shop** (www.lastminuteticketshop. nl) desk sells half-price seats on the day of performance. Available shows start posting online at 8am, though you can buy them in person only, starting at noon. Last Minute shops are also in the Centrale Bibliotheek Amsterdam (p69) and VVV Main Office (p98) at Centraal Station.

on the harbour, is a great place to see jazz, opera and classical performances at very affordable prices.

Theatre & Comedy

Felix Meritis
ARTS CENTRE
(Map p52; www.felix.meritis.nl; Keizersgracht 324; ☐13/14/17 Westermarkt) This wonderful arts and culture space hosts experimental theatre, music and dance, as well as lectures on politics, art and literature. The huge-windowed cafe is particularly hang-out worthy. The centre celebrated its 225th birthday in 2013 with a slew of special events.

Boom Chicago & Chicago Social Club
COMEDY, CLUB
(Map p56; ☎423 01 01; www.boomchicago.nl; Leidseplein 12; ☺box office 2-8.30pm Mon-Wed, from 1pm Thu-Sun ; ☐1/2/5/7/10 Leidseplein) Boom Chicago has branched out to become a trinity of Leidseplein entertainment: it's a comedy club, a late-night bar and a nightclub. The English-language improv troupe remains the mainstay, with inspiration culled from Chicago's legendary Second City. The topical shows riff on local and European issues and are a surprisingly good place to get the pulse of Amsterdam politics.

Amsterdams Marionetten Theater
THEATRE
(Map p46; ☎620 80 27; www.marionettentheater. nl; Nieuwe Jonkerstraat 8; adult/child €16/7.50) In

a former blacksmith's shop, the puppeteers put on a limited repertoire (mainly Mozart operas), but the fairy-tale stage sets, period costumes and singing voices enthral. Note from June to August the theatre only performs for groups.

Openluchttheater
THEATRE

(Open-Air Theatre; Map p56; www.openluchttheater.nl; Vondelpark 5a; ⊙Jun-Aug; 🚹; 🚋1 1e Constantijn Huygensstraat) Each summer the Vondelpark's intimate open-air theatre hosts free concerts and performances. Expect world music, dance, theatre, kids' programming and more. You can make a reservation (€2.50 per seat) on the website up to two hours in advance of showtime.

Stadsschouwburg
THEATRE

(City Theatre; Map p56; ☑624 23 11; www.stadsschouwburgamsterdam.nl; Leidseplein 26; ⊙box office noon-6pm Mon-Sat; 🚋1/2/5/7/10 Leidseplein) The regal, neo-Renaissance Stadsschouwburg, built in 1894, is used for large-scale plays, operettas, dance and major festival performances. Amsterdam's main ticket desk is also stashed inside, where you see what's on and can get half-price seats for shows around town.

Nightclubs

Most clubs close at 4am or so on Friday and Saturday (a few hours earlier the rest of the week). The party doesn't really fire up until after midnight. Many rock clubs, such as Melkweg (p92) and Paradiso (p92), also have awesome club nights.

Air
CLUB

(Map p56; ☑820 06 70; www.air.nl; Amstelstraat 16; ⊙Thu-Sun; 🚋4/9/14 Rembrandtplein) One of Amsterdam's It clubs, Air has an environmentally friendly design and a unique tiered dance floor. Though the place gets packed, its ultra-high ceilings make it feel like there's still plenty of room to get funky. Cover charges average between €9 and €15.

Studio 80
CLUB

(Map p56; ☑521 83 33; www.studio-80.nl; Rembrandtplein 17; ⊙Wed-Sat; 🚋4/9/14 Rembrandtplein) It's all about the (electronic) music at this raw space, which functions as much as a studio and radio station as a club. Bespectacled hipsters, glittering fashionistas and androgynous arty types mix it up on the dimly lit dance floor. Cheapish entry (usually between €6 to €16) guarantees a young crowd.

Cinemas

With Amsterdam's rainy weather and the city's abundance of gorgeous cinemas, you may well find yourself at a flick. Screenings are usually in the original language with Dutch subtitles.

Pathé Tuschinskitheater
CINEMA

(Map p56; www.pathe.nl/tuschinski; Reguliersbreestraat 26-34; 🚋4/9/14 Rembrandtplein) The sumptuous Tuschinski is a monument to art deco/Amsterdam School decor. It screens both Hollywood blockbusters (usually in the grote zaal, aka main auditorium) and arthouse films.

Movies
CINEMA

(☑638 60 16; www.themovies.nl; Haarlemmerdijk 161; 🚋3 Haarlemmerplein) Amsterdam's oldest cinema, an art deco gem dating from 1912, features indie films alongside mainstream flicks. Grab a pre-movie tipple at the inviting cafe-bar.

EYE Film Institute
CINEMA

(☑589 14 00; www.eyefilm.nl; IJpromenade 1) The Netherlands' uber-mod film cultural centre shows all manner of movies – new, old, foreign, domestic, child-oriented – and puts on film exhibits.

Sport

Ajax Amsterdam
FOOTBALL

(www.ajax.nl; Arena Blvd 1) Four-times European champion Ajax is the Netherlands' most famous football team. Ajax plays in Amsterdam Arena (about 7km southeast of the centre; take the metro to Bijlmer Arena), usually on Saturday evenings and Sunday afternoons from August to May. Fans can take a guided stadium tour (adult/child €12/10). Want more? The Ajax Experience (p64) museum in the Southern Canal Belt has exhibits for diehards.

🔒 Shopping

The capital's cupboards are still stocked with all kinds of exotica (just look at that Red Light gear!), but the real pleasure here is finding some odd, tiny shop selling something you'd find nowhere else. Specialities include Dutch-designed clothing and homewares, known for their cool, practical qualities. Antiques, art and vintage goodies also rank high on the local list. Popular gifts include tulip bulbs, bottles of jenever (Dutch gin) and blue-and-white Delft pottery.

MAGIC TRUFFLES & SMART SHOPS

Smart shops – which deal in organic uppers and natural hallucinogens – have long been known for selling 'magic' mushrooms. But in 2008, the government banned them after a high-profile incident in which a tourist died. Nearly 200 varieties of fungus then went on the forbidden list – though conspicuously missing was the magic truffle.

Truffles come from a different part of the plant, but they contain the same active ingredients as mushrooms. Truffles are now the smart shops' stock and trade. Counter staff advise on the nuances of dosages and possible effects, as if at a pharmacy. Listen to them. Every year, emergency-room nurses have to sit with people on bad trips brought on by consuming more than the recommended amount. Also, it seems obvious, but never buy truffles or other drugs on the street.

MEDIEVAL CENTRE & RED LIGHT DISTRICT

The big department stores cluster around the Dam. Chain stores line the pedestrian Kalverstraat.

TOP CHOICE Condomerie Het Gulden Vlies
SPECIALITY SHOP

(Map p46; www.condomerie.nl; Warmoesstraat 141; 4/9/16/24/25 Dam) Perfectly positioned for the Red Light District, the Condomerie stocks hundreds of hundreds of kooky condoms plus lubricants and saucy gifts.

American Book Center
BOOKS

(ABC; Map p46; www.abc.nl; Spui 12; 11am-8pm Mon, from 10am Tue-Sat, 11am-6.30pm Sun; 1/2/5 Spui) ABC's three-storey shop is the biggest source of English-language books in Amsterdam. It's the prime place to get your *New York Times* or next Lonely Planet guidebook.

PGC Hajenius
SPECIALITY SHOP

(Map p46; www.hajenius.com; Rokin 96; 4/9/14/16/24/25 Spui) Even if you're not a cigar connoisseur, this tobacco emporium is worth a browse. Inside is all art deco stained glass, gilt trim and soaring ceilings. You can sample your fresh Cuban stogie or other purchases in the handsome smoking lounge.

Hempworks
CLOTHING, ACCESSORIES

(Map p46; www.hempworks.nl; Nieuwendijk 13; 1/2/5/13/17 Martelaarsgracht) Hempworks' clothing and bags are all made with organic hemp, cotton and bamboo. Some of the clothes have special touches like hidden pockets for your stash.

Kokopelli
SMART DRUGS

(Map p46; www.kokopelli.nl; Warmoesstraat 12; 11am-10pm; 4/9/16/24/25 Centraal Station)

Were it not for its truffles trade you might swear this large, beautiful space was a fashionable clothing or homewares store. In addition to smart drugs, there's a coffee and juice bar.

Oudemanhuis Book Market
BOOKS

(Map p46; Oudemanhuispoort; 11am-4pm Mon-Fri; 4/9/14/16/24/25 Spui) Secondhand books weigh down the tables in the atmospheric covered alleyway between Oudezijds Achterburgwal and Kloveniersburgwal, where you'll rub tweed-patched elbows with University of Amsterdam professors. Most tomes are in Dutch.

Absolute Danny
EROTICA

(Map p46; www.absolutedanny.com; Oudezijds Achterburgwal 78; 11am-9pm Mon-Sat, from noon Sun; 4/9/16/24/25 Dam) Named by Dutch *Playboy* as Amsterdam's classiest sex shop, Absolute Danny specialises in fetish clothing, lingerie and leather, along with hardcore videos and dildos just for fun.

Hema
DEPARTMENT STORE

(Map p46; www.hema.nl; Nieuwendijk 174; 4/9/16/24/25 Dam) Once a Woolworths clone (and now akin to the USA's Target stores), Hema attracts as many design aficionados as bargain hunters. It has wide-ranging stock, including good-value clothing, homewares, wine and deli foods.

Chills & Thrills
SMART DRUGS

(Map p46; www.chillsandthrills.com; Nieuwendijk 17; 10am-10pm) Always packed with tourists, Chills & Thrills sells truffles, herbal trips, psychoactive cacti and novelty bongs. The life-sized, joint-smoking alien sculpture marks the spot.

NIEUWMARKT

Several good streets for typically eccentric local stores stripe the neighbourhood.

Droog
DESIGN, HOMEWARES

(Map p46; www.droog.nl; Staalstraat 7b; ⊙Tue-Sun; ⊠4/9/14/16/24/25 Muntplein) Droog means 'dry' in Dutch, and this local design house's products are strong on dry wit. Check out the cow chair and curtains with dress patterns. The shop is in the process of adding gallery space, a trippy courtyard garden and an inventively furnished cafe.

Het Fort van Sjakoo
BOOKS

(Map p46; ✆625 89 79; www.sjakoo.nl; Jodenbreestraat 24; ⊙11am-6pm Mon-Fri, to 5pm Sat; ⊠9/14 Waterlooplein) Get the low-down on the squat scene, plus locally produced zines and Trotsky translations, at this lefty bookshop, which has been in operation since 1977.

Juggle
SPECIALITY SHOP

(Map p46; www.juggle-store.com; Staalstraat 3; ⊙Tue-Sat; ⊠4/9/14/16/24/25 Muntplein) Wee Juggle puts more than just balls in the air: it also sells circus supplies, from unicycles to fire hoops to magic tricks.

JORDAAN & WESTERN CANAL BELT

At the top of the Jordaan, Haarlemmerstraat and Haarlemmerdijk are lined with hip boutiques and food shops. In the Western Canal Belt, the Negen Straatjes (Nine Streets) offers a satisfying browse among its offbeat, pint-sized shops.

Frozen Fountain
DESIGN, HOMEWARES

(Map p52; www.frozenfountain.nl; Prinsengracht 645; ⊠1/2/5 Prinsengracht) The city's best-

> **DON'T MISS**

AMSTERDAM'S BEST MARKETS

» **Albert Cuypmarkt** Soak up local colour and snap up exotic goods at Amsterdam's largest market (p66).

» **Waterlooplein Flea Market** Piles of curios, used footwear and cheap bicycle parts for bargain hunters (p51).

» **Bloemenmarkt** Bag beautiful bloomin' bulbs at the canalside flower market (p60).

» **Noordermarkt** It's morning bliss trawling for organic foods and vintage clothes (p54).

» **Dappermarkt** The Oost's multicultural bazaar reflects its diverse immigrant population (p69).

known showcase of furniture and interior design crams two canal houses full of the coolest, cleverest gadgets you're likely to come across, though they don't come cheap.

De Kaaskamer
FOOD & DRINK

(Map p52; www.kaaskamer.nl; Runstraat 7; ⊙noon-6pm Mon, 9am-6pm Tue-Fri, 9am-5pm Sat, noon-5pm Sun; ⊠1/2/5 Spui) The name means 'cheese room' and it is indeed stacked to the rafters with Dutch and organic varieties. You can try before you buy. The shop also makes sandwiches for take away.

Boekie Woekie
BOOKS

(Map p52; Berenstraat 16; ⊙noon-6pm; ⊠13/14/17 Westermarkt) This musty, one-of-a-kind shop sells books by artists, whether that means a self-published monograph or an illustrated story that's handcrafted right down to the paper.

De Looier Antiques Centre
ANTIQUES

(Map p52; www.antiekcentrumamsterdam.nl; Elandsgracht 109; ⊙11am-6pm Mon & Wed-Fri, to 5pm Sat & Sun; ⊠7/10/17 Elandsgracht) Anyone who likes peculiar old stuff might enter this knick-knack mini-mall and never come out. You're just as likely to find 1940s silk dresses as you are 1970s Swedish porn. Brasserie Blazer serves well-priced French fare inside to fuel the browsing.

Lady Day
CLOTHING

(Map p52; www.ladydayvintage.com; Hartenstraat 9; ⊠13/14/17 Westermarkt) Lady Day rocks for unearthing spotless vintage clothes. Leather jackets, swingin' 1960s and '70s wear, and woollen sailors' coats hang from the racks.

SOUTHERN CANAL BELT & DE PIJP

The Spiegel Quarter, along Spiegelgracht and Nieuwe Spiegelstraat, is ground zero for quality antiques and art.

Young Designers United
CLOTHING

(Map p56; www.ydu.nl; Keizersgracht 447; ⊙Mon-Sat; ⊠1/2/5 Keizersgracht) It's a showcase for newbie Dutch designers, each of whom gets their own rack. The range is huge, from asymmetrical sheaths to flowy frocks, all fairly well priced.

Heineken City Store
SOUVENIRS

(Map p56; Amstelstraat 31; ⊙11am-8pm Mon-Sat; ⊠4/9/14 Rembrandtplein) This multistorey concept store carries more wares than the brewery's shop in De Pijp. Some of the logoed gear is over the top (the chic jackets), but the art-decorated beer bottles in the huge refrigerator make groovy souvenirs.

Ajax Experience Store   SOUVENIRS
(Map p56; www.ajaxexperienceamsterdam.com; Utrechtsestraat 9; ⊙11am-7pm; 🚊4/9/14 Rembrandtplein) Own a piece of the glory that is Amsterdam's beloved football club. The shop, attached to the Ajax museum, stocks red-and-white team-logoed hats, shirts and other souvenir items.

Eduard Kramer   ANTIQUES
(Map p56; www.antique-tileshop.nl; Nieuwe Spiegelstraat 64; ⊙Tue-Sun; 🚊16/24/25 Keizersgracht) Specialising in antique Dutch tiles, this tiny store is crammed with old jewellery, pocket watches, silver candlesticks and crystal decanters. Stroll a few doors down to browse the expanded selection at Prinsengracht 807, an addition set in a refurbished old grocery store.

Fietsfabriek   BICYCLES
(Map p56; www.fietsfabriek.nl; 1e Jacob van Campenstraat 12; ⊙1-6pm Mon, 9am-6pm Tue-Fri, 10am-6pm Sat; 🚊16/24 Stadhouderskade) Wessel van den Bosch trained as an architect, and now he makes custom bicycles that are sold at this wild and crazy shop, one of several in Amsterdam. Peruse the *bakfiets* (cargo bike), *familiefiets* (bike with covered 'pram') or standard *omafiets* (one-gear city bike).

Concerto   MUSIC
(Map p56; Utrechtsestraat 52-60; 🚊4 Keizersgracht) You could spend hours browsing this rambling shop that has Amsterdam's best selection of new and secondhand CDs and records. It's often cheap, always interesting, and has good listening facilities.

Stadsboekwinkel   BOOKS
(Map p56; www.stadsboekwinkel.nl; Vijzelstraat 32; ⊙Tue-Sun; 🚊16/24/25 Keizersgracht) Run by the city printer, this is the best source for books about Amsterdam's history, urban development, ecology and politics. It's in the Stadsarchief (Municipal Archives) building.

Apple Store   ELECTRONICS
(Map p56; ☎530 22 00; www.apple.com; Leidseplein 25; ⊙9am-9pm Mon-Wed, to 10pm Thu-Sat, 10.30-7.30 Sun) Clued-up, multilingual staff roam the airy white space to help with all your iPhone, iPad and other iNeeds.

DON'T MISS

AIRPORT ART

The Rijksmuseum has a free mini-branch at Schiphol Airport that hangs 10 to 15 stellar Golden Age paintings. It's located after passport control between E and F Piers, and is open from 7am to 8pm daily.

OLD SOUTH & VONDELPARK
PC Hooftstraat unfurls Chanel, Gucci, Lacoste and scads of other fancy-pants brand-name shops.

Museum Shop at the Museumplein   SOUVENIRS
(Map p56; Hobbemastraat; 🚊2/5 Hobbemastraat) The Van Gogh Museum and Rijksmuseum jointly operate the Museum Shop at the Museumplein, so you can pick up posters, note cards and other art souvenirs from both institutions in one fell swoop.

Pied à Terre   BOOKS
(Map p56; www.jvw.nl; Overtoom 135-137; ⊙Mon-Sat; 🚊1 1e Constantijn Huygensstraat) Order a cappuccino and dream up your next trip at this classy travel-book shop, with hiking and cycling guides and maps.

❶ Information
Internet Access
Several cafes offer free wi-fi, including all branches of the ubiquitous **Coffee Company** (www.coffeecompany.nl). Many coffeeshops have internet terminals for customers. Internet cafes are scattered around Centraal Station. Expect to pay €3 per hour.

Internet City (Nieuwendijk 76; ⊙9am-midnight) More than 100 terminals; not far from the main coffeeshop drag.

Media
Het Parool (www.parool.nl) Amsterdam's favourite newspaper, with the scoop on what's happening around town.

Time Out Amsterdam (www.timeoutamsterdam.com) Monthly English-language magazine with good eating, drinking and entertainment listings.

Medical Services
Dam Apotheek (☎624 43 31; Damstraat 2; ⊙8.30am-5.30pm Mon-Fri, 10am-5pm Sat, noon-5pm Sun) Pharmacy just off the Dam.

Onze Lieve Vrouwe Gasthuis (☎599 91 11; www.olvg.nl; 1e Oosterparkstraat 1; ⊙24hr) At

STAYING ON TRACK: AMSTERDAM'S NEW METRO LINE (NOORD/ZUIDLIJN)

It's only 9.7km long, but the new Noord/Zuidlijn (north–south metro line) has stretched into a challenge of far greater size. Begun in 2003 and originally targeted for completion in 2011, the project deadline has now been pushed back to 2017.

It's no wonder, given the massive task at hand. To build the metro's route between Amsterdam-Noord and the World Trade Centre in the south, engineers must tunnel under the IJ river and the centuries-old buildings of Amsterdam's city centre. The first part went OK, but when some of the historic monuments in the centre started to shift off their foundations, engineers halted construction.

Debates flared over what to do. Continue, even though the budget was running skyhigh? Quit, and lose the millions of euros already spent? How much longer would residents tolerate the inconvenience of their main streets being torn to bits?

The city ultimately decided to proceed. Engineers added additional support beams beneath the affected buildings. And so far, so good. Take a peek at the epic project at the subterranean Noord/Zuidlijn Viewpoint (p45).

Oosterpark, near the Tropenmuseum. It's the closest public hospital to the centre of town.

Money

ATMs are easy to find in the centre, though they often have queues. To change money try **GWK Travelex** (☑0900 05 66; www.gwk.nl; Centraal Station; ⊗8am-10pm Mon-Sat, 9am-10pm Sun; ⏹Centraal Station), which also has branches at **Leidseplein** (Leidseplein 31a; ⊗9.30am-5.30pm Mon-Sat, 1.30-5.30pm Sun) and **Schiphol International Airport** (⊗24hr).

Post

Main Post Office (Singel 250; ⊗9am-6pm Mon-Fri, 9am-noon Sat) Large and well equipped.

Tourist Information

VVV Main Office (Stationsplein 10; ⊗7am-9pm Mon-Fri, 10am-6pm Sat & Sun) Located outside Centraal Station, this office can help with just about anything: it sells the I Amsterdam discount card, theatre and museum tickets, a good city map (€2.50), cycling maps, public transit passes (the GVB office is attached) and train tickets to Schiphol Airport. It also books hotel rooms for free. Queues can be long; be sure to take a number when you walk in.

VVV Leidseplein Office (Map p56; Leidseplein 26; ⊗10am-7pm Mon-Fri, 10am-6pm Sat, noon-6pm Sun) Run in conjunction with the Uitburo ticket shop.

Holland Tourist Information (⊗7am-10pm) A VVV-run office at Schiphol Airport.

Travel Agencies

Joho (☑517 13 57; www.joho.nl; Taksteeg 8; ⊗11.30am-5.30pm Mon-Sat) Sells travel services, guidebooks and offers advice on work and volunteering.

Websites

I Amsterdam (www.iamsterdam.com) City-run portal packed with sightseeing, accommodation and event info.

Overdose.am (www.overdose.am) Art, music and fashion to-do's.

ℹ Getting There & Away

Air

Most major airlines fly to **Schiphol Airport** (www.schiphol.nl), 18km southwest of the city centre. It has ATMs, currency exchanges, tourist information, car hire, train ticket sales counters, luggage storage, food and free wi-fi (for one hour).

Bicycle

It's easy to get to and from Amsterdam by bike. National bike routes radiate in all directions:

LF20/LF23 East to Muiden and beyond.

LF7 North via ferry across the IJ; before you know it you're in the rural wilds of Waterland.

LF20 West to Haarlem (25km) and on to the coast.

LF2 South to Gouda, Rotterdam and Belgium. For further route planning in the region, visit www.routecraft.com, which calculates the best bike paths; click on 'Bikeplanner' (there's an English version).

Bus

Eurolines (www.eurolines.com) connects with all major European capitals. Buses arrive at Amstelstation, south of the centre, which has an easy metro link to Centraal Station (about a 15-minute trip). The **Eurolines Ticket Office** (Rokin 38a) is near the Dam.

Car & Motorcycle

Motorways link Amsterdam to Den Haag and Rotterdam in the south, and to Utrecht and Amersfoort in the southeast. The Hoek van Holland ferry port is 80km away; IJmuiden is just up the road along the Noordzeekanaal.

Amsterdam's distance from some other European cities: Paris 480km; Munich 840km; Berlin 680k; Copenhagen 730km.

Train

National and international trains arrive at Centraal Station (CS) in the city centre. The station has ATMs, currency exchanges, tourist information, restaurants, shops, luggage storage (€5 per day), and national and international train ticket sales.

Amsterdam is the terminus of the new high-speed line south to Rotterdam and Belgium.

ℹ️ Getting Around

To/From the Airport

BUS Bus 197 (€4 one way, 25 minutes) is the quickest way to places by the Museumplein or Leidseplein. It departs outside the arrivals hall door.

DOOR-TO-DOOR VAN **Connexxion** (www.airporthotelshuttle.nl; one way/return €16/26) runs a shuttle bus (every 30 minutes from 6am to 9pm) from the airport to several hotels. Look for the Connexxion desk by Arrivals 4.

TAXI It takes 20 to 30 minutes to the centre (longer in rush hour), costing €45 to €50. The taxi stand is just outside the arrivals hall door

TRAINS Trains run to Amsterdam's Centraal Station (€4 one-way, 20 minutes) 24 hours a day. From 6am to 12.30am they go every 10 to 15 minutes; hourly in the wee hours. To buy tickets, you need cash or a credit card with chip (usually only Dutch ones work). Ticket machines accept coins only. To use euro bills, head past the machines to the ticket windows and purchase tickets from an agent for a €0.50 surcharge.

Bicycle

Cycling is the locals' main mode of getting around; 400km of bike paths make it easy. Many visitors rent a bike towards the end of their stay and wish they had done so sooner.

Rental shops are all over town; most open from 9am to 6pm (at least). Prices for single-speed 'coaster-brake' bikes average €12.50 per 24-hour period. Bikes with gears and handbrakes, and especially insurance, cost more. You'll have to show a passport or European national ID card, and leave a credit card imprint or pay a deposit (usually €50). Bike locks are typically provided; use them, as theft is rampant. Helmets are generally not available (the Dutch don't wear them). Most cycling tour companies also rent bikes (p70).

Bike City (☑626 37 21; www.bikecity.nl; Bloemgracht 68-70) There's no advertising on the bikes, so you can pretend you're a local.

Black Bikes (☑670 85 31; www.black-bikes.com; Nieuwezijds Voorburgwal 146) A sign-less company, with cargo bikes for toting kids.

MacBike (☑620 09 85; www.macbike.nl) You'll be conspicuous: the red bikes are equipped with big signs that say 'look out!' to locals. But the company has handy locations at Centraal Station (Stationsplein 5), Waterlooplein (Waterlooplein 195) and near Leidseplein (Weteringschans 2). It also sells great cycling maps.

Recycled Bicycles (☑06 5468 1429; www.recycledbicycles.org; Spuistraat 84a; ⊙Mon-Sat) Rents bikes rebuilt from scrap parts; the price is right at €5 per day. Reserve at least 24 hours in advance.

Boat

CANAL BUS The **Canal Bus** (www.canal.nl; day pass adult/child €22/11) offers a unique hop-on, hop-off service among its 17 docks around the city and near the big museums.

AMSTERDAM GETTING AROUND

TRAINS FROM AMSTERDAM

DESTINATION	PRICE (€)	DURATION (MIN)	FREQUENCY (PER HR)
Den Haag	11	50	4-6
Groningen	24	140	2
Maastricht	24	150	2
Rotterdam	14	65	5-6
Rotterdam (high-speed)	11-21	41	2-3
Schiphol Airport	4	20	6
Utrecht	7	30	3-6

ⓘ SIGHTSEEING BY TRAM

For a bit of passive sightseeing, look no further than the tram: the lines rattle through great cross-sections of the city. One of the best routes is tram 10. It starts near Westerpark, swings around the perimeter of the canal loop and heads out to the Eastern Docklands, passing 19th-century housing blocks, the Rijksmuseum and Brouwerij 't IJ windmill along the way. Another good route is tram 5, starting at Centraal Station and cutting south through the centre of town.

FERRIES Free ferries to Amsterdam-Noord depart from piers behind Centraal Station. Bicycles are permitted on all routes. The ride to Buiksloterweg is the most direct (five minutes) and runs 24 hours. Another boat runs to NDSM-werf (15 minutes) between 7am (from 9am weekends) and midnight. Another goes to IJplein (6.30am to midnight).

Car & Motorcycle

Parking is expensive and scarce. Street parking in the centre costs around €5/29 per hour/day. It's better to use a park-and-ride lot at the edge of town, at which a nominal fee (around €8 per 24 hours) also gets you free public transport tickets. For more information see www.bereik-baar.amsterdam.nl.

All the big multinational rental companies are in town; many have offices on Overtoom, near the Vondelpark. Rates start at around €35 per day.

Public Transport

The GVB operates the public transport system. You can pick up tickets, passes and maps at the **GVB Information Office** (www.gvb.nl; Stationsplein 10; ⊙7am-9pm Mon-Fri, 10am-6pm Sat & Sun). It's across the tram tracks from Centraal Station, and attached to the main VVV tourist information office.

BUS & METRO Amsterdam's buses and metro (subway) primarily serve outer districts. Fares are the same as trams. *Nachtbussen* (night buses) run after other transport stops (from 1am to 6am, every hour). A ticket costs €4.

TRAM Most public transport within the city is by tram. The vehicles are fast, frequent and ubiquitous, operating between 6am and 12.30am. On trams with conductors, enter at the rear; you can buy a disposable **OV-chipkaart** (www.ov-chipkaart.nl; €2.70, good for one hour) or day pass (€7.50) when you board. On trams without conductors (line 5, and some on line 24), buy a ticket from the driver. When you enter and exit, wave your card at the pink machine to 'check in' and 'check out'.

Most tram lines start at Centraal Station and then fan out into the neighbourhoods. Common routes:

Jordaan & Western Canals Tram 1, 2, 5, 13

Southern Canal Belt Tram 1, 2, 5 for Leidseplein; 4, 9 for Rembrandtplein

Old South & Vondelpark Tram 1, 2, 5

De Pijp Tram 16, 24

Nieuwmarkt & Plantage Tram 9

TRAVEL PASSES The GVB offers handy, unlimited-ride passes for 1/2/3/4/5/6/7 days (€7.50 /12/16/20.50/25/28.50/31), valid on trams, most buses and the metro. Passes are available at the GVB office, VVV offices (one- to four-day passes only) and from tram conductors (one-day passes only). The I Amsterdam Card (p60) also includes a travel pass.

Taxi

Taxis are expensive and not very speedy given Amsterdam's maze of streets. You'll find them at stands at Centraal Station, Leidseplein and a few hotels, or call one – **Taxicentrale Amsterdam** (TCA; ☑777 77 77; www.tcataxi.nl) is the most reliable.

Fares are meter-based. The meter starts at €2.65, then it's €1.95 per km thereafter. A ride from Leidseplein to the Dam runs about €12; from Centraal Station to the Jordaan is €10 to €15.

A nice alternative are the open, three-wheeled scooters of **TukTuk Company** (www.tuktuk company.nl; ⊙10pm-3am Fri & Sat) and **Bicycle Taxis** (www.fietstaxiamsterdam.nl). They often have lower rates, and can be flagged down in the street, especially near Leidseplein and Rembrandtplein.

Another alternative is **Hopper** (☑0900 8890; www.hopperamsterdam.nl; per ride €2.50; ⊙8am-8pm), a new fleet of lime-green, Vespa-style electric motor scooters. Flag them in the street, or call or book online.

Haarlem & North Holland

Why Go?

Wrapping around Amsterdam like a crown, Holland's north is thick with trad Dutch culture. West of the capital, elegant Haarlem is the region's crowning glory, a charming town of 17th-century grandeur. On its western outskirts are wide, sandy beaches.

Moving north, you'll be, yes, blown away by the iconic windmills at intriguing Zaanse Schans. Twee little Edam, Volendam and Marken hold a special place in Dutch culture for cheese, traditional customs, defiance of the sea, and tourism. The Golden Age ports of Hoorn and Enkhuizen have engaging old centres; the latter is also home to the Zuiderzeemuseum, a not-to-be-missed open-air extravaganza.

On the way to the Waddenzee island of Texel is Alkmaar, famous for its kitsch but oddly compelling traditional cheese auction. Texel itself is a gem, with long, fine beaches, busy little villages, sheep-swamped *polders* (strips of farmland separated by canals) and a forest or two.

When to Go

Haarlem, with its fine museums and indoor attractions such as good restaurants, is a year-round destination. The rest of North Holland is much more fair-weather country. Little burgs like Edam and Alkmaar all but hibernate in the winter. Think April to October for exploring this deeply Dutch region. Surprisingly the island of Texel actually makes a fascinating off-season destination as few things are moodier and more atmospheric as its deserted beaches when winds careen in off the North Sea (but on a sunny summer day, you can't beat time on the sand).

Best Places to Eat

» Kroft (p119)
» Freya (p128)
» Restaurant Topido (p128)
» Van Der Star (p129)

Best Places to Stay

» Stempels (p106)
» Posthoorn (p111)
» Hotel De 14 Sterren (p128)
» Bij Jef (p128)

NORTH HOLLAND

The iconic province of Noord Holland has enough cute little towns – in addition to Haarlem – to fill a week or more of touring.

History

The peninsula now known as Noord Holland was part of Friesland until the 12th century, when storm floods created the Zuiderzee and isolated West Friesland. By this time the mercantile counts of Holland ruled the area – or thought they did. One of the early counts, Willem II, became king of the Holy Roman Empire in 1247 but perished in a raid against the West Frisians (his horse fell through the ice). His son, Count Floris V, succeeded in taming his defiant subjects 40 years later.

Haarlem & North Holland Highlights

1 Explore the world-class museums of **Haarlem** (p103) and its charming Golden Age centre

2 Go nuts for cheese in the pastoral climes of cute little **Edam** (p112)

3 Experience the hardy life of North Holland's seafaring towns in the days before the Afsluitdijk (Barrier Dyke) at Enkhuizen's **Zuiderzeemuseum** (p120)

4 Wander the high sand dunes, quiet forests and pastures of **Texel** (p123)

5 Cycle the dykes of the region crowned by cosy old **Marken** (p111)

6 Be surprised by the fascinating **Museum Broeker Veiling** (p118) in Broek op Langedijk

7 Savour excellent smoked fish at **Oudeschild** (p129)

8 Take a trip to the captivating vast fortress at **Naarden** (p130), and enjoy an excellent lunch

West Friesland was now owned by the county of Holland, a founding member of the Republic of the Seven United Netherlands (1579). Northern Holland played a key role in the long struggle against Spanish domination, and the town of Alkmaar was the first to throw off the yoke. The era of prosperity known as the Golden Age ensued, and Noord Holland has its fair share of richly ornamented buildings from this period. The fishing and trading ports of Enkhuizen, Medemblik and Edam were at the centre of this boom.

Napoleon invaded Holland in 1795 and split it in two to break its economic power. Even after Holland came under the House of Orange in 1813, a divide remained and the provinces of Noord Holland and Zuid Holland were established in 1840.

Today Noord Holland's main business is agriculture, including cheese, lots of cheese.

❶ Getting There & Around

This is day-trip country: excepting Texel, all of the region is easily reached from Amsterdam, or you can set your own pace and go explore.

Noord Holland is well served by the national rail service, and where the train ends the bus networks take over.

Bike trails lace the province in almost every direction; you can cover the flat stretch from Amsterdam to Den Helder in two days at a very leisurely pace.

Haarlem

📝 023 / POP 152,000

This classic Dutch city of cobblestone streets, historic buildings, grand churches, even grander museums, cosy bars, fine cafes and the odd canal is a sure-fire stop. It's a perfect day trip from Amsterdam, but as a place with so much on offer in such a compact area, you may find yourself turning the tables on the capital and using Haarlem as a base to explore the surrounds.

History

The name Haarlem derives from Haarloheim, meaning a wooded place on high, sandy soil. Its origins date back to the 10th century when the counts of Holland set up a toll post on the Spaarne river. Haarlem quickly became the most important inland port after Amsterdam, but suffered a major setback when the Spanish invaded in 1572. The city surrendered after a seven-month siege but worse was yet to come: upon ca-

pitulation virtually the entire population was slaughtered. After the Spanish were finally repelled by Willem van Oranje, Haarlem soared into the prosperity of the Golden Age, attracting painters and artists from throughout Europe.

◉ Sights

Large **Grote Markt**, with its flanks of restaurants and cafes and a clutch of historical buildings, is literally and figuratively the centre of town (especially for the unmissable Monday and Saturday markets). Start your explorations here, a nice 500m walk from the train station.

Town Hall   HISTORIC BUILDING
At the western end of the Grote Markt stands the florid, 14th-century town hall, which sprouted many extensions including a balcony where judgements from the high court were pronounced. The counts' hall contains 15th-century panel paintings and is normally open during office hours.

Grote Kerk van St Bavo   CHURCH
(www.bavo.nl; Oude Groenmarkt 23; adult/child €2.50/free; ⊙10am-5pm Mon-Sat) Opposite the town hall looms the Grote Kerk van St Bavo, the Gothic cathedral with a towering 50m-high steeple. It contains some fine Renaissance artworks, but the star attraction is its stunning Müller organ – one of the most magnificent in the world, standing 30m high with about 5000 pipes. It was played by Handel and Mozart, the latter when he was just 10. Free **organ recitals** take place at 8.15pm Tuesday and 4pm Thursday during July and August.

De Hallen   GALLERY
(www.dehallen.nl; Grote Markt 16; adult/child €6/free; ⊙11am-5pm Tue-Sat, noon-5pm Sun) Haarlem's modern and contemporary art museum resides within two historic 'halls': the 17th-century Dutch Renaissance **Vleeshal**, a former meat market and the sole place that meat was allowed to be sold in Haarlem from the 17th through to the 19th century, and the neoclassical **Verweyhal** (Fish House). Eclectic exhibits rotate every three months and range from Dutch impressionists and CoBrA artists to innovative video, installation art and photography by cutting-edge international artists.

Statue of Laurens Coster   MONUMENT
On the square north of the Grote Kerk is a statue of Laurens Coster, whom Haarlemmers

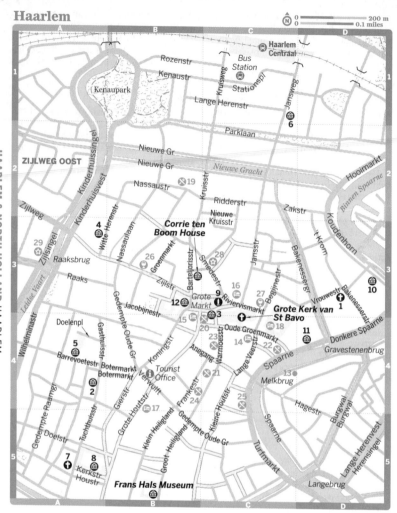

believe has a claim, along with Gutenberg, to be called the inventor of movable type.

Frans Hals Museum GALLERY
(www.franshalsmuseum.nl; Groot Heiligland 62; adult/child €7.50/free; ⊙11am-5pm Tue-Sat, noon-5pm Sun) A short stroll south of Grote Markt, the Frans Hals Museum is a must for anyone interested in the Dutch Masters. Kept in a poorhouse where Hals spent his final years, the collection focuses on the 17th-century Haarlem School; its pride and joy are eight group portraits of the Civic Guard that reveal Hals' exceptional attention to mood

and psychological tone. Look out for works by other greats such as Pieter Bruegel the Younger, and Jacob van Ruysdael. Among the museum's other treasures are the works of Hals' teacher, Flemish artist Carel van Mander: stunning illustrations of the human anatomy, all ceiling-high with biblical and mythological references.

FREE **Corrie ten Boom House** HISTORIC BUILDING
(www.corrietenboom.com; Barteljorisstraat 19; ⊙10am-4pm Tue-Sat Apr-Oct, 11am-3pm Tue-Sat Nov-Mar) Also known as 'the hiding place',

Haarlem

the Corrie ten Boom House is named for the matriarch of a family that lived in the house during WWII. Using a secret compartment in her bedroom, she hid hundreds of Jews and Dutch resistors until they could be spirited to safety. In 1944 the family was betrayed and sent to concentration camps where three died. Later, Corrie ten Boom toured the world preaching peace. There are daily tours in English.

Proveniershuis　　　HISTORIC BUILDING
(off Grote Houtstraat) To the southwest of Grote Markt stands the Proveniershuis, the former headquarters of St Joris Doelen (the Civic Guard of St George), which started life as a *hofje* (almshouse). This wonderful old building is one of Haarlem's prettiest.

Teylers Museum　　　MUSEUM
(www.teylersmuseum.eu; Spaarne 16; adult/child €10/2; ⊙10am-5pm Tue-Sat, 11am-5pm Sun) It's shocking, but depending on your tastes, the Teylers Museum may top Frans Hals Museum. It's the oldest museum in the country (1778) and contains an array of whiz-bang inventions, such as an 18th-century electrostatic machine that conjures up visions of mad scientists. The eclectic collection also has paintings from the Dutch and French schools and numerous

temporary exhibitions. The interiors are as good as the displays: the magnificent, sky-lighted Ovale Zaal (Oval Room) contains natural history specimens in elegant glass cases on two levels.

Bakenesserkerk　　　CHURCH
(cnr Vrouwestraat & Bakenesserstraat) Northeast of the Teylers Museum stands the striking Bakenesserkerk, a late 15th-century church with a lamp-lit tower of sandstone. The stone was employed here when the Grote Kerk proved too weak to support a heavy steeple – hence the wooden tower. It's closed to the public.

Nieuwe Kerk　　　CHURCH
(Nieuwe Kerksplein; ⊙10am-4pm Sun) Walk down charming Korte Houtstraat to find the 17th-century Nieuwe Kerk; the capricious tower by Lieven de Key is supported by a rather boxy design by Jacob van Campen.

Tours

Haarlem Canal Tours　　　CANAL TOUR
(www.haarlemcanaltours.com; Spaarne; per person €12.50; ⊙tours 10am-4pm, also 5.30pm & 7pm Jun-Aug) Fun hour-long tours in vintage open-top boats.

HAARLEM'S URBAN OASES

Haarlem has a surprising number of green spaces collectively known as *hofjes* – leafy courtyards enclosed by sweet little homes. They served as monastery gardens in the Middle Ages but eventually took on broader roles as hospitals and inns, or as refuges for orphans, widows and the elderly. These private squares also give clues about Dutch social concerns and the origins of the modern welfare state.

Most *hofjes* date from the 15th to the 18th centuries and are open for viewing on weekends only, but you can usually take a discreet peek any time. Ask the tourist office for its walking-guide brochure, *Hofjeswandeling*, which includes the following:

Brouwers Hofje (Tuchthuisstraat 8) Lodging for members of the brewers' guild (1472).

Frans Loenen Hofje (Witte Herenstraat 24) Almshouses built from a merchant's estate (1607).

Hofje van Loo (Barrevoetestraat 7) A women's hospital donated by mayor Sijmon Pieterszoon van Loo (1489); one of the most visible *hofjes* in Haarlem.

Hofje van Staats (Jansweg 39) One of the town's biggest, donated by a Haarlem merchant to poor women of the Reformed Church (1733), and still houses single, elderly women.

St Joris Doelen (Grote Houtstraat 144) A *proveniershuis* given as a donation; almshouse, later a gentlemen's inn (1591).

Teylers Hofje (Koudenhorn 144) Unusually grand affair, built by Pieter Teyler van der Hulst, founder of the Teyler Museum (1787).

🛏 Sleeping

TOP CHOICE Stempels HOTEL $$

(☑512 39 10; www.stempelsinhaarlem.nl; Klokhuisplein 9; r €95-160; @🖤) Haarlem's most interesting lodging has 17 spacious rooms (with high ceilings and stark, artful decor) in a gorgeous old printing house on the east side of the Grote Kerk. Small luxuries abound, including a computer in every room and collections of short stories on the bedside table. The on-site cafe may keep you from venturing far; the included breakfast is excellent.

Hotel Carillon HOTEL $$

(☑531 05 91; www.hotelcarillon.com; Grote Markt 27; s/d from €60/80; 🖤) Small but tidy white rooms in the shadow of the Grote Kerk are the hallmark here; eight have nice Grote Markt views. A couple share bathrooms and cost from €40. Breakfast (included) can be taken in wicker chairs on the sidewalk cafe.

Hotel Amadeus HOTEL $

(☑532 45 30; www.amadeus-hotel.com; Grote Markt 10; r €45-90; @🖤) Amadeus enjoys a brilliant spot nestled in a row of old gabled houses on the main square. Rooms are one step up from spartan, but they're comfy and have a few mod cons, and there's a small cafe on the 1st floor. Online deals are superb and breakfast is included.

Ambassador City Centre Hotel HOTEL $$

(☑512 53 00; www.acc-hotel.nl; Oude Groenmarkt 20; r €70-120; @🖤) More than 100 individual rooms spread over an entire block near the Grote Kerk; studios have kitchenettes. The hotel includes Joops Hotel, and the two function as one.

Haarlem Stayokay Hostel HOSTEL $

(☑537 37 93; www.stayokay.com; Jan Gijzenpad 3; dm/r from €21/52; @🖤) This 41-bed lakeside hostel has a 10pm silence rule but no curfew. The super-clean rooms are basic, but the bar-cafe is full of character. Take bus 2 (direction: Haarlem Noord) from the train station (10 minutes).

🍴 Eating

Haarlem has very good eating options. There are lots of cafes and restaurants along Zijlstraat, Spaarne and especially Lange Veerstraat, but you can find gems throughout town.

TOP CHOICE De Haerlemsche Vlaamse FRITES $

(Spekstraat 3; frites €2.10) Practically on the doorstep of the Grote Kerk, this *frites* (French fries) joint, not much bigger than a telephone box, is a local institution. Line up for its crispy, golden fries made from fresh potatoes. Choose from one of a dozen sauces including three kinds of mayonnaise.

De Lachende Javaan
INDONESIAN $$

(☎532 87 92; www.delachendejavaan.nl; Frankestraat 27; mains €10-20; ☺dinner Tue-Sun) An Indonesian restaurant that is almost as beautiful as its food. The interior of this old merchant's house glows from stained-glass windows and reflections off vintage art from Java. The menu traipses beyond standards and the *ristafel* (array of dishes served with rice) is great value at €22.

Vis & Ko
SEAFOOD $$$

(☎512 79 90; www.visenko.nl; Spaarne 96; menus from €35; ☺noon-2pm Tue-Fri, 6-9.30pm Tue-Sat, 1-9.30pm Sun) The sea isn't far and its seasonal bounty is given its own Golden Age at this bustling bistro with a fascinating open kitchen. Chef Imko Binnerts is a wizard with shellfish and finned delicacies; service is lavish without being stuffy (you have to love the faux seaman's uniforms).

Complimenti per Voi
ITALIAN $

(www.complimenti.nl; Nassaustraat 24; snacks from €3; ☺noon-6pm Wed-Fri, 10am-5pm Sat) Note the scent of garlic wafting over the street from this picknicker's heaven of a deli. Varieties of fresh Italian bread, pesto, cheese and more are arrayed in display cases.

Jacobus Pieck
INTERNATIONAL $$

(www.jacobuspieck.nl; Warmoesstraat 18; mains lunch €6-10, dinner €10-20; ☺lunch & dinner Tue-Sat) Touches such as freshly squeezed OJ put this tidy bistro on a higher plane. The menu bursts with fresh dishes, from salads and sandwiches at lunch to more complex pasta and seafood choices at dinner. Staff are welcoming; snag a sunny table on the back patio.

La Forca
ITALIAN $$

(☎532 25 00; www.laforca.nl; Frankestraat 17-19; mains €11-25; ☺lunch Tue-Sun, dinner daily) On a narrow quiet street, this trattoria (run by a charmer named Guiseppe) has tiled tables in a space as compact as the inside of a cannelloni. Perfect Tuscan and other Italian fare (the parmesan-crusted steak is superb) draws gaggles of locals. It sources from top local producers.

Grand Cafe Nobel
CAFE $

(Spaarne 36; dishes €6-15) Good waterside views from a sprawling patio should the sun break through. Look for the usual range of cafe standards: salads, soups and sandwiches.

🍷 Drinking

Haarlem's atmospheric cafes and bars are perfect spots to try Jopen beer, the local brew dating back to 1501. Jopen Koyt is dark, richly flavoured and has an alcohol content of 8.5%.

Proeflokaal in den Uiver
BROWN CAFE

(www.indenuiver.nl; Riviervismarkt 13) This nautical-themed place has shipping knick-knacks and a schooner sailing right over the bar. There's jazz on Thursday and Sunday evenings. It's one of many atmospheric places overlooking the Grote Markt.

Café Het Melkwoud
BROWN CAFE

(Zijlstraat 63) A fine place to nurse a beer (vast selection by the bottle) with ecofriendly locals in ancient wooden surrounds behind ceiling-high windows.

☆ Entertainment

Café Stiels
LIVE MUSIC

(www.stiels.nl; Smedestraat 21) For jazz and rhythm and blues, bands play on the back stage almost every night of the week from 10pm onwards to as late as 4am weekends.

Patronaat
LIVE MUSIC

(www.patronaat.nl; Zijlsingel 2) Haarlem's top music and dance club attracts bands with banging tunes. Events in this cavernous venue usually start around 9pm.

🛍 Shopping

Botermarkt has markets on Monday and Friday. **Grote Markt** also swarms on Monday as well as Saturday. Besides excellent produce and food from noted local producers there are food stalls selling all manner of freshly made Dutch treats. Think picnic.

On Wednesday Botermarkt has a book market. Haarlem has many antiquarian and used bookshops. Ask for a map at the tourist office. **Zijlstraat** becomes less upmarket and more funky as you head west.

ℹ Information

Suny Telecom (Kruisweg 42; per 20min €1; ☺10am-8pm) Internet access and cheap calls.

Tourist Office (☎0900 616 16 00; www.haarlemmarketing.com; Verwulft 11; ☺9.30am-6pm Mon-Fri, 9.30am-5pm Sat, noon-4pm Sun Apr-Sep, closed Sun Oct-Mar) Located in a modern glass house in the middle of the road.

TRAINS FROM HAARLEM

DESTINATION	PRICE (€)	DURATION (MIN)	FREQUENCY (PER HR)
Alkmaar	6.50	30-50	4
Amsterdam	4	15	5-8
Den Haag	8	35-40	4-6
Rotterdam	11	50	4

Staff will reserve local accommodation for €3.50; sells discount museum tickets. Good English-language tour brochures.

ℹ Getting There & Away

BICYCLE Haarlem is linked to Amsterdam by national route LF20 over a distance of 25km. Given the heavy urbanisation in the area this is not exactly a pastoral ride. Just west you can link up with the much more bucolic **LF1**, which follows the coast north and south. There's a large **bicycle shop** (531 70 66) at the train station.

TRAIN The city's stunning, restored art deco train station is served by frequent trains running between Amsterdam and Rotterdam. Lockers are up by track 3. Regular train services.

ℹ Getting Around

Bus 300 links Haarlem train station and Schiphol airport (40 minutes, 10 times hourly) between 5am and midnight.

Buses 2, 3, 4, 5 and 8 (and others) from the front of the train station stop at Zijlstraat, just east of Grote Markt (five minutes).

Around Haarlem

BEACHES

Just 5km west of Haarlem's peaceful outskirts lies **Zandvoort**, a popular seaside resort. It's not pretty as beach towns go, and drab apartment blocks line the main drag, but its proximity to Amsterdam ensures a steady flow of pleasure-seekers.

About 3km north of Zandvoort is Haarlem's second beach, **Bloemendaal aan Zee**, a much less developed spot with a handful of restaurants and cafes and uninterrupted beaches. It's frequented by those looking for a semblance of peace and quiet away from the hustle and bustle of its bigger neighbour to the south.

The closest accommodation to Bloemendaal is De Lakens, but Zandvoort is littered with accommodation.

Trains link Zandvoort to Amsterdam Centraal Station two times hourly (€5.50, 30 minutes) via Haarlem (€2.50, 10 minutes).

ZUID-KENNEMERLAND NATIONAL PARK

Some 3800 hectares of classic Dutch coastal dunes are being restored in this vast patch of nature in the midst of the busy Randstad. **De Zandwaaier** (023-541 11 23; www.npzk.nl; Zeeweg; admission free; ⊙10am-5pm Tue-Sun Apr-Oct, noon-5pm Tue-Sun Nov-Mar), the park's visitor centre, has nature displays and is a good source of information, with a range of detailed walking and cycling maps including a great 35km circuit. There are car parks at the Koevlak and Parnassia entrances, from where paths lead off into the reserve. Trails snake through hilltop copses of Corsican firs and valleys of low-lying thickets; at the western edge you come to a massive barrier of golden sand that's 1000 years old.

The dunes sprout an extra layer of colour in spring including desert orchids, the bright rosettes of the century weed and the white-blooming grass of Parnassus. Red foxes, fallow deer and many species of birds are native to the area. Bats slumber in the park's abandoned bunkers before appearing at dusk.

Among the main features, the **Vogelmeer** lake has a bird observation hut above the south shore. The artificial lake 't Wed teems with bathers in summer. Lookout points, with evocative names such as Hazenberg (Hare Mountain), are scattered throughout. At 50m, the **Kopje van Bloemendaal** is the highest dune in the country, just outside the eastern border of the park, with views of the sea and Amsterdam.

On a sombre note, the WWII cemetery **Erebegraafplaats Bloemendaal** (020-660 19 45; admission free; ⊙9am-6pm Apr-Sep, 9am-5pm Oct-Mar) is the resting place of 372 members of the Dutch resistance. Its walled compound in the dunes is isolated from the rest of the park and accessible only via the main road.

To reach the park, take bus 81 from Haarlem train station or cycle/drive the N200 towards Bloemendaal aan Zee. The distance is less than 5km.

Zaanse Schans

075

People come for an hour and stay for several at this open-air museum on the Zaan river, which is *the* place to see windmills operating. It's got a touristy element, but the six operating mills are completely authentic and are operated with enthusiasm and love. Visitors can explore the windmills at their leisure, seeing firsthand the vast moving parts that make these devices a combination of sailing ships and Rube Goldberg. As a bonus, the river-bank setting is lovely. To learn more about windmills, see p182.

The windmills include the following:

Spice mill De Huisman The air is redolent with the spices ground for the mustard sold here.

Sawmill De Gekroonde Poelenburg
See workers using wind power and lots of wooden gears to create lumber from logs.

Paint mill De Kat Grinds paint pigments using the same materials used to produce Renaissance masterpieces. Ask to see the storeroom of ground pigments for sale. Fascinating – and unchanged since Rembrandt's time.

Oil mill De Zoeker You'll delight in seeing how one central turning shaft operates a score of machines that extract oil from nuts and seeds.

Oil mill De Bonte Hen Another oil-producing windmill, this one dates to 1693.

Sawmill Houtzaagmolen Het Jonge Schaap 'The Young Sheep' is another sawmill, this one with a rare top-turning head.

The other buildings on the site have been brought here from all over the country to recreate a 17th-century community. There is an early Albert Heijn market, a cheesemaker and a popular clog factory that turns out wooden shoes as if grinding keys.

The site is free; entrance fees to the individual windmills average €3/1.50 per adult/child. At least a couple are open on any given day; hours tend to be 10am to 4pm. There are several cafes and restaurants on-site. Of course one sells pancakes – good ones too.

The impressive Zaans Museum (☏616 28 62; www.zaansmuseum.nl; adult/child €9/5; ⊗10am-5pm) shows how the harnessing of wind and water was done.

ⓘ Information

Zaanse Schans Information Desk (Zaans Museum; ⊗9am-5pm) An excellent resource.

ⓘ Getting There & Around

From Amsterdam Centraal Station (€3, 17 minutes, four times hourly) take the stop train towards Alkmaar and get off at Koog Zaandijk – it's a well-signposted 1km walk to Zaanse Schans.

After you tour the windmills, take the small boat (fare €1; ⊗9am-6pm May-Sep) across the Zaan river and walk back to the station through historic Zaandijk (15 minutes). The affable volunteers will give you a walking guide on the boat.

You can ride national bike route LF7 to the site from Amsterdam Centraal Station. The 22km route meanders through farmlands and lakes once it escapes the big smoke.

The site entrance closest to the bridge is the best way in. The entrance by the large car park and Zaans Museum has photo vendors and other irritations. You can rent a bike for €6.50 per hour.

Waterland Region

⏺ 075

Time moves slowly in this rural area that starts only 9km north of Amsterdam, which might as well be known as the Waterlogged Region. Fields of green are watched by herons standing motionless alongside watery

---

WORTH A TRIP

BEVERWIJK

Every weekend up to 80,000 visitors flock to the town of Beverwijk to visit the covered De Bazaar Beverwijk (www.debazaar.nl; Montageweg 35; adult/child €2.30/free; ⊗8.30am-6pm Sat & Sun), one of Europe's largest ethnic markets. Piled high are Arabian foods and spices, Turkish rugs, garments and handcrafted ornaments.

The liveliest of the three biggest halls is the Zwarte Markt, an enormous flea market with a carnival attitude. You can haggle with one of the 3000-plus vendors or just bask in the market chatter, live music and exotic aromas.

Parking (€3, free before 9am) becomes a problem after 9.30am. By train: Amsterdam Centraal Station to Beverwijk (€5.50, 40 minutes, two times hourly) and then walk 1km.

WATERLAND TICKET

If you're planning to day trip around the Waterland Region, Monnickendam, Marken, Volendam and Hoorn by bus, consider purchasing a Waterland Ticket (€10). Available from bus drivers, it allows a day's unlimited travel in the area north of Amsterdam (covered by buses including 110, 111, 115 and 311); it's excellent value.

furrows. Despite the proximity of the sea, you're most likely to smell cow dung from the many farms.

Broek in Waterland is a precious little burg in the heart of the region. Some 17th- and 18th-century houses are painted a particular shade of grey, known as *Broeker grijs* after the landscapes painted here by Monet and other masters. The village church was burned by the Spanish in 1573 but restored with a pretty stained-glass window recalling the tragic event. On the lake's edge stands the so-called Napoleonhuisje, a white pagoda where the French emperor and the mayor met in 1811. Rent a quiet little electric boat to explore the town by water from Waterland Recreatie.

ℹ Getting There & Around

BICYCLE The best way to experience the Waterland area is by bike; pick up a rental in Amsterdam and head north on the national bike route **LF7**.

BUS Buses 118, 311 and 315 among others serve Broek in Waterland from Amsterdam Centraal Station. Buy a Waterland Ticket.

Monnickendam

✆ 0299 / POP 10,800

Monnickendam, which gained its name from the Benedictines, who built a dam here, can trace its roots back to 1356. Since its fishing industry has gone belly up, it has transformed itself into an upscale port for yachts and sailors.

Today the beautiful old trawlers mainly catch pleasure-seekers. History still pervades the narrow lanes around the shipyards.

◉ Sights

Noordeinde is the main street and is enlivened by the drama of old brick houses tilting at crazy angles as they sink into the soggy ground.

As you stroll the lanes, look for **gable stones** on buildings – many have a story to tell. The one at Kerkstraat 32 dates to 1620, the one at Kerkstraat 12 tells of the five Jews succesfully hidden in the building for the duration of WWII.

Speeltoren   HISTORIC BUILDING

The town's trademark building is the 15th-century Speeltoren, an elegant, Italianate clock tower and former town hall. The tower's 17th-century carillon (glockenspiel) performs at 11am and noon on Saturday, when the four mechanical knights prance in the open wooden window twice before retiring.

Inside the clock tower you'll find the newly renovated **Museum De Speeltoren** (www. despeeltoren.nl; Noordeinde 4; adult/child €4.50/2; ◔11am-5pm Tue-Sun Apr-Oct, Sat & Sun only Nov-Mar). It shows the region through five eras of human occupation and allows you to see the amazing old mechanism that powers the clock tower.

FREE Grote Kerk   CHURCH

(De Zarken; ◔10am-4pm Tue-Sat, 2-4pm Sun & Mon Jun-Aug) The Gothic Grote Kerk, on the southern outskirts of town, is notable for its triple nave, tower galleries and a dazzling oak choir screen dating from the 16th century. It's impossible not to focus on the enormous organ in the nave; restoration of the edifice is ongoing.

Waag   HISTORIC BUILDING

A star in the architecture department includes the Waag (weigh house) on the central canal. Built in 1669, this focal point of local economic life was equipped in 1905 with grand Tuscan columns, a common trick of the day designed to make it look much older and more impressive.

In de Bonten Os   HISTORIC BUILDING

(Coloured Ox; Noordeinde 26) In de Bonten Os is the only house that's left in its original 17th-century state. In the days before proper glass, the curious vertical shutters at street level were made to let in air and light.

🏃 Activities

As elsewhere on the IJsselmeer, large pleasure boats are the thing in Monnickendam.

The harbour bristles with splendid old *tjalken*, *botters* and *klippers*, historic boats available for hire (as are skippers if need be). The *botters* can be hired out for a group from around €500 per day. The sky's the limit at the top end, for example three-masted clippers for as long as you (and your wallet) see fit.

Waterland Yacht Charter BOATING
(☑652 099; www.waterlandyacht.nl; Galgeriet 5a; daily rentals from €800) A large operation with a range of modern sail boats and yachts for hire.

Bootvloot BOATING
(☑06 5494 2657; www.bootvloot.nl; Hemmeland beach; half/full day rentals from €45/60; ☺10am-5.30pm Apr-Oct) Smaller two- to four-person sailboats can be found at Bootvloot. It's a 500m walk through the leafy Hemmeland recreation area northeast of Monnickendam marina – just follow the sign 'Zeilbootver-huur'.

Sleeping & Eating

Smoked eel (caught in the IJsselmeer) remains a local delicacy. Look for a remaining eel smokehouse on Havenstraat.

TOP CHOICE Posthoorn BOUTIQUE HOTEL $$$
(☑654 598; www.posthoorn.eu; Noordeinde 43; r from €150; ☎) This beautifully restored boutique hotel dates back to 1697 but the owners suspect it might be older. The five romantic rooms fuse trad comforts with modern style: bring on the pedestal sink. The restaurant (mains from €15; open dinner Tuesday to Saturday) uses local produce for solid mains of meats and seafood. Book rooms and courtyard dining on weekends.

't Markerveerhuis DUTCH $$
(www.hetmarkerveerhuis.nl; Brugstraat 6; mains €10-18; ☺lunch & dinner) Enjoy traditional Dutch fare while joining the old salts pondering the comings and goings in Monnickendam's harbour. Dutch folk music emanates from the stage at weekends while on the stylish rear cocktail terrace there's house music and much air-kissing.

Information

Tourist Office (VVV; ☑820 046; www.onswaterland.nl; Zuideinde 2; ☺10am-5pm) Small but excellent regional tourism office. Can recommend walks, obscure attractions and almost anything fun on the water.

Getting There & Around

BICYCLE Like the paths throughout Waterland, good bike routes abound, especially national route **LF21**, which starts in Amsterdam and follows rural dykes along the IJsselmeer. **Ber Koning** (☑651 267; www.berkonig.nl; Noordeinde 12; per day from €10; ☺10am-5pm Tue-Sat) rents bicycles.

BUS Buses 314, 315 and 317 (25 minutes, several hourly) link the centre of Monnickendam to Amsterdam Centraal Station, harbour side.

Marken
☑ 0299 / POP 500

Across Gouwzee Bay lies scenic Marken with a small and determined population. It was an isolated island in the Zuiderzee until 1957 when a causeway linked up with the mainland, effectively turning it into a museum-piece village. However, it still manages to exude a fishing-village vibe (well-used clogs sit outside houses), and the car-free centre helps keep *some* of the hordes at bay.

Sights & Activities

The colourful **Kerkbuurt** is the most authentic area, with tarred or painted houses raised on pilings to escape the Zuiderzee floods. A row of eel-smoking houses here has been converted to the **Marker Museum** (www.markermuseum.nl; Kerkbuurt 44; adult/child €2.50/1.25; ☺10am-5pm Mon-Sat, noon-4pm Sun Apr-Oct), which delves into the island's history and includes the recreated interior of a fisherman's home, with a wealth of personal odds and ends. It sells a walking tour brochure (€0.50), which will help guide you around the stout wooden structures that line the intricate pattern of lanes.

The **kerk** (Buurterstraat; ☺10am-5pm Mon-Sat, noon-4pm Sun Apr-Oct) is filled with ship models designed to attract God's good grace to local seamen. The lighthouse at the east end is a good 2km walk or ride.

Sleeping & Eating

TOP CHOICE Hof Van Marken HOTEL $$
(☑601 300; www.hofvanmarken.nl; Buurt II 15; r €80-155) Hof Van Marken has big beds, fluffy pillows and heavenly duvets that only a hard heart could resist. The seven cosy rooms have high-speed internet and are decorated with pastels natural to this region where land and water blend in the mists. The restaurant (mains €20 to €27; open lunch Saturday and Sunday, dinner Thursday to Monday) serves fresh and stylish takes on local produce and seafood. Bookings essential.

❶ Getting There & Away

BICYCLE The 8km ride along the dyke from Monnickendam is perfect for pondering the moody sea.

BUS Bus 311 links Marken with Amsterdam (40 minutes, half-hourly) via Monnickendam (12 minutes).

FERRY The **Marken Express** (www.markenexpress.nl; adult/child return €8/4.50; ⊘10.30am-6pm Mar-Sep) makes the 45-minute crossing from Volendam to Marken every half-hour. In Volendam the ferry leaves from the docks at Havendijkje.

Volendam
☑0299 / POP 20,700

Volendam is a former fishing port turned tourist trap. It's quaint all right, with its rows of wooden houses and locals who don traditional dress for church and festive events, but the harbour is awash with souvenir shops, fish stands and rapacious seagulls. On weekends it swarms with visitors. Here the ever-present regional smell of cow is replaced by fried fish. You'll enjoy Monnickendam, Marken or nearby Edam much more.

◉ Sights

Volendams Museum   MUSEUM
(Zeestraat 41; adult/child €3/1.75; ⊘10am-5pm mid-Mar–Oct) The Volendams Museum is a must for cigar aficionados. Local culture is covered with traditional costumes, prints, paintings of harbour scenes and even a cramped ship's sleeping quarters, but this place is really devoted to lovers of cheap cigars: some 11 million bands are plastered on its walls.

✖ Eating

Seafood is the undisputed king in Volendam, and the main street (and harbour) is lined with vendors offering smoked cod, eel, herring and tiny shrimp. But shop carefully as vendors are adept at making sandwiches look over-stuffed when the reality is all dough under the 'bursting' mound of seafood. This is a boon for bread-loving seagulls.

❶ Information

Tourist Office (VVV; ☑363 747; www.vvv-volendam.nl; Zeestraat 37; ⊘10am-5pm Mon-Sat year-round, 11am-4pm Sun Jun-Aug) Has regional accommodation info and is a good source of cycling maps.

❶ Getting There & Around

BICYCLE National bike route **LF21** passes right along the harbour; Monnickendam is 6km south. Amsterdam lies a mere 22km southwest.

BUS Buses 110 and 316 link Volendam to Amsterdam (25 minutes) and Edam (8 minutes) every 30 minutes until 1.30am.

Edam
☑0299 / POP 7500

Once a renowned whaling port – in its 17th-century heyday it had 33 shipyards that built the fleet of legendary admiral Michiel de Ruijter – this scenic little town is another of Noord Holland's hidden gems. With its old shipping warehouses, quiet cobblestone streets, hand-operated drawbridges and picture-perfect canals, you'd be hard pressed not to enjoy a stroll around. And it's quite astounding that so many tourists prefer Volendam, only 2km away – unless Edam's cheese market is on.

◉ Sights

Kaasmarkt   HISTORIC SITE
(Cheese Market; ⊘10.30am-12.30pm Wed Jul & Aug) In the 16th century Willem van Oranje bestowed on Edam the right to hold a Kaasmarkt, which was the town's economic anchor right through to the 1920s. At its peak 250,000 rounds of cheese were sold here every year. On the western side of Kaasmarkt stands the 1778 **Kaaswaag** (admission free; ⊘10am-5pm Apr-Sep), the cheese weigh house, which has a display on the town's chief product. The cheese market is smaller than the one in Alkmaar but equally touristy.

Gestam   CHEESE PRODUCER
(www.gestam.com; Voorhaven 127; ⊘10am-4pm Wed & Fri) Sample from an astonishing array of cheeses at the wonderful and barely commercial Gestam, a warehouse for regional cheese producers.

Edams Museum   MUSEUM
(www.edamsmuseum.nl; museum Damplein 8, annexe Damplein 1; adult/child €4/free; ⊘10am-4.30pm Tue-Sat, 1-4.30pm Sun Apr-Oct) The Edams Museum has a basic collection of old furnishings, porcelain and silverware, spread over three cramped floors. It's best known for its floating cellar, a remarkable pantry that rises and falls with the river's swell to reduce stress on the structure above. The ornate brick structure is Edam's oldest, dating from 1530. Just over the unusual

Edam

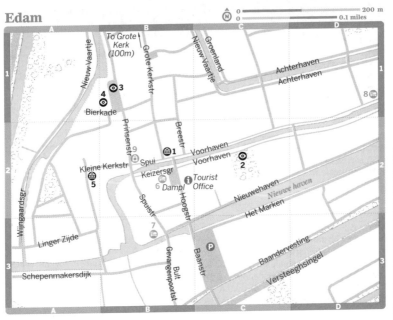

Edam

arched plaza across a canal, an annexe in the 1737 town hall, above the tourist office, has exhibits that include some famous paintings, including *Tall Girl*.

FREE Grote Kerk   CHURCH
(www.grotekerkedam.nl; Grote Kerkstraat; tower €2; ⏰1.30-5pm Apr-Sep) The 15th-century Grote Kerk has an unfortunate past that stands witness to the vagaries of Dutch weather. The stained-glass windows bearing coats of arms and historical scenes were added after 1602, when the church burned to a crisp

after a lightning strike. Its tower can be climbed for views of the surrounds.

Speeltoren   HISTORIC BUILDING
(Kleine Kerkstraat) The Speeltoren, leaning slightly over Kleine Kerkstraat about 100m south of Grote Kerk, is all that remains of the 15th-century Kleine Kerk.

⌂ Tours

The tourist office organises one-hour **boat tours** (adult/child €4/3; ⏰noon & 2pm Wed Jul & Aug) aboard a *tuindersvlet* (small, open-topped boat) in summer, weather permitting. It also organises one-hour **walking tours** (adult/child €4/3; ⏰1pm Wed Jul & Aug).

Fluisterbootjes   CANAL TOUR
(Whisper Boats; www.fluisterbootverhuur-edam. nl; VVV, Damplein 1; per hour €23; ⏰Apr-mid-Oct) Glide through Edam's canals in a small electric boat you pilot yourself.

⌂ Sleeping & Eating

In addition to the places reviewed here, the tourist office has a list of private accommodation and farmstays from €25 per person.

Along with the excellent Gestam there are several places to buy cheese and assemble picnics. **Edammer Kaaswinkel** (☎371 683;

cnr Spui & Prinsenstraat) has a wide variety and there's a good adjoining deli.

Dam Hotel
BOUTIQUE HOTEL $$

(☑371 766; www.damhotel.nl; Keizersgracht 1; r from €125; ☜) In the heart of Edam, this boutique hotel is a perfect romantic retreat, with a sultry blend of antiques and art. Some of the 11 rooms are a little on the small side, but this is counterbalanced by huge beds and thoroughly modern bathrooms. Its grand cafe (mains from €8) spills onto the main square. The bistro (menus from €35) serves modern French fare in elegant surroundings.

De Harmonie
BROWN CAFE $$

(☑371 664; www.harmonie-edam.nl; Voorhaven 92-94; s/d from €60/80; ☜) This barebones old brown cafe dates to the 17th century. It has five rooms upstairs at the back, which have views over neighbouring gardens. They are good value and have small kitchens; breakfast is included. It is just far enough away from the day trippers on Damplein and has nice tables along the canal. There is live music some nights and the excellent Budels beer on tap.

De Fortuna
HOTEL $$

(☑371 671; www.fortuna-edam.nl; Spuistraat 3; r from €88; ☜) An Edam gem, this place might have stood as a model for an old Dutch painting. Its 23 cute rooms have bathrooms best described as cosy. The restaurant (dinner mains from €20) serves classic Dutch dishes amid oil paintings, large bay windows and leather seats buffed shiny over the years. There are lush gardens and a waterside terrace for drinks and snacks; breakfast is included.

❶ Information

Tourist Office (VVV; ☑315 125; www.vvv-edam.nl; Damplein 1; ☉10am-3pm Mon-Sat Nov-Mar, 10am-5pm Mon-Sat Apr-Oct, 11am-1.30pm Sun Jul & Aug) Housed in the splendid 18th-century town hall. Pick up the good English-language booklet, *A Stroll Through Edam* (€2.50), for 90-minute self-guided tours.

❶ Getting There & Around

BICYCLE Bicycles can be rented at **Ton Tweewielers** (www.tontweewielers.nl; Schepenmakersdijk 6; per day from €8.50). Edam is on national bike route **LF21**; the many IJsselmeer dykes make for excellent riding.

BUS Buses 110 and 316 link Edam to Amsterdam (35 minutes) via Volendam every 30 minutes until 1.30am.

Alkmaar

☑072 / POP 94,000

If ever there was a cheese town, Alkmaar is it. Come Friday, its picturesque ringed centre is awash with tourists, all eager to catch a glimpse of the city's famous cheese market. It's a genuine spectacle and probably the best reason to visit. On other days Alkmaar's old charms are modest.

The city is more than just a purveyor of curdled milk. It holds a special place in Dutch hearts as the first town, in 1573, to repel occupying Spanish troops; locals opened the locks and flooded the area with sea water, forcing the perplexed invaders to retreat. The victory won the town weighing rights, which laid the foundation for its cheese market.

◉ Sights

Before beginning your exploration of the city, consider purchasing a copy of the *Walking Tour of the Town Among the Historic Buildings* booklet (€2.50) from the tourist office. It covers historical buildings such as the Renaissance **Stadhuis** (Town Hall; Schoutenstraat) in extensive detail.

Waaggebouw
HISTORIC BUILDING

(Weigh house; Waagplein 2; ☉carillon 6.30pm & 7.30pm Thu, 11am & noon Fri, noon & 1pm Sat mid-Apr–mid-Sep) Built as a chapel in the 14th century, the Waaggebouw was pressed into service as a weigh house two centuries later. This handsome building houses the tourist office and the Hollands Kaasmuseum. The mechanical tower **carillon** with jousting knights still springs to life.

Hollands Kaasmuseum
MUSEUM

(Dutch Cheese Museum; www.kaasmuseum.nl; Waagplein 2; adult/child €3/1.50; ☉10am-4pm Mon-Sat Apr-Oct) Housed in the Waaggebouw, this cheesy museum has a reverential display of cheese-making utensils, photos and a curious stock of paintings by 16th-century female artists.

Stedelijk Museum
MUSEUM

(www.stedelijkmuseumalkmaar.nl; Canadaplein 1; adult/child €8/free; ☉10am-5pm Tue-Sun) The Stedelijk Museum is overlooked by many who don't get past the cheese market. This

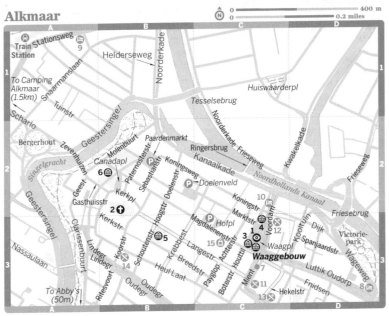

Alkmaar

is a shame because its collection of oil paintings by Dutch Masters, including impressive life-sized portraits of Alkmaar nobles, is alone worth the entry fee. Other works show the city in post–Golden Age decline; sombre scenes of almswomen caring for the poor recall how the church's role grew as trade declined. Modern works on display include Charley Toorop's odd oil painting of the Alkmaar cheese market; her cheese-bearers with grotesque features remain controversial.

Grote Kerk CHURCH
(Kerkplein; ⊙10am-5pm Tue-Sun Jul & Aug, Wed & Fri-Sun only Sep-Jun) The Grote Kerk reminds us that Noord Hollanders are organ lovers.

SCENIC DRIVE: DYKES & WINDMILLS

Midway between Edam and Alkmaar, the village of De Rijp on the N244 is at the south end of several good drives and rides along dykes that give an excellent feel for just how low the land is compared to the waterways coursing between the earthen walls. The Oostdijk–Westdijk road travels north 6km to the hamlet of Schermerhorn on the N243. Just west, another dyke road runs parallel and meanders past several windmills. Both are narrow and the domain of cyclists and sheep, so if you're in a car, go slow.

The most famous here is the little 'Swallow Organ' (1511) in the north ambulatory. The 17th-century organ built by Jaco van Campen dominates the nave. Organ recitals – which will thrill any fan of 1930s horror movies – take place on Wednesday evenings and at noon on days when the church is open. Be sure to get the English-language guide. The pastel stained-glass windows bathe the interior in the colours of spring.

Nationaal Biermuseum　MUSEUM
(www.biermuseum.nl; Houttil 1; admission €4; ☺1-4pm Mon-Sat) Housed in the attractive old De Boom brewery, the Nationaal Biermuseum has a decent collection of beer-making equipment and wax dummies showing how the suds were made. The video of Dutch beer commercials since the 1950s will have you in stiches. Choose from 30 beers (eight on draught) in the friendly bar after your tour.

☞ Tours

Grachtenrondvaart Alkmaar　CANAL TOUR
(www.rondvaartalkmaar.nl; Mient; adult/child €6/4.50; ☺from 11am Apr-Oct) Tours with multilingual commentary depart from Mient near the Waag and last 45 minutes.

🛏 Sleeping

Pakhuys City Centre Hotel　HOTEL $$
(☑520 25 00; www.hotelpakhuys.nl; Peperstraat 1; r €90-140; 🛜) A mini-empire spread over several buildings right in the centre, the hotel has 17 rooms that have artful interiors (some are blush-worthy vivid red, deluxe versions have luxurious loungers) and make the best of their historical surrounds. Some have ca-

nal views, all include breakfast. There's also a vibrant cafe.

Alkmaarse Bed & Breakfast　B&B $
(☑06 1111 6661; www.alkmaarsebedandbreakfast. nl; Wageweg 15; s/d from €40/70) Housed in a tidy building dating to 1630, this B&B is right across from a canal and close to the centre. There are rooms and larger apartments, the latter good for longer stays. The ground floor has an excellent bakery where you can buy breakfast and treats.

Hotel Stad en Land　HOTEL $$
(☑512 39 11; www.stadenland.com; Stationsweg 92; s/d from €65/85) Close to the train station, with 22 basic yet comfy rooms, Stad en Land is a good choice for those making a short overnight visit to Alkmaar. Of the four rooms those at the rear are the quietest and overlook a little pond.

Camping Alkmaar　CAMPGROUND $
(☑511 69 24; www.campingalkmaar.nl; Bergerweg 201; camp sites €21-26, cabins €40; 🛜) This campground lies in a pleasant copse convenient to the ring road, 1km west of the train station. Tent sites are sheltered and wooden cabins sleep two people. Take bus 6 to Sportpark (10 minutes).

✗ Eating

Charming restaurants and bars surround the Waag and the quay named Bierkade. Koorstraat and Ritesvoort are away from the cheesy madness and have many excellent bistros and cafes.

Cafe Restaurant De Buren　CONTEMPORARY DUTCH $$
(www.restaurant-deburen.nl; Mient 37; mains €6-20) Outside tables at this vintage cafe span the canal and wrap around to the old fish market. The menu is a fresh take on Dutch fare. There's a sprightly mustard soup and even Thai curries.

Eet Palais　GRAND CAFE $$
(www.eetpaleis.nl; Verdronkenoord 102; mains €8-20; ☺Tue-Sun) Chandeliers add class to this large cafe just around the bend from the greatest cheese market madness. Soups, salads, sandwiches, hot mains and more fill out the diverse menu. Enjoy a drink at tables along the canal but beware: the street name means 'drowned'.

Ijssalon W Laan　ICE CREAM $
(☑511 56 85; Koorstraat 45; treats €1.20; ☺noon-8pm) For more than six decades huge

industrial mixers have created soft ice cream at this tiled gem. There's one flavour: a tongue-titillating vanilla, but you can also have it in many sundaes.

De Vlaminck FRITES **$**
(Voordam; frites from €2) The fries are superb at this storefront counter. Feast on your paper cone of joy on benches in front along the canal and notice your new duck friends.

Abby's INTERNATIONAL **$$**
(511 11 11; Ritsevoort 60; meals €8-20) There's cool jazz inside and cool breezes outside on the terrace, which is in the shadow of an old windmill. Soups, salads and sandwiches please lunchtime diners.

🍷 Drinking & Entertainment

Alkmaar has a lively arts scene – pick up a copy of the monthly *Alkmaar Agenda* (free) from the tourist office to see what's on.

TOP CHOICE De Boom BROWN CAFE
(Houttil 1) The pub on the ground floor of the beer museum lives up to its location. The inside is unchanged since the 1930s – you expect to hear a scatchy 78rpm playing. Outside you can enjoy the fine selection of brews at seats on a moored old canal boat. On Thursday nights there is live jazz.

Theater De Vest PERFORMING ARTS
(548 98 88; www.theaterdevest.nl; Canadaplein 2) The centre for Alkmaar's highbrow entertainment, De Vest runs the gamut from traditional plays and puppet shows to avant-garde dance. In summer Canadaplein turns into a stage for the performing arts festival **Zomer op het plein** (Summer on the square).

🛍 Shopping

Langestraat is the pedestrianised shopping street with mainstream stores. Laat has a more interesting and diverse collection.

TOP CHOICE De Tromp Kaashuis CHEESE
(www.kaashuistromp.nl; Magdalenenstraat 11; ⊙10am-6pm Mon-Sat) If you're looking to grab some cheese after seeing so much of it, check out this quality-certified shop with Dutch and French cheeses stacked everywhere you look. Samples abound, and there's fresh bread for sale – perfect for making impromptu sandwiches with that delish two-year-old Gouda you just bought.

ℹ Information

Tourist Office (VVV; 511 42 84; www.vvvalkmaar.nl; Waagplein 2; ⊙10am-5pm Mon-Sat) In the Waaggebouw, the towering old weighhouse. Staff will book accommodation for €3.

ℹ Getting There & Away

BICYCLE There's a **bicycle shop** (511 79 07) at the train station. Pakhuys City Centre Hotel rents bikes (per day €10) and scooters (per day €50).

DON'T MISS

ALKMAAR'S CHEESE MARKET

Cheese is a big thing in the Netherlands; anyone who's breakfasted in a B&B or entered a supermarket can tell you this. But in Noord Holland's Schiereiland, cheese is a very serious business.

Alkmaar's traditional **cheese market** (Waagplein; ⊙10am-noon Fri Apr-early Sep) goes back to the 17th century. Around 30,000kg of waxed rounds of Gouda, Edam and Leiden *kaas* (cheese) are ceremoniously stacked on Waagplein, and soon the porters appear in their colourful hats, ready to spring into action. The dealers (looking official in white smocks) insert a hollow rod to extract a cheese sample and go into taste-test mode, sniffing and crumbling to check fat and moisture content. This is one of the few Dutch towns where the old cheese guilds still operate, and the porters' bright green, red and yellow hats denote which company they belong to. Once deals are struck the porters whisk the cheeses on wooden sledges to the old cheese scale in a stride reminiscent of someone hurrying to the toilet. It's primarily for show: nowadays the modern dairy combines have a lock on the cheese trade. Still, as living relics go it's a spectacle not to be missed, and it's fun to see so many people in a Wallace & Gromit state over cheese.

Ask at the tourist office for details on local cheese producers who give demonstrations and sell their wares. Or just go on a sampling binge at De Tromp Kaashuis (p117).

TRAINS FROM ALKMAAR

DESTINATION	FARE (€)	DURATION (MIN)	FREQUENCY (PER HR)
Amsterdam	7	30-40	4
Den Helder	7.50	35	2
Enkhuizen	7.50	50	2
Hoorn	5	25	2

National route **LF7** runs west 9km to link with the **LF1** coastal route. It runs east 28km to join the **LF21** which follows the IJsselmeer and links Edam and Hoorn.

TRAIN The train station has all services, including lockers and exchange. See the box above for services.

Getting Around

The town centre is focused on Waagplein, 500m southeast of the train station. Buses 2, 3 and 4 connect the train station to Kanaalkade (€1.80, five minutes). Cycling around town on cheese market days is very difficult due to the crowds, and bikes often 'disappear'.

Broek op Langedijk

📞 0226

Only in Holland! The vast water-logged area north of Alkmaar was once home to 15,000 tiny, yet productive, farms, each literally an island. Rather than tending to their crops by tractor or getting about by road, the farmers used rowboats. Most of the farms have been replaced by developments but in the town of Broek op Langedijk, about 8km northeast of Alkmaar, the fascinating **Museum Broeker Veiling** (www.broekerveiling.nl; 1721 BW Broek op Langedijk) recalls this way of life.

The centrepiece of this surprisingly unmissable attraction is a vast auction house where farmers would arrive with their boatloads of produce and then wait – afloat – inside, until they could paddle through an auction room where wholesale grocery buyers would bid on the load of carrots, turnips, cabbage etc. Built in 1878, it sits on 1900 piles. Visitors can still tour the immense interior and recreated auctions where the winning bid gets a bag of apples rather than a boatload. It's great fun.

A large striking new museum opened in 2012 shows some of the 15,000 islands on its exterior. Inside the exhibits on how the farms worked are a combination of high-tech wizardry and old-fashioned mechanised gadgets. It's even more fun.

The museum runs 45-minute traditional tours around some of the 200 surviving island plots nearby. On the grounds you can see some of the traditional crops in situ and there's a fine little cafe.

To get there by train, go to Alkmaar and change to bus 10 (30 minutes, hourly) and get off in front of the museum. A 9km bike route from Alkmaar follows canals and goes through the tiny old village of Sint Pancras

Hoorn

 0229 / POP 71,200

With a string of museums, a quiet affluent charm and a busy harbour, Hoorn attracts both weekend wanderers and skippers alike. It was once the capital of West Friesland and, thanks to the presence of the Dutch merchant fleet, a mighty trading city. As a member of the league of Seven Cities, it helped free the country from the Spanish who occupied the town in 1569.

Its most famous son, explorer Willem Schoutens, named South America's storm-lashed southern tip – Cape Horn – after his home town in 1616.

⊙ Sights

Perhaps Hoorn's greatest joy is simply strolling the streets where 16th- and 20th-century buildings mix, the older ones leaning forward as if they are hard of hearing. The scenic harbour is lined by stately gabled houses, especially along **Veermanskade**. Check out the old warehouses on **Bierkade**, where lager was brought from Germany.

Rode Steen   SQUARE

Hoorn's heyday as a shipping centre is long gone, but the imposing **statue of Jan Peterszoon Coen**, founder of the Dutch East India Company, still watches over the Rode Steen (Red Stone or Fortress), the square named for the blood that once flowed from the gallows. On the northeastern side of the square it's impossible to overlook the **Waag**, the 17th-century weighhouse that boasts a carved unicorn, the town symbol.

Westfries Museum   MUSEUM
(☏280 028; www.westfriesmuseum.nl; Rode Steen; adult/child €5/free; ☺11am-5pm Mon-Fri, 1-5pm Sat & Sun) This absorbing museum has a rich collection of historical paintings – so rich that it was the target of art theft in 2005. Some 20 paintings worth €10 million were stolen (and are still missing), but fortunately the four large group portraits of prominent *schutters* (civic guards) by Jan A Rotius (1624–66) were left in peace.

The museum is housed in the former seat of the Staten-College (States' Council), the body that once governed seven towns in Noord Holland. Its 1632 wedding-cake facade bears the coat of arms of Oranje-Nassau, the Dutch-German royal dynasty that the Dutch named as rulers when Napoleon left Holland. The rear courtyard has a number of curious stone tablets from local facades.

Hoofdtoren   HISTORIC BUILDING
Overshadowing surrounding historic buildings, the massive Hoofdtoren (1532) is a defensive gate that now hosts a bar and restaurant. The tiny belfry was an afterthought.

Museum of the 20th Century   MUSEUM
(Museum van de Twintigste Eeuw; www.museumhoorn.nl; Krententuin 24, Oostereiland; adult/child €6/3.50; ☺10am-5pm Tue-Fri, noon-5pm Sat & Sun) Housed in a vast new complex on Oostereiland, south of the Hoofdtoren, this fun museum is devoted mainly to household goods and modern inventions. Among the eye-openers are a 1964 Philips mainframe computer – a clunky bookcase-sized unit with a whole 1KB of memory – and a 30-sq-metre scale *maquette* (model) of Hoorn in 1650.

Speelgoed Museum de Kijkdoos   MUSEUM
(Toy Museum the Kijkdoos; Italiaanse Zeedijk 106; adult/child €4/2; ☺11am-5pm Tue-Sun) Not much larger than a toy box, this museum devoted to old toys will delight kids and old folks who once played with them. There's all manner of mechanical marvels, cute dolls and more.

Affiche Museum   MUSEUM
(Dutch Poster Museum; www.affichemuseum.nl; Grote Oost 2-4; adult/child €4/2; ☺10am-5pm Tue-Fri, noon-5pm Sat & Sun) If you weren't already

on a trip, this small museum would inspire you to take one. The proud graphic-arts traditions of the Netherlands are celebrated through the display of scores of posters. Many are beautiful and evocative old ones from the age of steamships and trains.

Museum Stoomtram   STEAM TRAIN
(☏214 862; www.museumstoomtram.nl; circle ticket adult/child from €20/15; ☺Apr-Oct) The Museum Stoomtram isn't a museum in the traditional sense but rather a historical steam locomotive that puffs between Hoorn station and Medemblik (22km; one hour). You can combine the train and boat for a route called the 'Historic Triangle': first from Hoorn to Medemblik by the steam train and then by boat to Enkhuizen and finally on a regular NS train back to Hoorn. Times vary by day, confirm in advance.

🛏 Sleeping

The tourist office has a list of B&Bs from around €30 per person.

Bed & Breakfast Grote Noord   B&B $$
(☏06 2871 9018; www.bedandbreakfastgrotenoord.nl; Grote Noord 3; r €55-150; 🛜) The Rode Steen is a wobbly roll of a cheese round away from this fine B&B. The two rooms come in two sizes: large and medium. Both are up high in the building and have exposed 17th-century timbers. Rooms are well appointed with stark furnishings that eschew twee. There are iPod docks and other luxuries.

Hotel de Keizerskroon   HOTEL $$
(☏212 717; www.keizerskroonhoorn.nl; Breed 33; s/d from €75/95; 🛜) Very much in the middle of things, this 25-room hotel-restaurant has stylish, comfortable rooms. Its insulated windows afford a view of the bustling market streets below. Rates include breakfast.

🍴 Eating

Open-air markets are held on Wednesday (June to August) and Saturday (year-round) along Breed.

🏆 Kroft   CONTEMPORARY DUTCH $$
(☏232 676; www.restaurantkroft.nl; West 52; mains €12-25; ☺lunch & dinner Wed-Sun) A tiny worker's cottage near the centre has been reborn as a vibrant and creative restaurant. From the open kitchen, skilled servers bring plates of seasonal fare. There are French and Asian influences but ultimately the seafood and meats are the best Holland produces.

Restaurant (B)eet CONTEMPORARY DUTCH $$
(☎214 659; www.restaurantbeet.nl; Veemarkt 8-10; menus lunch/dinner from €30/35; ⊙lunch Tue-Fri, dinner Tue-Sun) The gorgeous back garden is the place to be if a North Sea squall isn't pouring down. Otherwise this smart bistro outside the tourist zone yet close to the train station offers excellent seasonal fare. Dishes are a compelling combination of complex flavours.

Vishandel Leen Parlevliet SEAFOOD $
(snacks from €3, meals from €6; ⊙10am-7pm) Next to the Hoofdtoren at the harbour, this small glass pod sells wonderful seafood rolls and bigger seafood meals. It has a broad terrace with tables that enjoy three-way views.

Wormsbecher SEAFOOD $
(☎214 408; Wijdebrugsteeg 2; snacks from €3; ⊙11am-6pm) Turquoise tiles front this classic fresh-fish shop, which is the perfect place to enjoy the locally loved smoked eel. A fine seafood salad is a bargain at €5.

De Waag Café-Restaurant GRAND CAFE $$
(Rode Steen 8; mains €8-30) With pride of place on the main square in the stunning Waag building, this restaurant has always-popular outside tables and a bustling cafe. The restaurant is more formal and features top-notch takes on meaty Dutch staples.

ℹ Information

Tourist Office (VVV; ☎218 343; www.vvvhartvannoordholland.nl; Veemarkt 44; ⊙1-6pm Mon, 9.30am-6pm Tue-Fri, 9.30am-5pm Sat) Across from the train station with an ANWB office.

ℹ Getting There & Around

The old quarter begins about 1km southwest of the train station. From the station, walk south along broad Veemarkt to Gedempte Turfhaven, turn right and take the first left into Grote Noord, the pedestrianised shopping street. At the end is the scenic main square, Rode Steen, and the harbour area is a fishing net's throw further south, down Grote Havensteeg.

BICYCLE Hire your bikes at the **bicycle shop** (☎217 096) just to the right as you exit Hoorn train station. National bike route **LF21** runs 20km south to Edam and joins the **LF15** for the 25km coastal run to Enkhuizen.

BUS The bus station is outside the train station. Bus 135 goes once hourly to Den Helder (one hour). Change buses at Den Oever for trips across the IJsselmeer towards Leeuwarden. Buses 314 and 317 serve Edam (30 minutes, four times hourly).

TRAIN Regular train services include those covered in the box below.

There is a heritage route to Medemblik and Enkhuizen run by the Museum Stoomtram (p119).

Enkhuizen

☎0228 / POP 18,300

Enkhuizen may be a small, quaint town in the present day but during the Golden Age its strategic harbour sheltered the Dutch merchant fleet. It slipped into relative obscurity in the late 17th century but now possesses one of the largest fleets on the IJsselmeer – of recreational vessels. For most travellers, however, Enkhuizen's biggest drawcard is the Zuiderzeemuseum, one of the country's finest.

⊙ Sights

TOP CHOICE **Zuiderzeemuseum** MUSEUM
(☎351 111; www.zuiderzeemuseum.nl; adult/child €14.50/9; ⊙10am-5pm) This captivating and amazing museum consists of two parts: the open-air Buitenmuseum, with more than 130 rebuilt and relocated dwellings and workshops, and an indoor Binnenmuseum, devoted to farming, fishing and shipping. The two parts lie about 300m from each other. To relieve congestion visitors are encouraged to leave their vehicles at a car park (€5) off the N302 at the south edge of town. A ferry (fare included in your ticket; every 15 minutes April to October) links the car park with the train station (look for the red and blue flags by the VVV) and the Buiten-

TRAINS FROM HOORN

DESTINATION	PRICE (€)	DURATION (MIN)	FREQUENCY (PER HR)
Alkmaar	5	25	2
Amsterdam	8	40	2
Enkhuizen	4	22	2

museum. Plan to spend half a day for an unhurried visit to both sections.

Buitenmuseum
MUSEUM

Worth the trip alone. Opened in 1983, it was carefully assembled from houses, farms and sheds trucked in from around the region to show Zuiderzee life as it was from 1880 to 1932. Every conceivable detail has been thought of, from the fence-top decorations and choice of shrubbery to the entire layout of villages, and the look and feel is certainly authentic. An illustrated guide (in English), included in the ticket price, is an essential companion on your tour of the entire museum.

Inhabitants wear traditional dress, and there are real shops such as a bakery, chemist and sweet shop. Workshops run demonstrations throughout the day. Though varying in character, the displays join seamlessly: lime kilns from Akersloot stand a few metres from Zuidende and its row of Monnickendam houses, originally built outside the dykes. Don't miss the Urk quarter, raised to simulate the island town before the Noordoostpolder was drained. For a special postmark, drop your letters at the old post office from Den Oever. The Marker Haven is a copy of the harbour built in 1830 on what was then the island of Marken. There is a fun playground at the entrance.

Note that while the grounds are open all year, there are activities here only from April to October.

Binnenmuseum
MUSEUM

Occupying a museum complex adjoining the Peperhuis, this indoor museum is in the former home and warehouse of a Dutch shipping merchant. The displays include a fine shipping hall: paintings, prints and other materials relating the rise and fall of the fishing industry, and the construction of the dykes. Here too are cultural artefacts, such as regional costumes, porcelain, silver and jewellery, that indicate the extent of Holland's riches at the time. It is a 300m walk from the rear exit to the Buitenmuseum.

Drommedaris
HISTORIC BUILDING

Located between the Buitenhaven and the Oude Haven, the Drommedaris was built as a defence tower as part of the 16th-century town walls. Once a formidable prison, it now serves as an elevated meeting hall. Its clocktower carillon still tinkles a playful tune on the hour.

Bottleship Museum
MUSEUM

(www.flessenscheepjesmuseum.nl; Zuiderspui 1; adult/child €3.50/2.50; ⊙noon-5pm Tue-Sun) Almost as tiny as the boats in its collection, this museum has a surprisingly fascinating collection of ships in bottles carved by seamen through the ages. There are more than 1000 examples and a video shows the secret to their construction.

Waag
HISTORIC BUILDING

Follow Breedstraat north to the east end of Westerstraat where the 16th-century Waag (weigh house) overlooks the old cheese market. Nearby is the classical **town hall**, modelled after the Amsterdam town hall that once stood on the Dam. You can peek through the windows at the lavish Gobelins and tapestries.

Westerkerk
CHURCH

Moving east along Westerstraat you'll spy the remarkable Westerkerk, a 15th-century Gothic church with a removable wooden belfry. The ornate choir screen and imposing pulpit are worth a look. Opposite the church is the **Weeshuis**, a 17th-century orphanage with a sugary, curlicued portal.

🛏 Sleeping

Stedemaagd Hotel
BOUTIQUE HOTEL **$$**

(☑321 271; www.stedemaagd.com; Spoorstraat 10-14; r from €95; 🛜) A very appealing option 200m north of the train station along the waterfront. Rooms have vintage-style furniture in an art deco setting, and bathrooms have Jacuzzis; breakfast is included. The grand cafe downstairs is an excellent option for a pause whether you are staying here or not. It has a lovely terrace and long tables in the airy interior.

Hotel Garni RecuerDos
B&B **$$**

(☑562 469; www.recuerdos.nl; Westerstraat 217; s/d from €63/88; 🛜) Owned by a warm and welcoming music-society patron, this stately manor house is the picture of calm, with three immaculate rooms overlooking a manicured garden. Enjoy breakfast in the glassed-in conservatory where there are often live music performances.

Camping Enkhuizer Zand
CAMPGROUND **$**

(☑317 289; www.campingenkhuizerzand.nl; Kooizandweg 4; camp sites €15-26; ⊙Apr-Sep; 🏊) On the north side of the Zuiderzeemuseum's Buitenmuseum, this popular site is a model of self-sufficiency with sandy beaches, tennis courts and a grocery store.

ⓘ DYKE ROAD

The N302 between Enkhuizen and Lelystad deserves special mention because it runs along a 32km-long dyke, completed in 1976 as the first step of the reclamation of the Markerwaard. As you get under way you'll pass below a high-tech causeway that connects Enkhuizen harbour with the IJsselmeer, with ships floating surreally over the motorway.

Sights are few along the route, apart from the boats bobbing on the IJsselmeer and a stone monument at the halfway mark in the form of a chain link symbolising the joining of West Friesland with Flevoland.

✖ Eating

For a good cafe, try the Stedemaagd Hotel, which is on the waterfront.

De Drie Haringhe FUSION $$$
(☑318 610; www.diedrieharinghe.nl; Dijk 28; menus from €35; ☺lunch Wed-Fri, dinner Wed-Sun) This upmarket locale excels in Dutch- and French-inspired cuisine, and has been receiving rave reviews for years. Comfortably ensconced in an old East India company warehouse, it has a lovely walled summer garden. It's particularly noted for seafood.

De Smederij CONTEMPORARY DUTCH $$
(☑323 079; www.restaurantdesmederij.nl; Breedstraat 158; menus from €35; ☺dinner Thu-Tue) Cute as a button, this cosy restaurant was actually once a forge. Lavishly decorated (there are some beautiful old framed maps), it still evokes its rough-edged past. Hearty and creative seasonal fare is the perfect treat after you've spent the day pondering the past at the Zuiderzeemuseum.

**Grand Cafe Restaurant
Van Bleiswijk** GRAND CAFE $$
(☑325 909; www.vanbleiswijk.nl; Westerstraat 84-86; mains €8-25) There is a huge umbrella-protected terrace lined with outdoor tables at this very popular grand cafe on the town's main drag. All the standards are here, from salads to sandwiches to hot specials. Coffee drinks are fine and if the wind blows too hard the old wooden interior is a warm refuge.

ⓘ Information

Tourist Office (VVV; ☑313 164; www.vvvenkhuizen.nl; Tussen Twee Havens 1; ☺8am-5pm daily Jun-Aug, 8am-5pm Tue-Sat Sep-May) Just east of the train station; sells ferry tickets and a self-guided tour booklet in English (€1.50).

ⓘ Getting There & Away

There is a fun and historical trip between Enkhuizen and Hoorn and Medemblik on a steam train and boat combo (p119).

BICYCLE There is no bike shop in the station. Hoorn is 25km west along the coastal national routes **LF15** and **LF21**.

FERRY The **Enhuizen–Stavoren Ferry** (☑326 667; www.veerboot.nl; adult/child one way €11/7; ☺mid-Apr–Oct) plies the IJsselmeer connecting Noord Holland with Friesland. The 90-minute trips depart once or twice daily from near the tourist office, which sells tickets. Boats dock in Stavoren, which is on the train line to Leeuwarden via Sneek.

TRAIN The Enkhuizen train station is still an embarrassment. Services (such as lockers) are nil, although you may be able to sweet talk the fine station cafe into storing your bags while you visit town. Buying train tickets is diabolically difficult: there are no staff, only ticket machines, and the railway stopped allowing the tourist office to sell tickets.

For regular train services see the box opposite.

For Alkmaar, change at Hoorn. Den Helder means a train change at both Hoorn and Heerhugowaard, which is inconvenient but the fastest option for public transport.

Medemblik

☑0227 / POP 8000

About 12km northwest of Enkhuizen lies Medemblik, the oldest port on the IJsselmeer, dating back to the 12th century and the Hanseatic League. It's not a pretty town but its busy harbour, old waterfront streets and medieval fortress are worth a couple of hours of your time.

◉ Sights & Activities

The castle stands on the eastern side of town and is signposted from the harbour. The richly decorated facades on Kaasmarkt, Torenstraat, Nieuwstraat and along the Achterom canal are impressive.

Kasteel Radboud CASTLE
(www.kasteelradboud.nl; Oudevaartsgat 8; adult/child €5.50/3.50; ☺11am-5pm Mon-Sat May-Sep, 2-5pm Sun year-round) The pint-sized Kasteel Radboud at the head of the harbour is a more well-fortified mansion than the castle it once was. Built by Count Floris V in the

13th century to keep the feisty natives under his thumb, the fortress served as a prison before a 19th-century remodelling by Pierre Cuypers, the designer of Amsterdam's Rijksmuseum. The original floor plan has been preserved and the imposing Ridderzaal (Knights' Hall) still looks much as it did in the Middle Ages. The self-guided tour gives details of the castle's long history and the count's undoing.

Stoommachine Museum MUSEUM
(Steam Engine Museum; www.stoommachine-museum.nl; Oosterdijk 4; adult/child €5.50/4.25; ☉10am-5pm varying days) Ever wondered what drove the Industrial Revolution? Part of the answer lies at the Stoommachine Museum, in the old pump station outside Medemblik. Thirty handsome old steam engines from Holland, England and Germany are fired up for demonstrations on various days; check the website for dates.

The Museum Stoomtram (p119) departs from the old train station for Hoorn. You can also catch a boat to Enkhuizen as part of a triangle tour.

✖ Eating

De Driemaster SEAFOOD $$
(www.restaurantdedriemaster.nl; Pekelharinghaven 49; mains €11-20; ☉11am-9pm daily, Thu-Sun only Nov-Mar) Enjoy views of the harbour and IJsselmeer as you relish local fish while seated at the upstairs terrace. Watch large yachts drift under the drawbridge. The casual cafe is good for a relaxing drink outside.

ℹ Information

Tourist Office (VVV; ☏542 852; www.vvvmedemblik.nl; Kaasmarkt 1; ☉11am-4pm Mon-Sat Apr-Oct) A folksy all-in-one place, with a good stock of maps at the back of the local stationers, post office and tobacco store.

ℹ Getting There & Around

BICYCLE **Ted de Lange** (☏570 093; www.teddelange-ligfiets.nl; Vooreiland 1), on the eastern side of town, has a large selection of bicycles for hire from €7 per day. The national bike route **LF21** runs south and east along dykes 21km to Enkhuizen.

BUS The NS train station is in Hoorn, from where bus 239 (twice hourly) makes the 30-minute journey to Medemblik.

Den Helder
☏0223

Before you catch the ferry to Texel, the only attraction in the workman-like naval town of Den Helder is the **Marine Museum** (www.marinemuseum.nl; Hoofdgracht 3; adult/child €6/3; ☉10am-5pm Mon-Fri, noon-5pm Sat & Sun, closed Mon Nov-Apr). It's housed in the vast former armoury of the Dutch Royal Navy. The display covers naval history mainly after 1815, the year the Netherlands became a kingdom. You can run rampant through several vessels moored on the docks outside, including an ironclad ram ship and a submarine left high and dry. Check out the exhibits on modern-day pirates.

Driving through the town itself to/from the Texel ferry, the N250 passes a myriad ships new and old that together form their own living maritime museum.

There are trains to Den Helder and the ferry to Texel.

Texel
☏0222 / POP 13,700

Broad white beaches, lush nature reserves, forests and cute villages are the highlights of Texel, the largest and most visited of the Wadden Islands. About 3km north of the coast of Noord Holland, Texel (pronounced *tes*-sel) is 25km long and 9km wide. It actually consisted of two islands until 1835 when a spit of land to Eyerland Island was pumped dry.

Before the Noordzeekanaal opened in the 19th century, Texel was a main stop for ships en route to Asia, Africa and North

TRAINS FROM MEDEMBLIK

DESTINATION	PRICE (€)	DURATION (MIN)	FREQUENCY (PER HR)
Alkmaar	8	50	2
Amsterdam	10	60	2
Den Helder	11.50	90	2
Hoorn	4	22	2

Texel

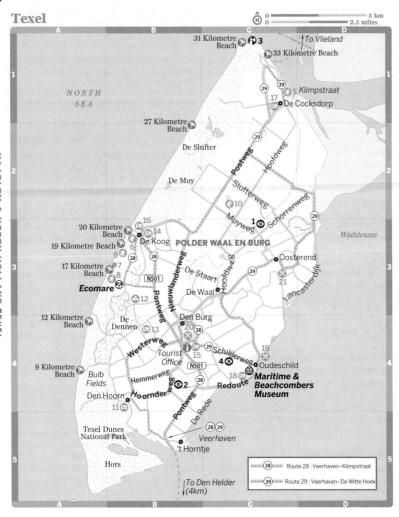

America: the first trade mission to the East Indies began and ended here. It was also the scene of a spectacular maritime disaster: on Christmas day 1593, hurricane-force winds battered a merchant fleet moored off the coast and 44 vessels sank, drowning about a thousand seamen.

Texel relies chiefly on tourism, with the majority of visitors being either Dutch or German. The local wool is highly prized and there are sheep everywhere, lazing, grazing or tippee-toeing along the dykes. It's the place to come if you want to find a beach, albeit a breezy beach, where you can wander for hours and not see a soul. Cyclists will be enchanted and there are just enough diversions – even a brewery – to keep you entertained for days on end.

Sights

Texel Dunes National Park PARK
(Nationaal Park Duinen van Texel; www.npduinen-vantexel.nl) For many nature lovers this patchwork of varied dunescape running along the entire western coast of the island is the prime reason for visiting Texel. Salt fens and heath alternate with velvety,

Texel

grass-covered dunes, and you'll find plants endemic to this habitat, such as the dainty marsh orchid or sea buckthorn, a ragged shrub with bright orange berries. Much of the area is bird sanctuary and accessible only on foot. There is an excellent **visitor centre** at the Ecomare wildlife reserve. Get info here about the informative ranger-led walks through the dunes.

De Slufter became a brackish wetland after an attempt at land reclamation failed; when a storm breached the dykes in the early 1900s the area was allowed to flood and a unique ecosystem developed. To the south, **De Muy** is renowned for its colony of spoonbills that are monitored with great zeal by local naturalists.

Only a stone's throw from the windswept beach lies the dark, leafy forest of **De Dennen** between Den Hoorn and De Koog. Originally planted as a source of lumber, today it has an enchanting network of walking and cycling paths. In springtime the forest floor is carpeted with snowdrops that were first planted here in the 1930s.

TOP CHOICE ⟩ Maritime & Beachcombers Museum
MUSEUM

(Kaap Skil Museum Van Jutters & Zeelui; ☑314 956; www.texelsmaritiem.nl; Heemskerckstraat 9, Oudeschild; adult/child €7.50/5.50; ☉10am-5pm Tue-Sat, noon-5pm Sun) Texel museums are a mixed bag, but the Maritime & Beachcombers Museum is a real winner. Its extraordinary variety of junk recovered from sunken ships and the shore is mind-boggling – and both tragic and comic. In the outdoor section there are demonstrations by ropemakers, fish-smokers and blacksmiths, while the indoor displays cover everything from underwater archaeology to windmill technology.

Reede van Texel, which the museum translates accurately as Texel Roads, has nothing to do with asphalt but rather is a vast and amazingly detailed model of the shipping lanes and ports as they existed in the 17th century. Two hours will float away here just like a lost bottle at sea. A new entrance opened in 2012 only makes this fine museum even better.

The maritime museum and Ecomare are covered by the **CombiKaart** (adult/child €13.50/9.50) ticket available from the tourist office.

Ecomare
WILDLIFE RESERVE

(www.ecomare.nl; Ruyslaan 92, De Koog; adult/child €10/6.50; ☉9am-5pm) Initially created as a refuge for sick seals retrieved from the Waddenzee, Ecomare has expanded into a nature centre devoted to the preservation and understanding of Texel's wildlife. It has displays on Texel's development since the last ice age and the islanders' interaction with the sea, as well as large aquariums filled with fish from the Waddenzee and the North Sea (including sharks and sea skates); outside there are marked nature trails.

The highlight for young and old, however, is the seals themselves. Their playful water

NAVIGATING TEXEL

Ferries from the mainland dock at **'t Horntje** on the south side of the isle, from where buses head north to Texel's six main villages:

» **Den Burg** The island's modest capital and main shopping destination; 6km north of 't Horntje.

» **De Koog** Texel's beachy tourist heart with a distinctly tacky streak; 5km north again.

» **Den Hoorn** A cute village handy to tulip fields and windswept sand dunes; 5km northwest of 't Horntje.

» **Oudeschild** The best harbour facilities on the island, a fine museum and splendid fish restaurants; 7km northeast of 't Horntje.

» **Oosterend** A quiet hamlet with distinctive architecture; 6km northeast of Den Burg.

» **De Cocksdorp** At the northern end of the island, this tiny village is a launch pad to the island of Vlieland and the rest of the Frisian Islands.

Beaches on the west coast are numbered by the kilometre from south to north.

ballet will delight all but the most jaded visitor. Try to catch feeding time at 11am or 3pm. Rescued birds are the other main tenants. The entire facility is impressive and despite the hype is definitely not a cheesy attraction. (Note that seals are rather delightfully called *zeehonden* in Dutch, which means 'sea dogs'.)

Lighthouse LIGHTHOUSE
(www.vuurtorentexel.nl; Vuurtorenweg 184, De Cocksdorp; admission €3.50) Battered not just by storms but by war as well, Texel's old lighthouse is a 45m crimson tower that has views across the islands and shallow waters. The climb to the top is 153 steps.

Eureka Orchideeën & Vogelbush GARDENS
(Eureka Orchids & Birds; www.eurekatexel.nl; Schorrenweg 20, Oosterend; ⊗8.30am-6pm Mon-Fri, 8.30am-5pm Sat) June is the time to see wild orchids on Texel, a rarity in the country; outside this month, dress lightly and head for the steamy Eureka Orchideeën & Vogelbush. Native orchid species can be viewed in all their tender, quivering glory alongside a menagerie of tropical birds in a large greenhouse. A large shop (silk orchids, oh dear) subsidises the free entrance.

Texelse Bierbrouwerij BREWERY
(www.speciaalbier.com; Schilderweg 214b, Oudeschild; tours adult/child €7.50/4; ⊗tours 2pm & 3pm, schedule varies) The isle's brewery gives tours on an erratic schedule that may drive you to drink (check the website). Fortunately this former dairy has a terrace ideal for downing a few from the bar. The nine beers brewed here (try the bock) are widely available across Texel and are always worth ordering first.

Kaasboerderijk Wezenspyk CHEESE FACTORY
(☑315 090; www.wezenspyk.nl; Hoondernweg 29, Den Hoorn; ⊗9.30am-5pm Tue-Sat Apr-Oct, closed Thu Nov-Mar) This small cheese farm between Den Hoorn and Den Burg is the place to scoop up tasty rounds produced from the local cows, sheep and goats. Opening hours vary widely through the year so just drop by and see if you can cut the cheese.

🏃 Activities

Although summer can be balmy, don't count on it. One local exclaimed without a trace of irony: 'It's going to be hot! 20°C!' Winds and squalls can blow in off the North Sea all year, although at these times the island is at its most evocative and atmospheric. Goosebump fetishists rejoice!

The tourist office sells maps and booklets of cycling routes and hiking trails that criss-cross the island. There are several horse-riding schools, which operate between April and October.

The well-marked 80km Texel Path takes you through the dunes and over the mudflats before veering inland through the island's villages; the circular local routes along the way make for nice one- to three-hour hikes or bike trips. All the roads are suitable for bikes, and you can circumnavigate the island following the dykes in the east and the trails behind the dunes in the west.

De Eilander BOATING
(☑06 2063 4413; www.deeilander.nl; Paal 33, De Cocksdorp; catamaran hire per hour from €55;

⊙May-Oct) Catamarans can be hired from near the Vlieland boat dock. Five-hour sailing courses cost €160.

Jutters Plezier
HORSE RIDING

(📞316 225; www.juttersplezier.nl; tours adult/child from €15/7.50; horse rides from €60) To gather your own beach treasure, board a horse-drawn wagon run by Jutters Plezier. The three-hour trips are really more for the journey than the treasure, and end at the owner's private residence for a round of herbal schnapps. Tours (minimum 15 people) depart from the lighthouse – check with the tourist office for times.

Tessel Air
SKYDIVING

(📞311 436; www.paracentrumtexel.nl; Texel Airport; scenic flight €38, tandem parachute jump €209) Tessel Air offers 15-minute pleasure flights over Texel (minimum two people), and for a bit more cash they'll explore the other Wadden Islands. To really feel the wind in your face, try a tandem jump; it includes all the thrill of free fall without the fear of screwing things up.

Kitesurf School Texel
KITESURFING

(📞06 1097 1992; www.kitesurfschooltexel.nl; Beach, De Koog; hourly rental from €15, lessons from €95) Kitesurf School Texel offers all manner of kitesurfing and windsurfing lessons and rentals.

Ozlines
SURF SCHOOL

(www.ozlines.com; Paal 17, De Koog; hourly rental from €8, lessons adult/child from €80/25; ⊙1-7pm Sat & Sun Apr-Oct, daily Jul & Aug) Rent boards and get lessons at this surf shop that sets up on groovy 17 Kilometre Beach.

Tours

In a perfect example of the modern economy, the harbour at Oudeschild is filled with former large prawn trawlers that found new life as tour boats. Competition is fierce and the best way to choose a boat is to just go down and wander around checking out itineraries and offers. The usual two-hour trip around Texel sails close to an endangered seal colony on the sandbanks.

Average prices for two-hour voyages is about €10. First sailings are usually 10am depending on tides.

Orion TX20
BOAT TOUR

(📞06 5104 4235; www.robbentochttexel.nl; Oudeschild; tours adult/child from €10/9) The *Orion* TX20 explores the mudflats between Texel and Den Helder. Seal-spotting is usual.

Emmie TX 10
BOAT TOUR

(📞313 639; www.garnalenvissen.nl; Oudeschild; adult/child from €10/9; ⊙departs 10.30am & 2pm Mon-Sat) Prawns caught on the *Emmie*'s journey are prepared fresh for passengers.

DON'T MISS

TEXEL'S BEACHES

Swimming, cycling, walking, boating, relaxing – Texel is an island to enjoy all these. Its pristine white beaches, lining the western shore in one unbroken ribbon, are numbered by the kilometre and marked with a *paal* (piling) from south to north.

The waters can be treacherous and lifeguards are on duty in summer from No 9 northeast of Den Hoorn to No 21 near De Koog. One told us they compete to see who has the fewest drownings (!).

No matter how crowded the island, with a little hiking you can always find a stretch of deserted sand. Among the notable beaches are the following:

» **No 9** Uncrowded, and popular with locals and nudists.

» **No 12** Uncrowded, with a sheltered cafe.

» **No 17** The party beach (www.paal17.com), where teens are on the make and there's always a groovy vibe. Lots of daytime *and* nighttime activities.

» **No 19** The beach (www.paal.nl) where the couples who met on No 17 go after they're married. The emphasis is on lounging with good food and drink.

» **No 20** Right in front of the tourist enclave of De Koog, and rather built up.

» **No 27** A fairly isolated beach popular with nudists.

» **No 31** Near the lighthouse; no swimming due to treacherous rip tides but lots of wind sports.

» **No 33** Also no swimming, but lots of beach sports and occasional seal-spotting.

Texel 44 BOAT TOUR
(📞06 5110 5775; www.tx44.nl; Oudeschild; tours adult/child from €10/9) A boat actually built for touring. It has a nice upper deck for seal-spotting.

⚜ Festivals & Events

Lammetjes Wandeltrocht FESTIVAL
(Lamb Walking Route) Popular walk around the island at Easter, attracting plenty of mainland Dutch and other baaaaaad folk.

Ronde om Texel CATAMARAN RACE
(www.roundtexel.com) The largest catamaran race in the world, held mid-June; spectators line the beaches for hours on end watching boats jive back and forth on the sea.

🛏 Sleeping & Eating

There are over 45,000 beds on the island, but it's essential to book ahead, especially in July and August. De Koog has by far the most options, but hamlets such as Den Hoorn or De Cocksdorp are more peaceful and relaxing.

The tourist office has a list of B&Bs from around €30 per person per night; otherwise hit the **VVV website** (www.texel.net) or pick up a copy of the *Texel Holiday Guide* and strike out on your own. Note that prices drop in the low season (October to April) when island life slips into a lower gear. Texel's 11 main campgrounds teem in summer; the tourist office can tell you which ones have vacancies. Many farms also offer rooms and camp sites.

With more than 27,000 sheep roaming the island, lamb naturally gets top billing on the menu, but seafood comes a close second. Asparagus season in the spring brings forth oodles of scrumptious local spears.

DEN BURG

TOP CHOICE Hotel De 14 Sterren HOTEL $
(📞322 681; www.14sterren.nl; Smitsweg 4, Dennenbos, Den Burg; r €60-75; 🐾) You couldn't wish for a nicer spot than this place, on the edge of De Dennen forest. Each of its 14 rooms is decorated in warm Mediterranean hues, and most have a terrace or balcony with garden views. The attached bistro, **De Worsteltent** (mains €9-25; ⏰11am-9pm) brings fine dining with an Italian accent to a barnhouse. Breakfast is served in your room.

Stayokay Texel HOSTEL $
(📞315 441; www.stayokay.com; Haffelderweg 28, Den Burg; dm €21-32, r €57-80; 🐾) Texel's modern HI hostel has 240 beds in clean, colourful rooms, and has a cafe on-site. You can rent bikes; the beach is 6km away.

TOP CHOICE Freya BISTRO $$
(📞321 686; Gravenstraat 4, Den Burg; set menu €27; ⏰dinner Tue-Sat) This petite restaurant serves outstanding French and Dutch cuisine, so it's no surprise that reservations are a must. The hosts are warm and welcoming, and you're never sure what seasonal delights await on the blackboard. Booking is essential.

Taveerne De Twaalf Balcken TRADITIONAL DUTCH $$
(Weverstraat 20, Den Burg; mains €12-20; ⏰lunch & dinner) The 'Tavern of the 12 Beams' is a locals' haunt that specialises in lamb dishes and cosy ambience. The front section is dark and subdued – perfect for sipping away on one of the many Trappist beers on offer, while the rear conservatory is light and airy.

Timmer BAKERY $
(Hogerstraat 4, Den Burg; treats from €1.50) Don't leave Texel without a bag of the addictive handmade cookies from Timmer.

DE COCKSDORP

This village has a large grocery store and a several appealing cafes along its tidy low-key streets.

't Anker HOTEL $$
(📞316 274; www.t-anker.texel.com; Kikkertstraat 24, De Cocksdorp; s/d from €47/92; @🐾) This small, family-run hotel is full of woodsy charm and cheer, and has basic yet comfy rooms set behind a solid brick facade. Its lush garden is just an appetiser for the Roggesloot nature reserve close by. Breakfast is hearty and included in the price.

TOP CHOICE Restaurant Topido SEAFOOD $$
(📞316 227; www.topido.nl; Kikkertstraat 21-23, De Cocksdorp; mains €8-25; ⏰lunch & dinner Tue-Sun) Each year the food producers on Texel concentrate on producing an ever-higher calibre of goods. The lamb and seafood are already famous but produce is rapidly gaining acclaim as well. This casual restaurant puts local foods to great advantage on a bistro menu that features many house-cured foods. Ask about cooking courses.

DEN HOORN

TOP CHOICE Bij Jef HOTEL $$$
(📞319 623; www.bijjef.nl; Herenstraat 34, Den Hoorn; r from €200; 🐾) The eight simple yet

stylish rooms here come with a bathtub, a lavish breakfast, views of the countryside and a sun-drenched balcony. However, the real star is the sumptuous restaurant (menus from €75), which has an ever-changing menu created from local produce, meats and seafood. Try for a garden table.

DE KOOG

The main drag of Dorpsstraat, Texel's tourist haven, is lined with cheap chipperies, bistros of uncertain provenance and the island's only gaggle of boisterous bars.

De Bremakker   CAMPGROUND $
(✑312 863; www.bremakker.nl; Templierweg 40; camp site €32, chalets per week from €300; ☺Apr-Oct) This leafy and serene campground is situated between Den Burg and De Koog at the forest's edge, about 1km from the beach. There's a laundry and snack bar, plus sports facilities.

Hotel Friends Texel   HOTEL $
(✑317 906; www.hotelfriendstexel.nl; Nikadel 5, De Koog; r €40-70; 🛜) The bargain of town, if you don't mind a little party noise. The 12 rooms have kitchenettes, share new bathrooms and are spotless. Get one at the back away from the merriment. There's a fun (!) adjoining cafe.

Strandhotel Noordzee   HOTEL $$
(✑317 365; www.strandhotelnoordzeetexel.nl; Badweg 200, De Koog; r per 3 nights from €410) This is the only hotel directly on Texel's sandy beaches. Its 10 rooms have a touch of colour and flair, and are suitably comfy; several have sweeping balcony views of the North Sea.

OUDESCHILD

This intriguing port town is home to an ever-growing number of places to get seafood. If the kids need to work up an appetite, take them to the pirate-themed playground at the north end of the harbour.

Texel Yurts   GUESTHOUSE $$
(✑322 100; www.texelyurts.nl; De Ruyterstraat 36, Oudeschild; 2-person yurt per 2 nights from €300) Feel the creak of the wind in your own fabric-sided yurt set in a shady clearing near town.

TOP CHOICE **Van Der Star**   SEAFOOD $
(www.vispaleistexel.nl; Heemskerckstraat 15, Oudeschild; mains €5-8; ☺11am-9pm Mon-Sat) The island's best fish is served at this seafood counter. The seafood soup is a garlicky delight while the many choices of smoked fish are simply sublime. An array of items fresh off the boats in the nearby harbour are available prepared in many ways. Seating is basic: go for a plastic chair on the terrace.

Cafe Veronica   SEAFOOD $
(www.veronicatexel.nl; Haven 9a, Oudeschild; meals €5-9; ☺10am-6pm Tue-Sun Apr-Oct, Sat & Sun only Nov-Mar) Part of a new cute little development down by the harbour with shops and cafes. This cheap and cheerful seafood hut specialises in fresh fare from the surrounding waters. Listen to the clang of lines against masts.

OOSTEREND

Rôtisserie Kerckeplein   LAMB $$
(www.rotisserie-texel.nl; Oesterstraat 6, Oosterend; mains €11-25; ☺dinner Wed-Sun) This cosy restaurant has got cooking local lamb down to a fine art, with seven choices in this category alone. You can sit in the loft and wash it all down with a dark Texels Speciaalbier. In high season it serves lunch – enjoy on the small front terrace.

ℹ Information

No one wants the local lifeblood – holidaymakers – to run short, so you'll find ATMs in every town. Den Burg has banks, bookshops, pharmacies and most other services.

Tourist Office (VVV; ✑314 741; www.texel.net; Emmalaan 66, Den Burg; ☺9am-5.30pm Mon-Fri, 9am-5pm Sat) Signposted from the ferry terminal; on the southern fringe of town. Has free internet access, plenty of information, and staff can book accommodation for a fee.

ℹ Getting There & Away

Trains from Amsterdam to Den Helder (€14, 75 minutes, twice hourly) are met by a bus that whisks you to the car ferry.

Teso (✑369 600; www.teso.nl; foot-passenger/car return €2.50/35) runs a service from Den Helder to 't Horntje. The crossing aboard the huge ferries takes 20 minutes and leaves at 30 minutes past the hour between 6.30am and 9.30pm; returning boats leave on the hour between 6am and 9pm. On some summer days there's a service every half-hour – check the timetable to be sure. In high season, show up at the docks 15 to 30 minutes before departure as there'll be a car queue.

There is a ferry to car-free Vlieland; see p205 for details.

ℹ Getting Around

BICYCLE Touring bikes can be rented in every town on Texel and at the ferry terminal for about €8 per day.

BUS Buses 28 and 29 operate throughout the year, supplemented with two more routes during summer months; day passes cost €6 from the bus driver. Bus 28 links 't Horntje with Den Burg (seven minutes) and De Koog (another 15 minutes) before returning via the Ecomare wildlife reserve, while bus 29 starts at the ferry jetty and goes to Den Hoorn and Den Burg before snaking its way along the eastern shore to De Cocksdorp via Oudeschild and Oosterend. Buses tend to run hourly, roughly during daylight hours (which means until 10pm in summer).

TAXI **Taxi Botax** (☑315 888; www.taxibotax texel.com) takes you between the ferry terminal and any destination on the island, including Den Burg (€16), De Koog (€24) and De Cocksdorp (€40). Book in advance.

Muiden
☑0294 / POP 3500

An ideal easy jaunt by bike from Amsterdam, Muiden is an unhurried historical town renowned for its red-brick castle, the Muiderslot. It's an idealised form of a castle and if you built it at the beach you'd be happy. Life otherwise focuses on the busy central lock that funnels scores of pleasure boats out into the vast IJsselmeer.

◉ Sights

Muiderslot   CASTLE
(Muiden Castle; www.muiderslot.nl; Herengracht 1; adult/child €12.50/7.50; ◷10am-5pm Mon-Fri, noon-5pm Sat & Sun Apr-Oct, noon-4pm Sat & Sun Nov-Mar) The town's draw is the Muiderslot, a fortress built in 1280 by the ambitious count Floris V, son of Willem II. The castle was one of the first in Holland to be equipped with round towers, a French innovation. The popular count was also a champion of the poor and a French sympathiser, two factors that were bound to spell trouble; Floris was imprisoned in 1296 and murdered while trying to flee.

In the 17th century historian PC Hooft entertained some of the century's greatest writers, artists and scientists here, a group famously known as the Muiderkring (Muiden Circle). Today it's the most visited castle in the country, with precious furnishings, weapons and Gobelin hangings designed to recreate Hooft's era. The interior can be seen only on guided tours; tours may be partly improvised in English. Reserve ahead if you want an English-only tour.

Pampus   HISTORIC SITE
(☑262 326; www.pampus.nl; adult/child ferry & tour €17.50/13.50; ◷Tue-Sun Apr-Oct) Off the coast lies a derelict fort on the island of Pampus. This massive 19th-century bunker was a key member of a ring of 42 fortresses built to defend Amsterdam and is great fun to explore. Rescued from disrepair by Unesco, the facility now receives preservation funds as a World Heritage site. Ferries to Pampus depart from Muiderslot port on a varying schedule during the opening season. Usually there is at least one morning departure which allows a couple hours to prowl the fort before a mid-afternoon return.

✖ Eating & Drinking

Café Ome Ko   CAFE
(www.cafeomekomuiden.nl; cnr Herengracht & Naardenstraat; ◷8am-2am) In warm weather the clientele of this little bar with the big green-striped awnings turns the street outside into one big party. When there's no party on, the cafe is a perfect spot to watch the comings and goings through the busy lock right outside. It serves Dutch snacks and sandwiches (meals from €6).

❶ Getting There & Around

BICYCLE National bike route **LF20** passes by Amsterdam's Leidseplein. Follow it east for 7km until it passes under the A10 and look for the start of the LF23 route. Cross the canal and follow the LF23 for 9km through parklands and over bridges southeast to Muiden.

BUS Bus 327 links Amsterdam's Amstel station (20 minutes, twice hourly) with Muiden. The castle is then a 15-minute walk.

Het Gooi

Along the slow-moving Vecht river southeast of Amsterdam lies Het Gooi, a shady woodland speckled with lakes and heath. In the 17th century this 'Garden of Amsterdam' was a popular retreat for wealthy merchants, and nature-hungry urbanites still flock to its leafy trails to hike and cycle today.

Naarden, on the Gooimeer to the north, has an intriguing fortress and is an excellent day trip. The main town, Hilversum, is really just an Amsterdam suburb with a few interesting early 20th-century buildings, most notably the Raadhuis (Town Hall, 1931) by Willem Dudok.

NAARDEN
☑035 / POP 17,000

Naarden is well worth a visit thanks to its remarkable fortress, **Naarden-Vesting**, on its northwest border. This military work of

AALSMEER FLOWER AUCTION

The town of Aalsmeer is home to the world's biggest **flower auction** (www.floraholland. com; Legmeerdijk 313; adult/child €5/3; ☺7-11am Mon-Fri, to 9am Thu), run by a vast posy conglomerate named FloraHolland. Make sure you're in the viewing gallery before 9am to catch the best action as the flower-laden carts go to auction. Selling is conducted – surprise! – by Dutch auction, with a huge clock showing the starting price. From the starting bell, the hand keeps dropping until someone takes up the offer and a deal is struck. There's a self-guided audiotour that will let you peek into the auction rooms and see arrangers fluffing the blooms for display.

Monday is the busiest time, Thursday the quietest. Come early for the best viewing.

Take bus 172 from Amsterdam Centraal Station to the BVFH Hoofdingang stop (55 minutes, four times hourly).

art has the shape of a 12-pointed star, with arrowheads at each tip. This defence system, one of the best preserved in the country, was (like closing a barn door after the horse has bolted) built only after the Spanish massacred the inhabitants in the 16th century. The bastions were staffed by the Dutch army until the 1920s, long after its strategic importance had become moot.

Today the walled town of Naarden-Vesting is an upmarket enclave with fine restaurants, galleries and antique shops.

◎ Sights

Roaming what is in effect a walled time capsule is a fine way to spend a few hours. Inside the fortress, most of Naarden-Vesting's quaint little houses date from 1572, the year the Spaniards razed the place during their colonisation of Noord Holland. The bloodbath led by Don Frederick of Toledo is commemorated by a stone tablet on the building at Turfpoortstraat 7.

TOP CHOICE **Vestingmuseum**　　　　MUSEUM
(Fortress Museum; www.vestingmuseum.nl; Westwalstraat 6; adult/child €6/4; ☺10.30am-5pm Tue-Fri, noon-5pm Sat & Sun) The Vestingmuseum brings context to the vast star-shaped fortress, which is thought to be the only one in Europe featuring a buffer of two walls and two moats. You can stroll around on the rolling battlements before descending into the casements for glimpses of a cramped soldier's life.

FREE **Grote Kerk**　　　　CHURCH
(www.grotekerknaarden.nl; Markstraat 13; ☺10.30am-4.30pm Tue-Sat, 1.30-4.30pm Sun & Mon mid-Jun–Sep) It's easy to spot the tall tower of the fort's central Grote Kerk, a Gothic

basilica with stunning 16th-century vault paintings of biblical scenes. You can climb the tower (265 steps) for a good view of the leafy Gooi and the Vecht river. Organ concerts are held throughout the year.

Comenius Museum　　　　MUSEUM
(www.comeniusmuseum.nl; Kloosterstraat 33; adult/child €5/free; ☺noon-5pm Tue-Sun) The 17th-century Czech educational reformer, Jan Amos Komensky (Comenius), is buried in the Waalse Kapel. His life and work (he promoted the concepts of universal eduction for rich and poor) are related next door at the Comenius Museum.

☞ Tours

Boat Tours　　　　BOAT TOUR
(www.vestingvaart.nl; adult/child €6.50/4.50; ☺1-4pm Apr-Oct) Enjoyable one-hour tours on vintage boats around the moats plus exploration of some of the reedy natural areas.

✗ Eating

Day trippers will find some excellent eating options inside the walls.

TOP CHOICE **Passionata**　　　　DELI **$**
(www.passionata-naarden.nl; Marktstraat 31; snacks from €3; ☺10am-6pm Tue-Sun) This stylish Italian deli is the perfect source for picnic supplies, which you can then enjoy out on the town walls. The grilled sandwiches are luscious.

Fine　　　　BRASSERIE **$$**
(☎694 48 68; www.restaurantfine.nl; Marktstraat 66; mains €20-25) A cosy bar and restaurant, this fine choice features canalside dining and regular art exhibitions. The menu highlights local seafood, and mussels in season. You can stop in just for a refreshing glass of wine and a cheeseboard.

DRAINING THE ZUIDERZEE

The Netherlands' coastline originally extended as far as the sandy beaches of Texel and its Frisian Island companions. The relentless sea, however, never seemed to be in agreement with such borders, and by the end of the 13th century storms had washed sea water over flimsy land barriers and pushed it far inland. The end result was the creation of the Zuiderzee (literally, South Sea).

The ruling Dutch had for centuries dreamed of draining the Zuiderzee to reclaim the huge tracts of valuable farmland. The seafaring folk of the villages lining the sea were of a different opinion, even though the shallow Zuiderzee constantly flooded their homes and businesses, and often took lives with it. A solution needed to be found, and the only way to tame the waves, it seems, was to block them off.

A huge dyke was proposed as early as the mid-17th century, but it wasn't until the late 19th century, when new engineering techniques were developed, that such a dyke could become reality. Engineer Cornelis Lely, who lent his name to Lelystad, was the first to sketch out a retaining barrier. A major flood in 1916 set the plan in motion, and construction began in 1927. Fishermen worried about their livelihood, and fears that the Wadden Islands would vanish in the rising seas were voiced, and while the former concerns were legitimate, the latter proved unfounded.

In 1932 the Zuiderzee was ceremoniously sealed off by the Afsluitdijk (Barrier Dyke), an impressive dam (30km long and 90m wide) that links the provinces of Noord Holland and Friesland. The water level remained relatively steady, but the fishing industry was effectively killed as the basin gradually filled with fresh water from the river IJssel – the IJsselmeer was born. However, vast tracts of land were created, and were soon turned into arable *polders* (strips of farmland separated by canals). A second barrier between Enkhuizen and Lelystad was completed in 1976 – creating the Markermeer – with the idea of ushering in the next phase of land reclamation, but the plan was shelved because of cost and environmental concerns.

For more information on this vast human endeavour, spend some time at Lelystad's Nieuw Land (p133) museum, which details the land reclamation.

ℹ Information

Tourist Office (VVV; www.vvvgooivecht.nl; Utrecht Gate, Westwalstraat 6; ⊘noon-3pm Tue-Sun) In the old barracks; has an English-language self-guided walking tour of the town and accommodation information. There's good parking right outside.

ℹ Getting There & Around

BICYCLE National bike route **LF23** passes right through Naarden-Vesting and is an ideal way to explore the extents of the star-shaped moat and nearby waters of the Gooimeer. The fort at Muiden is 11km northwest on the **LF23**.

TRAIN There are direct trains between Amsterdam Centraal Station and Naarden-Bussum (€5, 25 minutes, twice hourly). From the station, bus 110 (five minutes, twice hourly) runs to the fortress, otherwise it's a pleasant 20-minute walk.

FLEVOLAND

Flevoland, the Netherlands' 12th and youngest province, is a masterpiece of Dutch hydroengineering. In the early 1920s an ambitious scheme went ahead to reclaim more than 1400 sq km of land – an idea mooted as far back as the 17th century. The completion of the Afsluitdijk (Barrier Dyke) paved the way for the creation of Flevoland. Ringed dykes were erected, allowing water to be pumped out at a snail-like pace. Once part of Overijssel province, the Noordoostpolder was inaugurated in 1942, followed by the Eastern Flevoland (1957) and Southern Flevoland (1968). First residential rights were granted to workers who'd helped in reclamation and to farmers, especially those from Zeeland, who lost everything in the great flood of 1953.

The cities that sprang up bring to mind anything but the Golden Age. The main hubs – Almere, Lelystad and Emmeloord – are dull places, laid out in unrelieved grid patterns. However, Lelystad has some good attractions and a new train line means you can stop off on journeys to the northeast. The top highlights are the old fishing villages Urk and Schokland.

Lelystad

⏱ 0320 / POP 74,000

With unattractive modern architecture dominating its disjointed sprawl, Lelystad, the capital of Flevoland province, is a good example of urban planning gone awry. The main reason for visiting this expanse of steel and concrete is its three museums, which will keep parents and their hangers-on entertained for hours.

◎ Sights

Lelystad's two big sights, the Batavia exhibit and Nieuw Land museum, are next to Bataviastad, a mock fort containing a huge outlet shopping centre 3km west of the train station. Everything here is huge, even for the largest crowds. Bus 7 (10 minutes, two to four hourly) connects the museums with the train station. The parking system is infernal; it's accessed from the N302 as it heads across the IJsselmeer.

Bataviawerf   HISTORIC SITE
(Batavia Yard; www.bataviawerf.nl; Oostvaardersdijk 1-9; adult/child €11/5.50; ⏱10am-5pm) Bataviawerf is home to a replica of a 17th-century Dutch merchant frigate, the *Batavia*, which took 10 years to reconstruct. The original was a 17th-century *Titanic* – big, expensive and supposedly unsinkable. True to comparison, the *Batavia*, filled to the brim with cannon and goods for the colonies, went down in 1629 on its maiden voyage off the west coast of Australia. The replica, however, redeemed its predecessor in 2000 by sailing around the Pacific.

The huge weathered wooden skeleton alongside belongs to the *Seven Provinces,* a replica of Admiral Michiel de Ruijter's massive 17th-century flagship that's been under construction in fits and starts for years with no completion date in sight. In a separate building, the Netherlands Institute for Maritime Archaeology displays the remains of a 2000-year-old Roman ship found near Utrecht.

Nieuw Land   MUSEUM
(www.nieuwlanderfgoed.nl; Oostvaardersdijk 1-13; adult/child €7.50/3.50; ⏱10am-5pm Tue-Fri, 11.30am-5pm Sat & Sun, also 10am-5pm Mon Jul & Aug) Nearly half of the Netherlands was created by Brobdingnagian land reclamations. Nieuw Land has exhibits about *polder* reclamation aimed at kids, who can build model bridges or dams, and navigate ships through locks.

**Luchtvaart Themapark
Aviodrome**   MUSEUM
(www.aviodrome.nl; Dakotaweg 11a; adult/child €16/14; ⏱10am-5pm Tue-Sun) No expense has been spared for Luchtvaart Themapark Aviodrome. This huge museum has 70 historical aircraft on display, including a replica of the Wright Brother's 1902 Flyer, Baron von Richthofen's WWI triplane, a Spitfire and a KLM 747. You can also play air-traffic controller in a recreated flight tower or watch aviation films in the megacinema. It's at Lelystad Airport 4km east of town (bus 148 from the train station)

HAARLEM & NORTH HOLLAND LELYSTAD

DON'T MISS

SCHOKLAND

A bleak variation on the island theme, the community of Schokland eked out an existence for hundreds of years on a long, narrow strip of land in the Zuiderzee. By the mid-19th century the clock had run out: fish prices plummeted and vicious storms were literally eroding the island away. The plucky locals hung on, despite the appalling living conditions, prompting Willem III to order their removal in 1859. Schokland was eventually swallowed up by the Noordoostpolder in the 20th century, just like Urk.

The Schokland Museum (www.schokland.nl; Middelbuurt 3; adult/child €5/3.50; ⏱10am-5pm Tue-Sun Apr-Oct, daily Jul & Aug, Fri-Sun Nov-Mar) affords glimpses into this tortured past, describing the history of the island, now a Unesco World Heritage site, in detail with a good video in English. Views from the lower path hint at just how big the waves were here, at the prow-shaped barrier constructed from tall wooden pilings. Ironically, since the area was drained the foundations have begun to dry out. Schokland is sinking but, luckily, no longer into the sea.

There's no public transport to the museum. By bike, the LF15 from Urk 14km west passes right through and once here you can follow a 10km route around the old island.

✗ Eating

Chains and fast food dominate the Lelystad dining scene. The vast plaza by Nieuw Land has a few cafes.

❶ Getting There & Away

BICYCLE The national bike route **LF20** starts near Muiden and then runs across the reclaimed *polder* 44km to Lelystad before veering off to the waterfront and the museums. From here it continues northeast to Urk.

TRAIN Lelystad station is on the Hanze train line that has been extended to Kampen and Zwolle. There are now through trains serving Groningen, Leeuwarden, Zwolle and Amsterdam (€9, 40 minutes, two hourly) via Lelystad.

Urk

☏0527 / POP 18,400

This pious village was once a proud little island (not unlike Marken across the IJsselmeer), home to a sizeable fishing fleet and an important signal post for ships passing into the North Sea. In the 1940s Urk reluctantly joined the mainland when the surrounding Noordoostpolder was pumped dry.

Although now cut off from the North Sea, the town is still a centre of the seafood industry. Penetrate past the irksome modern housing developments and you'll find a knoll with the old town, interesting sights and views of the fishing harbour.

Dozens of historical fishing boats are moored around the **harbour**. At the western end of town, take the coastal walk around the **lighthouse** for a pinch of local folklore. Just 70m off the shore lies the Ommelebommelestien, a slippery rock said to be the birthplace of all native Urkers. Legend also has it that, far from receiving the delivery by stork, dad had to take a rowboat to pick up his newborn.

The supports of the village church, **Kerkje aan de Zee** (Wijk 3), are made entirely out of masts of VOC (Dutch East India Company) ships that brought back exotic goods from the East Indies. Inside are ship models and, at times, haunting recitals by the choir. Nearby you'll find the **Fishermen's Monument**, a lonely statue of a woman in a billowing dress gazing seaward where her loved ones were lost. Marble tablets around the perimeter list the Urk seafarers who never returned – name, age and ship's ID number – with new names still being added.

Bus 141 runs between Urk and Kampen (50 minutes, four hourly) and Zwolle. On Sunday, however, service is sparse.

Urk is 34km northwest of Lelystad on the national bike route **LF20**. Zwolle in Overijssel is 50km southeast on the **LF15**, a scenic ride of dykes, rivers and Schokland.

Utrecht

Includes »

Best Places to Eat

» Blauw (p141)

» Polman's (p141)

» Deeg (p141)

» Corazon Coffee (p144)

Best Places to Stay

» B&B Utrecht (p140)

» Mary K Hotel (p140)

» Grand Hotel Karel V (p141)

Why Go?

Don't underrate the petite province of Utrecht. Its famous namesake city – with its throngs of students, tree-lined canals and medieval quarter – deserves the limelight. No set piece, it has a plethora of edgy, fun bars and cafes. Those with calmer tastes can visit more than a dozen museums big and small. At the very least, Utrecht is an easy and evocative day trip from Amsterdam. Wandering the back streets you can revel in reminders of the 17th century.

And this is no mere city-state. By bike you can explore impressive castles and tiny towns in under a day. The splendid Kasteel de Haar on Utrecht's doorstep is one of the country's most beautiful castles. Amersfoort oozes medieval character but also honours native son Piet Mondrian and his minimalist, angular palette. Then there's Oudewater in the southwest, synonymous with witchcraft (Monty Python fans will dig it).

When to Go

At the heart of the country, Utrecht's weather is perfectly average: cold and wet in the winter, with the potential for chilly, wet days the rest of the year as well. However, you can get perfectly clear and sunny days any time, especially from April to October. These are prime times for day trips on bikes around the province. In Utrecht city, there are tasty bock beer fests in the autumn when many cafes and bars have the seasonal brew on tap.

UTRECHT CITY

♪030 / POP 317,000

Utrecht is one of the Netherlands' oldest cities, with a compact medieval centre set out around canals unique to the country. There's a lower level where warehouses were located in the 13th century, giving the canals a split-level character and meaning that diners and drinkers can nip off the street and enjoy a snack or a drink down at water level.

Of course a drink is what many people need after arriving in Utrecht, as the train station feeds into a vast enclosed mall, the Hoog Catharijne shopping centre, which goes on and on in all its unattractive glory until you are spat out at ground level in what seems to be a construction site. Wandering east you find the old town and suddenly you realise why you came.

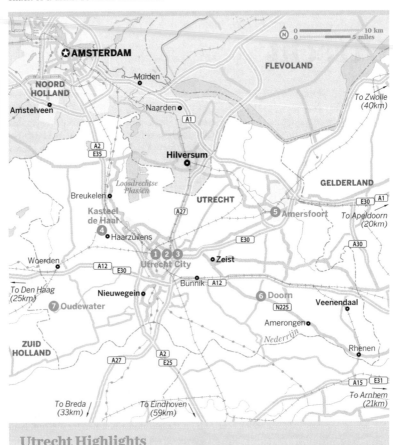

Utrecht Highlights

① Look out towards Amsterdam, 50km northwest, from the top of Utrecht's 14th-century cathedral tower, the **Domtoren** (p137)

② Find your own favourite spot along Utrecht's unique **bilevel canals** (p136)

③ Plunge into Utrecht's vibrant student culture and revel in the **nightlife** (p142)

④ Feel the weight of history at the imposing **Kasteel de Haar** (p143)

⑤ Discover narrow canals and medieval confines at **Amersfoort** (p143)

⑥ Get a bike and peddle out to Doorn's **Huis Doorn** (p145), a palace that was once a castle

⑦ Find out if a witch weighs the same as gravy at **Oudewater** (p145)

Fortunately, the entire train station region is undergoing the kind of rebuilding that will please anyone who thought the area needed to be blown up. Roads such as Catharijnebaan are being turned back into the canals they once were and the tatty station is being replaced by something that will both inspire and complement the old town. One downside: the vast project will last until 2019 (www.nieuwhc.nl).

Meanwhile, Utrecht's student population of 40,000 is the largest in the country, making the city a very vibrant place.

History

In Roman times the Rhine passed through present-day Utrecht, then called Trajectum. In the following centuries the town had religious ties and was part of various empires. From the 11th century it was a centre of culture and learning while Amsterdam was still just a grubby fishing town to the west.

In 1579 several regions of today's Netherlands united under the Union of Utrecht. The Protestant religion was made official but, in an early nod to tolerance, it was decreed that Catholics would not be persecuted. Utrecht's university was founded in 1636, the year after René Descartes, a local, wrote *Discourse on Method.*

In 1702 centuries of simmering animosity between the bishops of Utrecht and the Roman Catholic Church came to a head when the bishop was booted out of his job for failing to recognise the pope's infallibility. This caused a schism that resulted in the creation of the Old Catholics Church in Utrecht. The religion grew in popularity and peaked in 1889 when scores of disgruntled Catholics had a huge meeting in Utrecht. After that the Old Catholics lost following, and there's well under 10,000 members of the church in the Netherlands today.

⊙ Sights

Most of the interesting bits of the city lie within 500m of the Domtoren (Cathedral Tower), although the museum quarter is a pleasant stroll a couple of hundred metres further south. Utrecht likes its museums, and has over a dozen, some quirkier than a bag of cats, such as the one devoted to old grocery items.

Focus your strolling on the two canals which bisect Utrecht, the **Oudegracht** and the **Nieuwegracht**, the old and new canals from the 11th and 14th centuries. A third canal, the **Singel**, surrounds the old core.

Scene of many a wedding photo, the photogenic bend in the Oudegracht is illuminated by lamplight in the evening; hundreds sit at outside cafes here by day. South of this point is where the canal is at its most evocative, and the streets are quieter, stretching 1km to the southern tip of the old town.

A section of the Singel called the Stadsbuitengracht has its own turn as a lovely canal on the southeastern side of the old quarter, where it follows many parks built on the site of the old fortifications. Stroll down beside this canal and back north through Nieuwegracht, a peaceful stretch of plush canal houses and towering, grand old elms.

⌜TOP⌝
⌞CHOICE⌟ Domtoren HISTORIC BUILDING
(Cathedral Tower; www.domtoren.nl; Domplein; adult/child €9/5; ⊙11am-4pm) The Domtoren is 112m high, with 465 steps and 50 bells. It's a tough haul to the top but well worth the exertion, given that the tower gives unbeatable city views; on a clear day you can see Amsterdam. The guided tour, in Dutch and English, is detailed and gives privileged insight into this beautiful structure.

Finished in the 14th century, the cathedral and its tower are the most striking medieval landmarks in a city that once had 40 cathedrals. Appreciate the craft: it took almost 300 years to complete. In 1674 the North Sea winds reached hurricane force and blew down the cathedral's nave, leaving the tower and transept behind.

Domkerk CHURCH
(Cathedral; www.domkerk.nl; Achter de Dom 1; ⊙10am-5pm May-Sep, 11am-4pm Oct-Apr) Immediately north of the Domtoren, find the row of paving stones that mark the extents of the nave – across this extent is the Domkerk, the surviving chancel of the cathedral, with a few tombs within. A **tour** (adult/child €8/4.50; ⊙11.45am & 2.45pm Sat, noon & 2.45pm Sun) includes a look at the **treasury** (Schatkamer), which is slowly being excavated and reopened; tickets are sold at the tourist office (see p142). Back outside, look for new markers showing extents of the Roman town.

Behind the church is the most charming component of this ecclesiastical troika: **Kloostergang**, a monastic garden and peaceful refuge.

Utrecht University HISTORIC BUILDING
The 19th-century buildings on the eastern side of Domplein are the ceremonial buildings of Utrecht University, surrounding the

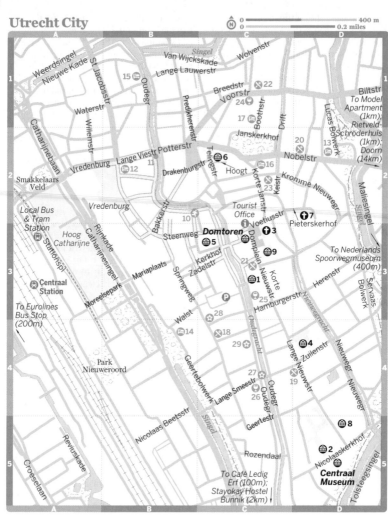

0   400 m
0   0.2 miles

old church chapterhouse where the Treaty of Utrecht was signed in 1579. The Treaty formed a military alliance of the northern provinces.

Centraal Museum   MUSEUM
(www.centraalmuseum.nl; Nicolaaskerkhof 10; adult/child €9/4; ⊙11am-5pm Tue-Sun) The Centraal Museum has a wide-ranging collection. It displays applied arts dating back to the 17th century, as well as paintings by some of the Utrecht School artists and a bit of De Stijl to boot – including the world's most extensive Gerrit Rietveld collection, a dream for all minimalists. There's even

a 12th-century Viking longboat that was dug out of the local mud, plus a sumptuous 17th-century dollhouse. Admission includes entry to the Dick Bruna House and Rietveld-Schröderhuis.

Dick Bruna House   MUSEUM
(www.dickbrunahuis.nl; Nicolaaskerkhof 10; ⊙11am-5pm Tue-Sun) One of Utrecht's favourite sons, author and illustrator Dick Bruna is the creator of beloved cartoon rabbit Miffy and she naturally takes pride of place at his studio across from the museum. Kids get a

Utrecht City

UTRECHT

huge kick out of it, but so do adults who appreciate superlative graphic design.

Rietveld-Schröderhuis   HISTORIC BUILDING
(⊘reservations 236 23 10; Prins Hendriklaan 50; admission surcharge €3; ⊙11am-5pm Wed-Sun) This Unesco-recognised landmark house is just outside the city centre. Built in 1924 by Utrecht architect Gerrit Rietveld, it is a stark example of 'form follows function'. Only six colours are used: red, blue, yellow, white, grey and black. Visits are by mandatory tour, which should be booked in advance at the Centraal Museum (see website for details); the museum will give you a map for the pleasant 25-minute stroll to the house or loan you a free bike.

Museum Catharijneconvent   MUSEUM
(www.catharijneconvent.nl; Lange Nieuwegracht 38; adult/child €12/7; ⊙10am-5pm Tue-Fri, 11am-5pm Sat & Sun) Museum Catharijneconvent is the pick of Utrecht's museums, with the finest collection of medieval religious art in the Netherlands – virtually the history of Christianity, in fact – housed in a Gothic former convent and an 18th-century canalside house. Marvel at the many beautiful illuminated manuscripts, look for the odd Rembrandt and hope for one of the often salacious special exhibitions.

Pieterskerk   CHURCH
(www.kerkenkijken.nl; Voetiusstraat; ⊙noon-4pm Tue-Sun Jul-Sep) Walk down Voetiusstraat from behind the Domkerk to Pieterskerk, built in 1048 and the oldest Romanesque church in the Netherlands. Much damage was caused during the storm in 1674 and again during a dodgy 1965 restoration. Opening hours are sporadic, but try visiting on Friday or Saturday.

Universiteitsmuseum   MUSEUM
(⊘253 87 28; www.museum.uu.nl; Lange Nieuwstraat 106; adult/child €7/3.50; ⊙11am-5pm) The Universiteitsmuseum has interactive science exhibits and traces Utrecht University's research through the centuries. There's a recreated late 19th-century classroom, historic dentistry tools and way too many models of medical maladies. Take refuge out the back in **De Oude Hortus**, the old botanical garden, along with all the other dentophobes, who'll be quivering amid venerable trees and plants collected by the Dutch during their world exploits. The garden is an oasis of calm, sheltering numerous rare flowers and plants such as the ancient *Ginkgo biloba* tree.

Nederlands Spoorwegmuseum   MUSEUM
(Dutch Railway Museum; www.spoorwegmuseum.nl; Maliebaanstation; admission €14.50; ⊙10am-5pm

MIFFY & DICK

The illustrator Dick Bruna was born in Utrecht in 1927 and has lived there all his life. His most famous creation is of course Miffy, or Nijntje as she's known in the Netherlands, an adorable best-selling cartoon rabbit with dots for eyes and a cross for a mouth that's a clear inspiration for Japan's famous Hello Kitty character.

But there's much more to Dick Bruna than Miffy (wonderful as she is). Our man from Utrecht has written and illustrated more than 120 children's books and designed more than 2000 book covers, as well as hundreds of other books, posters, postcards and prints. Today, Bruna still rises to go to work early every day at his Utrecht studio and is still every bit as obsessive in his search for perfect design. As he says: 'I'll never do 3-D illustration. I haven't simplified 2-D enough'.

His most recent Miffy book is 2007's *Queen Miffy*. Learn more at www.miffy.com.

Tue-Sun) The national railway museum features historic trains and thematic displays in an old station building; a high-speed minitrain takes kids around the grounds. To get there, take bus 3 from Utrecht CS to Maliebaan and walk southeast for about five minutes.

Aboriginal Art Museum   MUSEUM
(www.aamu.nl; Oudegracht 176; adult/child €9/5; ☺10am-5pm Tue-Fri, 11am-5pm Sat & Sun) A bit of a surprise in Utrecht, the Aboriginal Art Museum, devoted to contemporary Australian Aboriginal art, is sure to delight those bored with Rembrandt and Van Gogh.

Museum voor het Kruideniersbedrijf   MUSEUM
(Grocer's Museum; www.kruideniersmuseum.nl; Hoogt 6; ☺12.30-4.30pm Tue-Sat) This charming replica of an old grocery store isn't a museum per se. It's more like a sweetshop with lovely ladies in old-fashioned aprons selling sweets and tea (plus lentils, mustard and more) in decorative containers. Pick up a block of white liquorice candy to add to hot milk – an old Dutch tradition.

Museum Speelklok   MUSEUM
(Musical Clock Museum; ☎231 27 89; www.museumspeelklok.nl; Steenweg 6; adult/child €9.50/5.50; ☺10am-5pm Tue-Sun) This museum has a colourful collection of musical machines from the 18th century onwards. Hourly tours demonstrate them with gusto, and the restoration workshop lets you see how the mechanical marvels work.

🏃 Activities

Canal Tours   CANAL TOUR
(www.schuttevaer.com; Oudegracht a/d Werf 85; adult/child €10/7; ☺11am-4pm May-Aug) Hour-long canal tours are a fine way to see the old town and the old water-level warehouses.

The landing is on Oudegracht just south of Lange Viestraat.

Canal Bikes   BOATING
(www.canal.nl; per person per hr €8) You can rent canal bikes (pedal boats) from in front of the municipal library.

⭐ Festivals & Events

Holland Festival Oude Muziek   MUSIC FESTIVAL
(Holland Festival of Ancient Music; www.oudemuziek.nl) Held in late August, this festival celebrates music from the Middle Ages through to the baroque period.

Nederlands Film Festival   FILM FESTIVAL
(NFF; www.filmfestival.nl) The Dutch film industry may be tiny, but its output is generally good. Find out for yourself at the NFF in late September, culminating in the awarding of the coveted Golden Calf.

🛏 Sleeping

🔝 **B&B Utrecht**   GUESTHOUSE $
(☎06 5043 4884; www.hostelutrecht.nl; Lucas Bolwerk 4; dm/r from €21/60; @📶) Straddling the border between hostel and hotel, this spotless inn in an elegant old building has an internal Ikea vibe. Breakfast, lunch and dinner ingredients are free! Internet access (in a computer room with scanners, printers etc) is also free as is use of a huge range of musical instruments and DVDs.

📑 **Mary K Hotel**   HOTEL $$
(☎230 48 88; www.marykhotel.com; Oudegracht 25; r €120-180; 📶) A bevy of Utrecht artists decorated the rooms at this creative new Utrecht hotel in an ideal location. Rooms come in three basic sizes (small, medium and large)

but no two are alike. All make use of details in this old canal house and you may find an ancient timber running through your bathroom or a stuffed animal snoozing in the rafters.

Grand Hotel Karel V
HOTEL $$$

(☎233 75 55; www.karelv.nl; Geertebolwerk 1, off Walsteeg; s/d from €120/240; ❄@⊛) The lushest accommodation in Utrecht can be found in this former knights' gathering hall from the 14th century. The service and decor are understated, and the 117 rooms are split between the old manor and a modern wing. Taking tea in the walled garden is sublime.

Sandton Malie Hotel
HOTEL $$

(☎231 64 24; www.maliehotel.nl; Maliestraat 2; r from €110; ❄@⊛) Tucked away in a beautiful tree-lined avenue, this elegant and comfortable 19th-century house offers 45 large rooms and old-world charm. There's a nice garden out the back, and the hotel is away from the city centre for a bit of peace and quiet.

Strowis Budget Hostel
HOSTEL $

(☎238 02 80; www.strowis.nl; Boothstraat 8; dm from €18, r €65; @⊛) This 17th-century building is near the town centre and has been lovingly restored and converted into a hostel (with four- to 14-bed rooms). There's a fine rear garden and bikes available to rent.

NH Centre Utrecht Hotel
HOTEL $$

(☎231 31 69; www.nh-hotels.com; Janskerkhof 10; r €100-200; ❄@⊛) Traditional style trumps modernity at this atmospheric old hotel (1870). The 47 rooms (with minibars, trouser press etc) are comfortable, with good church views and modern, stylish decor.

Stayokay Hostel Bunnik
HOSTEL $

(☎656 12 77; www.stayokay.com; Rhijnauwenselaan 14; dm/r from €24/67; ☉Mar-Oct; ⊛) This charming old mansion overlooks a canal on the fringes of a nature reserve, 5km east of the city centre in Bunnik. There are three dining halls, a traditional bar and a lovely terrace. It's right on national bike path **LF4** or you can take bus 40 or 41 from Utrecht CS. Wi-fi in the cafe.

Apollo Hotel Utrecht City Centre
HOTEL $$

(☎233 12 32; www.apollohotelresorts.com; Vredenburg 14; r €90-200; ⊛) A low-key business hotel, the Apollo has 90 spacious, comfortable rooms. Those in the back are dead quiet, those in the front have views of the town centre reconstruction. Those enormous red lips hovering over you are not a dream but a print above the headboard.

✗ Eating

Do as the discerning locals do: avoid the cluster of wharfside restaurants on the Oudegracht in the dead centre of the old town near the town hall. It's a pretty spot better known for its views than culinary delights. Utrecht's best restaurants lie elsewhere.

TOP CHOICE Blauw
INDONESIAN $$$

(www.restaurantblauw.nl; Springweg 64; set menu from €25; ☉dinner) Blauw is *the* place for stylish Indonesian food in Utrecht. Young and old alike enjoy superb *rijsttafels* (array of spicy dishes served with rice) amid the red decor that mixes vintage art with hip minimalism.

Polman's
GRAND CAFE $$

(www.polmanshuis.nl; cnr Jansdam & Keistraat; mains €12-25) Diners at this grand cafe are welcomed in an elegant former ballroom with ceiling frescoes and extravagant floral displays. French and Italian flavours dominate the menu *and* the extensive wine list.

Deeg
FUSION $$$

(☎233 11 04; www.restaurantdeeg.nl; Lange Nieuwstraat 71; set menus from €35; ☉dinner) A charming corner location in the museum quarter is but the first draw at this casual bistro, which has nightly set menus that change regularly. Fresh local produce gets a Mediterranean accent and many items – such as the cheeses – are organic.

Opium
ASIAN $$

(☎231 55 15; www.restaurant-opium.nl; Voorstraat 80; mains €15-20; ☉dinner) A high-concept Asian restaurant with a stunning modern interior, Opium takes flavours from across the continent and mixes them with locally sourced ingredients. Everything is presented with an eye for drama and the vibe is backed by a pulsing DJ-driven beat. There's nice pavement tables up front (with heaters!) and some bright ones inside under an atrium.

Café Springhaver
CAFE $$

(www.springhaver.nl; Springweg 50-52; mains €12-14) The cafe next to the cinema is a fine place for a drink, snack or meal especially if you aren't debating the merits of a film. It's a little spot of charm on this sinuous old street away from the bustle. Much of the food is sourced from local organic farms and there's a wide range of seasonal dishes.

Lokaal de Reunie
CAFE $$

(☎231 01 00; www.lokaaldereunie.nl; t Wed 3a; mains €12-30) One of many atmospheric cafes

TRAINS FROM UTRECHT CITY

DESTINATION	PRICE (€)	DURATION (MIN)	FREQUENCY (PER HR)
Amsterdam	7	30	4
Den Haag	10	40	6
Groningen	25	115	2
Maastricht	24	120	2
Rotterdam	10	40	4

near the cathedral tower, Lokaal de Reunie is distinguished by its attractive, airy interior.

Florin BROWN CAFE **$**
(www.florinutrecht.nl; Nobelstraat 2-4; mains €9-15) Battered benches and scarred wooden tables are the hallmarks of a good brown cafe and Florin nicely fits the bill. There's more emphasis on food here than at some brown cafes, but the burgers, salads and more on the menu appeal to scores of students nightly.

🍷 Drinking

TOP CHOICE **'t Oude Pothuys** BROWN CAFE
(Oudegracht 279) Small and dark, this basement pub has nightly music – jam sessions with locals trying their hand at rock and jazz. Enjoy drinks on the canalside pier.

TOP CHOICE **ACU** BAR
(www.acu.nl; Voorstraat 71) Billing itself as a 'political cultural centre', ACU is a classic student dive. It combines bar, venue, lecture hall and more. Argue about whether Trotsky was too conservative while downing organic vegan food. Note: 'Racism, sexism, homophobia are not tolerated'.

Café Ledig Erf BAR
(Tolsteegbrug 3) This classy pub overlooks a confluence of canals (and other cafes) at the southern tip of town. The terrace vies with the beer list in offering the most joy, and the autumn bock beer fest is a winner.

Kafé België BAR
(Oudegracht 196) This lively bar is an absolute must for beer-lovers. It has 20 Benelux brews on tap and cheap food for absorption. There's a couple of canalside tables out front.

☆ Entertainment

Cees Place LIVE MUSIC
(www.ceesplace.nl; Oudegracht a/d werf 275; ⊘Wed-Sun) A lively venue with a sense of wit. Wednesdays are open stage nights, Thursdays are jazz and Sundays are a bluesy rock jam session. You'll hear all of that and more from performers other nights. Located on the lower level by the canal.

Tivoli LIVE MUSIC
(☑231 14 91; www.tivoli.nl; Oudegracht 245) This former monastery, now a cavernous dance hall with medieval chandeliers, is a fixture on Utrecht's student-oriented music scene. There's everything from big band jazz to new Brit bands.

Springhaver Theater CINEMA
(☑231 37 89; www.springhaver.nl; Springweg 50-52) This art-deco complex houses intimate cinemas that screen art-house and independent films.

🛍 Shopping

Once rebuilt, the Hoog Catharijne shopping centre may again be an Utrecht highlight. Between here and the town hall are pedestrian streets with lots of chains and mainstream shops. For more interesting choices, wander down Voorstraat and Oudegracht.

Huge markets take place on Vredenburg on Wednesday, Friday and Saturday. Most unusual, however, is the Saturday fabric market on Breedstraat.

ℹ Information

Tourist Office (VVV; ☑0900 128 87 32; www. utrechtyourway.nl; Domplein 9; ⊘noon-5pm Sun & Mon, 10am-5pm Tue-Sat) Useful stop for info and Domtoren tickets.

ℹ Getting There & Away

Utrecht is a travel hub: bike routes, train lines and motorways converge on the city from all directions.

BICYCLE National bike route **LF9** runs north through farmlands for 23km to a junction with **LF23**, which covers both Muiden and Flevoland.

To the south it runs through rich farmlands towards Breda. Marathon route **LF7** passes through Utrecht on its 350km route from Alkmaar to Maastricht; Amsterdam is about 50km northwest. **LF4** runs east 80km to Arnhem.

BUS Eurolines (www.eurolines.nl; Stationsplein 57; ☺9.30am-5.30pm Mon-Fri, 10am-4pm Sat & Sun) has a ticket office opposite the tram station. Regional buses stop on the west side of the train station on Jarbeursplein.

TRAIN As part of the rebuilding/resurrection of the quarter by the train station, the entire station will be replaced with a light and airy structure that will no longer be grafted onto the mall; expect a fair bit of chaos. Lockers, the bike shop and all other services will be moving about. Utrecht CS (Centraal Station) is the national hub for Dutch rail services, so you'll probably change trains here at some point.

❶ Getting Around

Local buses and trams leave from a station underneath the passage linking Utrecht CS to Hoog Catharijne.

AROUND UTRECHT CITY

Loosdrechtse Plassen

The town of Breukelen is 10km northwest of Utrecht. Although the town in itself is unremarkable, it was actually the namesake for the New York district of Brooklyn. Breukelen is also the gateway to the Loosdrechtse Plassen, a large series of lakes formed from the flooded digs of peat harvesters.

There are all manner of bike paths around the waters and quite a bit of interesting scenery. Parts of the lakes are somewhat desolate, while others are surrounded by lovely homes on small islands joined to the road by little bridges.

The best way to visit is by bike from Utrecht; it's 15km northwest by national route **LF7**. Follow the signs to Breukelen. Otherwise, it's just a short run by train to Breukelen from Utrecht CS (€3, 13 minutes, four per hour).

Kasteel de Haar

Feast your senses on one of the most imposing castles in the country, **Kasteel de Haar** (677 85 15; www.kasteeldehaar.nl; Kasteellaan 1; adult/child tour €12.50/9, gardens only €3.50/2.50; ☺park 10am-5pm, tours 11am-4pm Mon-Fri, 10am-5pm Sat & Sun mid-Mar–Dec), which was re-

stored in a fit of nostalgia little more than a century ago, long after its Gothic turrets ceased to have any defensive purpose. But architect PJ Cuypers (of Rijksmuseum fame) misjudged the weight on the centuries-old foundations; big cracks can be seen above moat level.

What you see now is a spiffed-up version of the fortress as it was believed to look around 1500, but (understandably) equipped with all the creature comforts available in the late 19th century. The project was so extensive that the church and the nearby hamlet of Haarzuilens became involved. The castle's owner, Baron Etienne van Zuylen, spared little expense and had the entire village moved so there'd be adequate space for the park and hunting grounds.

The castle is surrounded by a large English landscaped garden with broad paths, canal-like stretches of pond and statues throughout. The French baroque garden near the entrance bears the stamp of Hélène de Rothschild, the baron's wife and heir of the renowned Rothschild banking family – it was her fortune that paid for the 19th-century restoration. You can also just wander the grounds.

To get to the castle from Utrecht, take the A2 north to exit 6 (Maarssen) and drive 2km east to Haarzuilens. Alternatively, take bus 127 from Utrecht CS towards Breukelen and get off at Castle or Brink, from where it's a 15-minute walk. The castle is right on national bike route **LF4**, 15km west of Utrecht.

Amersfoort

☎033 / POP 149,000

Beer, wool and tobacco made Amersfoort an exceedingly rich town from the 16th century onwards. Well-heeled with a touch of the provincial, the town has many striking merchants' homes that have been lovingly restored. And the egg-shaped old town offers quiet, wonderfully evocative strolls along canals and narrow alleys that still ooze medieval atmosphere.

Amersfoort makes for a good break on a train journey to/from Friesland or Groningen. You can have an interesting stroll for an hour and then get a good meal.

◎ Sights & Activities

Much of Amersfoort's appeal comes from wandering the old centre, which has attractive little canals and more than 300 pre-18th-century buildings.

TRAINS FROM AMERSFOORT

DESTINATION	PRICE (€)	DURATION (MIN)	FREQUENCY (PER HR)
Amsterdam	8	35	4
Deventer	10	37	3
Utrecht	4.50	19	6

Kade Museum
MUSEUM

(www.kunsthalkade.nl; Smallepad 3; adult/child €7/3.50; ⊙11am-5pm Tue-Fri, noon-5pm Sat & Sun) All angles, this bold museum has all manner of modern art, sculpture and installations. The cafe is excellent.

Mondriaanhuis
MUSEUM

(www.mondriaanhuis.nl; Kortegracht 11; adult/child €6/free; ⊙10am-5pm Tue-Fri, noon-5pm Sat & Sun) The famous De Stijl artist Piet Mondrian was born in Amersfoort. This small but absorbing museum, in the house where he was born, honours his life and work with a detailed retrospective of prints, reproductions and some originals. His iconic primary – and square! – colours dominate the complex.

OLD TOWN

Zuidsingel is a fine place to start: the inner ring on the north side of town along Muurhuizen is quaint and good for walks. Langestraat is the mainstream shopping strip but Krommestraat is the street for interesting and offbeat choices. Don't miss the old houses on Krankeledenstraat just north of Langestraat.

The town has three surviving gateways, either to the city roads or over the canals:

Koppelpoort guards the north and was built in the 15th century.

Kamperbinnenpoort is at the eastern side and dates from the 13th century.

Monnikendam, in the southeast, is picturesque, and was built in 1430.

TOP CHOICE Onze Lieve Vrouwe Toren
HISTORIC BUILDING

(Lieve Vrouwekerkhof; adult/child €4/3; ⊙tours 11am-5pm Tue-Sun Jul & Aug, 2pm Tue & Thu, 12.30pm & 2pm Sat Apr-Jun & Sep-Oct) Onze Lieve Vrouwe Toren is the surviving 15th-century Gothic tower (346 steps, fine views) of the church that used to stand on this spot. Like so many of the Netherlands' churches, it was destroyed by tragedy – in this case a gunpowder explosion in 1787. The square in front, Lieve Vrouwekerkhof, is Amersfoort's most charming spot. A flower market is held here on Friday morning.

Sint Joriskerk
CHURCH

(www.sintjoriskerk-amersfoort.nl; Hof 1; admission €1; ⊙11am-5pm Mon-Sat mid-May–Sep) Amersfoort's surviving old church is Sint Joriskerk. It was rebuilt in a sort of Gothic-cum-aircraft-hangar style in the 16th century after the original Romanesque church burnt down (obviously, insuring Dutch churches has never been a lucrative proposition).

Museum Flehite
MUSEUM

(www.museumflehite.nl; Westsingel 50; adult/child €7/3.50; ⊙11am-5pm Tue-Fri, noon-5pm Sat & Sun) The collections at the Museum Flehite cover local geology, history and decorative arts. The building is attractively set at a junction of canals, and you enter the museum courtyard over a bridge. It has a fantastic free map showing historical highlights around town and an illustrative painting showing Amersfoort in 1671.

Drie Ringen Bierbrouwerij
BREWERY

(www.dedrieringen.nl; Kleine Spui 18; ⊙1-7pm Fri-Sun) Possibly the most fun you will have in Amersfoort is touring Drie Ringen Bierbrouwerij. You can wander enjoyably around this much-heralded microbrewery and try one of the five beers on tap.

☞ Tours

Canal Tours
CANAL TOUR

(☑465 46 36; www.amersfoort-rondvaarten.nl; Krommestraat 5; tours from €4; ⊙May-Oct) Sail around the old canals on four different routes that each take 45 minutes.

✕ Eating & Drinking

Both Hof and Lieve Vrouwekerkhof groan or – depending on the time of day – shriek with cafes and pubs.

TOP CHOICE Corazon Coffee
CAFE $

(www.coffeecorazon.nl; Krommestraat 18; snacks from €3; ⊙10am-6pm) Excellent choice for a pause while you wander the old quarter of Amersfoort. The coffees, teas and fresh juices are superb. The baked goods delight and you can lunch on sandwiches, salads and more. It has a children's play area and menu.

Café Kade CAFE **$**
(Smallepad 3; meals from €5; ⊙11am-5pm Tue-Sun) The fab cafe in the cutting-edge Kade Museum has a fine terrace with views of passing trains, a canal and the Koppelpoort gateway.

Blok's FUSION **$$$**
(☑461 02 22; www.bloksrestaurant.nl; Krommestraat 49; menus from €44; ⊙dinner Thu-Mon) On a street with many good choices, Blok's has a kitchen with a big window onto the street. Watch as all manner of contemporary, fresh creations stream forth to the stylish dining room. Look for seasonal menus.

❶ Information

Tourist Office (VVV; ☑0900 112 23 64; www.vvvamersfoort.nl; Breestraat 1; ⊙11am-5pm Mon-Fri, also 11am-4pm Sat Apr-Oct) Excellent cycling maps, across from the Onze Lieve Vrouwe Toren.

❶ Getting There & Around

BICYCLE There's a bicycle shop at the train station. Utrecht is 23km southwest on a beautiful ride through forests and farms on national bike route **LF9**. It also runs north 23km to meet **LF23**, and both continue into Flevoland.

TRAIN Amersfoort's train station is an easy 500m walk west of the centre. It has lockers and currency exchange services and regular train services:

Doorn

☑0343 / POP 10.500
Around 20km southeast of Utrecht lies Doorn, a wealthy little burg with a claim to an oddment in 20th-century Dutch history: **Huis Doorn** (www.huisdoorn.nl; Langbroekerweg 10; adult/child €9/free; ⊙10am-5pm Tue-Sat, 1-5pm Sun Apr-Oct, 1-5pm Tue-Sun Nov-Mar), a 14th-century castle that was turned into a sort of indefensible mansion during the 1700s. It had numerous owners during its time, but none of them was more infamous than Kaiser Wilhelm II of Germany, who inhabited Huis Doorn in exile from 1920 until his death in 1941.

There's a fine collection of German art that it seems the Kaiser brought with him from various German palaces. Afterwards, stroll the grounds and ponder the fate of the Kaiser, who had been allowed into exile by the Dutch as long as he remained under 'house arrest' (some house, eh?). Catch a local train from Utrecht CS to Driebergen-Zeist, then take bus 50, 56 or 81. It will take about 45 minutes. On national bike route **LF4**, ride 24km southeast from Utrecht.

Amerongen

☑0343 / POP 5200
The countryside around the small town of Amerongen on the Nederrijn River is dotted with old wooden tobacco-drying sheds. It's also home to **Kasteel Amerongen** (☑454 212; www.kasteelamerongen.nl; Drostestraat 20; adult/child €10/5; ⊙11am-5pm Tue-Sun Apr-Oct, Sat & Sun only Nov-Mar), a fortified castle built in the 13th century that took on its present twee appearance in the late 1600s; it was originally owned by Europe's old aristocracy. It's 38km southwest from Utrecht on national bike route **LF4**. Combine it with a visit to Doorn.

Oudewater

☑0348 / POP 10.100
There's one real reason to visit the sweet little town of Oudewater in the province's southwest: witchcraft. Until the 17th century the **Heksenwaag** (Witches' Weigh House; www.heksenwaag.nl; Leeuweringerstraat 2; adult/child €4.25/2; ⊙11am-5pm Tue-Sun Apr-Oct, Wed, Sat & Sun only Nov-Mar) in the town centre was thought to have the most accurate scales in the land; women were brought here from all over the place on suspicion of being witches.

The house has a modest display of witchcraft history in the loft upstairs, and at the end of your visit you'll be invited to step onto the old scale. If you feel light on your feet it's because your *certificaet van weginghe* (weight certificate) makes your weight shrink – an old Dutch pound is 10% heavier than today's unit.

Several bewitching cafes line the tiny canal here and you can see Holland's oldest in-use stork nest on the town hall.

Oudewater is on the route of bus 180, which runs in either direction between Gouda (33 minutes) and Utrecht CS (53 minutes) every half-hour. The town is 10km by a cycling route across canal-laced fields south of Woerden and national bike route **LF4**, which is 26km from Utrecht and 11km further southwest from Kasteel de Haar.

UTRECHT DOORN

Rotterdam & South Holland

Best Places to Eat

» De Dames Proeverij (p151)
» Spijshuis de Dis (p167)
» Z&M (p177)
» De Ballentent (p177)
» De Stroper (p185)

Best Places to Stay

» Het Paleis Hotel (p158)
» Hotel de Emauspoort (p166)
» Hotel New York (p173)
» Hotel Auberge Provençal (p188)

Why Go?

Think Holland and you're thinking of the region southwest of Amsterdam where tulips, cheese, Vermeer and plucky Dutch people standing up to the sea avoid cliché simply by their omnipresence.

South Holland's major cities are the biggest attractions. Mighty Rotterdam is blessed with an edgy urban vibe, surprising cultural scene and striking architecture. Leiden has its university culture and old town (and proximity to the bulbfields). Den Haag has museums, a stately air, luxe shopping and a kitsch beach, while charming, beautiful Delft is a medieval time capsule. Smaller places are also worth your time: Gouda is a perfect old canal town, while Dordrecht has its own surprises amid canals and charm.

Further south, Zeeland (Sea Land) is the dyke-protected province that people often associate with the Netherlands when they're not thinking of tulips and windmills. Cycling in this flat, mostly sub-sea-level region is unparalleled.

When to Go

The heart of Holland can be enjoyed year-round. Rotterdam is full of museums and nightlife, so you can ignore the weather while indoors. The same can be said to a certain extent for the main towns and cities such as Leiden, Den Haag and Delft. However, from spring through autumn, you'll find many more attractions open and the odds of enjoying a balmy canal stroll that much greater. Spring is the time for the explosion of colour at Keukenhof and summer means the beaches might actually be warm.

SOUTH HOLLAND

Along with North (Noord) Holland and Utrecht, South (Zuid) Holland is part of the Randstad, the economic and population heart of the Netherlands. Two of the nation's most important cities are here: Den Haag, the seat of the royal family and the government; and Rotterdam, Europe's busiest port. You could easily make a trip just exploring the classic Dutch destinations of the region.

Leiden

♩ 071 / POP 118,700

Lovely Leiden is a refreshing, vibrant town, patterned with canals and attractive old buildings. It also has a few claims to fame: it's Rembrandt's birthplace, and it's home

Rotterdam & South Holland Highlights

❶ Appreciate the architecture and verve of Holland's second city, **Rotterdam** (p168)

❷ Pop off for spectacular spring posies at **Keukenhof Gardens** (p156)

❸ Get your Art 101 in splendid form at Den Haag's **Mauritshuis** (p155)

❹ Look for girls wearing pearl earrings in old-world **Delft** (p163) home of Vermeer

❺ Go for a spin at Holland's best collection of windmills at **Kinderdijk** (p181)

❻ Feel the spray on your face riding a fast ferry to surprising medieval **Dordrecht** (p183)

❼ Have a meal at a genteel canalside cafe in **Leiden** (p147)

❽ Discover everything that's not cheesy about quaint **Gouda** (p161)

Leiden

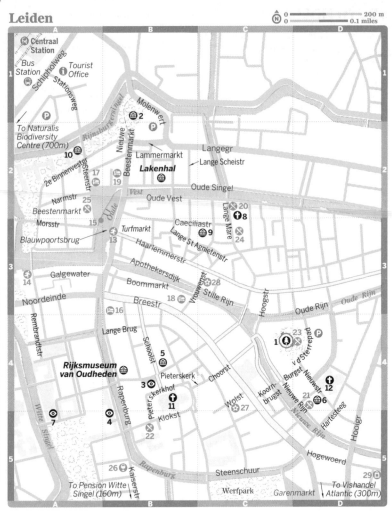

to the Netherlands' oldest university (and 20,000 students), the Alma Mater of René Descartes.

The university was a gift from Willem the Silent for withstanding two Spanish sieges in 1574. It was a terrible time, ending when the Sea Beggars arrived and repelled the invaders. According to lore, the retreating Spanish legged it so quickly, they abandoned a kettle of *hutspot* (hotchpotch, stew) – today it's still a staple of Dutch menus in restaurants and in homes.

Decades later, Protestants fleeing persecution elsewhere in the Low Countries,

France and England arrived in Leiden to a somewhat warmer welcome. Most notable was the group led by John Robinson, who would sail to America and into history as the pilgrims aboard the *Mayflower*.

Wealth from the linen industry buttressed Leiden's growing prosperity, and during the 17th century the town produced several brilliant artists, most famously Rembrandt van Rijn – better known by his first name alone. Rembrandt was born in Leiden in 1606, and remained here for 26 years before achieving fame in Amsterdam.

Leiden

◉ Sights

Leiden is right up there with the great historic cities of the Netherlands. As you walk five minutes south from its striking Centraal Station, the city's traditional character unfolds, especially around the Pieterskerk and south. Leiden's district of historic waterways is worth at least half a day of wandering.

TOP CHOICE Lakenhal   MUSEUM
(www.lakenhal.nl; Oude Singel 28-32; adult/child €7.50/free; ⊗10am-5pm Tue-Fri, noon-5pm Sat & Sun) Get your Rembrandt fix at the 17th-century Lakenhal, which houses the Municipal Museum, with an assortment of works by old masters, as well as period rooms and temporary exhibits. The 1st floor has been restored to the way it would have looked when Leiden was at the peak of its prosperity.

Rijksmuseum van Oudheden   MUSEUM
(National Museum of Antiquities; www.rmo.nl; Rapenburg 28; adult/child €9/free; ⊗10am-5pm Tue-Sun) This museum has a world-class collection of Greek, Roman and Egyptian artefacts, the pride of which is the extraordinary Temple of Taffeh, a gift from former Egyptian president Anwar Sadat to the Nether-

lands for helping to save ancient Egyptian monuments from flood.

Museum Volkenkunde   MUSEUM
(National Museum of Ethnology; www.volkenkunde.nl; Steenstraat 1; adult/child €8.50/6; ⊗10am-5pm Tue-Sun) Cultural achievements by civilisations worldwide are on show at the Museum Volkenkunde. More than 200,000 artefacts span China, South America and Africa, much like Amsterdam's Tropenmuseum. There's a rich Indonesian collection; watch for performances by the museum's gamelan troupe. Recent renovations have made exhibits more engaging.

De Valk   MUSEUM
(The Falcon; ☑516 53 53; 2e Binnenvestgracht 1; adult/child €3/2; ⊗10am-5pm Tue-Sat, 1-5pm Sun) Leiden's landmark windmill museum receives loving care (another restoration commenced in 2012), and many consider it the best example of its kind. Its arms are free to turn 'whenever possible' and can still grind the grain.

Museum Boerhaave   MUSEUM
(www.museumboerhaave.nl; Lange St Agnietenstraat 10; adult/child €7.50/free; ⊗10am-5pm Tue-Sat, noon-5pm Sun) Leiden University was an early centre for Dutch medical research.

This museum displays the often-grisly results (five centuries of pickled organs and surgical tools and skeletons) plus you can have a gander at the anatomical theatre with skeletons in stiff relief.

Leiden University UNIVERSITY

(www.leiden.edu) The oldest university in Europe was a gift to Leiden from Willem the Silent for withstanding two Spanish sieges in 1574. The campus comprises an interesting mix of modern and antique buildings that are scattered around town.

Hortus Botanicus GARDEN

(www.hortus.leidenuniv.nl; Rapenburg 73; adult/child €6/3; ☺10am-6pm daily Apr-Oct, 10am-4pm Tue-Sun Nov-Mar) The lush Hortus Botanicus is Europe's oldest botanical garden (1590), and home to the country's oldest descendants of the Dutch tulips. It's a wonderful place to relax, with explosions of tropical colour and a fascinating steamy greenhouse.

Naturalis Biodiversity Centre MUSEUM

(www.naturalis.nl; Darwinweg 2; adult/child €11/8; ☺10am-5pm) A stuffed elephant greets you at this large, well-funded collection of all the usual dead critters and, notably, the million-year-old Java Man discovered by Dutch anthropologist Eugène Dubois in 1891. It's 300m west of the town centre.

OLD LEIDEN

FREE De Burcht PARK, MONUMENT

(☺sunrise-sunset) De Burcht, an 11th-century citadel on an artificial hill, lost its protective functions as the city grew around it. Now it's a park with lovely places to view the steeples and rooftops, with a wonderful cafe at its base.

St Pancraskerk CHURCH

(Nieuwstraat) This huge pile of bricks is the 15th-century St Pancraskerk, an agglomeration of styles.

Pieterskerk CHURCH

(Pieterskerkhof; ☺10am-4pm Mon-Fri, 1.30-4pm Sat & Sun May-Sep, 1.30-4pm daily Oct-Apr) Follow the huge steeple to Pieterskerk, which is often under restoration (a good thing as it has been prone to collapse since it was built

PILGRIMS' PROGRESS

In 1608 a group of Calvinist Protestants split from the Anglican church and left persecution in Nottinghamshire, England, for a journey that would span decades and thousands of miles. Travelling first to Amsterdam under the leadership of John Robinson, they encountered theological clashes with local Dutch Protestants.

In Leiden they found a more liberal atmosphere, thanks to the university and some like-minded Calvinists who already lived there. They also found company with refugees who had escaped from persecution elsewhere. However, the group's past was to catch up with them. In 1618 James I of England announced he would assume control over the Calvinists living in Leiden. In addition, the local Dutch were becoming less tolerant of religious splinter groups.

The first group of English left Leiden in 1620 for Delfshaven in what is now Rotterdam, where they bought the *Speedwell* with the intention of sailing to the New World. Unfortunately, the leaky *Speedwell* didn't live up to its name; after several attempts to cross the Atlantic, the group gave up and, against their better judgement, sailed into Southampton in England. After repairs to their ship and a thwarted attempt to restart their journey, the group joined the much more seaworthy *Mayflower* in Dartmouth and sailed, as it were, into history as the Pilgrims.

This legendary voyage was actually just one of many involving the Leiden group. It wasn't until 1630 that most had made their way to the American colonies founded in what is today New England. Some 1000 people made the voyages, including a number of Dutch who were considered oddballs for their unusual beliefs.

In Leiden today, traces of the Pilgrims are elusive. The best place to start is the **Leiden American Pilgrim Museum** (☏512 24 13; www.leidenamericanpilgrimmuseum.org; Beschuitsteeg 9; admission €3; ☺1-5pm Wed-Sat), a fascinating restoration of a one-room house occupied around 1610 by the soon-to-be Pilgrims. The house itself dates from 1375, but the furnishings are from the Pilgrims' period. Note the tiles on the floor, originals from the 14th century. The curator is Jeremy Bangs, an author with vast knowledge of the pilgrims.

in the 14th century). The precinct here is as old Leiden as you'll get and includes the gabled old **Latin School** (Schoolstraat), which – before it became a commercial building – was graced by a pupil named Rembrandt from 1616 to 1620. Across the plaza, look for the **Gravensteen**, which dates to the 13th century and was once a prison. The gallery facing the plaza was where judges watched executions.

Marekerk   CHURCH

(Lange Mare) The Marekerk dates back to 1639 and has a beautiful eight-sided wooden interior. Try to sneak a peak during Sunday services.

🏃 Activities

Cycling enthusiasts can take a 50km to 60km looping bike route from Leiden through the bulbfields and Keukenhof Gardens that ends at the beach.

Bootjes en Broodjes   BOATING

(www.bootjesenbroodjes.nl; Blauwpoortsbrug 1; electric boat rental per hr €45, canal tours adult/child €8.50/4.50; ☺10am-6pm Apr-Oct) As the name implies, you can get snacks to go with your voyage. Rent a quiet electric boat or join a tour. Private tours available.

Botenverhuur 't Galgewater   BOATING

(Boat Hire Galgewater; www.galgewater.nl; Galgewater 44a; per hr from €6 ; ☺noon-7pm mid-Apr–Sep) Rent a canoe or kayak from Botenverhuur 't Galgewater and explore the canals.

☞ Tours

You can take three-hour cruises of the waterways and lakes around Leiden. Ask the tourist office for details.

Rederij Rembrandt   BOAT TOUR

(☑513 49 38; www.rederij-rembrandt.nl; Beestenmarkt; adult/child €10/6.50; ☺tours 11am-4pm Mar-Oct) There are leisurely one-hour canal boat tours of the channel around the old town centre with Rederij Rembrandt with commentary (English available).

✨ Festivals & Events

Leidens Ontzet   FESTIVAL

Leiden grinds to a halt on 3 October for Leidens Ontzet, commemorating the day the Spanish-caused starvation ended in 1574. The revelry is undiminished more than four centuries later, and there is much eating of the ceremonial *hutspot,* herring and white

bread. A beer-fueled time is had by all – especially the night before.

🛏 Sleeping

TOP CHOICE **Hotel Nieuw Minerva**   HOTEL **$$**

(☑512 63 58; www.hotelleiden.com; Boommarkt 23; s/d from €75/80; @🖥) Located in six 16th-century canalside houses, this central hotel has a mix of 40 regular (ie nothing special) and some very fun themed rooms, including a room with a bed in which King Lodewijk Bonaparte (aka Louis Bonaparte) slept. We prefer the thematic 'room of angels', a luminous vision of white.

Hotel de Doelen   HOTEL **$$**

(☑512 05 27; www.dedoelen.com; Rapenburg 2; s/d from €85/105; @🖥) It has a slightly faded air of classical elegance; some canalside rooms in this regal building are larger and better appointed than others. There are 128 rooms overall, some on the ground floor.

Rembrandt Hotel   HOTEL **$$**

(☑514 42 33; www.rembrandthotel.nl; Nieuw Beestenmarkt 10; r €90-130; @) Light pouring in the windows makes the white decor of the 20 rooms that much brighter at this historic but well-cared-for inn. Rooms have high-speed internet and work desks, although the furniture is dated.

Pension Witte Singel   GUESTHOUSE **$**

(☑512 45 92; www.pension-ws.demon.nl; Witte Singel 80; r €50-100; @🖥) Seven bright rooms (some sharing bathrooms) with large windows overlooking agreeable scenery: the perfectly peaceful Singel canal at the front and a typically Dutch garden out the back. Breakfast is included.

Hotel Mayflower   HOTEL **$$**

(☑514 26 41; www.hotelmayflower.nl; Beestenmarkt 2; s/d from €75/95) The 25 large rooms are bright but are something of a throwback to another era of lodging – say the 1980s. But the hotel is well located and a short walk from the station. Apartments are also available. Good breakfast buffet.

🍴 Eating

TOP CHOICE **De Dames Proeverij**   CAFE **$$**

(www.proeverijdedames.nl; Nieuwe Rijn 37; meals €12-20) Run by two women who have excellent taste, this cafe seems to have just what you want at any time of day. There is an excellent range of coffee drinks as well

HOLLAND'S BEST RAW HERRING

In 1989, two Turkish brothers started a fish stand, **Vishandel Atlantic** (www.vishandelatlantic.nl; Levendaal 118; fishy treats from €3; ☺9am-6pm). Since then their fanatical attention to quality has propelled them to the top ranks of seafood vendors in the Netherlands. Their raw herring scores 10 out of 10 in contests where 5.5 is considered a good score. They also sell all types of smoked fish and you can try them all, plus simple meals such as fish and chips. The corner location is a 10-minute walk southeast from St Pancraskerk.

as dozens of top wines by the glass. Enjoy your sips at the tables out the front overlooking the canal. House-made baked goods are treats and there is a long list of small plates for nibbling, sharing or combining into a meal. Desserts are also good.

Mangerie De Jonge Koekop　　BISTRO $$$
(Lange Mare 60; mains from €20-25; ☺dinner Mon-Sat) Always popular, this bistro has fresh and inventive fare. Dine under the stars at outside tables in summer. Look for the sculpted cow's head on the front, which is as narrow as the first stalk of spring asparagus. Dishes change seasonally.

Fresh 'n Fast　　CAFE $
(www.freshnfast.nl; Kloksteeg 7; mains €8-12; ☺5pm-midnight) A fabulous find near Pieterskerk, everything here is sourced from the best local and organic producers. The cheeses are from famous nearby dairies. Salads, burgers, hot dishes, pasta, soup and much more fill the appealing menu. Get a bench at a table out the front.

De Brasserie de Engelenbak　　CONTEMPORARY DUTCH $$
(www.brasseriedeengelenbak.nl; Lange Mare 38; lunch €6-9, menus from €32; ☺noon-4pm & 5-10pm) Right in the shadow of the 17th-century octagonal Marekerk, this elegant bistro serves a seasonally changing menu of fresh fare that takes its cues from across the continent. Local organic produce features in many of the dishes. Tables outside enjoy views of the hoi polloi. An adjoining cafe serves snacks until midnight.

Het Koetshuis　　CAFE $$
(www.koetshuisdeburcht.nl; Burgsteeg 13; mains €15-20) On a sunny day, it's hard to beat the terrace tables just outside the grand Burcht gate, where all of humankind gathers for an afternoon coffee or *borrel* (alcoholic drink of your choice).

Oudt Leyden　　PANCAKES $
(Steenstrat 49; pancakes €6-13; ☺11.30am-9.30pm; 🚼) Get ready to meet giant Dutch-style pancakes with creative fillings that make kids and adults alike go wide-eyed and giddy. Whether you're feeling savoury (marinated salmon, sour cream and capers), sweet (warm cherries and vanilla ice cream) or simply adventurous (ginger and bacon, anyone?), this cafe hits the spot every time.

🍷 Drinking

De Dames Proeverij (p151) and Het Koetshuis (p152) are good for a drink, as well as a snack.

TOP CHOICE Café L'Esperance　　BROWN CAFE
(www.lesperance.nl; Kaiserstraat 1) Long, dark and handsome, all decked out in nostalgic wood panelling and overlooking an evocative bend in the canal. Tables abound outside in summer; it has good meals too.

☆ Entertainment

Café de WW　　LIVE MUSIC
(www.deww.nl; Wolsteeg 4) On Friday and Saturday, live rock in this glossy scarlet bar can expand to an impromptu stage in the alley with crowds trailing up to the main street. On other nights there's a DJ. Though the emphasis is on the music, there's a great beer selection.

Hunky Dory　　LIVE MUSIC
(☎514 63 86; Vrouwensteeg 6) Locals swarm to this cool music bar to see some of the best touring bands from Holland and beyond. Music ranges from jazz to rock 'n' roll.

🛍 Shopping

Haarlemmerstraat has all the mainstream chain stores. Big department stores spill across to Breestraat. Look for more interesting shops on side streets such as Vrouwenstraat and in the lanes around Pieterskerk.

Mayflower Bookshop BOOKSHOP
(www.themayflowerbookshop.nl; Hogewoerd 107)
Compact selection of new and used classics,
fine fiction and travel guides.

❶ Information

Stationsweg has numerous banks and ATMs.

Internet Access

Centrale Bibliotheek (Central Library; Nieuwstraat; internet per hour €3, free wi-fi; ⊙10am-
6pm; 🛜)

Telecom (Steenstraat; internet per hour €2)
Cheap calls.

Tourist Information

Tourist Office (☑516 60 00; www.vvvleiden.nl;
Stationsweg 41; ⊙8am-6pm Mon-Fri, 10am-
4pm Sat, 11am-5pm Sun) Across from the train
station, this office has good maps and historic
info.

❶ Getting There & Away

Bicycle

The **bike shop** in Centraal Station is on the west
side.

Head west from the station on bike paths
along Geversstraat and then via Rijnsburg for
10km to the beach at Katwijk. There you can
pick up national route **LF1**, which connects with
the **LF20** for the 34km ride north to Haarlem.
Head south on the **LF1** 20km along the shore to
Scheveningen and Den Haag.

Bus

Regional and local buses leave from the **bus station** directly in front of Centraal Station.

Train

Centraal Station (Train Station) is bold and
modern. It has full services and many shops;
lockers are up near platform No 1. Sample fares
and schedules in the box below.

❶ Getting Around

Leiden is compact and you'll have a hard time
walking for more than 20 minutes in any one
direction.

Around Leiden

This is the very heart of Holland's tulip-
growing land. In spring you may get lucky
and fly over the impossibly brightly coloured
fields as you land a Schiphol. It's definitely
worth getting a bike and touring the region
from either Leiden, Haarlem or the gardens
themselves.

LISSE

Located 1km east of Keukenhof Gardens, the
tourist office (☑0252-414 262; www.vvvlisse.nl;
Grachtweg 53a; ⊙noon-5pm Mon, 9am-5pm Tue-
Fri, 9am-4pm Sat) in the village of Lisse can
give you many options for bulbfield touring. Also in town, the small **Museum de
Zwarte Tulp** (Museum of the Black Tulip; ☑0252-
417 900; www.museumdezwartetulp.nl; Grachtweg
2a; adult/child €5/3; ⊙1-5pm Tue-Sun) displays
everything you might want to know about
bulbs, including why there's no such thing
as a black tulip, a mythical posy that helped
drive Tulipmania in 1636.

Den Haag (The Hague)

☑ 070 / POP 501,000

Den Haag is a stately, regal place filled with
palatial embassies and mansions, green
boulevards and parks, a brilliant culinary
scene, a clutch of fine museums and a syba-
ritic cafe culture. It's the kind of place where
the musky aftershave of suave men wearing
pink cravats mingles with the frilly scents
of sachets sold in pricey boutiques. More
elemental, the seaside suburb of Scheveningen boasts lively kitsch and a long stretch
of beach.

Den Haag, officially known as 's-Graven-
hage (the Count's Hedge), is the Dutch seat
of government and home to the royal family. Prior to 1806, Den Haag was the Dutch
capital. However, that year, Louis Bonaparte
installed his government in Amsterdam.
Eight years later, when the French had been
ousted, the government returned to Den

ROTTERDAM & SOUTH HOLLAND AROUND LEIDEN

TRAINS FROM LEIDEN

DESTINATION	PRICE (€)	DURATION (MIN)	FREQUENCY (PER HR)
Amsterdam	8	34	6
Den Haag	3.50	10	6
Schiphol Airport	6	15	6

Den Haag (The Hague) Centre

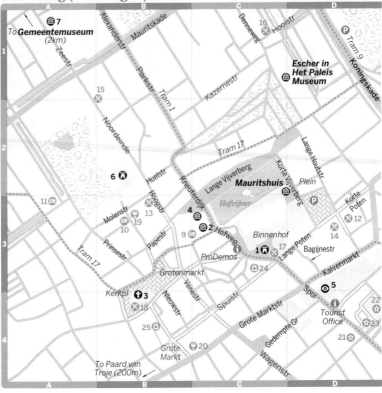

Den Haag (The Hague) Centre

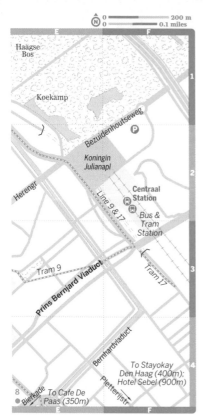

Girl with a Pearl Earring. Rembrandts include a wistful self-portrait from the year of his death, 1669, and *The Anatomy Lesson of Dr Nicolaes Tulp*.

The building was constructed as a mansion in 1640 in classical style; all its dimensions are roughly the same (25m), and the detailing shows exquisite care. In 1822 it was made the home of the royal collection. The collection is displayed in 16 rooms on two floors – almost every work is a masterpiece.

Even if you're just passing Den Haag on the train, it's well worth hopping off to visit.

Binnenhof   PALACE

(☉10am-4pm Mon-Sat) The Binnenhof is surrounded by parliamentary buildings that have long been at the heart of Dutch politics, though parliament now meets in a modern building on the south side.

The central courtyard looks sterile today but was once used for executions. A highlight of the complex is the 13th-century **Ridderzaal** (admission €4; ☉10am-4pm Mon-Sat). The Gothic dining hall has been carefully restored.

The North Wing is still home to the Upper Chamber of the Dutch Parliament, in 17th-century splendour. The Lower Chamber used to meet in the ballroom, in the 19th-century wing. It all looks a bit twee and you can see why the politicians were anxious to decamp to the sleek new extension nearby.

To see the Binnenhof buildings you will need to join a tour. **ProDemos** (www.prodemos.nl; Hofweg 1; Ridderzaal tours €4, government tours €6; ☉10am-5pm Mon-Sat, 11am-4pm Sun) is the visitor organisation for the government centre that is also charged with promoting democracy. It leads the **Ridderzaal tour** (€4; ☉10am-4pm Mon-Sat) as well as various **government tours** (from €6; ☉schedule varies, usually Mon-Sat mornings) that take in the two chambers of parliament.

After your walk, stroll around the **Hofvijver**, where the reflections of the Binnenhof and the Mauritshuis have inspired countless snapshots.

Museum de Gevangenpoort   MUSEUM

(Museum of Prison Gate; www.gevangenpoort.nl; Buitenhof 33; adult/child €7.50/5.50; ☉10am-5pm Tue-Fri, noon-5pm Sat & Sun) Across the Hof-vijver from the Binnenhof, the Gevangenpoort is a surviving remnant of the 13th-century city fortifications. It has hourly tours showing how justice was dispensed

Haag, but the title of capital remained with Amsterdam.

In the 20th century Den Haag became the home of several international legal entities, including the UN's International Court of Justice, which regularly holds trials that put Den Haag in the headlines.

◉ Sights

Den Haag has no true city centre; instead you'll find there are several areas of concentration, including the Binnenhof and the nearby Kerkplein. All are easily reached by tram or bike.

TOP CHOICE Mauritshuis   MUSEUM

(www.mauritshuis.nl; Korte Vijverberg 8; adult/child €13.50/free; ☉11am-5pm Tue-Sun) For a painless introduction to Dutch and Flemish Art 101, visit the Mauritshuis, a small museum in a jewel-box of an old palace. Highlights include the Dutch *Mona Lisa*: Vermeer's

ROTTERDAM & SOUTH HOLLAND DEN HAAG (THE HAGUE)

KEUKENHOF GARDENS

Covering some 32 hectares, the **Keukenhof Gardens** (www.keukenhof.nl; adult/child €15/7.50, parking €6; ☺8am-7.30pm mid-Mar–mid-May, last entry 6pm) are the world's largest bulb-flower extravaganza, attracting 800,000 visitors during a mere eight weeks every year.

The gardens stretch on and on, and there are greenhouses full of more delicate varieties of flowers besides the ephemeral tulips. You'll forgive the presence of thousands of other tourists – little can detract from the rainbow of natural beauty. Wandering about can easily take half a day. From the edges of the gardens, you can see the stark beauty of the commercial bulbfields stretching in all directions.

Opening dates vary slightly from year to year, so check before setting out. Buses 50 and 54 travel from Leiden Centraal Station to Keukenhof (30 minutes, four times per hour). All tickets can be purchased online, which helps avoid huge queues. The gardens are 4km inland from the coastal national bike route LF1. You'll need a map.

Bicycles (€10) can be rented at the gardens to explore the posy-filled region. You can also take a 50km to 60km looping bike route from Leiden through the bulbfields and Keukenhof Gardens that ends at the beach.

back in the day and new displays bathe the torture tools in radiant light.

Galerij Prins Willem V
GALLERY

(www.mauritshuis.nl; Buitenhof 35; adult/child €5/2.50; ☺noon-5pm Tue-Sun) Part of the Gevangenpoort complex, this gallery was the first public museum in the Netherlands when it opened in 1773. Paintings (including ones by Steen and Rubens) are hung in the manner popular in the 18th century.

Grote Kerk
CHURCH

(Rond de Grote Kerk 12) The Grote Kerk, dating from 1450, has a fine pulpit that was constructed 100 years later. The neighbouring 1565 **old town hall** (*oude raadhuis*) is a splendid example of Dutch Renaissance architecture.

New Town Hall
ARCHITECTURE

(Spui 170) The huge modern town hall is the hotly debated work by US architect Richard Meier. The 'official' nickname of the building is the 'white swan', but locals prefer the 'ice palace'.

Paleis Noordeinde
PALACE

The king's and queen's official quarters at Paleis Noordeinde is not open to the public. The Renaissance formality of the structure bespeaks regal digs.

Escher in Het Paleis Museum
MUSEUM

(www.escherinhetpaleis.nl; Lange Voorhout 74; adult/child €8.50/6; ☺11am-5pm Tue-Sun) The Lange Voorhout Palace was once Queen Emma's residence. Now it's home to the work

of Dutch graphic artist MC Escher. The permanent exhibition features notes, letters, drafts, photos and fully mature works covering Escher's entire career, from his early realism to the later phantasmagoria. There are some imaginative displays, including a virtual reality reconstruction of Escher's impossible buildings.

Gemeentemuseum
ART MUSEUM

(Municipal Museum; www.gemeentemuseum.nl; Stadhouderslaan 41; adult/child €13.50/free; ☺11am-5pm Tue-Sun) Admirers of De Stijl, and in particular of Piet Mondrian, mustn't miss the Berlage-designed Gemeentemuseum. It houses a large collection of works by neoplasticist artists and others from the late 19th century, as well as extensive exhibits of applied arts, costumes and musical instruments.

Mondrian's unfinished *Victory Boogie Woogie* takes pride of place (as it should: the museum paid €30 million for it), and there are also a few Picassos and other works by some of the better-known names of the 20th century. Take tram 17 from CS and HS.

Madurodam
AMUSEMENT PARK

(www.madurodam.nl; George Maduroplein 1; adult/child €15/11; ☺9am-7pm) Complete with 1:25 scale versions of Schiphol, Amsterdam, windmills and tulips, Rotterdam harbour and the Delta dykes, Madurodam is a miniaturised Netherlands. It's an enlightening example of the Dutch tendency to put their world under a microscope. It reopened in

2012 after a large expansion added many more tiny things. Kids love it.

Take tram 9 from CS and HS.

Photography Museum   MUSEUM
(Foto-Museum Den Haag; www.fotomuseumden haag.nl; Stadhouderslaan 43; adult/child €6/free; ⊙noon-6pm Tue-Sun) Adjoining the Gemeentemuseum, the Photography Museum has several major exhibitions a year.

Panorama Mesdag   GALLERY
(www.panorama-mesdag.com; Zeestraat 65; adult/child €8.50/4.50; ⊙10am-5pm Mon-Sat, noon-5pm Sun) Just past the north end of Noordeinde, the Panorama Mesdag contains the *Panorama* (1881), a huge 360-degree painting of Scheveningen that was painted by Hendrik Willem Mesdag. The panorama is viewed from a constructed dune, with real sand and beach chairs; birdsong and wave sounds are piped through. Masterful achievement aside, you could just head 4km west to the real thing.

Vredespaleis   HISTORIC SITE
(Peace Palace; www.vredespaleis.nl; Carnegieplein 2; visitor centre admision free, tours adult/child €8.50/free; ⊙10am-5pm Tue-Sun) The UN International Court of Justice is housed in the Vredespaleis. The grand building was donated by American steelmaker Andrew Carnegie for use by the International Court of Arbitration, an early international body whose goal was the prevention of war, which proved elusive as WWI broke out one year after it opened in 1913.

A new **visitor centre** details the work of the organisations within. Hour-long guided tours are sometimes offered, but if the courts are in session they are cancelled –

check first; you need to book ahead (security is strict). Take tram 1 from HS.

SCHEVENINGEN

The long **beach** at Scheveningen, pronounced – if possible – as s'CHay-fuh-ninger, attracts nine million visitors per year. It's horribly developed: architects who lost hospital commissions have designed all manner of modern nightmares overlooking the strand. Scads of cafes elbow each other for space on tiers of promenades by the beach, their themes taken from resorts with more reliable weather worldwide. It's tacky, but you might just find pleasure in the carnival atmosphere.

Better yet, you can escape to wide-open beaches and nature with just a bit of effort, especially to the south where the hype tapers off as you pass the harbour.

Most Den Haag streets heading west reach Scheveningen, 4km away, but it's more pleasantly approached at the end of a 15- to 20-minute bike ride that will take you past the lush homes of some of the most well-heeled residents.

Tours

The tourist office offers excellent walking and cycling guides (€2) in English with a variety of themes, including 'The Royal Kilometres'.

De Ooievaart   BOAT TOUR
(☑445 18 69; www.ooievaart.nl; Bierkade 18b; adult/child €10/6; ⊙Tue-Sun May-Sep, Mon-Sun Jul & Aug) Offers boat tours over various 1½-hour routes, taking in Den Haag's most interesting sights at canal level. Confirm times in advance.

WORTH A TRIP

ESCAPE TO THE DUNES

Open sand, endless beach, hillocks of dunes, the sounds of seagulls and shore; all this is easily accessible from Den Haag and Scheveningen.

To the south, a mere 1km past the harbour puts you in the heart of nature. From here you can continue along the coast for pretty much as long as you've got the fortitude, with only the odd simple beach cafe for relief. Take tram 12 from Hollands Spoor station (HS) to the end of the line right in the heart of the dunes.

Heading north, follow the beach past the end of tram lines 1 and 9. Here the dunes are pristine and the further you walk or cycle, the greater the rewards. You'll also pass a series of WWII bunkers, part of the Nazi Atlantic Wall defence system and an eerie reminder of the Netherlands' place in European history.

National bike route LF1 follows the coast throughout the region. Tellingly, it only diverts inland near Scheveningen when it passes through parks to avoid the chaos.

✨ Festivals & Events

Parkpop MUSIC
(www.parkpop.nl) Parkpop in late June draws some 350,000 pop-music fans to town for free concerts by big names in Zuiderpark.

🛏 Sleeping

Besides chains, Den Haag has some interesting smaller hotels scattered around its sprawl. There are numerous beachfront possibilities in Scheveningen.

TOP CHOICE Het Paleis Hotel LUXURY HOTEL $$$
(362 46 21; www.paleishotel.nl; Molenstraat 26; r from €200; ❄@📶) Near the Noordeinde palace, its location alone is atmospheric, but the antique trimmings in the room match it superbly. The 20 rooms are traditionally luxurious with thick drapes and carpet that will swallow your toes. Fabric patterns are unique to the hotel and richly elegant.

Hotel Sebel BOUTIQUE HOTEL $$
(385 92 00; www.hotelsebel.nl; Prins Hendrikplein 20; r €80-150; 📶) This 33-room boutique hotel is in a proud art nouveau corner building. Everything has been tastefully updated and the lobby is downright minimalist. The cheapest rooms let you touch the walls – all at once. It's on tram line 17 from CS and HS.

Hotel La Ville HOTEL $$
(346 36 57; www.hotellaville.nl; Veenkade 5-6; r €50-120; 📶) The 21 rooms here are the best deal close to the centre. The decor is a minimalist white, grey and maroon; some rooms share bathrooms. Apartments have basic cooking facilities and there's a small cafe. Book ahead.

Corona Hotel HOTEL $$
(363 79 30; www.corona.nl; Buitenhof 39-42; r from €110-180; ❄@📶) This pleasant hotel is across from the Binnenhof and is located in three vintage townhouses, which were renovated in 2011. It has all the usual business facilities and amenities. The 36 rooms span a range of styles that mix classic details with modernity.

Boulevard Hotel HOTEL $$
(354 00 67; www.boulevardhotel.nl; Seinpostduin 1, Scheveningen; r €85-150; 📶) A classic old beach hotel that's more attractive than its modern neighbours, the Boulevard is unpretentious. Rooms are seashore simple, but you can take your breakfast in the conservatory or patio with views down to the surf.

Stayokay Den Haag HOSTEL $
(315 78 88; www.stayokay.com; Scheepmakerstraat 27; dm from €25, r from €66; @📶) This branch of the Stayokay hostel chain has all the usual facilities, including a bar, a restaurant, internet and games. It's around 15 minutes' walk from HS station.

🍴 Eating

Den Haag's gastronomic scene is very good, with quality matched by the variety you'd expect in an international city. The cobbled streets and canals off Denneweg are a excellent place to stroll hungry.

An **organic farmers market** (Hofmarkt; ⊙11am-6pm Wed) offers a dazling array of local foods including a stall selling excellent crêpes.

TOP CHOICE Bloem CAFE $
(www.bloemdenhaag.nl; Korte Houtstraat 6; mains €5-8; ⊙10am-6pm Mon-Sat) A cute little cafe across the Plein from the Binnenhof. There are white tables, chairs and flowers out the front. House-made tartes are superb and sandwiches include a tasty club. Smoothies will give you a dose of healthy goodness. Stop by for afternoon high tea.

Les Ombrelles SEAFOOD $$$
(365 87 89; www.lesombrelles.nl; Hooistraat 4; mains €15-30; ⊙lunch Mon-Fri, dinner Mon-Sat) At a confluence of canals in one of the city's most charming districts, this long-running favourite sets up tables across the shady plaza. The tank with live crabs tells you that this is seafood country and the very long menu abounds with choice.

Brasserie 't Ogenblik BISTRO $$
(Molenstraat 4c; mains €6-15) Servers zip about at this ever-popular cafe at the confluence of several pedestrianised shopping streets (in summer, tables are set up along voyeur-friendly Hoogstraat). Coffees and teas offer refreshment, and a creative line-up of salads, sandwiches, soups and more offer sustenance.

Zebedeüs CAFE $
(Rond de Grote Kerk 8; meals from €8) Built right into the walls of the Grote Kerk, this bright cafe is a day tripper's dream, with huge, fresh sandwiches served all day. Grab one of the many chestnut-tree-shaded tables

outside or relax with a coffee and a newspaper at the big tables within.

Cloos GRAND CAFE **$$**
(☑363 97 86; Plein 12a; mains from €9) One of a gaggle of swank cafes on the vast Plein. Rest your gentrified butt on the comfy wicker chairs and watch the pigeons bedevil the solemn statue of Willem the Silent, hero of the Spanish war. No telling what the famous nationalist would have thought about Cloos' Italian menu.

It Rains Fishes SEAFOOD **$$$**
(☑365 25 98; www.itrainsfishes.nl; Noordeinde 123; mains from €22; ☉noon-2.30pm Mon-Fri, 6-11pm Mon-Sat) It's the 'restaurant on the sunny side of the street', a multi-award-winning seafood place serving grilled, fried and poached fish, mussels and scallops. The menu reflects what's fresh.

Mero BISTRO **$$$**
(☑352 36 00; www.merovis.nl; Vissershavenweg 61, Scheveningen; mains €20-30; ☉noon-2pm, 6-9.30pm Wed-Fri, 3-9.30pm Sat & Sun) Industrial chic is the style at this harbourside brasserie serving the best fish in the area. The bold crustacean art on the walls is matched by the bold flavours on the plate. Near tram 11.

🍷 Drinking

Cafe De Paas BAR
(www.depaas.nl; Dunne Bierkade 16a) A highly atmospheric old bar with a huge selection of Dutch, Belgian and other beers. The 17 taps rotate often and unusual seasonal beers are offered. Sit outside on a canalboat.

De Zwarte Ruiter GRAND CAFE
(The Black Rider; Grote Markt 27; snacks from €4) The Rider faces off with the competing Boterwaag across the Markt like rival kings of cool. We call this one the winner, with its terrace and art deco mezzanine – light-filled, split-level and cavernous – and boisterous crowds of commoners, diplomats and, no doubt, the odd international jewel thief.

Café De Oude Mol BROWN CAFE
(Oude Molstraat 61; snacks from €3) Some of the *oude* (old) *National Geographics* piled in the window actually predate the crusty yet genial characters arrayed around the bar. Pass through the ivy-covered door and you'll find Den Haag without the pretence.

Strandclub Doen BAR
(Strandweg 9, Scheveningen; ☉May-Sep; ☎) A vision of white, Doen is one of the least tacky of the plethora of beach bars lining the sands. Palm trees shivering in the North Sea breeze add atmosphere to sofas, loungers and other good chillin' and drinkin' spots. Some tables have charcoal fires for warmth.

☆ Entertainment

TOP CHOICE Paard van Troje CLUB
(www.paard.nl; Prinsegracht 12) This emporium has club nights and live music, as well as a cafe. The program's eclectic: everything from booty-shaking DJs to cutting-edge State-X New Forms.

Nederlands Dans Theater DANCE
(www.ndt.nl; Schedeldoekshaven 60) This world-famous dance company has two main components: NDT1, the main troupe of 32 dancers; and NDT2, a small group of 12 dancers under 21. The company is slowly emerging from the vast creative legacy of Jiří Kylián.

Cinematheek Haags Filmhuis CINEMA
(☑365 60 30; www.filmhuisdenhaag.nl; Spui 191) Screens foreign and indie movies.

Dr Anton Philipszaal VENUE
(☑360 98 10; www.dapz.ldt.nl; Spui 150) Home to the Residentie Orkest, Den Haag's classical symphony orchestra.

🛍 Shopping

Den Haag is brilliant for shopping, with several good districts for browsing.

Grote Marktstraat is, fittingly enough, where you'll find all the major department stores and chains. Going north things get much more interesting.

Hoogstraat, Noordeinde and Huelstraat are all good for interesting and eclectic shops and galleries. But the real treats are along Prinsestraat.

Denneweg is celebrated for its off-beat boutiques, with some fine antique galleries and shops. Wander north over a canal and the street becomes Frederikstraat, with some excellent delis and bakeries.

De Passage ARCADE
(www.depassage.nl; cnr Spuistraat & Hofweg) De Passage, off Hofweg ad Spuistraat, is a 19th-century covered arcade built to give locals an option for luxury goods from Paris.

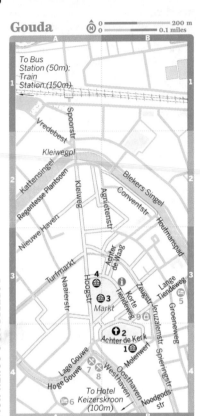

Gouda

Stanley & Livingstone BOOKS
(☏365 73 06; Schoolstraat 21) An excellent travel bookshop.

❶ Information

Tourist Office (VVV; www.scheveningenden haag.com; Spui 68; ◷10am-8pm Mon-Fri, to 5pm Sat, noon-5pm Sun; ☏) On the ground floor of the public library in the landmark New Toen Hall, this large office covers both Den Haag and Scheveningen.

❶ Getting There & Away

Bicycle

The **bicycle shop** (☏385 32 35) in CS is under the terminal. The HS **bicycle shop** (☏389 08 30) is at the southern end of that station. Both shops rent out bikes. The coastal national bike route **LF1** runs just inland of Scheveningen. Leiden can be reached by going 20 miles north and heading inland. **LF11** runs southeast 11km to Delft.

Bus

Eurolines long-distance buses and regional buses depart from the **bus and tram station** above the tracks at CS.

Train

Den Haag has two main train stations. **Centraal Station** (CS) – a terminus – is close to the centre. It is a hub for local trams and buses (and is under long-term reconstruction). **Hollandes Spoor Train Station** (HS) is about 1km south of the centre and is on the main railway line between Amsterdam and Rotterdam. Both have lockers and a full array of services.

Den Haag is meant to have high-speed Fyra rail services via Rotterdam, once that service starts running. Current sample train services opposite.

❶ Getting Around

Most tram routes converge on Centraal Station (CS), at the tram and bus station above the tracks and on the western side. A number of routes also serve Hollandes Spoor station (HS), including the jack-of-all-trades tram 1, which starts in Scheveningen and runs all the way to Delft, passing through the centre of Den Haag along the way. Trams 1, 9 and 11 link Scheveningen with Den Haag. The last tram runs in either direction at about 1.30am.

Den Haag is spread over a fairly large area. CS is near the heart of town; HS, on the main line from Amsterdam to Rotterdam and destinations further south, is 1km south of the town centre.

Tram and bus operator **HTM** (www.htm.net; single ride €2.50, day pass adult/child €7.50/5) sells a highly useful day pass, but you can only buy it from windows with often-long lines in CS and HS. There are no ticket machines.

Call **ATC Taxi** (☎317 88 77) for a cab.

Gouda

☎ 0182 / POP 71,200

Gouda's association with cheese comestibles has made it famous – the town's namesake fermented curd is among the Netherlands' best-known exports. But Gouda, the town, has a lot more to it than that.

Gouda enjoyed economic success and decline in the same manner as the rest of Holland from the 16th century onwards. Its cheese has brought recent wealth, as has the country's largest candle factory, which stays busy supplying all those Dutch brown cafes. The acclaimed 16th-century stained-glass windows in its church are a highlight.

Gouda makes a fine day trip, easily accessible from any city in South Holland or Amsterdam. The compact centre is entirely ringed by canals and is a mere five minutes' walk from the station.

◎ Sights

Most of the notable sights are within 10 minutes' walk of the trapezoidal Markt, but wander off down little side streets such as Achter de Kerk and Lage Gouwe, which pass quiet canals and seem untouched by the centuries. Or try the Lange Tiendeweg and Zeugstraat with its tiny canal and even tinier bridges.

MARKT

The central Markt is one of the largest such squares in the Netherlands. It is the focus of the old Gouda.

TOP CHOICE Waag   HISTORIC BUILDING

On the north side of the Markt, you can't miss the Waag, a former cheese-weighing house built in 1668. If you have any doubt about its use, check out the reliefs carved into the side showing the cheese being weighed. It houses the Kaaswaag (www.goudsewaag.nl; adult/child €4/3.50; ⊙1-5pm Tue-Sun Apr-Oct, Thu-Sun Nov-Mar), a museum that follows the history of the cheese trade in the Netherlands, especially its history in Gouda. There is also a cool model of the Markt c 1990.

Cheese Market   MARKET

(www.goudakaas.nl; ⊙10am-12.30pm Thu late Jun-Aug) A traditional cheese market on the Markt draws plenty of tourists and there are dozens of stalls selling dairy goods and souvenirs. A few locals dress up in costume and pose for countless photos.

Town Hall   HISTORIC BUILDING

(Markt; admission €1.50; ⊙10am-4pm Mon-Fri, 11am-3pm Sat) Right in the middle of the Markt is the mid-15th-century town hall. Constructed from shimmering sandstone, this regal Gothic structure bespeaks the wealth Gouda enjoyed from the cloth trade when it was built. The red-and-white shutters provide a fine counterpoint to the carefully maintained stonework. The ceremonial rooms inside are worth a look.

SINT JANSKERK & AROUND

Sint Janskerk   CHURCH

(Achter de Kerk; adult/child €4.50/2; ⊙10am-5pm) Just to the south of the Markt is Sint Janskerk. The church itself had chequered beginnings: it burned down with ungodly regularity every 100 years or so from 1361 until the mid-16th century, when what you see today was completed. At 123m it is the longest church in the country.

Architecturally, Sint Janskerk is an attractive late-Gothic church in need of a better steeple, but its huge windows set it apart, especially those created by Dirck Crabeth, his brother Wouter, and Lambert van Noort from around 1550 to 1570. Their works,

TRAINS FROM DEN HAAG (THE HAGUE)

DESTINATION	PRICE (€)	DURATION (MIN)	FREQUENCY (PER HR)
Amsterdam	11	50	4
Leiden	3.50	15	4
Rotterdam	5	25	4
Schiphol	8	30	4
Utrecht	10	40	4

TRAINS FROM GOUDA

DESTINATION	PRICE (€)	DURATION (MIN)	FREQUENCY (PER HR)
Amsterdam	11	55	2
Den Haag	6	20	4
Rotterdam	5	19	6
Utrecht	6	20	6

which are numbered, include highlights such as window No 6 (John the Baptist; the folks on either side paid for the window) and No 22 (Jesus purifies the temple; note the look on the face of the moneychanger).

Museum Gouda   MUSEUM
(www.museumgouda.nl; Achter de Kerk 14; adult/child €7/free; ☺10am-5pm Wed-Fri, noon-5pm Sat & Sun) To the immediate southwest of the Sint Janskerk church and near a small canal, the city museum is housed in an old hospital, Catherina Gasthuis. It covers Gouda's history and has a few artworks. In the basement there's a ghoulish section on local torture in the Middle Ages, including devices for the condemned (men were hanged but women were strangled to avoid people looking up their skirts). Outside, there's a nice walled garden.

Activities

There's a good circle ride through, well, the heart of the region, which bills itself as the Groene Hart (Green Heart). It begins just south of the centre and runs 42km through the canal-laced farmlands south of Gouda. Called the Krimpenerwaard Route after the region it covers, it includes stops at dairies where cheese is made. Get the brochure from the tourist office, which can also help with the detailed maps needed for the ride.

🛏 Sleeping

Given that Gouda is such a natural day trip, you might not think of staying here, but you may just appreciate its charms more after the buses are gone.

Hotel Keizerskroon   HOTEL $$
(☑528 096; www.hotelkeizerskroon.nl; Keizerstraat 11-13; r €50-110; ☜) Centrally located, cosy, comfortable, warm and welcoming (with attractive rooms with contemporary decor). The cheapest rooms share showers and you can rent bikes. Take your included breakfast in the restaurant at ground level.

Hotel de Utrechtsche Dom   HOTEL $
(☑528 833; www.hotelgouda.nl; Geuzenstraat 6; r €65-85; ☜) Neat, clean and on a quiet street, this is a lovely, low-key place to stay, with good amenities. Breakfast is included, the cheapest rooms share bathrooms. The complex has been an inn for more than 300 years, although the stables get little use from coachmen these days.

Eating & Drinking

Lekker Gouds   DELI $
(Hoogstraat; snacks from €3; ☺10am-6pm) An appealing deli right off the Markt, it's run by a longtime local cafe owner. There's a vast array of cheeses – try your old Gouda here, or create a picnic.

Kamphuisen   BROWN CAFE $$
(☑514 163; www.kamphuisen.com; Hoge Gouwe 19; mains €16-20; ☺5pm-midnight Tue-Sun, kitchen till 10pm) As brown a cafe as you'll find: a blackboard of drinks overlooks ancient wooden tables and light fixtures. Outside, there are tables under the eaves of the old fish market. The bar menu is ambitious: lamb, steak, fish and more. Book for dinner.

Scheeps   SEAFOOD $$
(☑517 572; www.restaurantscheeps.nl; Westhaven 4; mains €19-25; ☺noon-2.30pm & 5-9pm Mon-Sat) The flawless cream facade and potted olive trees suggest this place is special, and it is. The dining room is lined with art and features a contemporary menu of seasonal items prepared with a Mediterranean flair. Nice garden out the back, too.

Brunel   BISTRO $$
(☑518 979; www.restaurantbrunel.nl; Hoge Gouwe 23; mains €18-23; ☺dinner Tue-Sat) Classic top-end Dutch fare with a few creative twists: Look for produce and seafood of the region used as both mains and accents plus the odd truffle here and there. In summer, dine along the canal in the old colonnaded fish market.

Shopping

Kleiweg on the way from the train station has the usual chains. Better are the idiosyncratic shops in and around Jeruzalemstraat and Zeugstraat. Did we mention you can buy cheese?

Lekker Gouds (p162) is also a good cheesy stop.

TOP CHOICE 't Kaaswinkeltje   CHEESE
(www.kaaswinkeltje.com; Lange Tiendeweg 30) A cheese shop filled with fabulous smells; it's here that you can sample some of the aged Goudas that the Dutch wisely keep for themselves. The older the cheese, the sharper the flavour: some of the very old Goudas have a Parmesan-like texture and a rich, smoky taste. With a little mustard smeared on, a hunk is great with beer. Also try the locally made farm-style soft cheeses.

ⓘ Information

Tourist Office (VVV; ☏0182-589 110; www.welkomingouda.nl; Waag, Markt 35; ◷10am-6pm Apr-Oct, reduced hours in winter) In the historic Waag with the cheese museum and shop; sample cheese while you browse brochures.

ⓘ Getting There & Around

Gouda's **train station** is close to the city centre and all you'll need are your feet for local transport. The lockers are near track 8. Sample fares and schedules in the box opposite.

The **bus station** is immediately to the left as you exit the train station on the Centrum side. The one bus of interest here is bus 180 to Oudewater and on to Utrecht.

The **bicycle shop** (☏519 751) is in the train station on the far side from the centre.

National bike route **LF2**, which links Amsterdam and Rotterdam, runs right through the Markt. Follow its twisting route 12km north along dramatic dykes across several large bodies of water to the village of Bodegraven, where you can join the **LF4** for the farm-filled 38km run west to Den Haag.

Delft

☏ 015 / POP 98,700

Ah, lovely Delft: compact, charming, relaxed. It's a very popular tourist destination – day trippers (and lovers of beauty and refinement) clamour to stroll Delft's narrow, canal-lined streets, gazing at the remarkable old buildings and meditating on the life

VERMEER'S DELFT

Johannes Vermeer, one of the greatest of the Dutch old masters, lived his entire life in Delft (1632–75), fathering 11 children and leaving behind just 35 incredible paintings (the authenticity of two more is debated). Vermeer's works have rich and meticulous colouring and he captures light as few other painters have ever managed to. His scenes come from everyday life in Delft, his interiors capturing simple things such as the famous *Girl with a Pearl Earring*, giving a photographic quality to his compositions.

Vermeer's best-known exterior work, *View of Delft*, brilliantly captures the play of light and shadow of a partly cloudy day. Visit the location where he painted it, across the canal at Hooikade, southeast of the train station. Unfortunately, none of Vermeer's works remain in Delft, although the Vermeer Centrum Delft (p165) is a fine resource and the tourist office has a good walking tour brochure. The two works mentioned above can be seen at the Mauritshuis (p155) in Den Haag, while arguably his most famous painting, *The Milkmaid*, resides in Amsterdam's Rijksmuseum (p65).

Vermeer's life is something of an enigma. What little is known about him is not flattering. His wife wrote this after he died:

'...as a result and owing to the great burden of his children, having no means of his own, he had lapsed into such decay and decadence, which he had so taken to heart that, as if he had fallen into a frenzy, in a day or day and a half had gone from being healthy to being dead.'

His fame grows by the year, however. The 2003 film *Girl with a Pearl Earring* (based on Tracy Chevalier's novel) speculated on his relationship with the eponymous girl. The following year, a work long thought to be a forgery was finally confirmed as authentic – *Young Woman Seated at the Virginals* was the first Vermeer to be auctioned in more than 80 years, selling to an anonymous buyer for €24 million.

The excellent website www.essentialvermeer.com has exhaustive details on the painter and his works including where they are on exhibit at any given time.

and career of Golden Age painter Johannes Vermeer.

The artist was born in Delft and lived here – *View of Delft,* one of his best-loved works, is an enigmatic, idealised vision of the town. Delft is also famous for its 'delftware', the distinctive blue-and-white pottery originally duplicated from Chinese porcelain by 17th-century artisans.

Delft was founded around 1100 and grew rich from weaving and trade in the 13th and 14th centuries. In the 15th century a canal was dug to the Maas river, and the small port there, Delfshaven, was eventually absorbed by Rotterdam.

◉ Sights

Delft is best seen on foot: almost all the interesting sights lie within a 1km radius of the Grote Markt (p165). Much of the town dates from the 17th century and is well preserved.

Beestenmarkt is a large open space surrounded by fine buildings. Further east, **Oostpoort** is the sole surviving piece of the town's walls. **Koornmarkt**, leading south from the Waag, is a quiet, tree-lined canal. Look for the opulent facade of the **Gemeenlandshuis van Delfland** on Oude

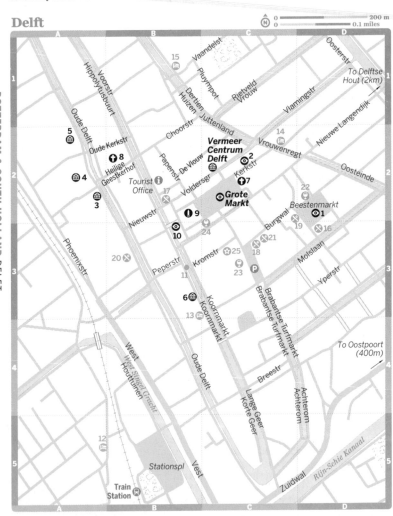

Delft across the canal from the Oude Kerk. It dates from 1505.

The town's ubiquitous blue-and-white china is almost a cliché. Given that the process was first developed in China, it's ironic that the mass of fake delftware sold in tourist shops also comes from China. The real stuff is produced in fairly small quantities at four factories in and around Delft. There are three places where you can actually see the artists at work.

TOP CHOICE **Vermeer Centrum Delft** MUSEUM
(www.vermeerdelft.nl; Voldersgracht 21; adult/child €7/3; ⊙10am-5pm) As the place where Vermeer was born, lived, and worked, Delft is 'Vermeer Central' to many art-history and old-masters enthusiasts. Along with viewing life-sized images of Vermeer's oeuvre, you can tour a replica of Vermeer's studio, which gives insight into the way the artist approached the use of light and colour in his craft. A 'Vermeer's World' exhibit offers biographical insight into his environment and upbringing, while temporary exhibits showcase the ways in which his work continues to inspire other artists.

Grote Markt SQUARE
(Koornmarkt 67) The pedestrian city plaza is worth a stroll for its pleasant collection of galleries, antique stores, clothing boutiques and quirky speciality shops.

Before you leave the crowded Markt, note the **town hall** (Markt), with its unusual combination of Renaissance construction surrounding a 13th-century tower. Behind it, the **Waag** is a 1644 weigh house.

Nieuwe Kerk CHURCH
(www.nieuwekerk-delft.nl; Markt; adult/child €3.50/1.50, includes entry to Oude Kerk; ⊙9am-6pm Apr-Oct, 11am-4pm Nov-Mar, closed Sun) Nicknamed 'Oude Jan' (Old Jan) by Delft's citizens in homage to its most famous resident (Johannes Vermeer is buried here), this beautiful church was built in 1246. It houses the crypt of the Dutch royal family. Note the striking white interior and the 27 stained-glass windows, which cast their brilliantly coloured lights on the walls on sunny days. You can climb the **tower** for views.

Oude Kerk CHURCH
(www.oudekerk-delft.nl; Heilige Geestkerkhof 25; adult/child €3.50/1.50, includes entry to Nieuwe Kerk) The Gothic Oude Kerk, 800 years old, is a surreal sight: its tower leans 2m from the vertical. One of the tombs inside is Vermeer's.

Municipal Museum het Prinsenhof MUSEUM
(www.prinsenhof-delft.nl; St Agathaplein 1; adult/child €7.50/free; ⊙10am-5pm Tue-Sat, 1-5pm Sun) Opposite the Oude Kerk, the former convent

Delft

where Willem the Silent was assassinated in 1584 (the bullet hole in the wall is preserved) is now a museum displaying various objects telling the story of the Eighty Years' War with Spain, as well as 17th-century paintings. An artist-in-residence paints interpretations of Dutch masterpieces; relax in the serene gardens.

Museum Paul Tetar van Elven MUSEUM
(www.museumpaultetarvanelven.nl; Koornmarkt 67; adult/child €4/2; ⏲1-5pm Tue-Sun) This off-the-radar museum has surprising delights within. A former studio and home of the 19th-century Dutch artist Paul Tetar van Elven, the museum features several Rembrandts and a Vermeer, along with many reproductions of notable paintings by the artist himself. Yet the most interesting thing about this museum might be the evocative 17th-century interior, with its original furnishings and lived-in feel.

Museum Nusantara MUSEUM
(☎260 23 58; www.nusantara-delft.nl; St Agathaplein 4; adult/child €3.50/free; ⏲10am-5pm Tue-Sat, 1-5pm Sun) The Museum Nusantara shines a light on the Netherlands' colonial past. There's a collection of furniture and other lifestyle artefacts from 17th-century Batavia (now Jakarta), as well as a 'colonial department' detailing the beginnings of Dutch rule in Indonesia.

Museum Lambert van Meerten MUSEUM
(www.lambertvanmeerten-delft.nl; Oude Delft 199; adult/child €3.50/1.50; ⏲11am-5pm Tue-Sun) The Museum Lambert van Meerten has a fine collection of porcelain tiles and delftware dating back to the 16th century, all displayed in a 19th-century mansion.

Tours

Canal Boat Tour CANAL TOUR
(www.rondvaartdelft.nl; adult/child €6.75/3; ⏲11am-5pm Apr-Oct) See Delft on a 45-minute canal boat tour departing from Koornmarkt 113.

Sleeping

Note that in summer Delft's accommodation is heavily booked. Reserve well ahead, or visit the town as a day trip. Conversely, Delft's small size and the proximity of the train station make it a great base for exploring the rest of Zuid Holland. Rates at many places shoot up on weekends in summer.

TOP CHOICE **Hotel de Emauspoort** HOTEL $$
(☎219 02 19; www.emauspoort.nl; Vrouwenregt 9-11; s/d from €90/100; @📶) Couples, singles, and business travellers alike rave about this sweet well-priced little hotel near the Markt. Spacious rooms strike a nice balance of old-world antique and totally modern comfort. Extras include a bountiful breakfast, an outdoor terrace and on-site bakery. The lofted Vermeer room is a bargain of a splurge.

Hotel de Plataan HOTEL $$
(☎212 60 46; www.hoteldeplataan.nl; Doelenplein 10; s/d from €105/115; 📶) Enjoy the clever surrounds at this hotel on a canal. Standard rooms are small but elegant and have fridges. Then there are the wonderfully opulent theme rooms, including the 'Garden of Eden'; the 'Amber', based on Eastern stylings; or the jaw-dropping 'Tamarinde', themed after a desert island. The included breakfast buffet is suitably clever.

Delftse Hout CAMPGROUND $
(☎213 00 40; www.delftsehout.nl; Korftlaan 5; campsites €24-28, cabins from €80 per night; @📶🏊) This well-equipped campground is just northeast of town. Take bus 80 or 82 from the bus station or use the campground's shuttle. It has 160 sites and is a 15-minute walk from the Markt.

Soul Inn B&B $
(☎071-215 72 46; www.soul-inn.nl; Willemstraat 55; s/d from €60/70; @📶) This funky bed and breakfast is a cool antidote for those who've experienced an overload of Delft quaintness; rooms play themes and colour schemes such as hot pink and retro 1970s, along with several African-themed suites. It is a 10-minute walk to the centre.

Hotel Coen HOTEL $$
(☎214 59 14; www.hotelcoendelft.nl; Coenderstraat 47; s/d from €72/90; @📶) Just behind the train station construction site, this family-run hotel has 55 beds in a variety of rooms, from budget singles as thin as your wallet to grander doubles. The included breakfast is tasty.

Hotel de Ark HOTEL $$
(☎215 79 99; www.deark.nl; Koornmarkt 65; s/d from €120/150; @📶) Four 17th-century canal-side houses have been turned into this gra-

cious and luxurious small hotel. Rooms are reached by elevator and have vintage beauty that isn't stuffy. Out back there's a small garden; nearby are apartments for longer stays.

Eating

Spijshuis de Dis CONTEMPORARY DUTCH **$$**
(www.spijshuisdedis.com; Beestenmarkt 36; lunch €5-15, dinner €16-25; ☺noon-2pm, 5-9.30pm Tue-Sun; 🖉🏿) Foodies, romantics and oenophiles flock to this cosily elegant restaurant, where fresh fish and amazing soups served in bread bowls take centre stage. Meat eaters and vegies are both well catered for. Don't skip the creative, mouthwatering starters or the Dutch pudding served in a wooden shoe.

Barrique CAFE **$**
(Beestenmarkt 33; meals from €8) Just east of the Markt, cafes sprawl across the shady Beestenmarkt. A place where pigs were once sold (1449–1972), look for the plaque nearby on the square, it's now home to joyous consumption. This slick cafe specialises in wine for the beer weary, tapas and smooth jazz.

't Walletje CAFE **$**
(🖉214 04 23; Burgwal 7; mains €7-12; 🕿) Tables front this small bistro on a pedestrian street near the town centre. Lunch has good smoothies, sandwiches and salads. At night three-course specials (€21) are artfully prepared and feature nice accents such as pesto side dishes with seafood and steaks.

Natuurlijk 015 CAFE **$**
(www.natuurlijk015.nl; Burgwal 11; mains from €5; ☺10am-6pm Tue-Sat; 🖉) This organic cafe delights travellers and locals alike, who congregate on the terrace for creative sandwiches, smoothies and salads.

De Visbanken SEAFOOD **$**
(Camaretten 2; snacks from €3; ☺10am-6pm) People have been selling fish on this spot since 1342. The present vendors line the display cases in the old open-air pavilion with all manner of things fishy. Enjoy marinated and smoked treats or go for something fried.

Stadys Koffyhuis CAFE **$**
(www.stads-koffyhuis.nl; Oude Delft 133; mains €7-12) Savour Delft from seats on a terrace barge moored out the front. Savour drinks, sandwiches and pancakes while admiring possibly the best view in Delft – the Oude Kerk, just ahead at the end of the canal.

Drinking

TOP CHOICE **Locus Publicus** BROWN CAFE
(Brabantse Turfmarkt 67) Glowing from within, this beer cafe has more than 200 beers. It's charming and filled with cheery locals who are quaffing their way through the list. Good people-watching can be enjoyed from the front-terrace tables.

Belgisch Bier Café Belvédère BAR
(www.bbcbelvedere.nl; Beestenmarkt 8) We dare you to try saying the name of this Belgian beer temple three times after a couple of cold La Chouffes. The cafe is located inside an old historic house, and you can choose from six beers on tap and many more by the bottle.

Stadcafe de Waag GRAND CAFE
(www.de-waag.nl; Markt 11; ☺10am-1am) With a sprawling terrace on the Markt, this is a perfect spot for a post-sightseeing beer or a light meal.

☆ Entertainment

Low-key Kromstraat has coffeeshops and boozers.

Bebop Jazzcafé LIVE MUSIC
(Kromstraat 33) Dark and small, with moody music and a great selection of beers.

🛍 Shopping

Most stores are open to 9pm on Friday, a rarity in small-town Holland. On Thursday you'll find the General Market on the Grote Markt (p165), while on Saturday from April to September, the Antiques, Bric-a-Brac and Book Market draws in visitors seeking treasures and deals alike.

Given the popularity of **delftware**, many visitors leave town treating their bags much more gently than when they arrived (although the factory shops will ship).

De Koninklijke Porceleyne Fles PORCELAIN FACTORY
(Royal Delft; www.royaldelft.com; Rotterdamseweg 196; adult/child €12/free; ☺9am-5pm, closed Sun Nov-Mar) Pottery fans, and even those new to the iconic blue-and-white earthenware, will enjoy this factory-meets-gallery-meets-shopping experience. The truly Delftware-obsessed will want to take a workshop (€46) in which you get to paint your own piece of Delft blue. Regular tickets include an audio tour which leads you through a painting demonstration, the company museum and

the factory production process. For many, of course, the real thrills begin and end in the gift shop.

Royal Delft is a 15-minute walk from the train station.

De Candelaer PORCELAIN STUDIO
(www.candelaer.nl; Kerkstraat 13; ⊘9am-5.30pm Mon-Fri, to 5pm Sat year-round, 9am-5pm Sun Mar-May) The most central and modest Delftware outfit is de Candelaer, just off the Markt. It has five artists, a few of whom work most days. When it's quiet they'll give you a detailed tour of the manufacturing process.

De Delftse Pauw · PORCELAIN FACTORY
(The Delft Peacock; ☑212 49 20; www.delftsepauw. com; Delftweg 133; tours free; ⊘9am-4.30pm Apr-Oct, 9am-4.30pm Mon-Fri, 11am-1pm Sat Nov-Mar) De Delftse Pauw employs 35 painters who work mainly from home. It has daily tours, but you won't see the painters on weekends. Take tram 1 to Vrijenbanselaan.

❶ Information

Tourist Office (VVV; ☑215 40 51; www.delft. nl; Hippolytusbuurt 4; ⊘10am-4pm Sun-Mon, 9am-6pm Tue-Fri, 10am-5pm Sat) Free internet access and excellent walking-tour brochures.

❶ Getting There & Around

Bicycle

The **bicycle shop** will move around the station area as construction continues. National bike route **LF11** goes right through town: Den Haag

---

❶ NAVIGATING ROTTERDAM

Rotterdam, split by the Nieuwe Maas shipping channel, is crossed by a series of tunnels and bridges, notably the Erasmusbrug. The centre is on the northern side of the water, and new neighbourhoods are rising to the south. Centraal Station (CS) will be a vast building site for the next few years as a striking new station (www. rotterdamcentraal.nl) rises along with new subways and underground parking. In the meantime, a 15-minute walk along the canal-like ponds leads to the waterfront. The commercial centre is to the east and most museums are to the west. The historic neighbourhood of Delfshaven is a further 3km west.

---

is 11km northwest (after about 8km you pass a windmill) and Rotterdam is 28km southeast on a meandering route that enters Rotterdam from the west at pretty Delftshaven.

Train

The train station is a vast chaotic construction site through to 2018 as the tracks are moved underground and a new station is built (www. spoorzonedelft.nl). Services are few, eg no lockers. Sample train service in the box opposite.

Den Haag is also linked to Delft by tram 1, which takes 30 minutes.

Rotterdam

☑010 / POP 616,000

Rotterdam bursts with energy. Vibrant nightlife, a diverse, multiethnic community, an intensely interesting maritime tradition and a wealth of top-class museums all make it a must-see part of any visit to Holland, especially if you are passing by on a high-speed train on your way to Amsterdam or the south.

The Netherlands' 'second city', Rotterdam was bombed flat during WWII and spent the following decades rebuilding. You won't find much classic Dutch medieval centre here – it was swept away along with the other rubble and detritus of war. In its place is an architectural aesthetic that's unique in Europe, a progressive perpetual-motion approach to architecture that's clearly a result of the city's postwar, postmodern 'anything goes' philosophy. (A fine example of this is the Paul McCarthy statue titled 'Santa with Butt Plug' that the city placed in the main shopping district.)

History

Rotterdam's history as a major port (it's Europe's busiest) dates to the 16th century. In 1572, Spaniards being pursued by the rebel Sea Beggars were given shelter in the harbour. They rewarded this generosity by pillaging the town. Needless to say, Rotterdam soon joined the revolution and became a major port during this time.

With its location astride the major southern rivers, Rotterdam is ideally suited to service trading ships. Large canals first constructed in the 1800s and improved ever since link the port with the Rhine River and other major waterways.

On 14 May 1940 the invading Germans issued an ultimatum to the Dutch govern-ment: surrender or cities such as Rotterdam will be destroyed. The government capitulated;

TRAINS FROM DELFT

DESTINATION	PRICE (€)	DURATION (MIN)	FREQUENCY (PER HR)
Amsterdam	12	60	2
Den Haag	3	12	4
Rotterdam	3.50	12	4

however, the bombers were already airborne and the raid was carried out anyway.

◎ Sights

Notable museums and good walking through interesting neighbourhoods are the highlights of the city's sights.

Rotterdam is easy to navigate, with so many memorable buildings and landmarks with which to orientate yourself. The city centre is also a lot smaller than it seems for such a bustling metropolis – you might never need to use the efficient public transport system. The best way to see the city is by bike, though the trams make for good sightseeing.

TOP CHOICE Museum Boijmans van Beuningen
MUSEUM

(www.boijmans.nl; Museumpark 18-20; adult/child €12.50/free, Wed free; ⊙11am-5pm Tue-Sun) Among Europe's very finest museums, the Museum Boijmans van Beuningen has a permanent collection spanning all eras of Dutch and European art, including superb old masters. Among the highlights are *The Marriage Feast at Cana* by Hieronymus Bosch, the *Three Maries at the Open Sepulchre* by Van Eyck, the minutely detailed *Tower of Babel* by Pieter Brueghel the Elder, and *Portrait of Titus* and *Man in a Red Cap* by Rembrandt. Renaissance Italy is well represented; look for *The Wise and Foolish Virgins* by Tintoretto and *Satyr and Nymph* by Titian.

Paintings and sculpture since the mid-19th century are another strength. There are many Monets and other French Impressionists; Van Gogh and Gauguin are given space; and there are statues by Degas. The museum rightly prides itself on its collection by a group it calls 'the other surrealists', including Marcel Duchamp, René Magritte and Man Ray. Salvador Dalí gained a special room in the recent expansion and the collection is one of the largest of his work outside Spain and France. All in all, the surrealist wing is utterly absorbing, with ephemera and paraphernalia rubbing against famous works.

Modern modes are not forgotten, and the whole place is nothing if not eclectic: a nude or an old master might be nestled next to a '70s bubble TV, some kind of installation or a vibrating table.

There's also a good cafe and a pleasant sculpture garden (featuring Claes Oldenburg's famous *Bent Screw*, among others).

Kunsthal
GALLERY

(www.kunsthal.nl; Westzeedijk 341; adult/child €11/2; ⊙10am-5pm Tue-Sat, 11am-5pm Sun) At the southern end of Museumpark, the Kunsthal hosts around 20 temporary exhibitions (including art and design) each year. As the publicity says, everything from 'elitist to popular' gets an airing. It was the victim of a major theft in 2012 when several masterpieces were stolen.

Euromast
OBSERVATION DECK

(www.euromast.com; Parkhaven 20; adult/child from €9/6; ⊙10am-11pm) A shimmy up the 185m Euromast offers unparalleled 360-degree views of Rotterdam from the 100m-high observation deck. There are all manner of extra diversions here and a bevy of combo tickets with other attractions around town.

Het Park
PARK

You can escape the madness of the city surprisingly easily among the lakes of Het Park. In summer locals love to barbecue here on the grassy expanses. Just east is Tuin Schoonoord (Kievitslaan; ⊙8.30am-4.30pm Mon-Fri, from 11am Sat & Sun), a hidden re-creation of an idealised Dutch wilderness that seems to have been taken right from a Renaissance painting.

TOP CHOICE Delfshaven
HISTORIC AREA

One of Rotterdam's best districts for strolling, quaint Delfshaven (it survived the war) was once the official seaport for the city of Delft. A reconstructed 18th-century windmill

Rotterdam Central

(Voorhaven 210; ⊙1-5pm Wed, 10am-4pm Sat) overlooks the water at Voorhaven 210. One of the
area's claims to fame is that it was where the
Pilgrims tried leaving for America aboard the
leaky *Speedwell*. **Oude Kerk** (Voorhaven 210;
⊙10am-noon Mon-Sat, 2-4pm Sun) on Voorhaven
is where the Pilgrims prayed for the last time
before leaving on 22 July 1620. Models of
their vaguely seaworthy boats are within.

Just south, **De Dubbelde Palmboom**
(☏476 15 33; www.hmr.rotterdam.nl; Voorhaven
12; adult/child €6/free; ⊙11am-5pm Tue-Sun) is a
branch of the Rotterdam Museum housing
an excellent collection of items relating to
Rotterdam's history as a port. Displays are
spread throughout the 1826 warehouse, and
many have a sociological bent.

Delfshaven Info (Voorstraat; ⊙9am-4pm
Mon-Fri) has a good walking-tour brochure.
Just west on Schiedamseweg are all manner
of ethnic groceries and eateries; Delfshaven

is wonderfully un-twee. It is best reached by
taking trams 4 and 9 or the Metro.

Maritiem Museum Rotterdam   MUSEUM
(Maritime Museum; www.maritiemmuseum.nl;
Leuvehaven 1; adult/child €7.50/4; ⊙10am-5pm
Tue-Sat, 11am-5pm Sun year-round, plus 10am-
5pm Mon Jul & Aug) This comprehensive museum looks at the Netherlands' rich maritime traditions and is more fun than a trip
to the poop deck. There's an array of models that any youngster would love to take
into the tub, plus interesting and explana-
tory displays.

FREE **Haven Museum**   OPEN-AIR MUSEUM
(Leuvehaven 50; admission free; ⊙visitor centre
10am-5pm Tue-Sun) Just south of the Maritime
Museum, the Haven Museum comprises all
manner of old and historic ships moored
in the basin. You can always wander the
quays; when the visitor centre is open you

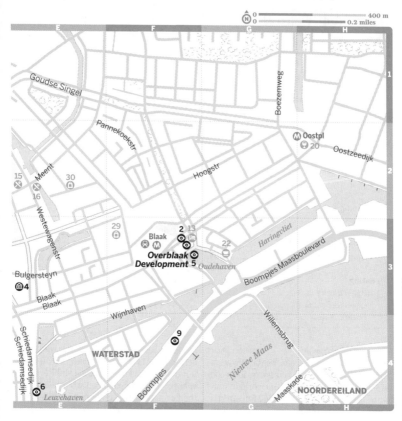

can learn more about what's tied up. Government budget cuts have threatened this fascinating site.

Rotterdam Walk of Fame   DISPLAY

(Schiedamsedijk) In front of the Haven Museum, the Rotterdam Walk of Fame features handprints from C-grade luminaries who've been to town plus the odd A-lister (Dizzy Gillespie).

Oude Haven   NEIGHBOURHOOD

The Oude Haven area, near the Overblaak development and the Blaak train, metro and tram station, preserves the oldest part of the harbour, some of which dates from the 14th century. It's a decent place for a stroll, especially if you pause at one of the waterside cafes.

Check out the **Openlucht Binnenvaart Museum** (Outdoor Ship Museum; Koningsdam 1; ⊙varies), which has a collection of historic inland waterway boats that fills much of the basin. Restorations are ongoing; sit on a shady wall and watch.

Museum Rotterdam   MUSEUM

(www.hmr.rotterdam.nl; Korte Hoogstraat 31; adult/child €6/free; ⊙11am-5pm Tue-Sun) The city's history is preserved at one of the centre's few surviving 17th-century buildings, now the Historisch Museum het Schielandhuis. Exhibits focus on everyday life through the ages, such as the (purportedly) oldest surviving wooden shoe. It has a branch at the De Dubbelde Palmboom (p170) in Delfshaven.

Wereldmuseum   MUSEUM

(World Museum; www.wereldmuseum.nl; Willemskade 25; adult/child €12/free; ⊙10am-8pm Tue-Sun) The Wereldmuseum celebrates multiculturalism, focusing on rituals, stories and sacred objects. Closed for several years of renovations, it has reopened with much new glitz to the displays. Major exhibits change regularly; the cafe is excellent.

Rotterdam Central

Miniworld Rotterdam　　MODEL TRAINS
(www.miniworldrotterdam.com; Weena 745; adult/child €10/7.50; ☺weekday hours vary, 10am-5pm Sat & Sun) The Dutch love of the world in miniature is celebrated at the vast Miniworld, a ginormous 500-sq-metre model railroad recreating Rotterdam and the Randstad.

War & Resistance Museum　　MUSEUM
(Oorlogs Verzets Museum; www.ovmrotterdam.nl; Coolhaven 375; adult/child €4/2; ☺10am-5pm Tue-Fri, noon-5pm Sun) The sounds of German bombers greet you at this small museum fittingly sheltered under a bridge. Displays recount life in Rotterdam during WWII; the fear in the faces of people fleeing the bombing in a 1940 photo is raw.

Unbroken Resistance　　MONUMENT
Unbroken Resistance, the statue at the start of the Westersingel, recalls WWII. It shows an enigmatic man, unbowed and calmly searching the skies. Many more statues line the water as you walk south, part of the city's commitment to public art of all forms.

Nederlands Fotomuseum　　MUSEUM
(www.nederlandsfotomuseum.nl; Wilhelminakade 332; adult/child €7/free; ☺10am-5pm Tue-Fri, 11am-5pm Sat & Sun) Down on the waterfront across the Maas, the Nederlands Fotomuseum mainly has large, special exhibitions; the value of a visit depends on what's on. Bits of the permanent collection (which is magnificent but hidden) can be accessed by various form-over-function gizmos. Take tram 20, 23 or 25 or the water taxi.

Tours

During the summer, the Nederlands Architectuur Instituut (p175) may offer bike tours that cover Rotterdam's eye-popping architecture. Check to see if they are on.

Spido　　BOAT TOUR
(www.spido.nl; Willemsplein 85; adult/child €11/7; ☺9.30am-5pm Jun-Sep, shorter hours Oct-May) Daily harbour tours are offered by Spido. Departures are from the pier at Leuvehoofd near the Erasmusbrug, the Leuvehaven metro stop and tram 7 terminus. Longer trips are possible in the high season.

You can also bob around the harbour on various themed dining boats, including one serving pancakes.

Line 10　　TRAM TOUR
(☏06 5351 3630; www.lijn10.nl; adult/child €5/3.50; ☺departures 10.30am-3.30pm Tue-Sun

Jul-Aug) Ride a historic tram throughout the city on Line 10. Staff are charming and there's an excellent guidebook in English. It's a great way to see some of the far reaches out of the centre. Trams depart from near the Spido dock on Willemsplein, at the terminus of tram 7 from the train station (also a scenic ride).

★ Festivals & Events

Rotterdam has festivals and events big and small all summer long.

International Film Festival Rotterdam   FILM
(www.filmfestivalrotterdam.com) Late January. A top-notch selection of independent and experimental films.

Poetry International Festival   POETRY
(www.poetry.nl) Mid-June. Hosting top-notch poets, don't ya know it, from all over the world.

North Sea Jazz Festival   MUSIC
(www.northseajazz.nl) Mid-July. One of the world's most-respected jazz events. Rooms throughout the region are at a premium as thousands of fans descend on the city. A lot of the acts organise unofficial jams outside the festival dates, a kind of pre-festival festival.

Rotterdam Unlimited   CARNIVAL
(Summer Carnival; www.zomercarnaval.nl) Last weekend of July. A carnival-like tropical bash with music, parades, dancing and parties.

Wereld Havendagen   HARBOUR FESTIVAL
(World Harbour Festival; www.wereldhavendagen.nl) Early September. Celebrates the role of the harbour, which directly or indirectly employs more than 300,000 people. There are lots of open houses, ship tours and fireworks.

🛏 Sleeping

Rotterdam has a good array of lodging, from scads of hostels to hotels grand and modest, many with views of the water.

The **tourist office** (Weena; ☺9am-5.30pm Mon-Sat, 10am-5pm Sun) makes room reservations, as does Use-It (p180), the latter with discounts.

TOP
CHOICE **Hotel New York**   LUXURY HOTEL $$$
(☑439 05 00; www.hotelnewyork.nl; Koninginnenhoofd 1; r €110-280; @🛜) The city's favourite hotel is housed in the former headquarters of the Holland-America passenger-ship line, and has excellent service and facilities. It's noted for its views, cafe and water taxi that takes guests across the Nieuwe Maas to the city centre. The 72 art nouveau rooms – with many original and painstakingly restored decorative items and fittings – are divine and come in various styles, from standard to rooms in the old boardrooms complete with fireplaces. Watch for deals.

Maritime Hotel Rotterdam   HOTEL $$
(☑411 92 60; www.maritimehotel.nl; Willemskade 13; r €50-140; @🛜) Popular with shore-leave-seeking seamen and travellers who appreciate the fine value here. The modern facility offers attentive service, a big breakfast buffet, a cheap bar with pool table, and oodles of models and posters featuring modern ships. The 135 rooms are small and the cheapest share bathrooms, but spend a little extra and you can enjoy the best waterfront views in town.

Hotel Bazar   HOTEL $$
(☑206 51 51; www.hotelbazar.nl; Witte de Withstraat 16; r €70-130) Bazar is deservedly popular for its 27 Middle Eastern-, African- and South American-themed rooms: lush, brocaded curtains, exotically tiled bathrooms and more. Top-floor rooms have balconies and views. Breakfast is spectacular: Turkish bread, international cheeses, yoghurt, pancakes

---

LOCAL KNOWLEDGE

JOSKA MOSMAN: PROUD ROTTERDAMER

West Kruiskade is a multicultural street with thousands of tastes, flavours and colours, where nationalities come together. Besides delicious food, there are bars, galleries, jewellery stores, Asian supermarkets, a park and many other stores. The street is pretty cheap; meals will only set you back a couple of euros. Rotterdam is still working on the development of the West Kruiskade. Already there are lovely, cosy streetlights in the evening and the facades have been thoroughly renovated. It is a great place to walk.

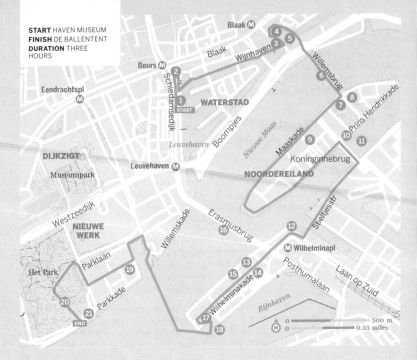

START HAVEN MUSEUM
FINISH DE BALLENTENT
DURATION THREE HOURS

Walking Tour
Rotterdam

> Start at the ❶ **Haven Museum** and the ❷ **Maritiem Museum Rotterdam** for a maritime history lesson, before making your way over the pedestrian bridge, along Wijnhaven and past the ❸ **Witte Huis** to ❹ **Oude Haven**.

Follow the walkways clockwise around the water and view the vessels at the ❺ **Openlucht Binnenvaart Museum**, then cross the ❻ **Willemsbrug**, drinking in the superb views, before in ❼ **Noordereiland**, a residential island that was once all shipping warehouses. To the left is ❽ **De Brug**, an apartment block.

Walk southwest, admiring watery views before stopping in at the maritime-themed ❾ **Cafe de Willemsbrug** for a beer and singalong.

Emerging into the light, walk southwest to the tip of the island, then make your way up Prins Hendrikkade. At the corner with Van der Takstraat look for ❿ **Observator Watersports**, a dealer in all things maritime, especially books and antiques. Across the Koninginnebrug look to the left as you cross the water:

❶❶ **De Hef** is a magnificent railway bridge from the 1920s that's been preserved as a National Monument.

Walk west along Stieltjesstraat and pass the country's tallest building, the ❶❷ **MaasToren**, before walking down to the old port, Wilhelminakade, and its new developments such as ❶❸ **De Rotterdam**, overshadowing ❶❹ **old shipping warehouses** with 'Celebes, Borneo, Java, Sumatra' carved into its facade. Pause at the art deco ❶❺ **Café Rotterdam** for refreshment and great views of the iconic ❶❻ **Erasmusbrug**.

At the southeast tip of the peninsula, take in the grand old maritime hotel, the ❶❼ **Hotel New York**, from where generations of people sailed to America. Board the scheduled ❶❽ **water taxis** and enjoy a quick run across the Nieuwe Maas to ❶❾ **Veerhaven**. Walk through this gentrified neighbourhood with its many old maritime offices and then meander around the lakes of ❷⓿ **Het Park** before settling in for a fine meal at ❷❶ **De Ballentent**, which has views of the grand old liner, the SS *Rotterdam*, permanently moored across the water and now used as a hotel.

ARCHITECTURE HIGHLIGHTS

Rotterdam is one vast open-air museum of modern architecture. The much-loved, 800m-long bridge, the 1996 **Erasmusbrug**, designed by Ben van Berkel, is a city icon. With its spread-eagled struts, it's nicknamed 'The Swan'.

To the south of Erasmusbrug is **KPN Telecom headquarters**, built in 2000 and designed by Renzo Piano, who also designed Paris' Pompidou Centre. The building leans at a sharp angle, seemingly resting on a long pole. Nearby are two other notables among many: the tallest building in the Netherlands, the **MaasToren** (2009, 165m) and **De Rotterdam**, which will be the largest building in the country when completed in 2014.

Retrace your steps across the river and walk northeast alongside the water on Boompjes, where you'll see the three distinctive **Boompjestorens** – apartment blocks built in 1988. Continue along the water until you see the striking 1998 **Willemswerf**. Note the dramatic lines casting shadows on its sleek, white surface.

Another 100m will bring you to Rotterdam's other signature bridge, the 1981 Willemsbrug (p179), which makes a bold statement with its red pylons. Turn north at Oude Haven on Geldersekade. The regal 12-storey building on the corner is the 1897 **Witte Huis** (White House), a rare survivor of the pre-war period, giving an idea of the wealth Rotterdam achieved thanks to the shipping industry.

Nederlands Architectuur Instituut (NAI; www.nai.nl; Museumpark 25; adult/child €10/free; ⏲10am-5pm Tue-Sat, 11am-5pm Sun) With one side surrounded by a dirty green moat and the other comprising a sweeping flow of brick along Rochussenstraat, this museum is striking. However, exhibits change regularly; there is nothing permanent on Dutch architecture so its value as a sight depends on what is on.

Included in the admission price is a ticket to **Huis Sonneveld** (Jongkindstraat 25), designed by Brinkman and Van der Vlugt and an outstanding example of the Dutch New Building architectural strain (also known as Dutch functionalism). This 1933 villa has been lovingly restored, with furniture, wallpaper and fixtures present and correct – it is an astonishing experience, almost like virtual reality.

Overblaak Development This development, designed by Piet Blom and built from 1978 to 1984, is near Blaak metro station. Marked by its pencil-shaped tower and up-ended, cube-shaped apartments, it seems plucked straight from the novels of JG Ballard. One apartment, the renamed **Kijk-Kubus Museum-House** (www.kubuswoning.nl; adult/child €2.50/1.50; ⏲11am-5pm), is open to the public. Look for the tiny chess museum in the cube complex, with all kinds of chess pieces on display – everything from ancient Hindu examples to likenesses of Jabba the Hut.

and coffee. The ground-floor bar and restaurant is justifiably popular.

Stayokay Rotterdam HOSTEL $
(☎436 57 63; www.stayokay.com; Overblaak 85-87; dm from €20, r from €55; @📶) Those odd angles you see at this hostel may not be to do with what you just smoked; this hostel is in the landmark Overblaak development. There are 245 beds in oddly shaped rooms that sleep two to eight. Some have air-con and those on the top floor have cool views.

Hotel Stroom BOUTIQUE HOTEL $$$
(☎221 40 60; www.stroomrotterdam.nl; Lloydstraat 1; r €90-350; ❄📶) Stroom is so modern and alternative it hurts. Housed in a converted power station, its designer studios come in a range of configurations, such as the *videstudio* option, a jaw-dropping split-level abode under a glass roof with an open bathroom. It's all sleek, white and metallic. During slow times these luxury rooms are priced cheap.

Home Hotel STUDIO $$
(☎411 21 21; www.homehotel.nl; Witte de Withstraat 81a; r from €85) More than 85 studio apartments are available for rent in various buildings in one of Rotterdam's most appealing neighbourhoods. Some have wi-fi and others don't, but all have cooking facilities. Rates fall for multiple nights and many people stay by the week or month.

Nieuwe Werk, Middelland and Delfshaven (Rotterdam)

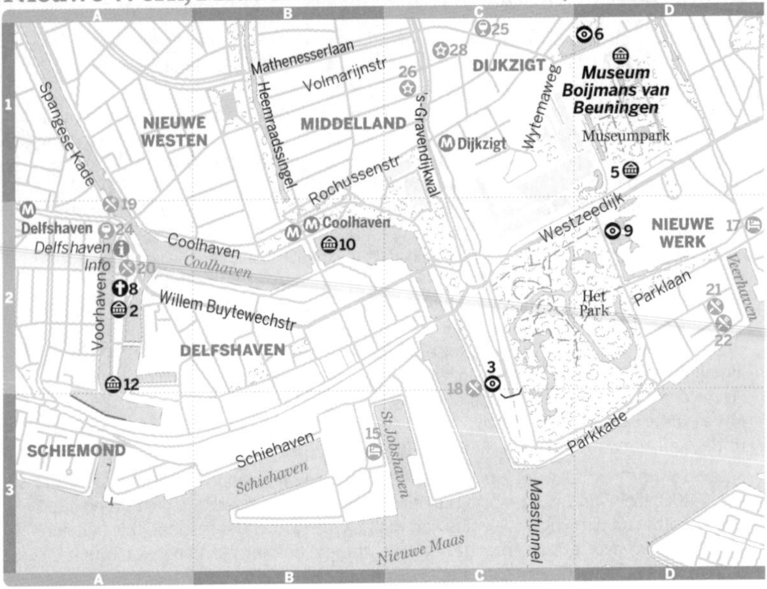

Nieuwe Werk, Middelland and Delfshaven (Rotterdam)

Top Sights

Museum Boijmans van Beuningen D1

Sights

1 Boompjestorens E1
2 De Dubbelde Palmboom A2
3 Euromast C2
4 KPN Telecom Headquarters F2
5 Kunsthal D1
6 Nederlands Architectuur Instituut D1
7 Nederlands Fotomuseum E2
8 Oude Kerk A2
9 Tuin Schoonoord D2
10 War & Resistance Museum B2
11 Wereldmuseum E2
12 Windmill A2

Activities, Courses & Tours

13 Rebus E1
14 Spido E2

Sleeping

15 Hotel Stroom B3
16 Maritime Hotel Rotterdam E2
17 Room Rotterdam D2

Eating

18 De Pannenkoekenboot C2
19 Het Eethuisje A2
20 Stadsbrouwerij De Pelgrim A2
21 Z&M D2
22 Zee Zout D2

Drinking

23 Cafe de Willemsbrug F1
24 De Oude Sluis A2
25 Westerpaviljoen C1

Entertainment

26 Dizzy C1
27 LantarenVenster E2
28 Nemo C1

Hotel Emma HOTEL **$$**

(☎436 55 33; www.hotelemma.nl; Nieuwe Binnenweg 6; r €60-150; @☎) Nicely refurbished, the Emma is a modern place with 24 rooms close to the city centre. Touches include posh bathrooms and double-glazed windows. The decor is bright and simple, although it does boast a breezy roof terrace with good views. The free breakfast includes fresh-baked goods.

around Veerhaven, Witte de Single, Nieuwe Binnenweg and Oude Haven. The city's (always growing) multicultural population keeps choices exciting.

De Ballentent

CAFE **$**

TOP CHOICE

(www.deballentent.nl; Parkkade 1; meals from €6; ⊙9am-11pm) Rotterdam's best waterfront pub-cafe is also a great spot for a meal. Dine on one of two terraces or inside. Mussels, schnitzels and more line the menu but the real speciality here are *bals*, huge home-made meatloafy meatballs. The plain ones are tremendous, but go for the house style with a piquant sauce of fresh peppers, mushrooms and more. Waiters and customers alike enjoy a good laugh.

Z&M

BISTRO **$$**

(436 65 79; www.zenmdelicatessen.nl; Veerhaven 13; lunch mains from €7, dinner mains from €20; ⊙noon-10pm Tue-Sun) A cosy, chic French/Mediterranean bistro revered for using only organic produce from small farms, a rarity in the factory-farm-laden Netherlands. The busy little kitchen overlooks the street and outside tables. Open through the day, you can get snacks beyween meals and linger over a drink. Some of its food is sold as takeaway from a deli area.

Bazar

MIDDLE EASTERN **$$**

(Witte de Withstraat 16; mains €7-15) On the ground floor of the creative Hotel Bazar, this vast and popular eatery comes up with creative Middle Eastern fusion fare that complements the stylised decor. Dolmades haven't tasted this good any place west of Istanbul. The outside tables are *the* neighbourhood meeting spot day and night.

Zee Zout

SEAFOOD **$$$**

(www.restaurantzeezout.nl; Westerkade 11b; menus from lunch/dinner €35/45; ⊙noon-2.30pm Tue-Sat, 6-9.30pm Tue-Sun) The name means sea salt and that's all you need to know. Well, actually, details such as the superbly prepared fresh fish, wraparound windows, outside seating with waterfront views and polished service are also key. It's a modern and beautiful room with some fine tiles decorated with fish.

Dudok

BRASSERIE **$$**

(Meent 88; dishes €6-20) There are always crowds at this sprawling brasserie near the city centre. Inside it's all high ceilings and walls of glass. Outside, you have your pick of an array of tables lining the street. Meals

Hotel Baan

HOTEL **$**

(477 05 55; www.hotelbaan.nl; Rochussenstraat 345; r €55-90) A family-run hotel close to Delfshaven, the Baan is in a modern building overlooking a canal. It's a bit stark inside and out but the prices are excellent as is the location. Rooms are smallish but clean, and at breakfast (included) you can look out to the garden in the back. Staff are very helpful.

Hotel Bienvenue

HOTEL **$$**

(466 93 94; www.hotelbienvenue.nl; Spoorsingel 24b; r €55-85; @ 🛜) In a quiet though central area; basic rooms with Ikea accents. There's a typical Dutch breakfast served in a typical Dutch breakfast room. Everything is quite clean if a bit uninspired; you can't beat the location.

Room Rotterdam

HOSTEL **$**

(282 72 77; www.roomrotterdam.nl; Van Vollenhovensraat 62; dm from €20; @ 🛜) A popular hostel with 16 dorm rooms, each with two to 10 beds. Each has its own decor, ranging from 'Dutch Delight' to 'Love'. It's a lively, young place and rocks much of the night right up until the free breakfast is served.

Eating

Rotterdam is an excellent place for dining. Good places abound, especially in and range from breakfasts to snacks to cafe fare such as soup and pasta. The name comes from noted architect WM Dudok who designed these former insurance offices.

Bagel Bakery
CAFE $

(Schilderstraat 57; meals from €4; ⊘breakfast & lunch Tue-Sun, dinner Thu-Sat) Excellent bagel sandwiches to takeaway. Dine in (or under the trees out the front) and enjoy excellent breakfasts, fresh lunches and inventive dinners. Lots of vegie options.

Burger Trut
CAFE $

(Meent 129; mains from €6; ⊘5-10pm Tue, 11.30am-10pm Wed-Sat, 2-8pm Sun; 🖉) Support the arts by enjoying a meal at this uniquely hybrid cafe that mixes vegetarian sensibilities with both meatless and meaty burgers. The menu is mostly Mediterranean (except for the burgers) but a hummus side with a carrot and oat burger covered in smoked cheese is fine indeed. The supported galleries adjoin.

Bagels & Beans
CAFE $

(🖉217 52 87; Lijnbaan 150; snacks from €3; ⊘9.30am-6pm Mon-Sat, noon-5pm Sun) On the 5th floor of the Selexyz & Donner bookshop; excellent coffees and a huge terrace with views and sun lounges.

Kiem Foei
ASIAN $

(West Kruiskade 29; mains from €5; ⊘8am-late) The woks rarely cool at this bustling fast food Asian place near the start of the multicultural West Kruiskade strip. Choose from Indonesian and Chinese favourites, which are cooked up quick. The dining-room ambience is two cuts above the standard.

De Pannenkoekenboot
TRADITIONAL DUTCH $$

(Pancake Boat; www.pannenkoekenboot.nl; Ms van Riemsdijkweg; adult/child from €23.50/18.50; ⊘8-10.30pm Sat) All-you-can-eat pancakes in a variety of flavours served aboard a boat touring the harbour. Departs across from Euromast.

DELFSHAVEN

On balmy days there are many choices of places to eat along the canals. At any time the main drag of Nieuwe Binnenweg offers a plethora of ethnic eateries, most very cheap.

Het Eethuisje
TRADITIONAL DUTCH $

(Mathenesserdijk 436; mains €8-10; ⊘4-9pm Mon-Sat) Traditional meaty, filling Dutch food is served from this little storefront near a canal. Utterly tourist free.

Stadsbrouwerij
De Pelgrim
TRADITIONAL DUTCH $$

(www.pelgrimbier.nl; Aelbrechtkolk 12; mains €12-22) It's named for the religious folk who passed through on their way to America, and you can take your own voyage through the various beers brewed in the vintage surrounds. Meals range from casual lunches to more ambitious multicourse dinners.

🍷 Drinking

In the city centre, Karel Doormanstraat is lined with shady cafes. Most of the places listed below also serve good food.

TOP CHOICE Rotown
BAR

(www.rotown.nl; Nieuwe Binnenweg 17-19) A smooth bar, a dependable live-rock venue, an agreeable restaurant, a popular meeting place. The musical program features new local talent, established international acts and crossover experiments.

De Witte Aap
BROWN CAFE

(Witte de Withstraat 78) Fine corner boozer that's always crowded with locals from this artist-filled 'hood. The front opens right up and a huge awning keeps inclements at bay.

Westerpaviljoen
GRAND CAFE

(Nieuwe Binnenweg 136; meals €6-16) A huge buzzy cafe with a very popular terrace, it's the perfect spot for a respite in this prime shopping district. Breakfast is served until 3pm and the long menu has many vegie options and even some Mediterranean flair.

Weimar
CAFE

(Haringvliet 637) Named for the Hotel Weimar that stood here and was blasted to rubble in 1940, this is one of scores of waterside cafes in Oude Haven. Have a wander and pick one or several, depending on your mood. The Weimar is one of the more gracious.

Café Rotterdam
CAFE

(🖉290 84 42; Wilhelminakade 699; mains from €10) In a soaring, light-filled space in the old ship-passenger terminal, the real draw here is the huge terrace with its views of the water and the Rotterdam skyline.

De Oude Sluis
BROWN CAFE

(Havenstraat 7, Delfshaven) The view up the canal from the tables outside goes right out to Delfshaven's windmill at this ideal brown cafe filled with crunchy locals. Inside you'll find peanut shells littering the floor; the perfect accompaniment/inducement for beer.

The Belgian cherry beer (*kriek*) on tap is a bargain.

Locus Publicus   BROWN CAFE
(www.locus-publicus.com; Oostzeedijk 364) With more than 200 beers on its menu (including 12 always on tap), this is an outstanding specialist beer cafe.

Cafe de Willemsbrug   BAR
(Maaskade 95) This old-time, maritime-themed pub attracts salty sea dogs from the island. However, it's all bark and no bite. There's an underlying genial charm that finds full throat when impromptu singing starts. Tables on the water are the best.

Apollo Rotterdam   BAR
(www.apollo-rotterdam.nl; Zwarte Paardenstraat 91a; ⊘from 6pm Fri, from 9pm Sat) A cool cafe and bar for gays, lesbians and bisexuals who are under 26. On Friday nights it's more cafe than bar, with discussion groups. On Saturday nights it's more club than bar, with DJs and more.

☆ Entertainment
Nightclubs

TOP CHOICE **Corso**   CLUB
(www.corsorotterdam.nl; Kruiskade 22) This is where it's at: bleeding-edge local and international DJs mashing up a high-fibre electronic diet of bleeps 'n' beats. Art displays provide diversions at this prototypical Rotterdam club.

Gay Palace   CLUB
(www.gay-palace.nl; Schiedamsesingel 139) And here we have Rotterdam's only weekly gay nightclub, with four floors of throbbing gay action – with different scenes on each floor – to work you into a lather and get you sweaty.

Worm   CLUB
(www.worm.org; Boomgaardsstraat 71) Music here has a try-anything, do-anything vibe. Media mash-ups, performance art and experimental music are some of the more mundane events.

Live Music

TOP CHOICE **De Unie**   VENUE
(www.deunie.nu; Mauritsweg 35) Truly cultural, this venue is a vision in white, which provides a blank slate for events from cabaret to forums about taxation and the middle class to acoustic folk. It's safe to say that the high-brow debates here continue right out

to the tables out front. The cafe has excellent food.

Dizzy   LIVE MUSIC
(www.dizzy.nl; 's-Gravendijkwal 127) Live concerts Monday and Tuesday nights and Sunday afternoons. The evening performances are scorching: everything from hot jazz to fast and funky Brazilian and salsa. There are regular jazz jam sessions. Excellent Scotch collection.

De Doelen   CLASSICAL MUSIC
(✆217 17 17; www.dedoelen.nl; Schouwburgplein 50) Home venue of the renowned Rotterdam Philharmonic Orchestra, a sumptuous concert centre that dates from 1935 and seats 1300.

Coffeeshops

There's a huge number of coffeeshops in Rotterdam, probably the highest concentration outside the capital.

Nemo   COFFEESHOP
(www.coffeeshop-nemo.nl; Nieuwe Binnenweg 181) Disney would not approve of the logo at this slick yet cheery shop. Browse the 15 kinds of weed on offer before you visit.

Pluto   COFFEESHOP
(www.pluto.nl; Nieuwe Binnenweg 54) Space, not the Disney dog, is the inspiration at this head shop, which sells every kind of pot accessory and goods to fill them.

Theatre

Schouwburg   THEATRE
(✆411 81 10; www.schouwburg.rotterdam.nl; Schouwburgplein 25) The main cultural centre, the Schouwburg has a changing calendar of dance, theatre and drama. Note the intriguing light fixtures with red necks out the front.

Cinema

Rotterdam's annual International Film Festival (p173) has been described as the 'European Sundance'.

LantarenVenster   CINEMA
(✆277 22 66; www.lantarenvenster.nl; Gouvernestraat 133) Great art-house cinema that spices up the screen with live jazz and house. Good bar and cafe too.

🛍 Shopping

An afternoon strolling the length of **Nieuwe Binnenweg** yields a captivating mix of stylish cafes, coffeeshops and shops selling used CDs, vintage clothing and plastic/fluorescent club wear. The odd local designer hoping for more adds spice.

Lijnbaan and side streets stretching to **Coolsingel** and **Mauritsweg** are lined with mainstream stores, chains and the big department stores. Every other bag says C&A or H&M. Dart further south to **Witte de Withstraat** for boutiques, galleries and general funkiness.

You can literally buy the salt of the earth at the ethnic groceries on **West Kruiskade**, which has a welter of ethnic groceries and stores.

Rotterdam has gone for Sunday shopping in a big way. Most stores in the centre are open noon to 5pm.

Blaak Market   MARKET
(⊙8am-5pm Tue & Sat) This huge market is the city's best and sprawls across its namesake square across from the cube houses. A striking new indoor market is set to open here by 2015. Stalls sell all manner of foods great and small, gadgets, clothes, antiques, fake antiques, snacks and a lot more.

Gorilli Concept Store   CLOTHES, LIFESTYLE
(www.gorilli.com; Oppert 296-298)   A top local brand, Gorilli does its best to be the anti-brand. There's a swank yet casual cool here with street clothes and pretty much every other accessory to go with them.

Selexyz & Donner   BOOKS
(☑413 20 70; Lijnbaan 150; ⊙9.30am-6pm Mon-Sat, noon-5pm Sun) The largest bookshop in the country has a nearly secret rooftop cafe.

❶ Information
Discount Card
Rotterdam Welcome Card (from adult/child €10/7) Offers discounts for sights, hotels and restaurants and free local transit. Buy it from the tourist office.

Internet Access
The library and tourist offices have free internet access. Many cafes have free wi-fi.

Centrale Bibliotheek (☑281 61 14; Hoogstraat 110; ⊙1-8pm Mon, 10am-8pm Tue-Fri, 10am-5pm Sat) An attraction in itself, with a cafe, an indoor life-sized chessboard and 30 minutes of free internet access each day.

Tourist Information
Tourist Office (VVV; ☑790 01 40; www.rotterdam.info; ☎) City (Coolsingel 197; ⊙9am-6pm Mon-Fri, to 5pm Sat & Sun) Groothandelsge-

bouw (p173) Free internet. The main (city) branch is located in the City Information Centre, with a good display on architecture since the war and a huge town model. A second location is near the train station in the landmark Groothandelsgebouw. There are excellent walking guides.

Use-It (www.use-it.nl; Schaatsbaan 41-45; ⊙9am-6pm Tue-Sun mid-May–mid-Sep, to 5pm Tue-Sat mid-Sep–mid-May; ☎) Offbeat independent tourist organisation all but lost amid the station construction. Has free wi-fi, books cheap accommodation and publishes the invaluable *Simply the Best* local guide. Free lockers.

❶ Getting There & Away
Air
Rotterdam The Hague Airport (RTM; www.rotterdamthehagueairport.nl) has limited service. But if you can get a deal, it's a low-key, hassle-free ingress to the country.

CityJet (www.cityjet.com) Flies to London City Airport.

Transavia (www.transavia.com) Mediterranean destinations.

Bicycle
Two important national bike routes converge just east of Het Park. **LF2** runs north through Gouda to Amsterdam and south through Dordrecht to Belgium. **LF11** runs from Den Haag through Rotterdam and on to Breda. Although the city seems large, 15 minutes of fast pedalling will have you out in the country.

Boat
The Waterbus (p182) is a fast ferry service linking Rotterdam with Dordrecht via Kinderdijk and is an enjoyable option for day trips, or in place of the train. Boats leave from Willemskade every 30 minutes.

Bus
Rotterdam is a hub for Eurolines bus services to the rest of Europe. The **Eurolines office** (☑412 44 44; Conradstraat 16; ⊙9.30am-5.30pm Mon-Sat) is in the Groothandelsgebouw by Centraal Station. Long-distance buses stop nearby.

Train
Rotterdam Centraal Station (CS) is a major hub. Regular rail lines radiate out in all directions. In addition it is a stop on the high-speed line from Amsterdam south to Belgium used by Thalys and Fyra fast trains.

Sample fares and schedules in the box opposite:

Until at least 2014 the trip won't be the adventure; however, the station will be. The entire CS area is being massively rebuilt. Until at least

TRAINS FROM ROTTERDAM

DESTINATION	PRICE (€)	DURATION (MIN)	FREQUENCY (PER HR)
Amsterdam (regular)	14	65	5
Amsterdam (high-speed)	11-21	43	2
Breda	9	32	3
Schiphol	11	47	3
Utrecht	10	40	4

2013 CS services are in what's literally a pile of containers near a temporary tunnel to the tracks; the lockers are by track 1 etc. All should be forgotten, however, when the new station opens (see www.rotterdamcentraal.nl). In keeping with local culture it will be an architectural stunner with a broad metallic roof arrowing towards the huge new plaza running south along Westersingel.

❶ Getting Around

To/From the Airport

Bus 33 makes the 20-minute run from the airport to CS every 15 minutes throughout the day. A taxi takes 10 minutes to get to the centre and costs around €22.

Bicycle

The **bicycle shop** at CS is in the backside of the Groothandelsgebouw during construction.

Public Transport

Rotterdam's trams, buses and metro are provided by **RET** (www.ret.nl). Most converge near CS. The **RET information booth** (⊙7am-7pm) sells tickets and is down in the Centraal metro station. There are other information booths in the major metro stations.

Day passes are sold for varying durations: 1/2/3 days costs €7/10.50/14. A single-ride ticket purchased from a bus driver or tram conductor costs €3. Ticket inspections are common.

Trams are the best way to get around the city. They go virtually everywhere and you get to sightsee along the way. The metro (subway) is geared more for trips to the suburbs.

Taxi

Call the **Rotterdamse Taxi Centrale** (☑462 60 60).

Water Taxi

Fast black and yellow **water taxis** (☑403 03 03; www.watertaxirotterdam.nl) are the Ferraris

of the Nieuwe Maas and cost about €30 per 15 minutes.

Enjoy water-taxi service for a fraction of the cost on two handy fixed routes (two to four times per hour from 11am to 9pm Monday to Thursday and 9am to midnight Friday to Sunday), travelling between:

» Hotel New York and Veerhaven (€3)

» Hotel New York and Leuvehaven (€3.60)

Around Rotterdam

KINDERDIJK

The **Kinderdijk** (www.kinderdijk.nl; free) is a great spot to see windmills out in the countryside. A Unesco World Heritage site, it has 19 windmills strung out on both sides of canals, which you can wander by foot or bike.

This spot has been a focus of Dutch efforts to claim land from the water for centuries. Indeed the name Kinderdijk is said to derive from the horrible St Elizabeth's Day Flood of 1421 when a storm and flood washed a baby in a crib with a cat up onto the dyke. Stories aside, it is a starkly beautiful area, with the windmills rising above the empty marshes and waterways like many sentinels.

Several of the most important types of windmill are here, including hollow post mills and rotating cap mills. The latter are among the highest in the country as they were built to better catch the wind. The mills are kept in operating condition and date from the 18th century. In summer tall reeds line the canals, lily pads float on the water and bird calls break the silence. If you venture past the first couple of mills, you leave 90% of the day trippers behind. You can also visit an old pumping station where a film is shown about Kinderdijk.

BLOWING IN THE WIND

Long before they appeared in a billion snapshots, the earliest known windmills appeared in the 13th century, simply built around a tree trunk. The next leap in technology came 100 years later, when a series of gears ensured the mill could be used for all manner of activities, the most important of which was pumping water. Hundreds of these windmills were soon built on dykes throughout Holland and the mass drainage of land began.

The next major advancement in Dutch windmill technology came in the 16th century with the invention of the rotating cap mill. Rather than having to turn the huge body of the mill to face the wind, the operators could rotate just the top, which contained the hub of the sails. This made it possible for mills to be operated by just one person.

In addition to pumping water, mills were used for many other industrial purposes, such as sawing wood, making clay for pottery and, most importantly for art lovers, crushing the pigments used by painters.

By the mid-19th century there were more than 10,000 windmills operating in all parts of the Netherlands. But the invention of the steam engine soon made them obsolete. By the end of the 20th century there were only 950 operable windmills left, but this number has stabilised and there is great interest in preserving the survivors. The Dutch government runs a three-year school for prospective windmill operators, who must be licensed.

Running one of the mills on a windy day is as complex as being the skipper of a large sailing ship, and anyone who has been inside a mill and listened to the massive timbers creaking will be aware of the similarities. The greatest hazard is a runaway, when the sails begin turning so fast that they can't be slowed down. This frequently ends in catastrophe as the mill remorselessly tears itself apart.

It's sad to see abandoned mills stripped of sails and standing forlorn and denuded, especially since these days you're more likely to see turbine-powered wind farms in the Dutch countryside than rows of windmills. However, there are opportunities to see healthy examples throughout the country.

To see oodles of windmills in a classic *polder* setting (with strips of farmland separated by canals), visit Kinderdijk (p181) near Rotterdam. To see mills operating and learn how they work, head to Zaanse Schans (p109) near Amsterdam.

Just about every operable windmill in the nation is open to visitors on National Mill Day, usually on the second Saturday of May. Look for windmills flying little blue flags.

On Saturdays in July and August, from 2pm to 5pm, most of the windmills are in operation, an unforgettable sight that was once common but is now impossible to find anywhere else.

❶ Information

You can wander the canals of Kinderdijk year-round. The second mill from the main entrance functions as a **visitors centre** (admission €3.50, combo ticket with film & pumphouse €6; ☺9.30am-5.30pm mid-Mar–mid-Oct). On most days this windmill operates, which is good as most of the others don't. Note: of the maps sold at Kinderdijk, only the one bearing the Unesco logo is of value.

❶ Getting There & Around

A visit to Kinderdijk is an ideal day trip.

It's close to Rotterdam (16km) or Dordrecht (11km) on national bike routes **LF2** and **LF11**.

The most enjoyable way to visit is by the **Waterbus** (www.waterbus.nl; Willemskade; day pass adult/child €12.50/9) fast ferry. From either Rotterdam or Dordrecht it takes about an hour and costs €4, with a transfer to a small ferry at Ridderkerk (€1.50). The connection runs every half-hour but the Kinderdijk ferry takes a long lunch break (10am until 11.30am). Bikes are carried for free; the ferry dock is 1km from the Kinderdijk entrance.

Rebus (www.rebus-info.nl; adult/child €14/11.50; ☺10.45am & 2.15pm Tue-Sun Apr-Sep) runs three-hour boat tours from Rotterdam that allow a fairly quick visit to the mills.

By train from Rotterdam CS, get off at Rotterdam Lombardijen station, then catch the hourly bus 90 (one hour) which runs to Utrecht.

A small cafe near the entrance, **De Molenhoek** (www.kantinedemolenhoek.nl; bike rental per 2hr €2.50; ☺9.30am-6pm Apr-Sep), rents bikes which are the best way to explore the basic 7km round-trip on the main paths.

Dordrecht

🎵 078 / POP 119,000

Underappreciated Dordrecht, with its lovely canals and busy port, sits at the confluence of the Oude Maas river and several tributaries and channels. This strategic trading position (precipitating a boom in the wine trade), along with the fact that it is the oldest Dutch city (having been granted a town charter in 1220), ensured that Dordrecht was one of the most powerful Dutch regions until the mid- to late-16th century. Accordingly, in 1572, it was here that town leaders from all over Holland met to declare independence from Spain.

Dordrecht and its evocative historical centre is a good stop on busy train lines or is a fun day trip by fast ferry from Rotterdam.

◉ Sights

See Dordrecht on foot: it's eminently suited to it, most of the sights are on or near the three old canals – the **Nieuwehaven**, the **Wolwevershaven** and the **Wijnhaven**.

Begin at the **Visbrug** (Bridge; over Wijnhaven), the bridge over Wijnhaven that gives fine views of the dignified town hall, which is built over the canal. At the northern end of Visbrug, turn right onto Groenmarkt. As you walk northeast you'll pass the oldest houses in town, many from the early 1600s.

At the next square, Scheffersplein, cross diagonally to Voorstraat, the main retail street. The canal runs under this area, which is home to numerous markets.

The **Augustinerkerk** (Voorstraat), an old church with a facade dating from 1773, is a little further along on the right. Just past it, watch carefully for a passage leading to **Het Hof** (⊙1-5pm Tue-Sun), where the setting alone – especially at night – is moody and evocative. It was here that the states of Holland and Zeeland met in 1572. The complex is home to the **Diep Museum** (www.erfgoed centrumdiep.nl; Het Hof; ⊙11am-5pm Wed-Sat, 1-5pm Sun), which has displays on the history and is undergoing a revamp until 2014.

Back on Voorstraat, continue north to the next bridge over the canal: Nieuwbrug. Cross over to Wijnstraat and turn right, continuing north. Many of the lopsided houses along here date from the peak of the wine trade, when the nearby canals were filled with boats bearing the fruits of the fermented grape.

The street ends at an attractive bridge. Pass along the west or left side of the canal to the river – and the **Groothoofdspoort**, once the main gate into town and truly a grand entrance. Here there's a small square with fine riverfront views of the busy confluence of waterways and a few cafes with leafy seating.

Circling to the south you'll see the Kuipershaven, the street along the Wolwevershaven, another old canal lined with restored wine warehouses and filled with interesting historic boats. On warm days boys complete the timeless tableau by plunging into the waters. At the tiny drawbridge, cross over to the north side of the Nieuwehaven. On the right, watch for the small **Museum 1940-1945** (www.dordrechtmuseum19401945. nl; Nieuwehaven 28; adult/child €2/1; ⊙10am-5pm Tue-Wed, Fri-Sat, 1-5pm Sun). It shows the privations of the region during WWII, residents from that era are often chatting in the lobby.

Just south, the **Museum Simon van Gijn** (www.dordrechtmuseum.nl; Nieuwehaven 29; adult/child €7/3.50; ⊙11am-5pm Tue-Sun) depicts the life of an 18th-century patrician, with vintage knick-knacks, furnishings and tapestries engagingly displayerd.

Continue southwest to the Engelenburgerbrug over the Nieuwehaven's access to the Oude Maas. Take an immediate right onto narrow Engelenburgerkade. At No 18, **Beverschaep** (Beaver & Sheep House) is a 1658 structure that takes its name from the bucktoothed critters supporting a coat of arms over the door.

At the end of the street is **Blauwpoort** (Engelenburgerkade), an old trading gate from 1652. Enjoy the views of the busy Oude Maas.

Grote Kerk   CHURCH
(🎵614 46 60; www.grotekerk-dordrecht.nl; Lange geldersekade 2; church admission free, tower adult/child €1/0.50; ⊙10.30am-4.30pm Apr-Oct, 1-4pm Sat & Sun Nov-Mar) The massive tower of the 14th- to 15th-century Grote Kerk was originally meant to have been much higher, but it took on a lean during its 150-year-plus construction. You can climb to the top – 275 steps – to enjoy excellent views of the town. Inside, the choir stalls are finely carved and there are a few stained-glass windows depicting local historical scenes.

Dordrechts Museum   MUSEUM
(www.dordrechtsmuseum.nl; Museumstraat 40; adult/child €10/free; ⊙11am-5pm Tue-Sun)

Dordrecht

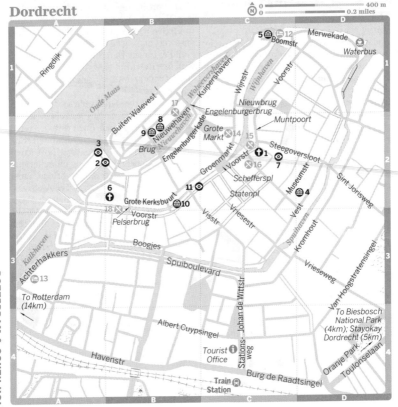

Away from the old town, the flashy Dordrechts Museum has works by local artists. Most noteworthy are pieces by Jan van Goyen (1596–1656) and Albert Cuyp (1620–91). Van Goyen was one of the first Dutch painters to capture the interplay of light on landscapes – look for his *View of Dordrecht* – while Cuyp, who lived in Dordrecht his entire life, is known for his many works painted in and around his hometown. These included, in his early career, landscapes featuring, inevitably, the town mascot: sheep.

Tours

De Stroper   CANAL TOUR
(www.destroper.com; Wijnbrug 1; adult/child €6.50/5; ☺departs 2-5pm Apr-May & Sep-Oct, 11am-5pm Jun-Aug) The excellent restaurant De Stroper runs boat tours that are a fine way to see Dordrecht's many delights.

Sleeping

Bellevue Groothoofd   BOUTIQUE HOTEL **$$**
(☏633 25 00; www.bellevuegroothoofd.nl; Boomstraat 37; r €125-155; ☞) You can't beat the location of this small hotel right at the river confluence. Views for the some of the 10 rooms are sublime. Decor is a nice palette of creams, grey and charcoal. There is a fine cafe and restaurant.

Hotel Dordrecht   HOTEL **$$**
(☏613 60 11; www.hoteldordrecht.nl; Achterhakkers 72; s/d from €90/110; ✳☞) A lovely option with excellent, spacious rooms that feature four-poster beds with curtains. Some rooms have private balconies; breakfast is included. There's parking and a garden terrace.

Stayokay Dordrecht   HOSTEL **$**
(☏621 21 67; www.stayokay.com; Baanhoekweg 25; dm/r from €23/47; ☞) The hostel, which has a bar and restaurant and rents bicycles, is in a modern building right next to Biesbosch

Dordrecht

National Park. It is 10km east of Dordrecht and easily reached by bike.

✖ Eating & Drinking

Dordrecht has some excellent eating. Schefersplein, a large central square built over a canal, has good cafes.

⊤ᴏᴘ De Stroper   BISTRO $$$

(☑613 00 94; www.destroper.com; Wijnbrug 1; menus €25-50; ⊘noon-2pm Mon-Fri, 6-10pm daily) Gaze out on the canal or in summer dine on a floating platform at this superb fish restaurant. The menus change daily; the six-course option at dinner is a culinary tour de force. Try the surprise menu (€35).

't Vlak   TAPAS $

(Vlak 11; dishes from €5; ⊘4pm-midnight) A lively tapas bar in a building from 1616. Sit under trees canalside and enjoy one of Dordrecht's best views: gaze over two old canals while drinking excellent riojas.

Zusjes   CAFE $

(Voorstraat 431; meals from €4; ⊘10am-5pm Tue-Sat) A gem of a little lunchroom run by namesake sisters where all the dishes are vegie and most of the produce is local and organic. Try a tasty baguette with a pot of fine tea or kick back with a fairtrade coffee. Outside tables are on a restful stretch of street.

Christa's Cookies   BAKERY $

(☑843 75 89; 'S-Heer Boeijnstraat 2; treats from €1; ⊘10.30am-6pm Wed-Sat) Fantastic organic bakery where the owner is as sweet as her delectable cookies and cupcakes.

Pim's Poffertjes en
Pannekoekenhuis   PANCAKES $

(www.pimspofenpan.nl; Nieuwstraat 19; mains from €6; ⊘noon-7.30pm Wed-Sun) Beautiful large and thin pancakes are filled with dozens of choices of ingredients from savoury to sweet. Kids and adults love this place inside a vintage building with atmospheric time-worn wooden booths.

🛍 Shopping

Voorstraat is the street for shopping. To the north it has interesting galleries and boutiques, while in and around Visbrug there is a fascinating stretch of ethnic grocery stores. As it curves to the west there are lots of new and creative shops.

❶ Information

The vast **tourist office** (VVV; ☑0900 46 36 888; www.vvvdordrecht.nl; Spuiboulevard 99; ⊘noon-5.30pm Mon, 9am-5.30pm Tue-Fri, 10am-5pm Sat) is midway between the train station and old town (of which it has a fascinating model).

❶ Getting There & Away

Buses leave from the area to your right as you exit the train station.

Bicycle

The **bike shop** is in a sparkling building to the left as you exit the train station. National routes **LF2** and **LF11** run north 27km to Rotterdam along pleasant countryside that includes Kinderdijk. South, **LF11** runs 43km to Breda. Biesbosch National Park is just a 10km ride east by a number of good routes.

Boat

The **Waterbus** (☑0900 899 89 98; www.waterbus.nl; day pass adult/child €12.50/9) is a fast ferry service linking Dordrecht with Rotterdam via Kinderdijk and is an enjoyable alternative to the train. The boat leaves from Merwekade every 30 minutes and takes one hour to Rotterdam (€4.20). The ferry stop is in the old town.

TRAINS FROM DORDRECHT

DESTINATION	PRICE (€)	DURATION (MIN)	FREQUENCY (PER HR)
Amsterdam	16	72-90	4
Breda	6	18	3
Rotterdam	4	14	6

Train

The train station has currency exchange and lockers and is on the old main line from Rotterdam south towards Belgium. The centre is a 700m walk from the station, a journey that passes through some less interesting, newer areas.

Sample fares and schedules in the box above.

Biesbosch National Park

Covering 7100 hectares, Biesbosch National Park encompasses an area on both banks of the Nieuwe Merwede river, east and south of Dordrecht. It's so big that it sprawls across a provincial border; there's a region known as the Brabantse Biesbosch, further east, while the part in this province is the Hollandse Biesbosch.

In 1970 the Delta Project shut off the tides to the area. Reeds, which had been growing wild, began to die, focusing attention on what is one of the largest expanses of natural space left in the Netherlands.

The park is home to beavers (reintroduced to the Brabant area of the park in 1988) and voles, along with scores of birds. The **visitors centre** (www.biesbosch.org; Biesboschweg 4; ⊙10am-5pm Tue-Sun) has displays and is where you can book the very interesting **boat tours** of this vast natural area and rent kayaks and canoes. There's an observation point near here where you can see beavers.

ⓘ Getting There & Away

The **Waterbus** (☑0900 899 89 98; www.waterbus.nl; day pass adult/child €11/6.75) has an hourly boat from Dordrecht to a dock 500m north of the visitors centre (€2, 25 minutes). Bus service is nonexistent. Good bike routes run the 10km east to the park from Dordrecht.

Slot Loevestein

Near the tiny, beautiful little walled town of **Woudrichem** you'll find the 14th-century castle, **Slot Loevestein** (☑0183-447 171; www.slotloevestein.nl; Loevestein 1; adult/child €9/6; ⊙11am-5pm Tue-Fri, 1-5pm Sat & Sun May-Sep, 1-5pm Sat & Sun Oct-Apr). The ancient keep is wonderfully evocative, perhaps more so for the difficulty involved in getting there. It has been a prison, residence and toll castle, though more recently it has hosted a varied calendar of cultural events.

It's best accessed by the **ferry** (www.veerdienstgorinchem.nl) from Woudrichem (€1.70) or nearby Gorinchem (€2.55), where there is a train station. National bike route **LF12** passes through between Dordrecht and Den Bosch.

ZEELAND

The province of Zeeland consists of three slivers of land that nestle in the middle of a vast delta through which many of Europe's rivers drain. As you survey the calm, flat landscape, consider that for centuries the plucky Zeelanders have been battling the North Sea waters, and not always with success. In fact the region has suffered two massive waterborne tragedies.

In 1421 the St Elizabeth's Day flood killed more than 100,000, irrevocably altering the landscape – and some say the disposition – of the Netherlands and its people.

In 1953, yet another flood took 2000 lives and destroyed 800km of dykes, leaving 500,000 homeless and leading to the Delta Project, an enormous nearly 50-year construction program that it is hoped will finally ensure the security of these lands. It ranks among the world's greatest engineering feats.

Middelburg is the somnolent historic capital, while the coast along the North Sea is lined with beaches. Many people visit this place of tenuous land and omnipresent water just to see the sheer size of the Delta Project's dykes and barriers.

ⓘ Getting There & Away

Middelburg is easily reached by train, but for most other towns you'll need to rely on the bus network. The most important includes bus 395, which makes a one-hour journey every hour between Rotterdam's Zuidplein metro station and Zierikzee, where you can transfer to buses for the rest of Zeeland.

National bike route **LF1**, which follows the entire North Sea coast of the Netherlands, is a vital link in Zeeland, as is **LF13**, which runs from Breda in the east to Middelburg and on to the coast (and LF1). However, it is also easy to explore on your own as the vast dyke-webbed farmlands make for easy, mellow riding. Re-

gional bike routes are also numbered and maps are widely available.

Middelburg

🎵 0118 / POP 47,600

Pleasant and prosperous Middelburg, Zeeland's sedate capital, is a perfect base for exploring the region and for getting to know the stolid, obliging Zeelanders.

Although Germany destroyed much of the town's historic centre in 1940, many

Middelburg

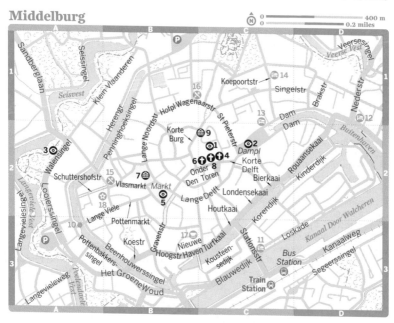

parts have been rebuilt and you can still get a solid feel for what life must have been like hundreds of years ago. The fortifications built by the Sea Beggars in 1595 can still be traced in the pattern of the main canals encircling the old town.

⊙ Sights

This pretty, airy little town is eminently suitable for walking, with cobblestones and snaking alleyways leading in and away from the Markt.

TOP CHOICE Abdij   HISTORIC SITE

This huge abbey complex dates from the 12th century and houses the regional government as well as three churches. It features a vast inner courtyard, the **Abdijplein**, unlike anything elsewhere in the Netherlands; it echoes with history.

The three churches are all in a cluster and reached through a tiny entrance (no ostentations for the Zeelanders!). The Wandelkerk (admission free, tower €4; ⊙10.30am-5pm Mon-Fri, 1.30-5pm Sat & Sun mid-Apr–Oct, tower 10am-5pm) dates from the 1600s and holds the tombs of Jan and Cornelis Evertsen, admirals and brothers killed fighting the English in 1666. It encompasses Lange Jan (Long John; it has its own locally brewed beer named after it), the 91m **tower** (207 steps).

The other churches are reached through the Wandelkerk. Just east, the Koorkerk (abbey complex) has parts that date from the 1300s. Just west is Nieuwe Kerk (Abbey Complex), which has a famous organ and dates from the 16th century. All surround a gem of a cloisters with a tiny herb garden.

The Zeeuws Museum (www.zeeuwsmuseum.nl; adult/child €8.50/free; ⊙11am-5pm Tue-Sun) is housed in the former monks' dormitories, and was given a recent massive revamp. Its collection was excellent, especially the traditional garb, which must have been an expensive burden for people barely eking out a living farming.

Markt   SQUARE

The Markt is the focus of commercial life; it's the location of a famous market on Thursdays.

Town Hall   HISTORIC BUILDING

(☑675 452; adult/child €4.25/3.75; ⊙tours 11.30am & 3.15pm Mar-Oct) Dominating the Markt, the town hall grabs the eye. It's ornately beautiful, and a pastiche of styles: the Gothic side facing the Markt is from the 1400s; the more-classical portion on Lange Noordstraat dates from the 1600s.

Inside there are several sumptuous ceremonial rooms that boast treasures such as the ubiquitous Belgian tapestries. Visits to the building are by 40-minute guided tours organised by the tourist shop.

Damplein   SQUARE

The area around the elongated Damplein (east of the Abdij) preserves many 18th-century houses, some of which have been turned into interesting shops and cafes.

Jewish Cemetery   CEMETERY

There is a fairly large old Jewish Cemetery on the Walensingel. It has the all-too-common stark memorial to the many Middelburg Jews taken away to their deaths by the Nazis.

☞ Tours

Canal Tours   CANAL TOURS

(☑643 272; www.rondvaartmiddelburg.nl; Achter de Houttuinen 39; adult/child €6.50/3.50; ⊙from 10.30am Apr-Oct) Has 40-minute tours along the southern canal.

★ Festivals & Events

Ringrijdendagen   FESTIVAL

(Ring Riding Days) The Ringrijdendagen are held on two separate days, the first in July around the Abbey square, the second in August at the Molenwater. 'Ring riders' charge about on horseback in fancy dress carrying big sticks towards a target, with the aim of trying to tilt it.

🛏 Sleeping

Accommodation rates can be much less in the low season.

TOP CHOICE Hotel Auberge Provençal   HOTEL $$

(☑627 659; www.auberge-provencal.nl; Koepoortstraat 10; s/d from €60/100; @☎) Dating from 1530, this building has eight comfortable rooms that were recently remodelled with stylish colours that accent the historic room details. It's a small, family-run establishment, a pleasant walk away from the centre on a beautiful old cobbled street. There's a nice garden and good breakfast buffet.

Hotel Aan De Dam   HOTEL $$

(☑643 773; www.hotelaandedam.nl; Dam 31; s/d from €90/110; ☎) An opulent 1652 mansion (built by the guy who did the palace on the Dam in Amsterdam) is now an appealing hotel. The nine rooms vary widely in size and view but all have period decor that's been tricked out with modern conveniences – such as luxurious bathrooms as opposed to pots. It overlooks a canal and small park.

Het Princenjagt
HOTEL **$**

(📞613 416; www.hotelhetprincenjagt.nl; Nederstraat 2; r €40-85; 📶) This eight-room B&B has a kitchen for guests to use and a jaunty location by the marina. Touches include a little toaster on each table at breakfast and nice chairs for slouching in the rooms. Four rooms share bathrooms.

Grand Hotel du Commerce
HOTEL **$$**

(📞636 051; www.hotelducommerce.nl; Loskade 1; r from €90; @📶) In a building that would look at home on the Cannes beachfront, this hotel has gaudy red awnings juxtaposed against whitewashed walls. The sum is less than the parts, however, as the rooms are a mixed bag in size and decor. Some singles are like closets and wi-fi is sporadic. The location is ideal for the train station.

✖ Eating & Drinking

On Sunday nights look for pizza and fast food by the Markt; at other times you'll do very well.

TOP CHOICE De Mug
PUB **$$**

(www.demug.nl; Vlasmarkt 54-56; mains €16-21; ⏱dinner Tue-Sat) Don't be fooled by the Heineken signs; the beer list is long and boasts many rare Trappist varieties. Also try the Mug Bitter, heavy on the hops. The menu goes well with the brews: hearty seafood and meat plus more simple fare for snacking. Nice soundtrack of 50s crooners.

De Gouden Bock
CONTEMPORARY DUTCH **$$**

(www.degoudenbock.nl; Damplein 17; mains €12-25; ⏱11am-9.30pm Tue-Sat) The colours of the coastal dunes add warmth to one of the town's most attractive restaurants. Gaze out over the square from the comodious wicker chairs outside or settle into the smart interior, a mix of creams and blues. The food is from the region and the menu changes regularly; seafood is a speciality.

St John
CAFE

(St Jaanstraat 40; snacks from €2; ⏱8.30am-6pm Mon-Sat) A perfect, creaky little old spot for a coffee. Woodsy inside and shady outside on the lovely square near the old fish market.

Restaurant De E etkamer
CONTEMPORARY DUTCH **$$$**

(📞635 676; www.restaurantdeeetkamer.nl; Wagenaarstraat 13-15; meals €35-70; ⏱noon-2pm & 5.30-9.30pm Tue-Sat) So prim and tidy out the front that you just have to step in. Produce is sourced locally and the menu changes with the seasons. Meats are house-cured and this attention to detail continues throughout your meal.

☆ Entertainment

De Spot
LIVE MUSIC

(www.despotmiddelburg.nl; Beddewijkstraat 15; ⏱10pm-4am Fri & Sat) A wide-ranging venue with everything from jazz to rock to rap (or even a South Park festival). Enter through an ancient arch.

❶ Information

There's no official VVV tourist office; there is a **tourist shop** (📞674 300; www.touristshop. nl; Markt 51; ⏱9.30am-5.30pm Mon-Sat), a counter inside the excellent local bookshop, De Drvkkery. It sells tours but has little info otherwise.

Free wi-fi blankets the Markt.

❶ Getting There & Around

Regional buses stop along Kanaalweg close to the train station.

Bicycle

The train station has a bike shop. National bike route **LF1** passes right through town; it crosses the many delta barriers to the north. Head east on **LF13** to Breda (140km) via the fertile coun-

TRAINS FROM MIDDELBURG

DESTINATION	PRICE (€)	DURATION (MIN)	FREQUENCY (PER HR)
Amsterdam	27	150	1
Roosendaal	11	45	2
Rotterdam	19	60	1

tryside and detour to charming villages such as Goes (36km).

Train

Middelburg is near the end of the train line in Zeeland, and the austere train station has that end-of-line feel. Services are limited: store your bags (€5) at the bicycle shop.

The station is only a five-minute walk from the centre.

Around Middelburg

The Walcheren peninsula is a very enjoyable place for bicycling: combine journeys to old towns with time at the beach.

VEERE

☑ 0118 / POP 1600

Veere is a former fishing village that found a new catch – tourists – when its access to the sea on the Veerse Meer (Veere Lake) was closed as part of the Delta Project. The town now boasts a busy yacht harbour. Much of Veere dates from the early 16th century and is a lovely place to stroll around.

The **tourist office** (VVV; ☑506 110; Oudestraat 28; ⊙10am-5pm daily Jul & Aug, noon-4pm Tue-Sun Apr-Jun & Sep) is in a small building near the Grote Kerk. Staff can advise on boat rentals and bike routes. It has free wi-fi.

⊙ Sights

Here, you'll feel like you're in a Vermeer painting: rich Gothic houses abound, a testament to the wealth brought in by the wool trade with the Scots, and at the waterfront, the **Campveerse Toren** was part of the old fortifications. Look for the indications on the side showing the levels of various floods.

The **town hall** on the Markt dates from 1474, but was mostly completed in 1599. Its tower is still stuffed with bells – 48 at last count.

At the south end of town is the 16th-century **Grote Kerk**, another edifice that never matched its designer's intentions – its stump of a steeple (42m) looms ominously.

🛏 Sleeping & Eating

Hotel 't Waepen van Veere   HOTEL **$$**
(☑501 231; www.waepenvanveere.nl; Markt 23-27; r €90-140; 🛜) On the central square and with a fine outdoor cafe (mains €12 to €25, closed Monday and Tuesday November to March), the 16 rooms here are comfy and stylish. It also has an elegant restaurant.

ℹ Getting There & Away

Veere is an easy ride from Middelburg on national bike route **LF1** (8km). Otherwise, bus 54 makes the 11-minute run every hour (every two hours on Sunday).

DOMBURG

☑ 0118 / POP 1300

Although Domburg is a low-key seaside town by Dutch standards (meaning 'not very tacky'), it's still jammed in summer. The **beach** is the main event. To escape the urban crowds, head south along the tall dunes. You can keep going past the golf course for a good 4km.

The **tourist office** (VVV; ☑583 484; www. vvvwnb.nl; Schuitvlotstraat 32; ⊙9am-6pm Mon-Sat, 11am-3pm Sun Jul & Aug, shorter hours other times) is near the entrance to town on Roosjesweg. The staff are experts at ferreting out accommodation.

The tourist office can steer you to one of many bike rental shops and provides maps of the popular 35km Mantelingen bicycle route, which begins and ends at Domburg. It takes in beaches, countryside and atmospheric little villages such as Veere.

🛏 Sleeping & Eating

The tourist office has myriad accommodation options, including holiday apartments and campgrounds.

Stayokay Domburg   HOSTEL **$**
(☑581 254; www.stayokay.com/domburg; Duinvlietweg 8; dm/r from €24/65; ⊙Apr-Oct; 🛜) A hostel notable for its location in a 13th-century castle, complete with moat, 2km east of Domburg and 1km from the beach. Reserve in advance, as it's very popular. Bus 52 from Middelburg stops along the N287 near the entrance.

TOP CHOICE Het Badpaviljoen   SEAFOOD **$$**
(☑582 405; www.hetbadpaviljoen.nl; Badhuisweg 21; mains €12-30; ⊙11am-midnight Thu-Mon) Perched on the grassy dunes of Domburg, this legendary restaurant is housed in a large and beautiful 19th-century bath house with a huge porch and terrace. You can opt for splendidly prepared seafood dishes in the restaurant or enjoy drinks and nibbles outside while savouring the seashore views.

ℹ Getting There & Away

Bus 52 links Domburg to Middelburg directly every hour, while bus 53 goes via the southern beaches.

The area is laced with ideal bike paths along dykes and through the green countryside. Get a map and start exploring. Middelburg is about 13km via various routes.

Waterland Neeltje Jans

Travelling the N57, you are on the frontlines of the Dutch war with the sea as you traverse the massive developments of the Delta Project: a succession of huge dykes and dams designed to prevent floods. Possibly the most impressive stretch is between Noord Beveland and Schouwen-Duiveland, to the north. The long causeway built atop the massive movable inlets is designed to allow the sea tides in and out of the Oosterschelde. This storm-surge barrier, more than 3km long and spanning three inlets and two artificial islands, took 10 years to build, beginning in 1976.

At about the midway point (Haringsvliet), the former visitors centre for the project has morphed into a theme park, complete with a busty mermaid mascot: **Waterland Neeltje Jans** (www.neeltjejans.nl; admission Nov-Mar €17, Apr-Oct €22; ☺10am-5.30pm, mostly weekends, only Nov-Mar). You can still see absorbing exhibits about floods, dams and plucky Dutch courage in battling the sea, but now the complex also includes seals, a water park, fake beach and the worrisomely named thrill ride: the Moby Dick. For a big blow, try the hurricane simulator. A boat trip takes you out onto the Oosterschelde for a panoramic view of the barriers and beyond. It's all a bit overblown and rather expensive if you just want to learn a little about the storm barrier.

The island on which Waterland is located has a long beach at the southern end, which is hugely popular with windsurfers. The entire region has coastal sections that are part of the **National Park Oosterschelde** (www.npoosterschelde.nl; Neeltje Jans; visitor centre admission free; ☺10am-5pm, to 9pm Jun-Aug); there are interesting displays in the visitors centre across the N57 from Waterland.

Bus 133 follows the N57 and stops at Waterland on its run from Middelburg train station (30 minutes, every 30 minutes to two hours) or Zierikzee (40 minutes). National bike route **NF1** passes right by.

Schouwen-Duiveland

The middle 'finger' of the Delta, Schouwen-Duiveland, is a compact island of dunes. Beaches and holiday developments can be

---

THE DELTA PROJECT

Begun in 1958, the Delta Project consumed billions of guilders, millions of labour hours and untold volumes of concrete and rock before it was completed in 1997. The goal was to avoid a repeat of the catastrophic floods of 1953, when a huge storm surge rushed up the Delta estuaries of Zeeland and broke through inland dykes. This caused a serial failure of dykes throughout the region, and much of the province was flooded.

The original idea was to block up the estuaries and create one vast freshwater network. But by the 1960s this kind of sweeping transformation was unacceptable to the Dutch public, who had become more environmentally aware. So the Oosterschelde was left open to the sea tides, and 3km of movable barriers were constructed that could be lowered ahead of a possible storm surge. The barriers, between Noord Beveland and Schouwen-Duiveland, are the most dramatic part of the Delta Project and the focus of Waterland Neeltje Jans, which details the enormous efforts to complete the barrier.

The project raised and strengthened the region's dykes and added a movable barrier at Rotterdam harbour, the last part to be completed. Public opinion later shifted, but large areas of water had already been dammed and made into freshwater lakes. At Veerse Meer the fishing industry has vanished and been replaced by tourists and sailboats.

The impact of the Delta Project is still being felt. At Biesbosch National Park the reduction of tides is killing reeds that have grown for centuries. But those who recall the 1953 floods will trade some reeds for their farms any day.

Although the entire, enormous project was finally completed more than 15 years ago, work is ongoing to strengthen and heighten portions to deal with rising water levels due to climate change.

found southwest from the village of Renesse. Buses hub at Zierikzee; from here you can catch bus 133 to Renesse and on for the ride over the Delta Works to Middelburg.

Bikes are the best mode of transit here. Routes abound, including national route **LF1** which runs north and south along the coast and over the various parts of the Delta Project.

ZIERIKZEE
📞 0111 / POP 10,500

Zierikzee grew wealthy in the 14th century from trade with the Hanseatic League, but things took a turn for the worse in 1576 when a bunch of Spaniards waded over from the mainland at low tide and captured the town, precipitating a long economic decline. There's good strolling along the long waterfront.

The tourist office (📞412 450; www. vvvschouwenduiveland.nl; Nieuwe Haven 7; ⊙10am-4pm Mon-Sat) can supply you with a list of local rooms for overnight stays, plus cycling maps.

At **Oude Haven** (Old Harbour), at the east end of town, the **Noordhavenpoort** and the **Zuidhavenpoort** are old city gates from the 16th and 14th centuries respectively. The **town hall** has a unique 16th-century wooden tower topped with a statue of Neptune. Hang out at a cafe and admire historic boats.

❶ Getting There & Away
The bus stop is north of the town centre, a five-minute walk across the canal along Grachtweg. Bus 395 runs to Rotterdam's Zuidplein metro station (the one-hour ride leaves at least every hour).

WESTERSCHOUWEN
📞 0111 / POP 18,000

Sheltered by tall dunes, this village at the west end of Schouwen-Duiveland adjoins a vast **park** set among the sands and woods. There are hiking and biking trails for outdoors enthusiasts and, although busy in summer, you can easily find solitude in some of the remoter parts of the park.

The tourist office (VVV; 📞0900-202 0233; www.vvvzeeland.nl; Noordstraat 45a; ⊙9am-5pm Mon-Sat), in the neighbouring town of Haamstede, can help with accommodation.

Bus 133 from Middelburg links the villages to Zierikzee.

Zeeuws-Vlaanderen

Running along the Belgian border south of the Westerschelde, Zeeuws-Vlaanderen is an unremarkable place with farms and a few chemical plants.

The many small villages, such as IJzendijk, all have their 'holy trinity' of the Dutch skyline: a church steeple, town hall tower and windmill.

No part of Zeeuws-Vlaanderen joins the rest of the Netherlands by land. The Vlissingen-Breskens ferry (www.veolia-transport. nl; adult/child €3/2; ⊙every 30 minutes) is a link for the Belgian channel ferry ports.

Foot passengers can travel to Brugge in Belgium by Veolia bus 42 from Breskens (€5.50, 75 minutes, hourly). From the port in Vlissingen, catch a bus or train to points beyond, such as Middelburg.

Friesland (Fryslân)

Best Places to Eat

» Restaurant By Ús (p197)

» Restaurant Eindeloos (p197)

» De Tjotter (p200)

» Café-Restaurant de Hinde (p202)

Best Places to Stay

» Hotel-Paleis Stadhouderlijk Hof (p196)

» Zeezicht Harlingen (p200)

» Hotel Pension van der Werff (p206)

Why Go?

At first, Friesland seems typically Dutch: it's flat, it's green and there are plenty of cows (the namesake Frisian black-and-white jobbies here). But explore a bit and you'll find its differences. For one, the province has its own language, as you'll see on road signs and other signage.

Even by Dutch standards, Frieslanders are a very self-reliant bunch. Here they didn't just have to build dykes to protect their land, they had to build the land as well. North Friesland segues into the Waddenzee in such a subtle way that the transition from watery mud to muddy water is elusive – albeit Unesco recognised.

At the province's centre is Leeuwarden, the sort of beguiling old Dutch town where you soon settle in and have a favourite cafe. Elsewhere, craggy old fishing villages like Hindeloopen are finding new life as evocative tourist destinations. This is the heart of the legendary Elfstedentocht, the sporadically held ice-skating race.

When to Go

Summer seems like the obvious time to visit Friesland. Watersports such as sailing on the Ijsselmeer are at their peak and offshore islands like Ameland have the most to offer. But the province rewards at other times too. Strolling its old towns such as Leeuwarden and Harlingen are rewarding at any time. The old fishing villages like Hindeloopen have a moody air to them and you can sense the tough lives once lived inside the sturdy little wooden cottages. And if conditions are just right in winter, the nation pauses for the Elfstedentocht ice-skating race.

History

Having dredged their home out of the Waddenzee armload by armload, the Frisians are no strangers to struggling with their natural environment.

Farming, fishing and nautical know-how (the building, repair and maintenance of ships) have been the area's principal activities for centuries, and made Friesland one of the wealthiest regions in the Netherlands in the pre-republic era. The Frisians became integrated further into Dutch society – not entirely willingly – in 1932 when the Afsluitdijk (Barrier Dyke) opened, closing the Zuiderzee. This provided better links to Amsterdam and the south but was devastating for small fishing villages, who suddenly found themselves sitting beside a lake.

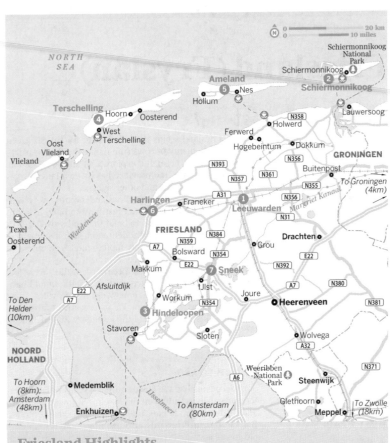

Friesland Highlights

1 Explore the excellent museums and shady back streets of **Leeuwarden** (p195)

2 Find your own little piece of island solitude on **Schiermonnikoog** (p205), which has a fine national park and countless trails amidst the quiet dunes

3 Kick back in **Hindeloopen** (p201), a cute coastal town almost forgotten by time

4 Mount a cycling trip through sand dunes and farmland on **Terschelling** (p203)

5 Spend your days enveloped in nature before a quiet night after sunset on **Ameland** (p204)

6 Watch boaters navigate the old canals of **Harlingen** (p199), which is worth a wander even if you're not catching a ferry

7 Take to the water around **Sneek** (p199), whether it be fresh, salty, in it, or on it

Language

Frisians speak Frisian, which is actually closer (in some ways) to German and Old English than Dutch; there's an old saying that goes 'As milk is to cheese, are English and Frise'. The majority of Frisians are, however, perfectly conversant in mainstream Dutch.

Don't worry if you can't make head nor tail of it – even the Dutch have difficulty deciphering Frisian. You'll usually see written examples, such as street signs, but you probably won't hear it much. You might, for example, see the word 'Snits', which is the Frisian version of Sneek, the region's second city.

A ruling in 2002 officially altered the spelling of the province's name from the Dutch 'Friesland' to 'Fryslân', the local version of the name.

❶ Getting There & Around

The capital, Leeuwarden, is easily reached by train from the south; trains can be caught from there to the coastal towns of the southwest, the port of Harlingen in the west, and Groningen in the east. The rest of the province requires more patience, but can be reached by bus or in the case of the islands, by ferry; various day passes are available.

Cycle paths crisscross Friesland. National bike route **LF3** bisects the province north and south through Leeuwarden; **LF10** cuts across Waddenzee on the Afsluitdijk (30km) from Noord Holland and takes in the north Frisian coast and all the ferry ports, while **LF22** covers the southern coast before heading inland towards Zwolle.

By car is also a good way to explore the entire province; the quickest route from Amsterdam is over the Afsluitdijk.

LEEUWARDEN (LJOUWERT)

🖉 058 / POP 95,300

While many visitors to Friesland head directly for the islands, don't pass through without making a stop in Leeuwarden, the province's capital. This compact, laid-back and pretty town is worth a visit, if only to explore its superb trinity of museums. Spending the night here will also allow time to wander its peaceful old streets and sample some of the northern hospitality, something easily found in its many bars and cafes.

◎ Sights

Most of Leeuwarden's sights are concentrated within a leisurely 10-minute walk

of Nieuwestad. The big news is that Zaailand, the huge central square otherwise known as Wilhelminaplein, has been reborn as the cultural centre of town: the Fries Museum occupies a landmark building at one end.

Look for historic ships of all kinds moored along the canals.

TOP
CHOICE ▶ **Fries Museum**   MUSEUM
(🖉255 55 00; www.friesmuseum.nl; Wilhelminaplein 92) New for late 2013, the show-stopping museum of the province will be in an imposing new glass-fronted building sporting a striking wood and steel roof 25m-tall that projects out over the square.

The huge collection of silver items – long a local speciality – is spectacular, as are the 19th-century period pieces from places like Hindeloopen. There is also a section on the efforts by locals to resist the Nazis and a sorrowful examination of the life of Mata Hari (p198). Temporary exhibits often feature cutting edge works by young artists.

Waag   HISTORIC BUILDING
The petite Waag dominates Waagplein, and is now surrounded by stores. It was the weigh house for butter and other goods from 1598 to 1884. The pedestrian zone includes the evocative old street **Weerd**.

Princessehof Museum   MUSEUM
(www.princessehof.nl; Grote Kerkstraat 11; adult/child €8/free; ◷11am-5pm Tue-Sun) Pottery lovers will adore the Princessehof Museum, the official museum for ceramics in the Netherlands. Here you'll find the largest collection of tiles on the planet, an unparalleled selection of Delftware, and works from around the globe – its Japanese, Chinese and Vietnamese sections are world class. It's all atmospherically housed in a 17th-century mansion.

Natuurmuseum Fryslân   MUSEUM
(www.natuurmuseumfryslan.nl; Schoenmakersperk 2; adult/child €6/4.50; ◷11am-5pm Tue-Sun) Even the most brow-beaten parent should let their angels run rampant in the Natuurmuseum Fryslân, a well-planned, interactive museum that's engaging for all ages. Covering Friesland's flora and fauna, highlights include spooky Captain Severein's collection of curiosities and a virtual bird-flight simulation (strap yourself into the hang-glider harness and away you go), but nothing tops the basement, where

Leeuwarden

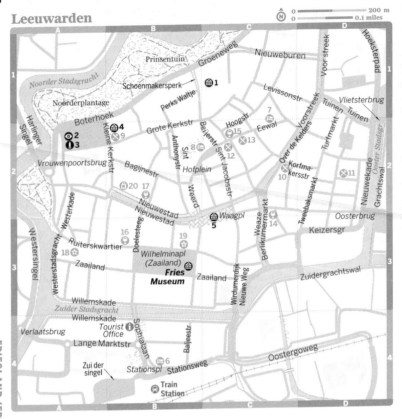

you can take in 'Friesland onder Water', an exploration of the bottom of a canal from a fish's perspective.

The museum's cafe, which occupies the inner courtyard, is topped by a glass roof, making it a cheery refuge on a cold day.

Oldehove   LANDMARK
(adult/child €2/1; ⊙1-5pm Tue-Sun May-Sep) Just past the west end of Bagijnestraat, the off-balance Oldehove dominates its unfortunate spot on the Oldehoofsterkerkhof parking lot. Things went wrong shortly after the tower was started in 1529. While by no means a Leaning Tower of Pisa, it presents a dramatic sight and is worth a climb for the views. Try to ignore the indignity of the attached cell phone tower. Compare the tilt to the very erect neighbouring **Pieter Jelles Troelstra statue**, a Dutch socialist who called for revolution after WWI.

🛏 Sleeping

Leeuwarden isn't swamped with accommodation options, but there's variety enough to suit everyone's tastes. For info on B&Bs at around €25 per person, try the tourist office (p198).

Hotel-Paleis Stadhouderlijk Hof   HOTEL **$$$**
(☑216 21 80; www.stadhouderlijkhof.nl; Hofplein 29; r €90-200; ❄❢) The plain pink facade of the Stadhouderlijk belies the plush interior of this one-time royal home. Inside, the red-carpeted stairwells lead to 24 rooms which have varying decors combining rich colours with wrought-iron details and canopied beds. The front entrance with a fountain contrasts with the regal courtyard garden.

Eden Oranje Hotel   HOTEL **$$**
(☑212 62 41; www.edenhotelgroup.nl; Stationsweg 4; r €60-150; ❄@❢) Directly opposite the train station, this business hotel has grand common spaces and comfy, large rooms

Leeuwarden

with a flash of style (ones in the far rear are leafy and quiet). Frequent discounts are excellent given the quality here.

Hotel 't Anker　　　　　　GUESTHOUSE **$**
(☏212 52 16; www.hotelhetanker.nl; Eewal 73; s/d from €50/70; ☎) This simple guesthouse is a fine bet for those just looking for a bed in a basic room (ask to see a couple) in an ideally located spot. It's surprisingly quiet as well, considering the ground floor contains a popular old pub, and a string of restaurants and bars line the street. The included breakfast is as simple as the rooms.

✕ Eating

Leeuwarden has a bevy of restaurants run by creative chefs offering finely prepared local foods at good prices.

TOP CHOICE Restaurant

By Ús　　　　　　CONTEMPORARY DUTCH **$$**
(☏215 86 63; www.restaurantby-us.nl; Over de Kelders 24; mains €19-23) Organic local foods are celebrated at this small little bistro with a nicely contrasting interior of simple wood and leather. Candles provide a nice glow for dishes on the ever-changing menu. Frisian-inspired dishes include soups and seafood. There is an excellent wine list and a young, effusive staff.

✎ Restaurant

Eindeloos　　　　CONTEMPORARY DUTCH **$$$**
(☏213 08 35; www.restauranteindeloos.nl; Korfmakersstraat 17; menus from €30; ◷noon-2pm Wed-Fri, 5-9.30pm Tue-Sat) Menus change con-

stantly at this perfect little restaurant; the precision to the decor of white and black matches the efforts in the kitchen. Local produce, seafood and lamb usually figure in the line-up.

Spinoza's　　　　　　BISTRO **$$**
(☏212 93 93; Eewal 50-52; mains €10-17; ◷lunch & dinner; ✎) This large eatery is great in summer when you can enjoy the tree-shaded tables out front or the private courtyard. In winter, huddle up in the candle-lit interior. The menu features regional specialties (soups and stews) and many vegetarian options.

De Brasserie　　　　　　GRAND CAFE **$**
(Grote Kerkstraat 7; mains from €6; ◷10am-8pm) A sprawling cafe popular with locals lounging and shoppers not shopping, it has a classic menu and absolutely fab coffees and teas. Knock back a few brews and head next door to the ceramics museum to do your bull act in the china exhibit.

Sems　　　　　　BISTRO **$$**
(www.semsleeuwarden.nl; Gouverneursplein 36; meals €10-28; ◷noon-midnight) On a balmy day the terrace in front of this stylish restaurant is one of the finest cafe-spaces in town. Tables shelter under huge umbrellas while patrons enjoy choices from the long wines-by-the-glass list and nibble on little delights, or tuck into casual fare like a burger. Inside the more formal restaurant you can have more traditional meals of meats and seafood.

FRIESLAND (FRYSLÂN) LEEUWARDEN (LJOUWERT)

MATA HARI

Born Gertrud Margarete Zelle, this daughter of Leeuwarden is best known by her acquired name: Mata Hari (Malaysian for 'sun'). An exotic dancer in Paris, her affairs and dalliances were legendary. She favoured rich men-in-uniform, and when WWI broke out she had high-ranking lovers on both sides. Things inevitably became tricky; French officers persuaded her to spy on her German lovers, and German officers managed to do the same. This web of intrigue was not helped by her keen imagination, and mistrust began to rise from both sides.

In 1917, at age 40, she was arrested by the French for spying. There was a dubious trial, during which none of her former 'pals' offered any assistance – probably out of embarrassment – and later that year she was sentenced to death and shot.

Today Margarete/Mata Hari is still – in a manner of speaking – alive and well in Leeuwarden. Her statue as a sultry dancer can be found on a bridge over the canal close to her birthplace at Over de Kelders 33; the Fries Museum also has a large and detailed exhibit on her life.

Drinking

A concentration of bars, clubs and coffee shops can be found around Doelesteeg, Kleine Hoogstraat and Grote Hoogstraat. Ruiterskwartier has a few clubs.

Grand Cafe De Brass GRAND CAFE
(www.cafedebrass.nl; Nieuwestad 71; meals from €8) Like mice in a cheese factory, outdoor tables fan out in all directions from this canalside cafe. When the weather is even vaguely sympathetic, half of Leeuwarden seems to be here – the other half is at other cafes nearby. Feeling faint from all the fun? Sprawl out on one of the huge bean bags sitting atop a canal bridge.

Café De Toeter PUB
(Kleine Hoogstraat 2) A fine place to chill out on faux wicker chairs and benches under a huge tree.

Doozo BAR
(213 60 69; Ruiterskwartier 93) Part club and part sushi bar, there are lots of sofas for lounging about and sucking down raw eel amidst the local beautiful folk.

Café de Ossekop BROWN CAFE
(Uniabuurt 8) The kind of timeless brown cafe where the installation of a women's toilet in 1970 is still recounted as a recent event. A loyal crowd of locals exchanges banter with the characterful bartenders while sipping lager and tossing back gin.

 ☆ **Entertainment**

De Harmonie THEATRE
(233 02 33; www.harmonie.nl; Ruiterskwartier 4) The local home to theatre performances, both mainstream and fringe. Last minute tickets are half price.

FilmHuis Leeuwarden CINEMA
(212 50 60; www.filmhuisleeuwarden.nl; Ruiterskwartier 6) The Filmhuis unspools art-house films.

 Shopping

Look along Turfmarkt and Tuinen for some of Leeuwarden's more interesting and edgy shops.

Van der Velde BOOKSHOP
(Nieuwestad NZ 57) An elegant bookshop with a smallish but decent selection of English-language and travel books.

 Information

GSM Clinic (Berlikumermarkt 21; internet per hr €2; ☉1-10pm) Good for cheap calls, SIM cards and printing.
Tourist Office (VVV; ☎0900-202 4060; www.vvvleeuwarden.nl; Sophialaan 4; ☉noon-5.30pm Mon, 9.30am-5.30pm Tue-Fri, 10am-3pm Sat) Stocks information on the province; to find it you'll have to paw your way through the jungle of souvenirs.

❶ Getting There & Around

Leeuwarden is at the end of the main train line from the south (trains often split at Meppel, so don't end up in the half going to Groningen); it's also the hub for local services in Friesland. Lockers can be found on platform No 8 and the **train station** has full services.

Buses are to the left as you exit the train station.

The **bicycle shop** (☎213 98 00) is to the right as you exit the train station. Leeuwarden is about 110km north of Kampen (near Zwolle) on the dairy cow–lined national bike route **LF3**. Otherwise, the region is laced with bike routes atop dykes and past lakes and farms.

AROUND LEEUWARDEN

The N357, which connects Leeuwarden with the Ameland ferry port at Holwerd, 23km to the north, passes some of the oldest settled parts of Friesland – it's an excellent route for touring. On bicycles, national bike route **LF3** covers the route in 28km.

At Ferwerd, 6km southwest of Holwerd, watch for a road northeast to **Hogebeintum**, 3km off the N357. Follow that road and you'll soon see the highest *terp* (mud mound) in Friesland with a lovely old church perched on top. There are some good displays explaining the ongoing archaeological digs. It's a 10km ride southwest of Holwerd on the coastal **LF10**.

Sneek (Snits)
☑ 0515 / POP 33,700

'All Frisians know how to sail, and all Frisians know how to fish', so the saying goes. This is certainly true of the residents of Sneek, but then again, they have no choice in the matter: Frisian lakes and rivers are linked to the IJsselmeer and decorate the land not unlike the spots on the local dairy cows. If you've got a hankering to get out under sail, this is the place.

Sights & Activities

You won't find many conventional sights here in Sneek, given its overwhelming bias towards the water. The **Waterpoort** dates from 1613 and is the former gateway to the old port. Its twin towers are local landmarks.

Across from the tourist office, the **town hall** (Marktstraat 15) is an excellent example of Dutch town halls of this era.

Fries Scheepvaart Museum MUSEUM
(☑ 0515-414 057; www.friesscheepvaartmuseum.nl; Kleinzand 16; adult/child €6/2; ⊙ 10am-5pm Mon-Sat, noon-5pm Sun) This maritime museum focuses on local seafaring life, especially the era when locals made their living off perilous voyages to the North Sea.

Sleeping & Eating

Cafes can be found by the harbour around Oosterkade and on Marktstraat.

De Wijnberg HOTEL/CAFE $
(☑ 412 421; www.hoteldewijnberg.nl; Marktstraat 23; s/d from €50/65) Opposite the tourist office, this standard hotel has 23 comfy-enough rooms with either bathtubs or showers. The cafe-pub on the ground floor is often lively.

ℹ Information

Tourist Office (VVV; ☑ 750 678; www.vvvsneek.nl; Marktstraat 18; ⊙ 10am-5pm Mon-Fri, 9.30am-1pm Sat) Has long lists of boat rental and charter firms, sailing schools and more, and shares its office with the ANWB.

ℹ Getting There & Around

From the decommissioned train station, which now sports a huge **model train museum** (www.modelspoormuseum.nl), the centre of town is a five-minute walk along Stationstraat. Trains to/from Leeuwarden cost €5 (22 minutes, two per hour).

Rijwielhandel Twa Tsjillen (☑ 413 878; Wijde Noorderhorne 8; per day from €8), 400m to the northeast of the station, rents bikes. You'll find that the area's cycling options are almost as bounteous as the fertile fields as you wend your way along the many small lanes in the countryside between Sneek and Leeuwarden (about 32km).

Harlingen (Harns)
☑ 0517 / POP 15,900

Of all the old Frisian ports, only Harlingen has kept its link to the sea. It still plays an important role for shipping in the area, and

FRIESLAND (FRYSLÂN) SNEEK (SNITS)

TRAINS FROM LEEUWARDEN

DESTINATION	PRICE (€)	DURATION (MIN)	FREQUENCY (PER HR)
Groningen	9	36	3
Utrecht	24	120	1
Zwolle	15	60	2

SNEEK'S WATER-SPORTS BOUNTY

Sneek is surrounded by water, and any activity associated with it – particularly if it involves wind, of which there is hardly ever a shortage – is big.

Several sailing and windsurfing schools, where you can learn from scratch or top up existing skills, operate in the area. One of the largest is **Zeilschool de Friese Meren** (☑412 141; www.zfm.nl; Eeltjebaasweg 7), which has a range of courses (a basic weekend sailing course costs €190).

There are also many boat rental companies, including:

» **JFT Watersport** (☑443 867; www.jft-watersport.nl; Henry Bulthuisweg 16; rentals from €250 per week)

» **Sail Charter Sneek** (☑439 413; www.sailchartersneek.nl; Jan Kuipersweg 5-7; rentals from €500 per week)

» **Zijda Yachting** (☑432 993; www.zijda.nl; Zoutepoel 2-4; ⊙rentals from €70 per day)

If you'd just prefer to watch sleek ships skip across the water, then cruise into town in early August to catch **Sneekweek** (www.sneekweek.nl), the largest sailing event on Europe's inland waters. You'll be treated to plenty of racing activity and lots of frivolity.

During the summer months there are **boat cruises** on the local waters. The schedules change according to whim and weather. Most leave from the Oosterkade, at the end of Kleinzand, so either wander over or inquire at the tourist office.

is the base for ferries to Terschelling and Vlieland.

Harlingen has also managed to retain a semblance of its architectural history; much of the attractive centre is a preserved zone of pretty 16th- and 18th-century buildings that make for a good hour or so of strolling as you wait for your sailing.

◉ Sights & Activities

Harlingen is best enjoyed on foot. Stroll along the canals, many with drawbridges that rise with rhythmic regularity, especially yacht-filled **Zuiderhaven** and **Noorderhaven**. The latter has been a place for ocean-going boats to dock since the 16th century. It is lined with houses from the rich era of trading.

Voorstraat is one of the country's more attractive main streets. It has shops (but few chains), attractions and cafes. It runs into a canal criss-crossed with bridges.

Museum Hannemahuis Harlingen MUSEUM (www.hannemahuis.nl; Voorstraat 56; adult/child €3.50/1.50; ⊙11am-5pm Tue-Fri, 1.30-5pm Sat & Sun) The Gemeentemuseum het Hannemahuis is housed in an 18th-century building and includes material on Harlingen's past as a whaling town.

Along with farming, whaling was one of the industries that made Friesland one of the most prosperous regions in the Netherlands in the 1700s. Hence the celebration of

flensing and flensers – the process of stripping blubber from a whale's carcass, and the lucky chaps who got to do it. It also has a *jenever* (Dutch gin) exhibit.

🛏 Sleeping & Eating

TOP CHOICE **Zeezicht Harlingen** HOTEL **$$** (☑412 536; www.hotelzeezicht.nl; Zuiderhaven 1; s/d from €85/110; ☎) Zeezicht (it means 'sea view' not 'sea sick') lives up to its name. The 22 rooms have been beautifully redone and many have gained balconies; you can watch the comings and goings of boats from bed, terrace or cafe.

TOP CHOICE **De Tjotter** SEAFOOD **$$** (☑414 691; www.detjotter.nl; St Jacobsrtraat 1-3; meals €12-35; ⊙noon-10pm) Opening onto Noorderhaven, this fishy empire has a fine restaurant that buys its fare right from the boats. Specials are listed on a board. The cafe out front is just the place to ponder passing boats and make trenchant comments about the skills of the skippers. There is a new oyster bar and a long menu of fresh and smoked seafood for take-away.

❶ Information

Tourist Information (VVV; www.harlingen friesland.nl; Grote Bredeplaats; ⊙11am-5pm Mon-Sat, noon-5pm Sun) An excellent resource located in a kiosk in the middle of the wide street just east of the town's main confluence of canals.

❶ Getting There & Away

Harlingen is connected to Leeuwarden (€5, 23 minutes) by two trains hourly. There is a harbour station (Harlingen Haven) 300m from the ferry terminal; it has lockers. Ferries serve Vlieland and Terschelling.

There is no ideal bike route between Harlingen and Leeuwarden; you'll have to meander over back roads (about 30km via Franeker). The ferry port is on national bike route **LF10**, which runs 8km south on the coast to the Afsluitdijk and the crossing to North Holland. Going northeast, **LF10** passes all the ferry ports.

Hindeloopen (Hylpen)

📞 0514 / POP 920

Huddled up against the banks of the IJsselmeer, Hindeloopen, a cloistered fishing town among the farms, has been set apart from Friesland for centuries. Today, as you approach across the fields of corn and groups of sheep that cover the flat Frisian countryside, the sudden appearance of a forest of yacht masts marks Hindeloopen in the distance.

With its narrow streets, tiny canals, little bridges, long waterfront and lack of traffic, Hindeloopen makes for an atmospheric afternoon escape. In extraordinarily cold winters it is one of the key towns on the route of the Elfstedentocht and has a quaint, yet reverent, museum devoted to the race.

Other coastal towns in the area worth a peek, if you have time, are pretty Makkum and busy Workum; both towns are north of Hindeloopen.

◉ Sights & Activities

Hindeloopen is best experienced at a slow pace.

Het Eerste Friese
Schaatsmuseum MUSEUM
(Frisian Skating Museum; www.schaatsmuseum.nl; Kleine Weide 1-3; adult/child €2.50/1.50; ⊙10am-6pm Mon-Sat, 1-5pm Sun) The icy spectacle that is the Elfstedentocht (p204) and ice skating in general are this museum's focus. Displays covering skating through the centuries are enthralling, as is the history of the Elfstedentocht. The shop seems to have every ice-skating book ever published.

Museum Hindeloopen MUSEUM
(📞521 508; Tuinen 18; adult/child €3/2; ⊙11am-5pm Mon-Fri, 1.30-5pm Sat & Sun Apr-Oct) Museum Hindeloopen has displays about the traditional lifestyles practised locally until quite recently. It has a good walking-tour flyer and other local info.

Grote Kerk CHURCH
(⊙9am-5pm Apr-Oct) The town's landmark church dates to 1632 and since then has had a dramatic history (recounted in its brochure) of war, fires and thievery. None of this is hinted at within the austere interior.

🛏 Sleeping & Eating

There's a sprinkling of restaurants and fish stands overlooking the town's harbour.

FRIESLAND (FRYSLÂN) HINDELOOPEN (HYLPEN)

WORTH A TRIP

FRANEKER (FRJENTSJER)

About 6km east of Harlingen, the quaint town of Franeker was once a big player in education, until Napoleon closed its university down in 1810. Today its well-preserved centre makes for a nice meander, but Franeker's real highlight is its planetarium.

The Eise Eisinga Planetarium (www.planetarium-friesland.nl; Eise Eisingastraat 3; adult/child €4.50/3.75; ⊙10am-5pm Tue-Sat, 1-5pm Sun year-round, 1-5pm Mon Apr-Oct) is the world's oldest working planetarium. The namesake owner was a tradesman with a serious sideline in cosmic mathematics and astrology, who clearly could have been a 'somebody' in the astronomical world. Beginning in 1774, he built the planetarium himself to show how the heavens actually worked. It's startling to contemplate how Eisinga could have devised a mechanical timing system built to a viewable working scale that could encompass and illustrate so many different variables of time and motion.

There's an artful cafe right next door and the ornate 1591 **Stadhuis** is right across the canal. Also close by is the very old (1421) **St Martin's Church**.

The Harlingen–Leeuwarden train stops in Franeker (from Leeuwarden €4, 16 minutes, two hourly), 500m from the centre. The town is a good reward for cycling the area's little lanes.

De Stadsboerderij
GUESTHOUSE $

(☎521 278; www.destadsboerderij.nl; Nieuwe Weide 9; s/d from €55/75; ☎) With comfy rooms in a leafy, quiet corner of town, De Stadsboerderij offers a peaceful night's sleep. There's also a restaurant-pub next door, with photos of boats sailing the IJsselmeer at uncomfortable angles.

Hotel De Twee Hondjes
B&B $$

(www.detweehondjes.nl; Paardepad 2; r from €80; ☎) Housed in a typical old weathered Hindeloopen building, this enjoyable B&B has simple rooms that share bathrooms. It cheerfully accommodates wind-surfers and cyclists. The included breakfast features local specialities such as smoked fish.

TOP CHOICE Café-Restaurant de Hinde
SEAFOOD $$

(☎523 868; www.dehinde.nl; 't Oost 4; mains from €15; ☺11am-9pm) A good place to while away the hours is the terrace at Café-Restaurant de Hinde, which has been in the same family for three generations. Its seafood specials are excellent.

There are several other cafes nearby as well.

❶ Information

The staff at the **tourist office** (VVV; ☎0514 52 25 50; www.vvvhindeloopen.nl; Nieuwstad 26; ☺10am-5pm Mon-Sat Apr-Oct) can help with accommodation and offer a useful walking map. For banks and shops, you'll have to go 4km north to Workum.

❶ Getting There & Away

The **train** station is a lovely tree-lined 2km walk from town. There is an hourly service to Leeuwarden (€8, 40 minutes) via Sneek (€4, 18 minutes). By bike, it's about 30km via country lanes from Sneek to Hindeloopen, which is also on the coastal national bike route **LF22**. Harlingen is about 32km north.

FRISIAN ISLANDS

Friesland's four islands – Vlieland, Terschelling, Ameland and Schiermonnikoog – are collectively known as the Frisian Islands. Despite being basically just raised bits of sand and mud (with plenty of introduced pine forests to stabilise them) amid the mudflats of the Waddenzee, they are popular with Dutch and German holiday-makers in search of a rural beach retreat in the warmer months (Noord Holland's Texel completes the island chain).

In 2009 much of the Waddenzee off both the coasts of the Netherlands and Germany was named a Unesco World Heritage site. Although the built-up portions of the islands were not included, the designation does include the windy, natural expanse of Schiermonnikoog's national park.

Each of the islands has been developed for tourism, and the number of hotels, B&B rooms and cottages for rent is staggering considering the size of the islands themselves. Even with the development, all have large open spaces where you can get close to the sea grasses or the water itself. Any one of the islands makes an interesting trip on its own and there are copious bicycle-rental options near the ferry ports. Paths suitable for hiking and biking circle each of the islands and, away from the built-up areas, you're rewarded with long sandy beaches on the seaward sides. Throughout the Waddenzee, you'll see opportunities to go *wadlopen* (mudflat-walking).

In summer, the islands are very crowded, so don't just show up and expect to find a room; populations routinely multiply by 10 on warm weekends. All the islands have a lot of campsites.

❶ Getting There & Away

Frequent ferries link the islands with the mainland and bikes are carried for free. Texel in North Holland is the only one of the Wadden Islands to allow people to bring cars. However, all the Frisian Islands have decent bus service as well as huge bike rental shops near the ferry docks. Always confirm ferry schedules in advance. For an adventure, try island-hopping your way from one to the next.

Vlieland
☎0562 / POP 1180

Historically the most isolated of the islands, Vlieland (4022 hectares) is still ignored by most tourists today. It's a windswept and wild place, but this is part of its charm. The sole town, Oost-Vlieland, is small, and only residents are allowed to bring cars across on the ferry.

The west end of the island is mostly nothing but sand at the mercy of the sea. Parts are used by the military and there are just a couple of lonely tracks across it.

◎ Sights & Activities

There's not much in the way of human-made attractions on Vlieland, and that's exactly the point: nature is the attraction. Most of the 72 sq km of island lies waiting to be explored by bike or on foot, including its 18km of beaches. Depending on how fit you consider yourself, cycling around Vlieland can be gentle or moderately gruelling; there are many unsealed tracks that confident off-roaders can opt to tackle. You can also rent sea kayaks to venture out on the usually sedate waters.

For nature hikes and bird-watching walks, consult the tourist office.

⌬ Sleeping & Eating

Vlieland has several cafes and restaurants, all with a basic sort of steak-seafood-bit-of-pasta menu. Sleeping options are many.

Hotelletje de Veerman   HOTEL **$$**
(☑451 378; www.hotelletjedeveerman.nl; Dorpsstraat 173; r €50-110; ⚋) The well-run Veerman has 12 simple rooms (some share bathrooms) that are a short walk from the ferry. Nothing is so fancy you won't want to get sand on it, and there are also apartments in the village.

❶ Information

The **tourist office** (VVV; ☑451 111; www.vlie land.net; Havenweg 10; ⊙9am-5pm Mon-Fri and 1hr after each ferry arrival daily) is opposite the ferry dock.

❶ Getting There & Around

Rederij Doeksen (☑0900-363 57 36; www. rederij-doeksen.nl)runs regular ferries from Harlingen to Vlieland (adult/child return €25/12, bicycle €14) that take approximately 90 minutes. Departures are typically at 9am, 2.15pm and 7pm. A fast service (€32/19) takes 45 minutes direct and 90 minutes via Terschelling. Schedules change often.

Ferries sail to nearby Texel over the summer months.

You can cycle (bike hire around €8) around the island, and a bus wanders the few roads of Oost Vlieland.

Terschelling

☑0562 / POP 4900

Terschelling (11,575 hectares) is the largest of the Frisian Islands; it's also the most visited and most commercial. Its small villages, of which West Terschelling is the largest, are strung out along the southern edge of the

island, while its northern coast is all sand dunes and white beaches. The eastern end of the island is a wild and isolated place, perfect for escaping the crowds. Overall, there are 250km of walking and cycling trails, many of them sandy.

The smaller villages of Hoorn and Oosterend are east of West Terschelling, and are much less commercial and closer to the very pretty natural parts of the island.

◎ Sights & Activities

De Boschplaat   PARK
This huge car-free natural reserve at the eastern end of the island is a highlight. It's a big bird-watching locale as there are at least 65 species that breed here; others just like to head off on the trails and get lost.

**Terschelling Museum 't
Behouden Huys**   MUSEUM
(www.behouden-huys.nl; Commandeurstraat 30-32; adult/child €3/2; ⊙10am-5pm Mon-Fri, 1-5pm Sat Apr-Oct, 1-5pm Sun Jul-Sep, 1-5pm Wed-Sat Nov-Mar) The Terschelling Museum 't Behouden Huys covers the island's maritime past.

✦ Festivals & Events

Oerol   FESTIVAL
(www.oerol.nl) The annual Oerol outdoor performance festival on Terschelling is revered nationally as a perfect excuse for going to sea. It started years ago with farmers letting their cows run loose one day each year (hence the name *oerol*, which means 'everywhere' or 'all over') – these days, *everybody* gets into the spirit of things. It's a wild, arty party, piercing the otherwise unflappable northern facade for 10 days in the latter half of June.

⌬ Sleeping & Eating

Stayokay Terschelling   HOSTEL **$**
(☑442 338; www.stayokay.com/terschelling; Burg van Heusdenweg 39; dm from €25, r from €60; ⊙Apr-Oct; ⚋) Just outside West Terschelling's borders, this typically well-run Stayokay hostel has a laundry, rents bikes, and has a small restaurant and kids playground.

**Hotel Eeetcafé 't Wapen
van Terschelling**   CAFE/HOTEL **$$**
(☑448 801; www.twapenvanterschelling.nl; Oosterburen 25; r €63-100, meals €5-20) A welcoming village cafe with the best beer list on the island. It has simple rooms; the cheapest share bathrooms while the better ones have balconies.

THE GREAT DUTCH RACE: ELFSTEDENTOCHT

Skating and Dutch culture are interwoven and no event better symbolises this than the **Elfstedentocht** (Eleven Cities Tour; www.elfstedentocht.nl). Begun officially in 1909, although it had been held for hundreds of years before that, the race is 200km long, starts and finishes in Leeuwarden, and passes through 10 more Frisian towns: Sneek, IJlst, Sloten, Stavoren, Hindeloopen, Workum, Bolsward, Harlingen, Franeker and Dokkum. The record time for completing the race is six hours and 47 minutes, set in 1985 (Evert van Benthem then won again in 1986, making him a living legend).

While it is a marathon, what makes the race a truly special event is that it can only be held in years when it's cold enough for all the canals to freeze totally; this has only happened 15 times since 1909. The last time was in 1997.

In the interim the huge Elfstedentocht committee waits for the mercury to plummet. When it looks as though the canals will be properly frozen, 48 hours' notice is given. All work effectively ends throughout the province as armies of volunteers make preparations for the race, and the thousands of competitors get ready.

On the third day, the race begins at 5.30am. The next few hours are a holiday for the rest of the Netherlands as well, as the population gathers around TVs to watch the live coverage.

De Heeren Van Der Schelling CONTEMPORARY DUTCH $$
(☎448 780; www.deheerenvanderschelling.nl; mains €11-22; ⏲11am-9.30pm Thu-Mon Apr-Oct, shorter hours other times) Owner Arno van Veen State is one of the Dutch promoters of the Slow Food movement; his lovely stone restaurant has a changing menu created from local produce, lamb and seafood. Book for dinner, especially for a terrace table.

Information

The **tourist office** (VVV; ☎443 000; www.vvv-terschelling.nl; Willem Barentszkade 19a; ⏲9.30am-5.30pm Mon-Fri, 10am-3pm Sat) has a great range of maps for cycling or walking. The ferry port is just over the road.

Getting There & Around

Rederij Doeksen (p203) runs regular ferries from Harlingen to Terschelling (adult/child return €25/12, bicycle €14) and take approximately two hours. Departures are several times daily aboard very large boats. A fast service (adult/child return €32/19) takes 45 minutes direct and usually goes three times daily. Note that these ferries have little deck space compared to the large ones. Schedules change often.

Ferries sail to nearby Vlieland over the summer months.

Hourly buses (day ticket €6) run the length of the main road. Bicycles can be hired for €8; some bicycle rental places will also deliver bikes to the ferry, and transport your luggage to your accommodation.

Ameland

☎0519 / POP 3600

If the Frisian Islands were given personalities, Ameland (8500 hectares) would be the person sitting on the fence. Its four peaceful villages – Buren, Nes, Ballum and Hollum – are less developed than those on Terschelling and Texel, but they provide enough social structure for the majority of tourists. Its large swaths of untouched natural splendour offer places to escape the crowds, but Mother Nature doesn't rule the roost as on Schiermonnikoog or Vlieland.

All in all, Ameland is an island for those looking for an idyll that's 'just right'.

Sights & Activities

At only 85 sq km in size, Ameland is easily tackled by pedal power. **Bicycle paths** cover the entire island, and include a 27km path that runs almost the full length of the northern shore just south of protective sand dunes. The eastern third of the island is given over to a combination of wetlands and dunes, with not a settlement in sight; it's by far the best place to take time out for yourself.

Of the villages, the 18th-century former whaling port of **Nes** is the prettiest and most carefully preserved (although all are interesting for a brief stroll), its streets lined with tidy little brick houses. **Hollum**, the most western village, has windswept dunes within an easy walk, and is in sight of a fa-

mous red and white lighthouse (adult/child
€5/2.50; ⊙10am-5pm & 7-9pm Tue-Sat, 1-5pm &
7-9pm Sun) with expansive views.

🛏 Sleeping & Eating

All four villages have accommodation options,
although Nes is the most convenient, being a
hop, skip and a jump from the ferry port.

Hotel Restaurant De Jong   HOTEL $$
(www.hoteldejong.nl; Reeweg 29, Nes; s/d from
€60/85; 🛜) Downtown Nes is really just a
cute little crossroads shaded by trees, with
the De Jong at the centre of the action. Its
cafe and pavement tables buzz during the
summer season as people watch the com-
ings and goings along the road leading to the
ferry pier 1km south. Rooms are straightfor-
ward and comfortable.

Stayokay Ameland   HOSTEL $
(📞555 353; www.stayokay.com/ameland; Oran-
jeweg 59, Hollum; dm/r from €25/75; 🛜) This
Stayokay establishment is 200m west of the
lighthouse outside Hollum. The atmosphere
is decidedly summer camp, the dorm rooms
are basic (four or six beds) but in great con-
dition, and sand dunes are literally outside
the doorstep. Meals, packed lunches and bi-
cycles are available.

ℹ Information

The island's main **tourist office** (VVV; 📞 546
546; www.vvvameland.nl; Bureweg 2, Nes;
⊙9am-5pm Mon-Fri, 10am-3.30pm Sat) is
seven minutes' walk, or one bus stop, from the
ferry terminal.

ℹ Getting There & Around

Wagenborg (📞0546 111; www.wpd.nl; adult/
child return €14/8, bicycle €9) operates ferries
between Nes and the large ferry port at Holwerd
on the mainland. The ferries run almost every
two hours (45 minutes) all year from 7.30am
to 7.30pm, hourly on Friday and Saturday from
June to August.

To reach the Holwerd ferry terminal from
Leeuwarden, take bus 66 (40 minutes, hourly).
By bike, it's 26km.

Taxis and a small network of public buses that
serve the island's four towns meet the ferries.
Bus day passes cost €6.

Schiermonnikoog
📞0519 / POP 1000

The smallest and most serene of the Frisian
Islands, Schiermonnikoog (7200 hectares) is
the place to get away from it all; the feeling
of sheer isolation as you move through its 40
sq kms, or along the 18km of beaches, can
be intoxicating. Its name means 'grey monk
island', a reference to the 15th-century cler-
ics who once lived here. However all traces
of these folk are long gone and the island
is mostly wild. The Dutch government made
Schiermonnikoog a national park in 1989.

The island's sole town, Schiermonnik-
oog (sound familiar?), is quiet, even when
crowded. Nonresidents are not allowed to
bring cars onto the island.

◉ Sights & Activities

The sights and activities on the island re-
volve around one thing – the great outdoors.

ISLAND-HOPPING

With a little planning, good weather karma (storms cause ferry cancellations) and some
plain old luck, you can travel between all five islands on the Waddenzee: Texel and the
four Frisians.

Going east, here's how to do it (after confirming all times):

Texel–Vlieland From the long beach north of De Cocksdorp, catch a boat with **De
Vriendschap** (www.waddenveer.nl; adult/child €15.50/9, bike €8.50). After a 30-minute trip
over the very shallow waters, you are met by a truck, which takes you across the military
reservation to Bomenland. Here you take a bus or cycle to Oost-Vlieland.

Vlieland–Terschelling Fast ferries are run by **Rederij Doeksen** (www.rederij-doeksen.
nl; adult/child €8/5.25, bicycle €14) usually once per day.

Terschelling–Ameland Options here are more adventurous. **Robbenboot** (📞0519-
720 550; www.robbenboot.nl; adult/child/bicycle one-way €28/18/5, 3½ hours) runs a boat
about once a week in summer.

Ameland–Schiermonnikoog About once a week in summer, **Robbenboot** (📞0519-
720 550; www.robbenboot.nl; adult/child/bicycle one-way €28/18/5, 3½ hours) runs a boat.

The best idea is to grab a map, rent a bike, pack a picnic, and head off in any direction that takes your fancy. Even when the ferry is packed on the way over, the endless beach absorbs like a sponge and you'll soon hardly see a soul.

It's easy to lose yourself (but not get lost) on the many trails. Near town there is a moving little cemetery filled with the young men whose damaged planes crashed here during WWII. Elsewhere, when the wind rustles through the trees and not another person is in sight, you could be just about anywhere.

And at night you may have no idea where you are. The island was named the darkest place in the country in 2012 for its almost entire lack of light pollution at night. Stargazing on a clear night is stunning.

The island is the most popular destination for *wadlopers* ('mud-walkers') from the mainland, see p213.

Schiermonnikoog National Park PARK

(www.nationaalpark.nl/schiermonnikoog) The national park, which encompases much of the island, includes beaches, dunes, slat marshes and woods. You can join a variety of tours, or head off on one of the many routes for walking and cycling. Book activities and learn more at the visitors centre (☏531 641; Torenstreek 20, Schiermonnikoog; ◷10am-noon, 1.30-5pm Mon-Sat, 10am-2pm Sun, no noon-1.30pm break Jul & Aug), located in an old power station in town.

🛏 Sleeping & Eating

Schiermonnikoog has very few hotels and B&Bs, but plenty of bungalows and apartments; cafes line the few streets of Schiermonnikoog town. Camping is not allowed in the national park.

Hotel Pension van der Werff HOTEL $$
(☏531 306; www.hotelvanderwerff.nl; Langestreek 70; r €80-125) Parts of this grand hotel date back 200 years. Rooms are modern, comfortable and some have balconies. The cafe out front is *the* spot for a long breakfast. Its own vintage bus meets the ferries.

ℹ Information

The **tourist office** (VVV; ☏531 233; www.vvvschiermonnikoog.nl; Reeweg 5, Schiermonnikoog; ◷9am-1pm & 2-5pm Mon-Fri, to 4pm Sat May-Oct) is in the middle of town. A good grocery store, an ATM, a pharmacy, a bicycle-repair shop and other services are in a tight little knot in town as well.

ℹ Getting There & Away

Wagenborg (☏0900-455 44 55; www.wpd.nl; adult/child return €14/8, bicycles €9) runs large ferries between Schiermonnikoog and the port of Lauwersoog in Groningen province. At least three ferries daily make the 45-minute voyage

Hotel and public buses (return €3) meet all incoming ferries, which arrive at the island's port, 3km from the town of Schiermonnikoog. There is a huge bicycle-rental facility at the port.

Bus 50 makes the one-hour run to Lauwersoog almost hourly from Leeuwarden.

Northeast Netherlands

Includes »

Best Places to Eat

» 't Feithhuis Grand (p212)
» Muller (p212)
» Brussels Lof (p213)

Best Places to Stay

» Hotel Schimmelpenninck Huys (p211)
» Auberge Corps De Garde (p211)

Why Go?

The Netherland's northeast is far from the tourist trails. Many travellers don't venture to this far corner, but they're missing out on the Netherlands' rural heart, a place where traditions are kept alive and relics of prehistoric residents dot the landscape.

Groningen is a buzzing, youthful city (thanks to its substantial student population). Museums, restaurants, bars, theatres, canals, festivals – you name it, the city has it. It's the centre of culture and entertainment in the north and makes a very good base for further exploration.

On the nearby coast you can try the strangely intriguing pastime of *wadlopen* (mudflat-walking). Or head to Bourtange, on the eastern border to Germany which makes the shortlist for 'Best Fortified Town in Europe'; its hefty defences are just as forbidding now as they were in the 16th century. To the south, look for *hunebedden*, prehistoric rock masses purportedly used as burial chambers.

When to Go

Summer is the time to visit the northeast of the Netherlands. The long days provide a surfeit of light that benefits both plants and people. The latter thrive on balmy nights when it seems to never get dark and the good times in an outdoor cafe never seem to end. Groningen punctuates this with Noorderzon, an August festival of arts and frolic. Spring and autumn have their own charms, when you'll see few other visitors. In winter everybody hunkers down and dreams of summer.

GRONINGEN CITY

♩050 / POP 192,800

Looking at a map of the Netherlands, Groningen seems a long way from anywhere – looks can be deceiving.

This vibrant, youthful city is very much part of the comings and goings of the country, and has all you'd expect of a progressive metropolis. Its student population (which has been around since 1614 when the university opened) of 20,000 ensures a healthy, hedonistic nightlife exists alongside the museums and other culture its more mature, established residents (think professors) demand. And like everywhere in this waterlogged country, you'll find gabled houses reflected in still canals.

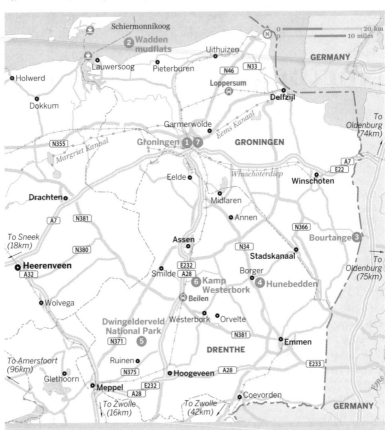

Northeast Netherlands Highlights

① Experience northern culture at its best in the museums, cafes, and bars of vibrant **Groningen** (p208)

② Join a *wadlopen* (mudflat-walking) excursion and stomp out a muddy trail on the **Wadden mudflats** (p213)

③ Walk the fortified ramparts of 16th-century **Bourtange** (p216)

④ Wonder at the **hunebedden** (p216), mighty stone constructions left behind by ancestors long since gone

⑤ Wander or cycle the beautiful boggy marshes of **Dwingelderveld National Park** (p218)

⑥ Ponder the role of everyday Dutch people at **Kamp Westerbork** (p218), where Jews like Anne Frank were held before being turned over to the Nazis

⑦ Climb the **Martinitoren** (p209) in Groningen for the view and see how many synonyms you can come up with for 'flat'

◉ Sights

The old centre, which can be crossed on foot in 15 minutes, is nicely compact and entirely ringed by canals. Virulent anticar policies dating from the 1970s mean that the centre is free of traffic.

⌐TOP⌐ Groninger Museum   MUSEUM
(www.groningermuseum.nl; Museumeiland 1; adult/child €13/3; ⊙10am-5pm Tue-Sun, to 10pm Fri) Arriving by train, it's impossible to miss the Groninger Museum. Occupying three islands in the middle of the canal in front of the station, the museum is, at the very least, a striking structure that will draw an opinion from any observer. The main collection is an eclectic mix of international artworks from throughout the ages. Look for the Asian porcelain.

The colourful, oddly shaped museum was the brainchild of architect Alessandro Mendini, who invited three 'guest architects' to each tackle a section. This explains why, to many, the museum has little consistency and appears thrown together at a whim. Inside, things are quite different; bright, pastel colours add life to the large, square exhibition rooms, and natural light seeps in from all angles.

The large spaces below the waterline, which have flooded in the past, are used for temporary exhibitions; like the curatorial direction, they are a wonderfully eccentric mix.

Noordelijk Scheepvaartmuseum   MUSEUM
(Northern Shipping Museum; www.noordelijkscheep vaartmuseum.nl; Brugstraat 24-26; adult/child €6/3.50; ⊙10am-5pm Tue-Sat, 1-5pm Sun) Well worth an hour or two, this maritime museum is an engaging look at the lives of seamen and the ships they sailed. It's laid out over several floors of buildings that once comprised a 16th-century distillery. Just getting through the labyrinth of 18 rooms is an adventure in itself and guarantees an excellent workout.

Highlights of the museum include an intricately carved replica of the church at Paramaribo – the capital of former Dutch colony Surinam – in a bottle (Room 3), showing just how much time sailors had to kill on long voyages, and detailed models demonstrating just how the many local shipyards operated throughout the centuries (Room 8). After Room 8, there are three rooms devoted to the Niemeyer Tabaksmuseum (Niemeyer Tobacco Museum), which is dedicated to the smoking habits of the Dutch through the ages. Some of the dummies aren't just toking on tobacco.

Grote Markt   SQUARE
The main square is a big, cafe-ringed public space with some 1950s duds that ruin the scene. Amid the yuck, the Stadhuis (town hall; Grote Markt), which dates from 1810, is a star.

Martinikerk   CHURCH
(www.martinikerk.nl; Grote Markt; admission €2.50; ⊙11am-5pm Mon-Sat Apr–mid-Nov, 2-5pm Sun year-round) This huge 16th-century church is at the northern corner of the Grote Markt. Its tower, the Martinitoren (adult/child €3/2; ⊙11am-5pm Mon-Sat Apr-Oct, from noon Nov-Mar), is 96m tall and is considered to have one of the most finely balanced profiles in the country. A climb to the top yields grand views.

Step around to the northeast where the Martinikerkhof is a large square surrounded by beautiful old houses. At the far corner, take take a breather at Prinsenhof, a 16th-century mansion with a gem of a little historic garden, the Prinsenhoftuin (Turfsingel; ⊙10am-dusk).

Other Sights

Just southwest of the Grote Markt, Vismarkt is a more intimate and attractive square, and not far south of Vismarkt is one of the few working synagogues (☑312 31 51; Folkingestraat 60; adult/child €4/free; ⊙1.30-5.30pm Tue-Fri & Sun) left in the country. It began life a century ago as a mosque (the light arches and minarets are dead giveaways) but now houses a school and a temporary exhibition space; its beautifully restored wooden ceiling is one of the interior's highlights.

Aa-kerk (A-Kerkhof) has parts dating to the 15th century and was a seaman's church, as this was the old harbour area. From most parts of town it is hard to miss the Academiegebouw (Broerstraat), the main building of the university. Its richly decorated exterior was completed in 1909. Around the corner on Oude Boteringestraat there are a number of appealing buildings dating from the 17th and 18th centuries.

☞ Tours

Groningen Bike Tours   BIKE
(☑301 18 81; www.fietsstadgroningen.nl; Meeting place: Bewaakte Rijwielstallingen, Ruiterstraat 1; €15; ⊙3pm Fri, 10.30am Sat) Take a 2½-hour tour of the city. Prices include bikes; book online ahead of time to arrange a meeting place; it's generally near the Pathé Cinema.

Canal Tours   CANAL TOUR
(☑312 83 79; www.rondvaartbedrijfkool.nl; adult/child €11/6) Tours of the city's largest canals

Groningen City

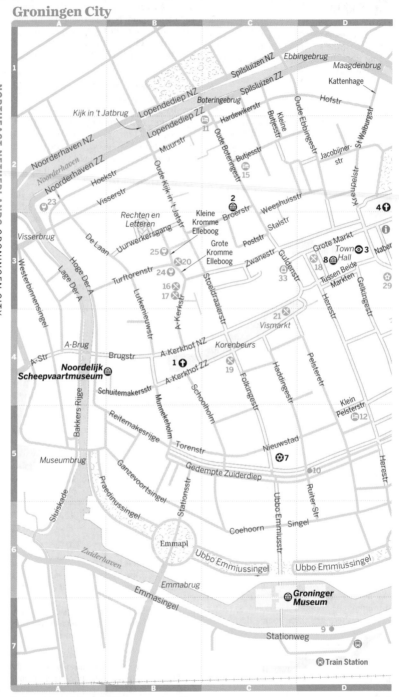

Spilsluizen NZ
Ebbingebrug
Maagdenbrug
Kattenhage
Spilsluizen ZZ
Hofstr
Boteringebrug
Kijk in 't Jatbrug
Lopendediep NZ
Hardewikerstr
Oude Ebbingestr
Lopendediep ZZ
Kleine Butjesstr
Oude Boteringestr
Jacobijner-str
St Walburgstr
Noorderhaven NZ
Muurstr
Butjesstr
11
Noorderhaven
Hoekstr
15
Kraneweelstr
Noorderhaven ZZ
Visserstr
Oude Kijk in 't Jatstr
2
Weeshuisstr
4
23
Rechten en Letteren
Broerstr
Kleine Kromme Elleboog
Stalstr
Visserbrug
De Laan
Uurwerkersgang
Poststr
Grote Markt
Naber
Westerbinnensingel
Hoge Der A
Grote Kromme Elleboog
Zwanestr
Guidenstr
Town Hall
3
25
20
Lage Der A
Turftorenstr
24
Stoeldraaierstr
33
18
8
Tussen Beide
Markten
29
16
Geikingestr
17
A-Kerkstr
21
Lutkenieuwstr
Vismarkt
Herestr
A-Brug
A-Kerkhof NZ
Korenbeurs
Pelsterstr
A-Str
Brugstr
1
Noordelijk
Scheepvaartmuseum
A-Kerkhof ZZ
19
Haddingestr
Klein
Pelsterstr
Schuitemakersstr
Schoolholm
Folkingestr
12
Bakkers Rijge
Reitemakersrijge
Munnekeholm
Torenstr
Nieuwstad
7
Museumbrug
Ganzevoortsingel
Gedempte Zuiderdiep
10
Herestr
Sluiskade
Praediniussingel
Stationsstr
Ubbo Emmiusstr
Ruiter Str
Coehoorn
Singel
Emmapl
Zuiderhaven
Ubbo Emmiussingel
Ubbo Emmiussingel
Emmabrug
Emmasingel
Groninger
Museum
9
Stationweg
Train Station

take approximately one hour and leave from out the front of the train station anywhere between one and six times daily, depending on the season.

✦✦ Festivals & Events

Eurosonic Noorderslag FESTIVAL
(www.festival.eurosonic-noorderslag.nl) A series of concerts by up-and-coming (they hope) bands. Mid-January.

Noorderzon FESTIVAL
(www.noorderzon.nl) Eleven-day arts festival featuring everything from theatre and music to children's entertainers and electronic installations. Huge fun. Mid-August in the Noorderplantsoen.

Bommen Berend FESTIVAL
Celebration of the day the city repelled the invading troops of the Bishop of Munster (28 August). Fireworks and drinking.

Studenten Cabaret Festival FESTIVAL
(www.gscf.nl) Draws performers from around Europe in late October.

🛏 Sleeping

The tourist office (p215) will book accommodation and carries a list of B&Bs and *pensions* starting at €25 per person.

TOP CHOICE ⧸ **Hotel Schimmelpenninck Huys** HOTEL **$$**
(🖉318 95 02; www.schimmelpenninckhuys.nl; Oosterstraat 53; r €70-120; 🛜) The Schimmelpenninck is Groningen's *grande dame,* and like a dowager of a certain age, it sprawls in several directions; in this case to three sides of its block. Antique-filled common areas lead to a serene courtyard and bistro, while the rest of the building features 60 rooms ranging from stylish standard doubles to suites with period pieces and chandeliers.

Auberge Corps De Garde HOTEL **$$**
(🖉314 54 37; www.corpsdegarde.nl; Oude Boteringestraat 72-74; r €85-150; 🌼🛜) Originally the town guard's quarters, the 17th-century building sports carved animal heads above the door (woodchucks?). The 19 rooms are a mix of vintage and contemporary decor. The 'historic rooms' feature ancient wooden beams that may delight or imperil depending on your height.

Martini Hotel HOTEL **$$**
(🖉312 99 19; www.martinihotel.nl; Gedempte Zuiderdiep 8; r €70-120; 🌼@🛜) Parts of the

Groningen City

Martini date to 1871, a time when people were smaller and rooms were too. But most of the hotel is housed in roomier modern wings lurking back from the street (some have air-con). The decor is cheery.

NH Hotel De Ville   HOTEL **$$**
(☏318 12 22; www.nh-hotels.com; Oude Boteringestraat 43-45; r €90-200; @🖘) Two 18th-century houses and a modern addition feature 66 luxurious rooms. Enjoy the fireplace and courtyard. Expect full four-star hotel services.

Citycamp Stadspark   CAMPGROUND **$**
(☏525 16 24; www.citycamps.com; Campinglaan 6; camp sites from €18; ⊙mid-Mar–mid-Oct) Stadspark is a spacious, green campground surrounded by a huge park, yet it's within easy shot of the city. Facilities include a shop, restaurant and playground but it's without frills like electricity at sites or cable TV. From the train station, take bus 4 (direction: Hoogkerk, stop Kranenburg) about 3km west.

Hotel Garni Friesland   HOTEL **$**
(☏312 13 07; www.hotelfriesland.nl; Kleine Pelsterstraat 4; r €40-100; 🖘) The Friesland is bare bones, but it's central and the prices are

unbeatable. Service is amenable, and the 17 rooms are adequate. Bathrooms are down the hall and a basic breakfast is included.

 Eating

Groningen may be a student city, but it has many fine restaurants.

TOP CHOICE **'t Feithhuis Grand**   CAFE **$$**
(www.restaurant-feithhuis.nl; Martinikerkhof 10; mains €8-16) In the leafy Martinikerkhof, just off the Grote Markt, this stylish grand cafe has a wide terrace outside and a sleek interior that is a study in woodsy materialism. The walls are lined with posters, and floral arrangements abound. Food ranges from bagels to complex sandwiches and Mediterranean-flavoured mains.

TOP CHOICE **Muller**   FUSION **$$$**
(☏318 32 08; www.restaurantmuller.nl; Grote Kromme Elleboog 13; menus from €65; ⊙6-10pm Tue-Sat) You can enjoy the show here for free by watching the artistry of Jean-Michel Hengge in the kitchen from the windows on the street. But really just be a voyeur? Menus change regularly and include delights such as lobster, scallops, lamb and much more.

One of the region's best; Hengge picks the vegetables from his own garden.

Brussels Lof
CONTEMPORARY DUTCH **$$**

(www.brusselslof.com; A-Kerkstraat 24; mains €15-25; ⊘5.30-9.30pm) When the menu says the fondue can be prepared with extra garlic, you know you've chosen a good spot. Casual in every way except when it comes to food, this bistro has an excellent menu that emphasizes local vegetables, seafood and, yes, fondue. Classical music gives the dining area an aural serenity.

Huis De Beurs
CAFE **$**

(www.huisdebeurs.nl; A-Kerkhof ZZ 4; mains €8-13) On a busy corner, this sidewalk cafe is a great place if you want to rubberneck for the inevitable speeding cyclist-dawdling shopper catastrophe. The casual menu of salads, sandwiches and hot specials is also served inside, which has an attractive and vaguely Victorian feel. On some nights there's live acoustic music.

Het Goudkantoor
TRADITIONAL DUTCH **$$**

(www.goudkantoor.nl; Waagplein 1; mains €12-20) The architecture of this restored historic cafe is amazing. Dating from 1635, the 'Gold Office' features a gold-tinted exterior and graceful interior, complete with striking paintings. The menu is, not surprisingly, traditional (eg steak with mustard).

Organic Food Market
MARKET

(Vismarkt; ⊘Tue) This market is a regional favourite.

🍷 Drinking

Groningen's student bar-hopping nightlife is centred on Poelestraat and its adjoining streets.

 De Pintelier
BAR

(Kleine Kromme Elleboog 9) Step back into the 1920s at this cosy bar where the selection of beer and *jenever* (Dutch gin) reads like an encyclopaedia. Its long wooden bar and thicket of candle-lit tables are timeless. Take in the breeze in the backside modern courtyard.

Café Mulder
LOUNGE

(☑314 14 69; Grote Kromme Elleboog 22) Artists, writers and musicians highlight a slightly older crowd that debates the events of the

---

POUNDING MUD: WADLOPEN

When the tide retreats across the Unesco-recognised mudflats off the north coast of the Waddenzee, locals and visitors alike attack it with abandon, marching, and inevitably sinking, into the sloppy mess. Known as *wadlopen* (mudflat-walking); it's an exercise in minimalism, forcing you to concentrate on the little things while you march towards the featureless horizon.

The mud stretches all the way to the Frisian Islands offshore, and treks across to the islands are popular. Because of the treacherous tides, and the fact that some walkers can become muddled and lose their way, *wadlopen* can only be undertaken on a guided tour. Proponents say that it is strenuous but enlivening; the unchanging vista of mud and sky has an almost meditative quality: the call of birds and the chance to focus on little details, such as the small crabs and cockles underfoot, puts one in touch with nature's finer points.

The centre for *wadlopen* is the coast north of Groningen, where several groups of trained guides are based, including:

Stichting Wadloopcentrum (☑0595-52 83 00; www.wadlopen.org; Haven 20, Lauwersoog)

Dijkstra's Wadlooptochten (☑0595-52 83 45; www.wadloop-dijkstra.nl; Hoofdstraat 118)

Guided walks have set rates and take place between May and October. Options range from a short 6km jaunt across the mudflats (€11, three hours) to a gruelling yet exhilarating 20km pound to Schiermonnikoog (€27, five hours); the latter, with its national park, is the most popular destination. The ferry ride back from the islands is included in the price.

It's essential to book around a month in advance. You'll be told what clothes to bring depending on the time of year. Note that you need good shoes for this but that they may be ruined.

WORTH A TRIP

RURAL CHURCHES

Stoic churches centuries old dot the flat countryside northeast from Groningen to the coast. They are a lasting testament to the pious and hardscrabble people who eked out lives in the muddy, sandy soil.

Reaching them can be difficult by bus and train, but they make for excellent touring by bike as you can use the distant steeples like points on a compass for navigating the tiny back roads and dykes (make sure to also get a map from the Groningen tourist office see p215). Doors may be open – or not.

A few favourites:

Zeerijp A large church with a high bell tower and an unusual fake brick motif inside. A 3km walk northeast from the Loppersum train station.

Kreward Surrounded by a tiny moat with ducks, this picture-perfect 16th-century church sits primly on a *terp* (mud mound). It's near the coast and the N33.

Bierum This 13th-century church's leaning tower was saved by adding a huge flying buttress in the 1800s. The town of Bierum is 24km northeast of Groningen and near the N33 and the coast. It's on the **LF10** national bike route.

day at this classy pub. The interior is both rich and intimate.

Café de Sleutel BROWN CAFE
(www.cafedesleutel.nl; Noorderhaven 72; ⊗4.30pm-1am Mon-Sat) In a 17th-century brewery (note the keg hanging outside bearing a gold *sleutel*, or key) in an old brewing district, this vintage bar has a local following for its €10 meals and cosy canalside vibe.

Roezemoes BROWN CAFE
(Gedempte Zuiderdiep 15) You can tell this gem of a brown cafe has been around a while; the bullet holes from the 1672 invasion attempt are a dead giveaway. Come evening, some enjoy trad Dutch fare (mains €15) while most are quaffing beers; there are occasional blues bands.

Stadlander GRAND CAFE
(www.eetcafestadtlander.nl; Poelestraat 35) Inside it feels like a large and bustling brown cafe, but outside, Stadlander is one of several popular cafes on a sort of impromptu square. If there's a hint of balmy, these places are heaving.

☆ Entertainment

To find out what's going on around town, check out the posters that appear everywhere, or check out the website www.groningeruitburo.nl.

The university ensures that there are a lot of talented students performing everything from jazz to rock.

TOP CHOICE **Jazz Café De Spieghel** LIVE MUSIC
(☑312 63 00; www.jazzcafedespieghel.nl; Peperstraat 11; ⊗music from 10.30pm) A perennial favourite, this lively brown cafe features nightly live jazz, a smooth sultry atmosphere, and a great bar.

Vera CLUB
(www.vera-groningen.nl; Oosterstraat 44; ⊗Thu-Sat) To see the next big rock act, head to this club; U2 played to 30-odd people in the early 1980s, and Nirvana later gave a performance to a crowd of about 60 people before going supernova. Maybe less is more?

Grand Theatre PERFORMING ARTS
(☑314 46 44; www.grandtheatregroningen.nl; Grote Markt 35) This is the city's premiere theatre and offers a thought-provoking array of musical and theatrical performances.

De Oosterpoort LIVE MUSIC
(☑368 03 68; www.de-oosterpoort.nl; Trompsingel) De Oosterpoort is *the* place in Groningen to catch many of the large musical acts passing through town. Jazz and classical concerts are the mainstay of its monthly program.

🔒 Shopping

Large markets are held on Grote Markt and Vismarkt Tuesday, Friday and Saturday. Galleries abound on the west side, especially on Visserstraat, Oude Kijk in 't Jatstraat, and Lopendediep NZ.

TOP CHOICE **Kaashandel van der Ley**   CHEESE

(Oosterstraat 61-63) The best cheese from the Netherlands and around the world is sold at this beautiful shop. Look for local organic varieties and some of the rare aged numbers that the Dutch never export. There are also deli items and a large array of olives so you can create a dreamy picnic.

Selexyz Scholtens   BOOKSHOP

(☑317 25 00; Guldenstraat 20) Has a large selection of English novels and travel titles.

❶ Information

Money
GWK (⊘8am-7pm) Currency exchange; located in the train station.

Tourist Information
Tourist Office (VVV; ☑313 97 41; www.toerisme.groningen.nl; Grote Markt 29; ⊘9.30am-6pm Mon-Fri, 10am-5pm Sat year-round, 11am-4pm Sun Jul & Aug) Offers advice and sells tickets, tours and excellent walking-tour maps in English. Buy your 'Er gaat niets boven Groningen' (There's no place like Groningen) T-shirt here. Has free internet.

❶ Getting There & Away

The regional **bus station** is to the right as you exit the train station.

Bicycle
Riding in Groningen province means a lot of back roads meandering; however, there are some key national bike routes. National bike route **LF9** runs south to Utrecht (about 200km) and beyond. It's been designed to follow what would be the Dutch coastline if there were no dykes. **LF14** heads 48km northwest to Lauwersoog, where you can get the ferry to Schiermonnikoog.

Train
The grand 1896 **train station**, restored to its original glory, is worth seeing even if you're not catching a train. Lockers can be found on platform 2b and there is a good range of services. Note that trains often split at Meppel, so don't end up in the half going to Leeuwarden.

Groningen is the hub for local services in the province. Sample train fares and schedules in the box below.

❶ Getting Around

Groningen is easily tackled on foot or by bicycle. The train station is just across from the Groninger Museum, and around a 10-minute walk from Grote Markt, the main town square.

Around Groningen

Meandering through the verdant countryside around Groningen by bike is rewarding by itself, but there are also numerous little delights to give you good reason to peddle away.

◉ Sights

Museum de Buitenplaats   MUSEUM

(☑309 58 18; www.museumdebuitenplaats.nl; Hoofdweg 76; adult/child €7/free; ⊘11am-5pm Tue-Sun) In the little town of Eelde, 5km south of Groningen, this charming museum is devoted to figurative art from around Europe. The main organic structure, which blends into its natural surroundings, features paintings from some of the Netherlands' more progressive 20th-century artists, such as Wout Muller, Henk Helmantel, Herman Gordijn and Matthijs Röling.

Its manicured gardens are peppered with sculptures and there's also a sun-bathed cafe. Poetry readings, storytelling and musical concerts (usually summer Sunday afternoons) are featured over the summer months on the museum's open-air stage.

From Groningen, take bus 52 (28 minutes, every half-hour). There's also a good bike route on the west side of Paterswolder Meer.

Zeehondencreche Pieterburen   NATURE CENTRE

(Seal Creche; ☑0595-52 65 26; www.zeehondencreche.nl; Hoofdstraat 94a, Pieterburen; admission €6; ⊘9am-5pm) Devoted to the rescue and rehabilitation of sick and injured seals, this centre normally houses 20 to 30 animals, which can be seen lounging and swimming

TRAINS FROM GRONINGEN CITY

DESTINATION	FARE (€)	DURATION (MIN)	FREQUENCY (PER HR)
Leeuwarden	9	36	3
Utrecht	25	120	1
Zwolle	16	69	3

in various pools. The most popular times to visit are the 11am and 4pm feeding times. More than 200 seals have been released back into the wild.

Back in 1972 Lenie 't Hart, a resident of the small coastal town of Pieterburen, began caring for seals in her backyard. Pollution and tourism were taking their toll on the local seal colonies, and it was her way of doing something about it. From this small start, the centre has grown. To get to Pieterburen on weekdays (the bus runs Monday to Friday only), take the train from Groningen to Winsum (€4, 15 minutes, hourly), and then bus 68 (20 minutes).

Menkemaborg   HISTORIC BUILDING
(☑0595-43 19 70; www.menkemaborg.nl; Menkemaweg 2, Uithuizen; adult/child €6/2; ☺10am-5pm Tue-Sun Mar-Sep, to 4pm Oct-Feb) Some 25km northeast of Groningen, in the small farming town of Uithuizen, is one of the Netherlands' most authentic manor houses, **Menkemaborg**. Originally a fortified castle dating back to the 14th century, Menkemaborg received its present gentrified appearance – a moated estate of three houses surrounded by immaculate gardens – early in the 18th century, and it has barely been altered since.

Inside, the rooms retain all the pomp and ceremony of 18th-century aristocratic life, complete with carved-oak mantelpieces, stately beds and fine china.

Hourly trains run between Uithuizen and Groningen (€6, 34 minutes). The train station is a 1km walk west of Menkemaborg. National bike route **LF10** passes right through.

Bourtange
☑0599 / POP 1200

Bourtange, a tiny town near the German border, is home to one of the best-preserved fortifications in the country. While rather small and best seen from the air, it is nonetheless a sight to behold, with its flooded moats, solid defences and quaint houses protected from all sides. The region around Bourtange is also worth exploring; off the beaten path, it consists of pretty countryside and tree-shaded canals, ideal for tackling by bike.

☉ Sights

Built in the late 1500s, Bourtange represents the pinnacle of the arms and fortification of the time. Behind its walls and moats, it could withstand months of siege by an invading army.

HUNEBEDDEN

People have been enjoying the quiet in Drenthe since as early as 3000 BC, when prehistoric tribes lived here amid the bogs and peat. These early residents began cultivating the land, a pastime still enjoyed by many in the province, and created what is arguably the most interesting aspect of Drenthe today, the *hunebedden*.

Hunebedden, which predate Stonehenge, are prehistoric burial chambers constructed with huge grey stones, some of which weigh up to 25,000kg. It is thought the stones arrived in the Netherlands via glaciers from Sweden some 200,000 years ago, but no one can be certain of the fact. Little is known about the builders of the *hunebedden*, except that they took burying their dead very seriously, burying people, along with their personal items and tools, under the monolithic stones. Theories as to how the chambers were constructed have been bantered about by the scientific community, but once again, a definitive answer is yet to be found. A total of 54 of these impressive groupings of sombre grey stones can be seen in Drenthe and Groningen.

The impressive **Hunebedcentrum** (☑0599-23 63 74; www.hunebedcentrum.nl; Bronnegerstraat 12, Borger; adult/child €7.50/3.50; ☺10am-5pm Mon-Fri, 11am-5pm Sat & Sun) in Borger, a little town 17km northwest of Emmen, is the centre for the *hunebedden*, and the logical place to start a tour. The website www.hunebedden.nl is also a good source of info.

The centre has many displays relating to the stones as well as excavated artefacts, and the largest *hunebed* is located just outside its doors. Maps of all the sites are also available; most are clumped around the villages of Klijndijk, Odoorn, Annen and Midlaren, which are strung out along the N34, a picturesque road linking Emmen and Groningen.

It's best to explore the *hunebedden* with your own transport; pick up a map from Hunebedden Centrum and look out for the large brown signs showing a pile of rocks while driving or cycling. Borger is 25km southeast of Assen on national bike route **LF14**.

In 1964 the regional government restored the battlements and the town itself to its 1742 appearance, when the fortifications around the citadel had reached their maximum size. It took three decades, during which time roads were moved and buildings demolished or reconstructed.

The results are impressive and Bourtange is stunningly pretty. The star-shaped rings of walls and canals have been completely rebuilt and the village has been returned to a glossier version of its 18th-century self. It's a cliché, but a visit to Bourtange is truly a step into the past, to a time when rogue armies wandered the lands, and villagers hid behind defences designed to keep them at bay.

From the parking area and tourist office, you pass through two gates and across three drawbridges over the moats before you reach the old town proper. From the town's central square, the Marktplein, cobblestone streets lead off in all directions; the pentagram-shaped inner fortification can be crossed in a matter of minutes by foot. The town's tourist office (☑35 46 00; www.bourtange.nl; William Lodewijkstraat 33; ☺10am-5pm Mar-Oct, noon-5pm Sat & Sun Nov-Feb) sells a handy English-language booklet. The museum (admission to Bourtange and museum: adult/child €6/3.50; ☺10am-5pm) has detailed displays showing the reconstruction and restoration. Aerial photographs show the remarkable changes between 1965 and 2004.

Inside the walls (which you can roam) at the core of the fortification, brick houses make good use of what little space the five bastions afford. Marktplein is a good spot to start exploring, with its cafes, small craft shops and tree-shaded benches.

Of the old buildings, six have been turned into exhibits that are part of the museum admission. Two – the Captain's Lodge and De Dagen van Roam – cover the life and times of the militia stationed at Bourtange in the 17th and 18th centuries, while the Museum de Baracquen displays artefacts and curios uncovered during the fort's reconstruction. De Poort has an excellent model of Bourtange; the town's synagogue, built in 1842, explains the life and times of its Jewish population, and includes a plaque listing the 42 locals taken away to their deaths by the Nazis.

🛏 Sleeping & Eating

It's possible to stay within the walls, in the original soldiers' (€77) or captains' (€87) quarters. Bookings are taken at the tourist office. Rooms are tidy, with polished wooden floors, and breakfast is included.

Two atmospheric cafes on Marktplein are the only places to eat within the old town.

❶ Getting There & Away

Bourtange is not easy to get to without your own wheels. From Groningen, the trip by train and bus takes about 90 minutes. The following connections can be made hourly and cost about €10: catch a train east to Winschoten, then bus 14 south to Vlagtwedde; transfer to bus 11 for Bourtange. But before you go, confirm this with the transport info website www.9292.nl.

If touring by bike, you can combine Bourtange with visits to the rural churches east of Groningen and the *hunebedden* in Drenthe, some 30km to the west, for a multiday ride. The area is laced with bike paths across farmlands but a cycling map is essential.

DRENTHE

If ever there was a forgotten corner of the Netherlands, this is it. With no sea access or major city to call its own (charm-starved Emmen is its largest) and few five-star attractions, Drenthe is as Vincent van Gogh described in 1833: 'Here is peace.' Of course, he later went mad.

But peace (and war) are exactly why this small backwater deserves some of your time, simply to experience something different in a land where one pretty town follows another and there's a growing collection of national parks. Plus, you get to explore the mysterious *hunebedden* and follow the legacy of Anne Frank.

Assen

☑0592 / POP 67,300

With a close proximity to Groningen, Drenthe's capital, Assen, brings up the rear in terms of appeal. The tourist office (VVV; ☑24 37 88; www.ditisassen.nl; Marktstraat 8; ☺1-6pm Mon, 9am-6pm Tue-Fri, 9am-5pm Sat) is a good source for bike maps of the region and info on the national parks.

The Drents Museum (☑37 77 73; www.drentsmuseum.nl; Brink 1; adult/child €12/free; ☺11am-5pm Tue-Sun), near the centre, has *hunebedden* artefacts and various artworks and furnishings from Drenthe's history.

The tourist office and museum are 500m from the station via Stationsstraat. Frequent

trains connect Assen with both Groningen (€6, 18 minutes) and Zwolle (€13, 50 minutes).

The station is the main regional bus stop and it has a bike shop. National bike route LF14 runs south 34km from Groningen and on to Emmen (about 40km southeast).

Kamp Westerbork

More than 107,000 Jews were deported from the Netherlands by the Nazis in WWII. Almost all died in the concentration and death camps of Central and Eastern Europe and almost all began their fateful journey here, a rural forest about 10km south of Assen, near the tiny village of Hooghalen.

Kamp Westerbork (0593-59 26 00; www.kampwesterbork.nl; Oosthalen 8; adult/child €6.50/3; ⊘10am-5pm Mon-Fri year-round, 1-5pm Sat & Sun Oct-Mar, 11am-5pm Sat & Sun Apr-Sep), ironically, was built by the Dutch government in 1939 to house German Jews fleeing the Nazis. When the Germans invaded in May 1940, they found Westerbork ideal for their own ends. Beginning in 1942 it became a transit point for those being sent to death camps, including Anne Frank.

A visit to the camp starts with the excellent museum at the car park. Displays trace the holocaust in the Netherlands and there is a moving timeline covering Anne Frank, her diary and her ultimate death at Bergen-Belsen in Germany in 1945. The bookshop has many excellent brochures and books.

The actual camp is a 2km walk through a forest from the museum (or a €2 bus ride that gets overcrowded in summer). There is little to see here today from the 1940s as the Dutch government rather incredibly used it as a refugee camp after the war, first for surviving Jews and later for immigrants such as the South Mollucans. However, displays show the location of Nazi-era features such as the punishment building and the workshops where internees worked as virtual slaves.

Monuments include a series of stones showing where Dutch Jews and Roma died (Auschwitz-Birkenau 60,330...).

❶ Getting There & Away

Despite the name, the camp itself is 7km north of Westerbork town (and 7km south of Assen).

By **train**, use the station at Beilen on the Zwolle–Assen–Groningen train line (at least two trains per hour). From here, take a *treintaxi* (special taxi for train passengers) to the site, which you summon at the station; it costs €5

and takes 10 minutes. By **bike**, use any of the many rural bike paths.

National Parks

Various national parks have been created amid the farmlands and natural areas of Drenthe. Drentsche Aa National Landscape (0592-36 58 64; www.drentscheaa.nl) takes in a varied 10,000 hectare landscape of ancient farms, fields of wildflowers, *hunebedden* and evocative country roads. It's mostly undeveloped but the park map, available from tourist offices, is a good guide. Cycling through this bell-shaped area just northwest of Assen is sublime. National bike route LF14 goes right down the middle.

Dwingelderveld National Park preserves 3700 hectares of the largest wet heathland in Europe. More than 60km of hiking paths and 40km of cycling paths wander amid the bogs, meadows and forest. It's a starkly beautiful place and very popular on summer weekends. Of several in the area, the best visitor centre (0522-472 951; Benderse 22, Ruinen; ⊘10am-5pm daily, Apr-Sep, Wed-Sun Oct-Mar) is in Ruinen, 7km west of the A28 on the N375. Get maps here.

Orvelte

0593

A foundation governs the tiny village of Orvelte, 17km south of Assen. Its goal – to preserve the feel of a 19th-century Drenthe community – is alive and well here, and visitors are welcome to join them in the past for a day, between Easter and the end of October.

No cars are permitted (aside from those of the residents) and owners cannot alter the old buildings in uncharacteristic ways. Residents mainly engage in traditional activities; there's the butcher, the baker...you get the idea. During summer there are lovely vegetable and flower gardens growing near every house.

The tourist office (32 23 35; www.orvelte. net; ⊘10am-5pm Apr-Oct) has brochures and maps of the village, and can inform you about what's on when. It can also arrange B&B accommodation in one of the traditional houses (from €30 per person).

To get to Orvelte, take the Beilen stop on the Zwolle–Assen–Groningen train line (at least two trains per hour); change to bus 22 (16 minutes, hourly Monday to Friday, less frequent on weekends) for Orvelte. Bike routes converge on Westerbork, just 3km west.

Central Netherlands

Includes »

Best Places to Eat

» Bouwkunde (p222)

» Cucina Italiana (p223)

» Poppe (p225)

» Restaurant de
Bottermarck (p227)

» Ijs van Co (p234)

Best Places to Stay

» Hotel de Leeuw (p221)

» Hotel Fidder (p225)

» Hotel Gilde (p221)

Why Go?

The 'forgotten' provinces of the Central Netherlands, Overijssel and Gelderland, compensate for a lack of blockbuster cities with natural beauty – forest, rivers, lakes, national parks – abundant history and compelling attraction. Hoge Veluwe National Park, containing the Kröller-Müller Museum (with the world's finest Van Gogh collection), should star in any Dutch itinerary.

Escape the hectic urban sprawl of the Central Netherlands and ride myriad bike routes among lush, watery scenery that will cleanse the soul. Weerribben-Wieden National Park sprawls across wetlands rife with otters, beavers, birds and eels.

Deventer, Zwolle and Kampen are centuries-old towns, filled with atmospheric historical buildings that recall a time in history when they were key members of the Hanseatic League. Nijmegen has a waterfront vibe, masses of students and an annual march that now takes the form of a weeklong party. On the other side of history, there are many WWII memorials and locations to contemplate around Arnhem.

When to Go

Rural Netherlands is at its best in summer when the fields are verdant, the waters are swimmable and the nights are long. Getting a bike and meandering the myriad bike lanes this time of year is a pleasure – you'll wish it was an 'endless summer'. Activities in places like Weerribben-Wieden National Park are at their peak and you can canoe and kayak for hours on end. The towns and cities, however, have longer seasons. Wandering the narrow streets of Deventer is an atmospheric pleasure at almost any time of year.

OVERIJSSEL

Overijssel means 'beyond the IJssel', named after the river forming much of the province's western border. The province is hilly in the east near Germany and flat and soggy in the west along the former coastline, now landlocked by Flevoland's Noordoostpolder.

You might like to anchor yourself in Deventer to explore Overijssel, though Zwolle also has its charms. Giethoorn in the north is a watery novelty, but beware of swollen summer crowds.

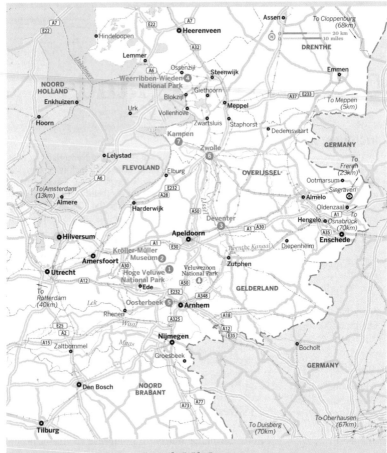

Central Netherlands Highlights

❶ Lose yourself while riding a free white bike in the verdant surrounds of **Hoge Veluwe National Park** (p234)

❷ Find your favourite masterpiece at the glorious **Kröller-Müller Museum** (p235)

❸ Discover hidden treasures along the ancient backstreets of Hanseatic **Deventer** (p221)

❹ Spook yourself in the otherworldly ambience of the **Weerribben-Wieden National Park** (p228), encompassing Overijssel's strange wetlands

❺ Consider the costs of war at Gelderland's war cemeteries and memorials in **Oosterbeek** (p234)

❻ Plunge into the past amidst the 14th-century buildings scattered along the streets of **Zwolle** (p224)

❼ See how many medieval monuments you can find amongst the 500 in **Kampen** (p227)

Deventer

🎵 0570 / POP 98,600

Deventer surprises. It's at its best on a beautiful August night, when you can wander alone among the Hanseatic ghosts along the twisting streets searching out the odd architectural detail in the ancient facades. What looks like a crack in the old architectural wonders is really a tiny passage to the IJssel.

Deventer was already a bustling mercantile port as far back as AD 800, and it maintained its prosperous trading ties for centuries, evidence of which you'll see everywhere in its sumptuously detailed old buildings. Think of it as the Delft of the east.

◎ Sights

The **Brink** is the main square and Deventer's commercial heart. This historic town is best enjoyed by randomly wandering the streets which radiate out from the Brink. Look for surprises.

The **Bergkwartier** has especially cute little houses jammed cheek to jowl and is home to a number of actors and artists.

The historic details are so rich that the WWII film *A Bridge Too Far*, which was essentially about Arnhem's role in the war, was filmed here (Arnhem, of course, had been levelled by the war).

Waag HISTORIC BUILDING
(🖉69 37 80; Brink; museum adult/child €5/2; ⊙museum 10am-5pm Tue-Sat, 1-5pm Sun) The town's famous Waag, the 1528 weigh-house in the middle of the square, was recently restored. Look for the cauldron on the north side – a gruesome and well-supported legend tells of a 16th-century clerk boiled alive in it after he was discovered substituting cheap metals for precious ones in the local money supply.

There's a small **museum** inside the Waag, with historical displays and the oldest bicycle in Holland. Check out the fish.

Grote of Lebuïnuskerk CHURCH
(admission €3; ⊙11am-5pm Mon-Sat) The Grote of Lebuïnuskerk is the city's main church. It stands on a site where other churches had been razed by flames and other catastrophes time and again; the present Gothic structure was built between 1450 and 1530. Climb the tower (220 steps) to see Deventer's old Hanseatic-era walled shape.

FREE **Bergkerk** CHURCH
(🖉61 85 18; ⊙11am-5pm Tue-Sun) At the top of Bergstraat, Bergkerk has landmark towers that date to the 13th century. The medieval equivalent of *Extreme Makeover* gave it a Gothic revamp in the 1400s.

🏃 Activities

The banks of the IJssel River are a scenic place for **cycling**. Green panoramas filigreed with water stretch in all directions. Riding national bike route **LF3** 36km north to Zwolle is a fine option, while a good 32km round-trip follows the riverbanks north to Olst, where you can take a ferry across and return along the other side to Deventer. You can do the same thing going south to Zutphen, a 47km loop.

🎭 Festivals & Events

Op Stelten FESTIVAL
On the first weekend of July, the old streets of Deventer are turned into a massive theatre with performances of all kinds. The festival name *op stelten* means 'on stilts', which refers to the scores of street performers who are part of the show.

Bookfest FESTIVAL
More than 800 dealers of used and rare books set up shop in the city on the first Sunday in August.

🛏 Sleeping

 Hotel de Leeuw HOTEL $$
(🖉61 02 90; www.hoteldeleeuw.nl; Nieuwstraat 25; r €80-140; @☎) One of the sweetest places to stay in the Netherlands, and not just because it has a bakery museum and old candy store. Every comfort you can think of, right down to the weather forecasts at breakfast (which you can take in the courtyard), is provided by the charming owner. The lovely building dates back to 1645; the simple rooms are comfy and many have kitchenettes.

Hotel Gilde HOTEL $$
(🖉64 18 46; www.hotelgilde.nl; Nieuwstraat 41; s/d from €80/100; ☎) This charming 36-room hotel, once a 17th-century convent, celebrates its former architectural glory. With all that weight of history on the trimmings and frills, you know that this is the swishest place in town (despite the austerity of its former tenants). Overlook a nice courtyard.

Deventer

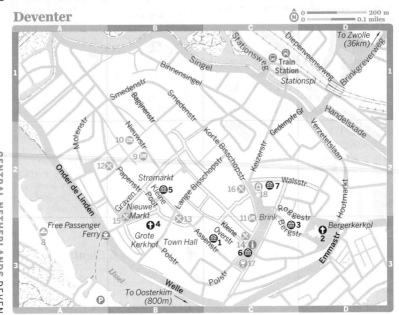

Deventer

◉ Sights
1	Assenstraat 67-79	C3
2	Bergkerk	D3
3	Bergstraat 29	C3
4	Grote of Lebuïnuskerk	B3
5	Oldest Stone House	B2
6	Waag	C3
7	Walstraat 20	C2

🛏 Sleeping
8	Camping De Worp	A3
9	Hotel de Leeuw	B2
10	Hotel Gilde	B2
11	Hotel Royal	C3

✗ Eating
12	Bouwkunde	B2
13	Cucina Italiana	B3
14	Eetcafé De Sjampetter	C3
15	't Arsenaal	B2
16	Talamini	C2

🍷 Drinking
17	Heksenketel	C3

🛍 Shopping
18	Kaashandel De Brink	C2

Camping De Worp　　　　　CAMPGROUND **$**
(☎61 36 01; www.stadscamping.eu; Worp 12; camp sites from €14; ◔Apr-Oct; ☎) Right across the IJssel from the centre of town, about two minutes north of the passenger ferry.

Hotel Royal　　　　　　　　　　HOTEL **$$**
(☎61 18 80; www.royal-deventer.nl; Brink 94; r €65-100; ☎) The 20 rooms here are spread over three floors and there is an elevator. Some overlook the Brink. The included breakfast buffet is quite nice.

✗ Eating

TOP CHOICE Bouwkunde　　　　　　　　BISTRO **$$**
(☎61 40 75; www.theaterbouwkunde.nl; Klooster 4; menus from €25; ◔6-10pm Tue-Sat) The best produce from the region is used at this superb brasserie located under a small theatre. The menu combines French accents with Dutch staples: expect fine preparations of simple seafoods and meats. Service is polished – like the silver. You can't beat the tables outside in summer. Book ahead.

Cucina Italiana   ITALIAN **$$**

(☎615 900; www.cucinadeventer.nl; Grote Poot 1; mains from €15; ☺5.30-10pm Tue-Sun) You'll swear that this excellent Italian restaurant must have been somehow tele-transported to Deventer from a piazza in Rome. The dishes are perfectly authentic, many sourced using local organic ingredients. Ask for the diverse antipasti plate to start for an unforgettable feast. Great wine list. Book outside in summer.

't Arsenaal   CONTEMPORARY DUTCH **$$$**

(☎61 64 95; www.restaurantarsenaal.nl; Nieuwe Markt 33-34; menus from €30; ☺5-10pm Mon-Sat) This stylish restaurant, next to the Grote of Lebuïnuskerk, comes into its own in summer, when the courtyard and alleyway, in the shadow of the old church, make for a grand setting. The seasonal menu has French influences for dishes such as lobster ravioli.

Talamini   ICE CREAM **$**

(www.talamini.nl; Brink 103; Treats from €2; ☺11am-9pm) This huge local institution has been dishing up ice cream since 1892. Choose (or *try* to choose) between over 50 freshly made flavours. Always crowded on a temperate day.

Eetcafé De Sjampetter   BROWN CAFE **$**

(☎61 71 55; Brink 81; mains from €8) The brownest of the gaggle of cafes on the main square. Long wooden tables inside are good for spreading out a map with your drink while the outside tables are oceanic in scope. Sandwiches are the thing at lunch, and dinner features globally inspired mains.

Drinking

Brink is lined with cafes and bars, facilitating hopping from one to the next.

 Heksenketel   BROWN CAFE

(Brink 63) At least a dozen brews (many hard to find elsewhere) are on tap at this local favourite where you'll find a jolly mix of regulars, students – and even guidebook writers.

Shopping

The local speciality is Deventer *koek,* a mildly spiced gingerbread made with honey and orange spices. It's widely available and so dense that it can sit undisturbed at the bottom of your bag for months.

The Saturday market on the Brink attracts food, flower and craft vendors.

Kaashandel De Brink   CHEESE

(Brink 2) You can see the rounds of cheese filling the windows at this exceptional shop devoted to the best curdled milk money can buy.

ℹ Information

Tourist Office (VVV; ☎71 01 20; www.vvvdeventer.nl; Brink 56; ☺10am-5pm Tue-Sat, 1-5pm Sun & Mon) Shares space with the **museum**; has good walking tour maps.

ℹ Getting There & Around

The **bus station** is located to the right as you leave the train station.

Bicycle

The bicycle shop is in the train station. National bike route **LF3** runs 36km north through lush farmlands to Zwolle. Going southwest, the **LF3** runs 55km to Arnhem and the gateway to Hoge Veluwe National Park, mostly following wide river banks and dykes.

Parking

There is parking around the town's periphery, but the best place to park is the free car park on the west bank of the IJssel. A **passenger ferry** (one-way/return €1/1.40; ☺8am-11pm) links the parking area to town. The voyage

DON'T MISS

HISTORIC STREETS

Deventer is so well preserved that most streets have something to see. These include:

» **Polstraat** Buildings with wall carvings and window decorations created over several centuries.

» **Assenstraat** Another street rich with carved details. The more contemporary carvings at **No 67-79** are especially artistic.

» **Walsstr No 20** shows a woman climbing down the wall while hanging by a sheet.

» **Bergstraat** A good street to marvel at the town's Hanseatic survivors (see Gothic-style **No 29**).

» **Kleine Poot** On a tiny alley just off this street, look for the **oldest stone house** in town, a much-modified 1100 AD vintage building with still-discernable Romanesque details.

THE HANSEATIC LEAGUE

Although primarily composed of northern German cities such as Lübeck and Hamburg, the Hanseatic League also included several Dutch towns. The powerful trading community was organised in the mid-13th century and its member towns quickly grew rich by the importing and exporting of goods that included grain, ore, honey, textiles, timber and flax. The league was not a government as such, but it did defend its ships from attack and it entered into monopolistic trading agreements with other groups, such as the Swedes. That it achieved its powerful trading position through bribery, boycotts and other methods shouldn't sound too unusual to business students today. The Hanseatic League members did work hard to prevent war among their partners for the simple reason that conflict was bad for business.

Seven Dutch cities along the IJssel River were prosperous members of the league: Hasselt, Zwolle, Kampen, Hattem, Deventer, Zutphen and Doesburg. It's ironic that the Hanseatic League's demise is mostly attributable to the Dutch. The traders of Amsterdam knew a good thing when they saw it and during the 15th century essentially beat the league at its own game, outmuscling it in market after market.

takes less than five minutes and operates most of the day and night.

Train

Deventer sits at the junction of two train lines; service is good in all directions. The train station has lockers up along track 3. Sample fares and schedules in the box text.

Zwolle

☑ 038 / POP 121,600

Zwolle, the capital of Overijssel province, is a compact town that can easily occupy a day of exploration – longer in summer, when the weekend market and a seemingly endless schedule of small festivals keep things bubbling.

In the 14th and 15th centuries Zwolle garnered wealth as the main trading port for the Hanseatic League and became a cultural centre of some repute. While those days are long gone, you can still step back in time, courtesy of the moat and ancient fortifications that surround the town.

◉ Sights & Activities

Standing on **Oude Vismarkt**, you have a good view of two main sights. The **Grote Kerk** is grand but was much grander before the usual series of disasters (three times struck by lightning – do you think it's cursed?) knocked down the tower. Much of what's left is from the 15th century. Next door, the **Stadhuis** has a typically Dutch old part (15th century) and a typically oddball (1976) new part.

Onze Lieve Vrouwetoren   CHURCH
(www.peperbus-zwolle.nl; Ossenmarkt 10; adult/child €2.50/1; ◷1.30-4.30pm Mon-Sat Nov-Apr, from 11am May-Oct) People from Zwolle say they know they're home when they see the Onze Lieve Vrouwetoren (also known as the *Peperbus*, or Peppermill), the huge former church that dominates the skyline as you approach town. You can climb the **tower**.

Museum De Fundatie   ART MUSEUM
(www.museumdefundatie.nl; Blijmarkt 20; adult/child €9/free; ◷11am-5pm Tue-Sun)   Housed in an old neo-classical courthouse, this art museum has works dating from the 15th century to the present from both Dutch and international artists. Being the recipient of a large grant means that the building is being greatly expanded with a stunning addition to its roofline. Set to reopen in late 2013, it should continue to be one of the country's most energetic small museums.

Stedelijk Museum Zwolle   MUSEUM
(☑421 46 50; www.stedelijkmuseumzwolle.nl; Melkmarkt 41; adult/child €7.50/2.50; ◷10am-5pm Tue-Sun) The Stedelijk Museum Zwolle has a fine collection of items, including a wealth of Hanseatic material. It also hosts numerous special exhibitions each year, ranging from high-art painting retrospectives to contemporary photography and multimedia. The wing in an elegant 16th-century mansion has good displays on local history.

Sassenpoort   HISTORIC BUILDING
The 15th-century Sassenpoort, situated at the corner of Sassenstraat and Wilhelminasingel, is one of the remaining town gates.

🛌 Sleeping

Accommodation is tight here, but then again, Zwolle is a good day trip destination so you may not care.

TOP CHOICE Hotel Fidder
HOTEL $$

(☑421 83 95; www.hotelfidder.nl; Koningin Wilhelminastraat 6; r from €105; ☎) Three grand late-19th-century homes have been combined into one 21-room family-run hotel. The gardens are pretty; inside antiques abound and many rooms have ornate four-poster beds. The included breakfast is lavish. The centre is a 500m walk to the northeast.

Hanze Hotel Zwolle
HOTEL $$

(☑421 81 82; www.hanzehotel.com; Rode Torenplein 10-11; s/d from €90/100; ☎) Virtually an island of vintage charm, the rooms here are simple but tidy. Sizes vary and those on the third floor are gut-busters for those who overpacked. Good breakfast buffet. Big cafe on the square out front.

Bilderberg Grand Hotel Wientjes
HOTEL $$

(☑425 42 54; www.bilderberg.nl; Stationsweg 7; r from €120; ☎) This stately establishment is a grand, sumptuous 56-room business hotel, with all the usual facilities and service to match. It has a chic cafe and is located just north of the station.

🍴 Eating

TOP CHOICE Poppe
CONTEMPORARY DUTCH $$

(☑421 30 50; www.poppezwolle.nl; Luttekestraat 66; menus from €32; ☺noon-2.30pm Tue-Fri, 5-10pm Tue-Sun) A former blacksmith's shop has been converted to this simple yet elegant restaurant. One of Zwolle's best, the open kitchen issues forth a steady stream of superb seasonal dishes. Spring brings asparagus, summer mussels; who knows what autumn will hold.

Van Orsouw
BAKERY $

(☑421 68 35; Grote Markt 6; treats from €2) This locally renowned bakery tempts with its olfactory siren song as you walk past. Get your *blauwvingers* (blue fingers, a local speciality of shortbread dipped in icing) here. The lunch room does not disappoint, with fine sandwiches, soups and more.

Public Grand Café & Terras
CAFE $

(☑422 66 00; www.grandcafepublic.nl; Blijmarkt 23; meals from €8) Housed in an 1817 bank building, this very popular cafe has tables out the front where you can take in the charms of the lovely square, or more intimate tables in the courtyard. The menu is classic: salads, soups, sandwiches, hot plates and more.

De Vier Jaargetijden
CAFE $$

(☑421 99 04; Melkmarkt 8; meals €8-20) Of the many cafes in the centre, this one is always the most crowded and for good reason: fast service, tasty chow and a long drinks list. This is *the* place in summer to let the long evening go on and on. Note the buttresses across the lane next door allowing neighbouring buildings to lean on each other for support.

☆ Entertainment

Swingcafé De Docter
LIVE MUSIC

(☑421 52 35; www.dedocter.nl; Voorstraat 3) A great place, dark and musty, this cafe hosts live rock bands a few nights per week, and has inviting open frontage. Other venues are nearby.

Odeon De Spiegel
THEATRE

(☑428 82 80; www.odeondespiegel.nl; Blijmarkt 25) This grand building is a multipurpose entertainment venue hosting everything from theatre and dance to live rock and electronica nights.

🔒 Shopping

Diezerstraat is the main shopping strip, now populated with chains and big stores. It leads to the Grote Markt.

TRAINS FROM DEVENTER

DESTINATION	PRICE (€)	DURATION (MIN)	FREQUENCY (PER HR)
Amsterdam	16	85	1
Arnhem	8	36	2
Nijmegen	101	61	2
Zwolle	6	24	2

Zwolle

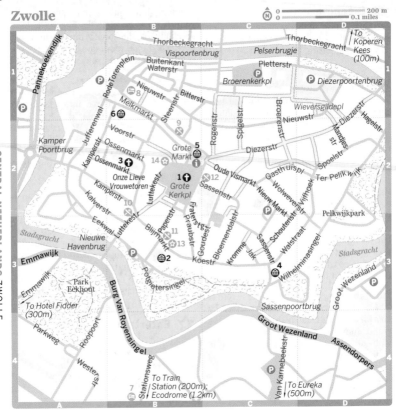

Zwolle

TOP CHOICE **Market**

MARKET

(⊕Fri & Sat) The market occupies most of the former Melkmarkt, Oude Vismarkt and the star-shaped centre. Fish, fresh fruit and vegetables, clothes – anything goes. You'll also find cheap cheese and bread. In summer crowds surge and it becomes a party.

ⓘ Information

Tourist Office (VVV; ☎421 61 98; www.vvvz wolle.nl; Grote Markt 20; ⊕10am-5pm Mon-Fri, 10am-4pm Sat) The tourist office is attached to the Stadhuis (with its distinctive architecture you can't miss it).

❶ Getting There & Around

Local buses leave from the right as you exit the station.

Bicycle

The bicycle shop is to the left of the station. Historic Urk in Noord Holland is 50km northwest on national bike route **LF15**, a scenic ride of dykes and rivers. Deventer is 36km south on **LF3** and there are a lot of optional routes along the IJssel. Hoge Veluwe National Park is a 40km ride through national forests, parklands and heath. Paths go in all directions so a map is essential for this ride.

Train

Zwolle is a transfer point for trains and has good connections. A new line linking Zwolle to Lelystad via Kampen opened in 2012 and it allows fast connections to Amsterdam.

Kampen

☑ 038 / POP 50,800

Picturesque Kampen, another lovely Hanseatic city, is a perfect day trip; 15km west of Zwolle, it's about 30 minutes by bicycle and well-linked to national bike routes. Its surrounding parklands are pretty and its historic centre is one of the country's best preserved, boasting no fewer than 500 medieval monuments, including houses, gates and towers. The closing of the Zuiderzee ended Kampen's status as an important port and the long economic decline that followed kept modernisation down and old buildings up.

It's difficult to get lost in Kampen, as it's small and laid out in a linear fashion, parallel to the IJssel.

❍ Sights & Activities

The major sights lie along Oudestraat.

Nieuwe Toren HISTORIC BUILDING
(Oudestraat) The Nieuwe Toren is immediately obvious: it's the 17th-century tower with the incredible lean. There's a little statue of

a cow here, linked to a rather ludicrous old story. Yet another renovation is ongoing.

Oude Raadhuis HISTORIC BUILDING
(Old Town Hall; Oudestraat 133) The Oude Raadhuis was – surprise, surprise – badly damaged by fire and rebuilt in 1543.

Bovenkerk CHURCH
(☑331 64 53; Koornmarkt 28) The 14th-century Gothic Bovenkerk features an organ with more than 3000 pipes.

Gotische Huis HISTORIC BUILDING
(Gothic House; Oudestraat 158) The Gotische Huis is a 15th-century merchant's house that's worth a look.

Stedelijk Museum MUSEUM
(☑331 73 61; www.stedelijkemuseakampen.nl; Oudestraat 133; adult/child €5/free; ☉10am-5pm Tue-Sat, 1-5pm Sun) This museum in the historic heart of town has local, historical relics plus a lot of artwork from the past 1000 years. Some of the portraits of rich old Kampens from the 17th century are quite unnerving.

Icon Museum MUSEUM
(www.ikonenmuseumkampen.nl; Buiten Nieuwstraat 2; adult/child €7/free; ☉1-5pm Tue & Wed, from 10am Thu-Sat) Icons, the images people of many faiths use to illustrate their faith, are the subject of this museum in a 17th-century monastery. Hundreds of icons from around the world are shown here and they span the centuries. Look for the vibrantly coloured figures on the Eastern Orthodox icons.

City Gates HISTORIC BUILDING
(Broederweg) Two 15th-century city gates, the Broederpoort, survive along the bucolic park on Kampen's west side.

✖ Eating

TOP CHOICE **Restaurant de Bottermarck** CONTEMPORARY DUTCH **$$**
(☑331 95 42; www.debottermarck.nl; Broederstraat 23; menus from €35; ☉noon-2pm Tue-Fri,

CENTRAL NETHERLANDS KAMPEN

TRAINS FROM KAMPEN

DESTINATION	PRICE (€)	DURATION (MIN)	FREQUENCY (PER HR)
Deventer	6	24	2
Groningen	16	67	3
Leeuwarden	15	60	2
Utrecht	14	60	3

5.30-9.30pm Tue-Sat) An innovative couple runs this fine bistro in an old building with thick exposed beams in the ceiling. A few tables out the front add a casual accent to the white tablecloths within. The changing menu is fresh and seasonal.

Petit Restaurant Efes CAFE $
(☑331 55 98; Plantage 2; meals from €6) On a cafe-filled square off Oudestraat; on a golden day, you may be tempted to stay long enough to join the list of local monuments. The casual food has a Mediterranean flair with lots of Greek dishes.

Banketbakkerij BAKERY $
(Oudestraat 148; treats from €2; ☺9am-6pm Mon-Sat) The goods on display are as lovely as this fine Art Nouveau building right beside the Nieuwe Toren.

❶ Information

Tourist Office (VVV; ☑038-331 35 00; www.vvvijsseldelta.nl; Oudestraat 41-43; ☺10am-6pm Mon-Fri, 10am-5pm Sat) Shares space with a good bookstore, Plantage Boekhandel.

❶ Getting There & Around

Bicycle

Kampen is a hub of national bike routes: **LF15** northwest to Urk and east to Zwolle (18km); **LF23**, which follows the old coast below Flevoland and goes 130km west to Amsterdam; **LF22**, which also follows the old coast north and west to Friesland; and **LF3**, which runs south via Zwolle to Arnhem.

Train

Kampen is a stop on the new line from Zwolle (€3, 10 minutes, two per hour) to Lelystad. The beautiful old station has been made 'efficient' by NS (Nederlandse Spoorwegen), which means no lockers or other services, although there is a small shop for tickets.

Weerribben-Wieden National Park

A serene and occasionally eerie landscape of watery striations, Weerribben-Wieden National Park covers 10,000 hectares, much of it marshy land. This entire area was once worked by peat and reed harvesters – backbreaking, muddy work. The long, water-filled stripes across the landscape are the result of peat removal: as one line of peat was dug, it was laid on the adjoining land to dry.

Reed harvesting was no easier, and still goes on today; you can see huge piles at many points in the park. Generations of harvesters lived out here with little contact with the outside world. Even now, their descendants live on some of the farms in the surrounding countryside in Ossenzijl and Blokzijl. Weerribben-Wieden is also an amazing natural landscape and an important stop for migratory birds in Europe.

SIGHTS & ACTIVITIES
As you ride along one of the isolated bike paths or row the channels, you might get the sense you're on another planet. A chief factor in creating this illusion is the sound of park: as you move through the sea of reeds, you'll hear the calls, clucks, coos and splashes of numerous birds, fish, frogs, otters, beavers and eels.

The park's visitors centre (☑0561-47 72 72; www.np-weerribbenwieden.nl; Hoogeweg 2, Ossenzijl; ☺10am-5pm Apr-Oct) is in Ossenzijl, a tiny village on the northern edge of the park. Pick up scads of maps of different cycling and walking routes. There's a small cafe here and a shop, De Gele Lis (The Yellow Iris; www.degelelis.nl; Hoogeweg 27a; ☺10am-5pm Apr-Oct), hires out bikes (€7 per day), canoes (from €15 for two hours) and kayaks (from €12 for two hours).

GETTING THERE & AWAY
To reach the visitors centre in Ossenzijl, take bus 76 from Steenwijk (38 minutes, hourly), a stop on the train line from Leeuwarden to Zwolle.

National bike routes LF3 and LF22 bisect the park and go right past the visitors centre. The former continues north towards Friesland and Leeuwarden. LCF3 follows a scenic and circuitous path south, 60km to Zwolle.

Northern Overijssel

Before the Noordoostpolder was created, the Northern Overijssel region was on the Zuiderzee. Today the former coastal villages are landlocked, but maintain their links to the water through the spider web of canals that criss-cross this marshy area. It's a difficult area to get around without a car or a bike and a set of energetic legs, as buses are infrequent and involve inconvenient connections.

THE GRASS IS ALWAYS GREENER...UP THE TOWER

Once upon a time a local farmer mistook moss growing atop Nieuwe Toren for grass and wondered aloud if he could get his cows up there to graze. So he hoisted one of his cows up to the top via a dodgy system of pulleys and ropes. The cheering townspeople below saw the cow's tongue protruding from its mouth and assumed it was indeed having a good old feed. And there was much rejoicing. Unfortunately, the poor animal was actually choking to death, a ridiculous episode that made Kampen the butt of Dutch jokes for many, many years.

GIETHOORN
☎0521 / POP 2500

Giethoorn, the region's highlight, is a town with no streets, only canals, walking paths and bike trails (inevitably it's tagged the 'Dutch Venice'). Contrary to most Dutch geography, Giethoorn is built on water crossed by a few bits of land, and farmers even used to move their cows around in row boats filled with hay. This is a sentimental place for the Dutch as it was the setting for *Fanfare*, a popular, funny 1958 film about the local folk, and one of the first to dissect the Dutch psyche.

Hugely popular in summer, at other times it has an almost mystical charm as you wander its idiosyncratic waterways.

The entire area is a joy for cycling or boating. Near the tourist office, you can rent an electric boat (€15 per hour), canoe (€8 per hour) or bike (€8 per day).

Giethoorn's tourist office (VVV; ☎0900 567 46 37; www.ervaarhetwaterreijk.nl; Eendrachtsplein 1; ⊙9.30am-5.30pm Mon-Sat Apr-Oct, 11am-3pm Sun Jul & Aug) is in the centre of things behind the Spar grocery store in the newish library. They can help navigate the maze of sleeping options: camping grounds, B&B and hotel rooms, and rental cabins.

Bus 70 serves Giethoorn on its route between Steenwijk (18 minutes) and Zwolle (one hour). Service is hourly.

To get around Giethoorn you'll need a boat, a bike or both. The area is about five scenic cycling kilometres off national bike routes LF3, LF9 and LF22.

GELDERLAND

The lush province of Gelderland has some gems amidst the green.

Nijmegen honours its past while Arnhem looks forward to escape its infamous WWII past; while Hoge Veluwe National Park is the star of the province, with its natural setting and superb museum.

Nijmegen
☎024 / POP 165,200

Nijmegen is enlivened by the 13,000 students at the Netherlands' only Catholic university. The centre – with its appealing and compact historic quarter – is only 10 minutes from the train station. The waterfront along the Waal River has cafes and boat tours. You can easily do the city justice in a couple of hours, and get ready for this: hills mean there are some actual climbs.

History

There's a minor rivalry between Nijmegen and Maastricht to claim the title as the oldest city in the Netherlands. Unfortunately the Romans, who could settle it once and for all, are long since dead. What is known is that the Romans conquered the place in 70 AD and promptly burnt it down. A sad taste of things to come.

Nijmegen built itself up as a trading and manufacturing town. It rolled with the many invasions through the centuries right up until WWII, which was devastating. A marshalling point for German forces, it was bombed heavily by the Americans in February 1944. Later that year, it was devastated during the Operation Market Garden fiasco. The postwar years have seen several rebuilding schemes, some better than others.

◎ Sights & Activities

TOP CHOICE Grote Markt — SQUARE

A few important bits of the old town either survived the war or have been reconstructed. The Waag (Weigh House; Grote Markt) on Grote Markt was built in 1612 and has a lovely interior. The market on Grote Markt is held Saturday and Monday.

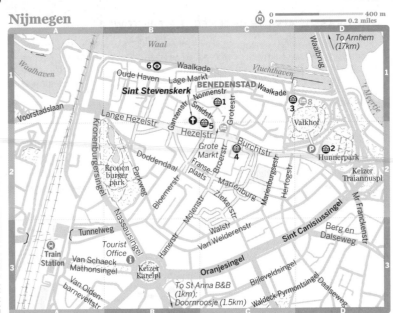

Nijmegen

Sint Stevenskerk   CHURCH

(www.stevenskerk.nl; off Grote Markt; tower climb adult child €4/2; ⊙church 10.30am-4.30pm daily, tower 2-4pm Wed & Sat) Through an arch from Grote Markt, this iconic church dates from the 14th century and has a classic reformist interior: no expense was spared for white-wash. It has 183 steps to the top.

Stadhuis   HISTORIC BUILDING

(Burchstraat) Just east of Grote Markt, the Stadhuis is a much-restored fairy tale in stone that dates to the 16th century. The dudes adorning the exterior are the various emperors who were good rulers in terms of the city (they didn't pillage, over-tax or slaughter the locals).

Commanderie van St Jan   HISTORIC BUILDING

(Franseplaats, cnr Grote Markt) North of the Grote Markt on Franseplaats, this was a 15th-century hospital for the knights of St John. Today it still gives life: it houses a brewery.

Museum het Valkhof   MUSEUM

(☎360 88 05; www.museumhetvalkhof.nl; Kelfkens-bos 59; adult/child €8/4; ⊙11am-5pm Tue-Sun) The Museum het Valkhof is housed in a strik-ing glass-clad building. The museum's rich collections cover regional history and art and there's a first-rate section of Roman artefacts.

Valkhof   HISTORIC SITE

The Valkhof is a lovely park and the site of a ruined castle (see it in its better days in the Jan Van Goyen painting in the museum across the way). At centre-stage is the 16-sided Sint Nicolaaskapel, which dates to the time of Charlemagne. It has been remodelled and reworked in a multitude of styles (depending on who held power in Nijmegen) during its 950-year lifespan. There are good views of the Waal from up here.

Nationaal Fietsmuseum
Velorama MUSEUM
(National Cycling Museum; ☎322 58 51; www.velorama.nl; Waalkade 107; adult/child €5/3, English guidebook €0.50; ☺10am-5pm Mon-Sat, 11am-5pm Sun) Follow the paths down the hillside to the riverfront Nationaal Fietsmuseum Velorama, a small but interesting museum with more than 250 bikes: everything from 19th-century wooden contraptions to hand-propelled bikes, to an entire room devoted to penny-farthings, plus more modern – and sane – machines. It's a must-see for anyone who's marvelled at the Dutch affinity for two-wheelers.

Waalkade PROMENADE
Even allowing for the usual air of frivolity commonly associated with such watery zones, strolling along the Waalkade, Nijmegen's waterfront, is enjoyable, especially if you're into boats and shipping. This stretch of river, Europe's busiest, sees a large barge or ferry plying the waters past Nijmegen every few minutes. Walk or ride a bike along the Waalbrug for breath-stealing sunset views of the old town, with the water and boats below.

★ Festivals & Events

TOP CHOICE Vierdaagse FESTIVAL
(Four Days; www.4daagse.nl) Nijmegen's big event is the annual Vierdaagse, a four-day, 120km- to 200km-long march held in mid- to late-July. It has a long history: the first one was held in 1909. Thousands walk it, even though the shortest or easiest route is a minimum of 30km a day. Many suffer debilitating blisters, while thousands more endure debilitating hangovers, as the Wandelvierdaagse is the city's excuse for a weeklong party. There are varying route classifications according to gender and age. Completing the walk is considered a national honour and comes with a medal.

⌸ Sleeping

Don't think about staying in the region during the time of the Vierdaagse.

A BRIDGE TOO FAR: OPERATION MARKET GARDEN

The battle they called Operation Market Garden was devised by British General Bernard Montgomery to end WWII in Europe by Christmas 1944. Despite advisers warning that the entire operation was likely to fail, Montgomery pushed on. He had often groused that the Americans under General George Patton were getting all the headlines in their charge across France. The plan was for British forces in Belgium to make a huge push along a narrow corridor to Arnhem in the Netherlands, where they would cut off large numbers of German troops from being able to return to Germany, thereby allowing the British to dash east to Berlin and end the war.

Everything went wrong. The British paratroops were only given two days' rations and the forces from the south had to cross 14 bridges, all of which had to remain traversable and lightly defended for the plan to work. The southern forces encountered some of the German army's most hardened troops and the bridges weren't all completely intact. This, in effect, stranded the Arnhem paratroops. They held out there and in neighbouring Oosterbeek for eight days without reinforcements. The survivors, a mere 2163, retreated under darkness. More than 17,000 other British troops were killed.

The results of the debacle were devastating for the Dutch: Arnhem and other towns were destroyed and hundreds of civilians killed. The Dutch resistance, thinking that liberation was at hand, came out of hiding to fight the Germans. But without the anticipated Allied forces supporting them, hundreds were captured and killed.

Finally, Montgomery abandoned the country. The winter of 1944–45 came to be known as the 'Winter of Hunger', with starvation rife as no food could be imported from Allied-held Belgium.

Most of the Netherlands was still occupied when the war ended in Europe in May 1945.

Besides the museums and memorials covered here, the Nationaal Oorlogs- en Verzetsmuseum (p245) in North Limburg covers the battle.

TRAINS FROM NIJMEGEN

DESTINATION	PRICE (€)	DURATION (MIN)	FREQUENCY (PER HR)
Amsterdam	15	70	2
Arnhem	4	15-20	8
Den Bosch	8	30-39	4

Hotel Courage
HOTEL $$

(☎360 49 70; www.hotelcourage.nl; Waalkade 108-112; r €85-130; ❊☏) This hotel has a superb location right on the waterfront – in the shadow of the Waalbrug – plus a nice restaurant and bar, and 27 cosy rooms with an appealing 1920s motif. The most expensive rooms have grand river views. All guests get direct access to the adjoining cycling museum.

St Anna B&B
B&B $$

(☎350 18 08; www.sintanna.nl; St Annastraat 208; s/d from €70/90; @☏) Perhaps Nijmegen's most charming accommodation. The two rooms at this welcoming B&B each have different themes. The Peace Room has a Japanese motif and sauna while the Liberation Room recalls when the Netherlands was freed near the end of WWII. The garden is lovely.

Hotel Atlanta
HOTEL/CAFE $$

(☎360 30 00; www.atlanta-hotel.nl; Grote Markt 38-40; s/d from €65/90; ☏) This place is a great-value option with 17 comfy rooms. It's also home to a popular cafe and is right on the Grote Markt. Be warned, though – the central location can get noisy at night.

✖ Eating & Drinking

The Waag and Waal are lined with cafes.

TOP CHOICE De Blauwe Hand
BROWN CAFE

(Blue Hand; ☎360 61 67; Achter de Hoofdwacht 3) The best bar in Nijmegen is also its oldest (1542), an ancient survivor that derives its name from its 17th-century customers: workers at a nearby dye shop. This corner spot is the perfect little Dutch bar (friendly and inviting) as evidenced by its motto: 'A frosty mug of rich beer gives you warmth, joy and sweet pleasure.'

De Waagh
GRAND CAFE $$

(☎323 07 57; www.de-waagh.nl; Grote Markt 26; lunch from €6, dinner from €18; ☉11am-10pm) This is an atmospheric place in which to eat, being as it is the town's 1612 former weigh house. The interior has been restored to a rich, sumptuous Burgundian ideal. In keeping with the traditional surrounds, the dinner menu is a hearty showpiece of roasts and more. The cafe menu is best enjoyed outside at the cafe with its commodious wicker chairs.

COMMANDERIE VAN ST JAN

The 15th-century hospital (Franseplaats 1) has several places for sustenance.

TOP CHOICE Plaats 1
FUSION $$

(www.plaats1.com; Franseplaats 1; mains €8-20; ☉5.30-10pm Tue, noon-10pm Wed-Fri, from 10.30am Sat & Sun) Fresh fare from the lush fields of the province is served much of the year at this very appealing restaurant. A bevy of tables sprawl around the beautiful courtyard while the interior has a chic, minimalist look. Order small plates, a sandwich or a lavish menu. Good wine list.

De Hemel
BREWERY

(Heaven; www.brouwerijdehemel.nl; Franseplaats; ☉noon-10pm Tue-Sun) A brewery with a few notable brews: Luna, a 5% lager and the 'hearty' Nieuw Ligt, which is anything but, being heavy in taste, body and colour, with a 10% alcohol quotient. It has a decent cafe with some shady outside tables in the courtyard.

Coffyn
CAFE

(Franseplaats; treats from €1; ☉10am-6pm Tue-Sun) Organic and free-trade coffees and teas are both served and roasted here.

☆ Entertainment

Doornroosje
LIVE MUSIC

(www.doornroosje.nl; Groenewoudseweg 322) Long-running, eclectic multipurpose venue, with live music ranging from electronica and house to indie-rock and world music.

ℹ Information

Tourist Office (VVV; ☎0900 112 23 44; www.vvvarnhemnijmegen.nl; Keizer Karelplein

32h; ⊙9.30am-5.30pm Mon-Fri, 10am-4pm Sat) Convenient to the train station.

ⓘ Getting There & Around

Regional and local buses depart from the area in front of the station.

Bicycle

The bicycle shop is underground in front of the station. Arnhem is 40km along the sinuous course of national bike route LF3, which follows rivers, including the Waal. Den Bosch is about 70km southwest along the equally curvaceous LF12. The rolling terrain means that you'll want a full range of gears on your bike.

Train

The train station is large and modern with many services. Lockers are near track 1A and are poorly marked.

Arnhem

☑026 / POP 149,300

With its centre all but levelled during WWII, Arnhem today is a nondescript, though prosperous, township with several museums and attractions around its northern outskirts.

⊙ Sights

There's no reason to linger in the area around the train station – it's a charmless commercial zone filled with chain stores.

John Frostbrug   HISTORIC SITE

Southeast of the Korenmarkt is the John Frostbrug, a modern and busy replacement for the infamous 'bridge too far'. It's not much to look at, but its symbolic value is immense. There are monuments and historical plaques at Kadestraat and Oranjewachstraat near the northwest corner of the bridge, about 1.2km southeast of the train station.

Nederlands Openluchtmuseum   MUSEUM

(Dutch Open Air Museum; www.openluchtmuseum.nl; Schelmseweg 89; adult/child €15/10.50; ⊙10am-5pm Apr-Oct) The Nederlands Open-

luchtmuseum is an open-air museum that showcases a collection of buildings and artefacts from all provinces with everything from farmhouses and old trams to working windmills. Volunteers in period costumes demonstrate traditional skills such as emptying chamber pots out windows – okay maybe not that one... Take bus 3 from the train station, direction: Alteveer.

⊟ Sleeping & Eating

Cafes and fast-food outlets crowd around the train station.

Stayokay Arnhem   HOSTEL $

(☑442 01 14; www.stayokay.com/arnhem; Diepenbrocklaan 27; d from €22, r from €55) This hostel, with 181 beds and a pub, is 2km north of town and inconvenient for the centre, but perfectly situated for seeing a lot of the sights on Arnhem's outskirts, especially by bike. Take bus 3 (direction: Alteveer) and get off at Ziekenhuis Rijnstate (hospital).

Hotel Old Dutch   HOTEL $$

(☑442 07 92; www.old-dutch.nl; Stationsplein 8; r €85-120; @) Conveniently located for transport connections, it's across the road from the main train station with 22 comfortable, striped rooms. Breakfast is included.

ⓘ Getting There & Around

Buses and public transport leave from in front of the station construction zone.

Bicycle

The train station has a large bike shop that moves with the construction. This area is one place to invest in a bike map – sights are ideal for visiting by bike and there is a thicket of bike routes. National bike route LF3 runs 55km northeast to Deventer; Nijmegen is a twisting 40km south along wide rivers; Utrecht is 40km west via LF4.

Train

Arnhem's train station is undergoing a massive reconstruction that will continue until 2015.

TRAINS FROM ARNHEM

DESTINATION	PRICE (€)	DURATION (MIN)	FREQUENCY (PER HR)
Amsterdam	15	70	2
Deventer	8	36	2
Nijmegen	4	15-20	8

DON'T MISS

ICE CREAM DREAM

Sure there are masterpieces inside Hoge Veluwe, but the real work of art may be what's sold at this simple storefront not far from the park entrance in Hoenderloo. IJs van Co (www.ijsvanco.nl; Krimweg 33d, Hoenderloo; treats from €2; ◷noon-5.30pm Mar-Oct) has been making delicious soft-serve ice cream for decades. Wildly popular, the creamy treat is firm, yet not too firm, sweet but not too sweet. There's options for toppings like syrupy fruit but we like ours straight.

Much of the new curvaceous facility will be underground; expect chaos in the interim. Train services are in the box on p233.

Around Arnhem

The tourist offices in Nijmegen and Arnhem can both provide specific information on visits and tours to the many sites in the region. Bike routes cover it all.

OOSTERBEEK

An old upscale suburb 5km west of Arnhem, Oosterbeek was the scene of heavy combat during Operation Market Garden.

◉ Sights

TOP CHOICE **Airborne Museum Hartenstein** MUSEUM
(www.airbornemuseum.nl; Utrechtseweg 232; adult/child €8/3.50; ◷10am-5pm Mon-Sat, noon-5pm Sun) Inside a mansion used by both the British and the Germans at different times as HQ during the battle, this museum is excellent. A modern six-storey addition has multimedia exhibits that do a good job of explaining the complex and confusing battle and putting it into context. A vast subterranean theatre luridly recreates a night battle in Arnhem. The museum lobby has a small but useful tourist office; it has battlefield and bike maps.

Oosterbeek War Cemetery CEMETERY
This somber cemetery and memorial is 500m east of Oosterbeek train station (follow the signs). More than 1700 Allied (mostly British and Free Polish) troops are buried here.

❶ Getting There & Away

Local trains on the line between Arnhem (€2.50, four minutes, every 30 minutes) and Utrecht stop at Oosterbeek station. Bus 1 serves the area from Arnhem train station (20 minutes). Bike routes lace the area.

GROESBEEK

The small town of Groesbeek, just inside Gelderland's southern border, 10km south of Nijmegen, is home to the National Liberation Museum 1944−45 (☑397 44 04; www.bevrijdingsmuseum.nl; Wylerbaan 4; adult/child €10.50/5.50; ◷10am-5pm Mon-Sat, noon-5pm Sun). Using interactive displays and historical artefacts, visitors 'relive' the campaign to liberate the Netherlands (which did not go so well). There's also a heavy dose about why people fight for freedom. Bus 5 runs here from Nijmegen every 15 minutes. By bike it's a pretty 8km.

Nearby, the Groesbeek Canadian War Cemetery is a mausoleum dedicated to the soldiers who fell here during Operation Market Garden. A memorial lists those killed but never found.

In the tiny township of Jonkerbos (a short distance from Nijmegen), Jonkerbos War Cemetery is the final resting place of mainly British servicemen.

Hoge Veluwe National Park

This park (www.hogeveluwe.nl; adult/child/car €8.20/4.10/6; ◷varies between 8am-10pm Jun & Jul, 9am-6pm Dec-Mar), the largest in the Netherlands, would be a fantastic place to visit for its marshlands, forests and sand dunes alone, but its brilliant museum makes it unmissable.

The park was purchased in 1914 by Anton and Helene Kröller-Müller, a wealthy German-Dutch couple. He wanted hunting grounds, she wanted a museum site – they got both. It was given to the state in 1930, and in 1938 a museum opened for Helene's remarkable art collection. A visit to the park can fill an entire day, and even if you don't have a bike, you can borrow one of the park's 1700 famously free white bicycles.

The ticket booths at each of the three entrances at Hoenderloo, Otterlo and Schaarsbergen have basic information and invaluable park maps (€3). In the heart of the park, the main visitors centre (◷9.30am-6pm Apr-Oct, to 5pm Nov-Mar) is an attraction itself. It has displays on the flora and fauna, including one showing the gruesome results of when a deer has a bad day and a crow has a good day. Book guided walks here.

Roads through the park are limited. There are myriad bike paths and 42km of hiking trails, with three routes signposted. The most interesting area is the Wildbaan, south of the Kröller-Müller Museum. At the north edge, Jachthuis St Hubert is the baronial hunting lodge that Anton had built. Named after the patron saint of hunting (but not the hunted), you can tour its woodsy interior.

Cyclists in particular will be interested in the camping ground (☎055-378 22 32; park plus adult/child from €7/3.50; ☺Apr-Oct), which is located at the Hoenderloo entrance. There are 100 sites; you can't reserve but you can call and see what's available.

TOP
CHOICE **Kröller-Müller Museum**   MUSEUM
(☎0318-59 12 41; www.kmm.nl; Houtkampweg 6; park admission plus adult/child €8.20/4.10; ☺10am-5pm Tue-Sun) Among the best museums in Europe, the Kröller-Müller Museum has works by some of the greatest painters of several centuries, from Bruyn the Elder to Picasso. The Van Gogh collection is world class, a stunning assortment of the artist's work that rivals the collection in the eponymous Amsterdam museum. Here you'll find *The Potato Eaters* and *Weavers* among many more, all arranged chronologically so you can trace his development as a painter. Impressionists include Renoir, Sisley, Monet and Manet.

A modern wing showcases contemporary sculpture. There's also a sculpture garden featuring works by Rodin, Moore and others. Art lovers can easily spend half a day here and they can recharge at the excellent cafe. If you are cycling to the museum from one of the three park entrances, it's 2.5km from Otterlo, 4km from Hoenderloo and 10km from Schaarsbergen.

ⓘ Getting There & Around

From Arnhem train station in the south, take bus 21 (20 minutes, every half-hour) to the Schaarsbergen entrance (stop: Museum 40 45). From

Apeldoorn train station in the north, take bus 108 to Hoenderloo (26 minutes, hourly). Various buses run inside the park to the museum.

There is car parking at the visitors centre and museum. It costs €6 to take cars into the park, €2 to park them at the entrances. Cars are not admitted after 8pm.

By bike, the park is easily reached from any direction; national bike route LF4 through Arnhem is the closest major route. You can also wait and use the famous free white bicycles, available at the entrances.

Apeldoorn

The rather featureless town of Apeldoorn has one attraction: the Paleis Het Loo (☎055-577 24 00; www.paleishetloo.nl; Koninklijk Park 1; adult/child €12.50/4; ☺10am-5pm Tue-Sun), built in 1685 for William III; Queen Wilhelmina lived here until 1962. Now it's a magnificent museum celebrating the history of the royal House of Oranje-Nassau. View the royal bed chambers, regal paintings, the lavish dining room dating from 1686 and the immense gardens with their maze of hedgerows and pathways.

Apeldoorn is a junction of train lines to Deventer, Zutphen and Amersfoort. The station now has lockers. Numerous local buses go near the palace.

Elburg

Gorgeous Elburg has a sculpted, cobbled 16th-century splendour. Compact and gridlike, its centre can be easily explored on foot. One highlight is the old harbour. Continue all the way down Jufferenstraat, through the 14th-century Vischpoort at the end of Vischpoortstraat and into the harbour itself, where a small flotilla of pleasure and fishing boats can take you on a boat tour.

ⓘ Getting There & Around

Take bus 100S from Zwolle train station (40 minutes, one to two per hour). Elburg makes a fine rest stop on national bike route LF23; it is a 16km ride south of Kampen.

Maastricht & Southeastern Netherlands

Best Places to Eat

» Artisan (p247)
» Gadjah Mas (p242)
» Bisschopsmolen (p242)
» Reitz (p242)

Best Places to Stay

» Kruisherenhotel (p241)
» Stadshotel Jeroen (p247)
» Eden Designhotel Maastricht (p241)

Why Go?

The Dutch southeast belies most clichés about the Netherlands: tulips, windmills and dykes are scarce. There is though plenty of beer, which is appropriate given the obvious Belgian and German influences.

Maastricht is a contender for the title of Finest Dutch City, and it even has – drum roll – hills. It's as different from Amsterdam as it is geographically distant except in one key area: its people are just as irreverent and fun. It's the true star of its province Limburg and fully embodies the southeastern concept of *bourgondisch*: eating and drinking with a verve worthy of the epicurean inhabitants of France's Burgundy.

The other province in the region, Noord Brabant, is a land of agriculture and industry peppered with a few pleasant towns; Den Bosch celebrates its namesake favourite son Hieronymous Bosch with a monument and a fantastic museum that gets to the heart of his idiosyncratic art. Breda is worth a look for its cathedral and small but interesting museums, while the Efteling theme park is the biggest domestic tourist attraction.

When to Go

Maastricht can be enjoyed in any season, although its cafes have such appeal that it would be a shame to miss their outdoor vibe from late spring to early autumn. Its famed art show is in March. Noord Brabant is striped by rivers which make for curvaceous – and bodacious – cycling along their banks during the fair-weather months. The southeast doesn't have the ascetic roots of the north, a fact made obvious during Carnaval in February when the streets fill with bands and impromptu parties, with fireworks overhead.

MAASTRICHT

♪ 043 / POP 121,000

Spanish and Roman ruins, sophisticated food and drink, French and Belgian twists in the architecture, a shrugging off of Dutch restraint – are we still in the Netherlands?

Maastricht is a lively and energetic place, with appeal and allure out of proportion to its size. The people are irreverent, there are hordes of university students and the streets are steeped in history. No visit to the Netherlands is complete without a visit.

History

Just like that other great afterthought, the appendix, Maastricht hangs down from the rest of the country, hemmed in on all sides by Belgium and Germany. It was this very precarious position that saved the town from war

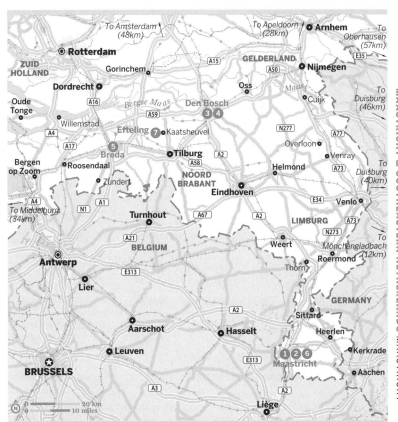

Maastricht & Southeastern Netherlands Highlights

① Thrill in the good life in **Maastricht** (p237), a world apart from the north

② Go bonkers at Maastricht's **Carnaval** (p241), one of the world's great festivals

③ Explore the unusual canals and charming cafes of lively **Den Bosch** (p245)

④ Decode the myriad messages in the paintings represented at Den Bosch's **Jheronimus Bosch Art Center** (p243)

⑤ Hop off your bike or train to tour **Breda** (p249) and its beautiful Gothic church

⑥ Have a sandwich made with flour ground in a 7th-century mill in **Maastricht** (p242)

⑦ See what the fuss is about at the tourist attraction the Dutch love most: **Efteling** (p248)

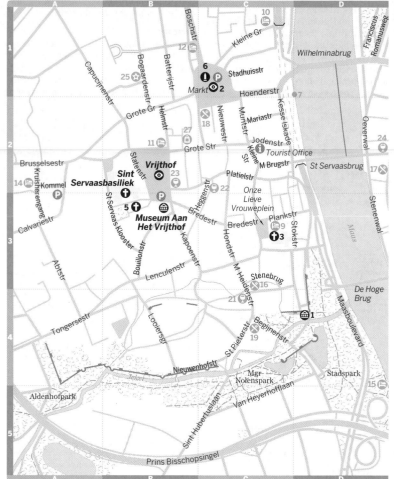

damage in the 20th century; the Dutch government didn't bother mounting a defence.

In the centuries before, however, Maastricht was captured at various times by most of Europe's powers. This legacy has helped give Maastricht its pan-European flavour. The average Maastricht citizen bounces between Dutch, English, French, German and Flemish with ease. This makes it all the more fitting that the city was the site of two seminal moments in the history of the EU. The first was the signature on 10 December 1991 by the 12 members of the then-European Community of the treaty for economic, monetary and political union. The following February, they gathered again to sign the treaty which created the EU.

⊙ Sights

Maastricht's delights dot a compact area on both sides of the bisecting Maas River. The area on the east side is known as **Wyck**, and to the south is **Céramique**.

The best approach is to just start strolling. The city's ruins, museums, cafes (and the odd surprise) reward walkers.

Streets not to miss include those south and east of **Vrijthof**: you'll enjoy a medieval

partments, each on its own floor: Old Masters and medieval sculpture are on one floor, contemporary art by Limburg artists on the next. A dramatic sweep of stairs beckons visitors to both floors. Make time for the world-class Neuteling collection of medieval art.

Space is devoted to special exhibitions and shows. The museum is the patron of the major biennial Vincent Van Gogh Award for Contemporary Art in Europe.

Vrijthof   SQUARE

This large square, a focal point of Maastricht, is surrounded by grand cafes, museums and churches.

Sint Servaasbasiliek   CHURCH

(www.sintservaas.nl; adult/child €4/free; ⊙10am-4.30pm) Sint Servaasbasiliek, a pastiche of architecture dating from 1000, dominates the Vrijthof. The Treasury is filled with gold artwork from the 12th century. Don't miss the shrine to St Servatius, a Catholic diplomat who died here in 384, and make sure to duck around the back to the entrance and serene cloister garden.

Museum Aan Het Vrijthof   MUSEUM

(☑321 13 27; www.museumspaansgouvernement.nl; Vrijthof 18; adult/child €8/2; ⊙10am-6pm Tue-Sun) Newly opened in 2012 on the south side of the Vrijthof, this museum combines local art, history and crafts to tell a compelling story tracing Maastricht's history and creativity. Artful objects made locally, such as antique pieces of silver, are shown along with rooms recreating various periods. The sky-lit lobby has a cool little cafe. The building dates to the 16th century and is where Philip II outlawed his former lieutenant Willem the Silent at the start of the Eighty Years' War.

Sint Janskerk   CHURCH

(church free, tower adult/child €1.50/0.50; ⊙11am-4pm Mon-Sat) This small 17th-century Gothic church is one of the most beautiful in the Netherlands. A remarkable red colour, it photographs beautifully. Climb to the top for sweeping views.

Onze Lieve Vrouwebasiliek   CHURCH

(treasury adult/child €3/1; ⊙10am-5pm) Onze Lieve Vrouweplein is an intimate cafe-filled square named after its church, the Onze Lieve Vrouwebasiliek, which has parts dating from before 1000 and may well be built on the foundations of a Roman cathedral. There is a separate treasury area that houses gaudy jewels and riches. The candle-filled

labyrinth punctuated by interesting shops and any number of places for a drink on a shady square.

The busy pedestrian Sint Servaasbrug dates from the 13th-century and links Maastricht's centre with the Wyck district.

TOP CHOICE **Bonnefantenmuseum**   ART MUSEUM

(www.bonnefantenmuseum.nl; Ave Cèramique 250; adult/child €9/free; ⊙11am-5pm Tue-Sun) The Bonnefantenmuseum features a 28m tower that's a local landmark. Designed by Aldo Rossi, the museum opened in 1995, and is well laid-out with collections divided into de-

Maastricht

shrine to Mary Star of the Sea near the entrance has been drawing pilgrims for more than 300 years.

Markt SQUARE
The Markt is the commercial heart of town. At the north end is a **statue of Johannes Petrus Minckelers**, who holds a flaming rod – he's the chap who invented gaslight.

Fortifications HISTORIC SITE
At the end of Sint Bernardusstraat, the **Helpoort** is the oldest surviving town gate in the Netherlands (1229); this area is laced with old walls. The remains of more 13th-century **ramparts** and fortifications are across the Maas in the Céramique district.

Fort Sint Pieter FORTRESS
(www.maastrichtunderground.nl; Luikerweg 80; tour adult/child €5.50/4.50; ⊘tour schedule varies) Much of Maastricht is riddled with defensive tunnels that had been dug into the soft sandstone over the centuries. The best place to see the tunnels is Fort Sint Pieter, which dates to Roman times and has now been restored to its 1701 appearance. It's 2km south of Helpoort.

The Romans built the Northern Corridor System Tunnels throughout the hills over a period of 2000 years; at one stage, the tunnels extended under the Netherlands–Belgium border.

This is a really beautiful area, pastoral despite the ominous walls – the fort is an arresting sight looming over the charming hillside – and it's a fine walk from town.

Maastricht Underground CAVES
(☑325 21 21; www.maastrichtunderground.nl; North Caves: Luikerweg 71, Zonneberg Caves: Slavante 1; tours adult/child €5.50/4.50; ⊘hours vary) Maastricht Underground, which also operates Fort Sint Pieter, runs spooky, thrilling, amusing and fascinating tours throughout the year on a constantly shifting schedule. The more popular tours are of the **North Caves**, the entrance is near the fort. You can also see the **Zonneberg Caves**, down near the river.

☞ Tours

The tourist office (p244) can arrange walking tours and cycling expeditions around town.

Stiphout Cruises BOAT TOUR
(☑351 53 00; www.stiphout.nl; Maaspromenade 58; adult/child from €8/5; ⊘daily Apr-Oct, Sat & Sun Nov-Dec) Runs a variety of boat cruises on the Maas.

✦ Festivals & Events

Three events stand out on the busy Maastricht calendar:

TOP CHOICE **Carnaval** FESTIVAL

(www.carnavalinmaastricht.nl) Celebrated with a gusto in Maastricht that matches Venice (Italy), Cologne (Germany) and Sitges (Spain). The orgy of partying and carousing begins the Friday before Shrove Tuesday and lasts until the last person collapses sometime on Wednesday. *Everything* stops for Carnaval.

TOP CHOICE **European Fine Art Fair** EVENT

(TEFAF; www.tefaf.com) The world's largest annual art show is held in mid-March. More than 200 exhibitors converge on Maastricht offering masterpieces to those with a few million euros to spare for the odd Rembrandt. The event is open to the public.

Preuvenemint FESTIVAL

(www.preuvenemint.nl) Each year Maastricht hosts this foodie festival, which takes over the Vrijthof for four days around the last weekend in August. It's touted as the 'largest open-air restaurant in the world'.

🛏 Sleeping

Maastricht is a popular weekend destination throughout the year, so reservations are a must. The tourist office (p244) has a list of private rooms travellers can book.

TOP CHOICE **Kruisherenhotel** BOUTIQUE HOTEL $$$

(☎329 20 20; www.chateauhotels.nl; Kruiserengang 19-23; r from €190; ✹@☎) This superb option is housed inside the former Crutched Friar monastery complex, dating from 1483. Where there are modern touches, such as moulded furniture and padded walls, they accent the historical surrounds. The 60 sumptuous rooms are all unique and designed to take advantage of their fabled surrounds.Some rooms have murals and artwork, others are in the rafters of the old church. Breakfast is suitably heavenly.

TOP CHOICE **Eden Designhotel Maastricht** HOTEL $$

(☎328 25 25; www.edendesignhotel.com; Stationsstraat 40; r €80-160; ✹@☎) On the main drag from the train station to the centre, this regal old hotel has been given a shot of youth and tarted up for a sprightly future. Small artful animal sculptures feature at the entrance. The 105 rooms have stark style with bold colours and details set against hardwood floors. You can go to sleep right under a print featuring an enormous nude butt. Breakfast is included.

Hotel Holla HOTEL $$

(☎321 35 23; www.hotelholla.nl; Boschstraat 104-106; r €65-100; @☎) In an elegant 1855 building, the 24 rooms here are smartly decorated and feature stylish linens. Adding to the fine value is the ground-floor cafe, which serves excellent coffee in stylish surrounds.

Hotel Derlon HOTEL $$$

(☎321 67 70; www.derlon.com; Onze Lieve Vrouweplein 6; r from €200; ✹@☎) The sleekly luxurious and smartly suave Derlon boasts 48 rooms with designer fittings and boldly coloured modern decor. The breakfast room in the basement is built around Roman ruins. A pampering and indulgent experience.

DARK AT THE END OF THE TUNNEL

The Romans developed the Sint Pietersberg tunnels by quarrying soft marlstone at a painstaking rate of just four blocks per day, creating an underground system that provided refuge during the numerous occasions when Maastricht found itself under attack.

The portion called the Northern Corridor System Tunnels (called the 'North Caves' on the tours) is an amazing feat of pre-industrial engineering: at one stage, there were 20,000 separate passages stretching past the Belgian border, adding up to a length of 200km.

Walking through the tunnels is an eerie experience and you'll feel a deep chill, not only from the thought of ghosts but also because it's cold (9°C) and dark. People hiding down here during sieges would often die of exposure.

One of the most fascinating aspects of the tunnels is the graffiti from throughout the ages. You can see generations of drawings on the walls, everything from ancient Roman stick figures to wartime depictions of movie stars such as Bette Davis, to '70s hippie nudes (the tunnels were barred from general access from the '80s on, before Dutch graffiti artists could lay down some murals).

Stayokay Maastricht
HOSTEL **$**

(☑750 17 90; www.stayokay.com/maastricht; Maasboulevard 101; dm from €22, r from €60; @⌂) A stunner of a hostel with a large terrace right on the Maas. Choose from one of the 199 beds in dorms and private rooms. It's just south of the centre in a park.

Hotel d'Orangerie
HOTEL **$$**

(☑326 11 11; www.hotel-orangerie.nl; Kleine Gracht 4; r €70-160; ⌂) There's a gracious elegance about this hotel in a stately building dating back to 1752. The 22 rooms come in various levels of ornate decor; all come with luxury beds and coffeemakers. Take the optional breakfast in the airy courtyard.

Hotel DuCasque
HOTEL **$$**

(☑321 43 43; www.amrathhotels.com; Helmstraat 14; r €80-160; ⌂) There's an air of faded art-deco intrigue about this 45-room hotel close to the shopping district and the Vrijthof. An elevator saves you from the stairs; some rooms on the 4th floor have terraces with views over town.

Hotel Le Guide
HOTEL **$**

(☑321 61 76; www.leguide.nl; Stationsstraat 17A; s €35-55, d from €64) Brilliant value close to the train station, with a popular cafe on the ground floor and six rooms upstairs. Some share bathrooms and all are dead simple.

✗ Eating

Maastricht has more than its share of excellent places to eat at every price range. Clusters of good places worth browsing include the eastern end of Tongersestraat, Rechtstraat, the little streets near the walls and up around the Vrijthof.

Onze Lieve Vrouweplein is easily the best place for a cafe interlude. Settle back under the trees at one of the many cafes that blend together into one.

TOP CHOICE ☞ Gadjah Mas
INDONESIAN **$$**

(www.gadjahmas.nl; Rechtstraat 42; mains €17-25; ⊙5-10pm) The Rechtstraat, east of the river, is one of the best streets for dining in Maastricht. This small, lovely Indonesian bistro has *rijsttafels* (array of spicy dishes served with rice) that break with the clichéd norm. Flavours are bright and there is no skimping on the spice. Good wine list.

TOP CHOICE ☞ Bisschopsmolen
BAKERY/CAFE **$**

(www.bisschopsmolen.nl; Stenebrug 1-3; meals €5-12; ⊙9.30am-6pm Tue-Sun) How cool is this? A working 7th-century water wheel powers a vintage flour mill that supplies an adjoining bakery. The loaves come in many forms and are joined by other tasty treats (direct from the ovens that are on view out the back). The cafe has sandwiches and other house-made creations, and you can self-tour the mill and see how flour's been made for eons.

Reitz
FRITES **$**

(Markt 75; frites €2; ⊙11am-6pm Tue-Sun) Join the queue at this iconic French-fries counter, which has been serving perfectly scrumptious *frites* under the classic neon sign for decades.

Sjieke
CONTEMPORARY DUTCH **$$**

(www.cafesjiek.nl; St Pieterstraat 13; meals €12-25; ⊙5pm-2am Mon-Fri, noon-11pm Sat & Sun, kitchen closes at 11pm; ⌂) This cosy corner spot turns out traditional Dutch fare, including hearty stews, roasts, fresh fish and more, with colour and flair. In summer there's a bevy of tables in the park across the street. Have a red beer and pick out the stars through the trees. Glorious.

▼ Drinking

Maastricht has a thriving cafe and bar scene and there are several for every taste. Most serve food. Maastricht was severely impacted by the change in coffeeshop rules in 2012. Several long-running places closed and the few remaining were made members-only. However public opinion soon supported a reversal in the policy and the situation remained in flux at time of research.

TOP CHOICE ☞ Take One
BROWN CAFE

(www.takeonebiercafe.nl; Rechtstraat 28) Cramped and narrow from the outside, this 1930s' tavern has well over 100 beers from the most obscure parts of the Benelux. It's run by a husband-and-wife team who help you select the beer most appropriate to your taste. The Bink Blonde is sweet, tangy and very good.

Zondag
CAFE

(www.cafezondag.nl; Wyckerbrugstr 42; mains €6-12) Funky mellow tunes during the day segue to jazzier, harder sounds at night. It's light, airy, beautifully tiled and the food couldn't be fresher. Choose from a huge range of sandwiches and baked goods by day. The creative drinks list is long.

EDD's
GRAND CAFE

(www.edds-cafe.nl; Heggenstraat 3; mains €12-25; ⊙11-2am) The acronym says it all: Eat, Drink and Dance. Match your mood to that of this humble-looking side street cafe with a striking post-industrial interior. There is a simple menu of Dutch standards with lots of fresh options. Sample the long beer, wine and drinks menu and then – on Saturday nights – wait for the dancing to begin.

In Den Ouden Vogelstruys   PUB
(www.vogelstruys.nl; Vrijthof 15) Overlooking the cathedral across the square, this antique bar is a little bit naughty and a little bit nice. The entrance has big, old, heavy, red curtains, while inside the bar there are photos of big, old, heavy men on the wall, big, old, heavy light fittings, and big, old, heavy Trappist beer. (But the local cheese is light and creamy...)

Cafe Forum   GRAND CAFE
(www.cafeforum.eu; Sint Pieterstraat 4) Settling into one of the plush wicker chairs outside, you may have a hard time mustering the energy to head inside – but you should. There's live music many nights a week, including jazz on Mondays. A simple lunch and tapas menu is complimented by a long beer and wine list.

☆ Entertainment

Cinema Lumiere   CINEMA
(☑321 40 80; www.lumiere.nl; Bogaardenstraat 40b) Offbeat and classic films are screened at a cinema located on a street with a name appropriate for films.

Derlon Theater   PERFORMING ARTS
(☑350 30 50; www.derlontheater.nl; Plein 1992 - 15) Near the library, Derlon has drama and music. The cafe has fine river views from the terrace.

🛍 Shopping

The **Markt** is the scene of a produce market Wednesday and a large mass-merchandise market on Friday. An **organic market** (⊘ 2-6.30pm Thu) fills the median of Stationstraat, while a used-everything market fills the same spot on Saturday.

The streets leading off Grote Straat are lined with mainstream stores. There's a clutch of luxury retailers around the **Entre Doux** (Helmstraat 3) shopping arcade. **Stokstraat** has galleries, boutiques and art stores, although you can find surprises all along the little streets in and around the old walls, such as **St Pieterstraat**.

In Wyck, **Rechtstraat** has the most compelling mix of boutiques and shops in the city. Happy browsing!

Selexyz n' Dominicanen   BOOKSHOP
(☑321 08 25; Dominicanenkerkstraat 1) A vast cathedral of books – literally.

DON'T MISS

DEN BOSCH'S OWN FANTASIST

Little is known about Hieronymus Bosch, the painter who lived in his namesake town from 1450 to 1516. However, much is known about the 125 paintings that survive today and are thought to be his: they show an enormous and wildly creative imagination at work. Or as Michael Connelly, the best-selling author whose main character in his central series is named after the painter, says, Bosch 'created richly detailed landscapes of debauchery and violence and human defilement'.

Although Bosch had a traditional moral sense of good and evil, one need only look at the couple flying on a fish in the *Temptation of St Anthony* to know that this wasn't your everyday painter of static Madonnas.

You can find traces of Bosch in his city today; there's a **statue** (Market) of him in front of the Stadhuis. Much more interestingly, the extraordinary **Jheronimus Bosch Art Center** (www.jheronimusbosch-artcenter.nl; Jeroen Boschplein 2; adult/child €6/3; ⊘10am-5pm Tue-Sun) re-creates all of his works and uses interactive exhibits to explore his work and life. Housed in an old church, it even has a modest thrill ride: an elevator takes you up 40m for a view over the town. This remarkable private musuem has reproductions of every Bosch painting and the story to go with it. It has numerous other wonders, as well as a lurid sculpture out front modelled on a part of *The Garden of Earthly Delights*.

Bosch's paintings have travelled far from his home town. The closest are *The Prodigal Son* and *The Marriage at Cana* at Rotterdam's Museum Boijmans Van Beuningen. His acclaimed *The Garden of Earthly Delights* is in Madrid's Prado (the Spaniards took a fancy to Bosch's work and sent a lot of it home in the 16th century).

TRAINS FROM MAASTRICHT

DESTINATION	PRICE (€)	DURATION (MIN)	FREQUENCY (PER HR)
Amsterdam	24	150	2
Den Bosch	19	85	2
Utrecht	23	120	2

❶ Information

Internet Access

The main tourist office (below) has a free terminal for a quick email check.

Centre Céramique Library (☎350 56 00; Ave Céramique 50; ⏰10.30am-8.30pm Tue & Thu, 10.30am-5pm Wed & Fri, 10am-5pm Sat, 1-5pm Sun) A multifaceted cultural centre with free internet access.

Tourist Information

Tourist Office (VVV; ☎325 21 21; www.vvvmaastricht.nl; Kleine Straat 1; ⏰9am-6pm Mon-Fri, to 5pm Sat year-round, 11am-3pm Sun May-Oct) In the 15th-century Dinghuis; offers excellent walking-tour brochures.

❶ Getting There & Away

Bicycle

Maastricht is one long ride from the rest of the Netherlands. National bike route **LF3** starts here and heads 220km north to Arnhem (where it continues to the north coast), staying east towards Germany much of the way. The initial route along the banks of the Maas is rather pretty, with good vistas as you swing through the innumerable turns.

LF7 runs along waterways northwest all the way to Alkmaar (350km) via Amsterdam. On this route the first major city you reach that's of interest to travellers is Den Bosch (140km northwest). Both **LF3** and **LF7** intersect more than a dozen national routes over their course. For an international trip, take **LF6** due east 35km to Vaals on the border with Germany. Attractive Aachen is just 5km further on.

Bus

The **bus station** is to the right as you exit the train station. Eurolines has buses to/from Brussels. Interliner has hourly buses to/from Aachen.

Train

The classic old **train station** has full services. Lockers are in an alcove off the main hall. Sample train fares and schedules in the box above.

There is an hourly international service to Liege (30 minutes), from where you can catch fast trains to Brussels, Paris and Cologne.

❶ Getting Around

It's about 750m from the train station to the Vrijhof.

The **bicycle shop** is in a separate building to the left as you exit the station.

Around Maastricht

This long, narrow province of Limburg at times barely seems part of the Netherlands, especially in the hilly south. There are all sorts of amusing notices on the A2 motorway warning drivers of impending 'steep grades' that would be considered mere humps in other countries.

The hills and forests of southern Limburg make for great hiking and biking. The **Drielandenpunt** (the convergence of the Netherlands, Belgium and Germany) is on the highest hill in the country (323m), in Vaals, 26km southeast of Maastricht. It's an excellent driving or biking destination.

Valkenburg to the east of Maastricht is an over-commercialized tour bus destination. It has no end of discount stores amidst some surprisingly serene forests.

NETHERLANDS AMERICAN CEMETERY & MEMORIAL

In Margraten, 10km southeast of Maastricht, this **war memorial** (⏰sunrise-sunset) is dedicated to US soldiers who died in Operation Market Garden and the general Allied push to liberate the Dutch. It's a sombre memorial with row after row of silent white gravestones – a stark but necessary testament to the futility of war.

Bus 50 runs from Maastricht's train station (20 minutes, four times per hour).

North Limburg

Clinging to the Maas river, the northern half of Limburg, barely 30km across at its widest point, is a no-nonsense place of industry and agriculture. **Venlo**, the major town, has a small historic quarter near the train station.

Venlo, along with **Thorn** and **Roermond**, are worth a quick look if you are changing trains for the hourly service to Cologne.

Nationaal Oorlogs- en Verzetsmuseum

(National War & Resistance Museum; ✆0478-641 820; www.oorlogsmuseum-overloon.nl; Museumpark; adult/child €13/8; ⊙10am-5pm) Overloon, a tiny town on the border with Noord Brabant, was the scene of fierce battles between the Americans, British and the Germans as part of Operation Market Garden in 1944. The heart of the battlefield is now the site of the sober **Nationaal Oorlogs- en Verzetsmuseum**, a thoughtful place that examines the role of the Netherlands in WWII and the fate of Dutch resistance fighters.

To reach the museum take the half-hourly train to Venray from either Roermond (€7.70, 40 minutes) or Nijmegen (€6.60, 35 minutes). Then take a taxi to the museum, 7km from the station (about €10). Make arrangements with the driver for your return. National bike route **LF3** passes by 6km to the east.

NOORD BRABANT

The Netherlands largest province, Noord Brabant, spans the bottom of the country, from the water-logged lands of the west to the hilly lands of the east. Den Bosch is its main city and well worth a visit; Breda also has its charms. However, despite its size, Noord Brabant won't fill your schedule. It's primarily a land of agriculture and industry.

Den Bosch ('s-Hertogenbosch)

✆073 / POP 142,000

The full name of Noord Brabant's capital is 's-Hertogenbosch (Duke's Forest), which is understandably not used often. Den Bosch has two dynamite sights: a remarkable church and a great museum dedicated to its namesake artist. It also has unique tunnel canals you can explore.

The significance of the city's full name held true in the 12th century when there was a castle and a large forest here. Both are long gone. It was hotly contested during the Eighty Years' War and you can still see where the lines of fortifications followed the shape of the canals. It's the birthplace of the 15th-century painter Hieronymus Bosch, who took his surname from the town.

◉ Sights

You can see the city in one large looping walk. There are many good bike rides around Den Bosch.

TOP CHOICE St Janskathedraal   CHURCH

(www.sint-jan.nl; Choorstraat 1; tower €4; ⊙8am-5pm) The main attraction is Sint Janskathedraal, one of the finest churches in the Netherlands. It took from 1336 to 1550 to complete, and there's an interesting contrast between the red-brick tower and the ornate stone buttresses. Take the time to loop around its exterior to appreciate the wizardry that went into its erection.

Look for a score of new angel statues added during a recent massive restoration; one is holding a cell phone.

The interior has late-Gothic stained-glass windows, an impressive statue of the Madonna and an amazing organ case from the 17th century. Unfortunately, Protestants destroyed the cathedral's paintings in 1566 – recent restorations uncovered a few 15th-century survivors.

Take the opportunity to climb the 73m **tower**, with its carillon and great views.

Stadhuis   HISTORIC BUILDING

The Stadhuis (town hall) was given its classical baroque appearance in 1670. It's the highlight of the vast, trapezoidal **Markt**.

Noordbrabants Museum   MUSEUM

(✆687 78 77; www.noordbrabantsmuseum.nl; Verwersstraat 41) The Noordbrabants Museum, in the 18th-century former governor's residence, features a sculpture garden and exhibits about Brabant life and art, a Van Gogh and – for those cafe-bound – an inspirational

TILBURG'S BIG PARTY

People usually only make a beeline to gritty Tilburg in the middle of July, when the **Tilburgse Kermis** (Tilburg Fair; www.tilburgsekermis.com) takes place for close to two weeks. Basically an enormous street party, it's a massive celebration of street fair and street fare. Rides, beer, bad music, sugary treats, stalls offering stuffed prizes for games of 'skill'... It's the biggest fair in Benelux, and for that reason alone it's remarkable.

Roman statue of Bacchus. A vast reconstruction is creating a large courtyard, the **Museumkwartier**, linking the revamped museum with the neighbouring modern-art venue, the **Stedelijk Museum**. It should be done by 2014.

Tours

Canals in Den Bosch are different from the others you've been seeing: many have long stretches where they pass under buildings, plazas and roads. These tunnels add spice to the usual canal tours and have inspired more than one Tunnel of Love moment.

TOP CHOICE **Binnendieze** CANAL TOUR
(www.binnendieze.nl; Molenstraat 15a; adult/child €7/3.50; ⊙tickets 9.30am-5pm Apr-Oct) Runs various fascinating 50-minute tours of the centre's canals. Boats usually leave hourly, but on busy summer weekends they depart with a frequency that rivals Disney's *Pirates of the Caribbean* ride.

Rederij Wolthuis BOAT TOUR
(☏631 20 48; www.rederijwolthuis.nl; adult/child €8/7; ⊙noon-3pm Tue-Sun May-Sep) Runs large boat tours in the old defensive and shipping canals that surround the old town (one hour).

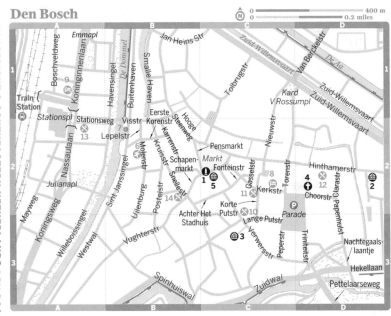

Den Bosch

0 — 400 m
0 — 0.2 miles

🛏 Sleeping

TOP CHOICE **Stadshotel Jeroen**   BOUTIQUE HOTEL **$$**
(☑610 35 56; www.stadshoteljeroenbosch.nl; Jeroen Boschplein 6; s/d from €100/130; 🖥) Right next to the Jheronimus Bosch Art Center, this small hotel is a gem. The six rooms are luxurious and each has a different artistic design. Guests enjoy the included breakfast in the stylish ground-floor cafe. Revel in the view – and inspiration – of the Bosch center's fountain which regularly climaxes.

Hotel Terminus   HOTEL **$**
(☑613 06 66; www.hotel-terminus.nl; Boschveldweg 15; s/d €38/70) As its name suggests, it's close to the station. The simple, brightly coloured rooms are decent enough and share bathrooms. There's a cheery bar with a good beer list and regular live folk music.

Eurohotel Den Bosch   HOTEL **$$**
(☑613 77 77; www.eurohotel-denbosch.com; Kerkstraat 56; s/d from €85/95; 🖥) This business hotel has generic but comfortable rooms that are right out of the Best Western catalogue (the franchiser here). Fans of generic blue will appreciate the corporate pastel palette. Good service and central location.

🍴 Eating & Drinking

Restaurant-lined Korte Putstraat is as crowded with diners as a Bosch painting is filled with little people.

Try the local speciality, a heart-failure calorie-fest known as the *Bossche bol* (Den Bosch ball). It's a chocolate-coated cake the size of a softball, filled with sweetened cream.

TOP CHOICE **Artisan**   CONTEMPORARY DUTCH **$$$**
(Verwerstraat 24; lunch menus from €29, dinner menu from €43; 🕐noon-10pm Tue-Sun) Fresh fare sourced locally. Lunches feature imaginative sandwiches, salads and specials. Dinner brings out the kitchen skills with seasonal menus that can range from mussels to roasts. Between meals enjoy a glass of wine in the courtyard.

TOP CHOICE **Jan de Groot**   BAKERY **$**
(Stationsweg 24; treats from €2; 🕐8am-6pm Mon-Fri, to 5pm Sat) The crowds know this is *the* place to get local speciality balls; join them! The rest of the bakery cases are filled with alluring goods and there's an excellent cafe for a coffee, snack or meal.

Koffiehuis Voltaire   CAFE **$**
(☑613 96 72; Stoofstraat 6; mains from €4; 🕐10am-6pm Mon-Sat; 🍴) The definition of funky. Settle into a table out front or amid the multicoloured shambles inside for some fab veggie fare. The affable owner cooks up a mean house special: a grilled sandwich of organic cheese, pesto, arugula, avocado and more. Great fruit shakes.

In de Keulse Kar   CAFE **$$**
(www.indekeulsekar.nl; Hinthamerstraat 101; lunch mains from €7, dinner mains from €15) Sit outside and enjoy beautiful views of the newly restored and radiant cathedral at this attractive corner cafe that proclaims its allegiance to *bourgondisch*. Fresh food sourced locally is appealing and there are many specials. The beer and wine list is good and goes nicely with the tapas menu.

In de Bossche Eetkamer   TRADITIONAL DUTCH **$$**
(☑613 28 28; Korte Putstraat 9; mains €21-25; 🕐dinner) Steaks and seafood are served in this traditional restaurant with cane chairs at the tables out the front.

🛍 Shopping

Thursday is the big night for shopping and many lunch places stay open to refresh the hordes. Wednesday and Saturday are the market days on Markt.

Uilenburg has antique shops, while Vughterstraat is lined with interesting boutiques. Hinthamerstraat going east is

MAASTRICHT & SOUTHEASTERN NETHERLANDS DEN BOSCH ('S-HERTOGENBOSCH)

TRAINS FROM DEN BOSCH

DESTINATION	PRICE (€)	DURATION (MIN)	FREQUENCY (PER HR)
Amsterdam	14	60	2
Breda	8	31-35	4
Maastricht	19	85	2
Nijmegen	8	30-39	4
Utrecht	8	30	4

TRAINS FROM EINDHOVEN

DESTINATION	PRICE (€)	DURATION (MIN)	FREQUENCY (PER HR)
Amsterdam	18	80	2
Maastricht	15	62	2
Rotterdam	17	70	2

another fine place for upmarket browsing and creative loafing.

ⓘ Information

Tourist Office (Markt 77; ☺1-6pm Mon, 9.30am-6pm Tue-Fri, 10am-5pm Sat)

ⓘ Getting There & Around

Buses leave from the area to the right as you exit the station.

Bicycle

The bicycle shop is located below the station. National bike route **LF12** heads due west over a twisting route through lush countryside, around rivers and through tiny villages some 70km to Dordrecht. It passes Slot Loevestein and the north side of Biesbosch National Park. **LF12** goes northeast 70km to Nijmegen along a twisting river route.

For some freelance fun head north 16km to the little old village of **Zaltbommel**, then cross the wide Waal and ride another 11km on rural paths north towards **Beesd**, where you can pick up **LF17** and ride **west** through the beautiful river valley of the Linge in Gelderland.

Train

The modern **train station** is 600m east of the Markt. It brims with services, including a good grocery store aimed at travellers. Lockers are on the concourse over the tracks.

Eindhoven

☏040 / POP 212,300

A mere village in 1900, Eindhoven grew exponentially thanks to Philips, founded here in 1891. During the 1990s, the electronics giant found it was having trouble recruiting employees to work in its home town; it solved the problem by moving to Amsterdam, although its research and engineering arms remain here. Electronics aside, Eindhoven is best known for its football team, **PSV**, although it could be said the many budget carriers serving its airport have also brought it frugal fame.

ⓘ Getting There & Around

Air

Eindhoven Airport (EIN; www.eindhovenairport. com) is 6km west of the centre. It's a hub for budget airlines. Most flights serve holiday spots in the south such as the Canaries.

Ryanair (www.ryanair.com) London Stansted, Dublin and cities in eastern and Mediterranean Europe.

Transavia (www.transavia.com) Berlin and other EU cities.

Wizzair (www.wizzair.com) Budapest, Prague

Bus 401 runs every 10 minutes between the airport and the train station (22 minutes).

Bicycle

Eindhoven is on the marathon national bike route **LF7**, which links Maastricht in the south with Amsterdam and on to the north coast. Den Bosch is 45km north.

Train

Budget fliers will easily find train connections to the rest of the Netherlands. The train station has lockers, money exchange and a full range of services.

Efteling

Near Tilburg, in the unassuming town of Kaatsheuvel, is **Efteling** (☏0416-288 111; www. efteling.nl; Europalaan 1; admission €32, parking €10; ☺10am-6pm year-round, longer hours during holidays), the Netherlands biggest domestic tourist attraction. This 'Dutch Disneyland' pulls more than three million visitors annually, proving its five-decade history as a family favourite is undiminished by the emergence of newer competitors, such as Flevoland's Six Flags.

All the usual suspects are here: huge, scary rides; walk-through entertainment with robots; scenes from popular stories and fairy-tales; live shows performed by 'talent'; sticky hands; crying kids… (And maybe it's us but the mascots all look a little peaked.)

To get to Efteling take 300 from Den Bosch (35 minutes, two times hourly) train station.

Breda

♬076 / POP 176,600

Breda makes for a good pause on a train or cycling journey. Enjoy interesting streets, flower-filled parks and a commanding main church. Its present peace belies its turbulent past, where its proximity to the Belgian border meant it has been overrun by invading armies many times.

The town centre is 500m southwest of the station through the leafy park, the Valkenberg.

◎ Sights & Activities

TOP CHOICE Valkenberg
PARK

The Valkenberg (Falcon Mountain) is the huge park between the train station and the centre. It's a good place to lounge around and listen to the splash of the fountains. On the south side is the 12th-century **Begijnhof** (admission to small museum €1; ◎noon-5pm Tue-

Sun), a home that once sheltered unmarried women. Breda has wonderfully preserved examples of these homes, which were found

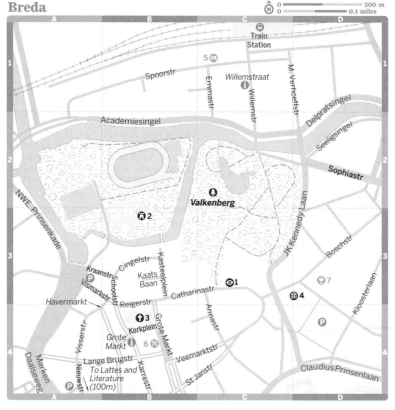

Breda

TRAINS FROM BREDA

DESTINATION	PRICE (€)	DURATION (MIN)	FREQUENCY (PER HR)
Den Bosch	8	31-35	4
Roosendaal	5	20	2
Rotterdam	9	32	3

throughout the Netherlands. This one has lovely traditional herbal gardens.

Breda Castle   CASTLE
Breda Castle is still an active military base and is off limits. However, the surrounds are worth a wander, especially the Spanjaards-gat (Spanish gate), a 16th-century survivor of the town's fortified era.

Grote Kerk   CHURCH
(www.grotekerkbreda.nl; ☺10am-5pm Mon-Sat, 1-5pm Sun) The white stones of the Grote Kerk gleam thanks to a recent restoration. This beautiful Gothic church was built between the 15th and 17th centuries. Its perfect tower is 97m tall and is occasionally open for a climb.

Museum of the Image   MUSEUM
(MOTI; www.motimuseum.com; Boschstraat 22; admission €7.50; ☺10am-5pm Tue-Sun) The Dutch tradition of clear visual communications is explored at this engaging museum. Among examples of 100 years of graphic design brilliance, the vintage Philips ads are timeless.

🛏 Sleeping

Apollo Hotel   HOTEL $$
(☎522 02 00; www.apollohotelsresorts.com; Stationsplein 14; r from €125; ❋🛜) Breda's main post office has been reborn as a stylish mid-range hotel. The 40 rooms are not huge but are colourful, and the hotel is close to everything, especially the train station.

🍴 Eating & Drinking

Breda is a great cafe town and on a sunny day it seems the entire population of the region is sitting around having a drink. Good ones can be found along all the pedestrian streets, with a classy bunch right on Kasteelplein.

TOP CHOICE Café de Bruine Pij   GRAND CAFE $
(☎521 42 85; Kerkplein 7; meals from €8; 🛜) Far enough away from the Markt madness by day; by night, you can enjoy the quiet of the square and the bells of the church unless there's a band on. There's a long list of regional beers.

Café De Beyerd   BEER CAFE $
(☎521 42 65; www.beyerd.nl; Boschstraat 26; meals from €8) The Beyerd is a highly regarded beer cafe, with more than 120 brews. It's also the perfect place to try some *bitterballen* (small, crumbed, deep-fried pureed meatballs) or other typical snacks to accompany your brew.

Lattes and Literature   CAFE $
(Nieuwstraat 18; drinks from €2; ☺10am-5pm) The perfect combo: an English-language bookshop and an excellent coffee bar.

❶ Information

Tourist Offices (VVV; ☎0900 522 24 44; www.vvvbreda.nl; 🛜) There are two tourist offices: Willemstraat (Willemstraat 17-19; ☺1-5.30pm Mon, 9am-5.30pm Tue-Fri, 10am-4pm Sat) and Grote Markt (Grote Markt 38; ☺10.30am-5.30pm Wed-Fri, 10.30am-5pm Sat). Both have maps and brochures for sale.

❶ Getting There & Around

Bicycle

The bicycle shop is right next to the station. National bike route **LF11** starts here and runs northwest 110km to Den Haag via Dordrecht and Rotterdam. **LF9** runs via Utrecht all the way to the north coast and **LF13** runs via Breda straight east from Middelburg to the German border.

Train

The **train station** has all the usual services; lockers are in the tunnel.

West Noord Brabant

Near the border with Zeeland, West Noord Brabant more closely resembles its soggy neighbour: canals and rivers criss-cross the land, and everything is absolutely flat.

Roosendaal is a major rail junction for lines north to Rotterdam, south to Belgium, east to Breda and west to Zeeland.

Bergen op Zoom's Carnaval is the most raucous west of Maastricht, drawing revellers from throughout Europe who basically go on a four-day bender.

Understand The Netherlands

population per sq km

NETHERLANDS	EUROPEAN UNION	USA

≈ 40 people

The Netherlands Today

Among the qualities the Netherlands is best known for is its famous tolerance. However, this idea of 'You don't bother me and I won't bother you' seemed under threat recently. Instead of a broad coalition government based near the centre of the political spectrum, the Dutch in 2010 shifted right. The coalition government formed that year included Geert Wilders, leader of the Party for Freedom, a far-right movement with a tough stance on foreigners living in – or immigrating – to the Netherlands.

During the next two years the government under prime minister Mark Rutte made a number of proposals that were a sharp break from previous Dutch policies. They weakened environmental regulations, slashed arts and culture funding and even passed what was thought to be a near-death sentence for the country's coffeeshops (where pot is sold legally). The formerly bedrock Dutch commitment to the European Union was openly debated.

But by the time an early election was called for in September 2012, it seemed that the Dutch political needle was heading back to the middle. Wilders' party went from 24 to 15 seats in the Dutch parliament and Rutte's centre-right Liberal party had to break bread with the left-leaning Labour party (led by a former Greenpeace activist) to form a government.

Coffeeshops Saved?

In 2011 the Dutch conservative government passed a law that would have banned foreigners from coffeeshops and restricted their customers to a limited number of card-carrying locals. There was general alarm among marijuana users and civil libertarians and indeed a majority of the Dutch public. However, one of the reasons for its passage was the complaints

---

Fast Facts

» Population: 16.7 million

» Area: 41,526 sq km

» Land in tulip bulbs: 110 sq km

» Per capita GDP: €40,040

» Unemployment rate: 6.5% (2009)

» Number of old windmills: 1200

Holland?

» Holland' is a popular synonym for the Netherlands, yet it only refers to the combined provinces of Noord (North) and Zuid (South) Holland. The rest of the country is not Holland, even if the Dutch themselves make the same mistake.

Best In Print

» *The Diary of Anne Frank* (Anne Frank; 1952) A moving account of a young girl's thoughts and yearnings while in hiding from the Nazis in Amsterdam. The book has been translated into 60 languages.

» *Netherland* (Joseph O'Neill; 2008) When a Dutch man faces the breakdown of his marriage in post–911 New York, memories of the Netherlands, cricket and a mysterious friendship complicate his life, yet repair his spirit, in this comically dark novel.

belief systems
(% of population)

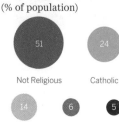

Not Religious	51
Catholic	24
Protestant	14
Muslim	6
Other	5

if The Netherlands were 100 people

81 would be Dutch
5 would be European
3 would be Indonesian
2 would be Turkish
2 would be Moroccan
7 would be Other

of southern cities like Maastricht which felt inundated by 'drug tourists' from neighbouring Belgium and Germany.

In May 2012 Maastricht was one of the first places where the new law was applied. Soon it fell victim to another law: the law of unintended consequences. Most of the city's coffeeshops closed due to a lack of customers and scores of people lost their jobs. Drug dealers returned to the streets, offering not just pot but also hard drugs, which caught the police unprepared. Soon Maastricht's mayor announced he no longer supported the new law.

Then when an election was called and Prime Minister Mark Rutte had to open talks with the Labour party to form a government, the odds that the law would be rolled out across the country (including Amsterdam and Rotterdam where the mayors opposed it) in 2013 fell like a first-time-space-cake eater who's had too many. Polls showed that the Dutch public (barely 5% of whom use pot) largely disliked the law and the requirement to register to enter the surviving coffeeshops was particularly hated because of privacy concerns (in the Netherlands one-third of people say they wouldn't shop online as they don't want to be tracked).

What now seems likely is that laws regarding coffeeshops will be reformed. One strange legal oddity is that while it's legal for coffeeshops to sell pot, it is technically illegal for them to buy it for resale. Politicians have seized on fixing – and taxing – this loophole to add an estimated €300 million in taxes to the €400 million the shops already pay.

Best on Film

» *Oorlogswinter* (Winter in Wartime; directed by Martin Koolhoven; 2008) Voted by Dutch critics as the top film of 2008. A young boy's integrity and loyalty is tested when he decides to help the Dutch Resistance shelter a downed British pilot.

» *Zwartboek* (Black Book; directed by Paul Verhoeven; 2006) This action-packed story explores some of the less heroic aspects of the Dutch Resistance in WWII. It launched the career of today's hottest Dutch actor, Carice van Houten.

History

While the Netherlands seems like a rather placid place now, you'd never guess the high drama of its history. It's like going into a cinema an hour after the last show: other than a few popcorn boxes lying on the floor, there's little evidence of the spectacles that played out just recently.

Greed, lust and war are prominent in the Dutch story, with doses of action that include pirates and high seas adventure. It's the story of land much invaded, whether by armies on land or water from the sea. At its highs it has produced astonishing art matched only by wretched excess.

Yet through it all, a society has emerged that has a core belief in human rights, tolerance and perhaps most surprising given the vicissitudes of its existence, consensus.

Invaders

The first invaders to take note of the locals in today's Netherlands were the Romans, who, under Julius Caesar, conquered a wide region along the Rijn (Rhine) and its tributaries by 59 BC. Celtic and Germanic tribes initially bowed to Caesar's rule and Utrecht became a main outpost of the empire.

As Roman power began to fade, the Franks, an aggressive German tribe to the east, began to muscle their way in. By the end of the 8th century, the Franks had completed their conquest of the Low Countries and began converting the local populace to Christianity, using force whenever necessary. Charlemagne, the first in a long line of Holy Roman emperors, was by far the most successful Frankish king. He built a palace at Nijmegen, but the empire fell apart after his death in 814.

For the next 200 years, Vikings sailed up Dutch rivers to loot and pillage. Local rulers developed their own fortified towns and made up their own government and laws.

Over time, the local lords, who were nominally bound to a German king, began to gain power. When one lord struggled with another for

TIMELINE	3000 -2000 BC	59 BC	AD 800
	People living in what is today's Drenthe province take to burying their dead under monolithic rocks called *hunebedden*. Long before Stonehenge, these people move enormous rocks and create structures.	The Romans extend their empire to what is today the Netherlands. Over the next four centuries, the Romans build advanced towns, farms and the roads that still shape the landscape.	Christianity arrives in the Low Countries by force. It replaces various Celtic belief systems – those who don't convert are killed. Charlemagne builds a church, parts of which survive in Nijmegen.

territory, invariably their townsfolk would provide support, but only in return for various freedoms (an equation familiar to any player of simulation games today), which were set down in charters. By the beginning of the 12th century, Dutch towns with sea access, such as Deventer and Zwolle, joined the Hanseatic League (a group of powerful trading cities in present-day Germany, including Hamburg and Rostock; p224). Meanwhile, the many little lords met their match in the dukes of Burgundy, who gradually took over the Low Countries. Duke Philip the Good, who ruled from 1419 to 1467, showed the towns of the Low Countries who was boss by essentially telling them to stuff their charters. Although this limited the towns' freedom, it also brought a degree of stability to the region that had been missing during the era of squabbling lords. The 15th century ushered in great prosperity for the Low Countries, the first of many such periods. The Dutch became adept at shipbuilding in support of the Hanseatic trade, and merchants thrived by selling luxury items such as tapestries, fashionable clothing and paintings, as well as more mundane commodities such as salted herring and beer.

The Dutch National Archive (www.nationaalarchief.nl) has almost a thousand years of historical documents, maps, drawings and photos.

The Fight for Independence

Philip II of Spain was a staunch Catholic; he'd gained the Low Countries and Spain from his father in 1555 after a period in which control of large swaths of Europe shifted depending on who was marrying who. Conflict with the Low Countries was inevitable; the Protestant reformation had spread throughout the colony, fuelled by the ideas of Erasmus and the actions of Martin Luther. However, before the Spanish arrived, the religious landscape of the Low Countries was quite diverse: Lutherans wielded great influence, but smaller churches had their places too. For instance, the Anabaptists were polygamists and communists, and nudity was promoted as a means of equality among their masses (in the warmer seasons). In the end it was Calvinism that emerged in the Low Countries as the main challenger to the Roman Catholic Church, and to Philip's rule.

Early residents of the soggy territory of Friesland built homes on mounds of mud (called *terpen*) to escape the frequent floods.

A big believer in the Inquisition, Philip went after the Protestants with a vengeance. Matters came to a head in 1566 when the puritanical Calvinists went on a rampage, destroying the art and religious icons of Catholic churches in many parts of the Netherlands. Evidence of this is still readily apparent in the barren interiors of Dutch churches today.

This sent Philip into action. The Duke of Alba was chosen to lead a 10,000-strong army to the Netherlands in 1568 to quell the unruly serfs; as the Duke wasn't one to take prisoners, his forces slaughtered thousands, and so began the Dutch War of Independence, which lasted 80 years.

The Prince van Oranje, Willem the Silent (thus named for his refusal to argue over religious issues), was one of the few nobles not to side

1150–1300	1200	1275	1287
Dams are built to retain the IJ River between the Zuiderzee and Haarlem, one of the first efforts in what becomes an ongoing tug-of-war with the sea.	The age of city-states is in full bloom as lords rule in many riverside towns. Trading between the towns is the source of wealth and a powerful inducement against war.	Amsterdam is founded after the count of Holland grants toll-free status to residents along the Amstel. The city gains its first direct access to the ocean via the Zuiderzee.	The Zuiderzee floods during a storm and upwards of 80,000 die. Except for a few port cities around its periphery, the sea is frequently regarded as a source of trouble.

DUTCH TRADERS

with Philip, and he led the Dutch revolt against Spanish rule. He was hampered by other Dutch nobles content to see which way the political winds blew. In 1572, Willem hired a bunch of English pirates to fight for his cause. Known as the Watergeuzen (Sea Beggars), they sailed up the myriad Dutch rivers and seized towns such as Leiden from the surprised and land-bound Spanish forces.

By 1579, the more Protestant and rebellious provinces in the north formed the Union of Utrecht. This explicitly anti-Spanish alliance became known as the United Provinces, the basis for the Netherlands as we know it today. The southern regions of the Low Countries had always remained Catholic and were much more open to compromise with Spain. They eventually became Belgium.

The battles continued nonetheless until the 1648 Treaty of Westphalia, which ended the Thirty Years' War, and included the proviso that Spain recognise the independence of the United Provinces.

The Golden Age

The Flying Dutchman is a mythical 17th-century ship cursed to sail the seas forever, unable to go home. The story has myriad variations, many added to by grog-addled seamen.

Throughout the turmoil of the 15th and 16th centuries, Holland's merchant cities (particularly Amsterdam) had managed to keep trade alive. Their skill at business and sailing was so great that, even at the peak of the rebellion, the Spanish had no choice but to use Dutch boats for transporting their grain. However, with the arrival of peace, the cities began to boom. This era of economic prosperity and cultural fruition came to be known as the Golden Age, which produced artistic and architectural masterpieces still loved today.

The wealth of the merchant class supported numerous artists, including Jan Vermeer, Jan Steen, Frans Hals and Rembrandt. It allowed for excesses such as 'Tulipmania' and the sciences were not left out: Dutch physicist and astronomer Christiaan Huygens discovered Saturn's rings and invented the pendulum clock; celebrated philosopher Benedict de Spinoza wrote a brilliant thesis saying that the universe was identical to God; and Frenchman René Descartes, known for his philosophy 'I think, therefore I am', found intellectual freedom in the Netherlands and stayed for two decades.

Tulipomania: The Story of the World's Most Coveted Flower by Mike Dash is an engaging look at the bizarre bulb fever that swept the nation in the 17th century.

The Union of Utrecht's promise of religious tolerance led to a surprising amount of religious diversity that was rare in Europe at the time. Calvinism was the official religion of the government, but various other Protestants, Jews and Catholics were allowed to practise their faith. However, in a legacy of the troubles with Spain, Catholics still had to worship in private, leading to the creation of clandestine churches. Many of these unusual buildings have survived to the present day.

1419	1452	1519	1535
The beginning of the end of the powerful city states. The dukes of Burgundy consolidate their power and unify rich trading towns under one geographic empire. Freedoms suffer under central rule.	Fire devours wooden Amsterdam. New building laws decree that only brick and tile be used in future. Similar conflagrations in other towns leads to the 'Dutch' look prized today.	Spain's Charles V is crowned Holy Roman Emperor. Treaties and marriages make Amsterdam part of the Catholic Spanish empire. Protestants are tolerated in Holland and the northeast.	A group of naked Anabaptists (motto: 'Truth is Naked') occupies Amsterdam's city hall; defeated by the city watch in a fierce battle, they are brutally executed.

MY FORTUNE FOR A BULB: TULIPMANIA

When it comes to investment frenzy, the Dutch tulip craze of 1636 to 1637 ranks alongside the South Sea Bubble of 1720, the Great Crash of 1929 and the internet boom of the late 1990s.

Tulips originated as wildflowers in Central Asia and were first cultivated by the Turks, who filled their courts with these beautiful spring blooms ('tulip' derives from the Turkish word for turban). In the mid-1500s the Habsburg ambassador to Istanbul brought some bulbs back to Vienna, where the imperial botanist, Carolus Clusius, learned how to propagate them. In 1590 Clusius became director of the Hortus Botanicus in Leiden – Europe's oldest botanical garden – and had great success growing and cross-breeding tulips in Holland's cool, damp climate and fertile delta soil.

The more exotic specimens of tulip featured frilly petals and 'flamed' streaks of colour, which attracted the attention of wealthy merchants, who put them in their living rooms and hallways to impress visitors. Trickle-down wealth and savings stoked the taste for exotica in general, and tulip growers arose to service the demand.

A speculative frenzy ensued, and people paid top florin for the finest bulbs, many of which changed hands time and again before they sprouted. Vast profits were made and speculators fell over themselves to outbid each other.

Of course, this bonanza couldn't last, and when several bulb traders in Haarlem failed to fetch their expected prices in February 1637, the bottom fell out of the market. Within weeks many of the country's wealthiest merchants went bankrupt and many more people of humbler origins lost everything.

However, love of the unusual tulip endured. To this day the Dutch continue to be the world leaders in tulip cultivation. They also excel in bulbs such as daffodils, hyacinths and crocuses.

So what happened to the flamed, frilly tulips of the past? They are now known as Rembrandt tulips because of their depiction in so many 17th-century paintings.

For an explosion of modern-day blooms, visit Keukenhof Gardens (p156) near Leiden in season. To see wealth in bloom, visit the flower market at Aalsmeer (p131).

Dutch Colonials

Wealth – and the need for more wealth – caused the Dutch to expand their horizons. The merchant fleet known as the Dutch East India Company was formed in 1602 and quickly monopolised key shipping and trade routes east of Africa's Cape of Good Hope and west of the Strait of Magellan, making it the largest trading company of the 17th century. It became almost as powerful as a sovereign state, with the ability to raise its own armed forces and establish colonies.

Its sister, the Dutch West India Company, traded with Africa and the Americas and was at the very centre of the American slave trade. Seamen

1555	1566–68	1579	1596
In the first major assault on Dutch tolerance, Philip II cracks down on Protestants. Religious wars follow and Calvinists pillage Catholic churches, stripping them of their decor and wealth.	The Low Countries revolt against a lack of religious freedom, launching the Eighty Years' War. In Friesland the rebels win their first battle, immortalised in the Dutch national anthem.	With scores of Dutch towns captured by Calvinist brigands, known as Watergeuzen (Sea Beggars), a Dutch republic made up of seven provinces is declared by Willem the Silent.	A Dutch trade expedition to Indonesia loses half its crew but brings back cargo that's sold for a profit. The Dutch East India Company is formed and the archipelago colonized.

COLONIALS

working for both companies discovered (in a very Western sense of the word) or conquered lands including Tasmania, New Zealand, Malaysia, Sri Lanka and Mauritius. English explorer Henry Hudson landed on the island of Manhattan in 1609 as he searched for the Northwest Passage, and Dutch settlers named it New Amsterdam.

Not surprisingly, international conflict was never very far away. In 1652 the United Provinces went to war with their old friend England, mainly over the increasing strength of the Dutch merchant fleet. Both countries entered a hotchpotch of alliances with Spain, France and Sweden in an effort to gain the upper hand. During one round of treaties, the Dutch agreed to give New Amsterdam to the English (who promptly renamed it New York) in return for Surinam in South America and full control of the Spice Islands in Indonesia.

And all of this outward focus coupled with the rich lives being enjoyed by the moneyed class at home caused a certain loss of focus. In 1672 the French army marched into the Netherlands and, as the Dutch had devoted most of their resources to the navy, found little resistance on land. During the decades of conflicts that followed, the Dutch could no longer afford their navy and foreign adventures. The English became the masters of the trade routes and keepers of the resulting wealth.

The Dutch managed to hold onto the Dutch East Indies (today's Indonesia) along with a smattering of spots in the Caribbean. The effectiveness of their rule in the East Indies ebbed and flowed depending on the situation at home. They never approached the intensive colonialism practiced by the British. (In Indonesia today it takes real effort to find traces of the Dutch rule or its legacy in most of the country.)

The Dutch East Indies declared itself independent in 1945, and after four years of bitter fighting and negotiations, the independence of Indonesia was recognised at the end of 1949. Surinam also became independ-

The Dutch *bought* (a concept foreign to North American tribes at the time) the island of Manhattan from the Lenape in 1626 for the equivalent of US$24 worth of beads.

CARIBBEAN NETHERLANDS

The Kingdom of the Netherlands shrunk even more with the end of the Netherlands Antilles. Really nothing more than a grab-bag of Dutch holdings in the Caribbean, islanders always saw themselves as residents of their island first. Aruba flew the coop first, in 1986, and never looked back. It is an independent country within the Netherlands, which effectively means it's autonomous but saves a lot of money on operating embassies, having its own military and the like. Curaçao and Sint Maarten have followed this route. Meanwhile, the relatively tiny islands of Bonaire, Saba and St Eustatius are staying much closer to the Netherlands and will effectively be municipalities within the nation – nice warm ones popular with Dutch tourists at that.

1600s	1600s	1602	1620
The Golden Age places Amsterdam firmly on the culture map. While Rembrandt paints in his atelier, the grand inner ring of canals is constructed. The city's population surges to 200,000.	The Golden Age spreads its wealth as new town halls, churches and other grand civic buildings are built. Many survive today as focal points of historic city centres.	Amsterdam becomes the site of the world's first stock exchange when the offices of the Dutch East India Company trade their own shares. Insider trading laws don't yet exist.	The pilgrims arrive in the New World aboard the leaky Mayflower, a voyage that began with many fits and starts in Leiden in the Netherlands.

THOSE 'DULL' DUTCH ROYALS

In power now for 200 years, the House of Orange has roots back to the 16th century. Unlike a certain royal family to the west across the Channel, the Dutch royals have proved to be of limited value to tabloid publishers or others hoping to profit from their exploits.

The most notable was Queen Wilhelmina, who took a page from Britain's Queen Victoria and approached her job as if she were a general. Although some faulted her for fleeing the Germans in WWII, she ended up winning praise for her stalwart support of her people.

During the postwar years, the family were a mostly low-key and benign presence (they have no substantive power within the Dutch government) with the exception of Prince Bernhard, who was caught up in a bribery scandal in the 1970s with the US defence firm Lockheed.

Queen Beatrix (born 1938) abdicated in 2013 in favour of her son, ending more than a century of female reign over the Dutch. King Willem-Alexander, father of three daughters, took the throne with his wife, Máxima Zorreguieta, a former banker he met at a party in Spain. Although her father's role in Argentine's Videla government raised a few eyebrows, Máxima has won praise for her work on immigrant issues and support of gay rights.

Despite being ranked among Europe's wealthiest royals, the family is considered by many as fairly modest. Beatrix was known for riding her bike in The Hague. The one day the Dutch think of the House of Orange is on Koningsdag when they wear the national colour and drink.

The celebrations were scarred in 2009 when a deranged man unsuccessfully attacked the family in Apeldoorn, killing himself and seven others in the process.

ent in 1975. In the Caribbean, the Netherlands Antilles disbanded but none of the islands severed ties completely.

The Foundation of Today's Netherlands

Wars with France proved the undoing of the Dutch in the 18th century. Shifting allegiances amongst Holland, the English, Spanish and various German states did their best to keep the uppity French contained. It was costly and the ties that bound the United Provinces together unravelled, beginning a spiral downwards. The population shrank due to falling fortunes and the dykes fell into a sorry state – there was little money to repair them, and widespread floods swept across the country. The Golden Age was long since over.

Politically, the United Provinces were as unstable as the dykes. A series of struggles between the House of Oranje and its democratic opponents led to a civil war in 1785. The situation reached a nadir

Hans Brinker, who supposedly stuck his finger in a dyke and saved the Netherlands from a flood, is an American invention and unknown in the Netherlands. He starred in a 19th-century children's book.

1642
Rembrandt paints the lauded *Night Watch*. However, many of the men portrayed didn't think it was that special as they'd paid to be in the picture and didn't like being in the back rows.

1650s
Oops! Big mistake. The Dutch infamously trade away the colony of New York to the British, killing all future likelihood that Broadway musicals will be sung in Dutch.

1700
The effective end of the Golden Age as wars empty the Dutch treasury, floods become common and the ruling class becomes caught up in conspicuous consumption instead of creating wealth.

» *Night Watch*, Rembrandt

DUTCH JEWS

The tale of Jews in Europe is often one of repression, persecution and downright hatred. In the Netherlands, it is more a tale of acceptance and prosperity, until the coming of the Nazis.

Amsterdam is the focus of Jewish history in the Netherlands, and Jews played a key role in the city's development over the centuries. The first documented evidence of Jewish presence in the city dates back to the 12th century, but numbers began to swell with the expulsion of Sephardic Jews from Spain and Portugal in the 1580s.

As was the case in much of Europe, guilds barred the newcomers from most trades. Some of the Sephardim were diamond cutters, however, for whom there was no guild. The majority eked out a living as labourers and small-time traders on the margins of society. Still, they weren't confined to a ghetto and, with some restrictions, could buy property and exercise their religion – freedoms unheard of elsewhere in Europe.

The 17th century saw another influx of Jewish refugees, this time Ashkenazim fleeing pogroms in Central and Eastern Europe. The two groups didn't always get on well and separate synagogues were established, helping Amsterdam to become one of Europe's major Jewish centres.

The guilds and all restrictions on Jews were abolished during the French occupation, and the Jewish community thrived in the 19th century. Poverty was still considerable, but the economic, social and political emancipation of the Jews helped their middle class move up in society.

All this came to an end with the German occupation of the Netherlands. The Nazis brought about the almost complete annihilation of the Dutch Jewish community. Before WWII, the Netherlands counted 140,000 Jews, of whom about two-thirds lived in Amsterdam. Fewer than 25,000 survived the war, and Amsterdam's Jewish quarter was left a ghost town. Many homes stood derelict until their demolition in the 1970s, and only a handful of synagogues throughout the country are once again operating as houses of worship.

Estimates put the current Jewish population of the Netherlands at around 45,000, almost half living in Amsterdam.

when Napoleon renamed it the Kingdom of Holland and installed his brother, Louis Bonaparte, as king in 1806. Fortunately Napolean's Russian debacle allowed the Dutch to establish a monarchy. Prince Willem VI landed at Scheveningen in 1813 and was named prince sovereign of the Netherlands; the following year he bumped up his Roman numeral and was crowned King Willem I, beginning a monarchy that continues to this day.

The Kingdom of the Netherlands – the Netherlands in the north and Belgium in the south – was formed in 1815. However, the marriage was

1795	1813–14	1830	1865–76
French troops install the Batavian Republic, named after the Batavi tribe that rebelled against Roman rule. The fragmented United Provinces become a centralised state, with Amsterdam as its capital.	The French are overthrown, and Willem VI of Orange is crowned as Dutch king Willem I. The protestant north and Catholic south combine as the United Kingdom of the Netherlands.	With help from the French, the southern provinces secede to form the Kingdom of Belgium. The remaining northern provinces form what continues to be the Netherlands of today.	A period of rapid economic and social change. The North Sea Canal is dug, the Dutch railway system expanded and socialist principles of government are established.

doomed from the start. The partners had little in common, including their dominant religions (Calvinist and Catholic), languages (Dutch and French) and favoured way of making money (trade and manufacturing). Matters weren't helped by Willem, who generally sided with his fellow northerners.

In 1830 the southern states revolted, and nine years later Willem was forced to let the south go. In a nice historical twist, Willem abdicated one year later so that he could marry – surprise! – a Belgian Catholic. It's not known if he ever spoke French at home.

His son, King Willem II, granted a new and more liberal constitution to the people of the Netherlands in 1848. This included a number of democratic ideals and even made the monarchy the servant of the elected government. This document remains the foundation of the Dutch government in the present day. Its role on the world stage long over, the Netherlands played only a small part in European affairs and concentrated on liberalism at home. It stayed out of WWI, but profited by trading with both sides.

In the 1920s growing affluence of the middle class fuelled desires for more liberalism. The Netherlands embarked on innovative social programs that targeted poverty, the rights of women and children, and education. Rotterdam became one of Europe's most important ports and the massive scheme to reclaim the Zuiderzee was launched in 1932.

The official website of the Dutch royal family (www.koninkli jkhuis.nl) features mini-biographies and virtual tours of the palaces.

WWII

The Dutch tried to remain neutral during WWII, but in May 1940 the Germans invaded anyway. The advancing Nazis levelled much of central Rotterdam in a raid designed to force the Dutch to surrender. They obliged.

Queen Wilhelmina issued a proclamation of 'flaming protest' to the nation and escaped with her family to England. The plucky monarch, who had been key in maintaining Dutch neutrality in WWI, now found herself in a much different situation and made encouraging broadcasts to her subjects back home via the BBC and Radio Orange. The Germans put Dutch industry and farms to work for war purposes and there was much deprivation. Dutch resistance was primarily passive and only gained any kind of momentum when thousands of Dutch men were taken to Germany and forced to work in Nazi factories. A far worse fate awaited the country's Jews.

The 'Winter of Hunger' of 1944–45 was a desperate time in the Netherlands. The British-led Operation Market Garden had been a huge disaster and the Allies abandoned all efforts to liberate the Dutch. The Germans stripped the country of much of its food and resources, and mass starvation ensued. Many people were reduced to eating tulip bulbs

Jewish Historic Sites

» Anne Frank Huis, Amsterdam
» Joods Historisch Museum, Amsterdam
» Kamp Westerbork, near Groningen

1873 Heineken is first brewed. The bland lager wins four awards in the next few years, honours still touted on the beer's label. It never adds to this number.

1890 Vincent van Gogh kills himself with no inkling that his brilliant work would one day command prices in the tens of millions and spawn museums and exhibitions.

1914–20 The Netherlands remains neutral in WWI while trading with both sides. Food shortages cripple the country, leading to strikes, unrest and growing support for the Dutch Communist Party.

» Self-portrait, Van Gogh

THE PROVOCATIVE PROVOS

The 1960s were a breeding ground for discontent and anti-establishment activity, and in the Netherlands this underground movement led to the formation of the Provos. This small group of anarchic individuals staged street 'happenings' or creative, playful provocations (hence the name) around the Lieverdje (Little Darling) on Amsterdam's Spui.

In 1962 an Amsterdam window cleaner and self-professed sorcerer, Robert Jasper Grootveld, began to deface cigarette billboards with a huge letter 'K' for *kanker* (cancer) to expose the role of advertising in addictive consumerism. Dressed as a medicine man, he held get-togethers in his garage and chanted mantras against cigarette smoking (all under the influence of pot). The movement grew.

The group gained international notoriety in March 1966 with its protests at the marriage of Princess (later Queen) Beatrix to German Claus von Amsberg. Protestors jeered the wedding couple as their procession rolled through Amsterdam.

In the same year the Provos gained enough support to win a seat on Amsterdam's city council. Environmental schemes and social schemes (such as giving everyone a free bike) proved unwieldy and the movement dissolved in the 1970s as some of its liberal policies became entrenched.

for their daily subsistence. Canadian troops finally liberated the country in May 1945.

After the war, the Netherlands was shattered both economically and spiritually. War trials ensued in which 66,000 were convicted of collaborating with the Nazis (with 900 receiving the death penalty). Yet the number of collaborators was much more and scores – such as the party or parties who ratted out Anne Frank and her family – never saw justice. And it should be noted: many Dutch people risked everything to help Jews, downed Allied airmen and others during the war.

WWII Museums

» War & Resistance Museum, Rotterdam

» Airborne Museum Hartenstein, Near Arnhem

» National Liberation Museum 1944–45, Groesbeek

Prosperity & Stability

The Dutch set about getting their house in order after the material and mental privations of WWII. During the 1950s a prosperous country began to remerge. After disastrous flooding in Zeeland and the south in 1953, a four-decades-long campaign began to literally reshape the land and keep the sea forever at bay.

The same social upheavals that swept the world in the 1960s were also felt in the Netherlands. Students, labour groups, hippies and more took to the streets in protest. Among the more colourful were a group that came to be known as the Provos. A huge squatters' movement sprung up in Amsterdam, and homeless groups took over empty

1919	1939	1940	1944–45
KLM takes to the skies, with a flight from London to Amsterdam. The airline eventually becomes the world's oldest still flying under its original name.	The Dutch government establishes Westerbork as an internment camp to house Jewish refugees. Eventually 107,000 Jews pass through this remote place in the east on their way to death camps.	Germany invades the Netherlands. Rotterdam is destroyed by the Luftwaffe, but Amsterdam suffers only minor damage before capitulating. Queen Wilhemina sets up a Dutch exile government in London.	The Allies liberate the southern Netherlands, but the north and west are cut off from supplies. The British Operation Market Garden fails and thousands perish in the 'Winter of Hunger'.

buildings – many of which had once belonged to Jews – and refused to leave.

Tolerance towards drug use and homosexuals also emerged at the time. The country's drug policy grew out of practical considerations, when a flood of young people populated Amsterdam and made the policing of drug laws impracticable. Official government policy became supportive of homosexuals who, since 2001, may legally marry.

Economically the Netherlands prospered more with each passing decade, allowing a largely drama-free middle class society to be the norm by the late 1980s.

All governments since 1945 have been coalitions, with parties mainly differing over economic policies. However, coalitions shift constantly based on the political climate, and in recent years there have been winds of change. Tension between different political colours and creeds had never been a problem in the Netherlands, until the murders of Theo van Gogh and Pim Fortuyn stirred emotions and struck fear into the hearts of some.

The leading political parties in the Netherlands responded with a shift to the right. In 2006 the government passed a controversial immigration law requiring newcomers to have competency in Dutch language and culture before they could get a residency permit. However despite some carping from the sidelines, the Netherlands continued its staunch support of the European Union, a role that goes back to the earliest days of the EU-predecessor organizations.

In the early 1600s, the Dutch East India Company flooded the local market with cheap porcelain from China. The Dutch responded with what's known today as Delftware. Today, most 'Delftware' is a cheap import from China.

The Legacy of Theo & Pim

If the 2004 assassination of Theo van Gogh rocked the Netherlands, it was the assassination of Pim Fortuyn two years earlier that gave the initial push.

The political career of the charismatic Fortuyn (pronounced foretown) lasted a mere five months, yet his impact on the Netherlands has proved indelible. His campaign for parliament in 2002 is best remembered for his speeches on immigration: particularly that the Netherlands was 'full' and that immigrants should not be allowed to stay without learning the language or integrating.

Just days before the general election in May 2002, Fortuyn was assassinated by an animal-rights activist in Hilversum, some 20km from Amsterdam. Fortuyn's political party, the Lijst Pim Fortuyn (LPF), had a number of members elected to parliament and was included in the next coalition, but without the dynamic Fortuyn it faded away by 2007.

Enter Theo van Gogh, a filmmaker and provocateur who made a short film claiming that Koranic verses could be interpreted as justifying violence against women. The film was a collaboration with Ayaan

The largest post-war political party in the Netherlands was the Christian Democratic Union (CDA). Nominally centre-right, it had a historic streak of pragmatism that served it well until 2010 when voters moved to other centrist parties.

HISTORY THE LEGACY OF THEO & PIM

1946	1958	1960s	1974
The UN-chartered International Court of Justice sets up shop in Den Haag, ensuring that the seat of Dutch government will grace the world's headlines for decades to come.	The Delta project is launched following the great floods of Zeeland in 1953 which cause widespread destruction and death. Vast construction projects continue for four decades.	Social upheaval sweeps the Netherlands leading to the creation of the Provos, a provocative underground countercultural movement. Squatting in empty buildings becomes widespread.	The Dutch World Cup soccer team finishes second. After doing so again in 1978 and 2010, they hold the record for the most second-place finishes without winning the final.

Hirsi Ali, a Muslim-born woman who had emigrated from Somalia to escape an arranged marriage and eventually became a member of parliament.

The film aired on Dutch TV in 2004, and Van Gogh was killed as he was cycling down an Amsterdam street. A letter threatening the nation, politicians, and Hirsi Ali in particular, was impaled on a knife stuck in Van Gogh's chest. The killing was all the more shocking to locals because the 27-year-old killer, while of Moroccan descent, was born and raised in Amsterdam. He proclaimed that he was acting in defence of Islam and would do the same thing again if given the chance (he was sentenced to life imprisonment). Meanwhile, Hirsi Ali has moved to the US and become a popular figure with American conservatives.

For the time being, politicians on the far right such as Geert Wilders have tried to trade on the legacy of Pim and Theo by stoking anti-Islamic feelings.

The newly-crowned King Willem-Alexander, and his wife Queen Maxima have three daughters: Catharina-Amalia, Alexia and Ariane.

1980
The coronation of Queen Beatrix is disrupted by a smoke bomb and riot on the Dam. The term 'proletarian shopping' (ie looting) enters the national lexicon as riotous behaviour becomes widespread.

2001
Same-sex marriage is legalised in the Netherlands, the first country in the world to do so. In the next few years Belgium, Spain, Canada and South Africa follow suit.

2004
Activist filmmaker Theo van Gogh, a critic of Islam, is assassinated, sparking debate over the limits of Dutch multiculturalism and the need for immigrants to adopt Dutch values.

2008
Amsterdam announces plans to clean up the Red Light District and close coffeeshops. Other cities follow suit and the 'smart shops' selling mushrooms are closed.

The Dutch Way of Life

Make no mistake, the Dutch have a flair for social engineering. The same nation that built its living rooms on a drained seabed also invented *verzuiling* (pillarisation), a social order in which each religion and political persuasion achieved the right to do its own thing, with its own institutions. This meant not only more churches, but also separate radio stations, newspapers, unions, political parties, sport clubs and so on. The idea got a bit out of hand with pillarised bakeries, but it did promote social harmony by giving everyone a voice.

Although the pillars are less distinct today, they left a legacy of tolerance. In fact tolerance is as Dutch as herring and ice skating, and what's more it's good for business, whether it be tourism or trade. The same applies to *gezelligheid* (conviviality), that easy intimacy that comes out at the drop of a hat. Where other nations struggle to get the words out, the Dutch are irrepressibly voluble. Sit alone in a pub and you'll soon have a few merry friends.

The Dutch also have a moralistic streak (coming from the Calvinists) and a tendency to wag the finger in disapproval. The Dutch may seem stunningly blunt, but the impulse comes from the desire to be direct and honest.

> About 2% (some 3100) of all Dutch deaths each year are caused by euthanasia. The practice is tightly controlled and is administered by doctors at the request of patients.

Dutch Lifestyle

Many Dutch live independent, busy lives, divided into strict schedules. Notice is usually required for everything, including visits to your mother, and it's not done to just 'pop round' anywhere. Socialising is done mainly in the home, through clubs and in circles of old friends.

Most Dutch families are small, with two or three children. Rents are high, so Junior might live with his family well into his 20s or share an apartment. (Liberal Dutch mortgage policies in recent years proved a problem during the global economic downturn when the otherwise thrifty Netherlands was caught up with a high percentage of defaults.)

On average the Dutch are fairly well off – they may not flaunt it, but they now earn more per capita than the Germans. Consumer spending is healthy, especially for travel to warm climates.

> Traditional Dutch toilets come with a shelf where deposited goods sit until swept away by a flush of water. The reason is tied to health and the supposed benefit of carefully studying what comes out. Not, as some wags say, because the Dutch can't bear to see anything underwater.

Sex & Drugs

On sex and drugs, the ever-practical Dutch argue that vice is not going to go away, so you might as well control it. Sex is discussed openly but promiscuity is the last thing on Dutch minds. It is perhaps revealing that only about 5% of customers frequenting the Red Light District are Dutch (traditionally, the biggest group has been the Brits).

By the same token, marijuana and hashish remain legal, despite efforts otherwise. Yet if you think everyone here gets stoned, you're wrong.

Only a fraction of the population smokes dope, a recent study showed that only 5.4% of Dutch people had used any form of marijuana in the previous year, less than the average for Europe (6.8%), America (7%) and Australia (15%), where drug policies are much stricter. On the other hand, the 'harder' drugs such as heroin, LSD, cocaine and ecstasy are outlawed, and dealers are prosecuted.

American author John Irving set his novel *A Widow for One Year* in Amsterdam's Red Light District; British novelist Irvine Welsh's *The Acid House* is a short-story collection about Amsterdam's drug underworld.

BY THE NUMBERS

The Dutch have a great love of detail. Statistics on the most trivial subjects make the paper (eg the number of pigeons on the Dam this year, incidence of rubbish being put out early), and somewhere down the line this feeds mountains of bureaucracy.

Last but not least, the Dutch are famously thrifty with their money – and they often don't know what to think of this. In one breath they might joke about how copper wire was invented by two Dutchmen fighting over a penny, and in the next, tell you that they don't like being called cheap.

Gay & Lesbian Rights

Gays and lesbians enjoy considerable freedom and respect among people of all ages. Discrimination on the basis of sexual orientation is not only illegal, but morally unacceptable; the police advertise in the gay media for applicants; the armed forces admit homosexuals on an equal footing. Most significantly, in 2001 the Netherlands became the first country in the world to legalise same-sex marriages, although this is a privilege reserved for local couples.

Religion

For centuries, religious preference was split between the two heavyweights of Western society, Catholicism and Protestantism, and if you were Dutch you were one or the other. Today, 51% of the population over the age of 18 claims to have no religious affiliation, and the number of former churches that house offices, art galleries and shops is an obvious sign of today's attitudes.

And faith is falling: 25% of the population follows Catholicism and 15% Protestantism, figures that decrease yearly. Vestiges exist of a religious border between Protestants and Catholics; the area north of a line running roughly from the province of Zeeland in the southwest to the province of Drenthe is home to the majority of Protestants, while anywhere to the south is predominantly Catholic.

Orange, as the national colour, has ties to the Dutch monarchy. The House of Orange traces its legacy back to Willem of Orange, leader of the resistance against the Spanish in the 16th century.

The church has little or no influence on societal matters such as same-sex marriage, euthanasia and prescription of cannabis for medical purposes, all of which are legal in the Netherlands.

The latest religion to have any great impact on Dutch society is Islam. Today, nearly 6% of the population classes itself as Muslim and the number is steadily increasing, especially in multicultural Rotterdam.

Population

The need to love thy neighbour is especially strong in the Netherlands, where the population density is the highest in Europe (405 per square kilometre). Nearly half of the country's 16.5 million residents live in the western hoop around Amsterdam, Den Haag and Rotterdam; the provinces of Drenthe, Overijssel and Zeeland in the southwest are sparsely settled, in Dutch terms at least.

More than 80% of the population are of Dutch stock; the rest is mainly made up of people from the former colonies of Indonesia, Surinam and the former Netherlands Antilles, plus more recent arrivals from Turkey, Morocco and countries throughout Africa.

COFFEESHOPS, MARIJUANA & HASHISH

Cannabis is not technically legal in the Netherlands – yet it is widely tolerated. The possession and purchase of small amounts (5g) of 'soft drugs' (ie marijuana, hashish, space cakes, and mushroom-based truffles) is allowed and users won't be prosecuted for smoking or carrying this amount.

Most cannabis products sold in the Netherlands used to be imported, but today the country has high-grade home produce, so-called *nederwiet*, developed by horticulturists. It's also a particularly strong product – some of the most potent variations contain approximately 20% tetrahydrocannabinol (THC), the active substance that gets people high. Many locals have switched to lower-potency imports. Newbies to smoking pot and hash should exercise caution.

Space cakes and cookies (baked goods made with hash or marijuana) are sold in a low-key fashion, mainly because tourists often have problems with what can be an intense (and long-lasting) experience.

Obviously the current uncertainty about the future of coffeeshops is of particular interest, for more information see p91 in the Amsterdam chapter.

SMOKING & SOFT DRUGS DOS & DON'TS

» If it's your first coffeeshop experience, do tell the coffeeshop counterperson – they're usually happy to give first-timers advice on how and what to consume.

» Don't ask for hard (illegal) drugs.

» Whether it is grass or hash, and smoked, eaten or inhaled through a vaporiser, most visitors admit it's much stronger than what they are accustomed to. Ask staff how much to take and heed their advice.

» Ask at the bar for the menu of goods on offer, usually packaged in small bags. You can also buy ready-made joints (€3 to €7). Most shops also offer rolling papers, pipes or even bongs to use.

» Don't drink alcohol or smoke tobacco in a coffeeshop – it's technically illegal.

» Herbal ecstasy – usually a mix of herbs, vitamins, and caffeine – is legal in the Netherlands and sold in 'smart shops'. Ask the smart shop employees what they recommend, as some varieties can have unpleasant speed-like side effects.

» Psilocybin mushrooms (aka 'magic mushrooms') are now illegal in the Netherlands, but many smart shops sell mushroom truffles, which have a similar effect.

THE DUTCH WAY OF LIFE MULTICULTURALISM

Multiculturalism

The Netherlands has a long history of tolerance towards immigration and a reputation for welcoming immigrants with open arms. The largest wave of immigration occurred in the 1960s, when the government recruited migrant workers from Turkey and Morocco to bridge a labour gap. In the mid-1970s the granting of independence to the Dutch colony of Surinam in South America saw an influx of Surinamese.

In the past few years, however, the country's loose immigration policy has been called into question. Politically, there has been a significant swing to the right and consequently a move towards shutting the door on immigration. The assassinations of Pim Fortuyn and Theo van Gogh (see p263) caused tensions to rise between the Dutch and Muslim immigrants, which also gave rise to far right anti-Islam politicians like Geert Wilders. However, when the former queen, Beatrix, wore a head scarf on a visit to a mosque in Oman and Wilders tried to make an issue out of it, she received overwhelming support from the population.

Still there is concern about immigrants not becoming 'Dutch' and there is a government Ministry of Large Cities and Integration. Strongly urging people to take classes in the Dutch language and culture, where concepts such as tolerance are emphasised, is official policy. And some

Arguably, no household item represents Dutch thrift better than the popular *flessenlikker* (bottle-scraper). This miracle tool has a disk on the business end and can scrape the last elusive smears from a mayonnaise jar or salad-dressing bottle.

HEAD & SHOULDERS ABOVE THE REST

The Dutch are the tallest people in the world, averaging 1.81m (5ft, 11in) for men and 1.68m (5ft, 6in) for women, according to Statistics Netherlands. Copious intake of milk proteins, smaller families and superior prenatal care are cited as likely causes, but researchers also suspect there is some magic fertiliser in the Dutch gene pool. Whatever the reason, the Dutch keep growing, as do their doorways. Today, the minimum required height for doors in new homes and businesses is 2.315m (7ft, 6in).

municipalities have gone further, suggesting that social benefits will be reduced for immigrants who don't take the classes.

How the paradoxical concept of forcing people to learn to be tolerant will play out remains to be seen.

Women in the Netherlands

Dutch women attained the right to vote in 1919, and by the 1970s abortion on demand was paid for by the national health service. Dutch women are a remarkably confident lot; on a social level, equality is taken for granted and women are almost as likely as men to initiate contact with the opposite sex. It's still a different story in the workplace – fewer women than men are employed full time, and fewer still hold positions in senior management. About 68% of Dutch women work part time, less than 25 hours a week.

Sport

The Netherlands is one sport-happy country. About two-thirds of all Dutch engage in some form of sporty activity, and the average person now spends 20 minutes more a week getting sweaty than in the 1970s. Sport is organised to a fault: about five million people belong to nearly 30,000 clubs and associations in the Netherlands.

Soccer, cycling and skating are favourites.

Football (Soccer)

In her book *Dutch Women Don't Get Depressed*, Dutch psychologist Ellen de Bruinand uses scientific studies to show that women in the Netherlands are a whole lot happier than women elsewhere in the world. She says that personal choice and freedom is the key.

Football is the Dutch national game, and they're pretty good at it. The national football team competes in virtually every World Cup (2010 saw them lose a heartbreaker final in overtime to Spain 1-0, their first trip to the final since 1978) and Euro Cup (2012 was a disaster as they lost all their group matches). 'Local' teams such as Ajax, Feyenoord and PSV enjoy international renown. The country has produced world-class players, such as Ruud Gullit, Dennis Bergkamp and the legendary Johan Cruyff. The unique Dutch approach to the game – known as Total Football (in which spatial tactics are analysed and carried out with meticulous precision) – fascinated viewers at its peak in the 1970s.

Passion for football runs very high. The National Football Association counts a million members, and every weekend professional and amateur teams hit pitches across the country. Many pro clubs play in modern, high-tech stadiums, such as Amsterdam Arena, assisted by a modern, high-tech police force to counteract hooligans.

Cycling

To say the Dutch are avid cyclists is like saying the English don't mind football. In sporting terms there's extensive coverage of races in the media, and you'll see uniformed teams whiz by on practice runs in remote quarters. Joop Zoetemelk pedalled to victory in the 1980 Tour de France after finishing second six times.

Leontien van Moorsel is one of the best Dutch athletes ever. She won scores of cycling championships in the 1990s. At the 2000 and 2004 Olympics she won a combined total of four golds, one silver and one bronze. At the 2012 Olympics Marianne Vos won the gold for the Women's road race.

Skating

Ice skating is as Dutch as *kroketten* (croquettes), and thousands of people hit the ice when the country's lakes and ditches freeze over. When the lakes aren't frozen, the Netherlands has dozens of ice rinks with Olympic-sized tracks and areas for hockey and figure skating. The most famous amateur event is Friesland's 220km-long *Elfstedentocht* (see p204).

The Dutch generally perform well in speed skating at the Winter Olympics; in 2010 seven of its eight medals (three of which were gold) were won on the ice.

Swimming

Swimming is the most popular sport when it comes to the raw number of practitioners, edging out even football and cycling. One-third of all Dutch swim in the pools, lakes or sea, and fancy aquatic complexes have sprung up in many cities to meet demand.

Legendary Dutch swimmer Inge de Bruin won a total of eight medals at the 2000 and 2004 Olympics. In 2008 the Dutch women's water polo team sunk all competition and took the gold. In 2012 Ranomi Kromowidjojo won two gold medals for the women's 50m and 100m freestyle.

The biggest Dutch cycling race is the Amstel Gold Race around hilly Limburg in mid-April. It is about 260km in length and features dozens of very steep hills. It is considered one of the most demanding races on the professional circuit.

THE DUTCH WAY OF LIFE SPORT

Dutch Art

Think 'Dutch Art' and you think of paintings: they don't call them the Dutch Masters for nothing. The line-up includes Rembrandt, Frans Hals and Jan Vermeer – these iconic artists are some of world's most revered and celebrated painters. And then, of course, there's Vincent van Gogh, the rock star of Impressionism, the jilted lover who cut off his ear, the artist who toiled in ignominy while supported by his loving brother, Theo. Understanding these quintessential Dutch painters requires a bit of history, as the roots of their respective styles go back to a time when Italy was the centre of the art world and painters would retreat there to study.

15th & 16th Century
Flemish School

Prior to the late 16th century, when Belgium was still part of the Low Countries, art focused on the Flemish cities of Ghent, Bruges and Antwerp. Paintings of the Flemish School featured biblical and allegorical subject matter popular with the Church, the court and to a lesser extent the nobility, who, after all, paid the bills and called the shots.

Among the most famous names of the era are Jan van Eyck (c 1385–1441), the founder of the Flemish School, who was the first to perfect the technique of oil painting; Rogier van der Weyden (1400-64), whose religious portraits showed the personalities of his subjects; and Pieter Bruegel the Elder (1525–69), who used Flemish landscapes and peasant life in his allegorical scenes.

Hieronymus (also known as Jeroen) Bosch (1450–1516) a namesake of Den Bosch created works for the ages with his macabre allegorical paintings full of religious topics. *The Prodigal Son*, which hangs in Rotterdam's Museum Boijmans Van Beuningen, is a study in motion and wit. Also there is *The Marriage at Cana*.

Dutch School

In the northern Low Countries, artists began to develop a style of their own. Although the artists of the day never achieved the level of recognition of their Flemish counterparts, the Dutch School, as it came to be called, was known for favouring realism over allegory. Haarlem was the centre of this movement, with artists such as Jan Mostaert (1475–1555), Lucas van Leyden (1494–1533) and Jan van Scorel (1494–1562). Painters in the city of Utrecht were famous for using chiaroscuro (deep contrast of light and shade), a technique associated with the Italian master Caravaggio.

17th Century (Golden Age)

When the Spanish were expelled from the Low Countries, the character of the art market changed. There was no longer the Church to buy

> **One-Artist Museums:**
> » Vermeer Centrum Delft, Delft
> » Jheronimus Bosch Art Center, Den Bosch
> » Museum Het Rembrandthuis, Amsterdam
> » Frans Hals Museum, Haarlem
> » Mondriaanhuis, Amersfoort
> » Escher in het Paleis, Den Haag

artworks (most of its art had been burned by rampaging Calvinists in 1566) and no court to speak of, so art became a business. Fortunately, there was wealth pouring into the Dutch economy and artists could survive in a free market. In place of Church and court emerged a new, bourgeois society of merchants, artisans and shopkeepers who didn't mind spending money to brighten up their houses and workplaces. The key: they had to make pictures the buyers could relate to.

Painters became entrepreneurs in their own right, churning out banal works, copies and masterpieces in factory-like studios. Paintings were mass-produced and sold at markets alongside furniture and chickens. Soon the wealthiest households were covered in paintings from top to bottom. Foreign visitors commented that even bakeries and butcher shops seemed to have a painting or two on the wall. Most painters specialised in one of the main genres of the day.

Rembrandt van Rijn

The 17th century's greatest artist, Rembrandt van Rijn (1606–69), grew up a miller's son in Leiden, but had become an accomplished painter by his early 20s.

In 1631 he came to Amsterdam to run the painting studio of the wealthy art dealer Hendrick van Uylenburgh. Portraits were the studio's cash cow, and Rembrandt and his staff (or 'pupils') churned out scores of them, including group portraits such as *The Anatomy Lesson of Dr Tulp*. In 1634 he married Van Uylenburgh's niece Saskia, who often modelled for him.

Rembrandt fell out with his boss, but his wife's capital helped him buy the sumptuous house next door to Van Uylenburgh's studio (the current Museum Het Rembrandthuis). There Rembrandt set up his own studio, with staff who worked in a warehouse in the Jordaan. These were happy years: his paintings were a success and his studio became the largest in Holland, though his gruff manner and open agnosticism didn't win him dinner-party invitations from the elite.

Rembrandt became one of the city's biggest art collectors. He was a master manipulator not only of images; the painter was also known to have his own pictures bid up at auctions. He often sketched and painted for himself, urging his staff to do likewise. Residents of the surrounding Jewish quarter provided perfect material for his dramatic biblical scenes.

NIGHT WATCH

In 1642, a year after the birth of their son Titus, Saskia died and business went downhill. Although Rembrandt's majestic group portrait *Night Watch* (1642) was hailed by art critics (it's now a prize exhibit at Amsterdam's Rijksmuseum), some of the influential people he depicted were not pleased. Each subject had paid 100 guilders, and some were unhappy at being shoved to the background. In response, Rembrandt told them where they could shove their complaints. Suddenly he received far fewer orders.

Rembrandt began an affair with his son's governess but kicked her out a few years later when he fell for the new maid, Hendrickje Stoffels, who bore him a daughter, Cornelia. The public didn't take kindly to the man's lifestyle and his spiralling debts, and in 1656 he went bankrupt. His house and rich art collection were sold and he moved to the Rozengracht in the Jordaan.

ETCHINGS

No longer the darling of the wealthy, Rembrandt continued to paint, draw and etch – his etchings on display in the Museum Het

DUTCH ART 17TH CENTURY (GOLDEN AGE)

For Dutch classical music, you can start with pianist Ronald Brautigam, who has international acclaim. Violinist-violist Isabelle van Keulen founded her own chamber music festival in Delft. The country's leading cellist is Pieter Wispelwey, known for his challenging repertoire, while Louis Andriessen is the leading composer now.

Great Art Museums

» Rijksmuseum, Amsterdam

» Van Gogh Museum, Amsterdam

» Mauritshuis, Den Haag

» Museum Boijmans Van Beuningen, Rotterdam

» Lakenhal, Leiden

10 GREAT OLD DUTCH PAINTINGS (AND WHERE TO SEE THEM)

Amsterdam

» *Night Watch*, Rembrandt (Rijksmuseum)

» *Self Portrait*, Rembrandt (Rijksmuseum)

» *The Merry Drinker*, Frans Hals (Rijksmuseum)

» *The Merry Family*, Jan Steen (Rijksmuseum)

» *Woman in Blue Reading a Letter*, Vermeer (Rijksmuseum)

Den Haag

» *Girl with a Pearl Earring*, Vermeer (Mauritshuis)

» *The Anatomy Lesson of Dr Tulp*, Rembrandt (Mauritshais)

Haarlem

» *Regents & the Regentesses of the Old Men's Almshouse*, Frans Hals (Frans Hals Museum)

Rotterdam

» *Tower of Babel*, Bruegel the Elder (Museum Boijmans Van Beuningen)

» *The Prodigal Son*, Hieronymus Bosch (Museum Boijmans Van Beuningen)

Rembrandthuis are some of the finest ever produced. He also received the occasional commission, including the monumental *Conspiracy of Claudius Civilis* (1661) for the city hall, although authorities disliked it and had it removed. In 1662 he completed the *Staalmeesters* (the 'Syndics') for the drapers' guild and ensured that everybody remained clearly visible, though it ended up being his last group portrait.

LATER WORKS

The works of his later period show that Rembrandt had lost none of his touch. No longer constrained by the wishes of clients, he enjoyed new-found freedom; his works became more unconventional yet showed an ever-stronger empathy with their subject matter, as in the *Jewish Bride* (1667). The many portraits of Titus and Hendrickje, and his ever-gloomier self-portraits, are among the most stirring in the history of art.

A plague epidemic between 1663 and 1666 killed one in seven Amsterdammers, including Hendrickje. Titus died in 1668, aged 27 and just married; Rembrandt died a year later, a broken man.

A new Rembrandt was 'discovered' in 2011 when the world's leading expert on the painter verified its origin thanks to new x-ray techniques. The *Old Man* (or *The Old Rabbi*) is in a private English collection and it is now thought to be a self-portrait.

Frans Hals

Another great painter of this period, Frans Hals (c 1581–1666), was born in Antwerp but lived in Haarlem. He devoted most of his career to portraits, dabbling in occasional genre scenes with dramatic chiaroscuro. His ability to capture his subjects' expressions was equal to Rembrandt's, though he didn't explore their characters as much. Both masters used the same expressive, unpolished brush strokes and their styles went from bright exuberance in their early careers to dark and solemn later on. The 19th-century Impressionists also admired Hals' work. In fact, his work *The Merry Drinker* (1628–30) in the Rijksmuseum's collection, with its bold brush strokes, could almost have been painted by an Impressionist.

Johannes Vermeer

The grand trio of 17th-century masters is completed by Johannes (also known as Jan) Vermeer (1632–75) of Delft. He produced only 35 meticulously crafted paintings in his career and died poor with 10 children; his baker accepted two paintings from his wife as payment for a debt of more than 600 guilders. Yet Vermeer mastered genre painting like no other artist. His paintings include historical and biblical scenes from his earlier career, his famous *View of Delft* (1661) in the Mauritshuis in Den Haag, and some tender portraits of unknown women, such as the stunningly beautiful *Girl with a Pearl Earring* (1666), also hanging in the Mauritshuis.

FAMOUS WORKS

Vermeer's work is known for serene light pouring through tall windows. The calm, spiritual effect is enhanced by dark blues, deep reds, warm yellows and supremely balanced composition. Good examples include the Rijksmuseum's *Kitchen Maid* (also known as the *Milkmaid*, 1658) and *Woman in Blue Reading a Letter* (1664), and, for his use of perspective, the *Love Letter* (1670).

The *Little Street* (1658) in the Rijksmuseum's collection is Vermeer's only street scene.

Other Golden Age Painters

Around the middle of the century, the focus on mood and subtle play of light began to make way for the splendour of the baroque. Jacob van Ruysdael (c 1628–82) went for dramatic skies while Albert Cuyp (1620–91) painted Italianate landscapes. Van Ruysdael's pupil Meindert Hobbema preferred less heroic, more playful scenes full of pretty bucolic detail. (Note that Cuyp, Hobbema and Ruysdael all have main streets named after them in the Old South and De Pijp districts, and many smaller streets here are named after other Dutch artists.)

The genre paintings of Jan Steen (1626–79) show the almost frivolous aspect of baroque. Steen was also a tavern keeper, and his depictions of domestic chaos led to the Dutch expression 'a Jan Steen household'. A good example is the animated revelry of *The Merry Family* (1668) in the Rijksmuseum; it shows adults having a good time around the dinner table, oblivious to the children in the foreground pouring themselves a drink.

18th Century

The Golden Age of Dutch painting ended almost as suddenly as it began when the French invaded the Low Countries in 1672. The economy collapsed and the market for paintings went south with it. Painters who stayed in business concentrated on 'safe' works that repeated earlier successes. In the 18th century they copied French styles, pandering to the fashion for anything French.

The results were competent but not groundbreaking. Cornelis Troost (1697–1750) was one of the best genre painters, and is sometimes compared to the British artist William Hogarth (1697–1764) for his satirical as well as sensitive portraits of ordinary people; Troost, too, introduced scenes of domestic revelry into his pastels.

Gerard de Lairesse (1640–1711) and Jacob de Wit (1695–1754) specialised in decorating the walls and ceilings of buildings – de Wit's *trompe*

THE MASTERS

DUTCH ART 18TH CENTURY

The Girl with a Pearl Earring, a dramatised account of the painting of Vermeer's famous work, is a highly readable 1999 novel by Tracy Chevalier. It was made into a movie in 2003.

GROUP PORTRAITS BY HALS

Frans Hals specialised in beautiful group portraits in which the participants were depicted in almost natural poses, unlike the rigid line-ups produced by lesser contemporaries – though he wasn't as cavalier as Rembrandt in subordinating faces to the composition. A good example is the pair of paintings known collectively as *Regents & the Regentesses of the Old Men's Alms House* (1664) in the Frans Hals Museum in Haarlem. The museum is a space that Hals knew intimately; he lived in the almshouse.

l'oeil decorations (painted illusions that look real) in the Bijbels Museum in Amsterdam are worth seeing.

19th Century

The late 18th century and most of the 19th century produced little of note, save for the landscapes and seascapes of Johan Barthold Jongkind (1819–91) and the gritty, almost photographic Amsterdam scenes of George Hendrik Breitner (1857–1923). They appear to have inspired French Impressionists, many of whom visited Amsterdam.

Jongkind and Breitner reinvented 17th-century realism and influenced the Hague School of the last decades of the 19th century. Painters such as Hendrik Mesdag (1831–1915), Jozef Israels (1824–1911) and the three Maris brothers (Jacob, Matthijs and Willem) created landscapes, seascapes and genre works, including the impressive *Panorama Mesdag* (1881), a gigantic, 360-degree cylindrical painting of the seaside town of Scheveningen viewed from a dune, painted by Mesdag.

For a moving window into the inner life of Vincent van Gogh, as well as a testimony to the extraordinary friendship and artistic connection he shared with his brother, Theo, read *Vincent Van Gogh: The Letters*. It contains all 902 letters to and from Van Gogh to his brother, friends, lovers, confidantes and fellow artists.

Vincent Van Gogh

Without a doubt, the greatest 19th-century Dutch painter was Vincent van Gogh (1853–90), whose convulsive patterns and furious colours were in a world of their own and still defy comfortable categorisation (a post-Impressionist? A forerunner of Expressionism?).

While the Dutch Masters were known for their dark, brooding paintings, it was Van Gogh who created an identity of suffering as an art form, with a morbid style all his own. Even today, he epitomises the epic struggle of the artist: the wrenching poverty; the lack of public acclaim; the reliance upon a patron – in this case his faithful brother, Theo; the mental illness; the untimely death by suicide. And of course, one of the most iconic images of an artist's self-destruction – which canonised him as the patron saint of spurned lovers everywhere – is the severed ear, sent to a woman.

THE ARTIST'S LEGEND: MYTHS & FACTS

But is any of this actually true? Was Van Gogh's suffering, his trials and tribulations for art, actually as bold and colourful as the inimitable brushstrokes that even art neophytes around the world can recognise?

Well, the answer is: yes and no. Despite how legend would have it, the facts remain. He did cut off his ear, but only part of it. He did give it to a woman, but it was in a fit of despair to a prostitute he knew, not to a lover who had rejected him.

And he did actually sell his work during his lifetime – but only a single painting, *Red Vineyard*, which now sits in Moscow. While in popular culture Van Gogh is often depicted as insane, he was in fact a depressive – contemporary medicine would probably diagnose him with bipolar disorder – who spent time in a psychiatric institution in Saint-Remy de Provence, where he kept a studio. Modern psychology makes a clear delineation between insanity and manic depression, and historians and doctors now believe Van Gogh suffered from this common illness, for which at the time there was no effective medicinal treatment (although

Van Gogh Films:

» *Vincent* (1987)

» *Vincent and Theo* (1990)

» *Lust for Life* (1956)

VAN GOGH'S LAST WORDS

Even Van Gogh's rumoured last words ring with the kind of excruciating, melancholic beauty that his best paintings express. With Theo at his side, two days after he shot himself in the chest after a manic fit of painting, he is said to have uttered in French '*la tristesse durera toujours*' (the sadness will last forever).

DUTCH GRAPHICS ARTS

It's not all paint on canvas, modern Dutch graphics arts win acclaim.

» Dick Bruna of Utrecht is famous for Miffy, an adorable cartoon character. He's written and illustrated more than 120 children's books and designed more than 2000 book covers, as well as hundreds of other books, posters, postcards and prints. The **Dick Bruna Haus** in Utrecht honours him.

» The Dutch tradition of clear visual communications has developed since the start of the 20th century. You see examples everyday, including on the national railway, which was an early trendsetter in graphic communication. See brilliant examples of Dutch graphics arts at the **Museum of the Image** in Breda.

some have countered that he suffered from epilepsy, lead paint poisoning, schizophrenia, or a host of other afflictions).

LEGACY OF A TORTURED GENIUS

Welcome to the stormy, torrid world of Vincent van Gogh, second only to Rembrandt in the lineage of Dutch artistic royalty. Who would have known, at his suicide in 1890, that the painter who once struggled to pay for basic food and art supplies would later sell a single painting (*A Portrait of Doctor Gachet*) at Christie's for $82.5 million? Probably no one.

Yet even among artists who become famous after their deaths, Van Gogh may be the most legendary – for his art, certainly, but also for his life. It takes remarkable energy and focus to produce over 900 paintings and over 1100 drawings and sketches in less than a decade, and art historians muse that it may have been his very intensity – the relentless energy that verged on mania and cycled into melancholy and despair – that fuelled his imagination even as it led to his demise. While his paintings continue to inspire the world with their artistry, and remain, to many, the most groundbreaking works of the highly lauded Impressionist era, it is also the legacy of his exquisitely tortured genius that survives, and serves as a reminder of the terrible price that artists sometimes pay for their talent.

20th Century

De Stijl

De Stijl ('The Style') was a Dutch design movement that aimed to harmonise all the arts by bringing artistic expressions back to their essence. Its advocate was the magazine of the same name, first published in 1917 by Theo van Doesburg (1883–1931). Van Doesburg produced works similar to Piet Mondrian's, though he dispensed with the thick, black lines and later tilted his rectangles at 45 degrees, departures serious enough for Mondrian to call off the friendship.

Throughout the 1920s and 1930s, De Stijl also attracted sculptors, poets, architects and designers. One of these was Gerrit Rietveld (1888–1964), designer of Amsterdam's Van Gogh Museum and several other buildings, but best known internationally for his furniture, such as the *Red Blue Chair* (1918) and his range of uncomfortable zigzag seats that, viewed side-on, formed a 'z' with a backrest.

Piet Mondrian

One of the major proponents of De Stijl was Piet Mondrian (originally Mondriaan, 1872–1944), who initially painted in the Hague School tradition. After flirting with Cubism, he began working with bold rectangular patterns, using only the three primary colours (yellow, blue and red) set

Van Gogh's Famous Five:

Amsterdam

» *Sunflowers* (Van Gogh Museum, Amsterdam)

» *Wheatfield with Crows* (Van Gogh Museum)

» *Self Portrait with Felt Hat* (Van Gogh Museum)

Hoge Veluwe National Park

» *The Potato Eaters* (Kröller-Müller Museum)

» *Weavers* (Kröller-Müller Museum)

against the three neutrals (white, grey and black). He named this style 'neo-Plasticism' and viewed it as an undistorted expression of reality in pure form and pure colour. His *Composition in Red, Black, Blue, Yellow & Grey* (1920), in the Stedelijk Museum's collection, is an elaborate example.

Mondrian's later works were more stark (or 'pure') and became dynamic again when he moved to New York in 1940. The world's largest collection of his paintings resides in the Gemeentemuseum (Municipal Museum) in his native Den Haag.

MC Escher

The favorite female pop singer in the Netherlands is Anouk, who was born in Den Haag. Although not well known outside Holland, it was hoped her performance in the 2013 Eurovision song contest would change that. The Dutch had failed to qualify for the finals eight years in a row.

One of the most remarkable graphic artists of the 20th century was Maurits Cornelis Escher (1902–72). His drawings, lithos and woodcuts of blatantly impossible images continue to fascinate mathematicians: a waterfall feeds itself; people go up and down a staircase that ends where it starts; a pair of hands draw each other. You can see his work at Escher in het Paleis Museum in Den Haag.

CoBrA

After WWII, artists rebelled against artistic conventions and vented their rage in Abstract Expressionism. In Amsterdam, Karel Appel (1921–2006) and Constant (Constant Nieuwenhuys, 1920–2005) drew on styles pioneered by Paul Klee and Joan Miró, and exploited bright colours and 'uncorrupted' children's art to produce lively works that leapt off the canvas. In Paris in 1945 they met up with the Danish Asger Jorn (1914–73) and the Belgian Corneille (Cornelis van Beverloo, 1922–2010), and together with several other artists and writers formed a group known as CoBrA (Copenhagen, Brussels, Amsterdam). It's been called the last great avant-garde movement.

Their first major exhibition, in the Amsterdam's Stedelijk Museum in 1949, aroused a storm of protest (with comments such as 'my child paints like that too'). Still, the CoBrA artists exerted a strong influence in their respective countries, even after they disbanded in 1951. The Cobra Museum in the Amsterdam suburb of Amstelveen displays a good range of their works, including colourful ceramics.

Contemporary Artists

Modern Dutch artists are usually well represented at international events and are known for mixing mediums. Look out for the installations of Jan Dibbets (1941–) and Ger van Elk (1941–), who mix photography, painting and sculpture, as well as the wry graphic illustrations of Marthe Röling (1939–). Among the younger generation, the artist duo Liet Heringa (1966–) and Maarten Van Kalsbeek (1962–) are known for their moody, free-form sculptures, Michael Raedecker (1963–) for his dreamy, radiant still lifes, and Roger Braun (1972–) for Industrial Realism.

Architecture

The Dutch are masters of architecture and use of space, but this is nothing new. Through the ages, few countries have exerted more influence on the discipline of art and construction than the Netherlands. From the original sober cathedrals to the sleek modern structures, their ideas and designs have spread not only throughout Europe but also to the new world.

The wonderful thing about Dutch architecture is that you can time-travel through a thousand years of beautiful buildings in one city alone. The odd thing about Dutch architecture – with all its influence, cleverness and internationally renowned architects – is that you're not going to find bombastic statements such as St Peter's Cathedral or the Louvre. But, then again, ostentation was never in keeping with the Dutch character. It's the little surprises that charm most: a subtle joke, a flourish on a 17th-century gable or that seemingly unending flight of stairs that feels far too tight to be at all practical but still manages to transport you to the 4th floor...

Romanesque

Romanesque architecture, which took the country (and Europe) by storm between 900 and 1250, is the earliest architectural style remaining in the country, if you discount the *hunebedden* (chamber tombs). Its main characteristics are an uncomplicated form, thick walls, small windows and round arches.

The oldest church of this style in the Netherlands is the Pieterskerk in Utrecht. Built in 1048, it's one of five churches that form a cross in the city, with the cathedral at its centre. Runner-up is Nijmegen's 16-sided Sint Nicolaaskapel, which is basically a scaled-down copy of Charlemagne's chapel in Aachen, Germany. Another classic example of Romanesque is the Onze Lieve Vrouwebasiliek in Maastricht.

Holland's countryside is also privy to this style of architecture. The windy plains of the north are filled with examples of sturdy brick churches erected in the 12th and 13th centuries, such as the lonely church perched on a manmade hill in Hogebeintum in Friesland.

Gothic

By around 1250 the love affair with Romanesque was over, and the Gothic era was ushered in. Pointed arches, ribbed vaulting and dizzying heights were trademarks of this new architectural style, which was to last until 1600. Although the Dutch buildings didn't match the size of the French Gothic cathedrals, a rich style emerged in Catholic Brabant that could compete with anything abroad. Stone churches with soaring vaults and buttresses, such as Sint Janskathedraal in Den Bosch and Breda's Grote Kerk, were erected. Both are good examples of the Brabant Gothic style, as it was later known. Note the timber vaulting and the widespread use of brick among the stone.

Stone is normally a constant fixture of Gothic buildings, but in the marshy lands of the western Netherlands it was too heavy (and too scarce) to use. The basic ingredients of bricks – clay and sand – were in abundance, however. Still, bricks are not exactly light material, and weight limits forced architects to build long or wide to compensate for the lack of height. The Sint Janskerk in Gouda is the longest church in the country, with a nave of 123m, and it has the delicate, stately feel of a variant called Flamboyant Gothic. Stone Gothic structures do exist in the western stretches of Holland, though: Haarlem's Grote Kerk van St Bavo is a wonderful example.

Mannerism

From the middle of the 16th century the Renaissance style that was sweeping through Italy steadily began to filter into the Netherlands. The Dutch naturally put their own spin on this new architectural design, which came to be known as Mannerism (c 1550–1650). Also known as Dutch Renaissance, this unique style falls somewhere between Renaissance and baroque; it retained the bold curving forms and rich ornamentation of baroque but merged them with classical Greek and Roman and traditional Dutch styles. Building facades were accentuated with mock columns (pilasters) and the simple spout gables were replaced with step gables that were richly decorated with sculptures, columns and obelisks. The playful interaction of red brick and horizontal bands of white or yellow sandstone was based on mathematical formulas designed to please the eye.

Hendrik de Keyser (1565–1621) was the champion of Mannerism. His Zuiderkerk, Noorderkerk and Westerkerk in Amsterdam are standout examples; all three show a major break from the sober, stolid lines of brick churches located out in the sticks. Their steeples are ornate and built with a variety of contrasting materials, while the windows are framed in white stone set off by brown brick. Florid details enliven the walls and roof lines.

The ultimate in early Functionalism, windmills have a variety of distinctive designs and their characteristic look makes them national icons.

Golden Age

After the Netherlands became a world trading power in the 17th century, its rich merchants wanted to splash out on lavish buildings that proclaimed their status.

More than anything, the new architecture had to impress. The leading lights in the architectural field, such as Jacob van Campen (1595–1657) and the brothers Philips and Justus Vingboons, again turned to ancient Greek and Roman designs for ideas. To make buildings look taller, the step gable was replaced by a neck gable, and pilasters were built to look like imperial columns, complete with pedestals. Decorative scrolls were added as finishing flourishes, and the peak wore a triangle or globe to simulate a temple roof.

A wonderful example of this is the Koninklijk Paleis (Royal Palace) in Amsterdam, originally built as the town hall in 1648. Van Campen, the

HOISTS & HOUSES THAT TIP

Many old canal houses deliberately tip forward. Given the narrowness of staircases, owners needed an easy way to move large goods and furniture to the upper floors. The solution: a hoist built into the gable, to lift objects up and in through the windows. The tilt allowed loading without bumping into the house front. Some properties even have huge hoist-wheels in the attic with a rope and hook that run through the hoist beam.

The forward lean also makes the houses seem larger, which makes it easier to admire the facade and gable – a fortunate coincidence for everyone.

architect, drew on classical designs and dropped many of De Keyser's playful decorations, and the resulting building exuded gravity with its solid lines and shape.

This new form of architecture suited the city's businessmen, who needed to let the world know that they were successful. As red sports cars were still centuries away, canal houses became showpieces. Despite the narrow plots, each building from this time makes a statement at gable level through sculpture and myriad shapes and forms. Philips and Justus Vingboons were specialists in these swanky residences; their most famous works include the Bijbels Museum (Biblical Museum) and houses scattered throughout Amsterdam's western canal belt.

The capital is not the only city to display such grand architecture. Den Haag has 17th-century showpieces, including the Paleis Noordeinde and the Mauritshuis, and scores of other examples line the picture-perfect canals of Leiden, Delft and Maastricht, to name but a few.

French Influence

By the 18th century the wealthy classes had turned their backs on trade for more staid lives in banking or finance, which meant a lot of time at home. Around the same time, Dutch architects began deferring to all things French (which reflected French domination of the country); dainty Louis XV furnishings and florid rococo facades became all the rage. It was then a perfect time for new French building trends to sweep the country. Daniel Marot (1661–1752), together with his assistants Jean and Anthony Coulon, was the first to introduce French interior design with matching exteriors. Good examples of their work can be found along the Lange Voorhout in Den Haag.

Neoclassicism

Architecture took a back seat during the Napoleonic Wars in the late 18th century. Buildings still needed to be built, of course, so designers dug deep into ancient Greek and Roman blueprints once more and eventually came up with Neoclassicism (c 1790–1850). Known for its order, symmetry and simplicity, neoclassical design became the mainstay for houses of worship, courtyards and other official buildings. A shining example of Neoclassicism is Groningen's town hall; of particular note are the classical pillars, although the use of brick walls is a purely Dutch accent. Many a church was subsidised by the government water ministry and so was named a Waterstaatkerk (state water church), such as the lonely house of worship in Schokland.

Late 19th Century

From the 1850s onwards, many of the country's large architectural projects siphoned as much as they could from the Gothic era, creating neo-Gothic. Soon afterwards, freedom of religion was declared and Catholics were allowed to build new churches in Protestant areas. Neo-Gothic suited the Catholics just fine as it recalled their own glory days, and a boom in church-building took place.

Nationwide, nostalgia for the perceived glory days of the Golden Age inspired neo-Renaissance, which drew heavily on De Keyser's earlier masterpieces. Neo-Renaissance buildings were erected throughout the country, made to look like well-polished veterans from three centuries earlier. For many observers, these stepped-gable edifices with alternating stone and brick are the epitome of classic Dutch architecture.

One of the leading architects of this period was Pierre Cuypers (1827–1921), who built several neo-Gothic churches but often merged the style with neo-Renaissance, as can be seen in Amsterdam's Centraal Station

Rotterdam's 12-storey Witte Huis (built 1898) was Europe's first 'skyscraper'. Today it looks almost squat compared to its neighbours; it somehow survived the destruction of Rotterdam in 1940.

Frank Lloyd Wright acolyte, William Dudok's stunning and vast town hall is the one good reason to visit Hilversum, west of Amsterdam.

and Rijksmuseum. These are predominantly Gothic structures but have touches of Dutch Renaissance brickwork.

Berlage & the Amsterdam School

As the 20th century approached, the neo styles and their reliance on the past were strongly criticised by Hendrik Petrus Berlage (1856–1934), the father of modern Dutch architecture. He favoured spartan, practical designs over frivolous ornamentation; Amsterdam's 1902 Beurs van Berlage displays these ideals to the full. Berlage cooperated with sculptors, painters and tilers to ensure that ornamentation was integrated into the overall design in a supportive role, rather than being tacked on as an embellishment to hide the structure.

Berlage's residential designs approached a block of buildings as a whole, not as a collection of individual houses. In this he influenced the young architects of what became known as the Amsterdam School, though they rejected his stark rationalism and preferred more creative designs. Leading exponents were Michel de Klerk (1884–1923), Piet Kramer (1881–1961) and Johan van der Mey (1878–1949); the latter ushered in the Amsterdam School (c 1916–30) with his extraordinary Scheepvaarthuis, which now houses a museum.

Brick was the material of choice for such architects, and housing blocks were treated as sculptures, with curved corners, oddly placed windows and ornamental, rocket-shaped towers. Their Amsterdam housing estates, such as De Klerk's 'Ship' in the west, have been described as fairytale fortresses rendered in a Dutch version of art deco. Their preference for form over function meant their designs were great to look at but not always fantastic to live in, with small windows and inefficient use of space.

Housing subsidies sparked a frenzy of residential building activity in the 1920s. At the time, many architects of the Amsterdam School worked for the Amsterdam city council and designed the buildings for the Oud Zuid (Old South). This large-scale expansion – mapped out by Berlage – called for good-quality housing, wide boulevards and cosy squares.

Functionalism

While Amsterdam School–type buildings were being erected all over their namesake city, a new generation of architects began to rebel against the school's impractical (not to mention expensive) structures. Influenced by the Bauhaus School in Germany, Frank Lloyd Wright in the USA and Le Corbusier in France formed a group called 'the 8'. It was the first stirring of Functionalism (1927–70).

Architects such as B Merkelbach (1901–61) and Gerrit Rietveld (1888–1965) believed that form should follow function and sang the praises

The *Guide to Modern Architecture in the Netherlands* by Paul Groenendijk and Piet Vollaard is a comprehensive look at architecture since 1900, arranged by region, with short explanations and photos.

The website of who's who in Holland's architectural scene is www.architectenweb.nl. It also showcases newly commissioned projects and those underway.

GABLES

Among the great treasures the old canals in Amsterdam, Haarlem and elsewhere are the magnificent gables – the roof-level facades that adorn the elegant houses along the canals. The gable hid the roof from public view and helped to identify the house, until 1795, when the French occupiers introduced house numbers. Gables then became more of a fashion accessory.

There are four main types of gable: the simple spout gable, with diagonal outline and semicircular windows or shutters, that was used mainly for warehouses from the 1580s to the early 1700s; the step gable, a late-Gothic design favoured by Dutch Renaissance architects; the neck gable, also known as the bottle gable, a durable design introduced in the 1640s; and the bell gable, which appeared in the 1660s and became popular in the 18th century.

of steel, glass and concrete. Their spacious designs were practical and allowed for plenty of sunlight; Utrecht's masterpiece Rietveld-Schröder-huis is the only house built completely along functionalist De Stijl lines.

After the war, Functionalism came to the fore and stamped its authority on new suburbs to the west and south of Amsterdam, as well as war-damaged cities such as Rotterdam. High-rise suburbs were built on a large scale yet weren't sufficient to keep up with the population boom and urbanisation of Dutch life. But Functionalism fell from favour as the smart design aspects were watered down in low-cost housing projects for the masses.

Modernism & Beyond

Construction has been booming in the Netherlands since the 1980s, and architects have had ample opportunity to flirt with numerous 'isms' such as Structuralism, Neorationalism, Postmodernism and Supermodernism. Evidence of these styles can be found in Rotterdam (see p175), where city planners have encouraged bold designs that range from Piet Blom's startling cube-shaped Boompjestorens to Ben van Berkel's graceful Erasmusbrug.

In fact the whole city is a modern architectural showcase where new 'exhibits' are erected all the time. The tallest building in the country, the MaasToren, topped out at 165m, and just a short distance away the rising De Rotterdam will be the largest building in the country. The latter is designed by Rotterdam's own Rem Koolhaas, one of the world's most influential architects.

Striking examples in Amsterdam include the NEMO Science Centre, which recalls a resurfacing submarine, and the recent Eastern Docklands housing estate, where 'blue is green' – ie the surrounding water takes on the role of lawns and shrubbery.

The shores along Amsterdam's IJ River are a good place to see the vaunted Dutch traditions of urban design in action. Northwest of Centraal Station lies the Westerdokeiland, an imposing clutch of flats, offices and cafes embracing a pleasure harbour; to the northeast is Oosterdokeiland, an A1 office location with housing and home to the Openbare Bibliotheek. Across the river in Amsterdam-Noord there's Overhoeks, a housing estate on the old Shell Oil compound that borders the EYE Film Institute. And so a new city rises where once there was marsh, the story of the Netherlands.

The Nederlands Architectuur Instituut (www.nai.nl) in Rotterdam is the top authority on the latest developments in Dutch buildings and design and it has good retrospective shows on the trends that have shaped the nation's architecture.

The Dutch Landscape

There's no arguing with the fact that the Netherlands is a product of human endeavour, and a well manicured one at that. Everywhere you look, from the neat rows of *polders* (strips of farmland separated by canals) to the omnipresent dykes, everything looks so, well, planned and organised. 'God created the world, but the Dutch created the Netherlands', as the saying goes.

Much of this tinkering with nature has been out of necessity – it's hard to live underwater for any length of time. But all this reorganisation has put a strain on the Dutch environment. Whether it's from pollution, deforestation or flooding, the cumulative dangers to natural and artificial environments are pressing. Nearly one-third of the country's surface is devoted to agriculture, while much of the rest serves towns and industry.

Since the mid-20th century Dutch awareness of the environment has grown considerably. Citizens dutifully sort their rubbish, avidly support pro-bicycle schemes, and protest over scores of projects of potential detriment. City-centre congestion has been eased by cutting parking spaces, closing roads, erecting speed bumps and initiating park-and-ride programs. Country roads favour bike lanes at the cost of motor vehicles.

A Land Created

Polders (areas of drained land) form 60% of the Netherlands' landscape – by far the highest percentage of any country in the world.

Flanked by Belgium, Germany and the choppy waters of the North Sea, the land mass of the Netherlands is to a great degree artificial, having been reclaimed from the sea over many centuries. Maps from the Middle Ages are a curious sight today, with large chunks of land 'missing' from North Holland and Zeeland. The country now encompasses over 41,500 sq km, making it roughly half the size of Scotland or a touch bigger than the US state of Maryland.

Twelve provinces make up the Netherlands. Almost all of these are as flat as a Dutch pancake, for want of a better term; the only hills to speak of in the entire country rise from its very southern tip, near Maastricht. The soil in the west and north is relatively young and consists of peat and clay formed less than 10,000 years ago. Much of this area is below sea level, or reclaimed land.

Dykes

The efforts of the Dutch to create new land – which basically equates to reclaiming it from the encroaching sea – are almost super-human. Over the past century alone four vast *polders* have been created through ingenious engineering: Wieringermeer in North Holland; the Noordoostpolder (Northeast *polder*) in Flevoland; and the Noordpolder (North *polder*) and Zuidpolder (South *polder*) on the province-island of Flevoland. Much of this, just over 1700 sq km, was drained after a barrier dyke closed off the North Sea in 1932. In total, an astounding 20% of the country is reclaimed land.

It's impossible to talk about the Dutch landscape without mentioning water, which covers 20% of the entire country. Most Dutch people shudder at the thought of a leak in the dykes. If the Netherlands were to lose its 2400km of mighty dykes and dunes – some of which are 25m high – the large cities would be inundated. Modern pumping stations (the replacements for windmills) run around the clock to drain off excess water.

The danger of floods is most acute in the southwestern province of Zeeland, a sprawling estuary for the rivers Schelde, Maas, Lek and Waal. The latter two are branches of the Rijn (Rhine), the final leg of a watery journey that begins in the Swiss Alps. The Maas is another of Europe's major rivers to cross the country. It rises in France and travels through Belgium before dropping its load in the North Sea in the Delta region.

The horrible floods of 1953 devastated Zeeland and the surrounding region. The resulting Delta Project to prevent future flooding became one of the world's largest public works projects.

Windmills

It's impossible to talk about the Dutch and their struggles with water without also mentioning windmills. These national icons were an ingenuous development that harnessed the nearly constant winds off the North Sea to keep the waters from the North Sea and elsewhere at bay. First used in the 13th century, windmills pumped water up and over the dykes from land below sea level. Later their uses became myriad.

Wildlife

Human encroachment has played a huge role in the wildlife of the Netherlands. Few wildlife habitats are left intact in the country, and more than 10% of species are imported. While the Netherlands' flora and fauna will always be in constant change, one thing remains the same – birds love the place. A great depth of species can be seen the entire year round, and birdwatching enthusiasts will be all aflutter at the abundance of spotting opportunities.

Animals

The Netherlands is a paradise for birds and those who love to follow them around. The wetlands are a major migration stop for European birds, particularly Texel's Duinen van Texel National Park, Flevoland's Oostvaardersplassen Nature Reserve and the Delta. Just take the geese: a dozen varieties, from white-fronted to pink-footed, break their V-formations to winter here.

Along urban canals you'll see plenty of mallards, coots and swans as well as the lovely grebe with its regal head plumage. The large and graceful blue heron spears frogs and tiny fish in the ditches of the *polder* lands, but also loiters on canal boats in and out of town. The black cormorant, an accomplished diver with a wingspan of nearly 1m, is another regal bird.

A variety of fish species dart about the canals and estuaries. One of the most interesting species is the eel, which thrives in both fresh and salt water. These amazing creatures breed in the Sargasso Sea off Bermuda before making the perilous journey to the North Sea (only to end up smoked and down someone's gullet). Herds of seals can be spotted on coastal sandbanks such as those around Texel.

Plants

Mention plant life in the Netherlands and most people think of tulips. Indeed, these cultivated bulbs are in many ways representative of much of

There are myriad small roads that follow the dykes – a good one is in North Holland near Alkmaar. You can appreciate just how far the land lies below the water in the canals and you can see the historic windmills once used to keep the water out.

Larger mammals such as the fox, badger and fallow deer have retreated to the national parks and reserves. Some species such as boar, mouflon and red deer have been reintroduced to controlled habitats.

the country's flora in that they were imported from elsewhere and then commercially exploited. A range of other flowers and fruits and vegetables – such as tomatoes and sweet peppers (capsicum) – fit this profile.

Of course the flowers of the Netherlands are not limited to exotic types. There are also thousands of wild varieties on display, such as the marsh orchid (with a pink crown of tiny blooms) or the Zeeland masterwort (with bunches of white, compact blooms).

Much of the undeveloped land is covered by grass, which is widely used for grazing. The wet weather means that the grass remains green and grows for much of the year – on coastal dunes and mudflats, and around brackish lakes and river deltas. Marshes, heaths and peatlands are the next most common features. The remnants of oak, beech, ash and pine forests are carefully managed.

Freshwater species such as white bream, rudd, pike, perch, stickleback and carp enjoy the canal environment. You can admire them up close at Amsterdam's Artis Royal Zoo, in an aquarium that simulates an Amsterdam canal.

National Parks

With so few corners of the Netherlands left untouched, the Dutch cherish every bit of nature that's left, and that's doubly true for their national parks (www.nationaalpark.nl). But while the first designated natural reserve was born in 1930, it wasn't until 1984 that the first publicly funded park was established.

National parks in the Netherlands tend to be small affairs – for an area to become a park, it must only be bigger than 10 sq km (and of course be important in environmental terms). Most of the 20 national parks in the country average a mere 6400 hectares and are not meant to preserve some natural wonder, but are open areas of special interest. A total of 1,200 sq km, or just over 3%, of the Netherlands is protected in the form of national parks; the most northerly is the island of Schiermonnikoog, and the most southerly is the terraced landscape of De Meinweg.

Some national parks are heavily visited, not only because there's plenty of nature to see but also because of their well-developed visitors centres and excellent displays of contemporary flora and fauna. Hoge Veluwe, established in 1935, is a particular favourite with its sandy hills and forests that once were prevalent in this part of the Netherlands.

Of the 19 remaining national parks, Weerribben-Wieden in Overijssel is one of the most important as it preserves a landscape once heavily scarred by the peat harvest. Here the modern objective is to allow the land to return to nature, as is the case on the island of Schiermonnikoog in Friesland, which occupies a good portion once used by a sect

---

BIRDWATCHING FOR BEGINNERS

Seen through an amateur birdwatcher's eyes, some of the more interesting sightings might include the following:

» **Avocet** – common on the Waddenzee and the Delta, with slender upturned bill, and black and white plumage.

» **Black woodpecker** – drums seldom but loudly. To see it, try woodlands such as Hoge Veluwe National Park.

» **Bluethroat** – song like a free-wheeling bicycle; seen in Biesbosch National Park, Flevoland and the Delta.

» **Great white egret** – cranelike species common in marshlands. First bred in Flevoland in the early 1990s.

» **Marsh harrier** – bird of prey; often hovers over reed beds and arable land.

» **Spoonbill** – once scarce, this odd-looking fellow has proliferated on coasts in Zeeland and the Wadden Islands.

» **White stork** – nearly extinct in the 1980s, numbers have since recovered. Enormous nests.

NOTABLE NATIONAL PARKS & NATURE RESERVES

NAME	FEATURES	ACTIVITIES	BEST TIME TO VISIT
Biesbosch NP	estuarine reed marsh, woodland	canoeing, hiking, bird-watching, cycling	Mar-Sep
Duinen van Texel NP	dunes, heath, forest	hiking, cycling, bird-watching, swimming	Mar-Sep
Hoge Veluwe NP	marsh, forests, dunes	hiking, cycling, art-viewing	year-round
Oostvaardersplas-sen NR	wild reed marsh, grassland	hiking, cycling, bird-watching, fishing	year-round
Schiermonnikoog NP	car-free island, dunes, mudflats	hiking, mudflat-walk-ing, birdwatching	Mar-Sep
Weerribben-Wieden NP	peat marsh	kayaking, canoeing, hiking, birdwatching	year-round
Zuid-Kennemerland NP	dunes, heath, forest	hiking, birdwatching, cycling	Mar-Sep

of monks and which is part of Unesco's 2009 recognition of the broader Waddenzee region. Biesbosch, near Rotterdam, was formerly inhabited by reed farmers.

Recently the national parks have become a part of public debate after the conservative government in 2011 proposed hiving off the parks and making them the responsibility of the provinces.

Environmental Issues

As a people, the Dutch are more aware of environmental issues than most. But then again, with high population density, widespread car ownership, heavy industrialisation, extensive farming and more than a quarter of the country below sea level, they need to be.

As early as the 1980s a succession of Dutch governments began to put in motion plans to tighten the standards for industrial and farm pollution. They also made recycling a part of everyday life, although this has become a subject of some debate after the right-leaning government in 2012 scrapped the plastic bottle deposit scheme following strong lobbying from the beverage industry. Local governments and environmental groups were vociferous in their opposition, claiming that litter would increase as happened in the UK when it scrapped a deposit scheme in the 1980s.

Car

While the Dutch are avid bike riders, they still like having a car at the ready. Despite good, reasonably cheap public transport, private car ownership has risen sharply over the past two decades. Use of vehicles is now about 50% above the levels of the late 1980s. Some critics warn that unless action is taken the country's streets and motorways will become gridlocked (as they already are at rush hour around the Randstad). Stiff parking fees (Amsterdam's, at €50 per day, are the highest in the world), the distinct lack of parking spaces, pedestrian spaces and outlandish fines have helped curb congestion in the inner cities.

Outside of town centres, minor roads are being reconfigured to put cyclists first, with drivers reduced to shared single lanes. Such schemes, plus the aggressive building plan for separate cycling routes, have made

The Dutch branch of Greenpeace won a court decision in 2012 allowing it to stage peaceful protests at petrol stations in the Netherlands operated by Shell. The oil company had sought to ban the protests of its oil drilling in the Arctic.

some headway in slowing the growth in car use. Although when a country driver blows past you on a dyke road doing 120km/h and scattering all before them, it's obvious that the concept of modest car use has not been universally adopted.

Water

The effects of climate change are obvious in the Netherlands. Over the past century the winters have become shorter and milder. The long-distance ice-skating race known as the Elfstedentocht may die out because the waterways in the northern province of Friesland rarely freeze hard enough (the last race was in 1997). The Dutch national weather service KNMI predicts that only four to 10 races will be held this century. Although damp and cold, winter in the Netherlands today is not the ice-covered deep freeze you see in Renaissance paintings.

The lack of ice over winter is simply annoying; a rise in sea levels would constitute a disaster of epic proportions. If the sea level rises as forecast, the country could theoretically sink beneath the waves, like Atlantis, or at least suffer annual flooding. Funds have been allocated to extend the dykes and storm barriers.

The possibility of a watery onslaught is very real, and not just from the sea. Glaciers in Switzerland are melting and that water finds its way into the Rhine, eventually becoming the Rijn in the Netherlands. River flows are expected to increase by 12.5% in the next decade.

In the coastal waters there are 12 crustacean species including the invasive Chinese mitten crab. Further out, the stock of North Sea cod, shrimp and sole has suffered from chronic overfishing, and catches are now limited by EU quotas.

Agriculture

The Dutch chicken population hovers around 100 million, one of the largest concentrations in the industrialised world (six chickens for every citizen; pigs are close to a one-to-one ratio). Such industrialised farming has been the cornerstone of Dutch agriculture since WWII and has brought much wealth to the country. Who hasn't seen the brilliant red Dutch tomato waiting to be sold in a supermarket in the dead of winter? (These tasteless lumps are gassed while green, which turns them red, and then flown at great expense all over the world.)

But with concerns about ground-water quality, intensive farming and all the artificial fertilisers, chemicals and animal waste that come with it are under scrutiny. The province of Noord-Brabant in the south was the first to limit farm size and ban antibiotics used in feed.

More attention is being paid to sustainable development. Organic (*biologische*) food is gaining in popularity and the huge agriculture industry is realising that profits can be made from more sustainable practices and by going green – and we don't just mean ungassed tomatoes.

A third of the dairy cattle in the world are Holstein Friesian, the black and white variety from the north of the Netherlands that are often used as iconic cows in ads worldwide.

Dutch Cuisine

The Netherlands is being transformed by a culinary revolution. Fresh winds are blowing through the Dutch traditional kitchen, breathing new life into centuries-old recipes by giving them a contemporary twist. Creative Dutch chefs are taking concepts from the rest of Europe and the world and melding them with excellent meats, seafood and vegetables sourced locally. You can find interesting and creative restaurants right across the country.

Of course, progress is needed; like many other countries in northern Europe, the Netherlands has never had a reputation for outstanding cuisine. Hearty, hefty, filling, stodgy – these are the adjectives with which Dutch cooking is usually tagged. This, however, has a historical context; traditionally, the Dutch never paid that much attention to food as there was too much work to be done and little time to cook. It is quite revealing that, during the Golden Age, spices such as pepper were more of a currency than a culinary ingredient.

On the Menu
Dutch

Van Gogh perfectly captured the main ingredient of traditional Dutch cooking in his painting *Potato Eaters*. Typically boiled to death, these 'earth apples' are accompanied by meat – and more boiled vegetables. Gravy is then added for flavour. It's certainly not fancy, but it is filling.

Few restaurants serve exclusively Dutch cuisine, but many places have several homeland items on the menu, especially in winter. Some time-honoured favourites:

» **stamppot** (mashed pot) – a simple dish of potatoes mashed with kale, endive or sauerkraut and served with smoked sausage or strips of pork. Perfect in winter.

» **hutspot** (hotchpotch; stew) – similar to *stamppot*, but with potatoes, carrots, onions, braised meat and more spices.

We list some of our favourite Dutch restaurants at the start of every chapter. Our recommendations cover the entire country and are in every price range and type of cuisine, from the best humble *frites* (French fries) to renowned restaurants.

PURELY DUTCH

The sight of a local slowly sliding a raw herring head first (thankfully headless) down their gullet never fails to get a double-take from visitors new to the Netherlands. But the Dutch love this salted delicacy and are eager for visitors to try it. If an entire fish is too much to stomach, it can be cut into bite-sized pieces and served with onion and pickles. You'll find vendors the length and breadth of the country – look for the words *haring* or *Hollandse nieuwe* and dig in. In fact, the arrival of new herring each May is a cause for celebration across the nation.

Another acquired taste in Holland is *drop*. This so-called sweet is a thick, rubbery liquorice root and Arabic gum concoction the Dutch go crazy for – a reputed 30 million kilos of the stuff is consumed each year. Its bitter taste is reminiscent of childhood medicine and some foreigners have trouble taking a second bite. There's also a liquid version; look for a bottle of Dropshot in supermarkets.

» **erwtensoep** (pea soup) – plenty of peas with onions, carrots, smoked sausage and bacon. And the perfect pea soup? A spoon stuck upright in the pot should remain standing. (Sadly not served in summer.)

» **asperge** (asparagus) – usually white and often crunchy; very popular when it's in season (spring); served with ham and butter.

» **kroketten** (croquettes) – dough balls with various fillings, crumbed and deep-fried; the variety called *bitterballen* are a popular pub snack served with mustard.

» **mosselen** (mussels) – cooked with white wine, chopped leeks and onions, and served in a bowl or cooking pot with a side dish of *frites* or *patat* (French fries); they're popular and best eaten from September to April.

The Dutch start the day with a filling, yet unexciting, breakfast of a few slices of bread accompanied by jam, cheese and a boiled egg. Many hotel breakfast buffets – often included in the rate – are far more lavish.

Lamb is prominently featured on menus, and when you are near the coast – really near – seafood is on every menu. It is also eaten as a snack, in which form it is everywhere. *Haring* (herring) is a national institution, eaten lightly salted or occasionally pickled but never fried or cooked; *paling* (eel) is usually smoked and can be rather oily. Many towns have fabulous smoked fish shops such as Van Der Star on Texel.

Typical Dutch desserts are fruit pie (apple, cherry or other fruit), *vla* (custard) and ice cream (try the phenomenal stuff from Ijs van Co in Hoenderloo near Hoge Veluwe see p234).

Many snack bars and pubs serve *appeltaart* (apple pie). Some Dutch eat *hagelslag* (chocolate sprinkles) on bread for breakfast.

Finally, most towns have at least one place serving *pannenkoeken* (pancakes), which come in a huge number of varieties. The mini-version, covered in sugar or syrup, is *poffertjes*. You can often find these fresh at markets.

Indonesian

Indonesian cooking, a piquant legacy of the colonial era, is a rich and complex blend of many cultures: chilli peppers, peanut sauce and curries from Thailand, lemon grass and fish sauce from Vietnam, intricate Indian spice mixes, and Asian cooking methods.

In the Netherlands, Indonesian food is often toned down for sensitive Western palates. If you want it hot (*pedis,* pronounced 'p-*dis*'), say so, but be prepared for watering eyes and burnt taste buds. You might play it safe by asking for *sambal* (chilli paste) and helping yourself. *Sambal oelek* is red and hot; the dark-brown *sambal badjak* is onion-based, mild and sweet.

The most famous Indonesian dish is *rijsttafel* (rice table), an array of spicy savoury dishes such as braised beef, pork satay and ribs served

---

DISTINCTLY CHEESY

Some Dutch say it makes them tall; others complain it causes nightmares. Whatever the case, the Netherlands is justifiably famous for its *kaas* (cheese). The Dutch – known as the original cheeseheads – consume 16.5kg of the stuff every year.

Nearly two-thirds of all cheese sold is Gouda. The tastier varieties have strong, complex flavours and are best enjoyed with a bottle of wine or two. Try some *oud* (old) Gouda, hard and rich in flavour and a popular bar snack eaten with mustard. Oud Amsterdammer is a real delight, deep orange and crumbly with white crystals of ripeness.

Edam is similar to Gouda but slightly drier and less creamy. Leidse or Leiden cheese is another export hit, laced with cumin or caraway seed and light in flavour.

In the shops you'll also find scores of varieties that are virtually unknown outside the country. Frisian Nagelkaas might be made with parsley juice, buttermilk, and 'nails' of caraway seed. Kruidenkaas has a melange of herbs such as fennel, celery, pepper or onions. Graskaas is 'new harvest' Gouda made after cows begin to roam the meadows and munch grass.

Lower-fat cheeses include Milner, Kollumer and Maaslander. One has to start somewhere: the stats show that the Dutch are gaining weight despite all that cycling.

FRITES

The national institution, *Vlaamse frites* (Flemish fries), are French fries made from whole potatoes rather than the potato pulp you will get if the sign only says *frites*. They are supposed to be smothered in mayonnaise (though you can ask for ketchup, curry sauce, garlic sauce or other gloppy toppings). Heed the words of Vincent Vega *(Pulp Fiction)*: 'You know what they put on French fries in Holland? Mayonnaise. And I don't mean a little bit on the side – they fuckin' drown 'em in it.'

Three favourite vendors: Haarlem's De Haerlemsche Vlaamse, Vleminckx in Amsterdam and Reitz in Maastricht.

with white rice. *Nasi rames* is a steaming plate of boiled rice covered in several rich condiments, while the same dish with thick noodles is called *bami rames*.

Surinamese

Dishes from this former colony have Caribbean roots, blending African and Indian flavours with Indonesian influences introduced by Javanese labourers. Chicken, lamb and beef curries are common menu items. *Roti*, a chickpea-flour pancake filled with potatoes, long beans, bean sprouts and meat (vegetarian versions are available), is by far the favoured choice of the Dutch. You will see a lot of Surinamese late-night snack bars in Rotterdam for instance; they specialise in slightly spicy deep-fried treats.

Drinks
Coffee & Tea

The hot drink of choice is coffee – after all, it was Amsterdam's merchants who introduced coffee to Europe. It should be strong and can be excellent if it's freshly made.

Ordering a *koffie* will get you a sizeable cup of the black stuff and a separate package or jug of *koffiemelk*, a slightly sour-tasting cream akin to condensed milk. *Koffie verkeerd* is similar to a latte, served in a big mug with plenty of real milk. If you order espresso or cappuccino, you'll be lucky to get a decent Italian version. Don't count on finding decaffeinated coffee; if you do it may be instant.

Tea is usually served Continental-style: a cup or pot of hot water with a tea bag on the side. Varieties might be presented in a humidorlike box for you to pick and choose. If you want milk, say *'met melk, graag'*. Many locals prefer to add a slice of lemon.

Beer

Lager beer is the staple drink, served cool and topped by a head of froth so big it would start a brawl in an Australian bar. Heineken tells us that these are 'flavour bubbles', and requests for no head will earn a steely response. *Een bier* or *een pils* will get you a normal glass; *een kleintje pils* is a small glass and *een fluitje* is a tall but thin glass – perfect for multiple refills. Some places serve half-litre mugs to please tourists.

Spirits

It's not all beer here: the Dutch also make the hard stuff. *Jenever* (pronounced ya-nay-ver; Dutch gin; also spelled *genever*) is made from juniper berries and drunk chilled from a tiny glass filled to the brim. Most people prefer *jonge* (young) *jenever*, which is smooth and relatively easy to drink; *oude* (old) *jenever* has a strong juniper flavour and can be an acquired taste. A common combination, known as a *kopstoot* (head butt),

At any given time the Netherlands has a population of about 14 million pigs against 17 million humans. Despite being small in size, it is Europe's largest exporter of pork and domestic consumption is huge.

The Dutch drink on average 140L of coffee each per year, more than any other Europeans except the highly caffeinated Danes.

GOOD BREWS

The Dutch love beer. It's seen as the perfect companion for time spent with friends in the sun or out partying till the small hours. And they've had plenty of time to cultivate this unquestioning love – beer has been a popular drink since the 14th century, and at one time the Dutch could lay claim to no fewer than 559 brewers. Most Dutch beer is pilsner (or lager), a clear, crisp, golden beer with strong hop flavouring.

Heineken is the Netherlands' (and possibly the world's) best-known beer. However, like Fosters in Australia, it has a poor name at home – 'the beer your cheap father drinks', to quote one wag. Amstel (owned by Heineken) is also well known, and Grolsch and Oranjeboom can also claim a certain amount of international fame. Most beers contain around 5% alcohol, and a few of those cute little glasses can pack a strong punch.

While the big names are ubiquitous, the Netherlands has scores of small brewers worth trying, including Gulpen, Haarlem's Jopen, Bavaria, Drie Ringen, Leeuw and Utrecht. La Trappe is the only Dutch Trappist beer, brewed close to Tilburg. The potent beers made by Amsterdam's Brouwerij 't IJ are sold on tap and in some local pubs – try the Columbus brew (9% alcohol).

Other local breweries worth trying include Texelse Bierbrouwerij on Texel, Rotterdam's Stadsbrouwerij De Pelgrim, Utrecht's Oudaen and De Hemel in Nijmegen. In addition almost every town has at least one cafe or bar serving a huge range of beers. One of the best is Take One in Maastricht.

If you're around in spring or autumn, don't pass up the chance to sample Grolsch's seasonal bock beers, such as Lentebok (spring bock) and Herfstbok (autumn bock). Sample many – and possibly suffer the consequences – at Utrecht's Café Ledig Erf, which has a bock beer fest over an autumn weekend.

And on a hot summer day, the seasonal fruity red beers by the major brewers are a refreshing treat.

---

is a glass of *jenever* with a beer chaser – few people can handle more than two or three of these. There are plenty of indigenous liqueurs, including *advocaat* (a kind of eggnog) and the herb-based Beerenburg, a Frisian schnapps.

Where to Eat & Drink

Restaurants abound and they cater to a wide variety of tastes and budgets. More casual are *eetcafés*, affordable pub-like eateries with loyal local followings. You'll also find a growing number of bistros and other types of eateries that draw their style from other cultures.

Where to Buy Cheese

» De Tromp Kaaswinkel, Alkmaar

» 't Kaaswinkeltje, Gouda

» Kaashandel De Brink, Deventer

» De Kaaskamer, Amsterdam

» Gestam, Edam

Cafes

When the Dutch say 'cafe' they mean a pub, and there are more than 1000 of them in Amsterdam alone. In a country that values socialising and conversation even more than the art of drinking itself, cafes aren't just places to drink: they're places to hang out for literally hours of contemplation or camaraderie. Every town and city has a variety of glorious cafes that regular customers or a certain type of clientele have considered a 'second home' for years, if not generations.

Many cafes have outside seating on a *terras* (terrace), which are glorious in summer, and sometimes covered and heated in winter. These are fetching places to relax and people-watch, soak up the sun, read a paper or write postcards. Most of these cafes serve food as well, ranging from sandwiches and fried snacks like traditional Dutch *bitterballen* (small, round meat croquettes) to surprisingly excellent full meals.

Of course the Netherlands will go down in cafe history for its historic *bruin cafés* (brown cafes). The name comes from the smoke stains from centuries of use (although recent aspirants slap on brown paint to catch up). You may find sand on the wooden floor or Persian rugs on the tables to soak up spilled beer.

Grand cafes are spacious, have comfortable furniture and are, well, just grand. A good tradition in many is an indoor reading table stacked with the day's papers and news magazines, usually with one or two in English. Another difference: they all have food menus, some quite elaborate. They're perfect for a lazy brunch or pre-theatre supper.

Theatre cafes are often similar to grand cafes, and are normally attached or adjacent to theatres, serving meals before and drinks after performances. Generally they're good places to catch performers after the show, though they're lovely any time of day.

Quick Eats

Broodjeszaken (sandwich shops) or snack bars proliferate. The latter offer multicoloured treats in a display case, usually based on some sort of meat and spices, and everything is dumped into a deep-fryer when you order.

FEBO-style snack bars have long rows of coin-operated windows à la the Jetsons and are the lifeblood of late-night partiers. The *frikandel* (a deep-fried skinless sausage) is worrisomely addictive. A *kaas soufflé* (cheese souffle) has a lavalike pocket of gooey cheesy goodness.

Lebanese and Turkish snack bars specialise in *shoarma*, a pitta bread filled with sliced lamb from a vertical spit – also known as a *gyros* or doner kebab.

Beer Bars
» 't Arendsnest, Amsterdam
» Locus Publicus, Delft
» Locus Publicus, Rotterdam
» De Mug, Middelburg
» De Pintelier, Groningen
» Take One, Maastricht

Vegetarians

For all their liberalism, it's surprising how few Dutch consider themselves vegetarians – only about 4% in most polls. Outside the major metropolises you'll be hard-pressed to find a strictly vegetarian-only restaurant in the small town you're visiting; in this case, you'll be relying on the couple of veg options available on most restaurant menus. Check their purity before ordering, though, as often you can't be sure whether they're 100% meat- or fish-free (meat stock is a common culprit).

Once you do track down a vegetarian restaurant, you'll be happy to find they rely on organic ingredients and often make everything in-house, from the bread with your starter to your cake for dessert.

Food Glossary

Dutch restaurants are skilled in serving foreigners, so bilingual or English menus are practically the norm.

appelmoes *a*·puhl·moos apple sauce

beenham *bayn*·ham leg ham

belegd broodje buh-*lekht broa*·chuh filled sandwich

biologisch bee·*yo*·*lo*·khees organic

boerenomelet *boo*·ruhn·oa·muh-*let* omelette with vegetables and ham

dagschotel *dakh*·skhoa·tuhl dish of the day

drop drop liquorice

frikandel free·kan-*del* deep-fried meat snack, like a sausage

hagelslag *haa*·khuhl·slakh chocolate sprinkles

Hollandse nieuwe *ho*·lant·suh *nee*·wuh salted herring, first of the season

hoofdgerecht *hoaft*·khuh·rekht main course

kaas kaas cheese

kroket kroa·*ket* meat croquette

nagerecht *naa*·khuh·rekht dessert

pannenkoek *pa*·nuhn·kook pancake

patat pa·*tat* French fries

poffertjes po·fuhr·tyuhs mini pancakes

speculaas spay·ku·laas spiced biscuit

tosti tos·ti toasted sandwich

uitsmijter öyt·smay·tuhr fried egg, ham and cheese on bread

Vlaamse frites vlaam·suh freet thick fries made from whole potatoes

vlammetjes vla·muh·tyuhs spicy spring rolls

voorgerecht voar·khuh·rekht starter

Cooking Terms

gaar khaar well done

gebakken khuh·ba·kuhn baked/fried

gebraden khe·braa·duhn roasted

gefrituurd khuh·free·turt deep fried

gegratineerd khuh·khra·tee·nayrt browned on top with cheese

gegrild khuh·khrilt grilled

gegrild aan 't spit khuh·khrilt aant spit spit-roasted

gekookt khuh·koakt boiled

gepaneerd khuh·pa·nayrt coated in breadcrumbs

gepocheerd khuh·po·shayrt poached

gerookt khuh·roakt smoked

geroosterd khuh·roas·tuhrt toasted

gesauteerd khuh·soa·tayrt sautéed

gestoofd khuh·stoaft braised

gestoomd khuh·stoamt steamed

gevuld khuh·vuhlt stuffed

half doorbakken half doar·ba·kuhn medium

rood roat rare

peper pay·puhr pepper

suiker söy·kuhr sugar

zout zowt salt

Desserts

amandelbroodje a·man·duhl·broa·chuh sweet roll with almond filling

appelgebak a·puhl·khuh·bak apple pie

cake kayk cake

ijs ays ice cream

slagroom slakh·roam whipped cream

taart taart tart, pie, cake

vla vlaa custard

wafel waa·fuhl waffle

Drinks

bier beer beer

brandewijn bran·duh·wayn brandy

jenever (or genever) yuh·nay·vuhr Dutch gin

jus d'orange/sinaasappelsap zhudo·ranzh/see·nas·a·puhl·sap orange juice

koffie ko·fee coffee

koffie verkeerd ko·fee vuhr·kayrt latte

melk melk milk

met melk/citroen met melk/see·*troon* with milk/lemon

rood/wit roat/wit red/white

spa blauw spaa blow brand of still mineral water

spa rood spaa roat brand of fizzy mineral water

thee tay tea

water *waa*·tuhr water

wijn wayn wine

zoet/droog zoot/droakh sweet/dry

Fruit, Vegetables, Staples & Spices

aardappel *aart*·a·puhl potato

appel *a*·puhl apple

artisjok ar·tee·*shok* artichoke

asperge as·*per*·zhuh asparagus

aubergine oa·ber·*zheen* eggplant/aubergine

boon boan bean

champignon sham·pee·*nyon* mushroom

courgette koor·*zhet* zucchini/courgette

erwt ert pea

groene paprika *khroo*·nuh *pa*·pree·ka green pepper (capsicum)

groente *khroon*·tuh vegetable

kers *kers* cherry

knoflook *knof*·loak garlic

komkommer kom·*kom*·uhr cucumber

kool koal cabbage

maïs *ma*·ees sweet corn

olijf o·*layf* olive

peer payr pear

perzik *per*·zik peach

peterselie pay·tuhr·*say*·lee parsley

pompoen pom·*poon* pumpkin

prei pray leek

pruim pröym plum

rijst *rayst* rice

rode paprika *roa*·duh *pap*·ree·ka red pepper (capsicum)

selderij *sel*·duh·ray celery

sinaasappel *see*·nas·a·puhl orange

sla slaa lettuce

spinazie spee·*naa*·zee spinach

spruitje *spröy*·chuh Brussels sprout

ui öy onion

witlof *wit*·lof chicory

wortel *wor*·tuhl carrot

Meat & Poultry

beenham *bayn*·ham ham on the bone

eend aynt duck

ei ay egg

everzwijn *ay*·vuhr·zwayn boar

fazant fa·*zant* pheasant

gevogelte khuh·*voa*·khuhl·tuh poultry

hert hert venison

kalfsvlees *kalfs*·vlays veal

kalkoen kal·*koon* turkey

kip kip chicken

konijn ko·*nayn* rabbit

lamsvlees *lams*·vlays lamb

lever *lay*·vuhr liver

paard paart horse

parelhoen *paa*·ruhl·hoon guinea fowl

ribstuk *rip*·stuk rib steak

rookworst *roak*·worst smoked sausage

rundvlees *runt*·vlays beef

schapenvlees *skhaa*·puhn·vlays mutton

slak slak snail

spek spek bacon

tong tong tongue

varkensvlees *var*·kuhns·vlays pork

vlees vlays meat

vleeswaren *vlays*·waa·ruhn cooked/prepared meats, cold cuts

wild wilt game

worst worst sausage

Seafood

ansjovis *an*·shoa·vis anchovy

baars baars bream

forel foa·*rel* trout

garnaal khar·*naal* shrimp, prawns, scampi

haring *haa*·ring herring

inktvis *ingt*·vis squid

kabeljauw kaa·buhl·*jow* cod

krab krap crab

kreeft krayft lobster

maatjes *maa*·chuhs herring fillets

makreel ma·*krayl* mackerel

oester *oos*·tuhr oyster

paling *paa*·ling eel

rivierkreeft ree·*veer*·krayft crayfish

roodbaars *roat*·baars red mullet

St Jacobsschelp sint·*yaa*·kop·skhelp scallop

schol skhol plaice

tong tong sole

tonijn to·*nayn* tuna

vis vis fish

zalm zalm salmon

zeebaars *zay*·baars bass/sea bream

Survival
Guide

Directory
A–Z

Accommodation

The country's wealth of hotels, homestays and hostels provides any traveller – whether they be backpacker or five-star aficionado – with plenty of choice. Hotels and B&Bs are the mainstay of accommodation in the country and, while most are fairly standard and highly functional, a few gems fly the boutique flag or are simply idiosyncratic.

Note that a good part of the country suffers from the 'Amsterdam effect': because transport is so efficient and the city is so popular, many visitors stay in the capital even if they're travelling further afield. Conversely, some savvy folk use easy-to-access charmers such as Haarlem or Delft as their base of operations, visiting the capital as a day (or night) trip (trains on key lines run all night).

B&Bs

Bed-and-breakfasts are an excellent way to meet the friendly locals face to face, and to see the weird, the wacky and the wonderful interior designs of the Dutch firsthand. While they're not abundant in cities, the countryside is awash with them. Local tourist offices keep a list of B&Bs on file; costs usually start from €25 to €30 per person.

Camping

The Dutch are avid campers, even within their own country. Campgrounds tend to be self-contained communities complete with shops, cafes, playgrounds and swimming pools. Lists of sites with ratings (one to five stars) are available from tourist offices.

A camp site, which costs anything between €10 and €20, covers two people and a small tent; a car is an extra €2 to €6. Caravans are popular – every one in 15 residents owns one – so there are oodles of hook-ups.

Simple bungalows or cabins (from €35) are also an option at many campgrounds.

Hostels

The Dutch youth-hostel association **Stayokay** (www.stayokay.com) still uses the Hostelling International (HI) logo, but the hostels now go under the name Stayokay. Most offer a good variety of rooms. Facilities tend to be impressive, with newly built hostels common. Some, like the Rotterdam Stayokay, are in landmark buildings.

Almost all Stayokay hostels and most indie hostels have dorm rooms that sleep up to eight people as well as private rooms for one to four people. Nightly rates normally range from €20 to €30 per person for dorm beds and from €60 for private rooms. Book ahead, especially in high season.

Amsterdam has scores of indie hostels. Some quiet, some shambolic, some party central filled with hijinks and stoners.

Hotels

Any hotel with more than 20 rooms is considered large, and most rooms themselves are on the snug side. You'll see a 'star' plaque on the front of every hotel, indicating its rating according to the Benelux Hotel Classification. The stars (from one to five) have to do with the existence of certain facilities, rather than quality. This means that a two-star hotel may be in better condition than a hotel of higher rank,

---

ACCOMMODATION PRICE RANGES

The following price ranges refer to a double room with bathroom in high season. Unless otherwise stated, breakfast is not included in the price.

€ under €80

€€ €80-160

€€€ over €160

though admittedly with fewer facilities.

AMENITIES

Wi-fi is nearly universal across the spectrum, but air-conditioning and lifts are not.

Top End Expect lifts (elevators), minibars and room service. At the top end of top end, facilities like air-conditioning and fitness centres are par for the course. Breakfast is often not included.

Midrange Most hotels in this category are big on comfort, low on formality and small enough to offer personal attention. Rooms usually have a toilet and shower, and a TV and phone. Not many hotels in this category over two storeys have lifts, and their narrow stairwells can take some getting used to, especially with luggage. Rates typically include breakfast.

Budget Lodgings in the lowest price bracket, other than hostels, are thin on the ground. Some are nothing short of run-down flophouses. The better options tend to be spick and span with furnishings that are, at best, cheap and cheerful. Rates often include breakfast.

Rental Accommodation

Renting a flat for a few days can be a fun part of a trip. In Amsterdam it gets you a kitchen and other amenities that make coming 'home' after a hard day having fun that much nicer, while out in the countryside it can be like your own retreat. (And rentals are often priced very competitively with hotels, which give you much less.)

Websites to check:

www.airbnb.com Everything from a couch in a closet to palatial apartments; especially good for Amsterdam.

www.vrbo.com (Vacation Rentals by Owner) Good for urban areas.

Climate
Amsterdam

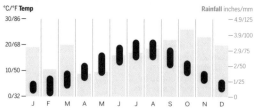

Business Hours

As a general rule, opening hours are as follows:

» **Banks & Government Offices** Open 9.30am to 4pm Monday to Friday.

» **Bars & Cafes** Open 11am to 1am, although some stay open longer at weekends and others won't open for service till the late afternoon.

» **Businesses** Hours are 8.30am to 5pm Monday to Friday.

» **Clubs** Hours vary, but in general clubs are open 10pm to 4am Friday and Saturday; some also open on Wednesday, Thursday and Sunday.

» **Museums** Most museums are closed on Monday.

» **Post offices** Open 9am to 6pm Monday to Friday.

» **Restaurants** Open 10am or 11am to 10pm, with a break in the afternoon from 3pm to 6pm.

» **Shops** Generally shops are open from noon to 6pm Monday, and then from 8.30am or 9am to 6pm Tuesday to Saturday. Most towns have *koopavond* (evening shopping), when stores stay open till 9pm on Thursday or Friday. Bigger supermarkets in cities stay open until 8pm. Sunday shopping is becoming more common these days; large stores are often open from noon to 5pm.

» We only list business hours in reviews when they differ from the standard ones outlined above.

Customs Regulations

For visitors from EU countries, limits only apply for excessive amounts. See www.douane.nl for details.

Residents of non-EU countries are limited to the following:

» **Alcohol** 1L spirits, wine or beer.

» **Coffee** 500g of coffee, or 200g of coffee extracts or coffee essences.

» **Perfume** 50g of perfume and 0.25L of eau de toilette.

» **Tea** 100g of tea, or 40g of tea extracts or tea essences.

» **Tobacco** 200 cigarettes, or 250g of tobacco (shag or pipe tobacco), or 100 cigarillos or 50 cigars.

Discount Cards

Visitors of various professions, including artists and teachers, may get discounts at some venues if they show accreditation.

Students regularly get a few euros off museum admission; bring ID.

Seniors over 65, and with partners of 60 or older, benefit from reductions on public transport, museum admissions, concerts and more. You may look younger, so bring your passport.

Many cities (eg Amsterdam, Den Haag and Rotterdam) offer discount card schemes that are good for discounts on museums, attractions and local transport. Ask at tourist offices.

Cultureel Jongeren Paspoort (Cultural Youth Passport; www.cjp.nl; card €15) Big discounts to museums and cultural events nationwide for people under the age of 30.

Holland Pass (www.holland pass.com; 2/5/7 attractions €28/44/54) You can visit sights over a prolonged period. Buy a pass usable for two, five or seven attractions that you pick from 'tiers' (the most popular/expensive sights are top-tier), from GWK Travelex offices and various hotels.

Museumkaart (Museum Card; www.museumkaart.nl; adult/child €45/22.50, plus €5 for first-time registrants) Free and discounted entry to some 400 museums all over the country for one year. Purchase at museum ticket counters or at Uitburo ticket shops.

Electricity

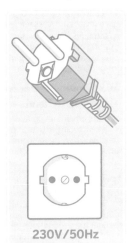

230V/50Hz

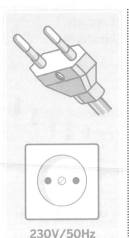

230V/50Hz

Embassies & Consulates

Amsterdam is the country's capital but, confusingly, Den Haag is the seat of government. So the embassies (including those for Australia, Canada, New Zealand and Ireland) are in Den Haag, but Amsterdam has several consulates.

Amsterdam

France (☎020-530 69 69; www.consulfrance-amsterdam. org; Vijzelgracht 2)

Germany (☎020-574 77 00; Honthorststraat 36-8)

UK (☎020-676 43 43; www. britain.nl; Koningslaan 44)

USA (☎020-575 53 09; http:// amsterdam.usconsulate.gov; Museumplein 19)

Den Haag

Australia (☎070-310 82 00; www.netherlands.embassy.gov. au; Carnegielaan 4, Den Haag)

Belgium (☎070-312 34 56; www.diplomatie.be/thehague; Alexanderveld 97)

Canada (☎070-311 16 00; www.netherlands.gc.ca; Sophialaan 7, Den Haag)

France (☎070-312 58 00;

www.ambafrance.nl; Smidsplein 1)

Ireland (☎070-363 09 93; www.irishembassy.nl; Dr Kuyperstraat 9)

New Zealand (☎070-346 93 24; www.nzembassy.com; Eisenhowerlaan 77, Den Haag)

UK (☎070-427 04 27; www. britain.nl; Lange Voorhout 10, Den Haag)

USA (☎070-310 22 09; http:// thehague.usembassy.gov; Lange Voorhout 102, Den Haag)

Food

Prices tend to be high by European standards. For more on Dutch food culture see Dutch Cuisine p287.

Gay & Lesbian Travellers

The best national source of information is COC (www. coc.nl). It has branches throughout the country that are happy to offer advice to newcomers.

Partisan estimates put the proportion of gay and lesbian people in Amsterdam at 20% to 30%. This is probably an exaggeration, but Amsterdam is certainly one of the gay capitals of Europe. In 2001, the Netherlands became the first country to legalise same-sex marriage.

Few countries are as gay-friendly. The government has long subsidised COC, the police advertise in the gay media for applicants, and homosexuals are admitted to the armed forces on an equal footing (in 2009 it was decided that members of the military could march in gay-pride parades in uniform).

In towns outside Amsterdam, however, gay and lesbian bars and clubs often operate behind dark windows. Rotterdam is an exception, as are the university towns with large gay and lesbian student populations.

Health

It is unlikely that you will encounter unusual health problems in the Netherlands, and if you do, standards of care are world-class. It is though important to have health insurance for your trip; for more information, see **Insurance**.

A few travelling tips:

» Bring medications in their original, clearly labelled containers.

» Bring a list of your prescriptions (photocopies of the containers are good) including generic names, so you can get replacements if your bags go on holiday – carry this info separately.

» If you have health problems that may need treatment, bring a signed and dated letter from your physician describing your medical conditions and medications.

» If carrying syringes or needles, have a physician's letter documenting their medical necessity.

» If you need vision correction, carry a spare pair of contact lenses or glasses, and/or take your optical prescription with you.

Recommended Vaccinations

No jabs are necessary for the Netherlands. However, the World Health Organization (WHO) recommends that all travellers should be covered for diphtheria, tetanus, measles, mumps, rubella and polio, regardless of their destination.

Insurance

Travel insurance is a good idea if your policies at home won't cover you in the Netherlands. Although medical or dental costs might already be covered through reciprocal health-care arrangements, you'll still need cover for theft or loss, and for unexpected changes to travel arrange-ments (ticket cancellation etc). Check what's already covered by your local insurance policies or credit cards.

Worldwide travel insurance is available at www.lonelyplanet.com/travel_services. You can buy, extend and claim online anytime – even if you're already on the road.

See also the insurance section of the Transport chapter on p303.

Internet Access

Wi-fi is common in hotels and can be found for free in many cafes, some tourist offices and other public places. Open your wireless device and you'll often find paid wi-fi access from **KPN** (www.kpn.com), the national phone company, and other providers such as **T-Mobile** (www.t-mobile.nl). Costs can be extortionate: upwards of €16 for a day pass.

Internet cafes have become less common, although storefronts selling cheap phone cards with a few terminals can be found near train stations in larger towns. Many libraries, tourist offices, coffeeshops and hotels provide internet terminals (sometimes free). Expect to pay anything from €2 to €4 per hour.

If you have a smartphone that works in the Netherlands, you can surf with that, although beware of possibly very high roaming charges.

Legal Matters

The Netherlands *politie* (police) are pretty relaxed and helpful unless you do some-thing clearly wrong, such as chucking litter or smoking a joint right under their noses.

Police can hold offenders for up to six hours for questioning (plus another six hours if they can't establish your identity, or 24 hours if they consider the matter serious). You won't have the right to a phone call, but they'll notify your consulate. You're presumed innocent until proven guilty.

ID Papers

Anyone over 14 years of age is required by law to carry ID. Foreigners should carry a passport or a photocopy of the relevant data pages; a driver's licence isn't sufficient.

Drugs

» Technically, marijuana is illegal. However, possession of soft drugs (eg cannabis) up to 5g is tolerated. Larger amounts are subject to prosecution.

» Don't light up in an establishment other than a coffeeshop without checking that it's OK to do so.

» Hard drugs are treated as a serious crime.

» Never buy drugs of any kind on the street.

Prostitution

Prostitution is legal in the Netherlands. The industry is protected by law, and prostitutes pay tax. Much of this open policy stems from a desire to undermine the role of pimps and the underworld in the sex industry.

In Amsterdam's Red Light District you have little to fear as the streets are well-policed, but the back alleys are more dubious.

FOOD PRICE RANGES

The following price ranges refer to a main course:

€ under €12

€€ €12-25

€€€ over €25

Maps

The best road maps of the Netherlands are those produced by Michelin and the Dutch automobile association ANWB. The ANWB also puts out provincial maps detailing cycling paths and picturesque road routes. You'll find a wide variety of maps for sale at any tourist office, as well as at bookstores and newsstands.

Tourist offices sell all forms of maps and often have local walking-tour maps in English for sale.

See p25 for sources of cycling maps.

Money

» The Netherlands uses the euro (€). Denominations of the currency are €5, €10, €20, €50, €100, €200 and €500 notes, and €0.01, €0.02, €0.05, €0.10, €0.20, €0.50, €1 and €2 coins (amounts under €1 are called cents).

» To check the latest exchange rates, visit www.xe.com.

ATMs

Automated teller machines can be found outside most banks and at airports and most train stations. Credit cards such as Visa and MasterCard/Eurocard are widely accepted, as well as cards from the Plus and Cirrus networks. Note that using an ATM can be the cheapest way to exchange your money from home – but check with your home bank for service charges before you leave.

You can use your ATM card to keep stocked up with euros throughout the Netherlands so there's no need for currency exchange. However, using your ATM card as a debit card, as opposed to a credit card, to pay for purchases is unlikely to work as the Dutch use PIN cards.

Cash

Cash is commonly used for everyday purchases throughout the Netherlands.

Credit Cards

All the major international credit cards are recognised, and most hotels and large stores accept them. But a fair number of shops, restaurants and other businesses (including Dutch Railways and supermarket chains) do not accept credit cards, or accept only European cards with security chips.

Some establishments levy a 5% surcharge (or more) on credit cards to offset the commissions charged by card providers. Always check first.

For a backup plan against any security chip issue, consider getting the **Chip and PIN Cash Passport** (http://www.travelex.com/us/products/cash-passport/), a preloaded debit MasterCard from Travelex that has the precious security chip embedded. You won't want to use the card much, as the exchange rates you get when you load it are pretty awful (read the regulations carefully). But it can be helpful to have in emergency situations when/if your home credit card won't work.

PIN Cards

In the Netherlands you'll notice people gleefully using 'PIN' cards everywhere, from shops to public telephones and cigarette-vending machines. These direct-debit cards look like credit or bank cards with little circuit chips on them, but they won't be of much use to visitors without a Dutch bank account.

Tipping

Tipping is not essential, as restaurants, hotels, bars etc include a service charge on their bills. A little extra is always welcomed though, and common in certain instances.

» **Hotel porters** €1-2
» **Restaurants** round up, or 5-10%
» **Taxis** 5-10%

Travellers Cheques

Travellers cheques are rare – you'll be hard-pressed to find a bank that will change them for you.

Post

The national post office in the Netherlands is privatised and has gone through two name changes.

The current operator is **PostNL** (www.postnl.nl). It has closed most city post offices and to mail a letter or package you'll need to go to a postal service shop which may be a supermarket or tobacco shop or something else. Use the website to find a location near you, although the website is only in Dutch. Note that if you're trying to mail a parcel abroad, the staff at the third-party shop may have no idea how to help you.

Public Holidays

People take public holidays seriously. Most museums adopt Sunday hours on the days below (except Christmas and New Year) even if they fall on a day when the place would otherwise be closed, such as Monday. Many people treat Remembrance Day (4 May) as a day off.

Carnaval is celebrated with vigour in the Catholic south. Huge lager-fed parties are thrown in the run-up to Shrove Tuesday and little work gets done.

The holidays:

» **Nieuwjaarsdag** (New Year's Day) Parties and fireworks galore.
» **Goede Vrijdag** (Good Friday)
» **Eerste Paasdag** (Easter Sunday)
» **Tweede Paasdag** (Easter Monday)
» **Koningsdag** (King's Day) 27 April
» **Bevrijdingsdag** (Liberation Day) 5 May. This isn't a

universal holiday: government workers have the day off, but almost everyone else has to work.

» **Hemelvaartsdag** (Ascension Day) Fortieth day after Easter Sunday.

» **Eerste Pinksterdag** (Whit Sunday; Pentecost) Fiftieth day after Easter Sunday.

» **Tweede Pinksterdag** (Whit Monday) Fiftieth day after Easter Monday.

» **Eerste Kerstdag** (Christmas Day) 25 December

» **Tweede Kerstdag** (Boxing Day) 26 December

Safe Travel

Much of the Netherlands is utterly safe, but caution is advised in the larger cities. Amsterdam and Rotterdam require a modicum of big-city street sense but nothing you wouldn't normally do at home. See p51 and p91 for more on safety and etiquette.

Bicycles can be quite a challenge to pedestrians. Remember when crossing the street to look for speeding bikes as well as cars; straying into a bike lane without looking both ways is a no-no.

Telephone

The Dutch phone network, **KPN** (www.kpn.com), is efficient, and prices are reasonable by European standards.

Collect Call (collect gesprek; ☑domestic 0800 01 01, international 0800 04 10) Both numbers are free.

International Directory Enquiries (☑0900 84 18; per number €1.15)

Operator Assistance (☑0800 04 10)

Costs

Calls are time-based, anytime and anywhere. Here is a rough guide to costs (note phones in cafes and hotels often charge more):

National call to land line €0.10 per 15 seconds.

National call to mobile phone €0.10 per nine seconds.

International call to Britain €0.058 per minute.

International call to USA €0.073 per minute.

Incoming calls to Dutch mobile phones are generally free to the recipient.

Domestic & International Dialling

To ring abroad, dial 00 followed by the country code for your target country, the area code (you usually drop the leading 0 if there is one) and the subscriber number.

Netherlands country code 31

Free calls 0800

Mobile numbers 06

Paid information calls 0900; cost varies between €0.10 and €1.30 per minute.

Drop the leading 0 on city codes if you're calling from outside the Netherlands (eg 20 for Amsterdam instead of 020). Do not dial the city code if you are in the area covered by it.

Internet Calls

Services such as **Skype** (www.skype.com) and **Google Voice** (www.google.com/voice) can make calling home cheap. Check the websites for details.

Mobile Phones

The Netherlands uses GSM phones compatible with the rest of Europe and Australia but not with some North American GSM phones. Smartphones such as iPhones will work – but beware of enormous roaming costs, especially for data (buy an international plan from your carrier before you leave home).

Prepaid mobile phones are available at mobile-phone shops, starting from around €35 when on special. You can also buy SIM cards (from €5) for your own GSM mobile phone that will give you a Dutch telephone number. Look for Phone House, Orange, T-Mobile and Vodafone shops in major shopping areas.

New prepaid phones generally come with a small amount of call time already stored. To top it up, purchase more minutes at one of the branded stores, newsagencies or supermarkets, and follow the instructions.

Phonecards

» For public telephones, cards are available at post offices, train station counters, VVV and GWK offices, and tobacco shops for €5, €10 and €20.

» KPN's card is the most common but there are plenty of competitors that usually have better rates.

» Train stations have Telfort phone booths that require a Telfort card (available at GWK offices or ticket counters), although there should be KPN booths nearby.

Time

The Netherlands is in the Central European time zone (same as Berlin and Paris), GMT/UTC plus one hour. Noon in Amsterdam is 11am in London, 6am in New York, 3am in San Francisco and 9pm in Sydney. For daylight savings time, clocks are put forward one hour at 2am on the last Sunday in March and back again at 3am on the last Sunday in October.

DUTCH WEBSITES IN ENGLISH

Many Dutch websites offer English as a language option. For those that don't, Google's translation service works like a charm: translate.google.com.

PRACTICALITIES

» The metric system is used for weights and measures.

» The Netherlands uses DVD region code 2.

When telling the time, be aware that the Dutch use 'half' to indicate 'half before' the hour. If you say 'half eight' (8.30 in many forms of English), a Dutch person will take this to mean 7.30.

Tourist Information

» Outside of the Netherlands, www.holland.com is a useful resource.

» Within the Netherlands, **VVV** (Vereniging voor Vreemdelingenverkeer, Netherlands Tourism Board; www.vvv.nl) is the official network of tourist offices around the country. Each tourist office is locally run and has local and regional info. Few VVV publications are free and there are commissions for services (eg €3 to €15 to find a room, €2 to €3 for theatre tickets). Tourist offices are a good place to buy maps and guides.

» **ANWB** (Dutch automobile association; www.anwb.nl) has maps and guidebooks for sale. It provides a wide range of useful information and assistance if you're travelling with any type of vehicle (car, bicycle, motorcycle, yacht etc). In some cities the VVV and ANWB share offices. You'll have to show proof of membership of your home automobile club to get free maps or discounts.

Travellers with Disabilities

Travellers with restricted mobility will find the Nether-

lands somewhat accessible despite the limitations of most older buildings.

» Most offices and larger museums have lifts and/ or ramps and toilets for the disabled.

» Many budget and midrange hotels have limited accessibility, as they are in old buildings with steep stairs and no lifts.

» Cobblestone streets are rough for wheelchairs.

» Restaurants tend to be on ground floors, though 'ground' sometimes includes a few steps.

» Train and other public transport stations sometimes have lifts.

» Most train stations and public buildings have toilets for the disabled.

» Trains have wheelchair access in most instances.

» The Dutch national organisation for the disabled is **ANGO** (Algemene Nederlandse Gehandicapten Organisatie, Dutch Society for the Disabled; ☎033-465 43 43; www.ango.nl).

Visas

Tourists from nearly 60 countries – including Australia, Canada, Israel, Japan, New Zealand, Singapore, South Korea, the USA and most of Europe – need only a valid passport to visit the Netherlands for up to three months. EU nationals can enter for three months with just their national identity card or a passport that expired less than five years ago.

Nationals of most other countries need a Schengen visa, valid within the EU member states (except the UK and Ireland), plus Norway and Iceland, for 90 days within a six-month period.

Schengen visas are issued by Dutch embassies or consulates overseas and can take a while to process (up to two months). You'll need a passport valid until at least three months after your visit, and will have to prove you have sufficient funds for your stay and return journey.

» **Netherlands Foreign Affairs Ministry** (www.minbuza.nl/en) Lists consulates and embassies around the world.

» **Immigratie en Naturalisatiedienst** (Immigration & Naturalisation Service; ☎per min €0.10 0900 123 45 61; www.ind.nl; Postbus 3211, 2280 GE Rijswijk) Handles visas and extensions. Study visas must be applied for via your college or university in the Netherlands.

Women Travellers

You should find little in the way of street harassment in Dutch cities, where most women will feel safe. Amsterdam is probably as secure as it gets among the major cities of Europe. Just take care in the Red Light District, where it's best to walk with a friend to minimise unwelcome attention.

Most women's organisations are based in Amsterdam. **Centrum voor Seksuele Gezondheid** (☎624 54 26; www.acsg.nl; Sarphatistraat 618; ⏰9am-6pm Mon-Fri, to 9pm Tue) is a clinic offering information and help with sexual problems and birth control, including morning-after pills. Appointments are necessary.

Transport

GETTING THERE & AWAY

The Netherlands is an easy place to reach. Amsterdam's Schiphol Airport has copious air links worldwide, including many on low-cost European airlines, and the links on high-speed trains are especially good from France, Belgium and Germany. Other land options are user-friendly and the border crossings are nearly invisible thanks to the EU. There are also ferry links with the UK and Scandinavia.

What's more, once you get to the Netherlands the transport stays hassle-free. Most journeys by rail, car or bus are so short that you can reach most regional destinations before your next meal. And with a country as flat as this, getting around by bicycle is a dream.

Entering the Country

Passport

In principle all passengers with passports are allowed entry to the Netherlands. There are relatively few nationalities that need visas.

Air

Airports

SCHIPHOL AIRPORT

Conveniently near Amsterdam, Schiphol Airport (AMS; www.schiphol.nl) is the Netherlands' main international airport and the fourth busiest in Europe. It's the hub of Dutch passenger carrier KLM and is serviced by most of the world's major airlines.

The airport is like a small city and is well-linked to the rest of the country by train, including the high-speed line south to Rotterdam and Belgium. It runs efficiently for its size, with a huge shopping mall, Schiphol Plaza, filled with travellers amenities. You can store luggage for up to a week. There are also airport hotels.

OTHER AIRPORTS

The other airports of interest to visitors are Rotterdam Airport and Eindhoven Airport. The former has limited service, the latter is served by some European budget carriers.

Tickets

Within Europe there are plenty of airlines connecting the Netherlands to other countries and these tickets are usually found online.

Land

Bicycle

» Bringing your own bike into the Netherlands will cause no problems. Ask your carrier to see what you need to do to check it on a plane; by train you usually have to remove the front wheel and put it in a carrier bag.

» Bicycle paths are called landelijke fietsroutes (LF) and retain that label in northern Belgium.

CLIMATE CHANGE & TRAVEL

Every form of transport that relies on carbon-based fuel generates CO_2, the main cause of human-induced climate change. Modern travel is dependent on aeroplanes, which might use less fuel per kilometre per person than most cars but travel much greater distances. The altitude at which aircraft emit gases (including CO_2) and particles also contributes to their climate change impact. Many websites offer 'carbon calculators' that allow people to estimate the carbon emissions generated by their journey and, for those who wish to do so, to offset the impact of the greenhouse gases emitted with contributions to portfolios of climate-friendly initiatives throughout the world. Lonely Planet offsets the carbon footprint of all staff and author travel.

BELGIUM

Long-distance cyclists can choose from a variety of safe, easy, specially designated routes to get to the Netherlands from Belgium and Germany. The **LF2** route runs 340km from Brussels via Ghent to Amsterdam.

GERMANY

Route **LF4** stretches 300km from Enschede near the German border to Den Haag.

The German fast ICE trains from Cologne and Frankfurt are not bike-friendly; use regular trains instead.

UK

Most cross-Channel ferries don't charge foot passengers extra to take a bicycle. You can also bring your two-wheeler on the connecting trains, where it travels for free if it fits into a bike bag as hand luggage.

Bus

Eurolines (www.eurolines. com), a consortium of coach operators, runs cheap international bus services to/from the Netherlands. Coaches have onboard toilets and reclining seats.

Busabout (☎020-7950 1661; www.busabout.com) operates buses that complete set circuits around Europe, stopping at major cities. The service is aimed at younger travelers; pricing is complex.

Car & Motorcycle

» Drivers need vehicle registration papers, third-party insurance and their domestic license. Get a Green Card

from your insurer to show you have coverage.

» ANWB provides information, maps, advice and services if you show a membership card from your own automobile association, such as the AA or AAA.

» Hitching is uncommon in the Netherlands.

» Ferries take cars and motorcycles to the Netherlands from several ports in the UK including Harwich to Hoek van Holland and Hull to Europoort (both near Rotterdam). There's also a service from Newcastle to IJmuiden near Amsterdam.

Train

BELGIUM

Trains between Amsterdam and Brussels have experienced much drama. Assuming the many problems are finally sorted out, there should be a reliable and frequent fast hourly service linking Brussels and Antwerp with Rotterdam, Schiphol and Amsterdam (two hours from Brussels, hourly) in 2013. Dubbed **Fyra** (www.fyra. com), the trains are operated by **Hispeed** (www.nshispeed. nl), the international arm of the Dutch railways. You can book online or visit the Hispeed counter at the largest stations.

Full fares are high (Amsterdam to Brussels €54), but advance fares are likely to be cheap (€25).

Thalys (www.thalys.com) operates trains between Paris, Brussels (where you can connect to Eurostar for the UK), Rotterdam and

Amsterdam (3½ hours from Paris). It also has good advance fares and there is a range of discount schemes.

In the south there is hourly service between Maastricht and Liege (30 minutes).

GERMANY

German ICE high-speed trains run six times a day between Amsterdam and Cologne (2½ hours) via Utrecht. Many continue on to Frankfurt (four hours) via Frankfurt Airport.

Advance purchase fares bought on the web are as little as €39. Buy your tickets in advance at either www.nshispeed.nl or www.bahn.de, print them out and present them on the train.

With connections in Cologne or Frankfurt, you can reach any part of Germany easily. Other direct services include several regular trains a day between Amsterdam and Berlin (6½ hours) and a local service from Groningen straight east across the border to tiny Leer, where you can get trains to Bremen and beyond.

From Maastricht you can reach Cologne via Liege in Belgium and Aachen in Germany (1½ to two hours).

UK

Eurostar (www.eurostar.com) takes two hours from London St Pancras to Brussels. There you can connect to a **Thalys** (www.thalys.com) or **Fyra** (www.fyra.com) high-speed train to the Netherlands and Amsterdam (two hours from Brussels). And there is speculation that Eurostar will soon extend its trains to Amsterdam, obviating the change.

Rail Europe (www.raileurope.co.uk) may not give you the best ticket options from the UK to the Netherlands. The excellent website **Seat 61** (www.seat61.com) explains all the options.

The **Dutch Flyer** (www. stenaline.co.uk) is one of the cheapest ways to reach the Netherlands from the UK.

THE ESSENTIAL TRIP PLANNER

The service **9292.nl** (☎0900 9292, per min €0.70; www.9292.nl) is an unrivalled planning resource for getting around the Netherlands. It has comprehensive schedules for every train, tram and bus in the country in English. There is a brilliant free smartphone app.

On the web or app, enter your start and end points (eg an address, train station, museum, hotel etc), the results include walking details and fares.

Trains from London (Liverpool Street Station), Cambridge and Norwich connect with ferries sailing from Harwich to Hoek van Holland, where a further train travels on to Rotterdam and Amsterdam. The journey takes around 9½ hours and costs as little as UK£34 one way.

Sea

UK

Several companies operate car/passenger ferries between the Netherlands and the UK. Most travel agents have details of the following services but might not always know the finer points. The ferry companies run frequent specials. There are also train–ferry–train services available.

Reservations are essential for cars in high season, although motorcycles can often be squeezed in. Most ferries don't charge for a bike and have no shortage of storage space.

Stena Line (www.stena line.co.uk) sails between Harwich and Hoek van Holland. The fast HSS ferries take only three hours 40 minutes and depart in each direction twice a day. Overnight ferries take 6¼ hours (one daily), as do normal day ferries (one daily). Foot passengers pay from UK£70 return. Fares for a car and driver range from UK£100 to UK£350 return depending on the season and the day of the week. Options such as reclining chairs and cabins cost extra and are compulsory on night crossings.

P&O Ferries (www.poferries.com) operates an overnight ferry every evening (11 hours) between Hull and Europoort (near Rotterdam). Return fares start at UK£50 for a foot passenger and UK£75 for a car with driver. Prices include berths in an inside cabin; luxury cabins are available. Prices are much higher in peak season.

FARES, TICKETS & OV-CHIPKAARTS

Local transport tickets are smartcards called the OV-chipkaart (www.ov-chipkaart.nl).

» Either purchase a re-usable one in advance at a local transport information office, or purchase a disposable one when you board a bus or tram.

» Some trams have conductors responsible for ticketing, while on others the drivers handle tickets.

» When you enter *and* exit a bus, tram or metro, hold the card against a reader at the doors or station gates. The system then calculates your fare and deducts it from the card. If you don't check out, the system will deduct the highest fare possible.

» Fares for the re-usable cards are much lower than the disposable ones (though you do have to pay an initial €7.50 fee; the card is valid for five years).

» You can also buy OV-chipkaarts for unlimited use for one or more days, and this often is the most convenient option. Local transport operators sell these.

» Stored-value OV-chipkaarts can be used on trains throughout the Netherlands.

DFDS Seaways (www.dfds.co.uk) sails between Newcastle and IJmuiden, which is close to Amsterdam; the 15-hour sailings depart every day. The earlier you book, the lower your fare: return fares start at UK£70 for a foot passenger in an economy berth, plus UK£100 for a car. Prices go up in peak season. The website is relentless in its efforts to upsell.

GETTING AROUND

The Netherlands is very easy to get around. If you are sticking to all but the most esoteric cities and sights, you won't need a car as the train and bus system blankets the country. Or you can do as the Dutch do and provide your own power on a bike.

Air

With a country as small as the Netherlands (the longest train journey, between Groningen and Maastricht, takes 4¼ hours), there is no domestic flying.

Bicycle

The Netherlands is extremely bike-friendly and a *fiets* (bicycle) is the way to go. Many people have the trip of a lifetime using nothing but pedal power. Most modes of transport such as trains and buses are friendly to cyclists and their mounts. Dedicated bike routes go virtually everywhere. For more on the fun you can have riding a bike in the Netherlands, see p24. For more information on cycling road rules, see p27.

Boat

Ferry

Ferries connect the mainland with the five Frisian Islands. Passenger ferries span the Westerschelde in the south of Zeeland, providing a link between the southwestern expanse of the country and Belgium. These are popular with people using the Zeebrugge ferry terminal and run frequently year-round.

The **Waterbus** (☎0900-899 8998; www.waterbus.nl; day pass adult/child €11/6.75) is an excellent fast ferry service that links Rotterdam and Dordrecht as well as the popular tourist destinations of Kinderdijk and Biesbosch National Park. Boats leave from Willemskade every 30 minutes.

Many more minor services provide links across the myriad of Dutch canals and waterways.

Hire

Renting a boat is a popular way to tour rivers, lakes and inland seas. Boats come in all shapes and sizes from canoes to motor boats to small sailing boats to large and historic former cargo sloops. Prices run the gamut and there are hundreds of rental firms throughout the country.

Bus

Buses are used for regional transport rather than for long distances, which are better travelled by train. They provide a vital service, especially in parts of the north and east, where trains are less frequent or nonexistent. The fares are zone-based. You can always buy a ticket from the driver (€2.70 to €5 for modest distances) but most people use the OV-chipkaart for payment.

There is only one class of travel. Some regions have day passes good for all the buses; ask a driver, they are usually very helpful.

Car & Motorcycle

Dutch freeways are extensive but prone to congestion. Those around Amsterdam, the A4 south to Belgium and the A2 southeast to Maastricht are especially likely to be jammed at rush hours and during busy travel periods; traffic jams with a total length of 350km or more aren't unheard of during the holiday season.

Smaller roads are usually well maintained, but the campaign to discourage car use throws up numerous obstacles – two-lane roads are repainted to be one-lane with wide bike lanes or there are barriers, speed-bumps and other 'traffic-calming schemes'.

Parking a car can be both a major headache and expensive. Cities purposely limit parking to discourage car use and rates are high: hotels boast about 'discount' parking rates for overnight guests of €30. Amsterdam has the highest parking rates in the world, averaging €50 per day.

Automobile Associations

ANWB (☎070-314 71 47; www. anwb.nl) is the automobile club in the Netherlands; most big towns and cities have an office. Members of auto associations in their home countries (the AA, AAA, CAA, NRMA etc) can get assistance, free maps, discounts and more.

Driving License

Visitors are entitled to drive in the Netherlands on their foreign licenses for a period of up to 185 days per calendar year.

You'll need to show a valid driving license when hiring a car in the Netherlands. An international driving permit (IDP) is not needed.

Fuel

Like much of Western Europe, petrol is very expensive and fluctuates on a regular basis. At the time of research

it was about €1.70 per litre (about US$8.50 per gallon). Gasoline (petrol) is *benzine* in Dutch, while unleaded fuel is *loodvrij*. Leaded fuel is not sold in the Netherlands but diesel is always available. Liquid petroleum gas can be purchased at petrol stations displaying LPG signs.

Hire

» The Netherlands is well covered for car hire; all major firms have numerous locations.

» Apart from in Amsterdam and Schiphol, the car-hire companies can be in inconvenient locations if you're arriving by train.

» You must be at least 23 years of age to hire a car in the Netherlands. Some car-hire firms levy a small surcharge for drivers under 25.

» A credit card is required to rent.

» Americans should note: less than 4% of European cars have automatic transmissions, if you need this, you'll pay a huge surcharge for your rental.

Insurance

Collision damage waiver (CDW), an insurance policy that limits your financial liability for damage, is a costly add-on for rentals but may not be necessary. Although without insurance you'll be liable for damages up to the full value of the vehicle.

Many credit cards and home auto insurance policies offer CDW-type coverage; make certain about this

---

HIDDEN TRAFFIC CAMERAS

More than 800 unmanned and hidden radar cameras (known as *flitspalen*) watch over Dutch motorways. Even if you are in a rental car, the rental company will track you down in your home country and levy a service charge while the traffic authority also bills you for the fine.

ROAD DISTANCES (KM)

	Amsterdam	Apeldoorn	Arnhem	Breda	Den Bosch	Den Haag	Dordrecht	Eindhoven	Enschede	Groningen	Haarlem	Leeuwarden	Leiden	Maastricht	Nijmegen	Rotterdam	Tilburg
Apeldoorn	86																
Arnhem	99	27															
Breda	101	141	111														
Den Bosch	88	91	64	48													
Den Haag	55	133	118	72	102												
Dordrecht	98	133	102	30	65	45											
Eindhoven	121	109	82	57	32	134	92										
Enschede	161	75	98	212	162	224	200	180									
Groningen	203	147	172	260	236	252	248	254	148								
Haarlem	19	117	114	121	103	51	94	136	184	204							
Leeuwarden	139	133	158	248	222	188	234	240	163	62	148						
Leiden	45	125	110	87	99	17	60	132	192	242	42	178					
Maastricht	213	201	167	146	124	223	181	86	274	348	228	334	239				
Nijmegen	122	63	18	101	44	135	98	62	134	208	135	194	131	148			
Rotterdam	73	128	118	51	81	21	24	113	195	251	70	206	36	202	114		
Tilburg	114	115	88	25	25	102	60	34	186	260	129	246	117	123	68	81	
Utrecht	37	72	64	73	55	62	61	88	139	195	54	181	54	180	85	57	81

before you decline the costly (from €10 per day) CDW.

At most car-rental firms, CDW does not cover the first €500 to €1000 of damages incurred, but still another add on, an excess cover package for around €10 to €20 per day, is normally available to cover this amount. Again, see what your credit card and home auto insurance cover, you may not need anything extra at all, making that bargain rental an actual bargain.

Road Rules

Rules are similar to the rest of Continental Europe. Full concentration is required because you may need to yield to cars, bikes that appear out of nowhere and pedestrians in quick succession.

» Traffic travels on the right.
» The minimum driving age is 18 for vehicles and 16 for motorcycles.
» Seat belts are required for everyone in a vehicle, and children under 12 must ride in the back if there's room.
» Trams always have the right of way.
» If you are trying to turn right, bikes have priority.
» At roundabouts yield to vehicles already travelling in the circle.
» Speed limits are 50km/h in built-up areas, 80km/h in the country, 100km/h on major through-roads and 120km/h on freeways (sometimes 100km/h, clearly marked). Speeding cameras are hidden everywhere.

Local Transport

Bicycle

Any Dutch town you visit is liable to be blanketed with bicycle paths. They're either on the streets or in the form of smooth off-road routes. For more on cycling see p24.

Bus, Tram & Metro

Buses and trams operate in most cities, and Amsterdam and Rotterdam have the added bonus of metro networks.

Taxi

Usually booked by phone – officially you're not supposed to wave them down on the street – taxis also wait outside train stations and hotels and cost roughly €12 for 5km. Even short trips in town can get expensive quickly. *Treintaxis*, which operate from many train stations, are a cheaper and more practical bet.

Train

Dutch trains are efficient, fast and comfortable. Trains are frequent and serve domestic destinations at regular intervals, sometimes five or six times an hour. It's an excellent system and possibly all you'll need to get around the country, although there are a few caveats.

» The national train company **NS** (www.ns.nl) operates all the major lines in the Netherlands. Minor lines in the north and east have been hived off to private bus and train operators, although scheduling and fares remain part of the national system.

» Bikes are welcome on the train system.

» Stations show departure information but the boards don't show trip duration or arrival times, so planning requires the web or a visit to a ticket or information window.

» The system shuts down roughly from midnight to 6am except in the Amsterdam–Schiphol–Rotterdam–Den Haag–Leiden circuit where trains run hourly all night.

» New **Fyra** (www.fyra.com) fast trains operate between Amsterdam, Schiphol, Rotterdam and Breda.

Stations

Medium and large railways stations have a full range of services: currency exchange, ATMs, small groceries, food courts, FEBO-like coin-operated snack food vending machines, flower shops and much more.

Smaller stations, however, often have no services at all and are merely hollow – often architecturally beautiful – shells of their former selves. At these there may only be ticket vending machines. This is especially true on non-NS lines.

LOCKERS

Generally these stations also have lockers, much to the delight of day-trippers. These are operated using a credit card. The one-day fee is €3.60 to €6 depending on size and location. If you return after more than 24 hours, you have to insert your credit card to pay an extra charge. If it's more than 72 hours, your goods will have been removed and you have to pay a €70 fine.

Note that some stations popular with day-trippers (eg Enkhuizen, Delft) do not have lockers.

Tickets

Train travel in the Netherlands is reasonably priced. Tickets cost the same during the day as in the evening and many discounts are available.

PURCHASING TICKETS

There is one important caveat to buying tickets in the Netherlands for visitors: non-European credit and debit cards are almost impossible to use.

Ticket windows Available at midsize to larger stations. Staff speak English and are often very good at figuring out the lowest fare you need to pay, especially if you have a complex itinerary of day trips in mind. But windows may be closed at night or the lines may be long.

Ticket Machines Most only take Dutch bank cards. About 25% do take coins, none take bills. All can be set for English.

If you are at a station with a closed ticket window and don't have the coins for the machines, board the train and find the conductor. Explain your plight (they know where this applies so don't fib!) and they will *usually* sell you a ticket without levying the fine (€35) for boarding without a ticket. If they do fine you, you can apply for a refund at a ticket window.

RESERVATIONS

For national trains, simply turn up at the station: you'll rarely have to wait more than 30 minutes for a train. Reservations may be required for some international trains.

TICKET TYPES

» *Enkele reis* (one-way) – single one-way ticket; with a valid ticket you can break your journey along the direct route.

» *Dagretour* (day return) – normal day return; 10% to 15% cheaper than two one-way tickets.

» *Weekendretour* (weekend return) – costs the same as a normal return and is valid from 7pm Friday to 4am Monday.

» *Dagkaart* (day pass) – costs €48/81.60 for 2nd/1st

TICKET TRIBULATIONS

Buying a train ticket is the hardest part of riding Dutch trains. Among the challenges:

» Only some ticket machines accept cash, and those are coins-only, so you need a pocketful of change.

» Ticket machines that accept plastic will not work with most non-European credit and ATM cards. The exceptions are a limited number of machines at Schiphol and Amsterdam Centraal.

» Ticket windows do not accept credit or ATM cards, although they will accept paper euros. Lines are often quite long and there is a surcharge for the often-unavoidable need to use a ticket window.

» Discounted tickets for Hispeed and Fyra trains sold on the web require a Dutch credit card. The cheap fares can't be bought at ticket windows.

» The much-hyped *Voordeelurenabonnement* (Off-Peak Discount Pass) yields good discounts, but only if you have a Dutch bank account.

class and allows unlimited train travel throughout the country. Only good value if you're planning extensive train travel on any one day.

» *Railrunner* – €2.50; day pass for children aged four to 11.

» Note that for delays in excess of half an hour (irrespective of the cause) you're entitled to a refund. Delays of 30 to 60 minutes warrant a 50% refund and delays of an hour or more a 100% refund.

» International trains require passengers to buy tickets in advance and carry surcharges, but also may have cheap fares available in advance.

TRAIN PASSES

There are several train passes for people living both inside and outside the Netherlands. These should be purchased before you arrive in the Netherlands. However, the passes don't offer good value even if you plan on a lot of train travel:

Eurail A Benelux pass is good for five days travel in a month on all trains within the Netherlands, Belgium and Luxembourg. It costs US$396/255 1st class/2nd class.

InterRail Benelux pass, good for six days in one month. It costs €308/201.

Trains
CLASSES

The longest train journey in the Netherlands (Maastricht–Groningen) takes about 4½ hours, but the majority of trips are far shorter. Trains have 1st-class sections, but these are often little different from the 2nd-class areas and, given the short journeys, not worth the extra cost.

That said, where 1st class is worth the extra money is during busy periods when seats in 2nd class are over-subscribed.

TYPES

In descending order of speed:

Thalys (www.thalys.com) Operates French TGV-style high-speed trains from Amsterdam, Schiphol and Rotterdam south to Belgium and Paris. Trains are plush and have wi-fi.

Fyra (www.fyra.com) Operates domestic high-speed trains on the line from Amsterdam south to Rotterdam plus service on to Belgium. Airline-style ticket pricing.

ICE (Intercity Express; www.nshispeed.com) German fast trains from Amsterdam to Cologne and onto Frankfurt Airport and Frankfurt. Carries a surcharge for domestic riders.

Intercity The best non-high-speed domestic trains. They run express past small stations on all major lines. Usually air-conditioned double-deck cars.

Sneltrein (Fast Train) Not an Intercity but not as slow as a *stoptrein*. May not be air-conditioned.

Stoptrein (Stop Train) Never misses a stop, never gets up to speed. Some have no toilets.

Treintaxi

More than 30 train stations offer an excellent *treintaxi* (train taxi) service that takes you to/from the station within a limited area. The cost per person per ride is €4.90 at a train station counter or ticketing machine, or €5.50 direct from the driver. The service operates daily from 7am (from 8am Sunday and public holidays) till the evening. There's usually a special call box outside near the normal taxi rank and there's a central information number (0900-873 46 82, per minute €0.35).

The *treintaxi* service can be very handy for reaching places far from stations that don't have useful local bus services, such as Kamp Westerbork in Drenthe. Unfortunately, most major stations are excluded.

Language

WANT MORE?

For in-depth language information and handy phrases, check out Lonely Planet's *Dutch Phrasebook*. You'll find it at **shop .lonelyplanet.com**, or you can buy Lonely Planet's iPhone phrasebooks at the Apple App Store.

Dutch has around 20 million speakers worldwide. As a member of the Germanic language family, Dutch has many similarities with English.

The pronunciation of Dutch is fairly straightforward. It distinguishes between long and short vowels, which can affect the meaning of words, for example, *man* (man) and *maan* (moon). Also note that aw is pronounced as in 'law', eu as the 'u' in 'nurse', ew as the 'ee' in 'see' (with rounded lips), oh as the 'o' in 'note', öy as the 'er y' (without the 'r') in 'her year', and uh as in 'ago'.

The consonants are pretty simple to pronounce too. Note that kh is a throaty sound, similar to the 'ch' in the Scottish *loch*, r is trilled and zh is pronounced as the 's' in 'pleasure'. This said, if you read our coloured pronunciation guides as if they were English, you'll be understood just fine. The stressed syllables are indicated with italics.

Where relevant, both polite and informal options in Dutch are included, indicated with 'pol' and 'inf' respectively.

BASICS

Hello.	*Dag./Hallo.*	dakh/ha·*loh*
Goodbye.	*Dag.*	dakh
Yes./No.	*Ja./Nee.*	yaa/ney
Please.	*Alstublieft.* (pol)	al·stew·*bleeft*
	Alsjeblieft. (inf)	a·shuh·*bleeft*
Thank you.	*Dank u/je.* (pol/inf)	dangk ew/yuh
You're welcome.	*Graag gedaan.*	khraakh khuh·*daan*
Excuse me.	*Excuseer mij.*	eks·kew·*zeyr* mey

How are you?
Hoe gaat het met u/jou? (pol/inf) — hoo khaat huht met ew/yaw

Fine. And you?
Goed. — khoot
En met u/jou? (pol/inf) — en met ew/yaw

What's your name?
Hoe heet u/je? (pol/inf) — hoo heyt ew/yuh

My name is ...
Ik heet ... — ik heyt ...

Do you speak English?
Spreekt u Engels? — spreykt ew *eng*·uhls

I don't understand.
Ik begrijp het niet. — ik buh·*khreyp* huht neet

ACCOMMODATION

Do you have a ... room?	*Heeft u een ...?*	heyft ew uhn ...
single	*éénpersoons-kamer*	eyn·puhr·sohns·kaa·muhr
double	*tweepersoons-kamer met een dubbel bed*	twey·puhr·sohns·kaa·muhr met uhn du·buhl bet
twin	*tweepersoons-kamer met lits jumeaux*	twey·puhr·sohns·kaa·muhr met lee zhew·*moh*
How much is it per ...?	*Hoeveel kost het per ...?*	hoo·*veyl* kost huht puhr ...
night	*nacht*	nakht
person	*persoon*	puhr·*sohn*

Is breakfast included?
Is het ontbijt inbegrepen? — is huht ont·*beyt* in·buh·khrey·puhn

bathroom	badkamer	bat·kaa·muhr
bed and breakfast	gasten-kamer	khas·tuhn·kaa·muhr
campsite	camping	kem·ping
guesthouse	pension	pen·syon
hotel	hotel	hoh·tel
window	raam	raam
youth hostel	jeugdherberg	yeukht·her·berkh

DIRECTIONS

Where's the ...?
Waar is ...? — waar is ...

How far is it?
Hoe ver is het? — hoo ver is huht

What's the address?
Wat is het adres? — wat is huht a·dres

Can you please write it down?
Kunt u dat alstublieft opschrijven? — kunt ew dat al·stew·bleeft op·skhrey·vuhn

Can you show me (on the map)?
Kunt u het mij tonen (op de kaart)? — kunt ew huht mey toh·nuhn (op duh kaart)

at the corner	op de hoek	op duh hook
at the traffic lights	bij de verkeers-lichten	bey duh vuhr·keyrs·likh·tuhn
behind	achter	akh·tuhr
in front of	voor	vohr
left	links	lingks
near (to)	dicht bij	dikht bey
next to	naast	naast
opposite	tegenover	tey·khuhn·oh·vuhr
straight ahead	rechtdoor	rekh·dohr
right	rechts	rekhs

EATING & DRINKING

What would you recommend?
Wat kan u aanbevelen? — wat kan ew aan·buh·vey·luhn

What's in that dish?
Wat zit er in dat gerecht? — wat zit uhr in dat khuh·rekht

I'd like the menu, please.
Ik wil graag een menu. — ik wil khraakh uhn me·new

Delicious!
Heerlijk/Lekker! — heyr·luhk/le·kuhr

Cheers!
Proost! — prohst

KEY PATTERNS

To get by in Dutch, mix and match these simple patterns with words of your choice:

When's (the next bus)?
Hoe laat gaat (de volgende bus)? — hoo laat khaat (duh vol·khun·duh bus)

Where's (the station)?
Waar is (het station)? — waar is (huht sta·syon)

I'm looking for (a hotel).
Ik ben op zoek naar (een hotel). — ik ben op zook naar (uhn hoh·tel)

Do you have (a map)?
Heeft u (een kaart)? — heyft ew (uhn kaart)

Is there (a toilet)?
Is er (een toilet)? — is uhr (uhn twa·let)

I'd like (the menu).
Ik wil graag (een menu). — ik wil khraakh (uhn me·new)

I'd like to (hire a car).
Ik wil graag (een auto huren). — ik wil khraakh (uhn aw·toh hew·ruhn)

Can I (enter)?
Kan ik (binnengaan)? — kan ik (bi·nuhn·khaan)

Could you please (help me)?
Kunt u alstublieft (helpen)? — kunt ew al·stew·bleeft (hel·puhn)

Do I have to (get a visa)?
Moet ik (een visum hebben)? — moot ik (uhn vee·zum he·buhn)

Please bring the bill.
Mag ik de rekening alstublieft? — makh ik duh rey·kuh·ning al·stew·bleeft

I'd like to reserve a table for ...	Ik wil graag een tafel voor ... reserveren.	ik wil khraakh uhn taa·fuhl vohr ... rey·ser·vey·ruhn
(two) people	(twee) personen	(twey) puhr·soh·nuhn
(eight) o'clock	(acht) uur	(akht) ewr

I don't eat ...	Ik eet geen ...	ik eyt kheyn ...
eggs	eieren	ey·yuh·ruhn
fish	vis	vis
(red) meat	(rood) vlees	(roht) vleys
nuts	noten	noh·tuhn

Key Words

bar	bar	bar
bottle	fles	fles

breakfast	ontbijt	ont·beyt
cafe	café	ka·fey
cold	koud	kawt
dinner	avondmaal	aa·vont·maal
drink list	drankkaart	drang·kaart
fork	vork	vork
glass	glas	khlas
grocery store	kruidenier	kröy·duh·neer
hot	heet	heyt
knife	mes	mes
lunch	middagmaal	mi·dakh·maal
market	markt	markt
menu	menu	me·new
plate	bord	bort
pub	kroeg	krookh
restaurant	restaurant	res·toh·rant
spicy	pikant	pee·kant
spoon	lepel	ley·puhl
vegetarian (food)	vegetarisch	vey·khey·taa·ris
with/without	met/zonder	met/zon·duhr

Meat & Fish

beef	rundvlees	runt·vleys
chicken	kip	kip
duck	eend	eynt
fish	vis	vis
herring	haring	haa·ring
lamb	lamsvlees	lams·vleys
lobster	kreeft	kreyft
meat	vlees	vleys
mussels	mosselen	mo·suh·luhn
oysters	oester	oos·tuhr
pork	varkensvlees	var·kuhns·vleys
prawn	steurgarnaal	steur·khar·naal
salmon	zalm	zalm
scallops	kammosselen	ka·mo·suh·luhn
shrimps	garnalen	khar·naa·luhn
squid	inktvis	ingkt·vis
trout	forel	fo·rel
tuna	tonijn	toh·neyn
turkey	kalkoen	kal·koon
veal	kalfsvlees	kalfs·vleys

Fruit & Vegetables

apple	appel	a·puhl
banana	banaan	ba·naan

beans	bonen	boh·nuhm
berries	bessen	be·suhn
cabbage	kool	kohl
capsicum	paprika	pa·pree·ka
carrot	wortel	wor·tuhl
cauliflower	bloemkool	bloom·kohl
cucumber	komkommer	kom·ko·muhr
fruit	fruit	fröyt
grapes	druiven	dröy·vuhn
lemon	citroen	see·troon
lentils	linzen	lin·zuhn
mushrooms	paddestoelen	pa·duh·stoo·luhn
nuts	noten	noh·tuhn
onions	uien	öy·yuhn
orange	sinaasappel	see·naas·a·puhl
peach	perzik	per·zik
peas	erwtjes	erw·chus
pineapple	ananas	a·na·nas
plums	pruimen	pröy·muhn
potatoes	aardappels	aart·a·puhls
spinach	spinazie	spee·naa·zee
tomatoes	tomaten	toh·maa·tuhn
vegetables	groenten	khroon·tuhn

Other

bread	brood	broht
butter	boter	boh·tuhr
cheese	kaas	kaas
eggs	eieren	ey·yuh·ruhn
honey	honing	hoh·ning
ice	ijs	eys
jam	jam	zhem
noodles	noedels	noo·duhls
oil	olie	oh·lee
pastry	gebak	khuh·bak
pepper	peper	pey·puhr

Signs	
Ingang	Entrance
Uitgang	Exit
Open	Open
Gesloten	Closed
Inlichtingen	Information
Verboden	Prohibited
Toiletten	Toilets
Heren	Men
Dames	Women

rice	*rijst*	reyst
salt	*zout*	zawt
soup	*soep*	soop
soy sauce	*sojasaus*	soh·ya·saws
sugar	*suiker*	söy·kuhr
vinegar	*azijn*	a·zeyn

Drinks

beer	*bier*	beer
coffee	*koffie*	ko·fee
juice	*sap*	sap
milk	*melk*	melk
red wine	*rode wijn*	roh·duh weyn
soft drink	*frisdrank*	fris·drangk
tea	*thee*	tey
water	*water*	waa·tuhr
white wine	*witte wijn*	wi·tuh weyn

EMERGENCIES

Help!
Help! help

Leave me alone!
Laat me met rust! laat muh met rust

Call a doctor!
Bel een dokter! bel uhn dok·tuhr

Call the police!
Bel de politie! bel duh poh·leet·see

There's been an accident.
Er is een ongeluk uhr is uhn on·khuh·luk
gebeurd. khuh·beurt

I'm lost.
Ik ben verdwaald. ik ben vuhr·dwaalt

I'm sick.
Ik ben ziek. ik ben zeek

It hurts here.
Hier doet het pijn. heer doot huht peyn

Where are the toilets?
Waar zijn de toiletten? waar zeyn duh twa·le·tuhn

I'm allergic to (antibiotics).
Ik ben allergisch voor ik ben a·ler·khees vohr
(antibiotica). (an·tee·bee·yoh·tee·ka)

SHOPPING & SERVICES

I'd like to buy ...
Ik wil graag ... kopen. ik wil khraakh ... koh·puhn

I'm just looking.
Ik kijk alleen maar. ik keyk a·leyn maar

Can I look at it?
Kan ik het even zien? kan ik huht ey·vuhn zeen

Do you have any others?
Heeft u nog andere? heyft ew nokh an·duh·ruh

How much is it?
Hoeveel kost het? hoo·veyl kost huht

That's too expensive.
Dat is te duur. dat is tuh dewr

Can you lower the price?
Kunt u wat van de kunt ew wat van duh
prijs afdoen? preys af·doon

There's a mistake in the bill.
Er zit een fout in de uhr zit uhn fawt in duh
rekening. rey·kuh·ning

ATM	*pin-automaat*	pin·aw·toh·maat
foreign exchange	*wisselkantoor*	wi·suhl·kan·tohr
post office	*postkantoor*	post·kan·tohr
shopping centre	*winkel-centrum*	wing·kuhl·sen·trum
tourist office	*VVV*	vey·vey·vey

TIME & DATES

What time is it?
Hoe laat is het? hoo laat is huht

It's (10) o'clock.
Het is (tien) uur. huht is (teen) ewr

Half past (10).
Half (elf). half (elf)
(lit: half eleven)

am (morning)	*'s ochtends*	sokh·tuhns
pm (afternoon)	*'s middags*	smi·dakhs
pm (evening)	*'s avonds*	saa·vonts

yesterday	*gisteren*	khis·tuh·ruhn
today	*vandaag*	van·daakh
tomorrow	*morgen*	mor·khuhn

Monday	*maandag*	maan·dakh
Tuesday	*dinsdag*	dins·dakh
Wednesday	*woensdag*	woons·dakh
Thursday	*donderdag*	don·duhr·dakh
Friday	*vrijdag*	vrey·dakh
Saturday	*zaterdag*	zaa·tuhr·dakh
Sunday	*zondag*	zon·dakh

Numbers

1	één	eyn
2	twee	twey
3	drie	dree
4	vier	veer
5	vijf	veyf
6	zes	zes
7	zeven	zey·vuhn
8	acht	akht
9	negen	ney·khuhn
10	tien	teen
20	twintig	twin·tikh
30	dertig	der·tikh
40	veertig	feyr·tikh
50	vijftig	feyf·tikh
60	zestig	ses·tikh
70	zeventig	sey·vuhn·tikh
80	tachtig	takh·tikh
90	negentig	ney·khuhn·tikh
100	honderd	hon·duhrt
1000	duizend	döy·zuhnt

January	januari	ya·new·waa·ree
February	februari	fey·brew·waa·ree
March	maart	maart
April	april	a·pril
May	mei	mey
June	juni	yew·nee
July	juli	yew·lee
August	augustus	aw·khus·tus
September	september	sep·tem·buhr
October	oktober	ok·toh·buhr
November	november	noh·vem·buhr
December	december	dey·sem·buhr

TRANSPORT

Public Transport

Is this the ...	*Is dit de ... naar*	is dit duh ... naar
to (the left bank)?	*(de linker-oever)?*	(duh ling·kuhr·oo·vuhr)
ferry	veerboot	veyr·boht
metro	metro	mey·troh
tram	tram	trem
platform	perron	pe·ron
timetable	dienst-regeling	deenst·rey·khuh·ling

When's the ...	*Hoe laat gaat*	hoo laat khaat
(bus)?	*de ... (bus)?*	duh ... (bus)
first	eerste	eyr·stuh
last	laatste	laat·stuh
next	volgende	vol·khun·duh

A ticket to ..., please.
Een kaartje naar ... graag. — uhn kaar·chuh naar ... khraakh

What time does it leave?
Hoe laat vertrekt het? — hoo laat vuhr·trekt huht

Does it stop at ...?
Stopt het in ...? — stopt huht in ...

What's the next stop?
Welk is de volgende halte? — welk is duh vol·khuhn·duh hal·tuh

I'd like to get off at ...
Ik wil graag in ... uitstappen. — ik wil khraak in ... öyt·sta·puhn

Is this taxi available?
Is deze taxi vrij? — is dey·zuh tak·see vrey

Please take me to ...
Breng me alstublieft naar ... — breng muh al·stew·bleeft naar ...

Cycling

I'd like ...	*Ik wil graag ...*	ik wil khraakh ...
my bicycle repaired	mijn fiets laten herstellen	meyn feets laa·tuhn her·ste·luhn
to hire a bicycle	een fiets huren	uhn feets hew·ruhn

I'd like to hire a ...	*Ik wil graag een ... huren.*	ik wil khraakh uhn ... hew·ruhn
basket	mandje	man·chuh
child seat	kinderzitje	kin·duhr·zi·chuh
helmet	helm	helm

Do you have bicycle parking?
Heeft u parking voor fietsen? — heyft ew par·king vohr feet·suhn

Can we get there by bike?
Kunnen we er met de fiets heen? — ku·nuhn wuh uhr met duh feets heyn

I have a puncture.
Ik heb een lekke band. — ik hep uhn le·kuh bant

bicycle path	fietspad	feets·pat
bicycle pump	fietspomp	feets·pomp
bicycle repairman	fietsenmaker	feet·suhn·maa·kuhr
bicycle stand	fietsenrek	feet·suhn·rek

GLOSSARY

abdij – abbey
ANWB – Dutch automobile association
apotheek – chemist/pharmacy

benzine – petrol/gasoline
bevrijding – liberation
bibliotheek – library
bos – woods or forest
botter – type of 19th-century fishing boat
broodje – bread roll (with filling)
bruin café – brown cafe; traditional drinking establishment
buurt – neighbourhood

café – pub, bar; also known as kroeg
coffeeshop – cafe authorised to sell cannabis

eetcafé cafes (pubs) serving meals

fiets – bicycle
fietsenstalling – secure bicycle storage
fietspad – bicycle path

gemeente – municipal, municipality
gezellig – convivial, cosy
GVB – Gemeentevervoerbedrijf; Amsterdam municipal transport authority
GWK – Grenswisselkantoren; official currency-exchange offices

haven – port
hof – courtyard

hofje – almshouse or series of buildings around a small courtyard, also known as begijnhof
hoofd – literally 'head', but in street names it often means 'main'
hunebedden – prehistoric rock masses purportedly used as burial chambers

jenever – Dutch gin; also genever

kaas – cheese
koffiehuis – espresso bar; cafe (as distinct from a coffeeshop)
klooster – cloister, religious house
koningin – queen
koninklijk – royal
kunst – art
kwartier – quarter

LF routes – landelijke fietsroutes; national (long-distance) bike routes
loodvrij – unleaded (petrol/gasoline)

markt – town square; market
meer – lake
molen – windmill; mill

NS – Nederlandse Spoorwegen; national railway company

OV-chipkaart – fare card for Dutch public transit

paleis – palace
polder – strips of farmland separated by canals

postbus – post office box

Randstad – literally 'rimcity'; the urban agglomeration including Amsterdam, Utrecht, Rotterdam and Den Haag
Rijk(s-) – the State

scheepvaart – shipping
schouwburg – theatre
sluis – lock (for boats/ships)
spoor – train platform
stadhuis – town hall
stedelijk – civic, municipal
stichting – foundation, institute
strand – beach

terp – mound of packed mud in Friesland that served as a refuge during floods
treintaxi – taxi for train passengers
tuin – garden
tulp – tulip

verzet – resistance
Vlaams – Flemish
VVV – tourist information office

waag – old weigh-house
wadlopen – mudflat-walking
weeshuis – orphanage
werf – wharf, shipyard
winkel – shop

zaal – room, hall
zee – sea
ziekenhuis – hospital

Behind the Scenes

SEND US YOUR FEEDBACK

We love to hear from travellers – your comments keep us on our toes and help make our books better. Our well-travelled team reads every word on what you loved or loathed about this book. Although we cannot reply individually to postal submissions, we always guarantee that your feedback goes straight to the appropriate authors, in time for the next edition. Each person who sends us information is thanked in the next edition – the most useful submissions are rewarded with a selection of digital PDF chapters.

Visit **lonelyplanet.com/contact** to submit your updates and suggestions or to ask for help. Our award-winning website also features inspirational travel stories, news and discussions.

Note: We may edit, reproduce and incorporate your comments in Lonely Planet products such as guidebooks, websites and digital products, so let us know if you don't want your comments reproduced or your name acknowledged. For a copy of our privacy policy visit lonelyplanet.com/privacy.

OUR READERS

Many thanks to the travellers who used the last edition and wrote to us with helpful hints, useful advice and interesting anecdotes:

Jeroen Bartol, Katie Bilodeau, Yuliono Budianto, Richard Campbell, Tara Cujovic, Nicole de Bruijn, De Jong, Bob den Hollander, Alexandra Di Oliveira, Marco Evenhuis, Stewart Fletcher, Wessel Franken, Marc Gebuis, Stefan Glasbergen, Jan Hansen, David Harmer, Jonathan Harrison, Juliette Hilders, Janine Hoogwerf, Kathryn Hughes, Marjolein Jansen, Norbert Janz, Frank Jochems, Jo Jones, Anneriek Joost, Klemens Karssen, Sjarka Kist, Wim Klumpenhouwer, Bouke Kroes, David Lacy, May Lee, Sam Lindley, Hannah Linnekamp, Alison Matthews, Ana Milosevic, Patrick Moffatt, Karim Mohamed, Joska Mosman, Karine Nellins, Mike Render, Tom Rice, Birgitte Schmidt, Olga Sin, Eline Thijssen, Annemarie van Nieuwamerongen-Oosterkamp, Niels van Os, Rob van Zutphen, Carlo Vandesteene, Joris Jan Voermans, Kim Ziesel.

AUTHOR THANKS

Ryan Ver Berkmoes

A double order of balls to Karla Zimmerman, who is a colleague, co-author and friend extraordinaire. Too many folks to thank in the Netherlands but I have to mention the incomparable Hortance van den Beld in Deventer. Then there's the linguist from whom I finally learned the meaning of my name: 'of the birch tree in the swamp' or something like that. And thanks to Floor van Abbema and Joachim Maurer for a splendid night out.

Karla Zimmerman

Many thanks to Jeremy Gray, Kimberley Lewis and crew from Randy Roy's, Roel and Martijn de Haas, and Manon Zondervan for your knowledge and help on the ground. Cheers to co-author Ryan Ver Berkmoes, who knows his Netherlands stuff, from best brews to Dutch ovens. Thanks most to Eric Markowitz, the world's best partner-for-life, who joined me in Amsterdam for steep stairs, beery brown cafes and windmill explorations.

ACKNOWLEDGMENTS

Climate Map Data (CRMS and Discover titles) Climate map data adapted from Peel MC, Finlayson BL & McMahon TA (2007) 'Updated World Map of the Köppen-Geiger Climate Classification', *Hydrology and Earth System Sciences*, 11, 163344.

Cover photograph: Field of tulips and traditional Dutch windmill, the Netherlands, Cornelia Doerr/Getty Images.

THIS BOOK

This 5th edition of Lonely Planet's *The Netherlands* guidebook was researched and written by Ryan Ver Berkmoes and Karla Zimmerman. The previous edition was also written by Ryan Ver Berkmoes and Karla Zimmerman, with research by Caroline Sieg and additional content by Simon Sellars. The 3rd edition was written by Neal Bedford and Simon Sellars. This guidebook was commissioned in Lonely Planet's London office, and produced by the following:

Commissioning Editors
Joanna Cooke, James Smart

Coordinating Editors
Elizabeth Harvey, Tasmin Waby

Coordinating Cartographers Hunor Csutoros, David Kemp, Laura Matthewman

Coordinating Layout Designer Kerrianne Southway

Managing Editors
Barbara Delissen, Bruce Evans

Senior Editor Andi Jones

Managing Cartographers Anita Banh, Amanda Sierp

Managing Layout Designer Chris Girdler

Assisting Editors Kellie Langdon, Jenna Myers, Kristin Odijk, Gabrielle Stefanos

Cover Research Naomi Parker

Internal Image Research Aude Vauconsant

Language Content Branislava Vladisavljevic

Thanks to Nigel Chin, Laura Crawford, Ryan Evans, Justin Flynn, Fayette Fox, Larissa Frost, Jouve India, Annelies Mertens, Trent Paton, Anthony Phelan, Raphael Richards, Gerard Walker

Index

NOTES

how to use this book

These symbols will help you find the listings you want:

👁 Sights	🚩 Tours	♀ Drinking			
🏊 Beaches	🎉 Festivals & Events	☆ Entertainment			
🏃 Activities	🛏 Sleeping	🔒 Shopping			
🎓 Courses	🍴 Eating	❶ Information/Transport			

Look out for these icons:

TOP CHOICE	Our author's recommendation
FREE	No payment required
🍃	A green or sustainable option

Our authors have nominated these places as demonstrating a strong commitment to sustainability – for example by supporting local communities and producers, operating in an environmentally friendly way, or supporting conservation projects.

These symbols give you the vital information for each listing:

☎	Telephone Numbers	🛜	Wi-Fi Access	🚌	Bus
⊙	Opening Hours	🏊	Swimming Pool	⛴	Ferry
P	Parking	✔	Vegetarian Selection	Ⓜ	Metro
⊝	Nonsmoking	📖	English-Language Menu	Ⓢ	Subway
✳	Air-Conditioning	👪	Family-Friendly	⊖	London Tube
@	Internet Access	🐾	Pet-Friendly	🚊	Tram
				🚆	Train

Reviews are organised by author preference.

Map Legend

Sights
- 🏖 Beach
- 🛕 Buddhist
- 🏰 Castle
- ✝ Christian
- 🕉 Hindu
- ☪ Islamic
- ✡ Jewish
- ❶ Monument
- 🏛 Museum/Gallery
- 🏚 Ruin
- 🍇 Winery/Vineyard
- 🐾 Zoo
- ⊙ Other Sight

Activities, Courses & Tours
- 🤿 Diving/Snorkelling
- 🛶 Canoeing/Kayaking
- ⛷ Skiing
- 🏄 Surfing
- 🏊 Swimming/Pool
- 🚶 Walking
- 🏄 Windsurfing
- 🔵 Other Activity/Course/Tour

Sleeping
- 🛏 Sleeping
- ⛺ Camping

Eating
- 🍴 Eating

Drinking
- ☕ Drinking
- ☕ Cafe

Entertainment
- 🎭 Entertainment

Shopping
- 🛍 Shopping

Information
- ✉ Post Office
- ❶ Tourist Information

Transport
- ✈ Airport
- ⊗ Border Crossing
- 🚌 Bus
- 🚠 Cable Car/Funicular
- 🚲 Cycling
- ⛴ Ferry
- 🚝 Monorail
- P Parking
- Ⓢ S-Bahn
- 🚕 Taxi
- 🚉 Train/Railway
- 🚊 Tram
- ⊖ Tube Station
- Ⓤ U-Bahn
- Ⓜ Underground Train Station
- • Other Transport

Routes
- Tollway
- Freeway
- Primary
- Secondary
- Tertiary
- Lane
- Unsealed Road
- Plaza/Mall
- Steps
-)=== Tunnel
- Pedestrian Overpass
- Walking Tour
- Walking Tour Detour
- Path

Boundaries
- International
- State/Province
- Disputed
- Regional/Suburb
- Marine Park
- Cliff
- Wall

Population
- 😊 Capital (National)
- ◉ Capital (State/Province)
- ● City/Large Town
- ○ Town/Village

Geographic
- 🏠 Hut/Shelter
- 🔦 Lighthouse
- 👁 Lookout
- ▲ Mountain/Volcano
- 🌴 Oasis
- 🌳 Park
-)(Pass
- 🧺 Picnic Area
- 💧 Waterfall

Hydrography
- River/Creek
- Intermittent River
- Swamp/Mangrove
- Reef
- Canal
- Water
- Dry/Salt/Intermittent Lake
- Glacier

Areas
- Beach/Desert
- + + + Cemetery (Christian)
- × × × Cemetery (Other)
- Park/Forest
- Sportsground
- Sight (Building)
- Top Sight (Building)

OUR STORY

A beat-up old car, a few dollars in the pocket and a sense of adventure. In 1972 that's all Tony and Maureen Wheeler needed for the trip of a lifetime – across Europe and Asia overland to Australia. It took several months, and at the end – broke but inspired – they sat at their kitchen table writing and stapling together their first travel guide, *Across Asia on the Cheap*. Within a week they'd sold 1500 copies. Lonely Planet was born.

Today, Lonely Planet has offices in Melbourne, London and Oakland, with more than 600 staff and writers. We share Tony's belief that 'a great guidebook should do three things: inform, educate and amuse'.

OUR WRITERS

Ryan Ver Berkmoes
Coordinating Author; all chapters except Amsterdam

Ryan worked on the first edition of Lonely Planet's *The Netherlands*, a country where they pronounce his name better than he can, possibly because his ancestors are lurking about there somewhere. Ryan is thrilled to see it continues to be the same charming, amusing, idiosyncratic place. He travels the world writing about great places to visit. Learn more at ryanverberkmoes.com or on Twitter: @ryanvb.

Read more about Ryan at:
lonelyplanet.com/members/ryanverberkmoes

Karla Zimmerman
Amsterdam

During her Amsterdam travels, Karla admired art, bicycled crash-free, ate an embarrassing quantity of *frites* and bent over to take her jenever like a local. She has been visiting Amsterdam since 1989, decades that have seen her trade space cakes for *stroopwafels*, to a much more pleasant effect. She never tires of the city's bobbing houseboats, cling clinging bike bells and canal houses tilting at impossible angles. Based in Chicago, Karla writes travel features for newspapers, books, magazines and websites. She has written several Lonely Planet guidebooks covering the USA, Canada, Caribbean and Europe.

Read more about Ryan at:
lonelyplanet.com/members/karlazimmerman.

Published by Lonely Planet Publications Pty Ltd
ABN 36 005 607 983
5th edition – May 2013
ISBN 978 1 74179 895 1
© Lonely Planet 2013   Photographs © as indicated 2013
10 9 8 7 6 5 4 3 2 1
Printed in China